# THE CAMBRIDGE HANDBOOK OF WESTERN MYSTICISM AND ESOTERICISM

Mysticism and esotericism are two intimately related strands of the Western tradition. Despite their close connections, however, scholars tend to treat them separately. Whereas the study of Western mysticism enjoys a long and established history, Western esotericism is a young field. *The Cambridge Handbook of Western Mysticism and Esotericism* examines both of these traditions together. The volume demonstrates that the roots of esotericism almost always lead back to mystical traditions, while the work of mystics was bound up with esoteric or occult preoccupations. It also shows why mysticism and esotericism must be examined together if either is to be understood fully. Including contributions by leading scholars, this volume features essays on such topics as alchemy, astrology, magic, Neoplatonism, Kabbalism, Renaissance Hermetism, Freemasonry, Rosicrucianism, number symbolism, Christian theosophy, spiritualism, and much more. This handbook serves as both a capstone of contemporary scholarship and a cornerstone of future research.

Glenn Alexander Magee is Professor and Chairman of the Department of Philosophy at the C. W. Post Campus of Long Island University. He is the author of *Hegel and the Hermetic Tradition* (2001) and *The Hegel Dictionary* (2011), as well as many articles on German philosophy and its connections with mysticism and esotericism.

# THE CAMBRIDGE HANDBOOK OF WESTERN MYSTICISM AND ESOTERICISM

Edited by

## GLENN ALEXANDER MAGEE

Long Island University

# CAMBRIDGE
## UNIVERSITY PRESS

University Printing House, Cambridge CB2 8BS, United Kingdom

One Liberty Plaza, 20th Floor, New York, NY 10006, USA

477 Williamstown Road, Port Melbourne, VIC 3207, Australia

314–321, 3rd Floor, Plot 3, Splendor Forum, Jasola District Centre, New Delhi - 110025, India

79 Anson Road, #06-04/06, Singapore 079906

Cambridge University Press is part of the University of Cambridge.

It furthers the University's mission by disseminating knowledge in the pursuit of education, learning and research at the highest international levels of excellence.

www.cambridge.org
Information on this title: www.cambridge.org/9780521734912

© Cambridge University Press 2016

This publication is in copyright. Subject to statutory exception and to the provisions of relevant collective licensing agreements, no reproduction of any part may take place without the written permission of Cambridge University Press.

First published 2016
First paperback edition 2019

A catalogue record for this publication is available from the British Library

Library of Congress Cataloging in Publication data
Magee, Glenn Alexander, 1966– editor.
The Cambridge handbook of western mysticism and esotericism / edited by Glenn Alexander Magee.
New York : Cambridge University Press, 2016. | Includes index.
LCCN 2015042979 | ISBN 9780521509831
LCSH: Mysticism – History. | Occultism – History.
LCC BF1999 .C3533 2016 | DDC 130–dc23
LC record available at http://lccn.loc.gov/2015042979

ISBN 978-0-521-50983-1 Hardback
ISBN 978-0-521-73491-2 Paperback

Cambridge University Press has no responsibility for the persistence or accuracy of URLs for external or third-party internet websites referred to in this publication, and does not guarantee that any content on such websites is, or will remain, accurate or appropriate.

*To Michael Murphy*

# CONTENTS

| | | |
|---|---|---|
| Acknowledgments | | *page* xi |
| Editor's Introduction | | xiii |
| List of contributors | | xxxvii |

|  | I ANTIQUITY | 1 |
|---|---|---|
| 1 | **Ancient Mysteries**<br>*Charles Stein* | 3 |
| 2 | **Pythagoras and Pythagoreanism**<br>*Joscelyn Godwin* | 13 |
| 3 | **Parmenides and Empedocles**<br>*Jessica Elbert Decker and Matthew Mayock* | 26 |
| 4 | **Plato, Plotinus, and Neoplatonism**<br>*Gwenaëlle Aubry* | 38 |
| 5 | **Hermetism and Gnosticism**<br>*Roelof van den Broek* | 49 |
| 6 | **Early Jewish Mysticism**<br>*Daphna Arbel* | 59 |
| 7 | **Early Christian Mysticism**<br>*April D. DeConick* | 69 |

|  | II THE MIDDLE AGES | 81 |
|---|---|---|
| 8 | **Sufism**<br>*William C. Chittick* | 83 |
| 9 | **Kabbalah**<br>*Brian Ogren* | 95 |
| 10 | **Medieval Christian Mysticism**<br>*Bruce Milem* | 107 |

| 11 | Hildegard of Bingen and Women's Mysticism<br>Anne L. Clark | 118 |

### III  THE RENAISSANCE AND EARLY MODERNITY — 131

| 12 | Renaissance Hermetism<br>Antoine Faivre | 133 |
| 13 | Christian Kabbalah<br>Peter J. Forshaw | 143 |
| 14 | Paracelsianism<br>Bruce T. Moran | 156 |
| 15 | Rosicrucianism<br>Hereward Tilton | 171 |
| 16 | Jacob Boehme and Christian Theosophy<br>Glenn Alexander Magee | 184 |
| 17 | Freemasonry<br>Jan A. M. Snoek | 200 |
| 18 | Swedenborg and Swedenborgianism<br>Jane Williams-Hogan | 211 |
| 19 | Mesmer and Animal Magnetism<br>Adam Crabtree | 223 |

### IV  THE NINETEENTH CENTURY AND BEYOND — 235

| 20 | Spiritualism<br>Cathy Gutierrez | 237 |
| 21 | H. P. Blavatsky and Theosophy<br>Michael Gomes | 248 |
| 22 | Rudolf Steiner and Anthroposophy<br>Robert McDermott | 260 |
| 23 | The Golden Dawn and the O.T.O.<br>Egil Asprem | 272 |
| 24 | G. I. Gurdjieff and the Fourth Way<br>Glenn Alexander Magee | 284 |
| 25 | C. G. Jung and Jungianism<br>Gerhard Wehr | 297 |
| 26 | René Guénon and Traditionalism<br>Mark Sedgwick | 308 |
| 27 | *Via Negativa* in the Twentieth Century<br>Arthur Versluis | 322 |

| | | |
|---|---|---|
| 28 | Contemporary Paganism<br>*Chas S. Clifton* | 334 |
| 29 | The New Age<br>*Olav Hammer* | 344 |

## V  COMMON THREADS — 357

| | | |
|---|---|---|
| 30 | Alchemy<br>*Lawrence M. Principe* | 359 |
| 31 | Astrology<br>*Kocku von Stuckrad* | 372 |
| 32 | Gnosis<br>*Wouter J. Hanegraaff* | 381 |
| 33 | Magic<br>*Wouter J. Hanegraaff* | 393 |
| 34 | Mathematical Esotericism<br>*Jean-Pierre Brach* | 405 |
| 35 | Panpsychism<br>*Lee Irwin* | 417 |
| 36 | Sexuality<br>*Hugh B. Urban* | 429 |

Suggestions for Further Reading — 441

Index — 463

# ACKNOWLEDGMENTS

The idea for this volume grew out of discussions over meals at a week-long academic conference on Western esotericism, held at the Esalen Institute in May 2007. I would therefore like to thank, first of all, conference organizers Jeffrey J. Kripal and Wouter J. Hanegraaff – particularly the latter. It was in conversation with Professor Hanegraaff that I originally floated the idea of proposing a volume on Western esotericism to Cambridge. He encouraged me to do so, but the scope of the volume was later widened to include mysticism as well. Thus, what began as a proposal for a modest collection of about a dozen or so essays grew into the large volume that you now hold in your hands.

Everything that happens at Esalen is due, directly or indirectly, to the generosity and inspiring influence of its "innkeeper," Michael Murphy. Without Mike, there would have been no conference, no conversations, and no book. Thus, I dedicate this volume to him.

For advice and guidance in the selection of authors and other matters, I must thank, again, Wouter Hanegraaff and Jeff Kripal, and also David Appelbaum, Antoine Faivre, Joscelyn Godwin, Lee Irwin, Peter Kingsley, Peter Manchester, Robert McDermott, Bernard McGinn, Barbara Newman, Frank Sinclair, and Arthur Versluis.

Thanks are also owed to Beatrice Rehl, my editor at Cambridge, for her support, good humor, and patience. Indeed, I must thank the contributors for their patience as well, since this project has been plagued by many setbacks and delays. Now that it has finally come to fruition, I hope that everyone involved will consider it worth the wait.

*G.A.M.*
**New York City**
*July 2015*

# EDITOR'S INTRODUCTION

## 1 A New Approach to the Hidden Intellectual History of the West

This handbook brings together articles on two subjects: Western mysticism and Western esotericism. These two areas are distinct, yet they are related so intimately that treating them together is not only possible but ultimately necessary if either is to be truly understood.

Mysticism in the West has tended to arise (as it has elsewhere in the world) within the context of a religious tradition, generally as a kind of deeper reflection on the inner meaning of the religion. This is obviously the case with Jewish, Christian, and Islamic mysticism. However, the origins of Western mysticism go back much further, to pagan polytheism in fact, and the mystery religions of Ancient Greece.

Scholarship on Western mysticism enjoys a long, established history and is almost as old as scholarship on the religions from which mysticism typically springs. The same is not true, however, for scholarship on Western esotericism. It is, in fact, a very young field. Defining "esotericism" is a difficult task, and one fraught with controversy. However, we may begin simply by noting that this is the word increasingly used today to designate currents of thought formerly referred to as "occultism" or as "the occult sciences" (terms that came into wide usage in the nineteenth century). These currents have a long history in the West, sometimes hidden and subterranean (as the word "occultism" implies) – at other times, in the Renaissance for example, as part of mainstream thought. Esoteric doctrines, schools, or practices include alchemy, astrology, magic, Kabbalism, Renaissance Hermetism, Freemasonry, Rosicrucianism, number symbolism, sacred geometry, Christian theosophy, spiritualism, mesmerism, and much else.[1]

---

[1] The terms "esotericism" and "esoteric writing" are also used by academics to refer to the practice of secrecy, of hiding one's meaning or intention behind an "exoteric" veneer. Here

The ideas and movements just mentioned are familiar, in one way or another, to most people. We know that they exercised a great influence in the past (and still do). We have encountered traces of them in literature, film, and fairy tales. They peek through the cracks of standard histories of philosophy, science, and literature when, for example, it is mentioned in passing that Renaissance art and science were influenced by hermetic and kabbalistic teachings; that Goethe was an alchemist, and Newton an astrologer; that Kant and Strindberg read Swedenborg, and Schelling was a spiritualist; that Blake and Hegel were influenced by Jacob Boehme; that W. B. Yeats was a member of the Hermetic Order of the Golden Dawn; and so on. These facts are mentioned, though not emphasized. They are seldom denied, but they are more or less avoided by most scholars. This began to change only recently.

In the 1930s, Paul Otto Kristeller became one of the first modern scholars to claim that the study of hermetic and esoteric literature was crucial for an understanding of the Renaissance. However, it was not until the publication of Frances Yates's *Giordano Bruno and the Hermetic Tradition* in 1964 that the academic study of esotericism really took off. Yates went on to write several other ground-breaking books, including *The Art of Memory, The Occult Philosophy in the Elizabethan Age*, and *The Rosicrucian Enlightenment*. Her work, in effect, spawned an entirely new discipline.

In 1965, an academic chair for the study of Western esotericism was established at the École Pratique des Hautes Études (Sorbonne) in Paris (currently held by Jean-Pierre Brach, and formerly by François Secret and Antoine Faivre). In 1999, a similar chair was established at the University of Amsterdam (currently held by Wouter J. Hanegraaff), where it is attached to a small department featuring several other specialists in esotericism and offering undergraduate and graduate-level degrees (see www.amsterdamhermetica.nl).[2] The European Society for the Study of Western Esotericism (www.esswe.org) held its first conference in July 2007, a major event, hosted

---

"esoteric" refers simply to "hidden doctrines" of any sort, including ones that are skeptical, atheistic, and materialistic. Leo Strauss and his school are famous for using the term "esoteric" in this manner. As should be obvious, the denotation of the word in this volume is quite different – though the two usages are related. For Strauss's views, see Leo Strauss, *Persecution and the Art of Writing* (Chicago: University of Chicago Press, 1952).

[2] In 2005, the University of Exeter in the United Kingdom became the world's third institution of higher learning to create a chair in esotericism. The position was held by Nicholas Goodrick-Clarke, who served as director of the Centre for the Study of Esotericism (EXESESO) within the College of Humanities at Exeter. However, following Goodrick-Clarke's untimely death in 2012, the university decided to close EXESESO.

by the University of Tübingen. Since 2001, the society has published a peer-reviewed journal, *Aries: Journal for the Study of Western Esotericism*.

In the United States, the Association for the Study of Esotericism (www.aseweb.org) was founded in 2002 by Arthur Versluis of Michigan State University, and has held biennial conferences. It publishes a web-based journal, *Esoterica*. There are now a number of scholars of esotericism teaching at American universities, many of them in religious studies departments. For many years now the meetings of the American Academy of Religion have included sessions on Western esotericism, beginning with the "Esotericism and Perennialism Group" in the mid-1980s. This group was an offshoot of the Hermetic Academy, an organization founded in 1980 by Robert A. McDermott, President Emeritus of the California Institute for Integral Studies.

The present volume includes contributions by many of today's leading scholars of Western esotericism, bringing them together with a number of prolific and talented scholars working in the area of Western mysticism. Treating these two fields together makes this *Handbook* unique. As we shall see, an understanding of the roots of esoteric currents almost always leads us back to the mystical traditions. Further, the work of many of the mystics was bound up with what today would be called esoteric or occult preoccupations.

Two things should be clear from what has been said thus far. First, these are fascinating subjects. Second, they constitute, in effect, the hidden intellectual history of the West, running like a dark thread through the fabric of the more conventional intellectual history we have all been taught. The influence of mystics and esotericists on science, philosophy, theology, literature, politics, and popular culture is immense, but it is a story scholars are only just beginning to tell. This volume constitutes a kind of *summa* of the present state of research.

However, the foregoing more or less presupposes that we know what the terms "mysticism" and "esotericism" mean. But how are we to define them, and to distinguish between them? And should we even attempt to? After all, on a certain understanding, these terms can be seen as virtually synonymous. The mystical has always been "hidden" – if only in the sense that it is difficult for most to access. The term "mysticism" itself is derived from the Greek adjective *mystikos*, meaning "pertaining to the mysteries (*ta mysteria*)," or the secret rites of Eleusis. This word ultimately derives from the Indo-European root *mu-*, meaning "to be silent." Yet, while everything that is mystical may be hidden (in the sense just mentioned), not everything that is hidden is mystical.

Gershom Scholem attempted to distinguish between the mystical and the esoteric as follows:

> Mysticism means a kind of knowledge which is by its very nature incommunicable. It cannot be directly transmitted; it can be made visible only indirectly, because its substance cannot be expressed in human language. Esoteric knowledge, on the other hand, means a kind of knowledge that may be communicable and might be communicated but whose communication is forbidden.[3]

But Scholem is using "esoteric knowledge" in a much narrower sense than is employed in this volume, and in the academic field of Western esotericism. As the reader will see, much of what currently falls under this rubric is not and never was "secret" or "forbidden," nor was it the property of an elite. To take merely one example, spiritualism was a populist movement with an egalitarian ethos, whose proponents were anything but secretive (see the essay by Cathy Gutierrez in the present volume).

Nevertheless, Scholem's understanding of mysticism is fundamentally correct and can be used as means not just to distinguish mysticism from esotericism (as the term is used by the authors herein) but also to discern how they are related.

## 2 The Nature of Mysticism

The essence of mysticism is to be found in the concept of *gnosis* (about which Wouter Hanegraaff has contributed an entire essay in this volume). *Gnosis* is precisely what was supposed to have been acquired by those who participated in *ta mysteria*: a direct perception of the ultimate truth of what is. This knowledge was life transforming and impossible to adequately express in words. If we examine all that is typically categorized as "mystical," we find that in one way or another it alludes to such an experience, or flows from the standpoint of one who has had it, and attempts to help others to be receptive to the same.[4] (It is, therefore, highly appropriate that the first essay in this

---

[3] Gershom Scholem, *Jewish Mysticism in the Middle Ages, The 1964 Allan Bronfman Lecture* (New York: Judaica Press, 1964), 3–4.
[4] A great many definitions of mysticism have been offered by scholars – too many to cite here. I recommend readers consult Bernard McGinn, *The Foundations of Mysticism*, Vol. 1: *The Presence of God: A History of Western Christian Mysticism* (New York: Crossroad, 1994), xv–xx. In many ways, William James's discussion of mysticism in *Varieties of Religious Experience* (1902) remains unsurpassed (see Lectures XVI and XVII in any unabridged edition).

volume, written by Charles Stein, introduces readers to what we know of the mystery rites of Eleusis.)

To be sure, there are significant differences between the mysticisms of Parmenides, Plato, Plotinus,[5] Pseudo-Dionysius, John Scotus Eriugena, the Kabbalists, the Sufis, the Rhineland mystics (Hildegard of Bingen, Meister Eckhart, etc.), and Christian theosophists such as Jacob Boehme – all of whom are discussed in this collection. Still greater differences are to be found between all the above and what those of us in the West call "Eastern mysticism": Vedanta, Shaivism, Tantra, Taoism, Zen, and so on. Nonetheless, there is an identity underlying these differences – a reason all of them have a "family resemblance" for us and lead us to group them under a single term, however inadequate that term may be.

All of the mystics – East and West – are concerned with knowledge of the transcendent source of all being, the object of *gnosis*. Since everything in our experience flows from this source, or owes its existence to it, the source itself cannot be understood in terms of the categories we employ in thinking or speaking about finite things. The doctrine that the source is "beyond the opposites" or that within it all conceptual oppositions meet or are left behind (the *coincidentia oppositorum*) is nearly universal to what we call mysticism. It follows that, according to mysticism's peculiar logic, the transcendent source transcends the distinction between transcendence and immanence. Further, if the being of all is to be found in a One that is beyond every duality, then in spite of appearances all really is one.

Thus, mysticism typically teaches that all finite things are connected; all are parts or aspects of a cosmic order – call it the *Tao*, the *Logos*, the Absolute, or what have you. We might also call it an "infinite whole," meaning a whole or One that is not limited by anything external to itself, thus making it simultaneously the most indeterminate being (since nothing determines it) and the most determinate one (since it is *the* One, subsuming all determinations). Usually, the mystics also hold that there is a fundamental identity between ourselves and the One. This doctrine is perhaps most starkly laid out in Vedanta, in the identity between *Atman* (one's true self or nature) and *Brahman* (the transcendent source of all being) – but the same teaching is to be found in Eckhart. Indeed, it is a perennial teaching and is often expressed as the identity of the macrocosm and the microcosm. Further, if the One/All is identical to the impersonal and universal soul of which each of us is a finite

---

[5] The first three figures listed here are commonly referred to as philosophers, and modern historians of philosophy would like to believe that there is a sharp distinction between mysticism and philosophy. The present volume – especially the essays dealing with these three figures – makes it clear that matters are not so simple.

inflection, then it would seem to follow that the being of all things is soul-like, or ensouled.

Now, the preceding is an attempt to describe what is typically taught by the mystics – with the usual caveat that there are countless variations and differences of emphasis. But it is crucially important to understand that when the mystics tell us these things, they are attempting to put into words the "information" conveyed wordlessly in the experience of *gnosis*. No such account can ever be fully adequate – yet the most brilliant writers and teachers among the mystics can give us a vivid glimpse. The typical mystical experience (the experience of *gnosis*) seems to involve several basic components. These include: a fundamental alteration in the *quality* of experience, as things seem to become more vivid or real; the sense that one is seeing into the true nature of things; the intuition that all is really one; the sense that the distinction between self and other has collapsed; and the overwhelming feeling of the *rightness* of things – that everything, just as it is, is fundamentally right. All of this is experienced at once, and in a form that is quite distinct from both thinking (in the sense of reasoning) and mundane sense experience. It is obvious how the doctrines of mysticism summarized earlier are an attempt to put the wordless into words; to convey in the form of communicable teachings, as far as possible, what is revealed in *gnosis*. (A classic, and highly personal, account of this attempt to render the "content" of *gnosis* in words is to be found in the writings of Jacob Boehme; see the essay on him in this volume.)

The foregoing account of the nature of mysticism should make it clear why it is necessary to distinguish it from esotericism. For what, after all, do astrology, magic, alchemy, and spirit-seeing have to do with what I have just discussed? Actually, as will slowly emerge, they have a great deal to do with mysticism. And yet they are distinct from it at the same time; esotericism is not mysticism. So what is it?

## 3 Approaches to Understanding Esotericism

Our first impulse is to try to identify what esoteric currents all have in common; to identify their essential characteristics. But when we speak of esotericism, we are speaking of a category that subsumes quite a lot of very different things. What can the four esoteric "sciences" just named – astrology, magic, alchemy, and spirit-seeing – all have in common? To say the least, it is not obvious. And so it has recently been suggested that instead of searching for the essential characteristics of esotericism, we should understand it instead through the history of how this catchall category was "constructed." This is the approach taken by Wouter Hanegraaff in his important book *Esotericism and the Academy: Rejected Knowledge in Western Culture*.

For Hanegraaff, the story of esotericism's construction begins in the Renaissance, when Florentine humanists argued for a fanciful "genealogy of wisdom" in which figures such as Plato, Plotinus, and Hermes Trismegistus were all seen as transmitting an ancient wisdom whose source, ultimately, was divine. This hugely influential "ancient wisdom narrative," as Hanegraaff refers to it, was in effect the first modern attempt at a history of philosophy. In the second half of the seventeenth century, however, Protestant German theologians went on the attack against the ancient wisdom narrative. Their aim was to "'purify' Christian theology from its contamination by pagan error."[6] Thus, they jettisoned the "Platonic orientalism" of late antiquity, Hermetism, Gnosticism, Kabbalism, theosophy, alchemy, and generally anything that seemed to somehow conflict with what they saw as true Christianity. Also cast out were the Renaissance purveyors of the ancient wisdom narrative – such as Ficino, Pico della Mirandola, and Bruno – as well as figures such as Paracelsus and Boehme.

The result was the creation of a kind of "wastebasket" of rejected knowledge (to use Hanegraaff's vivid description). Quite without intending to, these historians had created the category of what we call today "esotericism." From then on, these esoteric figures and movements – though they often had little in common – would be seen as all somehow belonging with one another in a "counter tradition." Secular Enlightenment historians basically adopted the approach of the Protestants, only this time esoteric currents were rejected not because of their apparent incompatibility with Christianity, but because they were considered "irrational." (Interestingly, both the Protestant theologians and the Enlightenment rationalists were united in their hostility to the esotericists' claims to "inner illumination."[7]) The result, to make a very long story short, was the construction of the history of science and philosophy that we are familiar with today. In both cases, Hanegraaff argues, what has occurred is that certain figures and schools of thought have been marginalized due to the prejudices of historians.

---

[6] Wouter J. Hanegraaff, *Esotericism and the Academy: Rejected Knowledge in Western Culture* (Cambridge: Cambridge University Press, 2012), 103.
[7] See Hanegraaff, Esotericism and the Academy, 137. It would be a gross error, however, to make a sharp distinction between the two groups. It was possible for someone to be both a Protestant theologian (or, at least, a Protestant) and an Enlightenment rationalist, and indeed many men saw themselves as such.

On the one hand, Hanegraaff has given us an account of the process by which different esoteric currents came to be understood as all belonging together under one rubric. On the other hand, he also argues that our modern conceptions of "real" science and "real" philosophy were formed in opposition to this discarded "other" – which was itself a construction of modern science and philosophy! There is thus a simple reason for the embarrassment of historians of philosophy and science when confronted with the facts mentioned earlier about Newton, Goethe, and Kant: To be rational and "modern" means *not* to believe in the esoteric.

This account of the construction of esotericism offers us a great deal of insight, but it does not follow from it that we cannot discern fundamental common features of things esoteric – and Hanegraaff does not claim otherwise. (Later on, I will very briefly discuss his own account of what characterizes esotericism.) A much more radical version of Hanegraaff's "constructivist" approach is to be found in the work of Kocku von Stuckrad, who, for all intents and purposes, denies that there is any such thing as esotericism with discernible, common features.[8] Instead, according to Stuckrad, we can speak only of "esoteric discourses," united solely by the fact that they are all "others" rejected by the cultural forces of modernity described earlier. Esotericism is, thus, merely a "construct."

This position invites a basic question: *In virtue of what* were esoteric thinkers, schools, and texts seen as belonging together? In virtue of what traits were they marginalized by modernity? We are faced with a question parallel to the one Socrates raises about piety in the *Euthyphro*: Is something esoteric because it was rejected by the Enlightenment; or was it rejected by the Enlightenment because it was esoteric (i.e., because it had certain specific features)? On most days, the items in my wastebasket have nothing in common other than that I no longer want them. But on the days I am pruning the house of specific sorts of things, the items in my wastebasket have a great deal in common – even though it might not be obvious to anyone other than myself.

If we turn, then, to attempts to identify the characteristic features of esotericism – the features that so enraged Enlightenment rationalists – we will find that the best place to begin is with the approach of Antoine Faivre, arguably the major figure in the academic study of esotericism now living. In *Access to Western Esotericism*, Faivre stipulates that there are four fundamental

---

[8] See Kocku von Stuckrad, *Locations of Knowledge in Medieval and Early Modern Europe* (Leiden: Brill, 2010). Stuckrad's approach is critiqued in Hanegraaff, *Esotericism and the Academy*, 361–367.

characteristics of esotericism (which he calls a "form of thought"), that is, four basic criteria for deciding whether something belongs to this category. He states, "By nature they are more or less inseparable, as we shall see, but methodologically it is important to distinguish between them."[9] These characteristics are:

1. "Correspondences." The entire universe is conceived in esoteric thought as an emblem book. "Everything is a sign," Faivre states.[10] The most fundamental of these correspondences is that of the macrocosm and the microcosm, which underlies, among other things, astrology.
2. "Living Nature." This is the notion of what is sometimes called "cosmic sympathies" (which is obviously related to the idea of correspondences). Nature is a living whole, whose finite members exist in relations of sympathy or antipathy to one another. As Faivre points out, it is the knowledge of these sympathies and antipathies that forms the basis of magic (as well as, just to mention two more examples, Paracelsism and animal magnetism).
3. "Imagination and Mediations." Faivre explains: "The idea of correspondences presumes already a form of imagination inclined to reveal and use mediations of all kinds, such as rituals, symbolic images, mandalas, intermediary spirits."[11]
4. "Experience of Transmutation." Esotericism tends to involve the attempt to effect a fundamental transformation of things in the world (as in alchemical transmutation or magic) and/or of the self. Of course, nuclear physics also deals with the fundamental transformation of things in the world, so here we must note the obvious, that esoteric transmutation involves, as Faivre puts it, "the passage from one plane [of reality] to another."[12] And the other plane, standing opposed to this mundane one, is not accessible by empirical science.

In addition to these four fundamental features of esotericism, Faivre also lists two other elements that are frequently, though not always, found together with those just discussed:

---

[9] Antoine Faivre, *Access to Western Esotericism* (Albany: State University of New York Press, 1994), 10. As I discuss shortly, Faivre actually lists six criteria on pp. 10–15 of *Access*. Faivre repeats the same list in *Modern Esoteric Spirituality*, ed. Antoine Faivre and Jacob Needleman (New York: Crossroad, 1995), xv–xx; and in *Theosophy, Imagination, Tradition* (Albany: State University of New York Press, 2000), xxi–xxiv.
[10] Faivre, *Access*, 10.
[11] Faivre, *Access*, 12.
[12] Faivre, *Access*, 13.

5. "The Praxis of the Concordance." This involves a tendency on the part of many esoteric thinkers to try and find links between different traditions or teachings, or among all of them. This praxis is itself conceived as a means to enlightenment: It is the identification of the one, true, universal tradition. One finds this feature displayed prominently in the "Traditionalist" school of René Guénon, and in C. G. Jung (both of whom are given their own essays herein), among others.
6. "Transmission." Esoteric teachings are "transmitted from master to disciple following a pre-established channel." The validity of esoteric knowledge somehow depends on this pedigree, and "initiation" into certain paths is only possible through an unbroken line of transmission.[13]

Of course, any attempt to define esotericism (or any other subject, for that matter) in terms of a set of necessary and jointly sufficient conditions will never please everyone. There will always be some scholar eager to assert that while we are quite willing to call *x* esoteric, it does not fit all the stipulated criteria. But part of the problem here is that many academics are so lost in minutiae and so wedded to ultra-fine-grained distinctions that they are often unable to see the proverbial forest for the trees. Indeed, some are so averse to generalizations that they brand any attempt to synthesize knowledge with the shopworn postmodern smear "essentialism." But it is the nature of the human mind to seek the "essence" of things, by which I mean simply a fundamental common trait, or set of traits. Speaking of essential traits is problematic only when there are none, or when we have misidentified them. (And postmodernists are oblivious to the irony of grouping their opponents under the rubric of essentialism — as if, after all, they shared some common essence.)

In the main, I think that Faivre's methodology is sound — and at least gives us a place to start.[14] It is difficult to think of any esoteric currents discussed in this book to which his four primary criteria do not apply. But in order to see those currents as they were seen by the Enlightenment zealots who, in Hanegraaff's account, marginalized them and thereby created an esoteric counter tradition, we have to go deeper.

---

[13] Faivre, *Access*, 14–15.
[14] Both Hanegraaff and Stuckrad have criticized Faivre's approach. I am not altogether persuaded by their criticisms, though I recognize that Faivre's account has its flaws. As will become apparent, I am using it as a means to reach what I regard as a deeper level of analysis.

## 4 The Nature of Esotericism – A Synthesis of Approaches

If one considers Faivre's first two criteria, "correspondences" and "living nature," one will realize that what is at work in both cases is a kind of "qualitative" approach to understanding nature. For instance, the Renaissance magus Marsilio Ficino (1433–1499) believed in a *spiritus mundi* permeating the entire universe, which human beings can draw on to improve their lot. This activity is magic, and it consists primarily in attracting the influences of particular planets through the use of various substances associated with them: precious stones, animals, scents, colors, and so forth. To draw on the influence of Jupiter, Ficino advises us to use "Jovial things" such as silver, sugar, and white honey; to think Jovial thoughts; and to bear in mind Jupiter's association with certain animals, such as eagles and lambs.[15]

Thus, correspondences are based on qualitative identities: Though silver, white honey, and eagles are quite different, they all possess a "Jovial quality" (or, we could say, they are qualitatively related to Jupiter). At the basis of the idea of "cosmic sympathies" is just this notion of qualitative ties. Needless to say, this way of thinking is now extremely alien to us, precisely because it was discarded in the modern period in favor of the *quantitative* approach to understanding nature. According to the modern outlook, all qualitative differences ultimately reduce to quantitative ones: to the combination and recombination, in quantifiable patterns and proportions, of basic material particles that are, in themselves, bereft of any of the qualities familiar to us from experience. This quantitative approach is, of course, still very much with us – and not just in science departments. It is at the basis of the modern worldview itself: our way of looking at life, at value, at being as such. It is not for nothing that René Guénon described modernity as "the reign of quantity" (see the essay on him in this volume).[16]

The qualitative approach to nature is not just a feature of esotericism: One finds it in what we normally categorize as ancient philosophy and science. So, for example, Aristotle in *On Generation and Corruption* speaks of what has come to be called the "four elements" – earth, air, fire, and water – but which

---

[15] See *Marsilio Ficino*, ed. Angela Voss (Berkeley: North Atlantic Books, 2006), 116.
[16] We find earlier esotericists explicitly aware of the conflict between their approach and modernity. To take but one example, Franz Josef Molitor (1779–1860) states: "Each really-existent creaturely essence exists thus in a living form. However, in our current fallen condition, it is no longer easily possible to know the inner qualitative essence of things ... which is possible via the holy language. We have become concerned only with the outward 'objective,' quantitative relationships among things; we have forgotten that the outer forms or signatures of things reveal the world of their inner, spiritual qualities." Quoted in Arthur Versluis, *Theosophia* (Hudson, NY: Lindesfarne Press, 1994), 77.

would be more accurately described as the four material qualities: the cold and dry, the hot and wet, the hot and dry, and the cold and wet. These four elements were, of course, bequeathed to alchemy. And it is partly on account of alchemy's qualitative approach that it was gradually divorced from chemistry.[17] (There are other major reasons for alchemy's marginalization, which I will come to in a moment.)

Consider next Faivre's category of "imagination and mediations." Faivre himself notes (as quoted earlier) that this way of thinking makes possible the worldview that contains correspondences and cosmic sympathies. And to the modern mindset, it is fatally and irredeemably "subjective." In the modern worldview, objectivity is virtually the same as measurability: Whatever cannot be measured, for all intents and purposes, may be said not to exist. Thus, the modern ideal of objectivity is inextricably tied to its emphasis on the quantitative. And this makes modernity fundamentally "extraverted," for only the "out there" can be measured. The "in here," my private world of thoughts, feelings, and (above all) imagination cannot be measured in any truly objective fashion. The idea that private intuitions, feelings, and imaginative reveries might be guides to truth is wholly anathema to the modern worldview. For modernity, the subjective is a dark realm; a source of falsehood and deception. Thus, any knowledge claims based on such subjective sources are simply ruled out. Even in modern psychology, which is supposed to be the science of subjectivity, strenuous efforts have been made to banish subjectivity. Behaviorism, of course, is the most extreme example.

One can easily see that a tremendous amount of what we classify as the esoteric is based on the subjective sources just described. After all, how did Ficino (and the older thinkers he relied on) arrive at the idea that there was some kind of sympathy between, for instance, the planet Jupiter and lambs? It was through the use of imagination: through getting a certain "feel" for the connections between things. Occultists such as Ficino will claim that others following the same path, and with a similar openness and sensitivity, will arrive at the same conclusions – and thus their assertions of correspondences and sympathies are genuinely objective, by virtue of intersubjective agreement. Needless to say, this position is not taken seriously by modern thinkers.

The same subjective element is to be found in alchemy – that is, the same reliance on felt or intuited connections. The essay on alchemy in this volume (by Lawrence Principe) discusses how the Jungian school, and others, have emphasized the "spiritual" element of alchemy virtually to the point of denying that laboratory alchemy took place. My own position is that

[17] See Versluis, *Theosophia*, 97.

alchemy was indeed a physical process, but inseparable – in the minds of most alchemists – from a spiritual one. (Heinrich Khunrath, 1560–1605, and Oswald Croll, ca. 1563–1609, are excellent examples.) This is arguably the primary reason it was banished from the discipline we now know as chemistry.

Needless to say, everything in esotericism that involves access to "higher worlds" (whether through visions, "astral projection," or what have you), spirit-seeing, mediumship, "psychic healing," precognition, telepathy, sympathetic magic, and so forth all depends on claims that flow from the authority of some supernormal aspect of subjectivity. This brings us directly to Faivre's fourth aspect of esotericism, "the experience of transmutation," which involves, as I have already quoted, "the passage from one plane to another." In the eyes of modernity, the greatest sin committed by esotericism is not specifically the subjectivism I have just discussed but rather the claim to have obtained (via special subjective powers) access to "other realities," which in principle cannot be reached by the empirical methods of modern science. As noted earlier, for modernity what is not measurable "out there" – directly or indirectly – is not real. There is not a single aspect of what is treated in this volume as esotericism that does not explicitly or implicitly challenge this modern conviction.

Finally, Faivre's fifth and sixth aspects of esotericism, treated together, bring us to a further and especially revealing insight into the unity of esotericism, from the perspective of modernity. Faivre speaks, again, of "the praxis of the concordance" and of "transmission." The common denominator of these two is reverence for the authority of tradition. And this is arguably not only the key element involved in modernity's rejection of esoteric currents – it may well give us the key feature of modernity as such.[18] Contempt for the authority of tradition is as central to the modern mindset as the "reign of quantity." For the esotericists, truth is to found in the oldest of old things; the new and original are generally viewed with suspicion.[19] For the moderns, only the new and the original are worthy of respect; the past is a record of mistakes, not a gold mine of eternal verities, and the more distant the past the darker the gloom of ignorance and irrationality.

Modernity was born in the reaction against authority of all kinds. In philosophy and the sciences, it was usually the authority of Aristotle, and

---

[18] August Heumann (1681–1764), often cited as the founder of the modern discipline of the history of philosophy, claimed that one of the worst sins of the esotericists was that they appeal to tradition rather than to logic. See Hanegraaff, *Esotericism and the Academy*, 131.

[19] A notable exception to this is Paracelsus, who often attacked tradition. Many Paracelsians did not follow him in this, however.

those who were taken (often erroneously) to be true to his thought. What is interesting, however, is that Aristotle himself never appeals to authority. He begins most of his works by explaining why his predecessors were wrong and is universally quoted as having said "Dear is Plato, dearer still truth" (and though no one can find this line in Aristotle's writings, it is nonetheless true to his spirit). Imagine, therefore, the outrage the fathers of modernity must have felt when sitting in judgment on esoteric traditions that not only explicitly appealed to authority in making truth claims but that – as per Faivre's praxis of the concordance – viewed the search for agreement among the authorities as a method for discovering truth! (An appeal to the majority of authorities, in other words.) Here, we have one of the principal factors in the separation of alchemy from chemistry – or, we might say, the construction of the modern discipline of chemistry. Modern chemistry accepts no appeals to authority, only testing, observation, and experiment. The alchemical tradition, on the other hand, abounds in such appeals.[20]

We have now discovered four fundamental features esoteric currents have in common, which led to their marginalization by the Enlightenment. Taken together, these elements constitute the antithesis of the spirit of modernity:

1. A qualitative approach to understanding nature – as opposed to the quantitative approach of modernity.
2. A reliance on subjectivity and subjective impressions of a highly rarefied nature – as opposed to the rejection of the subjective in favor of what is "objective" and measurable.
3. Knowledge claims regarding other aspects of reality (or other sorts of beings) accessible only by those subjective means – as opposed to the narrowly-defined empiricism of modernity.
4. Reverence for the authority of tradition as a source of truth – as opposed to modernity's rejection of tradition and insistence that history is the record of our emergence from darkness into the light.[21]

---

[20] See Hanegraaff, *Esotericism and the Academy*, 202–207, for a discussion of how preoccupation with the idea of recovering a lost tradition led to the marginalization of what we now call alchemy and the sharp divide between alchemy as pseudo-science and chemistry as legitimate science.

[21] These four fundamental characteristics are not meant to supplant the analysis offered by Faivre, but rather to deepen it. The four I have offered constitute an attempt to identify the root assumptions or attitudes that make possible the four (or, rather, the six) discussed by Faivre. Hanegraaff also perceives that what Faivre has offered as the characteristics of esotericism constitute, in effect, a repudiation of the modern worldview. His observations complement my own: "the notion of 'correspondences' is clearly an alternative to instrumental causality, 'living nature' stands against a mechanistic worldview, 'imagination/meditations' implies a multi-leveled neoplatonic cosmology as opposed to a

Understood in terms of these four features, what we know today as the different varieties of esotericism had to be rejected by the Enlightenment. One of the interesting things that emerges from this analysis is the ease with which one can identify the fundamental features of modernity (named as the second element in each numbered item above) precisely in terms of what it rejected (thus supporting Hanegraaff's thesis that the modern identity was partly constructed through what it disowned).

It would be far too simplistic, however, to say that these four characteristics constitute the essence of the "pre-modern worldview." Matters are much more complex than that, regardless of what early modern authors may have thought. As we have already seen, in certain ways Aristotle was much closer to the moderns than they thought he was. Indeed, of the four characteristics just summarized, only the first would be applicable to him, and then only with certain qualifications. Aristotle would, in fact, have vigorously repudiated claims to special, subjective revelations.[22] Whereas an argument can be made that Parmenides, though classed with Aristotle among the philosophers, fits all four (see the essay about him in this volume). In a certain sense, there have always been "ancients" and "moderns." Aristotle is much closer to the modern temperament than was, for example, C. G. Jung, who nonetheless dressed up his thought in the garb of modern science.

Still, while esotericism cannot be identified with the ancient worldview *simpliciter*, Hanegraaff makes an excellent point when he suggests that the "red thread" running throughout esotericism is paganism. He writes, "The factor of 'paganism' has been neglected by modern scholars of Western esotericism to an extent that seems amazing at first sight: While the importance of its specific historical manifestations (particularly hermetism) is obviously recognized, it plays no structural role in how the field has been constructed or defined."[23] The Protestant theologians who cast out all that we now call esotericism due to its "un-Christian" qualities were certainly bigoted, but they were not wrong. A little reflection on the esoteric topics and forms of thought discussed herein will suffice to reveal either their origin in the pagan, pre-Christian milieu, or their affinities with it. Astrology,

---

cosmos reducible to only matter in motion, and 'transmutation' implies the theosophical/ alchemical process of regeneration by which fallen man and nature are reunited with the divine." See Hanegraaff, *Esotericism and the Academy*, 254. As noted earlier, however, Hanegraaff is critical of Faivre's approach. See especially pp. 352–354.
[22] In the short treatise *De divinatione per somnum*, Aristotle expresses considerable skepticism about prophetic dreams.
[23] Hanegraaff, *Esotericism and the Academy*, 369.

magic, and number symbolism (think Pythagoras), spiritualism (think shamanism and necromancy), and panpsychism are obvious examples. And one has only to scratch the so-called Christians a bit – men such as Ficino, Pico, Paracelsus, and Boehme – to find the pagan.

It seems, therefore, that the features of esotericism discussed earlier are characteristic of a certain way of thinking that was indeed ubiquitous in the ancient world – but that is also perennial. We lack a good word for it and keep changing our minds. "Esotericism" is merely the term currently in vogue – though it is no better a choice than "occultism," and practically means the same thing. Historians such as Hanegraaff are correct to note that before modernity, and well into modernity's infancy, what we call esotericism not only coexisted with what we now think of as science and philosophy, but the lines between them were often unclear. Yet it is a fact that what has been lumped together under the rubric of esotericism has discernible common features that set it apart from the tendencies that were ultimately victorious in the modern period.

The picture that emerges is that the tapestry of Western intellectual history was woven out of a number of distinct and often antagonistic strands. But in the distant past, the figures in the tapestry – not surprisingly – often did not discern the individual strands themselves, or their antagonism. The effect of the Enlightenment was not to "construct" esotericism but to *reveal* it as a distinct current of thought, or worldview, with perceptible features. For the first time, we became aware of esotericism as a discernible tendency of the human spirit, when the stark contrast with the ideology of modernity finally made its outlines clear. Ironically, the Enlightenment did a far more rigorous job of delineating the nature of the esoteric than the Renaissance proponents of the ancient wisdom narrative. In doing so, the Enlightenment also inadvertently offered to those who felt repulsed and alienated by modernity a way to connect the dots between the different strains of archaic "irrationalism" to which they felt a passionate and intuitive attraction.

We are now in a position to sum things up. "Esotericism" refers to a number of theories, practices, and approaches to knowledge united by their participation in a premodern, largely pagan worldview. Central to this worldview is commitment to the idea of the unity of existence – that existence is an interrelated whole in which seemingly dissimilar things exist in qualitative correspondence and vibrant, living sympathy. The ruling correspondence is "as above, so below": The objects that surround us (and their relationships) mirror, in a fashion that can be called "emblematic," the fundamental features of the universe as a whole. Most important of all, we mirror those features in our own bodies and souls. These correspondences are discovered through the cultivation of supernormal aspects of human subjectivity, especially of the imagination. Esotericists typically hold that such knowledge can be utilized to effect changes in the world or in the self through causal mechanisms that empiricism finds inexplicable (and, therefore, rejects as impossible). This commitment usually goes hand in hand with the belief that the same supernormal aspects of the subject can reveal the existence of other dimensions of reality, usually hidden from view. Further, esotericists typically believe that the truths and practices just mentioned are of the greatest antiquity – perhaps once widely disseminated and openly proclaimed, but now (and for a great many centuries) hidden and preserved by a few special individuals or schools. Discovery in esotericism is almost always rediscovery.

## 5 The Relation of Mysticism and Esotericism

The preceding account should already have alerted readers to points at which esotericism and mysticism seem to converge. I have argued that a particular worldview is at the root of esotericism, one that asserts that existence is an interconnected whole shot through with correspondences and sympathies, and that the most fundamental of these correspondences is that of macrocosm and microcosm.

But this is precisely what I identified earlier as the core mystical teaching – the "doctrine" that emerges when mystics attempt to convey in words what the experience of *gnosis* has taught them. Thus, "esotericism" is founded on "mysticism." I have placed these words in quotes once again just to remind readers that the words themselves are inadequate, and that analysis of their literal meaning is not a reliable means to understand that to which they refer. It would be much more accurate to simply state that esotericism is founded on *gnosis*, either directly (when esotericists themselves have the experience of *gnosis*) or indirectly (when esotericists put their faith in the testimony of those who have had the experience). Everything treated in this book as esotericism – alchemy, astrology, magic, number symbolism, visions of other worlds, spiritualism, and so on – is founded in one way or another on the mystical teaching of *hen kai pan* (One and all), and everything that it entails.

It is useful in this context to recall one of the expressions that has been supplanted by the term "esotericism": the "occult sciences." This is normally regarded as loose talk, as a quaint, makeshift way of referring to our subject matter. But there is more to the term than meets the eye. Mysticism affords us with a special experience (if we are fortunate) or with the next-best thing: reports by those who have had the experience. The various items grouped together as esotericism, by contrast, mainly consist in techniques or practices or specialized areas of investigation (in other words, "sciences," to use the term charitably). Mysticism is *gnosis*; esotericism is *technē* (technique or art). And, as I have argued, this *technē* is founded on *gnosis*.

However, it would be highly misleading to gloss this as "mysticism is theory, esotericism is practice." When an astrologer creates a birth chart and attempts to thereby predict the course of an individual's life, this can certainly be described as a technique or practice. However, it is founded on the astrological *theory* that the stars exercise some kind of causal influence over individuals and events. There is thus both astrological theory and practice. However, the theory is founded on the deeper conviction that the universe is one, and that everything is connected to everything else, including microcosm to macrocosm. This conviction is the fruit of *gnosis*.

Believers in astrology will claim a kind of "empirical proof" for their art, asserting that astrological predictions are borne out by events. If this were true a significant amount of the time, it would constitute proof for astrological theory – and we could say that it would also offer proof of the deeper, mystical conviction of the unity of all things, and the correspondence of macrocosm and microcosm. But those mystical convictions were not arrived at as a result of observing the results of astrological practice, or as a result of inferences drawn from any esoteric practice. Indeed, they are not the result of inferences of any kind. The mystical worldview is the product of *gnosis*, and it is the deep assumption that is brought to esoteric practices of all sorts, not derived from them. Esotericism is founded on mysticism (i.e., esoteric *technē* is founded on mystical *gnosis*), not the other way around.

Magic provides us with yet another example. As Hanegraaff makes clear in the essay on magic in this volume, the term itself has been used and abused in a great variety of ways. But setting aside the checkered history of the word, when we use it today we are generally referring to a perennial phenomenon found in all cultures throughout all of history: the belief that it is possible for certain individuals, drawing on mysterious and supernormal powers of the soul and using such means as spells, incantations, amulets, and talismans, to manipulate cosmic sympathies or correspondences in order to effect changes in themselves, in the physical world, or even in the powers governing the universe.

Contrary to what is sometimes claimed, this use of the term "magic" is not of recent vintage. Whereas for the Greeks *mageia* was generally associated with the activities of Persian *magoi* (magi), for the Romans *magia* took on a broad meaning more or less identical to our use of "magic." In his *Naturalis historia*, Pliny the Elder (23–79) uses the term *magicae vanitates* ("magical vanities") to refer to the casting of spells, the making of amulets and talismans, and forms of divination. Understood in this way, magic is clearly a *technē* (as reflected in the familiar expression "magical arts," and in the literal meaning of "witchcraft"). And it is a *technē* that depends, once more, on the worldview that teaches that the universe is one, and that everything is related to everything else through complex patterns of correspondence and sympathy (thus, the species of sorcery scholars call "sympathetic magic"). Indeed, magic depends especially on one of the key revelations of *gnosis*: the identity of macrocosm and microcosm. In theory, magic is only possible through the felt experience, in the practitioner, of a literal sympathy, connection, or even identity with higher powers.

All of the foregoing should clarify why it makes sense to treat Western mysticism and esotericism together in one volume (again, construing these terms just in the senses stipulated earlier). Understanding esotericism leads us back to mysticism, as the fundamental theoretical groundwork for esoteric currents.[24] Indeed, esotericism is virtually unintelligible without an appreciation for its roots in mystic *gnosis*. And it can be plausibly argued that *gnosis* leads to esoteric *technē*, to the development of the various occult sciences, and the preoccupation with them. Thus, we frequently find mystics of all types engaged in esoteric practices. An excellent example would be the kabbalists – both Jewish and Christian – who, in addition to claiming to be recipients of *gnosis*, also engaged in astrology, magic, alchemy, and gematria.

A further area for inquiry, too complex to explore here, is the role of esoteric practices in leading one to *gnosis*. Western mystics are often quite silent concerning the techniques they use to obtain *gnosis*. But we know that this experience often led to the development of practices for repeating (or deepening) the experience, and for leading others to it. It is also quite true that some of the occult sciences, which depend ultimately on the wisdom conveyed in *gnosis*, may in turn have served as propaedeutic to the actual experience of *gnosis* itself.

Finally, I should note that there is a difficult philosophical issue surrounding the relationship between mysticism and esotericism – again, one too complex to be elaborated here, but on which the reader should reflect. Mystical *gnosis* typically has the effect of helping us accept reality *as it is*, of bringing us peace. (I noted earlier that the typical mystical experience involves the intuition of both the unity and rightness of existence.) So

---

[24] I would argue that the exact same relationship between esotericism and mysticism holds true for the non-Western equivalents of these. And, as already implied, I do believe that these categories, as I have defined them, are universal and cross-culturally valid. The present volume, of course, confines itself to their Western inflections.

much of esotericism, on the other hand, is concerned with changing reality: gaining knowledge or powers that might enable us to alter or control objects, situations, and events, either for selfish or selfless purposes. Magic, alchemy, astrology, and all other forms of divination are obvious examples.

## 6 Methodological Considerations

As noted earlier, Western esotericism as an academic discipline is very young. Consequently, at present there is a great deal of debate concerning methodological issues. To put the matter as starkly as possible, scholars of Western esotericism today are divided between those who see the careful study and documentation of esoteric currents as a means to discover important truths about the universe and human nature, and those who regard such an interest as incompatible with scholarly objectivity.[25] Some of the latter have described themselves as "methodological agnostics."[26] They tend to refer to the former approach, which they vigorously oppose, with the rather infelicitous term "religionism."[27] The agnostics reject religionism not just because they see it as an approach that tends to produce biased or inaccurate scholarship, but also because some of them are committed to postmodern relativism and historicism.

These issues are far too complex to be treated adequately in this Introduction. I will therefore limit myself to the observation that a middle ground between the religionist and methodological agnostic positions seems possible. There can be no rapprochement between their guiding philosophical assumptions: the conviction that there is timeless truth to be found in mysticism and esotericism (or in anything else) is completely incompatible with historicism. Nevertheless, I think it is possible to conceive of a methodology that combines the virtues of both approaches.

One should investigate mystical and esoteric texts and traditions in as unbiased a manner as possible, always with the willingness to abandon one's cherished presuppositions, if they prove untenable. But it is a *non sequitur* to assert that any interest in discovering truth through those sources makes scholarly objectivity impossible. After all, if it is truth that is sought through the study of mysticism and esotericism, it does not help us at all if we

---

[25] One can find the same difference among scholars of mysticism. But since esotericism is the younger and less familiar field, I will concentrate on it in this section.
[26] See Hanegraaff, *Esotericism and the Academy*, especially 357–358, for a description of this position, of which he is one of the major advocates.
[27] Major examples of "religionist" scholars of esotericism include Henry Corbin, Mircea Eliade, and C. G. Jung.

utilize (or generate) false historical claims or allow prejudice and wishful thinking to cloud our judgment.

A useful model here might be academic scholarship on the history of philosophy as it is practiced today, which can be seen as cutting just such a middle course as I am advocating here. Scholars who research the history of philosophy are all trained philosophers, teaching in university departments of philosophy. They all have their own philosophical views, and many tend to have very strong affinities for the historical figures and movements they write about. Thus, Plato scholars tend to be Platonists, Kant scholars tend to be Kantians, Hegel scholars tend to be Hegelians, and so on – all usually, it is important to say, in some more or less qualified sense. (No one believes that literally everything said by their favorite philosophers is true.)

All these scholars seek truth through the thinkers they study, but most are not only capable of objectivity concerning those thinkers, they are in fact their most perceptive critics. Thus, to take one example, Kantian Kant scholars analyze, reconstruct, and critique his arguments, pointing out their weaknesses and admitting when the great man's writings become too obscure for comment. Indeed, it is the Kantian Kant scholars who know the weaknesses of the philosopher best – precisely because their affinity for the spirit of the philosophy makes them especially attuned to the ways in which the letter is inadequate to it.

Of course, no one can be entirely objective. But if some scholars today have arrived at a point where they believe that objectivity demands we abjure the love of wisdom, then surely they have taken a wrong turn. Indeed, it may be the case that *only* a reflective or philosophical approach to esotericism will, in the long run, succeed in provoking widespread interest in these currents among serious thinkers. The simple reason is that such an approach can show us that not everything in esotericism is rubbish after all, and that some profound insights are to be found there. In other words, it can show us why this subject is genuinely worth our time. (It is difficult to see how a "purely empirical" approach such as that advocated by some, let alone a historicist approach, can do this.[28])

---

[28] On methodological agnosticism as an empirical approach, see again Hanegraaff, *Esotericism and the Academy*, 357; and Hanegraaff, "Empirical Method in the Study of Esotericism," *Method & Theory in the Study of Religion* 7:2 (1995), 99–129. As to historicism, it involves a troubling paradox. Implicitly, its adherents claim to speak from a privileged, ahistorical perspective that historicism itself declares impossible. They claim to stand on a higher level than, for example, the Enlightenment intellectuals who marginalized esotericism, and to be able to discern objective truths that they failed to see (e.g., that there is no such thing as objective truth). Indeed, the historicists implicitly claim to stand at the summit of the mountain itself, and to be able to make a judgment about the entire history of ideas – namely, that there is no truth to be

One of the great virtues of the methodological agnostics is that they have called for us to reassess intellectual history – to read, for example, the *Hermetica* alongside the works of Plato, Boehme alongside Bacon, and so on. We should do this, however, not just to have a richer and more complete account of the history of ideas, but also to have a richer and more complete understanding of ourselves and our world. Of course, we must separate the wheat from the chaff. The reader will find, on delving into these essays, that there are rather great differences between the truth claims made by esotericists. And some of what we classify as esotericism really is superstition and illusion, and thus merely of historical interest.

The authors featured in the present volume do not represent any one methodology or school of thought. The reader will find both "religionists" and "methodological agnostics" among them, as well as some who would reject both labels. Thus, there is a good deal of disagreement among the authors (though sometimes this is not superficially obvious). The essays in this volume are introductory and do not presuppose any prior knowledge of their subject matter. Needless to say, providing readers with an introduction to these subjects involves exposing them to differences of scholarly opinion.

Nevertheless, while these essays are introductory, they are anything but conventional. Many of the authors in the volume are taking bold, original, and controversial approaches to their subjects. Thus, readers will be introduced to scholarship on Western mysticism and esotericism that is at the cutting edge of research. This means that while the volume is primarily geared toward students and others with no prior knowledge, even those who are already well acquainted with these fields will find material here that is surprising and new.

---

had in any of it, save the absolute truth of historicism. One way out of this paradox would be for historicists to embrace the historical situatedness of their theory; to embrace, perhaps, the thesis that it is simply the perspective of modern, secular, European academics disillusioned by the carnage of two world wars and by the failure of progressivism. (And that, going a step further, historicism is exactly the sort of philosophy one would expect to emerge in an age of cultural decline.) Such an approach, which historicizes historicism, would see it merely as the perspective of a particular population within a certain culture, forged under a unique set of historical circumstances – and as simply one possible intellectual option among many. This approach has the virtue of making the *act* of asserting historicism consistent with *what* it asserts. But it also abandons any claim to the objective truth of historicism, thus inviting old-fashioned lovers of wisdom to simply step over it and go on climbing upward toward the sunlight. Finally, a specific difficulty for those methodological agnostics who endorse historicism is that historicism is not "empirically verifiable." On this point see Leo Strauss, "Natural Right and the Historical Approach," in *An Introduction to Political Philosophy*, ed. Hilail Gildin (Detroit: Wayne State University Press, 1989), 109–110.

A note about organization: The first four parts of the volume ("Antiquity," "The Middle Ages," "The Renaissance and Early Modernity," "The Nineteenth Century and Beyond") organize the essays in rough chronological order. Some essays, however, cover currents or schools of thought that span several historical epochs. In such cases, the essay is grouped in the historical division representing the period in which the particular current is thought to have originated or to have first come to light. For example, the Jewish Kabbalah is a tradition that continues to this day. However, as a distinct form of Jewish mysticism, it first appears in the Middle Ages and is hence to be found in that section of the volume. Part V, "Common Threads," is devoted to a number of more or less perennial facets of mysticism and/or esotericism, such as astrology, number symbolism, magic, and *gnosis*.

Full citations of the major sources (both primary and secondary) for the essays are given in footnotes accompanying each. Readers who wish to delve more deeply into these topics should consult those sources, as well as the material listed under "Suggestions for Further Reading" at the end of the volume.

For readers coming to these subjects for the first time, exploring this volume will be like discovering a lost continent of Western intellectual history. I envy them.

# CONTRIBUTORS

**Daphna Arbel** is Professor of Early Jewish Literature at the University of British Columbia, Vancouver, Canada.

**Egil Asprem** received his Ph.D. in 2013 from the University of Amsterdam. He is the author of *The Problem of Disenchantment: Scientific Naturalism and Esoteric Discourse, 1900–1939* (2014) and *Arguing with Angels: Enochian Magic and Modern Occulture* (2012).

**Gwenaëlle Aubry** is Researcher in Philosophy at the CNRS (Centre Jean Pépin, Paris-Villejuif). Her works include *Plotin. Traité 53 (I, 1)*, introduction, translation, commentary, and notes (2004); *Dieu sans la puissance. Dunamis et Energeia chez Aristote et chez Plotin* (2006).

**Jean-Pierre Brach** teaches the History of Esoteric Currents in Modern and Contemporary Europe at the École Pratique des Hautes Études, Paris. He is coeditor of *Politica Hermetica* and has published on topics ranging from early modern Christian Kabbalah and magic to number symbolism and contemporary occultism.

**Roelof van den Broek** is Emeritus Professor of the History of Christianity at Utrecht University, The Netherlands. His works include *Studies in Gnosticism and Alexandrian Christianity* (1996) and *Gnostic Religion in Antiquity* (Cambridge, 2013).

**William C. Chittick** is Professor of Religious Studies at Stony Brook University. He is author and translator of many books and articles on Muslim mystics and philosophers; the most recent is *The Unveiling of the Mysteries* (2015).

**Anne Clark** is Professor of Religion at the University of Vermont. She has published two books on Elisabeth of Schönau and articles on medieval mystics, gender, visual culture in medieval Christianity, and the use of cognitive theory to explore religious experience and expression.

**Chas Clifton** is editor of *The Pomegranate: The International Journal of Pagan Studies*, the only peer-reviewed journal in the field. His works include *Her*

*Hidden Children: The Rise of Wicca and Paganism in America* (2006) and, as coeditor, *The Paganism Reader* (2004). He teaches at Colorado State University–Pueblo.

**Adam Crabtree** is on the faculty of the Centre for Training in Psychotherapy in Toronto. He has published an annotated bibliography of animal magnetism and early hypnotism and psychical research and is the author of *From Mesmer to Freud: Magnetic Sleep and the Roots of Psychological Healing* (1993).

**Jessica Elbert Decker** is Assistant Professor of Philosophy at California State University–San Marcos, where she teaches courses in the Philosophy and Women's Studies Departments. Her work has been published in *Epoche: A Journal for the History of Philosophy*, *Philosophia: A Journal of Continental Feminism*, and *Women's Studies: An Interdisciplinary Journal*.

**April D. DeConick** is the Isla Carroll and Percy E. Turner Professor of New Testament and Early Christianity and Chair of the Department of Religion, Rice University. She is founding joint editor of *GNOSIS: Journal of Gnostic Studies* and author of *The Thirteenth Apostle: What the Gospel of Judas Really Says* (2nd ed., 2009).

**Antoine Faivre** is Professor Emeritus, Germanic Studies, and École Pratique des Hautes Études, Religious Studies (Chair of the History of Esoteric and Mystical Currents in Modern and Contemporary Europe). He is the author of ten books and more than one hundred articles in academic journals.

**Peter Forshaw** is Senior Lecturer in the History of Western Esotericism in the Early Modern Period at the University of Amsterdam's Center for the History of Hermetic Philosophy and Related Currents. He is editor in chief of *Aries: Journal for the Study of Western Esotericism*.

**Joscelyn Godwin** is Professor of Music at Colgate University. He has written, edited, or translated some thirty books on musical and esoteric topics, most recently *Atlantis and the Cycles of Time* (2010), *Upstate Cauldron* (2015), and a family memoir, *The Starlight Years* (2015).

**Michael Gomes**, Director of Emily Sellon Memorial Library, New York, has authored a number of studies on Helena Petrovna Blavatsky and her Theosophical movement, including abridgments of her major books *Isis Unveiled* and *The Secret Doctrine*. He is the recipient of Columbia University's Herman Ausubel Memorial Prize for historical achievement.

**Cathy Gutierrez** is Professor of Religion at Sweet Briar College, Virginia. She has published *Plato's Ghost: Spiritualism in the American Renaissance* (2009) and most recently edited the *Handbook of Spiritualism and Channeling* (2015).

**Olav Hammer** is Professor of History at the University of Southern Denmark, working in the field of history of religion. His main areas of research are new religious currents and post-Enlightenment Western esotericism. His most recent publication is *Western Esotericism in Scandinavia* (2016, coedited with Henrik Bogdan).

**Wouter J. Hanegraaff** is Professor of History of Hermetic Philosophy and Related Currents at the University of Amsterdam, and a member of the Royal Netherlands Academy of Sciences. He is the author or editor of twelve books, including *Esotericism and the Academy: Rejected Knowledge in Western Culture* (Cambridge, 2012).

**Lee Irwin** is Professor of Religious Studies at the College of Charleston, South Carolina. He is vice-president of the Association for the Study of Esotericism (ASE), coeditor of the peer-reviewed ASE book series on esotericism, and author of seven books and numerous articles related to esoteric studies.

**Glenn Alexander Magee** is Professor and Chairman of the Department of Philosophy at the C.W. Post Campus of Long Island University. He is the author of Hegel and the Hermetic Tradition (2001) and The Hegel Dictionary (2011), as well as many articles on German philosophy and its connections with mysticism and esotericism.

**Matthew Mayock** received his Ph.D. from Stony Brook University and is Instructor of Philosophy at College of the Desert, Palm Desert, California. His research explores the transition from religion to philosophy in Ancient Greece and its effect on the roles of body and extension in archaic thought.

**Robert McDermott**, President Emeritus and Chair of Philosophy and Religion at the California Institute of Integral Studies, was secretary of the American Academy of Religion and a Fulbright and NEH grantee. His books include *The Essential Aurobindo* (2001) and *The New Essential Steiner* (2009).

**Bruce Milem** is Associate Professor of Philosophy at the State University of New York at New Paltz. He is the author of *The Unspoken Word: Negative Theology in Meister Eckhart's German Sermons* (2002), as well as articles on negative theology and philosophy of religion.

**Bruce Moran** is Professor of History, University of Nevada–Reno. He is the author of *Distilling Knowledge: Alchemy, Chemistry, and the Scientific Revolution* (2005) and *Andreas Libavius and the Transformation of Alchemy: Separating Chemical Cultures with Polemical Fire* (2007).

**Brian Ogren** is the Anna Smith Fine Assistant Professor of Judaic Studies in the Department of Religion at Rice University. He is the author of *Renaissance and Rebirth: Reincarnation in Italian Renaissance Kabbalah* (2009) and editor of *Time and Eternity in Jewish Mysticism: That Which Is Before and That Which Is After* (2015).

**Lawrence M. Principe** is the Drew Professor of the Humanities in the Departments of the History of Science and Technology and of Chemistry at

Johns Hopkins University and author of *The Secrets of Alchemy* (2013) and *A Very Short Introduction to the Scientific Revolution* (2011).

**Mark Sedgwick** is Professor of Arab and Islamic Studies, Aarhus University, Denmark. He is the author of *Against the Modern World: Traditionalism and the Secret Intellectual History of the Twentieth Century* (2009).

**Jan A. M. Snoek** is Emeritus Professor of the study of religions at the University of Heidelberg. He is the author of *Initiating Women in Freemasonry* (2012) and coeditor of the *Handbook of Freemasonry* (2014).

**Charles Stein** is a poet and independent scholar. His publications include *Persephone Unveiled* (2006); a verse translation of *The Odyssey* (2008); and thirteen books of poetry, most recently *There Where You Do Not Think to Be Thinking* (2015).

**Kocku von Stuckrad** is Professor of Religious Studies, University of Groningen. He has published extensively on the themes of mysticism and esotericism, with a special focus on astrology. His most recent book is *The Scientification of Religion: An Historical Study of Discursive Change, 1800–2000* (2014).

**Hereward Tilton** has taught early modern German esotericism at the University of Exeter, the University of Amsterdam, and the Ludwig-Maximilians-Universität in Munich. His publications include *The Quest for the Phoenix: Spiritual Alchemy and Rosicrucianism in the Work of Count Michael Maier (1569–1622)* (2003).

**Hugh B. Urban** is Professor of Religious Studies at Ohio State University. He is the author of nine books, including *Magia Sexualis: Sex, Magic and Liberation in Modern Western Esotericism* (2006) and *New Age, Neopagan, and New Religious Movements: Alternative Spirituality in Modern America* (2015).

**Arthur Versluis** is Professor and Chair of the Department of Religious Studies at Michigan State University and author of numerous books, including *American Gurus: From Transcendentalism to New Age Religion* (2014) and *Magic and Mysticism: An Introduction to Western Esotericism* (2007).

**Gerhard Wehr** (1931–2015) was the author of numerous publications dealing with mysticism and esotericism. He was editor of the works of Jacob Boehme and of other Christian mystics. Wehr also wrote biographies of C. G. Jung, Rudolf Steiner, Martin Buber, and other figures.

**Jane Williams-Hogan**, Professor Emerita, teaches sociology, religious studies, and history at Bryn Athyn College, in Bryn Athyn, Pennsylvania. A specialist on Emanuel Swedenborg and his influence on individuals, movements, art, and literature, she is the author of *Swedenborg e le Chiese swedenborgiane* (2004) and editor of *Swedenborg and His Influence* (with Erland J. Brock et al., 1989).

# I
# *Antiquity*

# I

# ANCIENT MYSTERIES

CHARLES STEIN

## 1 Introduction

The institutions known as "mysteries" in Ancient Greece consisted of rites of initiation that offered individual access to the presence and power of the gods. Some of the mysteries were celebrated as early as Mycenaean times but had affinities with, and probable sources in, even earlier shamanic, goddess-cult, and Neolithic practices. In the Classical age, we find mysteries of Demeter and Persephone, The Great Mother, the gods at Samothrace and Andania. The mysteries of Dionysus were performed throughout Hellas, as were the mysteries of the ancient poet-prophet-hero Orpheus, probably in private settings. Later, in the Hellenistic period, there were mysteries of Isis and Osiris. And in Imperial times, mysteries of Mithras competed with Christianity for spiritual hegemony in the Empire. By far the most well known were the mysteries of Demeter and Persephone celebrated at Eleusis outside of Athens.

The ancient Greek language has two words for "that which is not to be spoken of": *arrheton* and *aporrheton*. The first translates as "the ineffable": that which, in principle, *cannot* be brought to speech; the second refers to that about which discourse is *forbidden*. The prohibition against speaking or writing of the ineffable may be statutory, as in classical Athens, or self-imposed, following from religious conviction.

The word "mysteries" (*ta mysteria*) comes to us directly from the Greek *mysterion*, "a secret rite," which derives from two linked verbs: *myo* and *myeo*. *Myo* means to close up or conceal, as in closing the eyes and stopping the ears or as when a flower closes itself at nightfall. *Myeo* means to initiate – for example, to initiate someone into the mysteries. The mysteries in Ancient Greece concealed initiatory secrets that were both incapable of being rendered verbally and of which the initiate was forbidden to speak. The secret or secrets of each had to do with the experience of the deity. At Eleusis, it seems that the celebration culminated in a theophany of Demeter and/or Persephone, in which the celebrants participated.

## 2 The Eleusinian Mysteries

The Eleusinian Mysteries (or, more specifically, their culminating events) occurred fourteen miles west of Athens on the Bay of Salamis and were framed as a festival of Demeter and Persephone. They were held annually until the Christian authorities destroyed all pagan rites and attempted to eradicate authentic knowledge of pagan traditions. Initiation took place in two phases: (1) The Lesser Mysteries, known as *myeisis*: initiation. Initiates were called *mystai* (singular, *mystes*); (2) the Greater Mysteries, the *epopteia*: "things seen." Persons who had completed them were *epopts*.

Prospective initiates came from everywhere and every walk of life. Even mythical personages such as Herakles were said to have sought initiation. There were two conditions for participation: knowledge of the Greek language and innocence of blood guilt. These conditions satisfied, all were welcomed who could afford the fees charged by the Eleusinian officials and the price of certain sacrificial animals.

What we actually know of the rites, beyond the archaeological remains, derives from fragmentary remarks in speeches, poems, and plays and from the writings of ancient scholiasts, Church Fathers, and philosophers. From these, we can learn something of the circumstances surrounding the mysteries, their mythology, and their history – along with a few tantalizing details about what *might* have occurred during the rite in the Telesterion, the temple hall where the *epopteia* took place. From hints, guesses, and hearsay remarks (by persons not necessarily sympathetic to Eleusis such as early Christian heresiologists), scholars have deduced that the Hierophant (the high priest) invoked the presence of the goddesses by removing certain sacred objects from the recesses of the temple, one of which was an ear of grain; that Persephone had given birth to an infant (possibly Dionysus) in the Underworld; and that at the decisive moment a special gong sounded, an enormous fire flared, the Underworld opened, and apparitions of Persephone and/or Demeter rose in the hall. All this transpired in an atmosphere of holy hush and pious expectation. We also know that in early Imperial times, as many as three thousand *mystai* celebrated together, and that the potential *epopts* imbibed a potion known as the *kykeon*.

It has been argued, with some plausibility, that the content of the *kykeon* was a psychotropic agent derived from the ergot on rye grown in Demeter's honor and pharmacologically similar to lysergic acid diethylamide.[1] An attempt to challenge the plausibility of this hypothesis has been offered by Walter Burkert in his *Ancient Mystery Cults*,[2] and I have attempted to rebut Burkert and restore its plausibility in *Persephone Unveiled*.[3] In any case, some synergy of mythic representations, physical exhaustion, fasting, dancing, theophanic dramaturgy, consumption of entheogens, not to mention a year and a half of training, would have made possible the transforming effect.

The most important single piece of evidence concerning the mysteries is a poem from approximately the seventh century BCE, written in the same poetic tradition as the Homeric texts and recounting the famous story of Demeter and Persephone, including Demeter's founding of the mysteries. (I give a translation and exegesis of the *Hymn* in *Persephone Unveiled*.) The founding of the mysteries appears toward the end of it, only after Demeter has attempted to bestow immortality on the son of the king of the Eleusinians. This fails when the king's wife sees Demeter working her magic on the child and fears for his life. Demeter interrupts the procedure, rages at mortals for their incapacity to recognize the presence of a deity, reveals herself as a goddess, and commands the people of Eleusis to build a temple in her honor. The lesson seems to be that if there is to be commerce between gods and humans, some special form of mediation must be devised. The mysteries are instituted to allow the overwhelming experience of divine immanence to occur without resulting in disastrous misunderstanding. As we shall see, it may be that true contact with the divine subverts the very basis of human values and must itself be contextualized so that it can be made to serve human institutions.

The *myesis*, the Lesser Mysteries, were celebrated in Classical times, not in Eleusis but in Agrai on the banks of the Illisos just outside of Athens. The Greater Mysteries, culminating with the *epopteia*, were performed in the Telesterion at Eleusis. The Lesser Mysteries were purificatory in character and began the initiates' training; to facilitate this, a *mystagog* (trainer) was assigned to each initiate. A year and a half elapsed between the two phases, during which time the *mystes* would have been occupied to some degree with the issues, myths, beliefs, and practices connected with initiation.

The Greater Mysteries consisted of a week-long series of events at Athens, followed by a procession on the Sacred Road to Eleusis, and finally the Holy

---

[1] See Gordon R. Wasson, Albert Hoffman, and Carl A. P. Ruck, *The Road to Eleusis: Unveiling the Secrets of the Mysteries* (Berkeley: North Atlantic Books, 2008).
[2] Walter Burkert, *Ancient Mystery Cults* (Cambridge, MA: Harvard University Press, 1987).
[3] Charles Stein, *Persephone Unveiled: Seeing the Goddess and Freeing Your Soul* (Berkeley: North Atlantic Books, 2006), 104ff.

Night during which the climactic *teletai* (the rites themselves) were performed. The *hiera*, the holy objects, stored during the year in the Anaktoron, the inner core of the Telesterion, were brought to Athens at the beginning of the week and then returned to Eleusis in the ritual procession along the Sacred Road. They were carried in mystical *kistai* or baskets on the heads of the priestesses of the mysteries. During the week in Athens, each initiate underwent special purifications and performed the sacrifice of a pig sacred to Demeter. In the procession, at the end of the week, the initiates were led back to Eleusis by Dionysus himself in the form of a wooden statue of Iacchus. On the road to Eleusis, the initiates sang energetic sacred songs and paid homage to various sacred sites along the way.

Just outside Eleusis, the procession crossed a long, narrow bridge over the river Kephisos, thought to be haunted by Underworld spirits, who assaulted the celebrants and attempted to impede their way to the temple grounds. As part of the effort to ward off these entities, various comic personages would accost the procession, relieving for a moment the solemn mood. This part of the mysteries was known as "bridge jests" and deployed a troop of actors impersonating and mocking well-known local dignitaries. Among the jesters would be Baubo, a portly, impish creature with a face painted on her belly, who ran about lifting her skirts and shouting lewd jokes. The entire event, both terrifying and bawdy, served to open the spirits of the celebrants to unimagined events to come. Their energy, piety, and enthusiasm for initiation merged with abject terror as the *mystai* walked along the haunted bridge. Then the initiates were further agitated by a spirit of mockery and hilarity.

On arrival at the temple grounds, the initiates passed under arches and in front of monuments, gazed at sculptures and painted scenes (depicting images from Eleusinian mythology), and visited a small temple dedicated to Hekate. The procession stopped at the Ploutonion, a shrine consecrated to Hades. The Ploutonion was a cave in the hillside thought to be an access to the Underworld and above which stood the citadel of Eleusis. Before entering the Telesterion, the *mystai* participated in sacred dances – initiatic processes in their own right, bringing the somatic energies of the *mystai* into both mimetic and dynamic alignment with events to come. At some point in these proceedings, the initiates imbibed the *kykeon*. After the dances, the *mystai* entered the temple, passing first through the outer and then the inner *propylaea* (monumental gateway). Within the latter were large statues of the priestesses with the *kistai* on their heads as caryatids about the entranceway.

Once on the temple grounds, the identification of the *mystai* with mythological figures and stories sacred to the mysteries would have grown ever richer and more compelling as image imitated image, and the concrete reality of what the *mystai* enacted became still more complexly represented by what they saw around them. Statues representing the timeless identities of the bearers of the holy objects were seen by the initiates as soon as they began to enter the inner chambers of the sacred precinct, each new entrance conducting them closer to the innermost recess of the Telesterion where the secret itself (perhaps revealed as the inner meaning of the sacred objects) awaited them.

Various other pedestals and friezes, some of which survive in fragments, depicted the procession itself, so that the ceremonial space, replete with such imagery, would have contributed to the identification of the *mystai* with the meaning of the procession. At the end of the sequence of these images would have been the two goddesses themselves, Demeter seated, Persephone on a dark throne behind her, so that there would have been a continuous flow of initiatory events leading directly to the goddesses. The *mystai* moved ever closer to the place where the mystical manifestation of the goddesses would occur, and this sense of approach would have been reinforced by the celebrants' relation to the imagery that appeared along the way.

Although identification with the images would have reached a crescendo of intensity in this manner, it is important to realize that it is not this identification that constituted the secret. The ordinary identities of the *mystai* were being exchanged for identities associated with the mysteries, so that, as we shall see, at the culminating moment, identity as such could be released or transformed.

We know something of the external events that induced this transformation from reports and surmises. The Hierophant, the leading official, whose name means "the one who causes the holy things to appear," is said to have revealed the *hiera*, the secret objects sacred to Demeter. A mighty light is reported to have arisen from the *Anaktoron* as a fire that could be seen for miles around. *Phantasmata* – ghostly appearances – are reported to have floated and trembled about the Telesterion, culminating in the phantasmic appearance of Persephone herself. Persephone also appeared among the flames with the infant Dionysus in her arms or with her mother, Demeter; or Persephone and Demeter appeared as one. The Hierophant showed a single ear of grain to the initiates. A special gong was struck, creating the effect of deep-echoing thunder bellowing from the Underworld. The Hierophant proclaimed in a high voice, "The Mistress has given birth to a holy child. Brimo [The Strong One] has given birth to Brimos [The Strong One]."

Undergoing the *epopteia* left the *epopt* in a state of profound awe of the gods and in some way possessed of a new confidence in his or her relation to existence beyond the grave. When the initiate entered the space of the gods – a world replete with divine figures, gestures, meanings, stories, attitudes – it would have become possible for the secret to be experienced directly.

3 The Secret of the Eleusinian Mysteries

Any attempt to theorize about the "the ineffable secret" must necessarily be highly speculative. Nevertheless, it is possible to formulate a reasonable conjecture as to what may have been imparted at Eleusis, based on the aforementioned testimonia, as well as knowledge of classical Greek thought and culture. The only rules governing such a conjecture are that it must not only accord with but also illuminate the available evidence – and it must offer some account of the secret that can shed light on why so many of the ancients found their experience at Eleusis to be profoundly life changing.

The Greeks, as is commonly known, valued clear forms in their art, clear concepts in their philosophy, fixed prerogatives for their gods, and determinate identities for themselves. "Count no man happy until he is dead," said Solon to Croesus, because the quality of one's existence – what we would call our true identity – could not be ultimately defined without the closure of death. In the most explicit rendition of the afterlife from the Hellenic world – the eleventh book of *The Odyssey* – we are shown a tableau of ghost-souls, each of whom has a well-defined identity, but each of whom also finds this condition an abject misery. The suffering of the dead is precisely the loss of the open possibilities of life that are cut off by fixed identity.

The mysteries offered to their initiates an experience that alleviated the fear of death. But what could this experience have been? Would it not have had to offer something beyond the grim termination of possibilities that *The Odyssey* so vividly portrays? The Eleusinian Mysteries culminated in a vision of the divine, the *seeing* of which transformed the initiate. It cannot be far from the mark to say that this seeing afforded a connection, even an identification, not simply with the figures of the Demeter/Persephone myth but also with the numinous background of all existence, which some of the later Greeks, in particular the Eleatic thinker Parmenides, knew as Being itself. Carl Kerenyi in his major study of Eleusis imagined that such an experience amounted to something like the Beatific Vision in Christian theology.[4] In

---

[4] Carl Kerenyi, *Eleusis: Archetypal Image of Mother and Daughter*, trans. Ralph Manheim (New York: Pantheon Books, 1967).

*Persephone Unveiled*, I develop the idea that the Parmenidean vision provides us with a better model for understanding the Eleusinian experience.

In general, the prospective initiate approached initiation familiar with the myths and provenances of the relevant gods. These myths would be quite exoteric, that is, associated with public festivals. But initiates came from all over Greece. Varying, contrasting, and contradictory versions of the myths would have been current among them. Stories about Persephone, for instance, existed in a plethora of variants; although participants would have most likely known at least one of them, no one myth fit all. The Eleusinian secret has been thought by some simply to have been the replacement of these mythic variants by a single version unique to Eleusis. But even if it could be proved that there was a unique Eleusinian myth (and it cannot), it could not have been this that constituted the secret of Eleusis.

We have various testimonies that the experience within the Telesterion involved great disorientation, to be alleviated only by the culminating moment when the secret was revealed. Certainly confusion and perplexity may have begun to be stimulated during the bridge jests and exacerbated by ecstatic dancing and the imbibing of the *kykeon*. Add to this the fact that the mythic imagery surrounding the initiate would have been unfamiliar to many, that hallucinatory phantasmata and strange sounds would have filled the darkened sacred temple interior. One can see that a state of spiritual darkness, disorientation, and perplexity would have been induced. The spiritual content of this perplexity would have involved both the nature of the divine and the nature of one's self, that is, the question of the identity of one's own being in relation to the gods would have been raised and brought to a fevered pitch. Perhaps for the first time, the initiates would have felt an unrelieved sense of inner darkness. This inner darkness would have corresponded to the physical darkness in the Telesterion prior to the moment of *epopteia*, and the confusion about the divine realm would have been emphasized by the dramatic, not to say chaotic events occurring there.

I wish to suggest that the essential sense of the initiatic darkness and perplexity was the breakdown of a fixed sense of personal identity with which the *mystes* would have entered the mysteries, and that the revelatory experience of *epopteia*, induced in such a context of psychic confusion, opened the initiate to the possibility of a state of being beyond fixed identity.

Given that Hellenic culture put such a high premium on the clear definition of character, the revelation of an experience beyond identity would have introduced certain values beyond those that Hellenic culture in general tended to affirm. It has often been asserted that Hellenic culture knew no experience of "unitive mysticism": the union of the individual soul with an all-embracing divine principle, such as is common in Indian religion and even in some forms of Islam, Judaism, and Christianity. Initiatic secrecy conceals an essential irony: The highest and most sacred experience offered by Hellenic mystery cults was subversive of Hellenic culture's principal values. If this is the case, one need look no further for why the experience of the mysteries had to be kept secret.

The mysteries also lent glory and legitimacy to the cities with which they were associated. Athens financed Eleusis and provided political protection, while Eleusis was allowed a free hand in all matters pertaining to the celebration of its rites. Athens, in turn, enjoyed prestige for its sponsorship of the rites. The numinous aura of the mysteries legitimized the Athenian state and its gods. As long as no one was permitted to speak or write of it, the holy character of the *epopteia* could benefit the very culture that it secretly subverted.

### 4 Other Mysteries

Space forbids a detailed treatment of the other mysteries of the ancient world. They were for the most part internally linked at least through the deities that were celebrated in them, and by the two-phase rhythm that characterizes their dramatic structure: one of veiling-dissolution-darkness, followed by revelation-reconfiguration-illumination.

Four unique gods were celebrated at Samothrace, but Dionysus, Hephaistos, Poseidon, and Demeter also had important roles. Dionysus himself, as we saw, is possibly the figure that was revealed in the Eleusinian *epopteia*. Samothrace seems to have involved an inversion of Eleusinian practice: In Eleusis, those who had committed violent crimes and/or could not speak Greek were excluded. Samothrace was founded by criminals, and initiates had to swear an oath that they had committed crimes against the gods and had to learn an indigenous tongue to participate in the mysteries. Thrace, just north of Samothrace, played a role in both Dionysian and Orphic mythology. Dionysian mysteries were celebrated throughout Greece and involved, mythologically, the dismemberment and rebirth of Dionysus himself. Their rites featured forms of psychic disintegration and rebirth brought on by inebriation probably associated with some pharmacological enhancement of ordinary wine. Orphic theogonies elevated Dionysus himself to a supreme divine principle and invoked concepts adopted from Persian cosmologies, bringing them into contact with the later Mysteries of Mithras. The Mysteries of Isis and Osiris were predicated on an assimilation of the legends of Demeter and Dionysus, Isis being identified with Demeter and Osiris with Dionysus.

The Mysteries of Orpheus deserve special mention. We know nothing of the sites where they were celebrated. It was once thought that they were not celebrated at all but came to us merely in the form of a latter-day literary fiction. Contemporary scholarship disputes this but provides little to elucidate the actual context of their performance other than to indicate that they were celebrated "privately," without either state support or proscription.

Orpheus himself is the legendary poet-magus who served in the Classical world as the archetypal author for cosmological poetry with possible initiatory relevance. More than with other cults, the Orphic Mysteries may have involved the study of poetic texts dealing with the origin, structure, and soteriological function of the cosmos. Indeed, pseudepigraphic writing that claimed to reveal such matters routinely appeared under the name of Orpheus. A series of such texts survive in later commentary, most frequently in a Neoplatonic context. Orphic cosmology in general is "solar" theology. Dionysus, Zeus, Helios, and a unique Orphic being known as Phanes were compounded into a demiurgic figure at the outer bounds of the cosmos. The human soul houses a struggle between higher (Dionysian) and lower (Titanic) forces that propel the individual through a series of incarnations and inter-incarnational periods, until, through proper purgations, ritual discipline, and other practices, the soul frees itself from bondage to the cosmic structure altogether and takes up its proper place beyond the solar sphere. Although an actual performance of these practices is no doubt indicated, I wish to suggest that the study of the Orphic theogonies themselves may have played a decisive role in the soteriological process.

The Orphic texts recapitulate, elaborate, and vary the Hesiodic theogony with an emphasis on situations that abuse temporal and logical order. "Night" precedes the generation of the anthropomorphic gods but is nevertheless generated by a specific divine pair. Dionysus precedes the creation of the "Orphic Egg" but then comes into being inside it. In Greek accounts of the gods, from Hesiod to Proclus, genealogical relations serve as metaphors for causally and logically genetic sequences. Ancient genealogy stands in for ontology: If X is the son of Y, this suggests that the principle that Y stands for, say cosmic space, is the source of the being of X, say the earth. When such arrangements are disordered, the mythologem suggests awareness of a deep mystery in the genealogical, that is, ontogenic process. To disrupt the order of temporal and logical sequence suggests a reality outside of time and cosmic being. Such genealogies are paradoxical in a way that expresses a feeling for an enigma at the heart of things. It is quite as the Emperor Julian remarked: "Concerning the myths of the Mysteries which Orpheus handed down to us, in the very things which in these myths are incongruous, he drew nearest the truth."[5] In the Orphic Mysteries, it may very well be as Henry Corbin writes of Islamic esotericism, "the text itself is the secret."[6]

---

[5] G. R. S. Meade, *Orpheus* (London: John M Watkins, 1965), 40. Quoted from the Emperor Julian, "Oration VII."

[6] Henry Corbin, *Avicenna and the Visionary Recital*, trans. Willard R. Trask (Princeton: Princeton University Press, 1960), 33.

# 2

# PYTHAGORAS AND PYTHAGOREANISM

## Joscelyn Godwin

## 1 Life and Work of Pythagoras

The giant figure of Pythagoras straddles the borderline between history and myth. As in the case of his approximate contemporaries Zoroaster, Mahavira, Confucius, Lao Tse, and Gautama Buddha, his followers created an idealized biography that cannot be checked against impartial sources.[1] Even then, they differ widely in their accounts, most of which date from the third century CE, eight centuries after their subject. Consequently, we cannot confirm any of the biographical data, nor even give firm dates for Pythagoras's birth and death.

Certainly his homeland was the Dodecanese island of Samos, and his birth occurred between 580 and 569 BCE. According to Iamblichus and Porphyry, he was born in Syria where his father Mnesarchus (a Phoenician by origin) was trading. After many travels, he settled in southern Italy, founding a school and community at Croton. Around 500 BCE, local opposition destroyed the school, and if Pythagoras did not perish then and there, he died in Metapontum during the following decade. This is the bare outline with which modern scholarship has to be content.

Turning to the legendary life of Pythagoras as reported by the same authors, we find him first studying with the Ionian philosophers Thales and Anaximander, and with Pherecydes of Syros. Next came his voyages to the Phoenician settlements in Syria, where he underwent mystery initiations. The early witness of Herodotus confirms his long residence in Egypt.

---

[1] Much of the source material is collected and translated in *The Pythagorean Sourcebook*, compiled by Kenneth Sylvan Guthrie (1919–1920), revised and expanded by David R. Fideler (Grand Rapids, MI: Phanes Press, 1987), including Iamblichus's *De Vita Pythagorica*. A clearer translation of Iamblichus, which divides his chapters by paragraphs, is *Iamblichus: On the Pythagorean Life*, trans. Gillian Clark (Liverpool: Liverpool University Press, 1989).

Having gone there on Thales's recommendation, Pythagoras visited the religious centers of Heliopolis, Memphis and Thebes and was admitted to initiations never before given to foreigners. A fourth, involuntary journey was to Babylon, as a captive following Cambyses's conquest of Egypt (525 BCE), but Pythagoras turned it to good use by studying astronomy and mathematics with the Magi. On his release, he returned to Samos but became increasingly at odds with his compatriots. He made a tour of the oracular centers of Delos, Samothrace, Eleusis, Grecian Thebes, Delphi, and Crete, and he visited Sparta to observe the system of government. After emigrating to Croton, he never returned to Samos.

Among the mythical aspects of Pythagoras's life, as distinct from the merely legendary ones, the third-century biographers report the Delphic Oracle's prediction of his birth; the golden thigh, which he sometimes displayed; his conversations with animals; the hailing of him "in a deep, penetrating voice" by the river Nessus; his descent into Hades and meeting with the souls there; and his bilocation, teaching simultaneously at Metapontum and at Tauromenium in Sicily.[2] These are all commonplaces of sacred biography, especially resembling events in the life of Apollonius of Tyana (first century CE). This is not surprising since Apollonius was a neo-Pythagorean and wrote a (lost) biography of the master, which served both as a source for the third-century biographers of Pythagoras and as a model for Flavius Philostratus's *Life of Apollonius of Tyana*.

More original are the claims that Pythagoras could recall his previous incarnations, and that he could hear the Harmony of the Spheres. Although these have become standard topoi with their own long histories, they have no pre-Pythagorean traditions in the Greek world, nor does reincarnation appear in the extensive Egyptian lore of the afterlife. The transmigration of a single soul into different bodies was taught in Orphism, but all that we know of Orphic teachings comes from the post-Pythagorean period. Walter Burkert suggests that Orphism itself may have been a reconstruction, claiming origin from its mythic founder but actually created by Pythagoreans,[3] just as the neo-Pythagoreans of the early centuries CE reconstructed their master's doctrines and biography. Burkert admits as a serious possibility that the doctrine of reincarnation came from India.[4]

---

[2] Chiefly Iamblichus and Porphyry, both of whom wrote a *Vita Pythagorae* (henceforth *VP*), and Diogenes Laertius's *Vitae philosophorum*.
[3] Walter Burkert, *Lore and Science in Ancient Pythagoreanism*, trans. Edwin L. Minar, Jr. (Cambridge, MA: Harvard University Press, 1972), 128–130.
[4] Burkert, *Lore and Science*, 133.

The first literary evidence for the Harmony of the Spheres is in Plato's *Republic* (617 b-c), which depicts Sirens singing on the planetary rings. In neo-Pythagorean and Neoplatonic doctrine, the soul hears this music as it passes through the planetary spheres on its way down to earth and back again. The harmony also has a metaphorical meaning that points to Pythagoras's achievement not as a mystic but as a proto-scientist. For if the planetary spheres are perceived to be harmonious, it must be because, like musical harmony, they obey the laws of number.

According to one of the best-known anecdotes, Pythagoras discovered the connection of harmony with number after hearing four smiths whose hammers rang on the anvil with different but consonant pitches.[5] After suspending the hammers on strings and weighing them, he found their proportions to be 12:9:8:6, namely those of an octave divided by its arithmetical and harmonic means, and thereby arrived at the quantification of musical intervals. (The fallacy in the experiment is mentioned later.) He thus anticipated both the quantitative worldview that only came into its own with the scientific revolution, and the experimental method inseparable from it, that uses mathematics as its tool.

Pythagoras's achievement in mathematics was to gather knowledge from Babylon and Egypt, civilizations already in decline, and to plant it in a Greek-speaking culture that was rising to intellectual prominence. Another possible source was Abaris, a priest of Apollo from Hyperborea (the Land beyond the North Wind), who traveled on a "golden arrow" and visited Pythagoras for a mutual exchange of wisdom.[6] Burkert, emphasizing the shamanic element in Pythagoras's character, interprets the arrow as a metaphor for the out-of-the-body flights of a Central Asian shaman.[7] Others think Abaris came from Britain and associate him with the geographer Pytheas of Massilia's report of a thriving, musical cult of Apollo in a circular temple there.[8] As Alexander Thom's research has shown, the megalithic temple builders of Britain used "Pythagorean triangles" (right-angled triangles based on whole numbers) as their principles of construction.[9] The principles of the five "Pythagorean solids" (later renamed "Platonic solids") were also known there in Neolithic times, as witness the many carefully carved specimens found in Scotland.[10]

[5] Iamblichus, *VP*, ch. 26, para. 115–121.
[6] Iamblichus, *VP*, 19, 90–93; 32, 215–218.
[7] Burkert, *Lore and Science*, 150, 162.
[8] Diodorus Siculus, *Bibliotheca Historica*, II, 3.
[9] See Alexander Thom, *Megalithic Sites in Britain* (Oxford: Oxford University Press, 1967), 27, 77–80.
[10] See Keith Critchlow, *Time Stands Still: New Light on Megalithic Science* (London, Gordon Fraser, 1979), 131–135.

For Pythagoras, numbers were the ultimate realities. While exoterically he enjoined piety to the gods and made bloodless sacrifices to them, it was against the esoteric background of a purely mathematical metaphysics. The primary and sacred symbol of this metaphysics was the Tetraktys, a triangle made from ten dots in rows of 1, 2, 3, and 4. The first ten numbers all carried metaphysical meanings, being similar to what Plato would later style the "forms" or "ideas" underlying all manifestation. The arithmetical series of the Tetraktys could be extended indefinitely to the whole realm of the limited or bounded (Gk. *peras*), as opposed to the unlimited or infinite (*apeiron*). These are the first pair of opposites into which the Pythagoreans divided the world of experience. Aristotle gives the list: Limited/Unlimited, Odd/Even, One/Many, Right/Left, Male/Female, Rest/Motion, Straight/Crooked, Light/Darkness, Good/Bad, Square/Oblong.[11]

Pythagoras's ethical teaching took the form of brief sentences or maxims and survives in three main collections: the "Symbols" (39 of which are explained in Iamblichus's *Exhortation to Philosophy*), the *Golden Verses* (preserved with a commentary by Hierocles of Alexandria, fifth century CE), and the "Sentences" (451 of which are collected in *The Sentences of Sextus*).[12] They range from statements such as "God dwells in the intellect of the wise man" and maxims, for example "Possess those things that no one can take away from you," to gnomic sayings: "Do not poke fire with a sword" and "Abstain from beans." The latter prohibition, for which the Pythagoreans were much mocked, has never been satisfactorily explained.

Although Diogenes Laertius reports that Pythagoras wrote several treatises, none survive. His chief method of teaching was oral, adapted to the various classes of listeners. The *akousmatikoi* or "auditors" assembled, perhaps by hundreds, to learn elementary precepts proclaimed by Pythagoras from behind a curtain. Five years of probation as silent auditors were required before disciples could progress to the status of *mathematikoi* or "those devoted to learning." These, also called the *esōteroi* ("initiates into secret matters") saw Pythagoras and learned his mathematical, cosmological, and musical principles.

Unusual for its time, the school was coeducational: Iamblichus names seventeen "illustrious Pythagorean women." The students lived a common life under a regime of abstinence from animal food and wine except in connection with sacred rites, the renunciation of fame and wealth, and sexual restraint. As a family man, Pythagoras encouraged monogamous marriage

---

[11] Aristotle, *Metaphysics*, 986a 25.
[12] Translations in Guthrie, *The Pythagorean Sourcebook*, 159–165, 267–274.

and the eugenic breeding of children. He controlled the emotions of his disciples by singing to the accompaniment of the lyre, adjusting the music to stimulate, calm, or cure body and soul. Porphyry adds that he danced, too. On occasion, he was able to avert disaster by knowing what kind of music would turn a man away from violence. But much as these tales enchanted later readers, it is impossible to disentangle Pythagoras's own practices from those of his later disciples, and difficult to distinguish reportage from invention.

From all the likely and unlikely stories, there remains the central ideal of the philosophic life, dedicated to the love of wisdom and to the benefits that this brings to the whole world.

## 2 Pythagoreans in the Classical World

After the destruction of the school in Croton, some of the survivors settled in mainland Greece and founded new schools. Others continued the tradition in Italy, including Philolaus of Croton or Tarentum (born ca. 470 BCE), who wrote the earliest surviving account of Pythagoras's metaphysical and astronomical teachings. Philolaus's student was Archytas of Tarentum, whom Plato visited in 388 BCE.

Plato's dialogue *Timaeus* is the earliest large-scale monument to the Pythagorean mentality, and the most lasting in its influence. In the *Republic*, Socrates prescribes for the Guardians of the ideal state the study of arithmetic, geometry (plane and solid, the latter called "stereometry"), astronomy, and harmony, adding: "These sciences are closely akin, as the Pythagoreans say, and we agree with them, Glaucon."[13] The Myth of Er at the end of the same dialogue presents reincarnation, if not as a doctrine, then as a plausible object of belief. According to Aristotle, the main differences between Plato's philosophy and that of "the Italians" (meaning the Pythagoreans) were (1) that Plato regarded numbers not as ultimate realities, but as intermediate between the sensible world and the forms and (2) that Plato's primary opposites were not the Limited and the Unlimited (as with the Pythagoreans), but the One and the Dyad, the latter producing all numbers.[14] Plato was reproached, as was Empedocles before him, for having disclosed the Pythagorean secrets, and he was excluded from the school.[15]

---

[13] Plato, *Republic*, VII, 530d.
[14] Aristotle, *Metaphysics*, I, 6, 987b.
[15] Diogenes Laertius, VIII, 27.

But were these secrets merely the mathematical disciplines just mentioned? Several recent researchers have given a glimpse of a formidable intellectual structure mostly unsuspected by mainstream classical studies. Musicologist Anne Macaulay (1924–1998), in a controversial work about Pythagoras's patron deity Apollo, analyses the Greek letters that make up the name of that god as comprising a geometrical diagram of circles and rectangles.[16] Among other surprises, these yield proportions that are the same as those of the seven strings of the cithara (large lyre). Macaulay thought that the Greeks had adopted a musical-mathematical-astronomical complex dating from megalithic times, which again recalls Abaris the Hyperborean.

David Fideler, following the Greek letter-number correspondences known as gematria, shows in *Jesus Christ, Sun of God* that the numbers of the names APOLLO (1061), ZEUS (612), LYRA (531), and HERMES (353) are related as a musical twelfth, divided by its geometric and harmonic means.[17] Moreover, the word TETRAKTYS sums appropriately to 1234, and PYTHAGORAS to 864 ($2^5 \times 3^3$, divisible by the important cosmological numbers 72 and 108). Such discoveries imply that the Greek alphabet and the orthography of divine names and other important terms were deliberately "rigged" to incorporate mathematical and musical theorems.

Ernest McClain, another musicologist, observes that "From a musician's perspective, Plato's *Republic* embodies a treatise on equal temperament."[18] In *The Pythagorean Plato*, he demonstrates that whenever Plato mentions a number, it conceals a reference to musical intervals and tuning systems. McClain traces analogous phenomena in Vedic, Babylonian, Egyptian, Hebrew, and early Christian texts, and he explains, "In this sea of restless change man discovered an island he could trust, the octave of ratio 1:2 – the 'basic miracle of music' – functioning as a matrix for all smaller intervals and providing a metric basis for a tonal algebra."[19]

The English polymath John Michell, in *The Dimensions of Paradise*, approaches the Platonic myths from a geometric viewpoint. Having established a connection between Greek gematria and the measurements of the earth and moon in traditional units, Michell shows that Plato was conversant

---

[16] Anne Macaulay, "Apollo: The Pythagorean Definition of God," in *Homage to Pythagoras: Rediscovering Sacred Science*, ed. Christopher Bamford (Hudson, NY: Lindisfarne Press, 1994), 245–270.

[17] David Fideler, *Jesus Christ, Sun of God: Ancient Cosmology and Early Christian Symbolism* (Wheaton, IL: Quest Books, 1993), 220–221.

[18] Ernest G. McClain, *The Pythagorean Plato, Prelude to the Song Itself* (Stony Brook, NY: Nicolas Hays, 1978), 5.

[19] Ernest G. McClain, *The Myth of Invariance: The Origin of the Gods, Mathematics and Music from the Rg Veda to Plato* (Stony Brook, NY: Nicolas Hays, 1976), 196.

with this secret system, which was passed on to the early Christians and incorporated into the Greek Testament.[20] Any of these discoveries, taken separately, might be ignored, but taken together they alert one to the possible existence of an early esoteric synthesis that demands further study.

As other philosophical schools came to prominence, the remaining Pythagoreans probably cultivated the more mystical and occult pursuits, such as resurfaced in the first neo-Pythagorean revival. Nigidius Figulus (98–45 BCE), a Roman praetor and friend of Cicero, founded a neo-Pythagorean order, which according to rumor practiced astrology and magic, using child mediums and other means of divination.[21] An underground meeting hall or chapel at the Porta Maggiore in Rome, built in the first century CE but only discovered in 1917, may have had some connection with Nigidius's order, and it certainly belonged to a kindred esoteric cult. The Roman historian Jérôme Carcopino, interpreting its stucco decorations as allegories of the soul's journey, did not hesitate to call the building a "Pythagorean basilica."

In a different vein, Philo of Alexandria (20 BCE–40 CE) applied Pythagorean mathematical concepts to the interpretation of his native Hebrew scriptures, making a synthesis of Jewish and Greek thought. For Philo, it was Moses who heard the Harmony of the Spheres and composed songs in every mode that replicated the heavenly motions, moving even the angels.[22] Philo's work on the Creation story of Genesis (*De Opificio Mundi*) celebrates the universal powers of the number seven in a way that comes as close as his theology allows to its deification. Although not classed as a kabbalist, Philo anticipated the later discipline of Kabbalah through his esoteric and arithmological reading of the Torah.

In the early centuries CE, neo-Pythagoreanism was indistinctly blended with Neoplatonism, with the Roman revival of the Orphic and Dionysiac mysteries, and even with elements of Christianity. However, it was Pythagorean mathematics, music theory, and metaphysics that had the most staying power and imbued the entire Neoplatonic movement. In the Middle Platonist period of the second century CE, Theon of Smyrna, Nicomachus of Gerasa, and Numenius of Apamea all wrote handbooks on mathematics and music in a Pythagorean vein. Of the third-century Neoplatonists, Plotinus (205–269/70) was less Pythagorean, his successor Porphyry (232/3–ca. 305) more so, and Iamblichus (ca. 250–ca. 325) most

[20] John Michell, *The Dimensions of Paradise: The Proportions and Symbolic Numbers of Ancient Cosmology* (London: Thames & Hudson, 1988), 33–35, 59–62, 101–106.
[21] *Magici pueri*, according to Apuleius, *Apologia*, 42.
[22] Philo, *De Somniis*, I, vi, 35; *De Virtutibus*, XI, 72.

of all. Yet Plotinus's ascetic leanings, his hierarchy of levels of being emanating from the One, and his own philosophic ecstasies continue typical Pythagorean themes. Porphyry and Iamblichus both wrote treatises on Pythagorean arithmetic; Porphyry also wrote lost works on geometry, astronomy, and harmonics. Boethius (ca. 480–524) would later name the four disciplines of arithmetic, geometry, music, and astronomy the *quadrivium* (crossroads), and they would survive as the backbone – or straitjacket – of scientific education into the Middle Ages and beyond.

Of the late Neoplatonists, Proclus (412–485) was a mathematician as well as one of the most profound commentators on Plato. By his time, the establishment of Christianity in the Roman Empire had provoked an angry reaction on the part of philosophers. They used Plato as the inspiration of an alternative theology, polytheist and emanationist rather than monotheist and creationist, and answered the need for religious experience through theurgy (the summoning of the gods through ritual and meditation).

St. Augustine (354–430), who had been a Platonist before his conversion, enthusiastically followed Philo's example in applying arithmology to biblical exegesis, and he validated elements of the Pythagorean-Platonic tradition for the Christian intellectual world. Other late classical writers under Pythagorean influence include Macrobius, Martianus Capella, Censorinus, Aristeides Quintilianus, and Calcidius. Last of all come Damascius and Simplicius, who emigrated to Persia in 529 CE when Emperor Justinian forbade pagans to teach philosophy and closed the Athenian Academy.

A well-received theory proposed by Michel Tardieu, of the Collège de France, states that Simplicius never returned to Athens but settled in Harran (the Roman Carrhae, now in southeast Turkey).[23] That would explain a missing link in the Pythagorean chain, for it was in Harran that the mysterious Sabians maintained a pagan cult with Hermes Trismegistus as its prophet and the worship of the seven planets as its principal rite. A century later, the Brethren of Purity (Ikhwān al-Safa') flourished in Basra (southern Iraq); although no direct connection with the Sabians of Harran exists, there is a suspicious community of interest. By the year 1000, the Brethren had completed an encyclopedia in fifty-two volumes that is still read in the Muslim world. The *quadrivial* disciplines play a large part in it, and the volume on music is especially Pythagorean, treating both music's influence on body and soul and planet-tone correspondences.

---

[23] Michel Tardieu, *Les paysages reliques, routes et haltes Syriennes d'Isidore à Simplicius* (Leuven: Peeters, 1990).

## 3 Later Pythagoreans

The Church Fathers approved of Pythagoras for promoting universal love, teaching the immortality of the soul, and founding the sciences of number. The Royal Portal of Chartres Cathedral (ca. 1160) includes him among ancient masters of the Seven Liberal Arts, and many manuscripts depict him experimenting with the four hammers or sounding the monochord. From this time onward, the dual Pythagorean themes of the Harmony of the Spheres and the power of music became commonplaces of literature and poetry.

The Florentine Platonists, with their access to Greek sources, could better appreciate Pythagoras's stature. Pico della Mirandola's *Conclusiones sive Theses DCCCC* (1486) contained fourteen extremely obscure "Pythagorean Conclusions, after Pythagorean Mathematics," mostly drawn from Proclus's commentaries on Plato. Marsilio Ficino included translations of the Pythagorean symbols and *Golden Verses* in his much-reprinted anthology of mystical and magical Neoplatonism.[24] In Venice, the friar Francesco Giorgi (1466–1540) wrote a tremendous work of kabbalistic and Pythagorean arithmology, *Harmonia Mundi* (1525), and advised the architects of the Venetian church of San Francesco della Vigna, whose plan is based on the number nine.

Johannes Kepler (1571–1630) spurned arithmology but shared Giorgi's conviction that the keys to understanding the cosmos lie in geometry and harmony. He had read in Pliny and Censorinus that Pythagoras measured the planetary distances according to musical intervals; even if Kepler had more accurate figures, he trusted the principle. Many years of calculation convinced him that the planetary distances accord with the five Pythagorean solids,[25] and, after many more, that God had designed the planetary orbits so as to create a splendid, ever-changing harmony.[26]

Kepler's laws of planetary motion opened the path for the discoveries of Isaac Newton (1643–1727), who revisited the story of the hammers and came to a radical conclusion.[27] As noted, the results of Pythagoras's reported experiment were false, for to produce tones in the ratio 12:9:8:6, the weights hung on equal strings would have had to be proportioned as the *squares* of

---

[24] *Iamblichus de mysteriis* [etc.], Venice, Aldus Manutius, 1497.
[25] The subject of *Mysterium Cosmographicum*, Tübingen, 1596.
[26] The subject of *Harmonices Mundi Libri V*, Linz, 1619.
[27] For Newton's text, from the Classical Scholia on the *Principia Mathematica*, see J. Godwin, *Harmony of the Spheres: A Sourcebook of the Pythagorean Tradition in Music* (Rochester, VT: Inner Traditions, 1993), 304–308.

those numbers. But by applying this principle to the heavens, it revealed the inverse square law of universal gravitation. Newton humbly concluded that he had only rediscovered a law that the Pythagoreans had concealed in the story of the hammers and the idea of the Harmony of the Spheres. In the field of optics, Newton made his own quasi-Pythagorean discovery. Through experimentation with sunlight shining through prisms, he found that the colors of the spectrum are related in the same proportions as the tones of the diatonic scale.[28]

After Newton, the Pythagorean current parted company with experimental science, because the latter no longer saw the cosmos as harmonized through sacred number, nor nature as ensouled. Pythagorean arithmology persisted in esoteric traditions, especially combined with Christian Kabbalah. It also figured in Freemasonry, notably in the Ancient and Accepted Scottish Rite, which treats arithmology in its twenty-eighth degree (Knight of the Sun, or Prince Adept).

Toward 1800, self-identified Pythagoreans appeared in London and Paris. The classical scholar Thomas Taylor (1758–1835) was notoriously neo-pagan, vegetarian, and anti-Christian and lived an austere philosophic life. He served English readers as Ficino had readers of Latin, by translating the Platonic and Neoplatonic corpus. This included Iamblichus's *Life of Pythagoras* (1818) and a compilation on *Theoretic Arithmetic* (1816). Taylor's passion for his material affected the English poets, including his friend William Blake. He was read and admired by the American Transcendentalists, the Theosophists, the Shrine of Wisdom,[29] and the circle around the English poet and Blake scholar Kathleen Raine (1908–2003).[30]

Antoine Fabre d'Olivet (1767–1825) is another example of a non-Christian esotericist. He published a French translation of the *Golden Verses* with long commentaries extolling the Pythagorean life and principles.[31] His posthumously published treatise on music is also thoroughly Pythagorean in spirit.[32] Toward the end of his life, he founded an esoteric order that taught

---

[28] See Penelope Gouk, *Music, Science and Natural Magic in Seventeenth-Century England* (New Haven: Yale University Press, 1999), 237–246, which also shows the fallacies in Newton's experiment.
[29] An anonymous group based near Godalming, Surrey, which published a journal and a number of translations of Neoplatonic and theosophic texts.
[30] Founder of the Temenos Academy, London.
[31] Antoine Fabre d'Olivet, *Les Vers dorés de Pythagore, expliqués*, Paris, 1813. English translation by Nayán Louise Redfield, *The Golden Verses of Pythagoras* (New York: G. P. Putnam's Sons, 1913).
[32] Antoine Fabre d'Olivet, *La Musique expliquée comme science et comme art*, Paris, Dorbon Aîné, 1928. English translation by J. Godwin, *Music Explained as Science and Art* (Rochester, VT: Inner Traditions, 1987). (Later entitled *The Secret Lore of Music*.)

the immortality of the soul, the science of number and sacred geometry, and the hierarchy of worlds and their inhabitants.[33] The French occult revival of the nineteenth century, strongly influenced by Fabre d'Olivet, saw many attempts to explain the cosmos through the sciences of number and harmony. The present writer has gathered and analyzed these in his study *Music and the Occult*.[34] They culminated in *L'architecture naturelle* (1949) by the pseudonymous author Petrus Talemarianus, which integrates Pythagoreanism with elements of Taoism, Tantrism, Kabbalah, and alchemy.

The Traditionalist René Guénon (1886–1951), in his study of Dante, recognized the importance for the poet of the *quadrivium*, and especially of arithmology as a guiding principle of the *Divine Comedy*. Guénon writes: "Though this symbolism [of numbers] is not uniquely Pythagorean, and can be found in other doctrines for the simple reason that Truth is One, we may still entertain the thought that from Pythagoras to Virgil and from Virgil to Dante, the 'chain of tradition' was probably never broken on Italian soil."[35] Some believe that the chain continued into modern times through ill-documented groups such as the Pednosophers, the Priseurs, and the Tabaccologists.[36]

Certainly it was in Italy that the most vigorous modern revivals of Pythagoreanism occurred, beginning around 1907 with the meeting of Arturo Reghini (1878–1946), a mathematics teacher and keen Freemason, with the musician Amedeo Armentano (1886–1966). Armentano initiated Reghini into a secret Pythagorean order, the Schola Italica, which claimed ancient roots. In 1909, the two of them founded the Rito Filosofico Italiano (Italian Philosophic Rite) in an attempt to reform Freemasonry from the inside, and in 1913 the Sodalizio Pitagorico (Pythagorean Association). Reghini was an outspoken neo-pagan, rejecting both Christianity and popular occultism in favor of self-transformation through inner alchemy and philosophic study. In 1927, he and Julius Evola (1898–1974) co-founded the magical Gruppo di Ur, and Reghini was a main contributor to its journal *Ur*.[37] In later life, marginalized by Fascism's alliance with the Catholic

---

[33] See Antoine Fabre d'Olivet, *La vraie maçonnerie et la céleste culture*, ed. Léon Cellier (Lausanne: La Proue, 1973).
[34] Joscelyn Godwin, *Music and the Occult: French Musical Philosophies, 1750–1950* (Rochester, NY: University of Rochester Press, 1995). First published as *L'ésotérisme musical en France, 1750–1950* (Paris: Albin Michel, 1991).
[35] René Guénon, *L'ésotérisme de Dante*, 4th ed. (Paris: Éditions Traditionnelles, 1957), 13.
[36] See Joscelyn Godwin, *The Real Rule of Four* (New York: Disinformation Company, 2005), 120–126, for a summary in English of the relevant documentation.
[37] Some of Reghini's essays, writing as Pietro Negri, are included in Julius Evola and the Gruppo di Ur, *Introduction to Magic*, trans. Guido Stucco (Rochester, VT: Inner Traditions, 2001).

Church and the suppression of Freemasonry, he devoted himself to symbolism and number theory.

Armentano had spent part of his youth in Brazil, where there was a flourishing neo-Pythagorean tradition as a result of the influence of French occultism and especially of Fabre d'Olivet. In 1909, Dario de Castro Vellozo (1869–1937) founded the Istituto Neo-Pitagorico (Neo-Pythagorean Institute) in Curitiba, enrolling many prominent members of society. It is still active in that city, where it has a Doric-style Templo das Musas (Temple of the Muses), and in other countries of South America.

Reghini and Armentano's activity rekindled awareness among Italian esotericists, hitherto more drawn to Theosophy or Anthroposophy, of their peninsular as the chosen home of Europe's first philosopher and his school. The result is a strong neo-pagan strain in contemporary Italian esotericism, vacillating between the two poles of adulation of ancient Rome and a more inward, Pythagorean path. While the former owes more to Reghini and Evola, the latter is strongly influenced by the Neapolitan Giuliano Kremmerz (Ciro Formisano, 1860–1931). In 1898, Kremmerz founded the Fratellanza Terapeutica Magica di Myriam (Magical Therapeutic Brotherhood of Myriam), a non-Masonic group (hence, including women), whose main purpose was healing through ritual magic and "Hermetic medicine." The branch in Bari, called Accademia Pitagora (Pythagoras Academy), was revived in the 1980s. On a more intellectual level, the traditions of Reghini and Kremmerz are maintained in the journal *Politica Romana*.

Pythagorean music theory has seen its strongest modern development in German-speaking countries. The Prussian parliamentarian and jurist Albert Freiherr von Thimus (1806–1878) influenced by the mythologist Georg Friedrich Creuzer, had the insight that the one unifying symbolic factor behind all ancient lore and learning might have been the discovery of the harmonic series and its association with mathematics. He applied this to a thesis of great density and erudition that embraced Chinese and Egyptian philosophy as well as the entire classical and Western tradition.[38] A main pillar of his argument is the "Pythagorean Table" or "Lambdoma," a grid or lattice with the harmonic series along one axis, the subharmonic along the other, and all tones, with their numbers, arranged in between. Among his many asides, von Thimus explained how Pythagorean harmonics concealed an esoteric knowledge of heliocentricity.[39]

---

[38] Albert von Thimus, *Die harmonikale Symbolik des Alterthums*, 2 vols. (Cologne: DuMont Schauberg, 1868, 1876); reprinted Hildesheim: Georg Olms, 1972.
[39] Translations of the relevant passages in Godwin, *Harmony of the Spheres*, 370–381.

Von Thimus's work, ignored in his lifetime, was taken up by Hans Kayser (1891–1964), who founded or, as he saw it, revived the essential Pythagorean science of *Harmonik* (Harmonics).[40] In his many writings, he applied the Lambdoma to such varied fields as architecture, anatomy, botany, crystallography, violin construction, composition, and, most importantly to him, theology and metaphysics. Of all the modern attempts at a "grand unified theory" on esoteric principles, Kayser's is the most wide ranging and the least infected by self-elevating claims to higher knowledge. It was continued by Rudolf Haase (b. 1920), who became a professor at the Vienna Hochschule für Musik und darstellende Kunst and in 1968 founded there the Hans-Kayser Institut für harmonikale Grundlagenforschung (Hans Kayser institute for research into harmonic principles). Haase's institute tests Kayserian Harmonics against recent developments in the natural sciences, hoping for a fruitful mutual exchange via the Pythagorean principles that (1) all is number and (2) number is best understood through the phenomenon of harmony.

[40] See Hans Kayser, *Lehrbuch der Harmonik* (Zurich: Occident-Verlag, 1950). English translation by Ariel Godwin, *Textbook of Harmonics*, n.p., Sacred Science Institute, 2006.

# 3

# PARMENIDES AND EMPEDOCLES

JESSICA ELBERT DECKER AND MATTHEW MAYOCK*

## 1 Introduction

To know the early Greeks, we must understand the lens through which we see them. That lens was powerfully shaped by later Greeks, foremost among them Plato and Aristotle, who developed the methods of ordered inquiry and formal argument that are foundational to Western rationalism. In the eyes of Plato and Aristotle, the works of their predecessors were fruitful but primitive, as they relied just as heavily on artful speech as they did on self-conscious argumentation, thereby demonstrating their inability to comprehend the difference. Thus, their notion of truth was contaminated by rhetoric. As a result, it became the distinct and primary task of the philosopher to explain how inquiry was to be purified from the irrationalities that plagued early Greek thought.[1]

This newfound concern marked a profound shift in mentality among the Greeks, giving rise to the faculty of critical distance (in contrast to the poetic association of images) as the accepted standard in making claims of truth.[2] While this development undeniably advanced the clarity and organizational power of the Western intellect, it also perpetuated a myopic view of the early Greeks by placing their works within a historical narrative that culminated in the achievements of rationalism.[3] Consequently, major features of their works were pushed aside, while others were disproportionately emphasized

---

* The authors would like to thank Peter Manchester for his helpful comments and suggestions on an earlier version of this article.
[1] Cf. Plato, *Republic* 601–602 on "imitators" of wisdom.
[2] Jean Pierre Vernant, *Myth and Thought Among the Greeks* (Brooklyn, NY: Zone Books, 1988), 218–226.
[3] Alexander P. D. Mourelatos, "Quality, Structure and Emergence," *Proceedings of the Boston Area Colloquium in Ancient Philosophy* 2 (1987), 127–194; see especially 127–128.

to accommodate the view that the earlier Greeks had been trying – and failing – to accomplish the same ends as the later Greeks.

Given this context, the task of reading Parmenides and Empedocles must address certain distortions, foremost among them the long-standing dictum that all religious or poetic content in their works was extraneous to their true concerns. Such conceptual partitioning, however, comes from an external agenda that caused such a restriction in focus among early readers that large sections of Parmenides's and Empedocles's poems were inadvertently left unpreserved for future generations.[4] The resulting damage to their works is extensive but fortunately does not preclude a more faithful reading, the goal of which would be to refrain from importing concepts – such as Plato's rigid distinction between reason and sense experience – that disrupt the natural flow of the texts. It is necessary to see how the materials conventionally deemed "peripheral" shed a tremendous amount of light on the "core" doctrines of these texts. Later Greeks sought to extract and embed these doctrines in a new conversation, which (in addition to the loss of meaning mentioned earlier) also stripped away any semblance of concord between Parmenides and Empedocles, painting them instead as dialectical adversaries.[5] Thus, the antithetical terms "monism" and "pluralism" classically serve to define their relationship, masking a tacit agreement that was too literary and esoteric for later philosophers to acknowledge.

In fact, there is significant evidence in the extant fragments that Parmenides and Empedocles were prophets of a mystical tradition endowed with a unique set of practices transmitted esoterically. This evidence is difficult to present simply, as it forms a complex web of symbolism, allusion, and intentional ambiguity spread throughout their writings. It is, therefore, best to begin by outlining the standard approaches to each figure to distinguish them from the "mystical" interpretation to follow. It is also necessary to show that the key passages containing their core doctrines may be presented in a way that does not conceptually insulate them from other material in the texts – material that is crucially important but has long been deemed merely peripheral. Then, it will be possible to introduce additional details, like spokes around the hub of a wheel, to extend the doctrines beyond the limits normally imposed on them. Lastly, it may be argued that, contrary to conventional intellectual history, Parmenides and Empedocles were solidly aligned with each other to the extent of forming an esoteric tradition.

[4] David Gallop, *Parmenides of Elea* (Toronto: University of Toronto Press, 2000), 4. Gallop estimates (p. 5) that as little as one-third remains.
[5] G. S. Kirk, J. E. Raven, and M. Schofield, *The Presocratic Philosophers* (Cambridge: Cambridge University Press, 2003), 285.

## 2 Parmenides

Parmenides was born approximately 515 BCE in Elea on the western coast of present-day Italy, a colony belonging to the Phocaeans, who originally lived on the coast of present-day Turkey and were widely known for their mastery of seafaring.[6] Parmenides's cultural affiliations illuminate the setting in which his doctrines had currency and, therefore, something of the *form* of the knowledge he sought to impart. The Phocaean emphasis on sea exploration, navigation, and travel cultivated an aptitude for supreme practicality, an alertness to the needs of the moment perhaps best described as "resourcefulness" or "cunning."[7] This particular brand of intelligence correlated with the Phocaeans' self-identification as seals (the Greek *phoce* means "seal"), since these amphibious mammals embodied the ambiguity and graceful agility needed to slip between worlds, under the surface and back again. In accordance with these defining virtues of Parmenides's culture, it is not surprising to find that his single work depicts a perilous journey beyond the surface of this world as we know it, one possible only through a divine level of resourcefulness. In this journey the *kouros* (boy, initiate[8]) is allowed to slip past the guardian of "the gates of Night and Day" (B 1.11), beyond the limits of mortality to the abode of an unnamed goddess who awaits a guest worthy of receiving her instruction on the "routes" available to thought.[9]

This initial journey comprises the mysterious Prologue to a poem in three parts and is followed by "The Way of Truth" and "The Way of *Doxa* [opinion]." Traditional readings focus exclusively on the arguments of "The Way of Truth," as they are deemed the earliest monument to "explicit and self-conscious argumentation"[10] in Western literature, but such efforts to embed Parmenides within a linear narrative of emergent Greek rationality often sacrifice historical and textual accuracy. The overarching and culturally vital theme of divine resourcefulness (which the Greeks called *mētis*) as well as many philologically salient details are sidelined from conventional studies of

---

[6] Herodotus, 1.164–168. Cf. Peter Kingsley, *Reality* (Inverness, CA: Golden Sufi Press, 2003), 17.

[7] Marcel Detienne and Jean-Pierre Vernant, *Cunning Intelligence in Greek Culture and Society*, trans. Janet Lloyd (Chicago: Chicago University Press, 1991), *passim*. Cf. Kingsley, *Reality*, *passim*.

[8] Peter Kingsley, *In the Dark Places of Wisdom* (Inverness, CA: Golden Sufi Press, 1999), 71–76.

[9] Diels's ordering adopted for all quotations of original text. Cf. Hermann Diels, *Die Fragmente der Vorsokratiker*, 6th ed, revised by W. Kranz (Berlin: Weidmann, 1951). The abbreviation "B" is a standard convention indicating that the numbering of the fragments follows that of Diels-Kranz.

[10] Gallop, *Parmenides of Elea*, 3.

the philosophical arguments that traditionally occupy center stage. A more hermeneutically faithful reading would allow the concept of "resourcefulness" to inform the whole of the text, not only as subject matter but as a virtue expected from the reader, thus correcting the biases of an overly rationalistic approach.

To give one example, the journey in the Prologue is classically depicted as an upward ascent to the heavens where the clear light of reason is bestowed on the *kouros*, but closer scrutiny and comparison with Homeric and Hesiodic traditions strongly suggest that the direction the *kouros* travels is not toward the celestial light, but rather the opposite: into the darkness of the Underworld.[11] This long-standing error is partly due to poetic ambiguities in the text but more importantly reflects the perennial philosophical paradigm that equates light and ascent with dialectical reason and sound understanding, so famously set forth one century later in Plato's allegory of the cave and his tale of the charioteer in the dialogue *Phaedrus*. The journey of Parmenides's *kouros*, however, is governed by a wholly different set of virtues and stipulations. These include the exploratory daring for which the Phocaeans were renowned; the power of cunning and trickery needed to circumvent traditional laws and make full use of ambiguities in expression; and, finally, a corporeal intelligence that does not abstract from the body in search of higher truths but plunges wholeheartedly, intuitively, into its physical surroundings and locates there a subtlety beyond that of the ratiocinative faculty. To draw from the symbolism of this example, Parmenides must be approached through a different paradigm that emphasizes practical urgency over academic argument and enables the recognition and cultivation of a "chthonic" (rather than "uranic") intelligence.[12]

At his destination, the *kouros* meets an unnamed goddess – most likely Persephone, in accordance with traditional piety and symbolism – who delivers an uncompromising logical exposition on a mysterious *eon* ("it") that "cannot not be" (B 2.3).[13] Thus begins the celebrated "Way of Truth" section (eighty-two out of roughly five hundred lines[14]) that has received the bulk of attention from commentators. The logic of "Truth" asserts that "what

---

[11] Gallop, *Parmenides of Elea*, 7. Cf. Alexander P. D. Mourelatos, *The Route of Parmenides* (Las Vegas, NE: Parmenides Publishing, 2007), 15.
[12] Kingsley, *Reality*, 26–48. See also M. Laura Gemelli Marciano, "Images and Experience: At the Roots of Parmenides' *Aletheia*," *Ancient Philosophy* 28 (2008), 21–48.
[13] Cf. Kingsley, Reality, 43. "*Eon*" is the controversial subject of the poem; it is a participle of *enai* and can be translated as "what-is" or "whatever-is," thus many commentators translate it as "Being." See Gallop, *Parmenides of Elea*, 42. Mourelatos, *Route of Parmenides*, treats *eon* as equivalent with *aletheia*; for his textual argument see pp. 74–78.
[14] Gallop, *Parmenides of Elea*, 29.

is" must be absolutely one (without parts) and eternal (without beginning or end) and complete (without lack) and motionless (without destination) and alone (without partners or associations of any kind), for all these "possibilities" would rely on the existence of "what is not" (or nothing) – which cannot exist. Mortals, explains the goddess (B 6.5), live in a fabricated world because they are unable to recognize or accept the radical *krisis* (decision) of this logic.[15] Instead, they choose a backward-turning (*palintropos*) path of compromise that attempts to combine the "what is" with the "what is not," because they consider them to be "both the same and not the same" (B 6.8–9). But such a combination misunderstands the nature of each: There cannot be a relation of sameness or dyadic pairing between them, for this would violate the definition of both members of the pair. There is nothing outside of "what is," and "what is not" cannot exist: A pairing or opposition between them is illusory. To underscore this truth, it is precisely the world of oppositions – of day and night, and so on – that has been left far behind by the *kouros* in his journey to the goddess.

The corruption of the goddess's logic is natural and inevitable for the whole of mortals who "ply an aimless eye and ringing ear" (B 7.4) along this habitual path, as they lack the alertness and resourcefulness to realize what they are doing. She demands that the *kouros*, on the other hand, accept the strife of her logic that what is cannot not be, nor what is not ever come to be. While she is conventionally construed as saying that the *kouros* ought to "judge by reason" (*krînai de logoi*), it has been noted that the Greek word *logos* did not take on the meaning of discursive rationality until the writings of Plato; in Parmenides's time, it was closer in meaning to "words spoken."[16] The goddess is essentially saying that the *kouros* has no choice but to accept what she is giving him. The context bears this out: She presents three paths as if to satisfy the mortal craving for choice, only to say that one does not exist and another folds back on itself. The third does not "go" anywhere as it is the unchanging *eon*, but she still ironically offers "a tale of a path" for it. In doing so, she mockingly requests consent while enforcing absolute obedience.

A note of irony and humor persists throughout the poem, reaching its peak at the goddess's announcement: "Here I stop my trustworthy speech to you and thought / about truth; from here onwards learn mortal beliefs (*doxas*), / listening to the deceitful ordering of my words" (B 8.50–52). Thus begins "The Way of *Doxa*," the third section that exists now only in fragments, a

---

[15] Kingsley, *Reality*, 177, 184–187.
[16] For *krînai* as "select," see Kingsley, *Reality*, 140; on *elenchos* and pathlessness, see Kingsley, *Reality*, 149–156.

tragedy understandable in light of the philosopher's dismissal of "mere" appearances. The problem with such dismissal in this context, however, is Parmenides's explicit announcement of his *doxa* as *doxa*, which creates a situation of instructive irony when reading them. The concept of irony has been almost universally neglected in studies of the third section of Parmenides's poem despite the fact that it explains perfectly the relationship between the second and third sections.[17] By humorously imitating the beliefs of mortals in "*Doxa*," the goddess "reveals the tension and conflict in their collective mind. For they cannot help feeling the presence of the *eon*: as a goal, as an intention, as an implicit commitment, as a half-forgotten memory of the ancient covenant with reality. Yet the terms they use are ambiguous in every case. If pressed they turn back on themselves."[18] The "*Doxa*" is thus a portrayal of their self-deception that undeceives by showing how the irony of their condition operates. It also creates a double audience: a community of those who understand, as well as a community of those unable to escape the irony of their condition because they insist on corrupting the logic of "Truth." Parmenides employs the path of irony or humor as a clue to ontological truth, since it is the nature of these devices to collapse on themselves suddenly and yield to a unity that bursts onto the scene. The prevalence of these textual devices suggests that they convey an experience analogous to realizing the nature of the *eon*, and thus that "The Way of Truth" depicts a revelatory event rather than a philosophical thesis.

There is no dialectical process of methodically arriving at the pure singularity of "what is." The interpretation that Parmenides intends us to "judge by reason" reflects a program of reading him that insists on limiting his focus. Beyond the fact that there was no such conception of "reason" in Parmenides's time and that reason only operates through a dialectic of "is" and "is not" that defies the logic Parmenides advances, this reading asserts that he consigns appearances to the category of "is not," an unacceptable outcome as it would eliminate the world of experiences in which we live and move. Nevertheless, the classical depiction of Parmenides's radical monism makes this assertion and can be traced back to Plato's reading in *Sophist*, which set the precedent of exclusively focusing on "Truth" without the surrounding context that would allow it to be recognized as the endpoint of irony. Having artificially banished appearances from Parmenides's account of what is, Plato retroactively generates the need to restore them to a role in philosophical inquiry, which he accomplishes by asserting them to be a

---

[17] Mourelatos, *Route of Parmenides*, 223.
[18] Mourelatos, *Route of Parmenides*, 226.

mixture of "is" and "is not." The irony in all this is that Plato ostensibly "saves" the appearances from Parmenides when it is the latter, in actuality, who gives them a higher ontological status by weaving them into his account of the *eon*. It would be absurd for Parmenides to say that sense experience "is not," while maintaining that what "is not" cannot be experienced, recognized, or pointed out. But Plato's interpretation prevailed, ensuring that the scope of what counted as a reading of Parmenides was all but permanently narrowed, and additionally that Empedocles could now only be seen as someone who tried – and failed – to resolve the problem generated by the Platonic reading of Parmenides.

## 3 Empedocles

In fact, the interpretation of Empedocles (born roughly 495 BCE in the city of Acragas in present-day Sicily) has never truly stepped out of the shadow of this false problem. His doctrine is conventionally seen as a compromise intended to rescue the natural world of change and motion from Parmenides's formidable challenge, while attempting to preserve the plenum (impossibility of void) and certain features of permanence from his predecessor's doctrine. From this perspective, which depicts their relationship in terms of a dialectical conflict, Empedocles appears to grossly misunderstand Parmenides's position, violating the stipulation of oneness (by positing multiple primary substances: earth, air, fire, and water), the stipulation of indivisibility (by asserting the Parmenidean sphere[19] to be a blend of them), and the stipulation of motionlessness (by having this sphere come together and separate endlessly).

Two forces accomplish the convergence and divergence of Empedocles's four elements: Love (the power of harmony, friendship, and creation) and Strife (the power of discord, enmity, and destruction). Empedocles is criticized for not providing arguments to justify his revision of Parmenides, as well as for not providing a principle that would explain why his cosmic cycle continues, and why all things must conform to it. The cycle is simply posited and expounded and appears to transfer theological forces onto the material plane and set them going with the same "givenness" that characterizes myth. He is also accused of naïvely mixing disciplines by rhetorically infusing natural philosophy with mystical significance. Later commentators follow Aristotle's judgment that Empedocles irrationally attempts to combine the

---

[19] At B 8.43, Parmenides compares the *eon* to a sphere.

incompatible: the role of the natural philosopher, on the one hand, and that of the religious prophet, on the other.[20]

Empedocles is open to charges of being dialectically primitive; he does not appear interested in making arguments for his doctrine. The dialectical deficiency of his writing, however, is explained by an altogether different intention. While the cosmic cycle appears as a primitive attempt at scientific explanation, a study of its poetics reveals that Empedocles, like Parmenides, strategically employs misdirection to reveal that various cosmic forces and events, including his own speech, have a far wider significance than is immediately apparent.[21] To begin with, the canonical reading has largely overlooked Empedocles's announcement that his account conforms to *themis* (propriety), which should put readers on their guard. He describes death as "miserable fate" (B 9.4), while adding that he only obeys convention in so describing it, since there is truly no such thing as birth or death (B 11). The bulk of his poetry, however, is devoted to biological descriptions of how things are born and die! He describes Love as "balance" and "harmony," the force responsible for "flourishing life," but he also calls it "Aphrodite," goddess of Love, and urges the listener not to be put "in a daze" by her seductive charms (B 17.21). Her deceitfulness was legendary among the Greeks.[22] When Empedocles labels her creation *thauma idesthai* (a wonder to behold), he alludes to prominent instances in Greek literature where the power of beauty conceals extreme danger.[23]

The force of Strife also plays a more ambivalent role than conventional interpretation admits.[24] The overwhelming majority of commentaries on Empedocles have unequivocally labeled Strife as "evil" and Love as "good," following the reading of Aristotle.[25] Recently, however, these monolithic descriptions have been challenged with regard to a key section where Empedocles speaks about placing his trust in "mad Strife" (B 115.14). This ill-advised trust in "evil" (the standard reading holds) explains why Empedocles – who presents himself as an exile from the company of the gods trying to earn his way back to them – was banished and sent to wander the earth until he purifies himself (presumably through acts of Love). This standard interpretation has been disputed, however, on the grounds that his

---

[20] Aristotle, *Rhetoric* 1407a 31–39.
[21] Kingsley, *Reality*, 323.
[22] Homeric *Hymn to Aphrodite*. Kingsley, *Reality*, 377–391.
[23] B, 35.17. Kingsley, *Reality*, 90; *Hymn to Demeter* 427.
[24] Kingsley, *Reality*, 370–371. For convention, cf. Kirk et al., *The Presocratic Philosophers*, 290.
[25] Aristotle, *Metaphysics* 1.4, 984b32–985a10. For criticism see Harold Cherniss, *Aristotle's Criticism of Presocratic Philosophy* (Baltimore: Johns Hopkins University Press, 1964), *passim*.

word for "trust" (*pisunos*) has the widespread connotation in Greek literature of trusting in something dangerous to get out of a difficult situation: "In short, he is not saying he is an exile because he trusted in Strife. He is saying the exact reverse, that he trusts in Strife because he is in exile."[26] Ironically, the conventional views of Empedocles's cosmic forces reverse the truth in accordance with propriety – just as he predicted through his observance of *themis*.

Empedocles is not a moralist. He does not ascribe a normative value to Love or Strife but views them objectively as the respective forces of binding and unbinding.[27] His ultimate purpose is to liberate the soul by destroying mortal habits and fixations that impede its renewal on a higher level. For this, something more powerful than the moral precept is needed: He wishes to transmit to his student the direct experience of an eternal reality that circumvents the need for prescriptions of any kind, to lead the student to a self-sufficient awareness of the proper role of the human being within the cosmos (B 112.10–12). Consequently, he must alter perception on every level. His method is the subtle language of the cosmic cycle, which is not a mechanism for scientific explanation but rather a means for portraying the nature of the exile (and homecoming) of the soul. This is able to occur through the magical principle of the attraction of "like to like" (B 109), as the attraction of a thing to its opposite is only accomplished by the deceptive power of Love. Left to its own devices, everything desires to return to its home among the purity of its kind. Mortal beings are mixtures of the four elements, which are themselves divine powers (B 6). If Love is able to lure reluctant divinities from their lofty state to become mortal beings, then she has no trouble convincing mortals that their lives, as they live them, are desirable and natural. In the midst of this pleasing illusion, however, the substance of life itself seems to yearn for something unattainable and unnameable. This vague longing tugs at mortals throughout their lives, producing an inexplicable feeling of exile – but they never imagine that this yearning for home originates not from them but from the primary substances of the cosmos itself.[28]

To awaken this vision, Empedocles taught a discipline of conscious participation in returning the divine roots to their homes, a service to the divine meant to restore the soul to its original stature, function, and capacity to lead others to the same realization, which is what Empedocles meant when

---

[26] Kingsley, *Reality*, 432. Cf. Kingsley, *Reality*, 588–589.
[27] Kingsley, *Reality*, 446–449.
[28] Compare Parmenides's use of *thumos* (longing) at B, 1.1. cf. Kingsley, *Reality*, 27.

he referred to himself as a *daimon*, or divinity (B 23.11). It calls for a specific way of being within the natural world, since nature is the repository for each immortal element – earth, air, fire, and water – and, therefore, provides the site for the exchange between mortal and divine. For Empedocles, this occurs through the act of perceiving the world consciously (B 106, B 110), since the perceptual faculties are none other than the active powers of the immortal roots.[29] In our daily experience, we are presented with a thoroughly convincing world of external objects, given all at once. To perceive each and every detail is tantamount to splitting perception into its original components, witnessing how they combine to form what we conventionally take for granted. Love's cosmos (illusion) continuously changes and thus offers no permanent rest or home for the things within it; yet, Empedocles hints that an elusive stillness (reminiscent of Parmenides's *eon*) is to be found at the heart of this motion, if perception can keep up with the changes (B 17.9–13). It is here that his complicity with Parmenides begins to be apparent.

## 4 The Tradition of Parmenides and Empedocles

For both men, stillness is the culmination of movement, a paradoxical truth that must be experienced to be understood. Their language is infused with a subtlety that demonstrates the necessary resourcefulness for this event to take place. Returning to the Prologue of Parmenides's poem, we find a depiction of a swift chariot ride to the Underworld, where absolute motionlessness is revealed to be the truth. The language of the Prologue especially emphasizes the constant revolution of wheels and the turning of the pins in the Gates as they open the way. There is a marked repetition of the word "carry," and the conspicuous use of assonance throughout the Prologue conveys a sense of continuous motion generated by the text itself.[30] Recent studies of the poetics of the Prologue provide parallels with other magical texts of Parmenides's time and show that its verbal strategies correlate exactly with the known examples of incantatory poetry that aim to produce an altered state of consciousness.[31] The motions of the language of the Prologue were intended to lead directly to an experience of motionlessness that is precisely the nature of the *eon* depicted in "Truth." Thus, only by following the poetics of the Prologue can the goddess's logical demonstration yield its

---

[29] Cf. Kingsley, *Reality*, 510–513.
[30] Kingsley, *In the Dark Places*, 127–133.
[31] Marciano, "Images and Experiences," 5; Kingsley, *In the Dark Places*, 109.

proper sense. The decontextualization of the latter by Plato and later philosophers left an impoverished (albeit intellectually stimulating) shell of a doctrine that has ever since mystified readers as to the identity of the "it is" that it depicts.

A statue of Parmenides was unearthed in 1962 from a buried building in Elea. The inscription on this statue is striking evidence that Parmenides was the founding figure in a lineage of healers who served Apollo and whose method was "stillness" (*hesychia*).[32] One manifestation of *hesychia* was the practice of "incubation," which entailed lying down in total stillness for extended periods to await contact from the divine.[33] In this context, the journey of the Prologue may be recognized as an account of an incubatory experience that yielded the revelation of "oneness" seen in "The Way of Truth." The association with Apollo is significant because the god's widely recognized cosmic function, to be the intermediary between gods and mortals, is noticeably served by the text. Just as Apollo was the god of mysterious prophetic utterance, Parmenides's and Empedocles's use of language is similarly bivalent, interfolded with depth and texture, employing a language of doubleness that was not simply expository but rather enacted a transformation on the listener; both of them refer to their words as a *muthos* (myth, or, more literally, speech-event), a genre of language over which Apollo notably presided.[34] Apollo's peculiar power to neutralize antitheses and escape constraints corresponds exactly to the nature of awareness they sought to teach. They are all liminal figures capable of crossing borders that conventionally remain closed.

For Apollo, escaping bonds was natural; for mortals to escape similar bonds and breach the laws of the cosmos, flawlessly constructed by Love, a countervailing acuity (which the Greeks called *metis*) needed to be developed.[35] For both Empedocles and Parmenides, mortals are defined by their lack of *metis* such that "helplessness in their chests steers their wandering minds as they are carried along in a daze, deaf and blind at the same time," "totally persuaded by whatever each of them happens to bump into while being driven one way, another way, all over the place."[36] The cultivation of *metis* fittingly lies

---

[32] Kingsley, *Reality*, 42. For the conventional rendering of "the quiet life" of contemplation, cf. Gallop, *Parmenides of Elea*, 4.
[33] Kingsley, *In the Dark Places*, 59, 77, 82, 139,142.
[34] Gregory Nagy, "The Name of Apollo: Etymology and Essence," in *Apollo: Origins and Influences*, ed. Jon Solomon (Tucson-: University of Arizona Press, 1994), 4.
[35] Detienne and Vernant, *Cunning Intelligence, passim*; Kingsley, *Reality*, 334–341. The epithet *polumetis* is applied throughout Homer to Odysseus, who also makes a rare journey to the Underworld.
[36] Parmenides, B 6.5–7, Empedocles, B 2.5–7.

in the background of their doctrines but serves as a defining thread in the tradition they jointly represent. Their texts are designed to provoke an awareness that could detect the subtle enchantments of Love, who proffers ten thousand items each moment to snag the attention and blunt the cares of mortals (B 110.7), and undo them in service to the divine. But this awareness does not struggle against the current of illusion. It works inside this current, slipping under the surface and returning in a way that thwarts rational expectation. Unlike the discipline of philosophy that appropriated parts of their works one century later, Parmenides and Empedocles do not dualistically contrast appearances with reality. Their continued relevance lies in their ability to unravel this distinction and present us with something fresh, entering inexplicably from beyond the borders of human thought to restore a vibrancy and resourcefulness for welcoming the sacred.

# 4

# PLATO, PLOTINUS, AND NEOPLATONISM

GWENAËLLE AUBRY

1. Introduction

Kant distinguishes between two philosophical schools: one in which knowledge is the fruit of rational labor and the other in which it is rather a kind of *ecstasy*, the mysterious "apotheosis" of intuition. It is in Plato that he finds the origin of the latter – referring to him as a *"Mytagogue,"* the founder of a sect, addressing himself only to initiates.[1] The truth is that the "Greek light" is not the same as Kant's "Enlightenment": It is not a brightness gradually winning the battle against darkness, but rather a flash, a sudden and powerful illumination.[2] This model certainly governs the Platonic tradition. It is for this reason that the question is not *whether* one can speak of mysticism and esotericism in relation to Platonism, but rather of *how* to do so.

It is well known that "mysticism" comes from the Greek term *mysteria*, which refers to the mystery cults, *mystes* meaning "initiate." But this linguistic fact leaves room for different inflections, depending on which aspect of the mysteric experience (i.e., the experience linked to mystery cults) is emphasized: the initiation, the revelation, the union with the divine, or the secret. These various inflections are precisely what we try to highlight. Thus, when Plato uses the "mysteric model," it is mainly as a model of the initiation, that is, of the break with ordinary ways of life and thought that philosophy both provokes and requires. We may, then, wonder whether Plato's philosophy is actually influenced by the mystery cults, and by the figures and trends of thought related to them (especially Orphism and Pythagoreanism). And we

---

[1] *Von einem neuerdings erhobenen vornehmen Ton in der Philosophie*, in *Kants Werke*, Vol. 7 (Berlin: Walter de Gruyter & Co, 1968).
[2] See Pierre Aubenque, "La découverte grecque de la rationalité" in *La naissance de la raison en Grèce*, ed. Jean-François Mattéi (Paris: Presses Universitaires de France, 1999), 407–417.

also have to ask whether Platonic philosophy is itself homologous to this tradition, insofar as it might be based on an esoteric teaching.

From Plato to Plotinus, the inflection changes: What prevails in the model of Neoplatonism is not so much the initiatic scheme, as the union with the divine. Indeed, Plotinus's philosophy proceeds from a founding experience – the union with the One-Good – and develops as an inquiry into the conditions of its occurrence and recurrence. It is in this manner that the philosophy of Plotinus inherits the mysteric tradition and also has a decisive influence on what is commonly called the "mystical tradition," particularly the Christian one. For this reason, we must also ask to what extent the mystical, in the modern sense of the term, derives from (or departs from) the original mysteric model.[3]

In any case, the transmission is anything but linear; from Porphyry and (especially) Iamblichus onward, the Neoplatonists are divided as to the conditions and means for achieving union with the divine. In opposition to the "long road" of Plotinus, involving spiritual exercises and discursive procedures, stands the "short road" of theurgy: ritual magic intended to invoke the presence of the divine. This theurgical turn in Neoplatonism coalesces with a theological turn. In terms of the mysteric model, it is the dimensions of revelation and secrecy that are here reactivated. This is accompanied by an appeal to some texts supposedly containing this revelation (e.g., the Chaldean Oracles), by a reading of Plato that connects him to Orpheus and Pythagoras, and finally by an effort to systematize these doctrines. Thus, it is as though the mysteric and esoteric model was received in an increasingly literal sense, and as though the Platonic project of transposing the mystical into the philosophic became transformed, in late Neoplatonism, into their *integration*.

2 Plato

In the *Symposium*, Diotima offers Socrates what she calls an "initiation." The outcome of this is uncertain, however: "The final and highest mystery" (*ta de telea kai epoptika*) may remain beyond reach.[4] While the mysteric reference and vocabulary here are explicit, Plato nonetheless dissociates initiation from revelation. The mystical discourse actually governs a double demystification: that of Eros and that of the figure of the philosopher shaped on the model of Eros.

---

[3] It is well known that the term "mystic" was substantivized only in the seventeenth century. This is why Michel de Certeau can write that "the mystic" is an invention of the modern ages. See "Mystique," in *Encyclopaedia universalis* t. 15 (Paris, 1989), 1031–1036.
[4] Plato, *Symposium*, 210a.

Eros is not a great god (as claimed, for instance, in the Orphic theogonies[5]), but a great *daimon*, an intermediary between the mortal and the immortal, mixing poverty and plenty. Like him, the philosopher is an intermediary between knowledge and ignorance. He is no more a superior being, sharing arcane knowledge, than Eros is a god. He is animated simply by a desire that is both a rupture with the common world and a passage to another. The projection of the figure of Eros onto that of Socrates indicates above all the *atopia*, the strangeness of the philosopher.[6] In the same way, Plato's reference to the mysteries aligns philosophy not so much with revelation of the final truth as with the dynamic of initiation. In initiation, it is the double dimension of rupture and passage that matters: rupture with *doxa* (opinion) and with appearance and passage to the intelligible forms (*eidē*), the basis of true knowledge.

In the *Phaedrus*, however, the mysteric model is associated with the actual contemplation of the forms, rather than merely the desire for such knowledge. True beauty is not presented as the goal of a journey that may never be completed but as the object of recollection. He who partakes of it is "always being initiated into perfect mysteries" and becoming himself perfect, even though he looks suspect, ridiculous, or insane in the eyes of the many.[7] Thus, the reference to the mysteries here associates the scheme of initiation with that of revelation.

Both are also simultaneously displayed in the allegory of the cave in the *Republic*, Book VII, which represents the passage from the sensible to the intelligible world as a journey from darkness to light. In this Platonic distinction between two worlds, which finds here its most famous illustration, some have seen a "transposition into rational terms of the antithesis between the visible and the invisible that is a feature of mythical thought."[8] The theory of forms could thus be seen as a remnant of the archaic mentality, with which it would share some fundamental features, such as belief in the participation of natural realities in a supernatural (or pre-natural) world, as well as belief in the possibility of mystical contact with it.

But Plato's intelligible world is not a "supernature" filled with mysterious forces or influences. It is the place of true being and identity and can only be

---

[5] Cf. Claude Calame, "Eros initiatique et la cosmogonie orphique," in *Orphisme et Orphée*, ed. Philippe Borgeaud (Genève: Droz, 1991), 227–247.
[6] See Pierre Hadot, "La figure de Socrate," in *Exercices spirituels et philosophie antique* (Paris: Etudes Augustiniennes, 1987).
[7] Plato, *Phaedrus* 249d.
[8] Yvon Lafrance, "Mythe et raison dans la théorie platonicienne des Idées," in Mattéi, *La naissance de la raison en Grèce*, 315.

reached through rigorous rational procedures, such as the passage from the particular to the universal or from the many to the One in the practice of definition. This intellectual discipline (and the ethical discipline it has as its condition) establishes a strict distinction between philosophical reason and ordinary modes of being and thought. The logic of distinction and definition is precisely what constitutes the difference between rational and mythical thought, the latter governed for its part by a logic of ambiguity and equivocity.[9] This ontological distinction is also an epistemic one: Indeed, in the "divided line" of the *Republic*, Book VI, we find Plato sharply delineating the cognitive states proper to the apprehension of the sensible and the intelligible, from *eikasia* to *noesis*.[10]

At this point, the question of the exact meaning of *noesis* must be raised. The traditional interpretation sees it as nonpropositional knowledge, or intellectual intuition. This intuitionist reading of Plato often goes together with a mystical one that assumes that *noesis* will involve an actual experience of ultimate reality, which Book VI of the *Republic* identifies with the Good. However, certain commentators have noticed that the experience of the Good is not explicitly associated by Plato with *noesis*, and that the identification of this term with intellectual intuition is not as clear in him as it will be in Neoplatonism.[11]

The experience of the Good could therefore only be termed "mystical" in the mysteric sense of the word, so long as it is described as a "dazzling vision" similar to the *epopteia*, the secret vision in which the initiatic journey of Eleusis culminated. But, even if this truth were considered an intellectual intuition, Kant's criticism of it is not well founded. Far from being immediate, it can only be received at the end of a philosophical and ethical journey, depicted in the images of the divided line and the cave. And far from being reserved only for initiates, according to Plato it must become the basis for a shared practice and a new political model, since those who reach it are destined to govern the just city. Finally, its condition, nature, and effects are no longer consigned to secrecy since they are the very object of the investigation carried out in the dialogues.

Beyond the echoes of the mysteric model, we must also examine the influence on Plato of certain trends of thought related to it, starting with

---

[9] As stressed by Jean-Pierre Vernant in his introduction to *Mythe et pensée chez les Grecs* (Paris: Editions La Découverte, 1988), 12.
[10] Plato, *Republic* VI, 509d–511e.
[11] See, for example, Julia Annas, *Introduction to Plato's Republic* (Oxford: Clarendon Press, 1991); Francesco Trabattoni, "L'intuizione intellettuale in Platone. In Margine ad alcune recenti pubblicazioni," *Rivista di storia della filosofia* 3 (2006), 609–719.

Orphism.[12] According to Olympiodorus, Plato "everywhere borrows from Orpheus."[13] This statement is characteristic, as we shall see, of late Neoplatonism. Orpheus is the legendary source of a group of writings, some of which, such as the Rhapsodies, were probably not composed prior to the first and second centuries CE. It is probable that the notion of Orphism was a vague one for the Greeks themselves. Aside from these writings, the term referred to the practices they founded, shared by some sectarian groups and constituting a kind of "alternative culture."[14]

Orphism involves first of all a complex account of the origin of the gods, peculiarly linked to an account of the origin of man.[15] This is grounded in the myth of the murder of Dionysus by the Titans: Man is made up partly of the ashes of the Titans struck by Zeus's lightning and partly of a divine spark of the Dionysian soul. It is as a consequence of this original murder that the soul finds itself locked up or buried in the body and caught in the cycle of rebirth, which it can escape only through purificatory practices such as fasting, vegetarianism, and abstaining from blood sacrifices.

Allusions to these ideas can be found in Plato. In the *Cratylus*, the word "body" is linked etymologically to "prison" and "grave."[16] In the *Phaedo*, we are told about the necessity of purification,[17] about reincarnation or the becoming of the soul after death,[18] and we are referred to an "ancient tradition."[19] For this reason, some modern historians have attributed to Orphism a decisive influence on Plato. More precisely, they have seen him as heir to a trend of thought born in the late seventh and early sixth centuries

---

[12] About the link between the name of Orpheus and the Mystery Cults (particularly those of Phlya and Eleusis), see Luc Brisson, "Orphée et l'Orphisme à l'époque impériale. Témoignages et interprétations philosophiques, de Plutarque à Jamblique," in *Aufstieg und Niedergang der Römischen Welt* II, 36.4, ed. by Wolfgang Haase (Berlin–New York: W. De Gruyter, 1990), 2867–3931.

[13] On Plato's *Phaedo* 7 §10.141 in *The Greek Commentaries on Plato's Phaedo*, Vol. 1, Olympiodorus, ed. Leendert G. Westerink (Amsterdam; New York: North-Holland Publishing, 1976).

[14] Cf. James Redfield, "The politics of immortality," in Borgeaud, *Orphisme et Orphée*, 103–117.

[15] A description of it can be found in Brisson, "Orphée et l'Orphisme"; see also Alberto Bernabé and Fransesco Casadesus, *Orfeo y la tradicion orfica. Un reencuentro* (Madrid: Akal, 2008).

[16] *Cratylus*, 400c; see also *Phaedrus* 250c2–4 and *Phaedo*, 62b; 83a–c, with the notes ad hoc of Monique Dixsaut, *Platon. Phédon, présentation et traduction* (Paris: Garnier Flammarion, 1991), 327–328, 356.

[17] *Phaedo*, 69c–d.

[18] 81a; 107d; see also *Epistle VII* 335a.

[19] *Phaedo*, 70c. This "ancient tradition" might as well be referred to Empedocles or Pythagoras; see Dixsaut, *Platon*, 339–340.

and associated with the semi-legendary, semi-historical figures of the "Seven Wise Men": Orpheus, Pythagoras, Empedocles, Aristeas, Abaris, Hermotimus, and Epimenides. These are supposed to have brought to Greece a kind of shamanism: practices aimed at freeing oneself from the particularity and limitation of the body.[20] This interpretation is now considered dubious, so much so that Pierre Hadot speaks of a veritable "myth of shamanism."[21] However, the fact remains that a new conception of the soul was developed at this time, a complete departure from the Homeric one: The soul was no longer considered as the life of the body, but rather as a distinct power, able to survive the death of the body, and recovering, through this separation, its own true identity.

Plato no doubt inherits this conception, but it could be attributed to Empedocles or Pythagoras as much as to Orpheus. Aside from the fact that it can be linked to an actual historical figure, Pythagoreanism differs from Orphism in its ethical and political dimensions, as well as in its marriage of magic and science, in particular mathematics.[22] Plato's doctrine of recollection is often associated with Pythagoreanism: It is well known that the Pythagoreans performed exercises to enhance memory and increase the soul's power of concentration. However, Platonic recollection did not aim at the remembrance of other incarnated lives but at the recovery of the knowledge of the forms present to the soul before (or outside) any incarnation.

Thus, far from being direct and linear as some late Neoplatonists and also some modern historians claim, Plato's relation to Orphism and Pythagoreanism is both mediated and problematic. Plato transforms the doctrine of the duality of soul and body into one that understands it not in terms of an original stain but in terms of the ontological division of the intelligible and the sensible worlds. Plato's aim is not really the salvation of the soul but the liberation of thought. Moreover, this is not the result of exterior obedience to a certain way of life (to prescriptions and prohibitions) but rather the result of conversion to the power of the intellect. It is perhaps in this sense that one must understand the sharp criticism in the *Republic* of those charlatans who claim to have power over the gods and those who

---

[20] This is why Henry Joly can call Socrates "the last shaman and the first philosopher" in *Le renversement platonicien* (Paris: Vrin, 1974), 67; see also Eric Robertson Dodds, *The Greeks and the Irrational* (Berkeley: University of California Press, 1951), ch. 5; Vernant, *Mythe et pensée chez les Grecs*, 123–125, 387–391.

[21] Pierre Hadot, "Shamanism and Greek Philosophy," in *The Concept of Shamanism: Uses and Abuses*, ed. Henri-Paul Francfort and Roberte Hamayon (Budapest: Akademiai Kiado, 2001), 389–401.

[22] See the tribute paid by Plato to the Pythagoreans in *Republic* VII, 530d.

present "a bushel of books by Musaeus and Orpheus," mistaking purification for a "pleasant sport."[23] Nevertheless, Plato's appropriation of Orphic-Pythagorean ideas transposes into philosophical discourse the powerful strangeness and enigmatic beauty of this ancient tradition. Moreover, it retains its essential core: rupture with common life and sense and striving to approach the divine. The philosophical transposition of the mythic and the mystical also appears in Plato's employment of Orphic and Pythagorean elements in his eschatological myths.[24] This goes together with a desire to persuade, to make the intelligible truths accessible to the many. This political use of the myth shows all the ambivalence of Plato's relation to esotericism, since, by employing it in his dialogues, he breaks with its essence: the secret. However, the question then remains of whether the Platonic doctrine is not itself built on an esoteric teaching. The specialists are divided on this point, but it is worth noting that even those who uphold the esotericist interpretation refer it to an initiatic scheme corresponding to progress in philosophical training.

## 3 Plotinus

Damascius (sixth century CE) sums up the complex relationship of Platonic tradition to mysticism and esotericism in the following way: "To some, philosophy is primary, such as with Porphyry and Plotinus and a great many other philosophers; to others, it is hieratic practice, as with Iamblichus; Syrianus, Proclus, and the hieratic school generally."[25] Plotinus (205–270) is here unambiguously associated with philosophy, as opposed to the "hieratic," that is, the observance and practice of sacred rituals. However, his philosophical style is very different from Plato's, in particular because he systematizes what in the latter is still expressed in the play of irony and image. Thus, we find in Plotinus a narrative in the first person of the experience depicted in the myth of the *Phaedrus*: that of the soul's ascent to the intelligible.[26] This experience is presented as proper to *noesis*, which is itself clearly identified with intellectual intuition, as opposed to *dianoia* (discursive knowledge). It can be called "mystical" in the sense that it has no propositional content but also because it is the experience of a union in which the distinction between subject and object vanishes.

---

[23] Plato, *Republic* 364b–365b. On this text, see F. Casadesus Bordoy, "Orfeo y el orfismo en Platon" in Bernabé and Casadesus, *Orfeo y la tradicion orfica*, 1239–1279.
[24] For a detailed description, see again Bernabé and Casadesus, *Orfeo y la tradicion orfica*, 1239–1279.
[25] *On Plato's Phaedo.* I, §172. 1–3 Westerink, *The Greek Commentaries on Plato's Phaedo.*
[26] *Enneads* IV, 8 [6], 1, 1–11.

However, this experience is only the first mystical one for Plotinus. He also admits the possibility of a union with the very source of the intelligible and of the whole of reality, the One-Good. The One-Good radically transcends both being and the intellect. As such, it has no common feature with what proceeds from it, and thus no quality can be attributed to it, making it ineffable. Nevertheless, for Plotinus the One-Good can be the object of a certain sort of experience. Following Pierre Hadot, one can enumerate its main features. The experience is that of an *ektasis* (ecstasy), brief but dazzling. It consists in the feeling of a presence and is compared sometimes to a luminous vision, sometimes to a blind touch. It is a union in which every distinction between soul and the One-Good vanishes; however, this absorption produces the feeling not of being destroyed, but of being expanded.[27]

Hadot has compared these characteristic features of the Plotinian experience to those of the Christian mystics.[28] However, we must ask whether one can legitimately speak of a Plotinian "mysticism" and, more precisely, whether such a designation does not amount to annexing Neoplatonism to Christianity, making it into a pagan forerunner.[29] The fact is that the word *mustikôs* appears only once in the *Enneads*, as a designation of the secret language and hidden meaning used in the mysteries and initiations – not as a description of a certain kind of experience.[30] It remains that Plotinus, although he does not apply the word *mustikôs* to the experience of the One-Good nor of the intellect, nonetheless utilizes expressions and images that evoke, sometimes explicitly, the mysteric model: that of purification, initiation, sanctuaries, the secret, and vision.[31]

Thus, the mysteric model actually is at work in Plotinus as it already was in Plato. However, it does not suggest only the dynamic of initiation but also its outcome as a union with the generative power of reality. And it is the nature of this experience that allows us to call it "mystical": One can indeed recognize in it the essential core of every mystical teaching, whether pagan or Christian. This is why we can admit a limited and legitimate use of the word "mystical," by which it would designate the direct and unitive experience of the principle of being. Such a use, nonetheless, leaves room to

---

[27] Cf. Pierre Hadot, *Plotin. Traité 38* (VI, 7) (Paris: Cerf, 1987), 58–66. See also *Plotin. Traité 9* (VI, 9) (Paris: Cerf, 1994), 44–53.

[28] See Hadot, *Plotin. Traité 38*.

[29] Cf. Luc Brisson, "Peut-on parler d'union mystique chez Plotin?" in *Mystique: la passion de l'Un, de l'Antiquité à nos jours*, ed. Alain Dierkens and Benoît Beyer de Ryke (Bruxelles, Editions de l'Université de Bruxelles, 2005), 61–72.

[30] *Enneads* III, 6 [26] 19, 26.

[31] Cf. *Enneads* I, 6 [1], 6. 1–5; 7. 1–11; 8. 1–6; en VI, 9 [9], 11; V, 3 [49] 14.

distinguish between different kinds of mystics, insofar as the conditions and the object of this experience can be conceived in various ways.

There is another essential core element in the Plotinian mystical experience: The union with the principle of being is also an escape from and transcendence of the ordinary self and ordinary consciousness. However, this supraconscious state is simultaneously the feeling of a presence and coincidence with one's true self.[32] Plotinus, when describing this state, formulates a paradox that can be considered paradigmatic of mysticism and is found again, for instance, in Meister Eckhart: *It is when one does not belong anymore to oneself that one is most oneself.*[33] This mystical paradigm certainly owes something to the mysteric model because this new identity occurs at the end of a process of purification modeled on the initiatic scheme.

However, this process also shows that the Plotinian path is indeed a philosophy, and not only a form of mysticism, insofar as this process of purification is an arduous intellectual and ethical path – an effort of conversion of consciousness, aimed at diverting it from the living body and turning it toward the "separate soul." Plotinus believes that the soul, in its essence, remains in the realm of the intelligible: Something in us (in fact, the essential part of ourselves) is always contemplating, in an unchanging, autarchic, and serene act, and that cannot be troubled by the tumult of the body. Plotinus's philosophy, then, appears as an inner journey, which, at its end, substitutes one identity for another: The immediate identification with the body must give way to the consciousness of the inward presence of the separate soul and, finally, to the identification with this soul.[34] Thus, while proceeding from a mystical experience, Plotinus unfolds it into a philosophy which, in order to elucidate the conditions for the possibility of that experience, constructs a new concept of the nature of the subject, as well as of the structure of reality.

## 4 From Porphyry to Damascius

Although he was counted by Damascius as a philosopher rather than a hieratic, Porphyry, the editor of Plotinus's *Enneads*, stands at the origin of a new evolution of Neoplatonism: the infusion into it of the Chaldean Oracles. This is a collection of texts from the second to third centuries CE, whose

---

[32] Cf. Pierre Hadot, "Les niveaux de conscience dans les états mystiques selon Plotin," *Journal de psychologie* 2–3 (1980), 243–266.
[33] Cf. Gwenaëlle Aubry, "L'impératif mystique: notes sur le détachement de soi chez Plotin et Maître Eckhart," in *Maître Eckhart* (Les Cahiers d'Histoire de la Philosophie), ed. Julie Casteigt (Paris: Cerf, 2012).
[34] See Gwenaëlle Aubry, *Plotin. Traité 53* (I, 1) (Paris: Cerf, 2004).

PLATO, PLOTINUS, AND NEOPLATONISM 47

redaction has been attributed (uncertainly) to Julian the Theurgist.[35] One finds in them, in an oracular form, a theoretical content very much influenced by Middle Platonism and Neoplatonism. But this metaphysical content mingles with ritual and liturgical prescriptions, presented as so many ways to reach the divine.

The Chaldean Oracles thus precipitate both a theological and a theurgical turn in Neoplatonism. The Oracles play the role of a revealed text, so much so that one may see in them the "Bible" of post-Plotinian Neoplatonists[36]: From Porphyry to Damascius, all will try to conciliate the content of the Oracles with the doctrines of Plato and Plotinus. This theological turn is also a theurgical one, for now rituals aiming at union with the divine come to the fore. In short, a new path to the mystical experience is introduced, distinct from the inner conversion prescribed by Plotinus.

It is with Iamblichus (240–325) that theurgy will make its claim as the exclusive path. This internal scission of Neoplatonism partly rests on a disagreement as to the nature of the soul. Iamblichus believes, as Aristotle did, that the soul is nothing else than the life of the body. He refuses to accept the idea of a separate soul whose power one would have to activate in oneself. Theurgy does not require any sort of human aptitude; rather, it is a kind of "technique of passivity," whose aim is to make oneself totally receptive to divine power. The theurgical turn of Neoplatonism, therefore, goes together with the dislocation of the peculiar conjunction between rationalism and mysticism, which appeared in the philosophies of both Plato and Plotinus.

It is also accompanied by a rereading of Platonism, intended to associate it not only with the Chaldean Oracles but also with the figures of Orpheus and Pythagoras. Iamblichus constructs a lineage from Orpheus to Pythagoras to Plato. He grounds it on a real philosophical myth, which all the Neoplatonists after him accept: that of Pythagoras's initiation into the Orphic Mysteries.[37] The result of such a construction is to ground philosophy in the Mysteries, so that it should finally appear as dependent on a revelation. In this way, Neoplatonism's theological and theurgical turns can be justified. In both cases, philosophy is taken away from human power (or from what, in man, is potentially divine) and made dependant

---

[35] For a clarification, see Pierre Hadot, "Bilan et perspectives sur les Oracles Chaldaïques," in *Plotin, Porphyre. Etudes néoplatonicienne* (Paris: Les Belles Lettres, 1999), 89–114.
[36] Cf. Pierre Hadot "Philosophie, exégèse et contresens," in Hadot, *Etudes de philosophie ancienne* (Paris: Les Belles Lettres, 1998), 3–11.
[37] Cf. Iamblichus, *On the Pythagorean Life*, §145–147; see Brisson, "Peut-on parler d'union mystique chez Plotin?" 118–125.

on divine power, "since it was originally handed down from the gods and can be understood only with the gods' help."[38]

Iamblichus's reconstruction of the Platonic tradition would be developed by the Neoplatonist school of Athens into a remarkable work of systematization. Even though Proclus (410/412–485) follows Iamblichus in his rejection of Plotinus's doctrine of the separate soul and in his adherence to theurgy, he nonetheless integrates Plotinus into the lineage of the initiated, describing this lineage as a "divine chorus" progressively rising up to the "mystical truth" concealed by Plato's writings.[39] Such a mysteric reading of Plato's philosophy presents it not only as the end of an initiation, as was already the case for Plotinus and Porphyry, but as the product of a revelation. It also dovetails with a theological reading, which, in particular, considers the second part of the *Parmenides* as a treatise of formal theology, by which the interpretation of the other dialogues should be guided. Plato's philosophy can then be ranked – along with Orphism, Pythagoreanism, and the Chaldean Oracles – as one of the four sources of revelation. More precisely, Proclus's aim is to show the correspondence between the Chaldean and the Orphic revelations, insofar as the latter includes Pythagoras's and Plato's teachings.[40] Space does not permit a discussion of how this project unfolds with Proclus as well as with Damascius, who will integrate Homer and Hesiod into the Neoplatonic system, in addition to Orphic theogonies,[41] and also revive the connection between mysticism and rationalism that was already at work in Plotinus.

---

[38] Iamblichus, *On the Pythagorean Life*, §1.
[39] *Théol. Plat.* I 1, p. 6.16–7.8 Saffrey-Westerink.
[40] Cf. Pierre Hadot, "Théologie, exégèse, révélation, Ecriture dans la philosophie grecque," in Hadot, *Plotin, Porphyre*, 27–58.
[41] Cf. Luc Brisson, "Damascius et l'Orphisme," in Borgeaud, *Orphisme et Orphée*, 157–209.

# 5

# HERMETISM AND GNOSTICISM

Roelof van den Broek

## 1 Introduction

The religious currents that are usually called Hermetism and Gnosticism flourished in the Greco-Roman world of the first centuries of our era, but their impact on Western culture is still being felt today. Both proclaimed a salvific spiritual knowledge (*gnosis*) about God, the world, and man meant only for an elite (i.e., those who were worthy of receiving it). Accordingly, both currents showed distinct esoteric features, but that did not prevent their adherents from writing numerous books propagating these ideas. Although their views on the origin and destiny of human beings have much in common, there are also considerable differences, especially regarding the nature of the material world and the manner of salvation. To a certain extent, Gnosticism shows a radicalization of ideas that are also present, though not dominant or structural, in Hermetism.

## 2 Hermetism

Late Antiquity left us an extensive literature attributed to Hermes Trismegistus. It consists of magical, astrological, and alchemical texts (the so-called technical or practical Hermetica) and philosophically inspired religious treatises (the philosophical Hermetica).[1] In the Greek world, Hermes Trismegistus was considered a sage of the remote Egyptian past, but originally he was the Egyptian god Thoth, the god of writing, culture, cosmic order, and magic. Already in the fifth century BCE, the Greeks identified

---
[1] On Hermes, hermetic literature, and Hermetism: Garth Fowden, *The Egyptian Hermes. A Historical Approach to the Late Pagan Mind* (Princeton: Princeton University Press, 2nd ed., 1993); Roelof van den Broek, "Hermes Trismegistus I: Antiquity," "Hermetic Literature I: Antiquity," "Hermetism," in *Dictionary of Gnosis and Western Esotericism*, ed. Wouter J. Hanegraaff (Leiden: Brill, 2005), 474–478, 487–499, and 558–570.

Thoth with their god Hermes, who faintly resembled the Egyptian god. The predicate "Trismegistus" ("Thrice-Great") derived from the Egyptian manner of expressing the superlative "greatest," by repeating the word "great" three times.[2]

There is no reason to assume that the technical and philosophical Hermetica once belonged together as successive parts of one great hermetic teaching program. But the adepts of religious-philosophical Hermetism had no objections to making use of magical practices and astrological calculations. The main sources for our knowledge of Hermetism are the following:

1. The Greek *Corpus Hermeticum* (= *CH*), a collection of seventeen treatises, of which *CH* I (*Poimandres*) and XIII (*On Rebirth*) are the most interesting.
2. The Latin *Asclepius*, the only complete hermetic text that was known during the Middle Ages. Some fragments of the Greek original have been preserved in later authors, and its final hymn is known from a Greek magical Papyrus. There are also Coptic translations of chapters 21–29 and of the final hymn, found in Nag Hammadi Codex (= NHC) VI.
3. A great number of hermetic *Testimonia*, literal quotations of now lost hermetic works and references to hermetic traditions, preserved in Greek and Latin authors of Late Antiquity.
4. The Coptic *Discourse on the Ogdoad and the Ennead*, a work that was completely unknown before its discovery in NHC VI. It shows that there was no strict borderline between the technical and the philosophical Hermetica, because it contains distinctly magical prayers (among other things, the seven vowels as the hidden name of God) and instructions with respect to the astrological constellation under which the treatise has to be preserved for future generations.
5. The *Definitions of Hermes Trismegistus*, a collection of short, often aphoristic summaries of the main points of hermetic doctrine, preserved in Armenian and partly in Greek.[3]

From Antiquity until the beginning of the seventeenth century, the hermetic treatises were generally thought to transmit authentic, ancient

---

[2] Patrick Boylan, *Thoth, the Egyptian Hermes. A Study of Some Aspects of Theological Thought in Ancient Egypt* (Oxford: Oxford University Press, 1922); Dieter Kurth, "Thot," *Lexikon der Ägyptologie* VI (1986), 498–523; Jan Quaegebeur, "Thot-Hermès, le dieu le plus grand!" in Hartwig Altenmüller et al., eds., *Hommages à François Daumas* (Montpellier: Institut d'Égyptologie–Université Paul Valéry, 1986), 525–544.

[3] Text editions and translations are given in the Suggestions for Further Reading at the end of the volume.

Egyptian ideas.[4] In reality, however, the philosophical Hermetica were all written in the first centuries of our era, under a strong influence of Greek philosophy and Jewish and Egyptian mythological and theological speculation. In the twentieth century, the strong emphasis on the Greek philosophical background led to an almost complete denial of any Egyptian influence on the Hermetica, but this has changed since the discovery of the *Discourse on the Ogdoad and the Ennead*.[5] This text put the question of the Egyptian roots of Hermetism on the scholarly agenda yet again, because it can only be explained within the context of the cultural and religious climate in Alexandria in the centuries around the beginning of our era.[6]

The basic doctrine of Hermetism is the idea of an indissoluble interrelationship between God, the cosmos, and man, which implies the unity of the universe. God is the source of being that encompasses everything that exists: "God is within himself, the world is in God and man in the world" (*Definitions* 7, 5; also *CH* VIII, 5; X, 14). The hermetists shared the Stoic idea that the beauty and perfection of the world prove the existence of a perfect creator. At the same time, however, they were convinced that true knowledge of God was only possible though divine illumination (*CH* V, 2; VI, 14; *Asclepius* 32). They were not primarily interested in abstract philosophy but rather in a pious and practical form of theology. In *Asclepius* 12, Hermes even declares that true philosophy "consists solely in the desire to know the deity by frequent contemplation and holy piety."

According to *CH* V, 9, God's essence exists in eternally creating everything; otherwise, he himself would not exist eternally. As such he is "completely filled with the fecundity of both sexes" (*Asclepius* 20), which means that he is an androgynous being (also *CH* I, 9 and 15). The final hymn of the *Asclepius*, in chapter 43, speaks about the creative activity of God in strong bisexual language, and its original Greek text says of the Father that he is

---

[4] Martin Mulsow, *Das Ende des Hermetismus: Historische Kritik und neue Naturphilosophie in der Spätrenaissance. Dokumentation und Analyse der Debatte um die Datierung der hermetische Schriften von Genebrard bis Casaubon (1567–1614)* (Tübingen: J. C. B. Mohr [Paul Siebeck], 2002).

[5] *Hermetica: The Ancient Greek and Latin Writings which contain Religious or Philosophic Teachings Ascribed to Hermes Trismegistus*, 4 vols., ed. Walter Scott (London: Dawsons 1924–1936); André-Jean Festugière, *La révélation d'Hermès Trismégiste*, 4 vols. (Paris: Gabalda, 1944–1954). See also *Corpus Hermeticum*, 4 vols., ed. A. D. Nock and A.-J. Festugière (Paris: Les Belles Lettres, 1945–1954).

[6] Egyptologists have always defended the Egyptian origin of the hermetic ideas; see François Daumas, "Le fonds égyptien de l'Hermétisme," in *Gnosticisme et monde hellénistique*, ed. Julien Ries (Louvain-la-Neuve: Université Catholique de Louvain, Institut Orientaliste, 1982), 3–25; Jan Zandee, "Der Hermetismus und das alte Ägypten," in *Die hermetische Gnosis im Laufe der Jahrhunderte*, ed. Gilles Quispel (Haarlem/Birnbach: Rozekruis Pers/DRP Verlang, 2000), 98–176.

eternally "pregnant" (*patros kyēphorountos*). The idea of God as an eternally creating androgynous being was closely connected with the view that God had been born out of himself. According to Lactantius, Hermes called God not only "without father" (*apatōr*) and "without mother" (*amētōr*) but also "his own father" (*autopatōr*) and "his own mother" (*autometōr*).[7] There is a general scholarly consensus that the idea of a primal, androgynous, self-created creator is not Greek but Egyptian, and the same holds for the bold sexual language to describe the process of creation.[8]

According to hermetic anthropology, the human being has a twofold nature: earthly and mortal, due to his body, but also divine and immortal, due to his possession of a rational soul or mind (*int. al. CH* I, 15; *Asclepius* 6 and 8; *Definitions* VI, 1). This leads in some cases to a negative evaluation of the material world in general and of the body and procreation in particular. Thus, the *Definitions* say: "Who behaves well towards his body, behaves badly towards himself" (IX, 5), and the *Poimandres* teaches that a mindful person understands everything if he knows "that he himself is immortal and that sexual desire is the cause of death" (*CH* I, 18). According to the latter text, all living beings had originally been created in androgynous bodies. It was only after a cycle of time had passed that they "were parted asunder together with the human being and part of them became male, part likewise female." However, the *Asclepius* voices a more positive view of the human condition: "Man is a great wonder (*magnum miraculum est homo*), a living being to be worshipped and honoured" (*Asclepius*, 6). The same text declares the sexual union of a man and a woman (which is accompanied by "the greatest affection, pleasure, gaiety, desire, and heavenly love") to be a divine mystery reflecting not only the fecundity and androgynous unity of God but also leading man and woman to the experience of their own original androgyny (*Asclepius*, 21).[9]

All hermetic writings aim to bring the reader to an intuitive, spiritual knowledge of himself, the world, and God, which is experienced as a divine

---

[7] Lactantius, *Divinae Institutiones* I, 7, 2; IV, 8, 5 (Nock-Festugière, *Corpus Hermeticum*, IV, 106–107; 112–113).
[8] This is already found in Scott, *Hermetica*, III, 135–138; Daumas, "Le fonds égyptien," 17–20; Jan Zandee, "Der androgyne Gott in Ägypten: Ein Erscheinungsbild des Welschöpfers," in *Religion im Erbe Ägyptens: Beiträge zur spätantiken Religionsgeschichte ze Ehren von Alexander Böhlig* (Ägypten und Altes Testament, 14), ed. Manfred Görg (Wiesbaden: Harrasowitz, 1988), 240–278; Zandee, "Der Hermetismus und das alte Ägypten," 120–125.
[9] Roelof van den Broek, "Sexuality and Sexual Symbolism in Hermetic and Gnostic Thought and Practice (Second–Fourth Centuries)," in *Hidden Intercourse. Eros and Sexuality in the History of Western Esotericism*, ed. Wouter J. Hanegraaff and Jeffrey J. Kripal (Leiden-Boston: Brill, 2008), 3–11.

gift and leads to the praise and worship of the supreme deity. The ultimate hermetic aim, however, is to become one with God, a goal that can be reached during one's lifetime through initiation into the divine mysteries, and definitively after death. In this respect, the most relevant texts are *CH* I (*Poimandres*), *CH* XIII (*On Rebirth*), and NHC VI, 6 (*Discourse on the Ogdoad and the Ennead*). *CH* XIII deals with the spiritual rebirth of Tat, Hermes's son and pupil. Under the guidance of his father, Tat eventually experiences union with the whole of creation, a cosmic omnipresence. He exclaims: "I am in heaven, in earth, in water, in air; I am in animals and plants, in the womb, before the womb, after the womb, everywhere" (*CH* XIII, 11).

*CH* I and NHC VI, 6 describe quite another kind of initiation, a visionary ascent through the seven spheres of heaven to the eighth and the ninth spheres. In *CH* I, 25–26, this heavenly ascent is pictured as a *post mortem* event, which brings the soul into the ninth sphere where it merges with God: "This is the final good for those who have received knowledge (*gnosis*): to be made God (*theōthēnai*)." NHC VI, 6 describes the same experience, but this time happening to a hermetic pupil during his lifetime, with Hermes acting as mystagogue. After a preparatory initiation of seven grades, the pupil comes to the vision of the divine powers in the Ogdoad and of God himself in the Ennead: "I see the Ogdoad and the souls that are in it and the angels singing a hymn to the Ennead and its powers. And I see him who has the power of them all" (NHC VI, 59, 24–60, 1). The experiences described in *CH* XIII and those of *CH* I and NHC VI represent two quite different forms of hermetic initiation, not, as has been argued, the successive stages of one and the same initiatory process.[10]

The hermetic texts not only speak about initiation with prayers and hymns but also about a brotherhood of initiates and sacred vegetarian meals, which suggests the existence of hermetic communities in Late Antiquity. In earlier scholarship, these references were mostly interpreted as merely literary devices without any basis in actual life. But since the discovery of the *Discourse on the Ogdoad and the Ennead*, this view has become untenable.[11] There is no reason to assume that the ancient world knew some kind of

---

[10] Wouter J. Hanegraaff, "Altered States of Knowledge: The Attainment of Gnōsis in the Hermetica," *The International Journal of the Platonic Tradition* 2 (2008), 128–163.

[11] Jean-Pierre Mahé, "L'hymne hermétique: une propédeutique du silence," in *L'hymne antique et son public*, ed. Yves Lehmann (Turnhout: Brepols, 2007), 275–289; Roelof van den Broek, "Religious Practices in the Hermetic 'Lodge': New Light from Nag Hammadi," in *From Poimandres to Jacob Böhme: Gnosis, Hermetism and the Christian Tradition*, ed. R. van den Broek and C. van Heertum (Amsterdam: In de Pelikaan, 2000), 77–95; A. van den Kerchove, *La voie d'Hermès. Pratiques rituelles et traités hermétiques* (Leiden: Brill, 2012); see also Hanegraaff's remarks on this point, "Altered States," 159–161.

hermetic "church" or a network of quasi-masonic groups. But there is also no reason to doubt that there were hermetic mystagogues who initiated their pupils into a visionary experience of unification with the divine, which at least presupposes small groups of hermetic devotees. The hermetic writings aimed to evoke similar experiences in their readers.

## 3 Gnosticism

Texts can be labeled "gnostic" if they express or presuppose a concept of salvation in which the possession of a specific, partly secret, spiritual knowledge (*gnosis*) is thought to be indispensable.[12] If used in this sense, the terms "*gnosis*" and "gnostic" are applicable to all ideas and currents that stress the necessity of esoteric knowledge. The term "Gnosticism," however, if used at all, should only be employed as a neutral term encompassing the various gnostic systems that flourished in the first centuries of our era.[13]

Until the middle of the twentieth century, our knowledge of the gnostic movement in Antiquity depended for the most part on anti-gnostic polemics by early Christian writers, such as Irenaeus of Lyons (ca. 180), Hippolytus of Rome (ca. 225), and Epiphanius of Salamis (ca. 375).[14] They described the many gnostic mythological systems they knew of and tried to refute them. Despite their biased approach, these works remain indispensable, even though we now have a great number of original gnostic works at our disposal. These sometimes transmit a complete Greek gnostic treatise, for instance Ptolemy's *Letter to Flora* on the Old Testament, in Epiphanius, *Panarion* 33, 3–7, or an extensive collection of literal quotations, such as the *Excerpts from Theodotus* by Clement of Alexandria (ca. 200).

Almost all complete gnostic works have been preserved in Coptic. Already in the eighteenth century, two Coptic gnostic codices were discovered, the Codex Askewianus (or Askew Codex; British Library, London) and the

---

[12] For more extensive discussions of gnostic literature, see Birger A. Pearson, *Ancient Gnosticism: Traditions and Literature* (Minneapolis: Fortress Press, 2007) and Roelof van den Broek, *Gnostic Religion in Antiquity* (Cambridge: Cambridge University Press, 2013), 25–125.
[13] Michael Allen Williams in *Rethinking "Gnosticism": An Argument for Dismantling a Dubious Category* (Princeton: Princeton University Press, 1996) has argued that the terms "*Gnosis*," "Gnosticism," and "gnostic" should be avoided, because they have lost any specific meaning; also Karen L. King, *What Is Gnosticism?* (Cambridge, MA and London: Harvard University Press, 2003), 213–216. Discussions of the problem of definition (and a rejection of Williams's proposal) in Pearson, *Ancient Gnosticism*, 8–12, and van den Broek, *Gnostic Religion in Antiquity*, 1–12.
[14] Werner Foerster, *Gnosis: A Selections of Gnostic Texts*, vol. I: *Patristic Evidence* (Oxford: Clarendon Press, 1972).

Codex Brucianus (or Bruce Codex; Bodleian Library, Oxford). The former contained the *Pistis Sophia*, the latter the *Books of Jeû* and the so-called *Untitled Treatise*. These works only became accessible in the second half of the nineteenth century and received little attention. At the end of that century, new gnostic texts were found in the Berlin Papyrus Codex 8502 (Berlin State Museums), of which the *Gospel of Mary* and the *Apocryphon of John* are the most important (published in 1955).[15] It was, however, the discovery in 1945 of a jar with thirteen Coptic codices near Nag Hammadi in Egypt that gave a new impetus to the study of the gnostic movement in Antiquity. The find contained fifty-one texts (and some unidentified fragments), of which forty had been completely unknown before.

Not all these texts are originally gnostic, but most of them are – and they must all have been of great interest to the gnostics who had the codices made. The diverse contents of the codices cannot be discussed here. The publication of the texts not only provoked an immense scholarly literature[16] but also aroused great public interest in the phenomenon of gnostic religion in general and in some texts in particular, for instance the *Gospel of Thomas* (NHC II, 2; the "hidden words" of Jesus), the *Gospel of Truth* (NHC I, 3; a Valentinian meditation on the meaning of Christ) and the *Apocryphon of John* (NHC II, 1; III, 1; IV, 1, and the Berlin Codex; the basic text of gnostic mythology). The most recently published Coptic gnostic codex is the Codex Tchacos (2007). It contains four writings, of which the *Gospel of Judas* is the most interesting.

Gnostic myths show a bewildering variety and complexity, but their message is simple. The human mind or rational soul originally belonged to a divine world of light, but it got entangled in the evil world of matter and became ignorant of its divine origin. Salvation is only possible through *gnosis*, that is, knowledge of one's origin, present situation, and destination, which is mediated by one or more divine revealers. *Gnosis*, therefore, is knowledge of God and self-knowledge in one. The *True Testimony* formulates what can be seen as a definition of *gnosis*: "When a person comes to know himself and God, who is over the truth, that person will be saved and crowned with the unfading crown" (NHC IX, 44, 30–45, 6). Clement of Alexandria quotes gnostics who said that *gnosis* means to know "Who we were, what we have become. Where we were, into what place we have been thrown. To what

---

[15] On the Coptic gnostic codices found before 1945, see M. Tardieu and J.-D. Dubois, *Introduction à la littérature gnostique*, I (Paris: Éditions du Cerf, 1986), 63–138.
[16] David M. Scholer, *Nag Hammadi Bibliography 1948–1969* (Leiden: Brill, 1971); Scholer, *Nag Hammadi Bibliography 1970–1994* (Leiden: Brill, 1997); Scholer, *Nag Hammadi Bibliography 1995–2006* (Leiden: Brill, 2009).

place we are hastening, from what we have been saved. What is birth, what rebirth" (excerpts from *Theodotus*, 78, 2). And in the *Book of Thomas*, the Savior Jesus says that he who does not know himself knows nothing, "but [he] who knows himself has also acquired knowledge about the depth of the All" (NHC II, 138, 16–18).

The origin and early development of the gnostic myths are matters of dispute, but the literary evidence leaves no doubt that they already existed around the middle of the second century in all their variegation. The antignostic writers complain that every gnostic teacher, even if he belonged to a specific school, taught his own brand of gnostic religion, a fact that is confirmed by the authentic texts. It is telling that not a single one of the Nag Hammadi writings completely fits the doctrines and schools that are described by the Church Fathers. Nevertheless, the great myths show a common pattern that recurs, or is presupposed, in many texts: the unknowable, completely transcendent God unfolds into a great number of personified divine entities, called "aeons," which together constitute the divine "Fullness" (*Plerōma*).

The highest divine beings are described as Father, Mother, and Son (in the *Apocryphon of John* and many other texts)[17] or as Man and Son of Man (e.g., Monoimos in Hippolytus, *Refutatio* VIII, 12–15) to which sometimes is added the Son of the Son of Man (*Eugnostus*: NHC III, 3; IV, 1) or the female Spirit (Ophites in Irenaeus, *Against Heresies* I, 30, 1).[18] Valentinus (ca. 140) and his followers taught that the highest divine principle, characterized as Depth and Silence, developed into a *Plerōma* of thirty aeons that are arranged into four, five, and six pairs.[19] Much more complex pleromatic systems were propagated by some gnostics who were active in the school of Plotinus around 250 CE. According to Porphyry, they appealed to such gnostic works as *Zostrianos* and *Allogenes*, which have been rediscovered in the Nag Hammadi Library (NHC VIII, 1; XI, 3). Plotinus sharply criticized them, just because they introduced such a great number of levels of being, whereas he only accepted three (the One, Mind, and Soul), and also because of their negative view of the material world (*Enneads* II, 9). His pupil Amesius

---

[17] Alastair H. B. Logan, *Gnostic Truth and Christian Heresy: A Study in the History of Gnosticism* (Edinburgh: T&T Clark, 1996); Karen L. King, *The Secret Revelation of John* (Cambridge, MA: Harvard University Press, 2006).

[18] Hans-Martin Schenke, *Der Gott "Mensch" in der Gnosis* (Göttingen: Vandenhoeck & Ruprecht, 1962); Jens Holzhausen, *Der "Mythos vom Menschen" im hellenistischen Ägypten. Eine Studie zum "Poimandres" (CH I), zu Valentin und dem gnostischen Mythos* (Bodenheim: Athenäum-Hain-Hanstein, 1994).

[19] Einar Thomassen, *The Spiritual Seed: The Church of the "Valentinians"* (Leiden: Brill, 2006).

even wrote forty books against *Zostrianos*, which, unfortunately, have all been lost.[20]

The observation that some elements of the gnostic myth as told in the *Apocryphon of John* and the *Holy Book of the Great Invisible Spirit* (NHC III, 2; IV, 2) recur in a number of other gnostic works has led to one of the most influential theories in modern gnostic scholarship: the thesis that these works testify to the existence of a specific gnostic group, called "Sethians," who adhered to a fixed set of doctrines called "Sethianism." The group's name derives from the figure of Seth, who in only some of these works plays a role of importance.[21] That certain elements of the basic gnostic myth recur in a number of texts is a correct observation, but that does not necessarily point to the existence of Sethianism as a specific gnostic current in Late Antiquity, comparable to that of Valentinianism. According to another, more recent theory, the Sethian texts were in fact the sacred writings of a specific group of gnostic Christians, called "the Gnostics."[22] It should be observed, however, that in many of these writings the influence of typically Christian ideas is only superficial or even completely absent.

The classic gnostic myth of the *Apocryphon* and that of the Valentinians gave different accounts of the origin of evil and the creation of the material world and human beings. But both agreed that it was Sophia (Wisdom), the lowest aeon, who had triggered the course of events that eventually led to the incarceration of the divine principle of man in the carnal body. She disturbed the tranquility and peace of the *Plērōma* by a reckless act against the will of the Father, which resulted in the birth of an abortion that she pushed outside the divine realm. This imperfect being became the Demiurge, the creator of the material world, who in the gnostic texts is often identified with the God of the Old Testament. It was this distinction between the unknown, transcendent God, revealed by the Savior, and the lower, imperfect, or even evil biblical creator that roused the greatest resistance from the non-gnostic Christians.

Through the intermediary of the Demiurge, who unconsciously blew something of his mother's spirit into their bodies (*Genesis* 2, 7), human beings possess a divine spark. However, they are kept in ignorance through the

---

[20] Porphyry, *Life of Plotinus*, 16.
[21] Hans-Martin Schenke, "The Phenomenon and Significance of Gnostic Sethianism," in *The Rediscovery of Gnosticism*, II: *Sethian Gnosticism*, ed. Bentley Layton (Leiden: Brill, 1981), 588–616; John D. Turner, *Sethian Gnosticism and the Platonic Tradition* (Quebec and Louvain: Les Presses de l'Université Laval/Éditions Peeters, 2001).
[22] Alastair H. B. Logan, *The Gnostics. Identifying an Early Christian Cult* (London and New York: T&T Clark, 2006); David Brakke, *The Gnostics. Myth, Ritual and Diversity in Early Christianity* (Cambridge, MA and London: Harvard University Press, 2010).

bonds of matter and the passions of the body. Nevertheless, from the beginning the pleromatic world launched a counterattack by sending one or more (often female) envoys to lift the veil of ignorance from those who were able to accept the salvific *gnosis* (already in *Genesis* 3, 1–7). In Christian gnostic texts, Jesus Christ is the revealer and Savior *par excellence*. The redemption delivered by the gnostic Christ is not the remission of sin but the deliverance from ignorance. For that reason and also because of their low esteem of the body, the gnostics ascribed almost no salvific meaning to the suffering, death, and resurrection of Jesus.[23] The Valentinians developed a rather complex doctrine of salvation, which distinguished between three Christs who imparted the salvific *gnosis* to three realms: the pneumatic Christ to the *Plerōma*, the Savior Jesus to the fallen Sophia in the psychic realm, and Jesus Christ to the spiritual seeds that had been sown in the world of matter. They were convinced that the pneumatics, who contained this spiritual seed, would be united after death with their heavenly counterparts, their "angels" in the divine *Plerōma*.

However, there were also gnostic systems in which Christ was not mentioned at all. In the *Paraphrasis of Seëm* (NHC VII, 1), it is a certain Dedekeas who fills the role of the Savior. In the *Holy Book of the Great Invisible Spirit* (NHC III, 2; IV, 2), the real Savior is Seth, who after several earlier incarnations was clothed with "the living Jesus" (NHC III, 64, 2; IV, 75, 16–7). The gnostic ideas about salvation had a strong impact on early Christianity, but the gnostic current was not an exclusively Christian phenomenon, let alone a typically Christian heresy. There were gnostic myths outside the sphere of Christian influence, for instance, in Mandaeism.[24] Moreover, gnostic ideas have always spontaneously emerged in Western culture, independent of early Christian Gnosticism.

---

[23] Van den Broek, *Gnostic Religion in Antiquity*, 198–205.
[24] Kurt Rudolph, "Mandaeans," in Hanegraaff, *Dictionary of Gnosis*, 751–756.

# 6

# EARLY JEWISH MYSTICISM

DAPHNA ARBEL

## 1 Introduction

In recent decades, attention has increasingly been paid to the shifting and multifaceted meanings of the "mystical" in a variety of cultural, historical, and linguistic contexts and discourses. As a result, scholars largely agree that the term "mysticism" can neither be uncritically imposed on ancient texts nor commonly utilized to connote a single, universal, timeless phenomenon.[1] With this in mind, this essay adopts a contextualized perspective and aims to elucidate the manner in which distinct notions, embedded in early Jewish sources, can be categorized as "mystical."[2] I discuss this topic with a focus on one heuristic model: the Merkavah mysticism of the Hekhalot literature.

## 2 Merkavah Mysticism of the Hekhalot Literature

Merkavah mysticism developed out of exegesis of, speculations on, and expansion of the vision of God's celestial chariot-throne (the Merkavah/ מרכבה) in Ezekiel 1, 10, as well as Daniel 7. Variants are found in diverse early Jewish sources, such as Qumranic texts, earlier apocalyptic and gnostic sources, the Talmud, and other rabbinic writings. The Hekhalot corpus includes its first developed expression. This literature derives its name from the Hebrew word for palaces or temples (Hekhalot/היכלות). This name corresponds with one of its key themes: the ascent of humans through divine celestial palaces or temples, and their visions of God and his chariot-throne.

---

[1] For a recent discussion, see Peter Schäfer, *The Origins of Jewish Mysticism* (Tübingen: Mohr Siebeck, 2009), 1–33.
[2] Here, "early Judaism" refers broadly to the Second Temple and Talmudic periods to Late Antiquity.

The Hekhalot corpus is distinctively multifaceted, composed of several pseudepigraphic compositions written primarily in Hebrew and Aramaic, and attributed to early rabbis of the second century CE. The precise historical date, provenance, social context, textual boundaries, and transmission of these compositions are ambiguous. The literature contains traditions from the Second Temple period and has strong connections with Qumranic, apocalyptic, rabbinic, and gnostic sources. However, it evolved through a long process of writing, editing, and redacting and is commonly assumed to have been formed in Babylonia and Palestine between the fourth and ninth centuries CE, perhaps even later. Despite its collective title, the Hekhalot literature is fluid and diverse, including a variety of texts, themes, practices, topics, and literary genres.[3]

## 3 A Paradigmatic Model

For a number of interrelated reasons, this remarkable cluster of writings serves as a highly suitable paradigm for the present investigation of early Jewish mysticism. Most scholars regard the Hekhalot corpus of Late Antiquity as embodying the first full-fledged and unchallenged manifestation of Merkavah mysticism (recognized as the first mystical movement within early Judaism).[4] Further, the Hekhalot literature is not a homogeneous body

---

[3] Hekhalot manuscripts from the fourteenth to the sixteenth centuries have been found in medieval Europe. Additional fragments, from the ninth century, have been found in the Cairo *Geniza*. Peter Schäfer and his team published several manuscripts in the *Synopse zur Hekhalot-Literatur* (Tübingen: Mohr Siebeck, 1981) and in the *Geniza-Fragmente zur Hekhalot-Literatur* (Tübingen: Mohr Siebeck, 1984), which form the primary textual basis for current scholarship. On the Hekhalot literature and its scholarship, see Ra'anan S. Boustan, "The Study of *Heikhalot* Literature – Between Religious Experience and Textual Artifact," *Currents in Biblical Research* 6 (2007), 135–167.

[4] On notions associated with mysticism in the Hekhalot literature, see the following studies, which have been consulted throughout this article: Philip S. Alexander, *Mystical Texts: Songs of the Sabbath Sacrifice and Related Manuscripts* (London: T&T Clark, 2006), 122–125; Vita Daphna Arbel, *Beholders of Divine Secrets: Mysticism and Myth in the Hekhalot and Merkavah Literature* (Albany: State University of New York Press, 2003); Ra'anan S. Boustan, *From Martyr to Mystic: Rabbinic Martyrology and the Making of Merkavah Mysticism* (Tübingen: Mohr Siebeck, 2005); James R. Davila, *Descenders to the Chariot: The People Behind the Hekhalot Literature* (Leiden: Brill, 2001); Joseph Dan, *The Ancient Jewish Mysticism* (Tel Aviv: MOD Books, 1993); April D. DeConick, "What Is Early Jewish and Christian Mysticism?" in *Paradise Now: Essays on Early Jewish and Christian Mysticism*, ed. April D. DeConick (Atlanta: Society of Biblical Literature, 2006), 1–24; Rachel Elior, *The Three Temples: On the Emergence of Jewish Mysticism* (Oxford: Littman Library of Jewish Civilization, 2004); Ithamar Gruenwald, *Apocalyptic and Merkavah Mysticism* (Leiden: Brill, 1980); David J. Halperin, *The Faces of the Chariot: Early Jewish Responses to Ezekiel's Vision* (Tübingen: Mohr Siebeck, 1988); Martha Himmelfarb, *Ascent to Heaven in Jewish and Christian Apocalypses* (New York:

of writings. Rather, it contains a wide array of overlapping traditions and outlooks. These probably emerged in various circles throughout several historical phases of early Jewish history and were incorporated into its literary framework. Of course, Merkavah mysticism of the Hekhalot literature certainly does not represent all early Jewish mystical traditions. However, it incorporates (and develops) models of thought, terms, themes, practices, and reported experiences that emerged in other contexts in early Judaism, both prior and contemporaneous. Among these are select apocalypses and Qumranic sources that are particularly important for this discussion.

## 4 Mysticism in the Hekhalot Corpus

Scholars have often adopted specific preconceived definitions of mysticism and thus included or excluded certain material from the category of the "mystical." Here, I embrace the wide-ranging and uncontroversial understanding of mysticism as broadly relating to attempts at bridging the gap between human beings and God. Rather than categorizing the Hekhalot material according to a strict, predetermined taxonomy of mysticism, it is necessary to approach the Hekhalot corpus without such preconceptions. Consideration of the parallel ways in which diverse Hekhalot descriptions and claims – both major and minor – convey this notion of overcoming the gap between the human and the divine provides a wider and more flexible view of the ancient tradition itself.

Oxford University Press, 1993), 29–46; Rebecca M. Lesses, *Ritual Practices to Gain Power: Angels, Incantations, and Revelation in Early Jewish Mysticism* (Harrisburg: Trinity Press International, 1998); Christopher Morray-Jones, *A Transparent Illusion: The Dangerous Vision of Water in Hekhalot Mysticism* (Leiden: Brill, 2002); Andrei A. Orlov, *The Enoch-Metatron Tradition* (Tübingen: Mohr Siebeck, 2005); Christopher Rowland and Christopher Morray-Jones, *The Mystery of God: Early Jewish Mysticism and the New Testament* (Leiden: Brill, 2009), 219–339; Peter Schäfer, *The Hidden and Manifest God: Some Major Themes in Early Jewish Mysticism* (Albany: State University of New York Press, 1992); Schäfer, *The Origins of Jewish Mysticism* (Tübingen: Mohr Siebeck, 2009) 243–350; Gershom Scholem, *Major Trends in Jewish Mysticism* (New York: Schocken 1941; reprint, 1974), 40–79; Scholem, *Jewish Gnosticism, Merkabah Mysticism, and Talmudic Tradition* (New York: Jewish Theological Seminary, 1960; reprint 1965); Alan F. Segal, *Two Powers in Heaven: Early Rabbinic Reports about Christianity and Gnosticism* (Leiden: Brill, 1977), 365–382; Segal, "Describing Experience" in *With Letters of Light: Studies in the Dead Sea Scrolls, Early Jewish Apocalypticism, Magic, and Mysticism in Honor of Rachel Elior*, ed. Daphna V. Arbel and Andrei Orlov (Berlin: De Gruyter, 2011), 365–382; Michael D. Swartz, *Scholastic Magic: Ritual and Revelation in Early Jewish Mysticism*. Princeton: Princeton University Press, 1996); Elliot R. Wolfson, *Through a Speculum That Shines: Vision and Imagination in Medieval Jewish Mysticism* (Princeton: Princeton University Press, 1997), 74–124; Wolfson, "Mysticism and the Poetic-Liturgical Compositions from Qumran: A Response to Bilhah Nitzan," *Jewish Quarterly Review* 85 (1994), 185–202.

At the outset, several issues must be acknowledged. First, the Hekhalot literature does not convey the bridging of the human and the divine in a methodical, comprehensible fashion. Rather, this idea is described through a layered tapestry of goals, spiritual stances, practices, and reported experiences. Further, these claims are presented in both theoretical or exegetical and experimental or practical terms, in varying degrees of detail. Accordingly, several descriptions refer to what may be actual ritual practices aimed at cultivating visions and experiences. Other segments include theoretical stances and theosophical speculations conveyed through exegesis, narratives, and conventional formulas. Collectively, these interrelated claims articulate principles and beliefs characteristic of early Jewish mysticism.

Finally, the Hekhalot literature often voices its mystical outlook in its language, imagery, and models of expression by employing and underscoring the import of several concepts: the ascent to heaven, ritual practice, visions of God and the Merkavah, participation in angelic liturgy, transformation into angelic form, attainment of divine secrets, and the performance of temple rituals in the celestial sanctuaries. While each notion is thematically and conceptually distinct, they all relate to the principal mystical idea of bridging the gap between humans and God.

*a The Ascent to Heaven*

In principle, the Hekhalot literature conveys the notion of crossing the boundary between the human and divine not by employing the model of *unio mystica* (union of the human soul with the divine), which scholars often treat as the essential characteristic of mysticism, but through the idea of human ascension to heaven. Accordingly, Hekhalot segments include diverse accounts of journeys to heaven, aimed at partaking in the celestial realm of God's chariot-throne, the Merkavah. This type of ascent (paradoxically, often referred to as "descent") involves a "round trip" from earth to heaven and back during the person's lifetime.

Several Hekhalot segments present the ascent as an accepted practice resulting from human initiatives and deeds. Accordingly, a number of descriptions portray the ascent as a viable option for all people. Other Hekhalot segments further emphasize the ascent's effortless and uncomplicated nature (e.g., §199: "It is like having a ladder in one's house and being able to go up and down at will"). Others present the ascent as the ultimate goal not only of the adepts, the "descenders to the chariot," but also of God (e.g., §218: "*Tutrusiai*, the Lord of Israel, longs and keeps watch, when will he descend, [the adept] who descends to the Merkavah?"). This material stands in sharp contrast both to standard biblical and rabbinical traditions – which typically disapprove of human attempts to cross such boundaries – and to apocalyptic traditions, which characteristically envision human ascension as initiated by God.

On the other hand, certain segments limit the ascent to select individuals who must prove their abilities and qualifications – for example, through knowledge of magical aids (seals, names), religious knowledge, dedication, ethical and moral behavior, and sometimes distinguished familial lineage. For example, §199: "This may be done by anyone who is pure of idolatry, sexual offences, bloodshed, slander, vain oaths, profanation of the Name, impertinence and unjustified enmity, and who keeps every positive and negative commandment." Moreover, several segments discourage unqualified adepts from attempting the ascent, emphasizing the terrifying dangers and devastating obstacles awaiting them on the journey to celestial palaces. For example, §213: "At the entrance to the seventh palace stand and rage all heroes, lordly, powerful and hard, frightening and terrible."

Most Hekhalot segments do not assume a clear separation between body and soul, and thus they portray the ascents as corporeal experiences taking place in celestial sites. Accordingly, these segments represent adepts as asking for directions in geographical locations and estimating distances in the celestial landscape (e.g., §546: "How many bridges [are there]? How many rivers of fire? How many rivers of hail?"). In contrast, some passages introduce the ascent as an inner, mental experience that capable adepts undergo on earth while focusing their minds upon heaven. Further, they present the mental and concrete journeys as inherently connected (e.g., §544: "Who is able to contemplate the seven palaces, and to ascend, and behold the heaven of heavens?"). Both models, however, reveal a fundamental view that validates human attempts to reach God and partake in his innermost sacred realm.

*b Ritual Practice*

The ascent to heaven – and the experiences and revelations it entails – is often associated with ritual practices. These are frequently introduced as preparatory methods aimed at inducing experiences that, in turn, lead humans to transcend their limits and attain divine visions and revelations. Because the only data available to us are Hekhalot texts in their present redacted form, it is impossible to either confirm the real effect of certain practices or validate the authentic nature of the experiences and revelations that adepts are said to have cultivated. Nonetheless, in this context it is impossible to disconnect an experience from its literal context, as the Hekhalot descriptions detail a wide array of ritual practices explicitly introduced as technical methods for attaining divine visions and revelations.

These practices involve techniques ranging from the magical to the contemplative. In fact, several segments seem to function as manuals, providing instructions and practices that may lead to revelatory experiences – for example, adopting specific postures, following fasts and special diets, repeating hymns, uttering prayers and incantations, pronouncing divine names, reiterating sounds and letters, actively visualizing, and employing "magical" formulas, seals, and incantations.

Needless to say, terms such as "trance" and "altered states of consciousness," which might explain, in modern terms, the impact of ritual practices, are never mentioned. Nonetheless, these concepts seem to be indirectly recognized, particularly in descriptions underscoring the effect of specific practices on human consciousness and the capacity to behold divine visions, experience the celestial realm, and acquire revelations. For example, §591: "Everyone who prays this prayer in all his power catches sight of the splendor of the Presence." And §81: "What is the meaning of the hymns that one must chant when he desires to gaze into the vision of the Merkavah?"

*c Visions of God and the Merkavah*

One of the main goals of the ascent is attaining visions of God in all his splendor and beauty, as well as visions of his celestial entourage and chariot-throne. This goal is often expressed in terms such as "ascend to heaven and behold the king in his palace," "gaze upon the vision of the Merkavah," "look at the *Shekhinah*," "view a glimpse of the chariot," "catch sight of the Mighty One," and "behold the King in His beauty."

Most accounts do not provide many details about what adepts actually see when they encounter the image of God and his Merkavah. Nonetheless, in various segments the act of beholding is perceived as the culminating stage of the journey toward the divine. This goal is presented theoretically through general descriptions but is also grounded in personal experience and presented in first-person statements of individual adepts (e.g., §556: "I saw the King of the Kings sitting on a high and exalted throne."). The import of the vision is particularly accentuated in several segments in which adepts are required to report what they saw above to people on earth (e.g., §169: "Heavenly decree [shall befall] you, you who descend to the Merkavah, if you do not ... testify what you have seen.").

## d  Participation in Angelic Liturgy

The Hekhalot literature envisions another way of narrowing the gulf between the human and the divine: joining the angels in their performance of the celestial liturgy and worship. Accordingly, several descriptions portray humans crossing the boundaries of space and time, becoming part of the heavenly realm, and participating in the angelic choir that sings hymns and utters praise before God in his heavenly palace.

Some segments depict adepts as standing before the throne of God and observing or joining the angelic liturgy – for example, §557: "Happy is the man who stands in all his power and brings songs before the cherubim of *Adonai* God of Israel . . . and sees all things that they do before the throne of glory." Other segments imagine the heavenly and earthly liturgical worship as mirroring each other and further portray the worshipers in their earthly houses of prayer partaking in the celestial temple rituals and praising God in unison with the ministering angels (e.g., §179: "When they [the angels] hear the sound of hymns and praises which Israel speaks from below, they begin from above.").

## e  Angelification

Several segments suggest that select individuals employing specific practices can ascend to heaven, partake in the celestial reality, and also be transformed into angelic or divine beings. This certainly constitutes a dramatic vision of closing the divide between human and divine. In these segments, the celestial journey culminates in the enthronement of adepts either on the chariot-throne itself or on a throne alongside the throne of glory. This enthronement alters the being of the adepts and changes them into angels or, alternatively, into divine beings. In turn, this angelification or deification enables them to behold divine visions normally withheld from both angelic and human beings.

A primary example of this metamorphosis is in the account of Enoch ben Yared (originally mentioned in Genesis 5:24), who was transformed into the supreme angel Metatron. In heaven, Enoch is said to have received a throne "like the throne of glory," as well as other divine attributes. He is even endowed with God's holy name, being entitled "the lesser YHVH." The description does not employ a model of *unio mystica*. Yet, the distance between human and God is minimal, since Enoch is depicted as a deified figure who then becomes godlike: "All mysteries of the world and all the orders of nature stand revealed before me as they stand revealed before the Creator" (§14). In several other texts, adepts are said to be enthroned in the seventh palace before God. This enthronement could imply angelification, consequently resulting in visions of God and his chariot.

### f Revelations

Several segments further propose that the gap between human and divine can be bridged by gaining esoteric knowledge of divine origin. This knowledge, normally hidden or inaccessible, is said to encompass diverse matters, such as astronomical, cosmological, and calendrical issues, matters related to primordial and eschatological times, the mysteries of the Torah, the names of God, and the secrets of wisdom, as well as information pertaining to God's everlasting accessibility and love for Israel.

Accordingly, in several descriptions, divine secrets concern, for example, the "letters by which the heaven and earth were created," "the curtain of the Omnipresent One on which are printed all the generations of the world, and all their deeds whether done or to be done," or "all the mysteries of wisdom, all the depths of the perfect Torah, and all the thoughts of human hearts" (e.g., §§ 14, 16, 59–68). In other descriptions, the attained divine mysteries include knowing the dimensions and, especially, the appropriate names of the limbs of God's gigantic body and, consequently, the magical use of these names – for example, §948: "I will tell you how great is the measure of the body of the Holy One ... the height of his soles is three thousand myriad *parsangs*: the name of his right sole is *PrmsyyhAtyarkny* and the name of the left is *Agtmz*." Still other segments present the revealed knowledge as pertaining to God's continuous presence in heaven and his care for Israel. These segments further emphasize the responsibility of those who made the celestial journey to disclose this knowledge to "God's children" – the earthly community – for example, §163: "I have no joy in the entire world that I created except at the hour in which your eyes are raised to my eyes and my eyes are raised to your eyes."

### g Temple and Priestly Rituals Above

Several segments also envision a peculiar link between the celestial and earthly realms, through transforming the ritual world of the destroyed earthly temple in Jerusalem – the focus of holiness and sanctity – into the heavenly sanctuaries. Accordingly, these passages describe the heavenly temple with architectural details of the earthly temple, presenting the various heavens (which adepts cross) as the *hekhalot*, the sanctuaries therein, and the highest heaven, wherein God resides, as the Holy of Holies.

Re-creating the priestly ritual of the destroyed or defiled Jerusalem temple, several passages further link the heavenly ritual of the angels with the earthly rituals of the priests. These segments align the earthly temple and its priests with the heavenly temple and its angels and describe a hierarchical group of celestial priests or angels as conducting temple worship in heaven: performing temple liturgies, uttering the *Kedusha*, presenting offerings to God, reciting thanksgivings and glorifications, and pronouncing the ineffable name of God, just as the high priest does on the day of atonement. Moreover, some descriptions present qualified adepts as partaking in these rituals themselves (e.g., §151: "Rabbi Ishmael said: Once I was offering a burnt-offering upon the altar, and I saw *Akhatriel* YH YHWH of Hosts.").

## 5 Conclusion: Multiple Expressions of "Mysticism" in Early Judaism

Unlike more dogmatic and orthodox sources, in which views were typically formulated to express a coherent message of a single authoritative group, different writers and redactors shaped the Hekhalot literature within separate and changing sociohistorical contexts in early Judaism. Consequently, the interest in moving beyond human restrictions toward the divine was conceptualized through different, but parallel methods: ascending to heaven, practicing rituals that lead to experiences and revelations, attaining visions of God and the Merkavah, participating in the celestial angelic liturgy, transformation resulting in angelification and visions, and reconstructing temple rituals in the heavens.

It would be misleading to claim that the same mentality and objectives that lie behind all the Hekhalot layers also motivate other traditions in the larger landscape of early Judaism. Yet, several of the Hekhalot eclectic notions are not altogether unique. Rather, they cohere and resonate with a number of views embedded in other Jewish traditions, both earlier and contemporaneous. Distinct traditions found in Qumranic and apocalyptic sources, such as the ascent apocalypses (e.g., *Similitudes of Enoch*, the *Book of the Watchers*, the *Testament of Levi*, *2 Enoch*, the *Apocalypse of Zephaniah*, the *Apocalypse of Abraham*, the *Ascension of Isaiah*, and *3 Baruch*), as well as the *Self Glorification Hymn*, the *Thanksgiving Scroll* (the *Hodayot*), and the *Songs of the Sabbath Sacrifice* from Qumran are particularly relevant.[5] Without claiming direct

---

[5] There are close relationships between the Hekhalot literature and other early Jewish sources, such as rabbinic traditions and the philosophical writings of Philo from Alexandria. Specific apocalypses and Qumranic texts, however, particularly share several mystical characteristics. See Alexander, *Mystical Texts*; James R. Davila, "The Ancient Jewish Apocalypses and the

links or an evolutionary continuity between Hekhalot mysticism and these sources, or harmonizing their idiosyncratic and sometimes ambiguous information, one can see verbal, thematic, and conceptual affinities between them. This is particularly noticeable in descriptions treating the idea of closing the gap between the human and the divine, and in how this idea is expressed, either implicitly or explicitly.

There is no doubt that distinct historical-cultural circles in early Judaism, as well as the literature they produced, reveal major ideological or theological differences as well as diverse attitudes, beliefs, and presuppositions. Yet, they all demonstrate a persistent interest in the attempt to transcend human boundaries and experience God during this lifetime. It is just in this broad sense that the ambiguous modern term "mysticism," can be effectively and critically employed to characterize these dimensions of early Jewish religious life and experience.

None of these early Jewish writings puts across mystical ideas in an orderly and comprehensive manner. Likewise, these writings do not comprise a unified mystical tradition. On the contrary, different sources throughout several historical phases in early Judaism present diverse models that can be characterized as mystical. These include undertaking the extraordinary journeys and undergoing the remarkable transformations and visions described earlier. While these paradigms have not evolved into a clear synthesis, they are all vital components of early Jewish mysticism. Beyond this, they are an expression of the perennial ideal of bridging the gap between the human and the divine.

Hekhalot Literature," in *Paradise Now*, 105–125; Davila, "The Dead Sea Scrolls and Merkavah Mysticism," in *The Dead Sea Scrolls in Their Historical Context*, ed. Timothy H. Lim, Larry W. Hurtado, A. Graeme Auld, and Alison Jack (Edinburgh: T&T Clark, 2000), 249–264; Elior, *The Three Temples*; Crispin H. T. Fletcher-Louis, *All the Glory of Adam: Liturgical Anthropology in the Dead Sea Scrolls* (Leiden: Brill, 2002); Gruenwald, *Apocalyptic and Merkavah Mysticism*; Martha Himmelfarb, "Heavenly Ascent and the Relationship of the Apocalypses and the Hekhalot Literature," *Hebrew Union College Annual* 59 (1988), 73–100; Himmelfarb, *Ascent to Heaven*; Carol Newsom, "Merkavah Exegesis in the Qumran Sabbath Shirot," *Journal for the Study of Judaism* 38 (1987), 11–30; Orlov, *The Enoch-Metatron Tradition*; Schäfer, *The Origins of Jewish Mysticism*, 53–153, 243–355; Rowland and Morray-Jones, *The Mystery of God*, 307–342; Michael D. Swartz, "The Dead Sea Scrolls and Later Jewish Magic and Mysticism," *Dead Sea Discoveries* 8 (2001), 182–193.

# 7

# EARLY CHRISTIAN MYSTICISM

## April D. DeConick

## 1 Introduction

Early Christian mysticism customarily has been understood as a relatively late Platonic philosophical product of patristic theology, marked particularly by Denys the Areopagite (also known as Pseudo-Dionysius, he is thought to have written ca. 500 CE). Denys taught the apophatic way, in which the soul escapes the world to unite with the Unknowable God. The first generations of Christians and their foundational narratives are often casually brushed aside as "background" to a mysticism arising later from Christianity's fusion with Neoplatonism.

Although it is true that a particular strand of Christianity fused with Neoplatonism produced the type of mysticism taught and practiced by Denys, it is also true that long before Denys lived, there was already a rich tradition of Christian mysticism, which grew out of even older Jewish traditions.[1] When historians of Christianity talk about mysticism, they usually define it narrowly in terms of the medieval Christian monastic tradition, in which the devotee, through spiritual practices, gradually purges darkness from the soul, experiences a spiritual death, and ascends to union with a God described as "love." Yet comparativists, studying mysticism across religions, have a less culturally restrictive definition. For example, they define mysticism as the direct experience of Ultimate Reality. I suggest that we set aside the monastic definition of mysticism and examine, as comparativists might, those claims to direct premortem experiences of God found in the foundational Christian sources. We will find that this approach

---

[1] For a treatment of the major characteristics of early Jewish and Christian mysticism, see April DeConick, "What Is Early Jewish and Christian Mysticism?" in *Paradise Now: Essays on Early Jewish and Christian Mysticism*, ed. April D. DeConick (Atlanta: Society of Biblical Literature, 2006), 1–24.

allows the texts themselves to define the phenomenon of early Christian mysticism.

## 2 Apocalyptic Experiences

To describe their immediate, premortem experiences of God, the early Christians did not use the word "mysticism," which derives from the Greek word *myeô*, "to be initiated." Although they do sometimes speak of the revelation of "mysteries" (*mysteria*), the first Christians call their direct immediate experiences of God "apocalypses" (*apocalypseis*) or "revelations." The most famous examples are the visions of the heavenly realm and the descriptions of eschatological events given to John of Patmos. These are described as "the revelation of Jesus Christ" (Rev 1:1). The Book of Revelation mimics the form of other contemporary Jewish apocalypses, in which the otherworldly journeys of seers are described, focusing on the premortem journey or vision, and the revelation of secret knowledge of world events and cosmic endings.

Among the early Christians, the claim to apocalyptic experience reaches far beyond the production of a "new" Jewish apocalypse such as Revelation. In Galatians, Paul writes that his gospel was not received from another person, but "through a revelation of Jesus Christ" (Gal 1:11–12). He bases the authority of his apostleship and mission on this experiential claim. In another letter, Paul describes a typical Jewish mystical ascent in which "a man in Christ fourteen years ago" ascended to the third heaven where Paradise is located and heard secrets that cannot be told. Paul introduces the story as an example of the ongoing "visions and revelations of the Lord," which he boasts of for himself (2 Cor 12:1–4, 7).

Ephesians mentions the revelation of Christ the Power, the fullness of God beyond measure – a mystery that had been hidden until it was revealed to the Apostles and prophets via the Spirit. This revelation occurs between the believer and God and involves the inner workings of the Spirit that effect the indwelling of Christ and his love. It is a profound mystery because it means that Christ and his church are wedded lovers. This testimony from Ephesians aligns with Paul's claim that his revelatory experience was one he thought all Christians would ultimately share. Paul sees this shared revelation as immediate and ongoing, as well as prescient and eschatological. These are constant gifts of the Spirit given to the community, and Paul understands himself to be a servant of Christ and a steward of the mysteries of God.

In the Synoptics, the mystery of God's kingdom is given only to the believer, while the unbeliever sees without perceiving and hears without understanding. The idea that the mystery is "revealed" to Christians and kept from unbelievers appears to have been a very old and prominent teaching known also to Paul. Only the believer is able to behold the Glory of the Lord face-to-face and gradually be transformed into that Glory, while the unbeliever stares absently at a veil concealing its splendor. This transformation is a mystery that will be completed at the eschatological moment when death is swallowed up in victory upon Jesus's return. Thus, in the Pauline traditions, the eschatological return of Jesus was framed as the last apocalypse, when Jesus would be revealed from heaven with his mighty angels. This teaching, like the revelation of what is hidden to believers, coheres with the words of Jesus that on the day when the Son of Man is revealed, God's fiery judgment will rain down from the heavens. His revelation in the other Synoptic narratives is described as a vision of the Son of Man coming on the clouds of heaven in power and glory. A vision of the coming Kingdom of God is also anticipated.

In 1 Peter, the experience of Jesus Christ takes a backseat to the eschatological revelation. Under the influence of the Holy Spirit the church leaders already had taught believers "the things that angels long to have a glance at," but it is only at the eschaton (the end of time) that believers will be able to possess their immortal fate, when Jesus is revealed to them in the skies (1 Pet 1:3–13). These mystical experiences were understood by the early Christians to guarantee the authority, legitimacy, and authenticity of the teachings of their leaders, a point that the Pauline author of Colossians tries to sink at least in terms of the visionary claims of his Christian-Jewish opponents. At the same time, the Christian-Jewish traditions preserved in the Pseudo-Clementine corpus, which understand Paul to be the Apostate, contain polemics against Paul's claims to visions and an authority based on them.

When we track early Christian testimonies about premortem experiences of God, we discover that these experiences were thought to be effected via the indwelling Spirit, and to be eschatological and visionary. They were perceived to be an effect of the power of Christ, and to transmit the mystery of immortal life.

## 3 The Appearances of Jesus

Jesus's postmortem "appearances" are a common feature in the literature, although even the vision of him before his death (as the Glory) is preserved in the transfiguration stories and allusions to them. The Christians also preserved traditions of apostolic visions associated with Jesus's call to the disciples, his prayer in Gethsemane, and his crucifixion. Paul transmits the earliest tradition of postmortem visions and speaks of his own ecstatic experiences as "visions and revelations of the Lord." There are also a number of secondary descriptions of Paul's initial revelation that provide embellishments Paul himself never mentions.[2] The early Christian literature is filled with similar claims to waking and dream visions of the postmortem Jesus.

The words of the postmortem Jesus delivered in visions serve several functions. They give authority to the leaders of various Christian communities. They are used to correct opinions that some Christians did not like, and to rebuke unwanted behaviors. They are also used to inculcate certain beliefs that were proving a challenge for conversion or adherence. Christological indoctrination seems to have been a priority. The words of Jesus delivered in visions are also words of comfort, particularly relevant at a time when the imminence of the eschaton and Jesus's return were being questioned. Jesus's words also sometimes reveal mysteries to those perceived worthy of them. In these cases, Jesus often delivers sectarian teachings as postmortem sayings and mythological instruction.

## 4 Christocentric Mysticism

The main object of the mystical experiences of God reported by the early Christians is the afterlife Jesus. When his appearance is described it is variable, often even shifting in the same vision. In some cases, these descriptions of Jesus are highly stylized, keying old scriptural passages to Jesus's appearance in order to make even more specific Christological statements. What is most significant about the Christocentric nature of these visions of Jesus is that they were understood to function as the *visio dei*. While God the Father remains shrouded and invisible, the afterlife Jesus appears in his stead. This Christology, in which Jesus's appearance stands in for God's, is particularly developed in the Johannine material, and by second-century Christian theologians fond of it.

This understanding of Jesus as the visible body of God on earth was built upon two related scriptural complexes. One complex includes a number of passages about the manifestation of YHWH, called his Glory (MT: *kavod*; LXX: *doxa*), particularly Exodus 33:20 and Ezekiel 1:26–28. A number of other passages associate the revelation of the *Kavod* with the future restoration of Israel and God's Judgment.[3] The complex that emerges is one focused

---

[2] See, for example, 2 Cor 12:1–4; 1 Cor 9:1. Acts 9:3–9; cp. Acts Thom 27: The Lord "appears" to a group of initiates, but they only hear his voice because they were not able to bear his light; Acts 22:6–11, 17–21; Acts 26:16.

[3] Isa 42:8; 43:6–7; 48:10–11; 58:8; 59:19; 60:1–3; Ezek 28:22; 39:13, 21.

on the hiddenness of God. Direct viewing of God will bring death to creatures who attempt to gaze upon him, so he manifests himself in a bodily form that is luminous, even angelic. The Glory and the Lord himself were indistinguishable, and God manifests as his Glory enthroned in heaven and seen by the prophets. The Glory will be revealed when God's Judgment comes on the world. The second scriptural complex includes a number of passages mentioning the Angel of YHWH as the humanlike divine being who bears the Name YHWH.[4] Like the *Kavod*, the YHWH angel was understood to be interchangeable with God or operating with God's power and authority and was associated with Judgment.

With reference to these scriptural complexes, Jesus was associated with the Glory. He was framed as the anthropomorphic manifestation of God and the Angel of the Lord, who bore God's Name and Image. It was in this way that Jesus became understood as the visible image of the invisible God. Thus, visions of Jesus were powerful mystical experiences of God himself, experiences that were understood by the early Christians to be life altering.

## 5 (Apo)theosis

Although the visions of Jesus appear to have fulfilled a number of social and religious functions, at the heart of the "revelation of Jesus Christ" was a soteriological assertion. The mystical encounter with Jesus transfigured the seer. Paul embraces the vision of Jesus Christ as life altering. He writes in 2 Corinthians 3:16–18 that at conversion a veil is lifted off the convert's face. With unveiled faces, Christians look into a mirror and see that their own reflections are being transformed into God's Image by degrees of glory. Paul says (1 Cor 13:12) that this gradual transformation into the Glory is made possible through the power of the Spirit of the Lord, who dwells in the faithful.

Since Paul had identified God's Spirit as the spirit of Jesus Christ, he understood Christians as those who were possessed by his spirit and had thus taken on "the same form as the Image of his Son" (Rom 8:29; cf. Gal 4:6). He addresses the struggling Galatians as a congregation he is suffering with "until Christ is formed in you" (Gal 4:19). Paul claims that because Christ dwells in him, he has been crucified with Christ. "It is no longer 'I' who live," he says, "but Christ who lives in me" (Gal 2:20). He applies this same rationale to other Christians, explaining that if the Spirit of Christ is in them, their bodies may be dead due to sin, but their spirits are alive due to

---

[4] Exod 23:20–21.

righteousness. Paul commands people to be transformed by remaking their minds. This gradual, ongoing process of *(apo)theosis* via Christ will not be completed until the eschaton, when the glorified body will replace the flesh as the fulfillment of the promise of resurrection. The glorified body was the body resurrected: the Image of the man from heaven, Jesus Christ.

The ongoing *(apo)theosis* that Paul experiences is possible not only because the visionary is identified with the Glory at which the faithful peer in the mirror. A possessive dynamic is also involved, in which the embodiment of the spirit of Jesus results in identification with him. Since he is YHWH-Manifest, the Glory of the Lord, and the Image of the invisible God, the indwelling of his spirit has a powerful transformative effect on the possessed. Its presence within the believer works to transfigure him or her into the same Image of God. The believer is glorified by degree, until the glorification is fully actualized at the eschaton, with the final transfiguration into a spiritual, resurrected body.

Even though the Johannine tradition features different emphases, it is very similar to the Pauline in understanding Jesus as God manifest on earth. While Paul emphasizes that *Jesus* is the manifestation of God, the Johannine tradition emphasizes that Jesus is the manifestation of *God*. This difference in emphasis has caused some confusion in scholarship and the advancement of the flawed view that Paul is advocating "Christ mysticism," centering on Christ as distinct from God the Father, while John is focusing on "God mysticism," which makes no such distinction.[5] This is not the case, however. For Paul, the most significant part of the *Kavod* Christology is that *Jesus* is where God has been manifested and localized. If we conform ourselves to Jesus, we experience a similar *(apo)theosis* and localization of God. The Johannine author wants to stress the second half of that equation: Jesus is *God revealed on earth*. Because of this emphasis, he is quite explicit that during the lifetime of Jesus, the historical vision of him was the vision of God (John 14:7). Even the angels in heaven must descend to earth to see the manifestation of God in the historical Jesus! According to John, as a *visio dei* the vision of the historical Jesus was immortalizing.

But how does one go about "seeing" Jesus after he is dead when the author of John is clear that flights to heaven are prohibited? Like Paul, the Johannine author understands that the Spirit of Jesus plays a role in the Christian community. Since Jesus is gone, the Spirit or Paraclete replaces the historical Jesus as God's manifestation on earth. At the end of the Johannine gospel,

---

[5] See Albert Schweitzer, *The Mysticism of Paul the Apostle*, trans. William Montgomery (Baltimore: The John Hopkins University Press, 1998).

Jesus blesses with eternal life those who have "not seen" but "believe" (John 20:29–31). Throughout the gospel, the concept of faith in Jesus is repeatedly linked with the visionary experience, so that faith replaces vision and functions as a form of transfiguration. This concept is developed in the Johannine epistles, which make clear that Jesus's appearance at the end of time will result in our ultimate transfiguration.

The type of mysticism that is developed in the Johannine literature appears to be directly responding to and critiquing another form of mysticism familiar to the author of the Gospel of Thomas. Thomasine mysticism was that of an "open heaven," which encouraged the faithful to ascend to heaven and gaze on the Living God and his Son before death in order to achieve immortality. The Syrian Christians who wrote the Gospel of Thomas transmitted traditions about the ascent through the spheres, the enjoyment of Paradise, visionary meetings with heavenly doppelgangers and the Living God and his Son, and transfigurations into the primordial Man. In order to commune with the Living God and his Son, these Syrian Christians combined this open-heaven mysticism with a call to self-discipline that would control the body of passions. The result was a practical theology that taught that the man or woman in whom the Spirit dwells could conquer the body of passions, and through righteous living re-create in its place the virtuous body of Adam before the Fall. It was believed that one could ascend and reside in Paradise and elicit visions of Jesus and God through a regime of self-discipline and meditation. Eventually this would bring one face-to-face with his or her own God-Image, a vision that restored the soul to its original glorious state. This form of mysticism is a precursor to that which pervades later Eastern Orthodoxy.

## 6 The Democratization of the Mystical

One of the most fascinating aspects of early Christian mysticism is the "democratization" of the mystical via the establishment of sacraments that make the presence of God available to *all* believers. Baptism, anointing, and the Eucharist were all understood to effect the transformation of the soul, and the integration of the Spirit and/or the Christ within it. As early as Paul, these rituals were understood to reintegrate the person into the being of the divine. Baptism washed one clean and made one righteous; it provided sanctification through the indwelling of the Spirit and the Name of the Lord Jesus Christ.

Paul develops this old baptismal theology by ruminating on the implications of being possessed by Christ's Spirit, which he understands to be the "transcendent power belonging to God." If we have Christ's Spirit in us and have become part of his body, then we have experienced everything that he experienced, including his death and resurrection. This is why Paul says (Rom 6:3–5) that when the faithful are baptized into Jesus Christ, they are baptized into his death, but they are also resurrected to walk a new life glorified. Accordingly, we carry within our bodies "the death of Jesus" so that "the life of Jesus may also be manifested in our bodies" (2 Cor 4:7–12). Paul has a similar interpretation of the Eucharist. He understands that drinking the blood of Christ and eating his body effect union with him, on the principle that the person who eats the meat of the sacrificed animal is united with the god to whom that sacrifice was offered (1 Cor 10:14–22).

The Johannine author knows that baptism and Eucharist are powerful mystical experiences that bring God's presence to the faithful, in the absence of the historical Jesus. For this community, entrance into the Kingdom of God is dependent on "water and spirit" that effect a personal rebirth (John 3:5; 4:10–14). Jesus is the "bread of life" that has "come down from heaven" (John 6:35, 41, 51).[6] This bread is his "flesh," which, when consumed, provides the faithful with immortality (John 6:51). The same is true of his blood. When Jesus's flesh and blood have been consumed, he is incorporated into the person. The text is clear, however, that believers are not eating the flesh or drinking the blood of the historical Jesus, because Jesus himself has ascended to heaven and his flesh has been transformed into a glorified body. What they are eating is "flesh" transfigured and made divine via the Spirit, which joins with it during the ceremony in the same way that the Logos did at the incarnation. Because the Spirit is made assimilable via Jesus's divinized flesh and blood, the faithful who have eaten it are mystically united with him. His spirit thus fuses with matter and begins the process of its divinization. Eating Jesus results in the immortalization or resurrection of the flesh of the faithful. In later traditions, including the Valentinian, this understanding of the Eucharist persists.

Christians believed that these rituals were effective because they relied on the power of the secret Name of God (YHWH) that had been given to Jesus, a tradition that appears to be part of the foundational Christian movement as early as Paul. The invocation of the Name effected forgiveness of sins, healing, and salvation. Its efficacy was based on principles common to ancient magic, in which the secret names of deities and angels were understood to carry tremendous power.

---

[6] John 6:35, 41, 51.

## 7  The Cosmic Drama Internalized

One aspect that cannot be overemphasized is the relationship between early Christian mysticism and the drama of cosmic endings that Christian Jews believed would play out in their lifetime. This drama depended on the Genesis story, which teaches that God created human beings in his Image, so that they enjoyed living directly in his presence. Ancient readers speculated about why exactly this was no longer the case, and what was needed to restore it. Most Jews thought that Adam had made a bad choice that had separated him from God, tarnishing his original state or causing him to lose it entirely. This meant that piety was the key to restoration and salvation. If one lived in obedience to God's Law, upon death or the eschaton one would be restored to the original created state and live again in Paradise. They taught this via their doctrine of the resurrection of the dead in a glorious, angelic body reflecting God's Image.

Jews such as the Therapeutae and the Qumranites believed that the lost Image could be restored, at least provisionally, before death; that the eschatological encounter with God and all the promises that went with it could be had *now*, including the promise of the glorified body. This meant that the rewards traditionally reserved for the Last Day became available to the faithful in the present, including the revelation of God's mysteries and encounters with God resulting in the *(apo)theosis* of the devotee. Mysticism and eschatology are not competing alternatives, however, but are instead opposite ends of the same apocalyptic continuum. Eschatology views salvation and transformation on a cosmic level as a future apocalyptic reality. Mysticism views salvation and transformation on a personal level, as an immediate apocalyptic reality. Eschatology is mysticism externalized and postponed. Mysticism is eschatology actualized in the present and on a personal, internalized level.

Mysticism and eschatology not only do not oppose each other, they work in tandem. Rarely if ever in early Christian literature do we find one without the other. The matter usually is one of focus or emphasis, with either the eschatological or the mystical dominating. In the earliest Christian literature, the two operate seamlessly as partners, beginning with the early memories of Jesus. He is remembered as a prophet, anointed with the Holy Spirit. In this way, he is recalled as the mystic par excellence, in whom God's Spirit dwelled at his baptism and who was transfigured into a luminous angel on the mountain. A major focus of his teaching was the immediacy of God. He was remembered as a teacher who spoke about the future but imminent end of the world, when God's Judgment would occur and his Kingdom would come. Simultaneously, Jesus was remembered as a teacher who taught that God's Kingdom was already accessible to believers, that it had been sown like a mustard seed in the earth. He had come to directly reveal to them what is hidden: the mystery of the Kingdom and knowledge of the Father.

This dual message allowed early Christian mysticism to develop in fascinating directions, especially when the immediacy of the eschaton was called into question after long years of waiting for an event that became the great Non-Event. When the Kingdom did not come, the early Christians reevaluated their traditions to explain the Non-Event and make their recollections of Jesus's apocalyptic words meaningful again. They tried several strategies, and all of them were successful to some extent. Paul appears to have emphasized that Christians were already experiencing a divine transformation as a result of the indwelling of Christ's Spirit at their baptism. Revelations of Jesus should be expected as part of their experience. The transformation, however, would be fully actualized at the eschaton, when the final revelation of Jesus in the clouds of heaven would occur. Paul's solution was to understand the restoration to God's image as occurring in stages, paving the way to the final moment of full actualization. In this way, both the mystical and the eschatological dominate religious experience. The authors of the Synoptic gospels assure their readers that they must prepare for the eschaton regardless of when it will happen. The eschaton is understood to be underway, although postponed. This meant that the cosmos was changing as God or his Spirit broke into the world, making possible direct encounters between him and the faithful. But the restoration of the Image was reserved mainly for the day of the resurrection. This solution allowed the eschatological to dominate while the mystical simmered in the background.

The early Christians also began to consider the implications of Jesus being the first to be resurrected from the dead. Did this mean that the end of the world had already started? Many thought so, which led them to believe that they were living in the era of the End, and that all the promises of the eschaton were theirs already. With the collapse of their eschatological expectations, the early Christians relied more and more on the mystical dimension of apocalypticism. Some, like the Syrian Christians represented by the Gospel of Thomas, shifted their theology away from a future-oriented, cosmic eschatology to a personal mysticism. This depended on a premortem ascent and vision attained through a regime of self-discipline that would transform their bodies, allowing them to enter Eden. The Johannine Christians went so far as to collapse the future eschatological drama back into the story of Jesus, so that the coming of the Son of Man, the Judgment, and the establishment of God's Kingdom already occurred during Jesus's lifetime.

Although there is still an expectation of a future coming of Jesus, this takes a backseat to the teaching that we have already been judged, saved, and had God revealed to us through Jesus and his Spirit. In this case, the mystical dimension trumped the eschatological and the cosmic drama was played out as an internalized pageant.

## 8 The Mystery Unveiled

The mysticism that pervades the foundational early Christian movement is Christocentric. It focuses on the "revelation of Jesus Christ," which is understood to be the disclosure of the mystery that has been hidden with God for the ages: that Christ Jesus is the Power and Fullness of God. It was taught that all Christians experienced this revelation in an ongoing manner beginning with baptism, which brought an indwelling of the Spirit. The experience continued in the life of the community and the sacraments, in which Jesus and the Spirit were encountered regularly. Christ's ultimate revelation would be a vision coming at the eschaton.

The revelation of Jesus functioned as a *visio dei*, in which the vision of Christ Jesus substitutes for the vision of God: Encounter with Jesus is encounter with God. The faithful are transfigured into the same Image that Christ is, which means that they too become God-manifest. Through this transfiguration, the faithful (eventually) achieved the "lot" of immortality. There is some speculation in the literature that the Father himself might be revealed at the end of time, but in the present it is Jesus as God's Image who is met by the faithful, and it is he that they become.

# II
# *The Middle Ages*

# 8

# SUFISM

## WILLIAM C. CHITTICK

### 1 Introduction

The Arabic word *ṣūfī*, the original sense of which has been much discussed, came into use in the second century AH/eighth century CE[1] to designate a certain sort of pious, usually ascetic, individual. Its derivative form "Sufism" (*taṣawwuf*, literally, "to be a *ṣūfī*") has been one of several terms used to designate those tendencies of Islamic thought and practice that focus on the inner domain of the human spirit rather than the outer domain of ritual activity, social rules, and creedal dogmatics. Many Western scholars have referred to Sufism as mysticism, esotericism, or spirituality, but there is no consensus as to what exactly it, or any of these words, designates. The difficulty of defining the word "Sufism" itself is partly the result of the historical and geographical vagaries of the word's usage and the frequent controversies over its legitimacy – controversies in which the two sides typically had radically different notions of what it denotes. Throughout Islamic history, numerous definitions have been offered by authors claiming to speak for it. These are rarely consistent with the notion that Sufism had a clearly defined identity, especially when we take into account the definitions offered by critics.[2] In what follows, I use the word as a designation for the focus on "interiority" that is found in the sources of the Islamic tradition and in countless authors down through the centuries, whether or not the term

---

[1] "AH" stands for the Latin *anno Hegirae* ("in the year of the Hijra") and designates a year or period in the Muslim calendar. Year one was 622 CE, in which Muhammad emigrated from Mecca to Medina, known as the Hijra.
[2] A century ago, the well-known Orientalist R. A. Nicholson published "A Historical Enquiry Concerning the Origin and Development of Sufism," *Journal of the Royal Asiatic Society* (1906), which included a list of seventy-eight early definitions by Sufi authors. A longer list is found in J. Nurbakhsh, *Sufism: Meaning, Knowledge, and Unity* (New York: Khaniqahi-Nimatullahi, 1981).

"Sufism" itself was employed in each case. I will discuss three broad issues: Sufism's relation to other fields of learning, its characteristic approach to theory, and its understanding of the role of praxis.

## 2 The Three Dimensions of Islam

The Koran and the Hadith (the sayings of Muhammad) are full of raw material for the disciplines that came to be called jurisprudence (*fiqh*), scholastic theology (*kalām*), philosophy, and Sufism, but these disciplines themselves appeared gradually. When scholars say that Sufism originated in the second/eighth or third/ninth centuries, they mean that before that time, the sources do not delineate the specific concerns that differentiate the Sufis of later times from other Muslims. The same is true, however, for the other approaches to Islamic thought and practice – not least jurisprudence and scholastic theology, which are often said to represent "orthodox" Islam.

We can attempt to unravel the interwoven strands of germinal Islam by differentiating among three dimensions of human concern: practice, understanding, and transformation. On the most outward, "exoteric" level, the Koran and Hadith lay down rules and regulations for right and wrong activity, such as the "five pillars," the essential acts of every Muslim. This strand of Islam became codified and institutionalized in the various schools of jurisprudence, all of which were trying to explicate what is commonly called the Shariah (*sharī'a*, literally "road leading to water"), a word that is usually translated as sacred or revealed law.

On a more subtle level, the Koran and the Hadith provide guidelines for right understanding and right thought. Both have a great deal to say about the "unseen" (*ghayb*), which includes God, angels, and the Last Day, and they mention that God has sent scriptures and prophets. Muslims are told to have "faith" (*īmān*) in all this, though the word's semantic field overlaps with that of knowledge (*'ilm*). Faith implies understanding the truth of these notions and committing oneself to the praxis that they entail. Schools of thought explicating the significance of faith and its objects began to appear in the second/eighth century and are typically classified as scholastic theology or as philosophy. Scholastic theologians attempted in a rather dogmatic way to clarify and rationalize the Koran's teachings about God, the universe, and human destiny; philosophers addressed the same subjects (and others as well) without limiting themselves to properly "Islamic" sources, taking much of their inspiration from the content and methodology of Greek thought, especially Aristotle, Plotinus, and the Corpus Hermeticum.

Parallel with these two approaches, a further approach was found in various saintly figures who relied on inner insight (*baṣīra*) and mystical "unveiling" (*kashf*). They claimed that the only way to acquire true understanding of God, the world, and the soul was to adhere assiduously to the outer and inner model of human perfection established by the Prophet. Their watchword was "Be truly pious, and God will teach you" (Koran 2:282). They respected rational thought but recognized its limitations, especially in its attempts to unravel the nature of the unseen. They sought to achieve what later was called "a stage beyond the stage of reason" (*ṭawr warā' ṭawr al-'aql*). Once this strand of thought and practice became differentiated from other strands, these figures were looked back on as the early Sufis. Every one of the many hagiographical accounts that talk about their lives and teachings traces their approach back to the Prophet himself and some of his outstanding companions, especially his cousin and son-in-law ʿAlī and the first caliph Abū Bakr.

Those who took this Sufi approach based themselves squarely on the Koran and the Hadith. In their view, the primary concern of these sources was to guide people in re-joining their Divine Source. They saw the prototype of their path in Muhammad's "ladder" (*miʿrāj*) or "night journey" (*isrā'*), during which the angel Gabriel took him up stage-by-stage to the highest heaven, from which he entered alone into God's presence. This was the second of the two defining moments of Islam's foundation, the first being God's revelation of the Koran – which also took place through the intermediary Gabriel. For the Sufi tradition down through the centuries, the goal of both right practice and right understanding has been to assimilate the Koranic revelation and, on that basis, to ascend the ladder in the footsteps of the path breaker, the Prophet himself.

By the time of al-Ghazālī (d. 505/1111), a scholar of great renown, there existed a variety of approaches to understanding God, the universe, and the human soul. Scholastic theologians gave pride of place to rational interpretation of the Koran; Hellenophile philosophers preferred rational interpretation of the universe and the soul in the context of a metaphysics of being; and Sufis claimed access to the unveiling of the esoteric meanings of the Koran, the cosmos, and the human self. Al-Ghazālī himself was a synthesizer, drawing from jurisprudence, theology, philosophy, and Sufism. The oft-repeated assertion that he brought Sufism into the Islamic mainstream means that he helped give it a high profile in the official religious establishment. What he was doing, however, was making explicit the Koranic stress on balance among practice, understanding, and transformation.

By "transformation," the third dimension of human concern, I mean achieving conformity with the Source of all, or what al-Ghazālī and others called "becoming characterized by the character traits of God" (*takhalluq bi akhlāq Allāh*). The competence of the jurists is limited to right and wrong activity, and that of the scholastic theologians to the rational defense of the articles of faith. What characterizes the specifically Sufi approach is the insistence that true understanding of and conformity to the Divine Reality depend on the soul's transformation. The philosophers also had a good deal to say about this issue – they spoke about achieving "conjunction" (*ittiṣāl*) with the Agent Intellect or "deiformity" (*ta'alluh*, from the same root as *Allāh*) – but with some exceptions, they tended to get bogged down in the rational preliminaries and had little to say about the Koranic path. In contrast, the Sufi masters spoke from the standpoint of having climbed the ladder to God in the Prophet's footsteps.

## 3 The Three Principles of Understanding

In a brief overview such as this, it would be impossible to do justice to the major authors who produced significant works on Sufi theory. Instead, I address a few of the basic themes, the contours of which can be summed up in what are commonly called the three "principles" (*aṣl*) of faith: the assertion of God's unity *(tawḥīd)*; prophecy (*nubuwwa*), or divine guidance; and the return (*ma'ād*) to God, or eschatology. When elaborated by scholastic theologians, philosophers, and Sufis, *tawḥīd* developed into various approaches to metaphysics and theology; *nubuwwa* yielded elaborate discussions of human perfection and spiritual anthropology; and *ma'ād* focused on the posthumous development of the soul and the means to achieve a happy resting place.

The first of the five pillars of Islamic practice is a speech act: "bearing witness" (*shahāda*) that there is no god but God and that Muhammad is God's messenger. Jurists have much to say about how and when one performs this act, but they have nothing to say about its meaning, which is the domain of theologians, Sufis, and philosophers. The first half, "(There is) no god but God" is known as the sentence declaring *tawḥīd*. The Koran says that God is designated by "the most beautiful names." The quickest way to grasp the implications of *tawḥīd* is to insert the divine names into the formula: God is One, so "None is one but God." God is Alive, so "None is alive but God." God is Knowing, so "None is knowing but God." God is Desiring, so "None is desiring but God." In short, every real quality, not least existence itself, pertains exclusively to God, for God is the Real (*al-ḥaqq*), and "There is nothing real but God."

The most sophisticated and prolific theoretician of the Sufi tradition was Ibn ʿArabī (1165–1240), who likes to point out that dogmatic theologians, focusing on one apparent meaning of *tawḥīd*, come to the conclusion that God is radically other, dwelling in transcendence and "incomparability" (*tanzīh*). Sufis say the same thing, but they add that transcendence does not contradict immanence and "similarity" (*tashbīh*), for the law of noncontradiction pertains to the created realm, not to God, whose very incomparability demands that he be the coincidence of opposites (*jamʿ al-aḍdād*). In Ibn ʿArabī's view, scholastic theologians reject immanence because of their overreliance on reason (*ʿaql*), the mental faculty that analyzes and systematizes. In contrast, Sufi teachers also use the faculty of imagination (*khayāl*), which, when cultivated and refined, provides access to "unveiling" or "mystical vision," in which the divine face is seen to be actually present in phenomenal appearances. For Ibn ʿArabī, true understanding of *tawḥīd* depends upon seeing with both eyes of the "heart" (*qalb*): the eye of reason and the eye of imagination.

Beginning with Avicenna (d. 1037), philosophers typically spoke of being or existence using the word *wujūd*. The existence of God is then necessary, and the existence of everything else is contingent upon God's existence. The literal sense of *wujūd*, however, is "to find and to be aware of," and the Koran mentions God as the subject of the verb, so theologians speak of God as *al-wājid*, the Finder. As al-Ghazālī explains, God is "the Finder in an absolute sense, and anything else, even if it finds some of the attributes and causes of perfection, also lacks certain things, so it can only find in a relative sense."[3] In other words, *tawḥīd* demands that, as al-Ghazālī likes to put it, "There is nothing in *wujūd* but God." This means not only that God's Being is the only true and real being, but also that his finding – his consciousness and awareness – is the only true and real finding.

The notion that God's Being is true and real and that its created analogues are "metaphors" (*majāz*) is a constant theme of Sufi teachings, whether or not the term *wujūd* is employed. Moreover, as the often quoted Arabic proverb puts it, "The metaphor is the bridge to the reality." As seen by the Sufis, the universe is a transparent metaphor, which is to say that all phenomena point back to the noumena that are God's most beautiful names. All things are theophanies or divine "self-disclosures" (*tajallī*), a term derived from the Koranic story of Moses. In truth, says Ibn ʿArabī, all of reality is two: the

---

[3] *al-Maqṣad al-asnā fī sharḥ maʿānī asmāʾ Allāh al-ḥusnā*, ed. Fadlou A. Shehadi (Beyrouth: Dar el-Machreq, 1971), 143.

Real *Wujūd* that is God, and the metaphorical *wujūd* that is God's self-disclosure.

Ibn ʿArabī's stress on the dual implications of *tawḥīd* – both transcendence and immanence – led Ibn Taymiyya (d. 1328), the great Hanbali polemicist, to ascribe to him the notion of *waḥdat al-wujūd*, "the oneness of Being," though Ibn ʿArabī never used the term. According to Ibn Taymiyya, this expression was outright unbelief, for it means that no distinction can be drawn between God and the cosmos. Everyone who took part in the heated debate that ensued (including Orientalists in modern times) has had in mind a specific meaning of *waḥdat al-wujūd* and has assumed that Ibn ʿArabī spoke of it in that meaning. In fact, at least seven distinct meanings can be discerned in the literature.[4] Few people actually took the trouble to read Ibn ʿArabī's books, not least because they are notoriously difficult. What becomes clear when one does delve into his writings is that he addressed the relationship between the Oneness of God and the manyness of the cosmos in scores of ways, none of which is reducible to a simple either/or statement. One of his refrains is "He/not He" (*huwa lā huwa*), a variant on the formula of *tawḥīd*, "No god but He." Things, phenomena, contingent beings, creatures are "He" inasmuch as they partake of *wujūd*, but "not He" inasmuch as they are simply themselves. Everything is a commingling of real and unreal, being and nonexistence, light and darkness, necessity and contingency.

Ambiguity, in short, defines our cosmic situation. This is what Ibn ʿArabī and others mean when they say that the universe is *khayāl*, a word that means both imagination and image. All things are God's imagination – images of both Real Being and nothingness. Like reflections in a mirror, they are what they appear to be, but they are also something else. In Ibn ʿArabī's formulation, the rational eye of the heart thinks in terms of either/or, but the imaginal eye sees that things can simultaneously be and not be. Seeing with either eye alone distorts the vision of *tawḥīd*, with its harmonious balance of transcendence and immanence. The general Sufi acknowledgment of cosmic ambiguity led to a vision of the cosmos as ranked in hierarchical degrees of intensity of *wujūd*. The basic insight is simply that some things are clearer images of the divine qualities than others – it is not a question of "yes or no" but rather "To what extent?"

The Koran refers to two basic realms of created existence, using terms such as unseen and visible, heaven and earth, high and low. Many Sufis and

---

[4] See William Chittick, "Rūmī and *Waḥdat al-wujūd*," in *Poetry and Mysticism in Islam*, ed. A. Banani, R. Hovannisian, and G. Sabagh (Cambridge: Cambridge University Press, 1994), 70–111.

philosophers spent a good deal of effort explaining that these are not sharp dichotomies but designations for the extreme points on a spectrum. Some of them discussed a third, intermediate realm, often calling it by the Koranic expression "isthmus" (*barzakh*). Its outstanding characteristic is that it is neither heaven nor earth, neither spirit nor body, neither high nor low; rather, it is low in relation to heaven and high in relation to earth, gross in relation to spirit and subtle in relation to body. Thus, we commonly find a three-world scheme: the World of Spirits at one extreme, the World of Bodies at the other extreme, and the Isthmus or World of Images in between – what Henry Corbin labeled the *mundus imaginalis*. The overall picture is that the divine qualities are infinitely present in the Real Being, and their properties and traces become manifest in ever-decreasing levels of intensity, much as light diminishes as it recedes from its source. Things dwelling at each lower level make manifest, or act as symbols for, those dwelling at higher levels: "As above, so below."

That the lower discloses the properties of the higher accords with two of the implications of *tawḥīd* mentioned in elementary Islamic catechisms: Everything comes from God, and everything is constantly sustained by God. The third implication is that everything goes back where it came from. God is the First *and* the Last. This going back is the already mentioned *ma'ād*, "return," the third of the three principles of faith. It helps explain why the first two principles, *tawḥīd* and prophecy, are so important: Our response to them determines the trajectory of our ultimate encounter with the One: "As below, so above." We will go back to God in keeping with the manner in which we live our lives and shape our souls.

Philosophers commonly described the Return to God as the necessary outcome of a prior movement, called "the Origin" (*mabda'*). Sufis used the same Koranic terminology, but they often preferred the word *qawsān*, which means "two bows" or "two arcs" (like Latin *arcus*, the word *qaws* means both bow and arc). The word derives from a Koranic verse that refers to the Prophet's proximity to God on his Night Journey: "He was two-bows-length away, or closer" (53:9). This is taken as an allusion to the fullness of human perfection that is reached when an individual, having descended into the world from God, returns voluntarily to him by achieving deiformity and becoming characterized by his traits. Through such a trajectory, man traverses the entire circle of existence and re-joins his Source.

Sufi theory also gives prominence to the notion of the universe as macrocosm (*al-'ālam al-kabīr*) and the human individual as microcosm (*al-'ālam al-ṣaghīr*). Both realms make manifest the same roots, for each is an all-embracing theophany, appearing in God's "form" (*ṣūra*). The macrocosm, however, is relatively externalized, dispersed, and differentiated (*mufaṣṣal*), and the microcosm relatively internalized, focused, and undifferentiated (*mujmal*). In this anthropocosmic vision, the human subject takes as its object, at least potentially, the entire cosmos. Sufis see Koranic reference to this teaching in many passages, not least the Creation story, according to which God taught Adam "the names, all of them" (2:31). These are the names of all things, whether manifest or non-manifest, visible or unseen, even of God himself. To say that Adam – a word that the Koran uses generically for human beings – was taught the names implies that awareness of God and the universe is innate to the human substance, no matter how obscured it may have become by the forgetfulness (*nisyān*) that is endemic to mankind ever since "Adam forgot" (Koran 20:115). The role of the prophets is "to remind" (*dhikr, tadhkira*), that is, to guide people in remembering what they already know because of their primordial nature (*fiṭra*), created in God's form.

The cosmos in its entirety is a self-disclosure of Being, an image of Infinity; it is what Ibn ʿArabī calls "Nondelimited Imagination." The *mundus imaginalis* discussed by Corbin is then the intermediary cosmic realm, situated between the intense luminosity of the spirits and the darkness of the bodies. In a similar way, the microcosm has three levels: spirit (*rūḥ*), soul (*nafs*), and body (*badan*). The soul is the isthmus between consciousness and forgetfulness, the image of light and darkness, life and death, activity and inertia. The human drama plays out in the soul, not in the spirit or body, for it is constantly pulled in two directions – upward toward greater awareness and downward toward deeper forgetfulness. The Persian poet Rūmī (d. 1273) offers some of the most down-to-earth depictions of this internal struggle in Sufi literature, as when he says, "The states of human beings are as if an angel's wing were stuck on a donkey's tail so that perhaps the donkey, through the radiance and companionship of the angel, might itself become an angel."[5]

Having descended into manifestation, the microcosm, unlike the macrocosm, is forced to take into account its own free will, however limited this may be. People have no choice but to return to God, because everyone dies and is resurrected, but their freedom to choose plays a major role in determining the manner in which they will experience posthumous becoming. Failure to make the right choices can lead to indefinite misery (although many Sufi authors, in contrast to the exoteric theologians, say that hell's suffering – as opposed to hell itself – cannot be everlasting).[6]

---

[5] *Fīhi mā fīhi*, ed. B. Furūzānfar (Tehran: Amīr Kabīr, 1969), 107.
[6] Ibn ʿArabī provides numerous arguments to prove the point. For a few of them, see William Chittick, *Ibn ʿArabī: Heir to the Prophets* (Oxford: Oneworld, 2005), ch. 9.

The function of the prophets is to guide people in making the choices that lead to a happy return. The divine root of prophecy is the name Guide (*al-hādī*), one of the many contrasting names of the Godhead. Its correlative is the name Misguider (*al-muḍill*), the most salient cosmic manifestation of which is Satan.[7] As in the microcosm, so in the macrocosm: People encounter the conflicting claims of right and wrong, truth and falsehood. The general Sufi position is that no one can tread the labyrinth of moral and cosmic ambiguity and achieve the goal of human life – transformation and deiformity – without prophetic guidance. Muslims are called specifically to follow Muhammad and climb the ladder in his footsteps.

Here a major discussion enters the picture, that of "the perfect human being" (*al-insān al-kāmil*), an ideal type embodied first and foremost by Muhammad and then by other prophets. There are numerous sides to the issue. Ibn ʿArabī's voluminous discussions of metaphysics, cosmology, and spiritual psychology can best be understood as an attempt to describe the full parameters of human perfection. Among the many prominent issues he and others address is the relationship between the prophets (*nabī*), the last of whom was Muhammad, and the "friends" (*walī*), those who achieve nearness to God by conforming to the prophetic model (the translation of this word as "saint" is problematic).[8]

## 4 Climbing the Ladder

The Sufis wrote myriad volumes on theory, and perhaps even more on practice. Sufi institutions – the so-called "orders" (*ṭarīqa*, literally, "paths") – began developing around the sixth/twelfth century and eventually spread throughout the Islamic world, always adapted to local circumstances. If esotericism is understood as something exclusive to initiates, and exotericism as suitable for the general public, then the weight of Islamic history suggests that later Sufism has been more exoteric than esoteric, for its teachings about interiority were assimilated into the most popular forms of religiosity. One can also say that in many cases, Sufi orders turned into a sort

---

[7] Some of the more interesting esoteric interpretations of Satan are provided by Sufis such as the famous al-Ḥallāj. See Peter J. Awn, *Satan's Tragedy and Redemption: Iblīs in Sufi Psychology* (Leiden: Brill, 1983). On Ibn ʿArabī's views, see William Chittick, "Iblīs and the Jinn in al-Futūḥāt al-Makkiyya," *Classical Arabic Humanities in Their Own Terms: Festschrift for Wolfhart Heinrichs on His 65th Birthday*, ed. Beatrice Gruendler and Michael Cooperson (Leiden: Brill, 2008), 99–126.
[8] A closely related discussion has to do with the relationship between "the Seal of the Prophets" (Muhammad) and "the Seal of the Friends." On this see Michel Chodkiewicz, *The Seal of the Saints* (Cambridge: The Islamic Texts Society, 1993).

of exoteric esotericism, and Sufi literature is full of criticisms of teachers who preserved the trappings of Sufism but lacked the prerequisite personal transformation. For similar reasons, calling Sufism "mysticism" is problematic, given that a mystic should be someone who has actually achieved some sort of divine intimacy or inner illumination. The vast majority of those affiliated with Sufi orders, however, are simply striving on the path, acknowledging that God's friends alone deserve to share in the divine mysteries. This is one reason why they have rarely referred to themselves as "Sufis," for, in most definitions, the word designates a high station of spiritual realization. Rather, they call themselves "the poor" (Arabic *faqīr*, Persian *darwīsh*). The expression is Koranic: "O people, you are the poor toward God, and God is the Rich, the Praiseworthy" (35:15).

In almost every case, the Sufi orders trace their origin by a chain of transmission (*silsila*) back to Muhammad. The Sufi teachers, commonly known as "elders" (*shaykh, pīr*) or "spiritual guides" (*murshid*), initiate disciples by means of a ritual, again going back to the Prophet, called "the swearing allegiance of good-pleasure" (*bay'at al-riḍwān*, alluded to in Koran 48:10). Sufi teachers also transmit specific practices, the most common of which is the "invocation" (*dhikr*) of a divine name or a Koranic formula. The word literally means reminder, remembrance, and mention; it is used in the Koran to designate not only the practice of invoking God's name but also the function of prophecy itself – "reminding" people of their rootedness in God. In communal meetings, Sufis engage in rituals centering on the recitation of Koranic verses and divine names (and rarely involving anything that might be called "dancing"). All of this is "esoteric" only in the sense that not all Muslims participate.

The notion that Sufism adds a dimension to ordinary, exoteric observance of Islam is found in the common teaching that there are three basic components of the Islamic tradition: the Shariah or revealed law; the Tariqah (*ṭarīqa*) or Sufi path; and the Haqiqah (*ḥaqīqa*) or "Reality," which is the source and goal of both Shariah and Tariqah. The Reality, in other words, is God himself, who revealed the Koran so that people could climb the ladder back to him in the footsteps of the Prophet.

Sufi writings call the final goal of the path – reaching the Reality – by many names and describe the process in numerous ways. All such works focus on overcoming the distance demanded by God's transcendence, and this helps explain the hostility toward Sufism that has often appeared among the exoterically minded jurists and theologians. According to al-Ghazālī and many others, the goal is simply the full actualization of *tawḥīd*. He explains this in his grand summa of the spirit of Islamic practice, *Iḥyā' 'ulūm al-dīn*,

"Revivifying the Sciences of the Religion": *Tawḥīd*, he says, has four levels. The first is to utter the formula "No god but God," while the heart is heedless of its meaning. The second is to acknowledge its truth, as in the belief of the common people. The third is to witness its truth by way of unveiling, as in the case of those brought near to God. The fourth is to see nothing in *wujūd* (existence, consciousness) but the One – this, he tells us, is what the Sufis mean when they speak of "annihilation" (*fanā'*) in *tawḥīd*."[9]

Al-Ghazālī's reference to four levels of *tawḥīd* follows the standard model of the ladder ascended by the Prophet. Discussion of the ladder's rungs – sometimes enumerated as 7, 10, 100, 300, or even 1001 – makes up a common genre of Sufi literature. A famous example is *Manṭiq al-ṭayr*, "The Language of the Birds," by the Persian poet Farīd al-Dīn 'Aṭṭār (d. 1221), in which a group of birds flies over seven mountains and achieves final union with its king. Each of the mountains – called seeking, love, recognition, independence, unity, bewilderment, and poverty – represents a transformation of the soul and a stage in becoming characterized by divine traits.

## 5 Conclusion

The distinction between the exoteric path of the jurists and theologians and the esoteric path of the Sufis can perhaps best be reduced to the focus on transformation, or to the notion that true understanding comes only through active and conscious participation in the very reality of the divine consciousness. This is why the two approaches have often been differentiated in terms of two basic sorts of knowledge: transmitted (*naqlī*) and intellectual ('*aqlī*). Transmitted knowledge underlies all learning, since it is the source of language, grammar, social norms, and, in the specifically Islamic context, the Koran and the Hadith. As for intellectual knowing, it is the consciousness of Reality, or a direct awareness of the way things are – *ma'rifa*, "self-recognition," a word often translated as "*gnosis*." This term's most often cited *locus classicus* is the Prophet's purported saying, "He who recognizes himself recognizes his Lord."

The distinction between these two sorts of knowledge is implicit in al-Ghazālī's four levels of *tawḥīd*. The first and second are based on what is technically called *taqlīd*, imitation, that is, following the authority of the transmitted learning. The third and fourth depend on inner transformation,

---

[9] *Iḥyā' 'ulūm al-dīn* (Beirut: Dār al-Hādī, 1993), vol. 4, 359. For a free translation of the passage, see David Burrell, *Al-Ghazali: Faith in Divine Unity & Trust in Divine Providence* (Louisville: Fons Vitae, 2001), 10ff.

or what is called *taḥqīq*, realization. The word *taḥqīq* derives from the same root as *ḥaqq* and Haqiqah (*ḥaqīqa*). As a Koranic divine name, *al-ḥaqq* designates the real, the true, the worthy; Haqiqah, as noted, designates the origin and final goal of both the Shariah and the Tariqah. As for *taḥqīq*, it means to establish and actualize what is real, true, and worthy, that is, to attain to the Haqiqah. Once realization has been achieved, there can be no more talk of imitation, for the distinction between knower and known has been effaced.

Sufi authors provide numerous depictions of the transformed selfhoods achieved by the friends of God. Ibn ʿArabī often calls the highest level of human perfection "the station of no station" (*maqām lā maqām*), because it represents the full realization of all divine attributes and character traits. Like the Divine Essence, this supreme stage cannot be designated by any specific name. Here are brief excerpts from his discussions:

> The people of perfection have realized all stations and states and passed beyond them to the station above both majesty and beauty, so they have no attributes and no description. It was said to Abū Yazīd, "How are you this morning?" He replied, "I have no morning and no evening; morning and evening belong to him who becomes delimited by attributes, and I have no attributes."[10]

The highest of all human beings are those who have no station, because the stations determine the properties of those who stand within them. But without doubt, the highest of all groups themselves determine the properties – they are not determined by properties. They are the divine ones, for the Real is identical with them.[11]

---

[10] Ibn ʿArabī, *al-Futūḥāt al-makkiyya* (Cairo: 1911), vol. 2, 133.
[11] Ibn ʿArabī, *al-Futūḥāt al-makkiyya*, vol. 3, 506. For these two passages and several more along with a discussion of their significance in the context of Ibn ʿArabī's teachings, see William Chittick, *Sufi Path of Knowledge* (Albany: State University of New York Press, 1989), ch. 20.

# 9

# KABBALAH

BRIAN OGREN

## 1 Introduction

"Kabbalah" is a multifaceted term which, in its most austere religious sense, denotes the "reception" of tradition from a higher source or an older generation. One of the earliest expressions of this sense of "Kabbalah" comes in a verbal form in the Mishnaic tractate *Avot*, which begins: "Moses *received* (kibbel) the Torah from Sinai, and transmitted it to Joshua; and Joshua to the elders; and the elders to the prophets; and the prophets transmitted it to the men of the great assembly."[1] This passage establishes an uninterrupted chain of transmission of Kabbalah, that is, of that which is "received," going back to the theophany at Sinai. In so doing, it lends a sense of direct divine sanction to Kabbalah, which in this passage is connected to both prophecy and religious adjudication. It has thus been understood for millennia to go beyond the reception of the Written Torah and to include the entire tradition of commentary, law, and ethics known as Oral Torah, thereby giving even seemingly innovative interpretations and practices an air of primordial authority.

Abraham Joshua Heschel has observed that "the term *kabbalah* denotes the act of taking an obligation upon oneself. The term in this sense has the connotation of strictness and restraint. Yet *kabbalah* in its verbal form means also: to receive, to welcome, to greet."[2] Heschel goes on to note that the obligatory usage has a legal meaning, whereas the welcoming connotation is spiritual, but that the two are inseparable from each other. In the traditional view, a binding commitment to established statutes goes hand-in-hand with a sense of personal sanctity and awe. It is from this standpoint that starting in the Middle Ages, the term "Kabbalah" came to denote a sacrosanct esoteric tradition fundamentally based

---
[1] *Avot* 1:1.
[2] Abraham Joshua Heschel, *The Sabbath: Its Meaning for Modern Man* (New York: Farrar, Straus and Young, 1951), 61.

within Jewish praxis. Kabbalah, in this view, was part of God's revelation through Torah to his people, Israel. In the words of the thirteenth-century *Zohar*: "There are three interconnected levels: the blessed Holy One, Torah, and Israel. Each is level upon level, concealed and revealed."[3] Kabbalah thus became associated not only with the revealed and received, but also with the received and concealed elements within what came to be three of the foundation stones for all of Judaism, namely, God, Torah, and Israel.

For medieval kabbalists, Kabbalah as esoteric lore is the heart of Oral Torah, received by Moses at Sinai on behalf of the entire people of Israel. It is thus a misconception to identify Kabbalah with Jewish "mysticism," which I take to denote a direct, individual, and novel experience of God.[4] Such mystical encounter is certainly one aspect of medieval Kabbalah, but it is only one part of the larger picture of reception that traces itself to divine revelation. In what follows, other aspects of kabbalistic tradition will be presented in an attempt to offer a fuller portrait. This essay will focus on a phenomenological exposition of some major kabbalistic concepts. I take this approach rather than a historical survey because influences are not always linear, corollary processes are rarely singular, and representative ideas often crop up in different periods and disparate lands. In addition, perceptions of kabbalists themselves are not always historically accurate, nor are they always chronologically conditioned. For example, works such as the twelfth-century *Bahir* and the thirteenth-century *Zohar* were attributed to ancient authors but were taken to contain eternal teachings. Kabbalists such as the sixteenth-century circle of Isaac Luria saw themselves in direct contact with the past and the future through means such as reincarnation and prophetic revelation. A nonlinear phenomenological exposition thus allows for a fuller, more complex portrayal of Kabbalah. Accordingly, it is to some of the timelessly perceived esoteric traditions that we now turn, as structured on the three, originally *Zoharic* foundations of God, Torah, and Israel.

## 2 God

### a *Transcendence and Immanence*

The relationship between transcendence and immanence is of special concern to Kabbalah. Is God wholly other, or is he personal and intimate? Does

---

[3] *Zohar* 3:73a.
[4] For more on this, see Joseph Dan, *Kabbalah: A Very Short Introduction* (New York: Oxford University Press, 2006), 3–4; Boaz Huss, "The Mystification of Kabbalah and the Myth of Jewish Mysticism" [Hebrew], *Pe'amim* 110 (2007), 9–30.

God, in all of his infinitude, somehow relate to his finite creation? If he is infinite and wholly other, then how did he possibly create that which is finite and dissimilar to his own essence? Kabbalistic attempts to grapple with such questions assume many forms, including expositions of classical midrashic and philosophical theories of the intermediary nature of language and the transcendent quality of intellectual abstraction. But perhaps the most distinctive and prominent kabbalistic manner of dealing with such questions is the doctrine of *Ein-Sof* and the *sefirot*.

*Ein-Sof* literally means "without end," and it denotes the transcendent, infinite, hidden aspect of God. The concept was developed from the *via negativa* as expounded by the likes of the eleventh-century Neoplatonist Bahya ibn Paquda and the twelfth-century rationalist Moses Maimonides. According to this doctrine, God is beyond all finite limitations, and thus all that can be said about him is what he is not. God's essence is beyond human comprehension, so any assertion about it is by nature false. Claiming that he is "infinite," however, is legitimate in that it asserts that he is "not" finite. Philosophers usually use the adjectival phrase *bilti ba'al takhkit* to denote this apophatic, negative attribute of God.

By contrast, the term *ein sof* (written here with a small "e" and "s" to denote its linguistic function) is usually used in an adverbial sense, denoting the infinite nature of God's various other attributes. The first known instance in which the term is used nominally as *Ein Sof* (written here with an uppercase "E" and "S" for distinction) comes from within the twelfth-century Provencal kabbalistic circle of Isaac the Blind.[5] Isaac's student Azriel of Gerona writes: "The boundless is called *Ein-Sof*, Infinite. It is absolute undifferentiation in perfect, changeless oneness.... The philosophers acknowledge that we comprehend it only by way of no."[6] Here *Ein-Sof* is an appellation for God's ultimate essence, which for Azriel and subsequent kabbalists paradoxically remains undefined by its very definition as infinite, undifferentiated oneness. It is thus beyond all comprehension.

Kabbalists bridge this abyss by positing that out of the unknowable *Ein-Sof* radiate knowable potencies called *sefirot*. This term first appears in the ancient cosmogonic text *Sefer Yetzirah*, although there it seemingly relates to primordial accounts rather than to God's manifestation. By contrast, medieval kabbalists cast the *sefirot* as ten divine hypostases that emanate from the clear

---

[5] For more on this, see Gershom Scholem, *Origins of the Kabbalah*, ed. R. J. Zwi Werblowsky, trans. Allan Arkush (Princeton: Princeton University Press, 1987), 261–289.
[6] Azriel of Gerona, "Commentary on the Ten Sefirot," in Me'ir ibn Gabbai, *Derekh Emunah* (Warsaw, 1850), 2b, quoted in Daniel C. Matt, *The Essential Kabbalah: The Heart of Jewish Mysticism* (San Francisco: HarperCollins, 1996), 29.

light of *Ein-Sof* in a sequential manner of increasing opacity. Paradoxically, the more opaque they become, the clearer they are to human comprehension. From the most abstract to the most tangible, they are:

(1) *Keter Elyon*, "Highest Crown": the least palpable, with indistinct borders alongside *Ein-Sof*.
(2) *Hokhmah*, "Wisdom": the beginning of God's ways, considered as the supernal father.
(3) *Binah*, "Understanding": the place of return, the upper Eden, the divine womb, the supernal mother.
(4) *Hesed*, "Mercy": associated with the right, the side of love and of the divine masculine.
(5) *Gevurah*, "Might": associated with the left, the side of judgment and of the divine feminine.
(6) *Tif'eret*, "Beauty": the mediating force of balance.
(7) *Netzah*, "Eternity": feminine triumphalism.
(8) *Hod*, "Splendor": masculine glory.
(9) *Yesod*, "Foundation": a righteous covenant.
(10) *Malkhut*, "Royalty": God's indwelling on earth.

Whether these *sefirot* are essentially divine or are mere instruments for God to break forth from his concealed essence in *Ein-Sof* is hotly debated among kabbalists, but all assert the ultimate unity of the ten, the need for harmony between them, and the inherent heresy in treating them as separate powers.

*b Bisexuality*

The *sefirotic* decad that is actually one and the apparent separation that actually demands harmony give rise to a remarkably polar, bisexual structure within the kabbalistic notion of the godhead itself. This is based on the bisexual nature of primordial man, as understood from a melding of the two seemingly contradictory accounts of creation in Genesis. According to Genesis 1:27: "God created man in His image, in the image of God He created him; male and female He created them." Man and woman are created simultaneously. Genesis 2:7, however, tells a different story. There "God formed man from the dust of the earth," and only later said to himself: "It is not good for man to be alone; I will make a fitting helper for him" (Gen. 2:18). To do this, God took from the side of man and formed it into woman, an act to which the first man proclaimed: "This one at last is bone of my bones and flesh of my flesh. This one shall be called Woman, for from man she was taken" (Gen. 2:23). In this account, the formation of woman is subsequent to the creation of man.

Rabbinic tradition noticed this discrepancy, and offered a theory of original androgyneity as an explanation, not unlike that of Aristophanes in Plato's *Symposium*.[7] Humanity, the rabbis explain, was indeed created simultaneously "male and female" as in the account in Genesis 1:27, but as a single entity that was then divided, as in Genesis, ch. 2. This is referred to in rabbinic literature as *du-partsufin*, which literally means "dual-countenance," and connotes a bisexual nature within primordial man.

Kabbalists took this notion a step further, noting that if (according to Genesis 1:27) "God created man in His image," and if that image was dually "male and female," then God too must have elements that are both male and female. The twelfth-century Abraham ben David of Posquieres was one of the first to make this link, equating the dual male and female countenances to divine mercy and divine sternness, respectively. Abraham ben David's oft-quoted statement is variously interpreted by scholars as a statement of an inseparable unity within God, a necessary separation for the sake of equal cooperation between the two powers, and a statement of the necessary incorporation of the female into the prioritized male.[8] Whatever the case may be, the godhead itself here is clearly cast as a bisexual polarity in need of unitive, or at least interactive, harmony.

For the thirteenth-century prophetic kabbalist Abraham Abulafia and other philosophically inclined authors such as the early sixteenth-century Yohanan Alemanno and Leone Ebreo, this bisexual polarity came to represent the intellect as a formal masculine element issued from God, which impregnates the material feminine body created by God.[9] In an idyllic state, these two elements are completely unified, with the feminine ultimately subordinate to the masculine. On various levels of both microcosmic and macrocosmic restoration, woman ideally returns to man, from whom she was taken.

---

[7] Genesis Rabbah 8:1; Leviticus Rabbah 14:1.
[8] See, respectively, Scholem, *Origins*, 217–218; Moshe Idel, *Kabbalah: New Perspectives* (New Haven and London: Yale University Press, 1988), 128–130; Idel, *Kabbalah and Eros* (New Haven and London: Yale University Press, 2005), 61–64; Elliot Wolfson, *Language, Eros, Being: Kabbalistic Hermeneutics and Poetic Imagination* (New York: Fordham University Press, 2005), 167–170.
[9] Abraham Abulafia, *Imrei Shefer* (Tel Aviv: Aharon Barzani and Son, 1999), 62; Yohanan Alemanno, *Einei ha-Edah* (ms. Paris BN 270), 42a; Leone Ebreo, *Dialogues of Love*, trans. Cosmos Damian Bacich and Rosella Pescatori (Toronto: University of Toronto Press, 2009), 281.

God's bisexuality becomes especially pronounced in relation to the *sefirot*. This is the case for each individual *sefirah*, which has the power to both receive and to overflow the divine influx, and for relations between the *sefirot*, which are usually coupled from the second (*Hokhmah*) onward. *Hokhmah* is often cast as the supernal father, while *Binah* is the supernal mother. *Hesed* is the masculine representation on the right, while *Gevurah* is the feminine divine on the left, and *Netzah* and *Hod* are a similar pair. *Tiferet* is the masculine body linked to *Malkhut*, the vaginal receptor, through *Yesod*, the divine phallus. In an idyllic state, these pairs all join together in both ecstasy and creation, allowing for the divine flow by the process of unity and integration.

## 3 Torah

### a Infinite Revelation

For kabbalists, not only are the *sefirot* divine manifestations, so too is the language of Torah. This idea derives from the assertion in *Sefer Yetzirah* that God formed the world with thirty-two paths of wisdom, namely, the ten *sefirot* and the twenty-two Hebrew letters. Such an assertion accords the Hebrew language a special divine status, and as noted by later kabbalistic interpreters, thirty-two is represented in Hebrew numerology by the combination of the very first letter and the very last letter of the Torah. The *sefirot* coupled with divine language thus become synonymous with the contents of the Torah, from its very beginning to its very end. Not only is Torah God's revelation, it is the divinity itself. As famously stated in the *Zohar*, "Torah is nothing but the blessed Holy One."[10] "Torah" here stands for Written Torah, while "the blessed Holy One" stands for *Tiferet*, the central masculine pillar in the sefirotic structure. This outlook, which hypostatizes Torah, fundamentally changes the process and meaning of reading the Torah in two primary ways.

First, if Written Torah itself is divine, then reading Torah becomes a way of directly encountering God. Reading itself becomes a mystical activity of direct relation, which functions as a path to union with *Tiferet*, the blessed Holy One through whom the light of *Ein-Sof* flows. As one eighteenth-century Hasidic master noted, "By the cleaving of man to the letters of the Torah ... he draws down onto himself the revelation of the light of *Ein-Sof*."[11] The divine letters act as channels for *Ein-Sof*, and the process of

---

[10] *Zohar* II, 60b.
[11] Mordekhai of Chernobyl, Liqqutei Torah, fol. 29d, quoted in Moshe Idel, *Absorbing Perfections: Kabbalah and Interpretation* (New Haven: Yale University Press, 2002), 184.

reading actively opens those channels and allows the reader to directly experience the flow of divine light. Reading directed toward God turns into actual immersion in the divine, and the author-text-reader nexus genuinely conflates into one.

Second, if Torah is perceived to be God, and (according to medieval Jewish thought) God is infinite, then Torah too must necessarily be understood as an infinite being. One medieval kabbalist explains that "the Torah has seventy aspects, and there are seventy aspects to each and every verse; in truth, therefore, the aspects are infinite."[12] This is based on a rabbinic statement from *Numbers Rabbah* 13:15 that "there are seventy modes of expounding Torah," but here it relates to the word "secret," which in Hebrew is *sod*, and which numerologically equals seventy. The secret tradition that is Kabbalah thus organically contains within itself the secret of a Torah that in its innermost "secret" aspect is at once absolutely divine yet dynamically multifarious.

Another expression of the infinitude of Torah was popular in Lurianic Kabbalah, and ties into the idea of reading as direct, experiential revelation. This is the idea that every letter of the Torah has six hundred thousand aspects in relation to the six hundred thousand children of Israel who stood at the foot of Mount Sinai. The idea came to be expanded beyond the six hundred thousand to all of the souls of Israel, as based on God's pronouncement: "I make this covenant, with its sanctions, not with you alone, but both with those who are standing here with us this day before the Lord our God and with those who are not with us here this day" (Deuteronomy 29:13–14). Accordingly, each soul of Israel individually received the Torah, and each thus has its own individual understanding. There is thus no one single meaning of divine revelation; there are instead infinite possibilities of subjective, albeit divinely authoritative meanings, based on personal experience of the divine.

### b Interpretive Hermeneutics

The multitude of individual understandings entails an infinity of possibilities for experience of the divine through the reading of Written Torah. Nevertheless, such reading is anchored in specific kabbalistic interpretive patterns of Oral Torah. The process of endless revelation is filtered through limited structures of discourse, an idea that relates to the embodiment of the infinite God in a seemingly finite text, and also to the dialectical nature of

---

[12] *Kaf ha-Ketoret*, quoted in Gershom Scholem, *The Messianic Idea in Judaism* (New York: Schocken Books, 1971), 42.

Kabbalah itself as subjective experience grounded in received tradition. Due to this dialectic, not all interpretations are equally valid – a fact that markedly distinguishes kabbalistic hermeneutics, in all of their multiplicity, from the postmodern approach to texts.

As the famous thirteenth-century kabbalist and exegete Nahmanides states regarding the biblical account of creation, "it is a profound secret that is not understood from a reading of the biblical verses alone, and it cannot be known completely except by way of the Kabbalah (i.e., the received tradition) going back to Moses our master, as received from the mouth of divine fortitude; and those who know it are obliged to conceal it."[13] This statement by a highly respected kabbalistic exegete is too complex to unpack here in its entirety, but in several ways it sheds great light on the kabbalistic understanding of biblical hermeneutics. First, profound secrets are understood to be contained within the text of the Bible, and personal revelation relates to an understanding of these secrets. Second, these secrets cannot simply be understood by all who read the text, even if the readers are intelligent and insightful. Rather, the revelation of secrets requires a tradition of transmission, an Oral Torah that is ultimately traced back to God himself. This is fundamentally related to the revelation at Sinai. Finally, individual revelation requires personal concealment, both to preserve the secrets for an esoteric elite and to conserve the dialectic of concealment and revelation that, by its very nature, constitutes the secret of the infinite contained within the finite that is contained within the infinite.

The idea of the concealed and the revealed as standing side-by-side in the Torah has been variously understood, but the most prevalent kabbalistic explication involves a fourfold method of interpretation. This method, which is dominant in the *Zohar* and in the writings of Moshe de Leon, came to be known as *Pardes*, which means "Paradise," and which is an acronym for the four layers of *peshat* or literal sense, *remez* or allegorical sense, *derash* or homiletical sense, and finally *sod* or secret sense. According to one reading, this is a hierarchical schema that at once preserves traditional modes of interpretation while asserting that the secret sense is their culmination.[14] According to another reading, these different layers are not absolutely distinct, and inasmuch as the Torah is dialectically both infinite and finite in its immanent transcendence and transcendent immanence, it follows that the literal sense comprehends all the other senses.[15] Whatever

---

[13] Nahmanides, *Commentary on Genesis 1:1*.
[14] See especially Idel, *Absorbing Perfections*, 429–437.
[15] For a nuanced analysis, see Elliot Wolfson, *Luminal Darkness: Imaginal Gleanings from Zoharic Literature* (Oxford: One World Publications, 2007), 56–110.

the case may be, both of these readings emphasize that the kabbalistic fourfold system preserves the rabbinic dictum that "a biblical verse cannot depart from its literal sense" (Babylonian Talmud *Shabbat* 63a). Indeed, it is important to note the inclusive character of the kabbalistic fourfold system, in which the esoteric does not eradicate the exoteric but necessarily preserves it. In this way, kabbalistic hermeneutics are at once conservative and innovative. They conserve traditional layers and variant methods of reading, while opening new possibilities for the revelation of the secret that needs to be concealed.

## 4 Israel

### a *Israel as the Divine Feminine*

Just as God is manifest in Torah, so is she hypostatized in the people of Israel. I utilize the feminine pronoun "she" deliberately here, as the hypostatization is of the divine feminine. Whereas Torah represents the masculine blessed Holy One in *Tiferet*, Israel represents his divine female cohort in *Malkhut*. The relationship between the two is perhaps best characterized by Isaac the Blind, commenting on the rabbinic statement that "the world was created exclusively for the sake of Israel."[16] Isaac writes: "This means 'due to the merit of Israel' – because of the unique qualities inherent in Israel. For [Israel] receives the divine overflow from the very root, core, and trunk of the Tree – from the middle pillar which draws from the branches."[17] Israel as receptacle is none other than the feminine *Malkhut*, while the middle pillar is *Tiferet*, who inseminates *Malkhut* with his divine overflow. The "Tree" is the sefirotic structure, but it seems to be no coincidence that the core and trunk are *Tiferet*, Written Torah. Based on the book of Proverbs, it has been likened to "a tree of life to those who behold it" (Proverbs 3:18). "Those who behold" are the pious of the people of Israel, who not only derive nourishment from the tree, but who also symbiotically provide fertile ground in which the tree can take root.

A key concept at work here is Israel's particularistic exclusivity, presented in the above quote by Isaac the Blind as "the unique qualities inherent in Israel." The idea of uniqueness as an inherent quality is further expressed by the seventeenth-century kabbalist Shabbetai Sheftel Horowitz: "The souls of the [non-Jewish] nations are from external forces, the forces of the husks ... but

---

[16] *Song of Songs Rabbah* 2:6; cf. *Leviticus Rabbah* 36:4.
[17] Isaac the Blind, "The Process of Emanation," trans. Ronald C. Keiner in *The Early Kabbalah* (New York: Paulist Press, 1986), 83.

the souls of the nation of Israel are emanated from Holiness."[18] Here we find an ethnocentric dichotomy cast in the very kabbalistic language of "husks" and of "emanated Holiness." The husks are those parts of emanated reality that went awry and became alienated from the divine essence, while the souls of Israel, like the *sefirot* and the divine Torah, are a manifestation of the light of *Ein-Sof* within existence.[19] The souls of Israel are the body of *Malkhut*, who through an attachment to Torah, or *Tiferet*, can channel the flow of *Ein-Sof* into the world. It is thus through Israel, and Israel alone, that God ultimately acts in the concrete world.

This way of thinking gives theosophical significance to Israel's biblical role as "a kingdom of priests, and a holy nation" (Exodus 19:6). Indeed, it is only because Israel is synonymous with *Malkhut* and thus hypostatically divine that it can receive Torah and become wedded to it. Torah needs Israel as its exclusive partner in order to be able to flourish in the world. Yet the relationship is reciprocally symbiotic; only through cleaving to Torah can Israel create an open channel and return to its Divine Source.[20] Just as *Malkhut* remains cut off from the sefirotic tree (the tree of life) when she does not cleave to her consort *Tiferet*, so too Israel, even with its inherent divinity, is cut off from its Divine Source without the medium of the divine Torah.

### b Israel as Oral Torah

Just as *Tiferet* becomes identified with Written Torah, so *Malkhut*, and by extension Israel, becomes identified with Oral Torah. This is perhaps best exemplified by a now famous statement by Isaac the Blind, commenting on an earlier text entitled *Midrash Konen*:

> *Malkhut* [is] the Oral Torah. It is the hue of black fire on white fire, which is the Written Torah. Now the forms of the letters are not ... shaped except through the power of black, which is like ink. So too the Written Torah is unformed in a physical image, except through the power of the Oral Torah.[21]

---

[18] Shabbetai Sheftel Horowitz, *Shefa Tal* (Brooklyn, 1960), fol. 1a–4c, quoted in Moshe Hallamish, *An Introduction to the Kabbalah*, trans. Ruth Bar-Ilan and Ora Wiskind-Elper (Albany: State University of New York Press, 1999), 268.

[19] For more on the history and implications of this essentially ethnocentric idea of Israel in medieval kabbalistic thought, see Elliot R. Wolfson, *Venturing Beyond: Law and Morality in Kabbalistic Mysticism* (New York: Oxford University Press, 2006).

[20] For more on this complex relationship, see Brian Ogren, *Renaissance and Rebirth: Reincarnation in Early Modern Italian Kabbalah* (Boston and Leiden: Brill, 2009), 80–84 and 204–211.

[21] Isaac the Blind, "The Mystical Torah – Kabbalistic Creation," trans. Ronald C. Keiner in *The Early Kabbalah*, 75–76.

Oral Torah gives expression to Written Torah, which is otherwise formless in this world. It is only through the black fire that the white fire becomes visible, only through the ink that the parchment takes on meaning. Only through the interpretive process that is Oral Torah does Written Torah have any significance in the world. Only as a lived Torah can it truly come to life.

In this regard, the Congregation of Israel functions not only as a community of interpreters but also as a living Torah society: a social expression of abstract theosophical ideas. The living God becomes manifest in his community through the medium of Torah, but Torah needs to be both interpreted and lived in order for this manifestation to actually occur. This is the true meaning of Israel as Oral Torah, which is one point of a triangle, the other points being Written Torah and God. Yet the societal aspect of this equation does not stop with earthly action. In fact, one of the most salient features of kabbalistic thought brings earthly action into the divine realm with a stratagem known as *ta'amei ha-mitzvot*, that is, "the reasons for the commandments." On the interpretive level, these give cosmic significance to even the most mundane of the commandments. While on the level of lived experience, Israel truly comes to embody metaphysical, and even divinely revelatory principles of Torah through entirely normative practices.

An interesting example of this is the seemingly obsolete biblical command to allow the land of Israel to lay fallow once every seven years (Leviticus 25). Indeed, not only is this a physical, time-bound and space-bound commandment, in a state of exile in medieval Europe, it no longer seems relevant. Yet Nahmanides comments that it is "one of the great secrets of the Torah,"[22] and then in his classical kabbalistic manner, he seems to conceal more than he reveals. He does, however, mention that the commandment alludes to "all of *the days* of the world,"[23] which thus makes it one of the most stringent commandments, whose transgression is punishable by exile. Such gravity was noticed by subsequent kabbalists, and "days" came to be interpreted as referring to the seven lower *sefirot*.[24] In the process of interpretation, time itself becomes hypostatized, and a seemingly mundane, outmoded commandment takes on cosmic meaning that here infuses not only the people of Israel, but also the land of Israel with theosophical significance. Not only in this example but throughout kabbalistic thought, Israel's state of exile is related to its neglect of Torah. This situation is to be remedied through Oral Torah, which Israel embodies through interpretation and the

---

[22] Nahmanides, *Commentary on Leviticus* 25.
[23] Nahmanides, *Commentary on Leviticus* 25.
[24] For more on this, see Haviva Pedaya, *Nahmanides: Cyclical Time and Holy Text* [Hebrew] (Tel Aviv: Am Oved Publishers, 2003), especially 207–466.

performance of the commandments, and by which Torah, God, and Israel can all be restored to their proper, integrative places.

## 5 Conclusion

I close with a quote from a late stratum of Zoharic literature, which brings together the various elements of God, Torah, and Israel and infuses them with righteousness in an attempt to define Kabbalah: "The *Shekhinah* [a synonym for *Malkhut*] is called *Righteousness*, and the blessed Holy One is the master, or husband of Righteousness." The passage continues regarding *Malkhut*: "She is certainly Oral Torah. And She is *Kabbalah* when she receives from [her husband] the master of Righteousness, which is Written Torah. When she [actively] goes to Him to receive, she is called *Halakhah*. When She [passively] receives from Him, she is called *Kabbalah*."[25] Kabbalah here is a hypostatic process that involves the union of the masculine and the feminine elements of God as manifest in Torah and in Israel, respectively. It is the subtle turning of *halakhah* (i.e., Jewish Law) on its head – yet without subverting it, and precisely by means of infusing it with righteous, cosmic meaning.

---

[25] *Tiqqunei ha-Zohar* 21, 58a; cf. Wolfson, *Venturing Beyond*, 275.

# 10

# MEDIEVAL CHRISTIAN MYSTICISM

## Bruce Milem

## 1 Introduction

"Mysticism" is a modern designation that became widespread in the late nineteenth and early twentieth centuries. The first scholars of mysticism, such as William James, Evelyn Underhill, and Rudolf Otto, focused on what they called mystical or religious experience, which they thought was the root of all religion. This emphasis on experience is characteristically modern, in harmony with doubts about tradition, authority, and institutions, and congruent with modernity's confidence in the experiential basis of science.

Because of the modern origins and character of the concept of "mysticism," we have to be careful when looking for mysticism in medieval Christianity. It is not that medieval people did not have, or were not interested in, extraordinary experiences of union with God. Rather, medieval people did not put the same weight on experience as an authority different from tradition, Scripture, and church that modern people do. They expected these authorities to agree. Moreover, medieval thinkers typically put experiences of God within the context of the Christian's gradual transformation into a perfected human being who enjoyed some sort of union or identity with God. This transformation, enacted in central Christian rituals such as baptism and communion, is what mattered, not the experiences. Still, some writers in the Middle Ages explored or emphasized the possibility that union with God is available in this life rather than exclusively in heaven, and they are the focus of this essay.[1] While some of

---

[1] Mystical women writers of medieval Christianity are discussed in another essay in this volume. Regrettably, space precludes discussion of Eastern Orthodox mystical theologians, such as Maximus the Confessor, Symeon the New Theologian, and Gregory Palamas. Two classic works on Eastern Orthodox mystical theology are Vladimir Lossky, *The Mystical Theology of the Eastern Church* (London: Clarke, 1957) and Jaroslav Pelikan, *The Christian*

these writers saw union as the basis for extraordinary experiences, others understood union as a permanent state of being that Christians could attain.

## 2 Two Early Influences: Augustine and Eriugena

Augustine of Hippo (354–430) had unparalleled influence on medieval Christian theology. Although he is not usually considered a mystic, he wrote extensively about how God is present to Christians on earth. One way is through visions. In his *Literal Commentary on Genesis*, Augustine explains that visions come in three kinds. First are visions in which one perceives God by means of the senses, such as when the Israelites saw and heard God descend to Mount Sinai. Second are imaginative visions, such as those given to the prophets. The third kind of vision is purely intellectual, without sense perception or images of any sort, in which one apprehends God by the mind alone. This is the kind of vision enjoyed by those in heaven.

However, Augustine believed one can have the third kind of vision in this life, and in his *Confessions*, he describes two that he himself had. Both experiences have a three-step structure, which Augustine probably borrowed from the pagan Neoplatonic philosopher Plotinus (204–270). First, one has to turn one's attention away from the senses and physical things. Second, one turns inward and searches within oneself. In Book 10 of the *Confessions*, for instance, Augustine finds traces of God's presence in his own memory. Another example is in the second half of his treatise *On the Trinity*, where he argues that the best analogy to the triune God is the soul's own faculties of memory, knowledge, and will, which have separate functions but make up one unified soul. In the third stage of the intellectual vision, one is lifted above oneself to perceive God directly, without the mediation of images. This last step happens only by God's grace, and in this life such experiences are partial and transient. Although they deliver knowledge unavailable by other means, Augustine does not regard them as more authoritative than the Bible or rational speculation.

Augustine's *Confessions* provides a model for mystical encounter with God in other ways as well. One aim of the book is to articulate Augustine's sense that God was with him at all times, even when Augustine himself was mired in sin or error. By looking back at his life, Augustine discovers God's presence at every turn. He also uses the Bible in an influential way. It is well known that Augustine presents the *Confessions* as a speech to God. But

*Tradition: A History of the Development of Doctrine*, Vol. 2: *The Spirit of Eastern Christendom (600–1700)* (Chicago: University of Chicago Press, 1977).

the conversation is not one-sided: God speaks too by means of the extensive quotations from Scripture that Augustine includes. Like Christian thinkers before and after him, Augustine believes that in reading the Bible, one encounters God. This does not commit him to a literalist interpretation of Scripture. Instead, he practices a "spiritual" or "mystical" style of interpretation that goes back at least as far as Origen (ca. 180–254). Indeed, the word "mystical" in the Middle Ages mainly referred to a level of meaning in the Bible hidden beneath the apparent literal meaning of the text. For instance, Augustine reads the Garden of Eden story in Genesis not so much as history but rather as an allegorical description of the human soul and its tendency toward sin. In depicting the self and the Bible as the best places for discovering the divine, Augustine influenced mystical thought in medieval Christianity.

Another early influence is John Scotus Eriugena (ca. 800–ca. 877). In the *Periphyseon*, he attempts to integrate Christian doctrine with Neoplatonic ideas gleaned from Pseudo-Dionysius the Areopagite (ca. 500) and other Greek authors. This leads him to develop the relationship between God and created things in new and original ways. Since creation involves giving being where there was none before, it follows that creatures are beings. God, on the other hand, utterly transcends the limitations that define creatures and needs to be conceived in a wholly different way. Consequently, if creatures are beings, then God is not one, and it is better to call God "nothing." This "nothing" is not the same as nonexistence, since it is more excellent than the being that creatures have. But Eriugena's equation of God with nothing shows that God is best described in negative terms rather than positive ones. In addition, it allows Eriugena to reinterpret the Christian idea that God creates everything from nothing: the nothing that God creates from is in fact God.

Eriugena also maintains that creatures are the means by which God expresses or reveals himself. The whole universe, then, is the manifestation of God. These claims led to suspicions that Eriugena was a pantheist who simply identified God with the universe and everything in it. His work was even condemned as heretical in the thirteenth century. But Eriugena's view of creatures as God's self-expression rests on the infinite difference between God and creatures. His treatment of God oscillates between apparently contradictory descriptions: God is identical with creatures in one sense but utterly different from them in another. In this way, his thought is dialectical. This aspect of his thinking, derived in part from Pseudo-Dionysius, influenced later writers. Although Eriugena did not write or apparently care much about mystical experiences, his understanding of ordinary things as the self-expression of an utterly transcendent God makes them in some sense divine and makes God present in everyday life.

## 3 Monastic Mysticism: Bernard of Clairvaux

Between the sixth and the thirteenth centuries, intellectual life in Western Europe was based in monasteries. It was there that manuscripts were copied, preserved, and studied. Many monasteries followed the rule of St. Benedict (ca. 480–543), which required monks to spend part of each day working, another part in prayer and worship, and a third part in study of the Scriptures and theology. Catholic monasticism thus encouraged the cultivation of spirituality, and monasteries produced several important mystical writers. Hugh (ca. 1090–1141) and Richard (d. 1173), both of St. Victor, a monastery outside Paris, offered the first systematic accounts of mystical contemplation, which, as Hugh wrote, could in the end provide a foretaste of the Beatific Vision of God in heaven. The greatest of the monastic writers is Bernard of Clairvaux (1090–1153). He is also one of the greatest mystics of love in the Christian tradition.

Famous in his own day as a preacher who helped to motivate the Second Crusade and to promote the Cistercian monastic order, Bernard wrote prolifically about the soul's ascent to God. Like Augustine, he interpreted the Bible mystically. This is clearest in his sermons on the Song of Songs, the most erotic text in the Bible, which Bernard, following old Christian tradition, interprets allegorically as an account of the soul pursuing and being pursued by God. He weaves many quotations and allusions to the rest of the Bible into his commentary on the Song. This merges Bernard's voice with the divine voice of the Scriptures and offers a literary enactment of the union with God that his sermons describe. Bernard combines his commentary on the Song of Songs with a keen interest in spiritual experience. In one sermon, he famously remarks that he will read from "the book of experience."[2] This book is the Song of Songs, but Bernard's description suggests that he reads it through the lens of contemplative experience. In this way, Bernard treats the Scripture and experience as mutually complementary. He occasionally alludes to his own experiences, though he does not claim any special authority from them.

In his treatise *On Loving God*, Bernard explains that one should approach God through love, which deepens by degrees as one progresses. He urges

---

[2] Sermon 3 on The Song of Songs, in Bernard of Clairvaux, *Selected Works*, trans. G. R. Evans (Mahwah: Paulist Press, 1987), 221.

devotion especially to the incarnate Christ, who shares in the physical woes of ordinary people. Bernard begins with the love that people commonly have for themselves, which he associates with the body. The next stage consists in loving God for the benefits that God gives. The third stage is loving God unselfishly, simply in response to what God is. Finally, in the fourth stage, all self-love fades away, and one views oneself as nothing apart from God's will. One's love for God motivates one's actions without hindrance by concern with the body or its welfare. Bernard admits to being unsure that anyone actually attains this love on earth, although he supposes that some of the martyrs did. Such union with God attained through love nevertheless leaves God and the soul as separate beings, just as love may be said to unite two people who yet retain distinct identities.

4 The New Mysticism: Francis of Assisi and Bonaventure

Bernard McGinn argues that the year 1200 marks a shift in mystical thought so profound that he calls it "the new mysticism."[3] Monastic life lost its place at the center of Christian spirituality. Western Europe was urbanizing rapidly, and people began working out new forms of spirituality. One example was offered by the new mendicant orders of Franciscans and Dominicans, who were not monks retired from the world but friars deliberately engaging it through preaching and works of service. Writers began to use vernacular languages rather than Latin, and they began to write in different genres as well: poems, allegories, spiritual biographies. Last but not least, women authors began to contribute their ideas and experiences.

The character of this "new mysticism" can be seen in the founder of the Franciscan order, Francis of Assisi (ca. 1181–1226). Born to a noble family, he chose to live as a beggar devoted only to preaching the word of God in imitation of Christ. Two years before his death, he reportedly had a vision of an angel, a six-winged seraph, nailed to a cross. When the vision passed, he discovered the marks of Crucifixion on his own body, in his hands, feet, and side. These marks, called "stigmata," were taken as signs of divine approval, and Francis was apparently the first of many to receive them. He wrote little, but among his writings is the "Canticle of Brother Sun," a song or poem that praises God for creating various natural phenomena that Francis addresses with winning familiarity: "Lord Brother Sun," "Sister Moon," "Brother

---

[3] Bernard McGinn, *The Flowering of Mysticism: Men and Women in the New Mysticism (1200–1350)*, Vol. 3 of *The Presence of God* (New York: Crossroad, 1998), 1–30.

Wind," even "Sister Bodily Death." The poem offers the natural world as one place for meeting God.

One of his followers in the Franciscan order was Bonaventure (1217–1274), who synthesized ideas and themes from Francis, Pseudo-Dionysius, Augustine, Bernard, and others in a superb work entitled *The Mind's Journey to God*. Inspired by Francis's vision of the crucified angel, Bonaventure sketches the path toward an experience of ecstatic union with God. His "journey" has seven steps, with the first six arranged in pairs, corresponding to the six wings of the crucified seraph. First, one looks at the natural world as evidence of God's creative activity. Then, second, one imaginatively considers those same natural things as embodying God's power and wisdom. Third, one turns within and considers how the mind, with its powers of memory, knowledge, and love, is an image of the Trinity. In the fourth step, one contemplates the mind after its purification by divine grace, brought through Christ. Fifth, one meditates on God as being or existence (*esse*). In the sixth step, one considers God as "good," which according to Pseudo-Dionysius is the highest and best of God's names. As Bonaventure explains, to be good is to overflow with love and gifts. It is because of this love that the one God spills over into the three persons of the Trinity. Out of love, God chose to become human and die on the cross. Like Francis, Bonaventure focuses on the crucified Christ. This vision arouses intense love, which in the seventh and final step makes one "pass over" into an ecstatic state of loving union with God. The mind is taken beyond itself, cannot grasp where it is, and plunges into darkness, where it finds deep peace. This state is temporary in this life, yet it gives a foretaste of heaven.

## 5 Rhineland Mysticism: Meister Eckhart

In the thirteenth and fourteenth centuries, the Rhineland of Holland, Belgium, eastern France, and western Germany proved to be a fertile area for mystical thought and writing. In this region were many communities of beguines, women interested in spirituality and ecstatic experience, who frequently lived together but without taking vows or receiving official church supervision. Some of these communities were eventually turned into convents under the watch of Dominican friars. A considerable number of writings survive from these beguinages and convents that show keen interest in union with God and unusual experience. In addition, the Dominicans ran a school in Cologne to educate its members. Founded by Albert the Great (ca. 1200–1280), it counted Thomas Aquinas (ca. 1224–1274) as an alumnus. Albert wanted to reconcile the doctrines of the church with new texts from the ancient Greeks that were then becoming available, including writings by Aristotle and Neoplatonic philosophers such as Proclus (ca. 410–485). This inspired a particular strain of speculative theology that merged the Aristotelian focus on being with the Neoplatonic idea of the ineffable One from which all things arise. The most famous representative of this school is Eckhart of Hochheim (ca. 1260–1328).

Born in Germany, Eckhart joined the Dominican order and was educated in Cologne and Paris, where he received a master's degree in theology and became known forever after as "Meister" Eckhart. He wrote biblical commentaries and other texts in Latin but also delivered sermons and penned devotional works in Middle High German. Eckhart was both an academic professor of theology and a devoted pastor. He was clearly aware of the ideas spreading among the nuns, beguines, and other pious women and may have been influenced by them. Eckhart interprets the relationship between God and creatures in a dialectical way reminiscent of Eriugena. All things are dependent on God the creator for everything that they are. In this sense, creatures in themselves are nothing apart from God, and the being that they have is God's own being. It follows that God is indistinct from creatures. But creatures are distinct and different from one another. This means that God, in being indistinct from all creatures, is for that very reason distinct from them. In this way, Eckhart shifts between contrary descriptions of God, who is both distinct and indistinct from creatures, both absolutely identical with and completely different from them. Nor does he strictly hold to the identification of God with being and creatures with nothing. One can also look at being as something that creatures have, in which case it makes more sense to speak of God as nothing, not a thing, "neither this nor that," as Eckhart often says.

While Bernard of Clairvaux understood union with God as a merging of love that left God and the soul separate beings, Eckhart sometimes describes a union in which God and the soul are fully merged. One recurring image in Eckhart's German works is the "ground" of the soul. This ground, which is the source of the intellect and the will, also turns out to be God's ground. Similarly, Eckhart often talks about a "light" or "spark" or "little castle" in the soul, where God and the soul are unified in such a way that no distinction between them can be drawn. Eckhart even says that God must put aside the persons of the Trinity in order to be one with the soul. One unresolved question is whether Eckhart understands this identity without distinction as a constant state of being, an occasional event, or some combination of the two.

Eckhart repeatedly urges the practice of what he calls "detachment." This requires giving up self-centered goals and recognizing that all things are nothing without God. It enables one to maintain equanimity in all circumstances whether good or bad. By letting things be rather than viewing them in terms of our self-interest, we can perceive them in their sheer created existence, which is wholly dependent on God. We then learn to serve others with genuine compassion and no expectation of any reward. All things become images of the divine, who is present in them and utterly transcendent at the same time. Eckhart sometimes even claims that the truly detached person compels God to come down and reside in him.

In developing these ideas, Eckhart relies in a special way on the Bible. Most of his works are interpretations of Scripture that attempt to unearth the hidden, spiritual meaning of particular passages. This mystical meaning is not a static truth but instead the Word, identical with Christ, more of a living presence than a doctrine. This Word is inexhaustible, and every verse in the Bible can be given multiple interpretations. In his Latin commentaries, Eckhart sometimes offers a dozen or more interpretations of a single verse. In a way, union with God is attained through mystical interpretation of Scripture, as the exegete works with God to draw out its inner meaning. Eckhart's sermons invite their listeners to share in this event too.

Toward the end of his life, Eckhart was accused of heresy and put on trial. He died of natural causes before the final verdict, which condemned twenty-eight propositions from his works as heretical or "badly-sounding." His judges worked from lists of suspicious propositions taken from Eckhart's writings without regard for their original context. This procedure ignores the often poetic movement of Eckhart's language and the dialectical character of his thought, which balances assertions of the identity of God and creatures against contrary statements of absolute difference. Eckhart insisted that even if he were in error, he was no heretic, because heresy involves an act of rebellion against the Church, to which he himself was unwaveringly loyal.

After Eckhart's condemnation, his writings continued to circulate surreptitiously or with his name removed. Two of his friends and students, John Tauler (ca. 1300–1361) and Henry Suso (ca. 1295–1366), defended and developed his ideas but were also careful to state them in more orthodox ways. Some later mystical writers, such as John Ruusbroec (1293–1381), drew on Eckhart but also kept a critical distance.

## 6 Late Medieval Mysticism: Jean Gerson and Nicholas of Cusa

By the late fourteenth century, mystical writing emphasized experiences of the divine and of love as the path to union. Jean Gerson's (1363–1429) famous definition of mystical theology exemplifies both trends. He defines it as the experiential knowledge of God achieved through loving union with God. Gerson distinguishes mystical theology from academic or scholastic theology, which proceeds by intellectual reflection on the Scripture and church doctrine. For Gerson, the experience of union with God attained through love is itself a source of knowledge distinct from that provided by conventional theology. His definition points the way toward the modern concept of "mysticism."

Writers in England in the fourteenth century also emphasize experience and love. Julian of Norwich (1342–ca. 1416) and Richard Rolle (ca. 1300–1349) recount visionary experiences that they use as the basis for theological reflection. Developing ideas from Thomas Gallus (ca. 1200–1246) and reinterpreting Pseudo-Dionysius, the anonymous *Cloud of Unknowing* (late fourteenth century) portrays love as the primary force in the ascent to God.

The last great mystical theologian of medieval Christianity is the bishop and cardinal Nicholas of Cusa (1401–1464). He is sometimes considered the first great modern thinker as well. Although medieval intellectuals thought the universe was finite, Cusanus proposed that it was infinite. He was fond of using mathematical images and examples to illustrate theological ideas. Some scholars maintain that his theory of knowledge resembles the one developed by Kant three centuries later.

Cusanus also looks back to the dialectical style of theology practiced by Eriugena and Eckhart. He portrays God as the "coincidence of opposites," in that contradictory terms apply equally well to the divine. God is both the absolute maximum and the absolute minimum, both being and nonbeing, and so on. Yet, while we are compelled to describe God in these contrary terms, we must also recall that God is absolutely one, beyond the duality implied by our paradoxical descriptions. Doing theology in this way, one gradually recognizes how little about God one actually knows, and one acquires what Nicholas calls "learned ignorance."

Cusanus's most important contribution to mystical thought is his treatise *On the Vision of God*. He sent the treatise to monks in Tegernsee, Germany, along with an icon (probably of Christ) painted in such a way that the icon's eyes appear to be looking right at viewers no matter where they stand. The treatise then takes off from the experience of contemplating the icon. One looks, of course, but seeing the icon means being seen by it. In seeing the icon, one sees the icon seeing and sees oneself being seen. Cusanus's treatise plays with this ambiguity throughout, which is signaled in the title *On the Vision of God*: Is God the subject seeing or the object seen? If several people are looking at the icon at once, then one also realizes that everyone else is having the same experience. Everyone in the room is enfolded into the one gaze of the icon.

This gaze is both particular and universal. It regards each person individually, but it also views them all in one. This strange gaze expresses the relationship between God and creatures, which Cusanus conveys in two linked terms: *explicatio*, or unfolding, and *complicatio*, enfolding. The created universe is the unfolding of all things in their multiplicity from the singularity that is God. Yet God is the absolute infinite that enfolds all things within itself. In this way, Cusanus identifies God with the created universe while also maintaining God's distinction from and transcendence of it. In addition, just as seeing the icon means being seen by it, so Cusanus argues that loving God coincides with being loved by God. Although the believer's love or desire for God could be taken as a longing for something absent, Cusanus makes it instead a sign of God's presence. His speculative theology urges Christians to reconsider their concept of God and think about their ordinary experience as believers in a new way.

## 7 Conclusion

Although the emphasis on experience in mysticism is characteristically modern, it is true that medieval Christian mysticism makes room for extraordinary experiences and visions. Bernard of Clairvaux and Bonaventure set out a path toward union with God culminating in an ecstatic experience, even if it is best described, as in Bonaventure, as a kind of darkness. Many writers give accounts of their visions. But some of the writers who are usually acclaimed as mystics, such as Eckhart, Eriugena, and Cusanus, do not emphasize experiences or visions. Their mysticism consists in a particular way of thinking about God that tries to articulate how God is present in ordinary things and everyday experience. All three use a dialectical or paradoxical mode of speech that balances contrary descriptions of God against each other. Although God is identical with ordinary things, God is also absolutely transcendent and unlike them. Following their path of thinking may not lead to any special, peak mystical experiences, but it can infuse all things with a new significance as expressions or images of God. Thus, mysticism in the medieval context includes not just ecstatic raptures but also abstract speculation and a quiet transformation of quotidian experience.

Christian mysticism of the Middle Ages existed for the most part in harmony with the institutions and doctrines of the Catholic Church. Augustine, Bernard, Bonaventure, Eckhart, and Cusanus all occupied important offices in the church or in their monastic or fraternal orders. Although Eriugena and Eckhart were ultimately condemned for espousing heretical views, both declared themselves loyal to the Church. Augustine played a crucial role in drawing the lines between orthodoxy and heresy. Bernard actively preached against heresy. They all put the Bible at the center of their reflection on God. For these reasons, it would be incorrect to suppose that mysticism in the Middle Ages flourished best in the margins. Instead, it can be found in the mainstream of medieval Catholic theology and spirituality. Toward the end of the Middle Ages, when writers began to speak of mystical theology in opposition to academic speculative theology, and when church authorities became concerned about new movements of popular spirituality, the harmonious accord between mysticism and church institutions started to break down. In this respect, the story of medieval Christian mysticism reflects the larger pattern of social fragmentation in Western Europe that helps set the scene for the modern period.

11

# HILDEGARD OF BINGEN AND WOMEN'S MYSTICISM

ANNE L. CLARK

1 *Frauenmystik* or "Women's Mysticism"

In the Middle Ages, Christian women as well as men committed themselves to the practices of prayer, meditation, and asceticism that were the conditions usually associated with the mystical life. Some of them also committed themselves to producing texts in which they strove to communicate what they learned through their practices. The history of scholarship on medieval Christian mysticism has traditionally privileged texts by male authors as representing the pinnacle or at least the mainstream of mystical accomplishment, thereby marginalizing texts by women as secondary or derivative. Recent attention to women's texts as representing "feminine" mysticism is usually marked by an insistence on their affectivity and on "paramystical" physical phenomena. These approaches obscure how thoroughly affective many mystical texts by men are, how male mystics were often influenced by women, and how male texts about female mystics tended to emphasize paramystical experience. "Women's mysticism" is thus a problematic category, and the attention to women's mystical texts in this essay is not an assertion of any inherently female essence to the subject matter. What is common to most if not all women's mystical literature is an awareness of the suspicion about women's authority to teach, or a discomfort with cultural assumptions about the nature of women and their religiosity. These commonalities are due, of course, not to an essential female nature but to women's awareness of cultural norms that ascribed to them a particularly carnal nature, and that positioned men as authoritative teachers, mediators of sacramental grace, and confessors of sins.

I offer here a characterization of mystical life that is relevant for the study of both male and female medieval mystics. It is a life structured by "tuning" the self — body, mind, and emotions — to seek the presence of the divine,[1] and preparing the self to be invaded or flooded or lifted up, thus losing a clear sense of the boundaries of the self. The emphasis here is on a structured life of practice, not a single type of "peak experience." Furthermore, where extraordinary psychological experiences are described, they are often not the primary focus of the authors' concerns; rather, mystical authors are often primarily concerned with praising God, teaching proper devotion, and leading the moral life.[2]

For most of the Middle Ages, the structure that supported mystical religion was monastic, a community life of moderate asceticism organized to minimize the importance of individual will. The primary activity of the monastery was the Divine Office, an elaborate course of shared ritual composed primarily of singing the psalms found in the Psalter of the Old Testament. The texts of these rituals as well as other books of the Bible provided the sustenance for lifelong meditation; that is, ruminative reading and reflection. Furthermore, the lifelong participation in the Divine Office, with its repetitive chanting of the psalms and other hymns, enabled the effects that Judith Becker ascribes to music in trance experience: "by enveloping the trancer in a soundscape that suggests, invokes, or represents other times and distant spaces, the transition out of quotidian time and space comes easier." Such a transition could involve "feelings of nearness to the sacred, loss of boundaries between self and other, experience of wholeness and unity," or sometimes feelings of anguish or pain, as well as *gnosis*.[3] The other principal ritual of the Middle Ages, the celebration of the Eucharist, seems to have been cultivated, especially by women, as an opportunity for intimate experience of the presence of God.[4] Thus, mystical practice was deeply rooted in the liturgical life of the medieval church, and this liturgical foundation is often apparent in the mystical texts.

Despite limited literacy throughout the Middle Ages, there is nonetheless a significant body of mystical literature associated with women. Some of this literature is hagiographical, that is, texts written about particular individuals that testify to their holiness. Women who were perceived by others to have extraordinary connections to God were often the subjects

---

[1] Cf. Bernard McGinn, *The Growth of Mysticism: Gregory the Great through the 12th Century* (New York: Crossroad Publishing Company, 1999), 81.
[2] Grace M. Jantzen, *Power, Gender, and Christian Mysticism* (Cambridge: Cambridge University Press, 1995), 5.
[3] Judith Becker, *Deep Listeners: Music, Emotion, and Trancing* (Bloomington: Indiana University Press, 2004), 27, 54–55.
[4] Caroline Walker Bynum, *Holy Feast and Holy Fast: The Religious Significance of Food to Medieval Women* (Berkeley: University of California Press, 1987).

of hagiographies, and sometimes these texts contain fascinating portraits of women engaged in mystical pursuits. However, hagiographies are heavily inflected by their (usually male) authors' perspectives. Because they offer idealized models of sanctity based on particular assumptions about female nature, they must be treated with caution as sources for women's mysticism. There are also many texts that more reliably transmit women's words about their own experience and their mystical thought, and these will be the primary focus of this essay. Within these texts, women's claims about their experience of divine presence vary widely, and no normative taxonomy is offered here to rank them.

## 2 The Life and Works of Hildegard of Bingen

Perhaps now the most famous religious woman of the Middle Ages, Hildegard of Bingen (1098–1179) was widely regarded in her own day as a prophet and visionary. From the age of fourteen, Hildegard lived in a monastic community, first in a small women's hermitage attached to a community of Benedictine monks in Disibodenberg, then in a monastery for women that she founded in Rupertsberg, against the initial wishes of her abbot. Hildegard claimed that from a young age she sensed in herself "the power and mystery of secret and wonderful visions," but the turning point in her life came at the age of forty-two when she suddenly experienced an outpouring from heaven: "A greatly flashing fiery light coming from the opened heavens poured down over my brain and inflamed my whole breast – not like a burning flame but a warming one, as when the sun warms whatever it shines its rays upon" (*Scivias*, Prologue).[5] Hildegard's sense of divine inspiration recalls the story in Acts of the Apostles, when the sound of a mighty wind filled the house where the disciples of Jesus were gathered together, and "tongues as if of fire" appeared above the head of each of them, "and they were filled with the Holy Spirit and began to speak in various tongues" (Acts 2:2–4). As the author of Acts portrays this fiery invasion loosening the tongues of the Apostles in a miraculous way, so Hildegard portrays her own fiery, tongue-loosening experience bringing immediate knowledge that must be shared: "And suddenly I tasted the understanding of the exposition of Scripture – namely, the Psalter, the Gospels and other catholic books from the Old Testament as well as the New" (*Scivias*,

---

[5] Hildegard of Bingen, *Scivias*, 2 vols., ed. Adelgundis Führkötter and Angela Carlevaris. Corpus Christianorum, Continuatio Mediaevalis 43, 43A (Turnhout: Brepols, 1978). Translations from Latin texts are my own.

Prologue). She hears a voice from heaven identifying itself as "living and dark light illuminating the person I have chosen," which commands her by words and by "the whip" of illness to write what she sees and hears. Hildegard emphasizes that what she describes as seeing, hearing, taste, and touch should not be confused with normal sensory perception and was not experienced in ecstasy or dreams. Yet her expression also suggests her sense of being invaded and changed by divine power, transforming her into a channel of the mysteries of God.

The noetic aspect of this initiatory experience continues in a series of visions that unfold for the rest of Hildegard's life. This was the basis for her composition of three major works, *Scivias* (*Know the Ways*), *Liber vitae meritorum* (*The Book of Life's Merits*), and *Liber divinorum operum* (*The Book of Divine Works*). Each of these works is presented as a vividly detailed record of her visions, which describe scenarios of movement and sound, including verbal explications of the visions provided by a voice from heaven. A copy of the *Scivias* produced in Hildegard's monastery included brilliant paintings of the visions, and an illuminated manuscript of the *Liber divinorum operum*. Although not produced at Rupertsberg, it was probably adapted from pictorial designs by Hildegard no longer extant.[6] These manuscripts attest to Hildegard's attempt to communicate the fullness of her experience, both visually and verbally.

Hildegard also wrote a long musical play, the *Ordo Virtutum* (*Order of Virtues*), several minor theological, pastoral, and hagiographic works, and a glossary of her own neologisms. She composed more than seventy pieces of liturgical music, mostly intended for use in the Divine Office, and gathered them into a collection entitled *Symphonia armonie celestium revelationum* (*Symphony of the Harmony of Celestial Revelations*). Hundreds of Hildegard's letters to a wide array of correspondents are also extant, attesting to her deep involvement in the affairs of her world, and to the keen desire of many people to seek her counsel, or occasionally to question her about her claims to divine revelation. Hildegard was also profoundly interested in the human body, medicine, and the natural world, and she produced two scientific texts. The first was the *Physica* or *Liber simplicis medicinae* (*The Book of Simple Medicine*), an encyclopedia of natural history, including works on the properties of plants, animals, stones, and other elements of nature. The other was the *Liber compositae medicinae* or *Causae et curae* (*Book of Compound Medicine or Causes*

---

[6] Madeline H. Caviness, "Hildegard as Designer of the Illustrations to Her Works," in *Hildegard of Bingen: The Context of Her Thought and Art*, ed. Charles Burnett and Peter Dronke (London: The Warburg Institute, 1998), 29–62.

*and Cures*), a treatise describing diseases and their cures. She understood her own physical suffering (diagnosed in modern times as migraine) as part of her experience of being used by God.

Hildegard's visionary mode of writing broke with the medieval tradition of citing textual authorities to support one's perspective. This style, combined with her claims of divinely infused knowledge, might suggest that she had a relatively limited education. However, as new scholarship continues to demonstrate, Hildegard seems to have absorbed much of the intellectual traditions available to a twelfth-century monastic. Although the written word (with its meaning sometimes enlarged by paintings and melodies) was Hildegard's primary means of expression, she also traveled to Trier and to Cologne to preach, an indication of how eager her contemporaries were to hear her message.

The mystical life for Hildegard was hardly one of withdrawal from the world or pursuit of solitary contemplation. Her astonishingly diverse corpus of writings, her preaching tours, the two monasteries she founded, her care and education of the nuns at Rupertsberg, her correspondence with kings, popes, bishops, abbots, abbesses, and laypeople – all of this shows that for Hildegard the mystical life was the source she drew on to shape the world as much as she could.

## 3 Hildegard's Vision

Although "holistic" is a word often associated with modern or postmodern sensibilities (especially those drawing on ecology or New Age spirituality), it is not at all anachronistic to use it to describe the worldview Hildegard created from what she perceived to be divine visions. Characteristic of her holistic vision of reality is the concept of *viriditas*, a "greenness" that is alive, powerful, moist and fresh, fertile.[7] In an early vision of the Trinity in which the figures seen are described as having the colors of sapphire, glowing fire, and bright light (none of which literally suggests green), Hildegard declares that what is conveyed is the *viriditas* of God that is the source of his creative work. Consequently, the work of creation enables human perception of God (*Scivias*, II.2.1). Hildegard's scientific interest in nature is part of this larger vision of the world as manifesting divine *viriditas*. Given that the earth's *viriditas* is literally the source of green plants that nourish animals, it both symbolizes human fertile physicality and points humanity beyond itself to the

---

[7] Constant Mews, "Religious Thinker," in *Voice of the Living Light: Hildegard of Bingen and Her World*, ed. Barbara Newman (Berkeley: University of California Press, 1998), 56–61.

creator (*Scivias*, II.1.2). *Viriditas* is most fully expressed in the incarnation of God in the body of the Virgin Mary, a belief that elicited Hildegard's most rapturous poetry. "In you blossomed the beautiful flower which gave fragrance to all the spices that were dry. / And at that, they all appeared in full viridity" ("O viridissima virga").[8] The redemption of a disordered cosmos through divine incarnation enabled the establishment of Ecclesia (Hildegard's personified image of the church), whose righteous members make her "burst forth with buds and spread out with blessed viridities" (*Scivias*, II.5.26).

Although Hildegard affirms *viriditas* as the foundation for divine, human, and cosmic correspondences, she also asserts that one particular type of human life is most exalted for maintaining this essential connection to God: the monastic life of virginity, best expressed by the life of virginal women (*Scivias*, II.5.1–26). For Hildegard, as winter dries out the *viriditas* of the grass, so marriage leads to human aridity. But the virgin "stands in the simplicity and beautiful integrity of paradise, which never will appear dry but will always remain in the greenness of flower" (Ep. 52 r).[9] Virginal bodies retain the qualities of earthly paradise; sexual bodies reflect the corrupted nature of a fallen world. Virginal bodies – especially, again, female ones – also are most fully capable of making the music that Hildegard wrote, music created for singing in the Divine Office.[10] Music, like *viriditas* itself, is something that binds heaven and earth together, bridging the gap between the present and the Edenic past, where the virginal bodies of Adam and Eve sang with the angelic choirs (Ep. 73).

Hildegard's visionary experience led her to articulate the presence of the divine in the form of powerful female entities, especially Sapientia or Caritas, the embodiment of God's eternal counsel. Barbara Newman has demonstrated how Hildegard's female figures express God's eternity and cosmic relations. But Hildegard's use of male figures, for example Father and Son, comes to the fore in her meditations on the particularities of history.[11] Thus, Hildegard enlarged biblical wisdom traditions to create a theology that gave full expression to her sense of divine fecundity and beauty, qualities also embodied in the earth and in Hildegard herself as revealer of this divinity

---

[8] Hildegard of Bingen, *Symphonia*, 2nd ed., trans. Barbara Newman (Ithaca: Cornell University Press, 1998), 126, translation modified.
[9] Hildegard of Bingen, *Epistolarium*, 3 vols., ed. L. Van Acker and Monica Klaes, Corpus Christianorum, Continuatio Mediaevalis 91–91B (Turnhout: Brepols, 1991–2001).
[10] Bruce Holsinger, "The Flesh of the Voice: Embodiment and the Homoerotics of Devotion in the Music of Hildegard of Bingen (1098–1179)," *Signs* 19:1 (1993), 92–125.
[11] Barbara Newman, *Sister of Wisdom: St. Hildegard's Theology of the Feminine* (Berkeley: University of California Press, 1987), 45–46.

(*Liber divinorum operum*, III.3.2).[12] Her sense of the divine as overwhelming all categories also led to images that overwhelm all verbal or visual logic. In the *Liber divinorum operum*, she described a fantastic hybrid figure: an image standing erect with a bright splendor obscuring its head, with lion's feet and six wings. The rest of its body was covered in fish scales, except for its belly, where there was a human head with white hair and a beard. This image simultaneously represents God, human beings created in God's image, the Son of God, the pregnant body of the Virgin Mary, and perhaps even the body of Eve holding within her the future generations of human beings. Whereas hybrids or monsters often convey a sense of impurity or threat, Hildegard's vision emphasizes the jubilant impossibility of maintaining consistent boundaries between human and divine. In spite of all her attention to the pastoral crises of her day, Hildegard's ultimate experience of the presence of the divine was cosmic harmony, whether expressed in music, *viriditas*, Sapientia, or a monstrous image of superabundant meaning.

## 4 Other Visionary Nuns

Hildegard of Bingen's mode of visionary writing had no exact imitators. Elisabeth of Schönau (1128/29–1164/65) knew Hildegard and was influenced by her visionary expression, but her own works are strikingly different. Elisabeth explicitly described her visions as occurring while she was in ecstasy, or rapture, or *mentis excessus*, outside of her normal cognitive process. Yet, although she was not afraid to admit her loss of normal consciousness, her texts retain a vivid personal voice. By contrast, those of Hildegard are dominated by an attempt to represent the voice of the Living Light rather than her own. These contrasts are linked to differing views of mystical experience. Whereas Hildegard saw herself as chosen by God to receive divine revelation, Elisabeth had a more complicated sense of mystical agency. She was aware of how her own actions, particularly devout prayer, could influence the course of her ecstatic experience. The monastic liturgy was often the setting and even the trigger for her ecstasies, and so it is not surprising that she affirmed that sometimes her trances and encounters with heavenly beings were shaped by the actions of other members of her community. Also, Elisabeth described her experiences as much more dialogic or interactive than Hildegard's. Elisabeth spoke with the various angels and saints she encountered, and she spoke with members of her monastic

---

[12] Hildegard of Bingen, *Liber divinorum operum*, ed. A. Derolez and P. Dronke, Corpus Christianorum, Continuatio Mediaevalis 92 (Turnholt: Brepols, 1996).

community. Mediating between these two areas of engagement was a powerful part of her life. Elisabeth claimed occasionally to hear the voice of the Lord, but her most frequent and important experiences are encounters with angels and saints, especially the Virgin Mary. This too sets her apart from Hildegard, who portrayed an exclusive relationship with the Living Light, despite her keen interest in the various ways in which the divine presence manifests itself.

The dialogic character and sense of mystical embeddedness in a liturgical community that mark Elisabeth's visionary works emerge even more forcefully in the works of Gertrude "the Great" (1256–ca. 1301–2), who lived in the monastery of Helfta and contributed substantially to its vibrant intellectual and devotional culture. *Legatus memorialis abundantiae divinae pietatis* (*The Memorial Herald of the Abundance of Divine Love*) is a collaboratively written work enshrining both first-person and third-person accounts of Gertrude's mystical life. It was part of a decades-long effort at Helfta to produce a literature of spiritual guidance that would foster within the community the kind of experience that Gertrude cultivated in herself.

The *Legatus* attests to a belief in a permeable sense of both the divine and human being. For example, a wound – the puncturing of the skin that opens up the body – is a powerful focus of attention for Gertrude. She prayed for her own heart to be inscribed with Christ's wounds and felt that she did actually receive the stigmata in her heart (*Legatus*, II.4.3).[13] Later she prayed for her heart to be transfixed by the arrow of Christ's love. When she received the Eucharist, she looked at the painting of the Crucifixion in her prayer book and saw coming out of the wound in Christ's side a ray of sunlight pointed like an arrow. This arrow moved toward her but retreated – arousing but not satisfying her desire. Three days later, Christ appeared to her, "inflicting a wound in my heart," which led Gertrude to acknowledge him as the one who "was made bone of my bone and flesh of my flesh" (*Legatus*, II.5.2–4). Evoking the words of Adam greeting his new spouse Eve, Gertrude acclaims Christ as her intimate partner who has made them one in substance.

This focus on wounding and mutual interpenetration is not a celebration of a spiritual height accessible to her alone. Gertrude described the Eucharistic ritual, the prayers spoken, the material stimulants (e.g., the painting in her prayer book), and even her own lukewarm devotion, all of which teach her audience about how to pursue this path. As she

---

[13] *Legatus divinae pietatis* in *Le Héraut*, 4 vols., ed. Pierre Doyère et al. Sources Chrétiennes 139, 143, 255, 331 (Paris: Éditions du Cerf, 1968–1986).

acknowledged, her book was written so that Christ would offer such benefits to many people (*Legatus*, II.10.1). Other testimonies in the *Legatus* portray Gertrude's penetration into Christ as directly connecting God to the world through her. For example, after receiving the Eucharist, Gertrude saw her soul "in the likeness of a tree having its root fixed in the wound in the side of Jesus Christ. Through that wound as if through the root, she felt herself penetrated in a marvelous new way by the power of the humanity and divinity passing through each of her branches and fruits and leaves, in such a way that the fruit of his whole life took on a greater splendor though her" (*Legatus*, III.18.16). Gertrude then prayed that others in heaven, on earth, and in purgatory might benefit from the divine grace she received. Whereupon she saw each of the fruits on her tree exude a most powerful liquid that flowed forth to increase the joy of those in heaven, to mitigate the punishments of those in purgatory, and to enhance both the sweetness of grace for the just and the bitterness of punishment for sinners on earth. As Anna Harrison has shown, the nuns of Helfta embraced the communal monastic liturgy as an ongoing opportunity to move into an intimacy with Christ. Feeling his divinity infused in them, they taught the members of their community how to feel Christ's proximity through their liturgy and through joining with Christ in the work of salvation.[14]

## 5 Beguines and New Possibilities

In the early thirteenth century, some women forged a new style of religious life embracing poverty, prayer, chastity, and often charitable work such as care for the sick and dying. They did not take formal monastic vows, although they sometimes lived together in informal communities. These women were known as "beguines," and their life in the world (instead of in a monastery) offered them new possibilities for creating mystical lives – yet it also made them the frequent target of suspicion about their lifestyle and their mystical claims.

Hadewijch, about whom little biographical detail is known, was a beguine living in thirteenth-century Brabant. She probably acted as an informal leader of a small group of beguines, and she wrote a substantial collection of poems, visions, and letters in her native Dutch. Some of her works show familiar elements such as the mystical possibilities of communal liturgy, especially the celebration of the Eucharist. Erotic imagery adapted

[14] Anna Harrison, "'I Am Wholly Your Own': Liturgical Piety and Community Among the Nuns of Helfta," *Church History* 78:3 (2009), 549–583.

from the Song of Songs, which can be seen in Gertrude of Helfta, explodes in Hadewijch's works as she takes over the language of *Minnesang*, German love poetry in the courtly tradition, to teach about the ecstasies and horrors of loving God.

Hadewijch's visions include some of the most explicit attempts to convey the extremity of desire. For example, she describes her tremulous presence at a service of morning prayer sung in church on Pentecost Sunday,

> My heart and my veins and all my limbs trembled and quivered with eager desire and, as often occurred with me, such madness and fear beset my mind that it seemed to me I did not content my Beloved, and that my Beloved did not fulfill my desire, so that dying I must go mad, and going mad I must die. (Vision 7)[15]

At a communal liturgy on the feast celebrating the infusion of the Holy Spirit into the world and into Christ's disciples, Hadewijch describes herself on the brink of frenzy as she wants her Beloved to "content" her in his godhead, holding nothing back. For this, she desires to "give satisfaction in all great sufferings ... to grow up in order to be God with God." She then sees her Beloved, first as a three-year-old child, coming to her with the Eucharistic bread and chalice, then as a man. After giving her the Eucharist, "he came himself to me, took me entirely in his arms, and pressed me to him; and all my members felt his full felicity, in accordance with the desire of my heart and my humanity." But then he seemed to dissolve, so that she could not see him outside of her or distinguish him within: "Then it seemed to me as if we were one without difference.... I wholly melted away in him and nothing any longer remained to me of myself" (Vision 7).

The divinizing experience of "being God with God" opens Hadewijch to a kind of knowledge that pierces her: the knowledge of damnation. In another vision, Hadewijch describes seeing the countenance of her Beloved, in which she recognized "all the countenances and all the forms that ever existed and ever shall exist" and saw the reason for the damnation or blessing of every one who had ever lived (Vision 6). Her vision pans out to encompass the mystery of divine judgment, causing her to fall out of this visionary ecstasy but into "fruition of his Nature, which is Love." This movement from a God's eye view of human wretchedness and beatitude to being engulfed in the enjoyment of God's nature ends with a return to the moral life, now transformed: she now must live "in conformity with my

---

[15] Quotations of Hadewijch are from Hadewijch, *The Complete Works*, trans. Columba Hart (New York: Paulist Press, 1980).

Divinity and my Humanity – back again into the cruel world, where you must taste every kind of death" (Vision 6). The suffering that Hadewijch experiences in the world is the agony of God's absence, the struggle to keep up the pursuit despite its seeming folly, and the torment of identifying with the damning, not just the loving, power of God (Vision 5). The struggle of the pursuit is most fully expressed in Hadewijch's poems, in which she becomes the lover-knight of *Minnesang*, pursuing *Minne*, Lady Love, who demands the impossible yet somehow entices her lover "to sally forth to meet my doom" (Poems in Stanzas, 9.1.10). Doom, enemy, battle, violence: For Hadewijch the mystical life requires the masculine aggression of the knight as he tries to conquer his fierce Lady. Love is not simply languishing in desire. As Barbara Newman puts it, for Hadewijch love demands "unfaith," "an angry, no-holds-barred demand for reciprocity ... a fierce determination to 'stand up to' infinite Being, demanding all of Love's love for all of one's own."[16] Hadewijch crafted a new language of love, ecstatic and agonistic, whereby the sweetness of enjoying the Beloved is never far from the terror of madness, the acceptance of suffering, and the bracing awareness that one is out to conquer God.

As Amy Hollywood has shown, Marguerite Porete (d. 1310), another beguine, rejected a mysticism grounded in visionary experience and the acceptance of suffering. Instead, she articulated a path of divinization through the annihilation of reason and the will. The courtly language of love is still used, but for Marguerite, love's demand is self-annihilation. Freedom is achieved by this annihilation: The soul is freed from the exhausting, inexhaustible demands of the virtuous life. Yet, being fully united with the divine, the soul becomes unable to sin and is returned to its natural, unfallen state.[17] Marguerite's book, *The Mirror of Simple Souls*, was condemned for the radicalism of her language of annihilation and her seeming amorality. When she refused to recant the teachings therein, she was burned at the stake.

## 6 Conclusion

Marguerite's fate points to the growing danger for women experimenting with new ways of expressing their experience of God's presence – especially

---

[16] Barbara Newman, *God and the Goddesses: Vision, Poetry, and Belief in the Middle Ages* (Philadelphia: University of Pennsylvania Press, 2003), 177, 182.

[17] Amy Hollywood, "Suffering Transformed: Marguerite Porete, Meister Eckhart, and the Problem of Women's Spirituality," in *Meister Eckhart and the Beguine Mystics: Hadewijch of Brabant, Mechthild of Magdeburg, and Marguerite Porete*, ed. Bernard McGinn (New York: Continuum, 1994), 87–113.

beguines and laywomen who did not have the protection of monastic communities. The sharply divided response to Margery Kempe (1373–1438), a married woman who claimed to marry Christ and be assured of her own salvation, drew on the increased cultural willingness to attribute women's mystical claims to demonic rather than divine inspiration.

Accusations of heresy or demonic possession, the rich symbolic environment of the liturgy, and the discipline of monastic practice – all of these cultural elements point to the social embeddedness of the mystical life. Medieval women – many more than have been discussed here – used the resources of their religion to develop means of perceiving, uniting with, and being transformed by the brilliant, sometimes scorching presence of their God. Their creativity and commitment to articulating their sometimes startling expressions of God and self are among the most vibrant aspects of medieval Christianity, and a crucial chapter in the history of Western mysticism.

# III
# The Renaissance and Early Modernity

# 12

# RENAISSANCE HERMETISM

## Antoine Faivre

### 1 Hermetism: A Definition

"Hermetism" (adjective: "hermetic") has two complementary meanings. First, it designates the works known as the Hermetica, written in Greek at the dawn of our era in the region of Alexandria. The term "Alexandrian Hermetism" is often used to refer to these works, which deal with matters such as cosmology, spiritual illumination, and theurgy. A collection dating from the second and third centuries CE, dubbed the *Corpus Hermeticum* (henceforth *CH*) at the beginning of the Renaissance, stands out within this body of works. It is composed of seventeen short treatises, which were oftentimes to be edited along with the *Asclepius*, and the fragments attributed to Stobaeus. Their "author" or inspirer is the legendary figure Hermes Trismegistus, or Hermes the "thrice great," associated in many different (and conflicting) mythical genealogies with the Egyptian Thoth and the Greek Hermes.

In the expression "Neo-Alexandrian Hermetism," however, Hermetism refers to the various works, adaptations, and commentaries that stand in the philosophical or religious wake of the Hermetica, particularly of the *CH*, in the Middle Ages but principally from the Renaissance until the present day. The term "Hermeticism," which is vague, is frequently used as a synonym for esotericism and also for alchemy.

### 2 Rediscovery and First Publication of the *CH* at the Dawn of the Renaissance

In the Middle Ages, there had been no dearth of literature following in the tradition of the Hermetica and/or inspired by the figure of Hermes Trismegistus, but the *CH* itself had been lost since around the fifth century (save for the *Asclepius*, originally known in Greek as *Logos Teleios*, which survived in an ancient Latin translation only). Around the year 1460, a monk named Leonardo da Pistoia discovered fourteen treatises of the *CH* in Macedonia. These had been gathered together in the eleventh century, and it was in this form that the Byzantine Platonist Psellus had known them. Pistoia brought the treatises to the ruler of Florence, Cosimo de' Medici the Elder, who had entrusted Marsilio Ficino with the creation of a Platonic Academy. Cosimo and Ficino had intended to have the available writings of Plato translated into Latin; however, when they learned of these fourteen treatises (*CH* I–XIV), Cosimo insisted that Ficino temporarily set aside his Latin translation of Plato and work on the hermetic texts instead. In 1463, Ficino completed his translation of the treatises, which was printed at Treviso in 1471 under the title *Mercurii Trismegisti Pimander Liber de potestate et sapientia Dei*, together with a prefatory argument (*Argumentum*) by Ficino himself. In his *Argumentum*, Ficino called attention to the *Asclepius*, which he called "the most divine" of this kind of literature (an edition of the *Asclepius* had just been printed in Rome in 1469 and inserted into Apuleius's *Opera*). He also described a "genealogy of wisdom," which he elsewhere called *prisca theologia* (ancient theology), consisting of six main figures: Mercurius (Hermes) Trismegistus, Orpheus, Aglaophemus (an Orphic teacher of Pythagoras), Pythagoras, Philolaus, and Plato. That list was later to undergo various changes depending on the authors who presented it.

The *CH* (often published under the title of the first treatise, *Poimandres*, or *Pimander* in Ficino's 1471 translation) and the *Asclepius* enjoyed considerable success throughout the Renaissance. Up to 1641, no fewer than twenty-four Latin editions appeared, not counting partial ones or translations into other languages. In addition, there were many commentaries. This literature was a central element in European culture, mostly among learned and prominent members of society. A large part of these commentaries constitutes Neo-Alexandrian Hermetism proper, one of the so-called modern esoteric currents.

## 3 Other Key Figures at the End of the Fifteenth Century: Giovanni Pico della Mirandola, Giovanni da Corregio, and Lodovico Lazzarelli

Anthony Woodville's English translation of several of the hermetic texts in the anthology *The dyctes or sayengis of the philosophers* bears witness to an early, albeit discreet presence of the *CH* in England. In fact, it was the first dated book in the history of English printing: published by William Caxton in Westminster in 1477. In Italy, the reception was much wider.

For example, Giovanni Pico della Mirandola's *Oratio de hominis dignitate* (1486) begins with a reference to the "Magnum, O Asclepi, miraculum" passage of the *Asclepius* (*Ascl.* 6). Pico synthesized the hermetic traditions advanced by Ficino with the Kabbalah, which he believed had been entrusted to Moses on Mount Sinai. Two years before, on Palm Sunday of 1484, there appeared in Rome a certain Giovanni da Correggio. On the banks of the Manara, he put on winged shoes and a crown of thorns topped with a crescent moon bearing the inscription: "This is my son Poimandres, whom I have chosen." Mounting a white donkey, he made a speech in which he called himself the "angel of Wisdom, Poimandres, in the highest and greatest ecstasy of the Spirit of Jesus Christ." He seems to have believed that Poimandres (*CH* I) had been identical with the Logos who had first appeared to Hermes, then incarnated in Christ, and had now reincarnated (so to speak) as Correggio, who was therefore the "Hermetic Christ" (Poimandres and Christ in one). Following his speech, he deposited various objects on the throne of Saint Peter in the Vatican. In 1496, he turned up again in Florence and then in Lyons.

Lodovico Lazzarelli saw in Giovanni a new and divine prophet whom he considered his mentor, and he left a vivid description of these events in a manifesto entitled *Epistola Enoch*, probably published in Milan ca. 1490. Another text by Lazzarelli, *Crater Hermetis* ("The Mixing-Bowl of Hermes") written around 1492 or 1494 – but not published until Lefèvre d'Etaples's edition in 1505 – is a fictitious conversation in the style of the dialogues contained in *CH*. The complete Latin subtitle of this work reads in English translation: "A Dialogue on the Supreme Dignity of Man, entitled the Way of Christ and the Mixing-Bowl of Hermes." The interlocutors in the dialogue are Lazzarelli himself, who plays the role of the initiator, and two other historical personalities: Ferdinand I of Aragon, King of Naples and Sicily, and Giovanni Pontano, his prime minister, who are cast in the role of pupils. The *Crater Hermetis* is one of the most interesting examples of hermetic-Christian syncretism written during the Renaissance.

Convinced that the Bible and hermetic writings were equiprimordial, in 1482 Lazzarelli dedicated to Correggio a manuscript in his own hand consisting of three parts, each one opening with a dedicatory preface. The first contains Marsilio Ficino's translation of the *Pimander* (1471, i.e., *CH* I–XIV); the second contains the *Asclepius*. The third contains the first Latin translation (by Lazzarelli himself) of *CH* XVI–XVIII: three treatises that he had apparently discovered in a separate manuscript (unfortunately not preserved). He entitled them *Diffinitiones Asclepii ad regem Ammonem*. This author is an even better exemplar than Ficino and Pico of Christian Hermetism in the Renaissance (in addition to being one of the first noteworthy authors instrumental in the early development of Christian Kabbalah). For many years, however, he was passed over in silence until the historians Wouter J. Hanegraaff and R. M. Bouthoorn recognized his contributions.[1]

Also at this time appeared Jacques Lefèvre d'Etaples's first edition of the *Pimander* (Paris, 1494). It contains, besides Ficino's translation of *CH* I–XIV, a series of commentaries or *Argumenta* of his own (long attributed to Ficino). The second edition (Paris, 1505) was augmented with both the *Asclepius* and an abridged version of Lazzarelli's *Crater Hermetis*.

Hermes Trismegistus also appeared in artworks of the Renaissance. He had already appeared in medieval art, for example, in alchemical treatises in which he was represented as a sage seated in a crypt, tomb, pyramid, or temple, holding the *Tabula Smaragdina*, or Emerald Tablet, in his hands. At the end of the fifteenth century, he appears in Bacchio Baldini's *Florentine Picture Chronicle* (1470–1475). The god Hermes-Mercurius in Botticelli's painting *Primavera* (1482) could be interpreted as an allusion to Hermes Trismegistus. One sees him looking upward and playing with clouds, touching them lightly as if they were beneficent veils through which transcendent truths might reach the seeker. Six years later, in 1486, an artist inlaid the pavement of Siena Cathedral with a panel representing Hermes Trismegistus as a tall and venerable bearded man, dressed in a robe and cloak, wearing a brimmed miter and in the company of two personages (possibly Moses and Plato). The panel bears the inscription "Hermes Mercurius Trismegistus Contemporaneus Moysi" (Hermes Mercurius Trismegistus Contemporary of Moses). Pope Alexander VI, the protector of Pico della Mirandola, commanded Pinturiccio to paint a great fresco in the Borgia Apartments of the Vatican. Abounding with hermetic symbols and zodiacal signs, the fresco depicts Hermes Trismegistus, young and beardless, in the company of Isis and Moses. Around 1500, he was painted on a wall of the church Sint-Walburgis in Zutphen in the Low Countries, in the company of Mary, the newly born Jesus, angels, and sibyls. Many such examples could be mentioned.

## 4 First Half of the Sixteenth Century: Hermetism and *philosophia perennis*

Many hermeticists of this period were instrumental in fostering what was to be called – mostly as of 1540 – *philosophia perennis* (perennial or eternal

---

[1] See especially W. J. Hanegraaff and R. M. Bouthoorn, *Ludovico Lazzarelli (1447–1500). The Hermetic Writings and Related Documents*, Medieval and Renaissance Texts and Studies, vol. 281 (Tempe: Arizona Center for Medieval and Renaissance Studies, 2005).

philosophy). Among them are to be counted Champier, Giorgio, and Agrippa. Symphorien Champier, an admirer of Ficino and disciple of Lefèvre d'Étaples, attempted to derive all of Greek philosophy from Hermes, incorporating into the tradition of *prisca theologia* (as Ficino had defined it) the supposed doctrines of the Druids, as well as elements drawn from the Kabbalah. His *Liber de quadruplici vita: Theologia Asclepii Hermetis Trismegisti discipuli cum commentariis* ... (Lyons, 1507) contains, among other texts, Lazzarelli's translation of *Diffinitiones Asclepii*. As exemplified by Lefèvre and Champier, the French were generally more cautious than their Italian or German counterparts regarding the "magical" elements of the *CH* and the *Asclepius*.

Francesco Giorgio (or Zorzi), who belonged to the Order of Friars Minor, authored *De Harmonia mundi totius Cantica tria* (Venice, 1525; Paris, 1545, 1546; French translation by Guy Lefèvre de la Boderie, Paris, 1578), and *In Sacram Scripturam Problemata* (Venice, 1536; Paris, 1622). These two works are an original construction aimed at making the *prisca theologia* coincide with Neoplatonism and Kabbalah, as well as astrological and alchemical elements. *De Harmonia mundi* was to enjoy a lasting success among representatives of esoteric currents.

Indeed, the Hermetic treatises were increasingly considered to be the expression of a philosophy transmitted over the course of many centuries, since the time of Moses or even before. What Ficino had called *prisca theologia* became – albeit in a slightly different sense – *philosophia perennis*. This expression was introduced by the Italian Augustinian and Vatican librarian Agostino Steuco (*De perenni philosophia*, Lyon, 1540, new ed. 1590). Although staunchly attached to the church's magisterium, he too tried to reconstruct the ancient philosophy as a foundation for restoring Christian unity. The *CH*, the *Asclepius*, and the figure of Hermes Trismegistus were thus thought to belong to a far distant past, namely to the age of Moses, or possibly earlier. Although pagan in character, they were considered to foreshadow Christian truths and were expected to give new depth to the Christian revelation.

Traces of Hermetic influence are also noticeable in Copernicus's *De Revolutionibus* (1543), wherein Hermes Trismegistus is identified with the sun considered as the visible God. But one of the most famous representatives of Hermetism at that time, who was also to remain an influential figure in the history of Western esotericism, was the German Henricus Cornelius Agrippa. Besides quite a few passages in his much celebrated *De Occulta Philosophia* (1533), several of his writings are devoted to a hermeneutics of the *CH*, particularly *Oratio in praelectionem Hermetis Trismegisti de Potestate et*

*Sapientia Dei* (Cologne, 1535); *Liber de triplici ratione congnoscendi Dei* (1516); and *Dehortatio gentiles theologiae* (ca. 1526, a text in which he distances himself from Hermetism).[2]

Sebastian Franck, another German, presented in his *Die Güldin Arch* (Augsburg, 1538) a collection of biblical sayings and paraphrases, together with extracts from "illuminated pagans and philosophers" such as Hermes Trismegistus. In Basel, Franck also made a German translation (1542) of both the *Asclepius* and *CH* I–XIV, illuminated by long commentaries dealing mostly with commonalities between the Bible and nature (a still-unpublished manuscript).

Almost all French adherents of the *prisca theologia* dealt with Hermetism from a perspective of Christian apologetics. This is reflected, for instance, in Gabriel du Préau's book *Mercure Trismégiste ancient Thelogien & excellent Philosophe, de la puissance & sapience de Dieu ... Auecq' un Dialogue de Loys Lazarel poëte chrestien intitulé le Bassin d'Hermès* (Paris, 1549; new ed. 1557). It contains, along with abundant commentaries, the first edition in French of *CH* I–XIV, of the *Asclepius*, and (as the title indicates) of Lazzarelli's *Crater Hermetis*.

Besides the presence of Agrippa and Franck, in general the Germanic countries had little part in this Neo-Alexandrian Hermetic current. This may be due partially to the fact that Humanism made only slight progress in those countries during this period, hampered by the barrier that Lutheranism had erected against it. Therefore, Hermetism, by its very nature a legacy of ancient Greek literature, remained mostly a subject of study for the humanists. As a consequence, during this period most commentators of the *CH* were French and Italian.

Any overview of Neo-Alexandrian Hermetism must also give attention to the so-called *Tabula Smaragdina*, a short text that belongs to the literature of the Hermetica and had circulated in a Latin translation as early as the twelfth century. In the period considered here, it was the subject of quite a few commentaries (e.g., in Johann Trithemius's correspondence with Germain de Ganay in 1505). But its first printed edition, also in Latin, appeared in Nuremberg in 1541 (part of a compilation of alchemical texts gathered under the title *De Alchemia*, 1541). The publication of this enigmatic prose poem caused torrents of hermetic, alchemical, and theosophical ink to flow – and still does.

---

[2] See W. J. Hanegraaff, "Better than Magic: Cornelius Agrippa and Lazzarellian Hermetism," *Magic, Ritual & Witchcraft* 4:1 (2009), 1–25.

## 5 Bearers of the Flame in the Latter Half of the Sixteenth Century

In the second half of the sixteenth century, Valentin Weigel, whose work is an adumbration of Christian theosophy, cites the name of Hermes Trismegistus more than that of any author of his time. The French Catholic scholar Adrien Turnèbe produced the first edition of the original Greek *CH* (Paris, 1554) based on the manuscript used by Ficino and accompanied by the latter's Latin translation, as well as by Lazarelli's translation of the additional treatises (i.e., *Diffinitiones Asclepii*, or *CH* XVI–XVIII). In the wake of such scholarly publications, François Foix-Candale, bishop of Aire, near Bordeaux, brought out another edition in 1574 (*CH* I–XIV, accompanied by some other hermetic texts). Five years later, he produced extensive commentaries of his own in French, in *Le Pimandre de Mercure Trismégiste: de la Philosophie Chrestienne, Cognoissance du Verbe Divin* ... (Bordeaux, 1579, new ed. Paris, 1587). Here, the hermetic texts serve as supports of meditation and reflection on a great variety of themes, such as the World Soul, the spirits of the elements, celestial bodies – themes that, for the most part, were part and parcel of the *philosophia occulta* of the Renaissance.

*De la vérité de la religion chrestienne* ... (Antwerp, 1581), by the Huguenot Protestant Philippe du Plessis-Mornay, was written at a time when William of Orange was trying to establish religious tolerance at Antwerp. The author employed Hermetism with a view to fashioning a position above all religious conflicts and close to that of Erasmus – but with an additional esoteric dimension. He compared the *CH* with the *Zohar* and made mention of Orpheus, Zarathustra, the sibyls – and especially of Hermes, "the source of them all." This work was published several times in Latin translation and proved to be influential in the development of Protestantism in France. Translated into English by Sir Philip Sidney and Arthur Golding in 1587, it counts as one of the main expositions of Hermetism in the tradition of Ficino.

Giordano Bruno may be counted among the most influential authors in terms of Hermetism in particular, and esoteric literature in general. He made frequent use of the hermetic texts (notably in *Spaccio della bestia triomphante*, 1584). In contrast to that of Ficino and the French, his Hermetism represents a kind of aggressive return to hermetic magic. Not a Christian, unlike most other hermeticists of his time, he did not identify the *intellectus* and *Filius Dei* of the *CH* with the second person of the Trinity, and he was less prone to share the hope nursed by others that a religious reconciliation might be effected by a general acceptance of Hermetism. In fact, Bruno did not desire a reformed Christendom but rather a return to the cults or beliefs of ancient Egypt as described in the *CH* and particularly in the *Asclepius*. In 1591 in Rome, he tried to win over Clement VIII to his views, but his radical ideas led him to the stake in 1600.

Hannibal Rossel's *Pymander Mercurii Trismegisti*, swollen to six volumes (Cracow, 1585–1590), is not so much a commentary on the *CH* as an encyclopedic roll call of a variety of philosophical themes, along with a presentation of *CH* I–VII and the *Asclepius*. Francesco Patrizi's *Nova de universis philosophia* (Ferrara, 1591) contains *CH* I–XIV (as established by Turnèbe and Foix de Candale), the *Asclepius*, and *CH* XVI–XVIII (*Diffinitiones Asclepii*), along with the medieval so-called *Theologia Aristotelis*, and a new Latin translation of these texts. He subjected the Aristotelian philosophy to sharp criticism and wanted to oust it from Jesuit-run colleges. Patrizi portrayed the true *magus* as one who is devoted to God, and true *prisca magia* as the true religion. He claimed that a single treatise of the *CH* contained more philosophy than all of Aristotle. In the dedicatory preface of his book, he asked Pope Gregorius XIV to place the *CH* on the academic curriculum as an alternative philosophy. He went so far as to suggest to the pope that Hermetic Platonism be assigned in all Christian schools as an aid to converting the Lutherans. In 1592, Clement VIII, won over to some of Patrizi's ideas, called him to Rome to hold the chair of Platonic philosophy at the University La Sapienza. Once there, however, Patrizi incurred the displeasure of the Inquisition and his book was placed on the Index. Alongside such reforming plans as Patrizi's, other works were to appear. In 1587, a painting appeared on a pilaster of a Sistine room in the Biblioteca Vaticana, showing Hermes Trismegistus with attributes of Mercurius. The caption informs us that he is "Mercurius-Thoth, inventor of the alphabets." Other examples of his presence in Roman Catholic buildings could be adduced.

Religious Hermetism is irenic by nature. The Puritanism then flourishing in England brought about a weakening of the theological syncretism that had favored such tendencies. With Edward VI, the English Protestants had already begun to break with the past, going so far as to destroy books and libraries. Under the reign of Mary, a Hispano-Catholic intolerance went even further in this direction. Later, Puritan Anglicanism under Elizabeth tended to be impervious to Erasmian tolerance. Hermetism continued to develop within private circles, however, such as those that formed around Sir Philip Sidney and Queen Elizabeth's astrologer, John Dee.

## 6 Reappraisals and Developments as of the Beginning of the Seventeenth Century

Isaac Casaubon, a Protestant minister in Geneva and one of the greatest philologists of his age, set out to prove (in a chapter of his *De rebus sacris ecclesiasticis exercitations XVI*, London, 1614) that the *CH* had not been written prior to the second or third century CE and was therefore a "forgery" of the early Christian era. Although Casaubon's name has long been attached to that new dating, since 1976 research (see especially Mulsow 2002) has shown that this discovery had already been made by other philologists as early as the 1560s. Be that as it may, the claim that the *CH* had been erroneously dated could only deal a heavy blow to its authority, since that authority depended largely on its age. Nevertheless, Neo-Alexandrian Hermetism did not disappear. Indeed, in the following centuries and up to the present day, many esoterically oriented people have preferred to ignore or downplay the significance of the new dating. The following are a few examples of concerns at the beginning of the seventeenth century.

One of the first highly sympathetic exegetes of the *CH* at this time in Germany was Heinrich Noll (author of *Theoria Philosophiae Hermeticae, septem tractatibus*, Hanover, 1617; *Theoria Philsophiae Hermeticae*, Copenhagen, 1617; and *Panergii Philosophici Speculum*, 1623, an initiatic novel that stands in the wake of early Rosicrucian literature). Noteworthy too is the Italian Livius Galante, who authored *Christianae theologiae cum platonica comparatio* (Bologna, 1627). Furthermore, a number of translations of the *CH* into European languages continued to appear. For example, Abraham Willemsz van Beyerland produced a Dutch version of sixteen treatises of the *CH*, based on Patrizi's text, under the title *Sestien boecken* ... (Amsterdam, 1643, new ed. 1652). Beyerland, who was also a translator of Jacob Boehme, added long strongly theosophical commentaries of his own (his translation was to be used in 1706 by the first translator of the *CH* into German, a Paracelsian). Alchemical treatises (e.g., Michael Maier's *Symbola aureae mensa duodecim nationum*, 1617) occasionally devoted an entire, laudatory chapter to Hermes Trismegistus. In addition, many such treatises of the seventeenth century are rich in illustrations in which he appears, usually on the front page, either alone or in the company of other personages such as Hippocrates, Galen, Aristotle, Geber, and Paracelsus. The first version of the *CH* in English was produced by John Everard and contributed greatly to the continuation of Neo-Alexandrian Hermetism throughout the following centuries. (Everard titled it *The Divine Pymander of Hermes Mercurius Trismegistus, in XVII Books. Translated formerly out of the Arabick into Greek* ..., London, 1650, new ed. 1657.)

The number of scholarly works on Hermetism has increased considerably since the middle of the twentieth century. With regard to Neo-Alexandrian Hermetism proper, Frances A. Yates's book *Giordano Bruno and the Hermetic Tradition* (1964) has been highly instrumental in calling the attention of historians to the significance of this current in the history of the Renaissance. Her groundbreaking book has paved the way for an ongoing academic recognition, even institutionalization, of modern Western esotericism as a specialty in its own right. In addition, it has caused a flurry of debates, in particular, over what Robert S. Westman has called the "Yates Thesis," according to which there is a close relation between Hermetism and the scientific revolution.[3]

In the wake of this, the scholar Wouter J. Hanegraaff introduced (in 2001) the expression "the Yates paradigm," referring to the presence in her work of a "grand narrative" that consists in presenting "the Hermetic Tradition" as a more or less autonomous movement, based on a covert reaction against Christianity and the rise of scientific worldviews. Yates also considers the tradition of "magic" – which she sees as essentially nonprogressive – as an important factor in the development of the scientific revolution. Hanegraaff and others have called this paradigm into question. Still, even if neither of these two claims made by Yates can withstand close scrutiny, her work and the debates that still surround it will probably continue to foster the interest of historians in this fascinating chapter of Western culture in general, and of Western esoteric currents in particular.

---

[3] See R. S. Westman and J. E. McGuire, *Hermeticism and the Scientific Revolution* (Los Angeles: William A. Clark Memorial Library, 1977).

# 13

# CHRISTIAN KABBALAH

PETER J. FORSHAW

GERSHOM SCHOLEM ARGUES THAT THE PRIMARY MOTIVATION for Christian kabbalists was a form of missionary activity: "Christian Kabbalah can be defined as the interpretation of kabbalistic texts in the interests of Christianity (or, to be more precise, Catholicism); or the use of kabbalistic concepts and methodology in support of Christian dogma."[1] As evidence, he points to the Christological speculations of Jewish converts, such as the *Pugio Fidei* (*Dagger of Faith*) of Raymund Martini (1220–1285), works that contributed to the growth of an incipient Christian Kabbalah.[2]

## 1 Giovanni Pico della Mirandola and the Dawn of Christian Kabbalah

Although the Majorcan mystic Ramon Lull (1225–1315) is sometimes credited with being the first Christian to show an acquaintance with Kabbalah in his *De auditu Kabbalistico*, the work actually shows little familiarity with the Jewish tradition. Christian speculation about the Kabbalah first took root in the Florentine Renaissance. While Marsilio Ficino (1433–1499) was busy translating and writing commentaries on the works of Plato, Plotinus, and Hermes Trismegistus, Giovanni Pico della Mirandola (1463–1494) began studying kabbalistic works. This was all part of Pico's project of creating his syncretic *philosophia nova*, his synthesis of Aristotelian and Platonic thought with esoteric doctrines gleaned from *prisci theologi* such as Zoroaster,

---

[1] Gershom Scholem, "The Beginnings of the Christian Kabbalah," in *The Christian Kabbalah: Jewish Mystical Books & Their Christian Interpreters*, ed. Joseph Dan (Cambridge, MA: Harvard College Library, 1997), 17–51, here 17.
[2] Scholem, "The Beginnings of the Christian Kabbalah," 18. See also Moshe Idel's "Introduction to the Bison Book Edition," in Johann Reuchlin, *On the Art of the Kabbalah*, trans. Martin and Sarah Goodman (Lincoln: University of Nebraska Press, 1983), v–xxix; Idel, *Kabbalah in Italy 1280–1510: A Survey* (New Haven: Yale University Press, 2011), 227–235.

Orpheus, Hermes Trismegistus, and Pythagoras. Pico is the first author raised as a Christian who is known to have read an impressive amount of genuine Jewish Kabbalah. He marks a watershed in the history of Hebrew studies in Europe.[3]

The fruit of Pico's studies can best be found in his famous nine hundred *Conclusiones Philosophicæ Cabalisticæ et Theologicæ* (1486). It was here that Pico first introduced the Kabbalah into the mainstream of Renaissance thought by means of forty-seven "Cabalistic Conclusions" according to "the secret teaching of the wise Hebrew Cabalists" and seventy-two "Cabalistic conclusions according to my own opinion," with further kabbalistic references in other groups of "Conclusions," including those on magic, Mercury Trismegistus, Zoroaster, and the Orphic hymns.[4]

Pico's two major kabbalistic influences were the Spanish kabbalist Abraham Abulafia (1240–ca. 1291) and the Italian rabbi Menahem Recanati (1250–1310). These men represent two quite different types of Kabbalah, the one ecstatic, the other theosophical-theurgical. Recanati is mainly concerned with the ten *sefirot* as divine emanations and engages in a symbolic exegesis of Scripture as the way to unravel their mysteries. On the other hand, Abulafia, the father of prophetic Kabbalah, tends to downplay the importance of the *sefirot* and concentrates on the names (*shemot*) of God and their permutations as a spiritual discipline by which man can attain union with the divine.[5] Though neither detailed nor systematic in his discussion, for example, of the *sefirot*, paths of wisdom, and gates of understanding, Pico nevertheless shows an awareness of these teachings and understands their relation to kabbalistic theories of creation and revelation.

Pico's alleged primary motivation for studying the Kabbalah is evangelizing against heretics and Jews. In the *Apologia* he composed in 1487 – following the condemnation of thirteen of his theses as heretical – he avows that his motive is "to do battle for the faith against the relentless slanders of the

---

[3] On Pico and Kabbalah, see François Secret, *Les Kabbalistes Chrétiens de la Renaissance* (Paris: Dunod, 1964), Cap. III; Klaus Reichert, "Pico della Mirandola and the Beginnings of Christian Kabbala," in *Mysticism, Magic and Kabbalah in Ashkenazi Judaism*, ed. Karl Erich Grözinger and Joseph Dan (Berlin: Walter de Gruyter, 1995), 195–207; *Pico della Mirandola: New Essays*, ed. M. V. Dougherty (Cambridge: Cambridge University Press, 2008), *passim*. On Pico as creator of the "first true Christian Cabala," see Bernard McGinn, "Cabalists and Christians: Reflections on Cabala in Medieval and Renaissance Thought," in *Jewish Christians and Christian Jews: From the Renaissance to the Enlightenment*, ed. Richard H. Popkin and Gordon M. Weiner (Dordrecht: Kluwer, 1994), 11–34.
[4] Steven A. Farmer, *Syncretism in the West: Pico's 900 Theses (1486): The Evolution of Traditional Religious and Philosophical Systems* (Tempe, AZ: Medieval & Renaissance Texts & Studies, 1998), 343, 421, 489, 497–503, 507, 511.
[5] On Abulafia and Recanati, see Idel, *Kabbalah in Italy, passim*.

Hebrews."[6] As his second set of "Cabalistic Conclusions" explains, his intention is one of "providing powerful confirmation of the Christian religion from the very principles of the Hebrew Sages," so that the Jews can be refuted by their own kabbalistic books.[7] He proposes to use the Kabbalah's own hermeneutical techniques to prove, for instance, the supremacy of the name of Jesus and the mystery of the Trinity.[8]

The significance of Pico's Kabbalah should not, however, be restricted simply to Christian polemic and apologetics. Chaim Wirszubski argues that the "Cabalistic Conclusions" "outgrew their original purpose" and that Pico viewed Kabbalah from an entirely new standpoint, being "the first Christian who considered cabbala to be simultaneously a witness for Christianity and an ally of natural magic."[9] Pico's interest goes far beyond the simple confirmation of Christianity when in his "Magical Conclusions" he famously asserts that the divinity of Christ is best demonstrated by the science of magic and Kabbalah.[10] Joseph Dan believes that with this thesis, Pico is less concerned with promoting traditional Catholicism than with implying that Christianity should discover a new meaning, one outlined in his nine hundred theses.[11] The extreme nature of the claims Pico makes, such as that "no magical operation can be of any efficacy unless it has annexed to it a work of Cabala," created a widespread interest in this Jewish tradition.[12] Pico's alliance between Kabbalah, magic, and theology produced a significant development in Christian Kabbalah: From then on, a Christian kabbalist could be a theologian or a magus or both.

## 2 Johann Reuchlin's Influential Formulations on the Word and the Art

During the time Pico was active in Florence, he was visited by the German scholar Johann Reuchlin (1455–1522), universally regarded as one of the key

---

[6] Brian P. Copenhaver, "The Secret of Pico's Oration: Cabala and Renaissance Philosophy," in *Renaissance and Early Modern Philosophy*, ed. Peter A. French and Howard K. Wettstein (Oxford: Blackwell, 2002), 56–81, here 75.
[7] Pico della Mirandola, *On the Dignity of Man*, trans. Charles Glenn Wallis, Paul J. W. Miller, and Douglas Carmichael (Indianapolis and Cambridge: Hackett Publishing, 1998), 29, 32.
[8] Farmer, *Syncretism in the West*, 523.
[9] Chaim Wirszubski, *Pico della Mirandola's Encounter with Jewish Mysticism* (Cambridge, MA: Harvard University Press, 1989), 151, 185.
[10] Farmer, *Syncretism in the West*, 497.
[11] Joseph Dan, "The Kabbalah of Johannes Reuchlin and Its Historical Significance," in Dan, *The Christian Kabbalah*, 55–95, here 57.
[12] Farmer, *Syncretism in the West*, 499.

figures of European scholarship and intellectual life at the turn of the sixteenth century. Reuchlin wrote two of the most influential books of Christian Kabbalah, the *De Verbo Mirifico* (*On the Wonder-Working Word*, 1494) and *De Arte Cabalistica* (*On the Kabbalistic Art*, 1517).[13] One of the main attractions of Kabbalah for him was the multiplicity of divine names in Hebrew. In his "Conclusions," Pico had briefly referred to the name of Jesus in a kabbalistic context; in *De Verbo Mirifico*, Reuchlin launched into a full-blown declaration of how the Jewish four-letter name the *Tetragrammaton*, YHVH, had been superseded by the five-letter Christian *Pentagrammaton*, the name "above all others," YHSVH.

Reuchlin's first kabbalistic work was significant for its ideas about language and the contribution it made to the Renaissance debate on the occult powers and properties of words and names. It contained extraordinary examples of marvelous deeds achieved through the wonder-working word, from feeding the hungry and curing the sick to exorcizing demons and reviving the dead.[14] By the time he published *De Arte Cabalistica*, Reuchlin was the leading Christian Hebraist of his age and had become involved in the controversy with the Cologne Dominicans over the Talmud, sometimes referred to as the "Battle of the Books." Reuchlin wrote his second kabbalistic work "as a form of special pleading for the protection of Hebrew books against burning because of their 'Christian' content." This was a particularly courageous stance to take and a radical departure from the standard theological antagonism toward the Talmud.[15]

An important aspect of the new concept of language found in kabbalistic sources was a set of exegetical techniques having no counterpart in the Christian interpretation of Scripture. In *De Arte Cabalistica*, Reuchlin provides examples of the Jewish techniques of gematria (or arithmetic),

---

[13] On Reuchlin, see Karl E. Grözinger, "Reuchlin und die Kabbala," in *Reuchlin und die Juden*, ed. Arno Herzig and Julius H. Schoeps (Sigmaringen: Jan Thorbecke Verlag, 1993), 175–187; Bernd Roling, "The Complete Nature of Christ: Sources and Structures of a Christological Theurgy in the Works of Johannes Reuchlin," in *The Metamorphosis of Magic from Late Antiquity to the Early Modern Period*, ed. Jan N. Bremmer and Jan R. Veenstra (Leuven: Peeters, 2002), 213–266; Wilhelm Schmidt-Biggemann, "Einleitung: Johannes Reuchlin und die Anfänge der christlichen Kabbala," in *Christliche Kabbala*, ed. Schmidt-Biggemann (Ostfildern: Jan Thorbecke Verlag, 2003), 9–48.

[14] Charles Zika, "Reuchlin's De Verbo Mirifico and the Magic Debate of the Late Fifteenth Century," *Journal of the Warburg and Courtauld Institutes* 39 (1976), 104–138.

[15] Joseph Leon Blau, *The Christian Interpretation of the Cabala in the Renaissance* (New York: Columbia University Press, 1944), 50; Joseph Dan, "Christian Kabbalah in the Renaissance," in *Dictionary of Gnosis and Western Esotericism*, ed. Wouter J. Hanegraaff (Leiden: Brill, 2006), 991; Reichert, "Pico della Mirandola and the Beginnings of Christian Kabbala," 197.

CHRISTIAN KABBALAH 147

*Notariacon* (manipulation of letters), and *Themura* (commutation of letters), all for the sake of proving the supremacy of the Christian religion. Somewhat incongruously, Reuchlin's Jewish representative, Simon ben Eleazar, promotes Christian Trinitarian doctrine with his explanation of how the twelve-letter name *Ab Ben Veruach Hakadosh* (Father, Son, and Holy Spirit) flows from the Jewish *Tetragrammaton* YHVH.[16] So informative was Reuchlin's exposition that from his time, no writer who touched on Christian Kabbalah with any thoroughness did so without using him as a source.

## 3 Other Significant Sources for Early Christian Kabbalah

One of the central figures in sixteenth-century Christian Kabbalah is undoubtedly the Venetian scholar Francesco Giorgio (ca. 1460–1540),[17] author of two large volumes on Kabbalah that were widely read: *De Harmonia mundi totius cantica tria* (*Three Canticles on the Harmony of the Whole World*, 1525) and the *Problemata* (1536). In both books, the Kabbalah was central to the themes developed, and the *Zohar*, for the first time, was used extensively in a work of Christian origin. Elaborating on the works of Pico and Reuchlin, in *De Harmonia mundi* Giorgio presents the major ideas of Renaissance kabbalists. In the process, he takes the Christianization of Kabbalah far beyond that found in Pico's theses. One of Giorgio's disciples, Arcangelo da Borgonuovo (d. 1571), borrowing extensively from the works of his teacher and Reuchlin, published a *Dechiaratione sopra il nome di Giesu* (*Declaration on the Name of Jesus*, 1557), essentially an expansion of the final chapters in Reuchlin's *De Verbo Mirifico*. This was later followed by a commentary on Pico's kabbalistic theses, *Cabalistarum selectiora, obscurioraque dogmata* (*More select and obscure dogmas of the Cabalists*, 1569).[18]

The German Jewish convert Paulus Ricius (1470–1541) likewise discovered in Kabbalah the mysteries of the Trinity, the eternal generation of the Son of God, redemption through the passion and blood of the Messiah, and his resurrection. Rici was widely read in Hebrew sources, and with the zeal of a convert he published a series of short tracts under the title *Sal Fœderis* (*Salt*

---

[16] Blau, *The Christian Interpretation of the Cabala*, 57–59.
[17] Giulio Busi, "Francesco Zorzi: A Methodical Dreamer," in Dan, *The Christian Kabbalah*, 97–125; Frances A. Yates, *The Occult Philosophy in the Elizabethan Age* (London: Routledge and Kegan Paul, 1979; reprinted 2001), 33–44.
[18] Chaim Wirszubski, "Francesco Giorgio's Commentary on Giovanni Pico's Kabbalistic Theses," *Journal of the Warburg and Courtauld Institutes* 37 (1974), 145–156.

*of Covenant*) in 1507, intended to defend Christianity against the calumnies of the Jews. In 1514, Rici became physician to Emperor Maximilian I, for whom in 1519 he prepared a new Latin translation of the Talmud, with commentary. In 1516, he published what was to become an influential translation of Joseph Gikatilla's *Gates of Light* (1516), containing the first depiction of the Tree of Life outside a Jewish text. The most famous of his kabbalistic works is the four-part religio-philosophical synthesis of kabbalistic and Christian sources, *De Cœlesti Agricultura* (*On Celestial Agriculture*, 1541). Book Four consists of an introduction to the Kabbalah in a series of fifty theorems, as well as a translation of main passages from Gikatilla's *Gates of Light*. Ironically, despite his Jewish origins and obvious erudition, and despite the orthodox, non-magical nature of Rici's Kabbalah, he was accused by a priest of not propounding true Kabbalah "because he presented this doctrine in another light than that of Pico."[19]

The individual responsible, however, for providing the most enduring image of early modern Christian Kabbalah is the German theologian Heinrich Cornelius Agrippa (1486–1535), in his encyclopedia of esoteric thought, *De Occulta Philosophia libri tres* (*Three Books of Occult Philosophy*, 1533). This work was to became one of the most widely consulted sources for Kabbalah in the Christian world – despite (or perhaps because of) the fact that Agrippa only shows knowledge of the works of Christian kabbalists such as Pico, Reuchlin, Rici, and Giorgio, rather than direct engagement with Hebrew or Aramaic sources. Agrippa presents a similar intermingling of Pythagorean, Neoplatonic, and kabbalistic ideas to Reuchlin, iterating the same claims to Hebrew being the "original language" and the significance of its twenty-two letters as the foundation of the world. Scholem observes that the place of honor in *De Occulta philosophia* is accorded to practical Kabbalah and arithmology, for it is a rich source of information on the occult and kabbalistic significance of numbers; at the same time, we should not neglect the importance of Kabbalah for Agrippa's notion of a sacralized magic.[20]

---

[19] Secret, *Les Kabbalistes Chrétiens*, 89. On Ricius, see also François Secret, "Notes sur Paolo Ricci et la Kabbale chrétienne en Italie," *Rinascimento* 11 (1960), 169–192; Crofton Black, "From Kabbalah to Psychology: The Allegorizing Isagoge of Paulus Ricius, 1509–1541," *Magic, Ritual, and Witchcraft* 2:2 (2007), 136–173.

[20] Gershom Scholem, *Kabbalah* (New York: Meridian Books, 1978), 198; Zika, "Reuchlin's *De Verbo Mirifico* and the Magic Debate," 138. See also Christopher I. Lehrich, *The Language of Demons and Angels: Cornelius Agrippa's Occult Philosophy* (Leiden: Brill, 2003), 149–159. On Christian Kabbalah's relations with occult philosophy, see Secret, *Les Kabbalistes Chrétiens*, ch. 11.

## 4 A Cabalchemical Hybrid: Experimental Fusions of Kabbalah and Alchemy

During the course of the sixteenth century, a pronounced trend emerged toward the permeation of Christian Kabbalah with alchemical symbolism.[21] This convergence of alchemy and Kabbalah was perhaps to be expected as both arts were concerned with knowledge of creation. Both arts, too, advocated a secret transmission of knowledge from master to pupil, with initiations, ordinations, and revelations from God and his angels. To a certain extent, the kabbalists' reduction of language to its elemental letters corresponded to the alchemists' reduction of matter to its primal state; the permutation of letters and words corresponding to the circulation and combination of elements and substances.

The first known combination of alchemy and Kabbalah can be found in the works of the Venetian priest Giovanni Agostino Panteo (d. 1535), who develops a hybrid "Kabbalah of Metals" in two works: the *Ars transmutationis metallicae* (*Art of metallic transmutation*, 1519) and *Voarchadumia contra alchimiam* (*Voarchadumia against alchemy*, 1530).[22] In the most kabbalistic-sounding chapter of the *Voarchadumia*, concerned with the "Mixture at the roots of the Unity of the 72 Voarchadumic elements," Panteo numerically analyzes a small collection of words connected with alchemical substances. We learn that the mysterious substance *Risoo* is called *Thélima* in Greek, and in Hebrew *Reçón*, both terms appearing in Panteo's list of synonyms for gold. Both words translate literally as "Will," but the alchemico-kabbalistic significance lies in the realization that the Hebrew *Reçón* shares the same letters as *Eretz*, one of the Hebrew words for "earth."[23] In this opaque way, Panteo attempts a kabbalistic elucidation of the secrets of the powers of alchemical substances and processes. He makes no direct reference to Jewish texts, but he does mention Pico and provides three magical alphabets derived from Hebrew, one of which subsequently appears in Agrippa's *De occulta philosophia*. Another is the Enochian alphabet, well known to those familiar with John Dee's communications with spirits.

---

[21] Gershom Scholem, *Alchemy and Kabbalah* (Dallas: Spring Publications, 2006); Raphael Patai, *The Jewish Alchemists: A History and Source Book* (Princeton: Princeton University Press, 1994), 152–169.

[22] On Pantheus, see Lynn Thorndike, *A History of Magic and Experimental Science*, 8 vols. (New York: Columbia University Press, 1941), Vol. 5, 537–40; Hilda Norrgrén, "Interpretation and the Hieroglyphic Monad: John Dee's Reading of Pantheus's *Voarchadumia*," *Ambix* 52:3 (2005), 217–245.

[23] Nicolas Séd, "L'or enfermé et la poussière d'or selon Moïse ben Shémtobh de Léon (c. 1240–1305)," *Chrysopoeia*, Tome III, fasc. 2 1989, 121–134, at 131.

The French Paracelsian David De Planis-Campy (1589–ca. 1644) identified Dee, the Elizabethan magus, as one "most versed in Chymical Cabala." This is doubtless because of the composite alchemical symbol "mathematically, magically, cabbalistically, and anagogically" elucidated by Dee in his *Monas Hieroglyphica* (1564).[24] Dee is familiar with the kabbalistic exegetical techniques of "the Tziruph (or Themura) of the Hebrews" and speaks of the "cabbalistic expansion of the quaternary," thereby introducing a Reuchlinian reference to the Pythagorean *tetraktys*. It is evident, however, that he is less convinced of the importance of Hebrew than Pico or Reuchlin. Dee also shows a marked tendency to forge his own Kabbalah of Greek and Roman letters and geometrical, astrological, and alchemical symbols to discover the secrets of God and creation. Despite being classed by Méric Casaubon as "a Cabalistical man, to his ears," Dee gives the distinct impression that he is not particularly interested in kabbalistic textual interpretation. In the *Monas*, he pointedly makes a distinction between a "Kabbalah of the Real" and a "Kabbalah of the Word," the former relating to the Book of Nature, the latter to the Book of Scripture. Dee turns from an exclusively "literal" kabbalistic reading of printed books to one connected with natural magic and deciphering the hieroglyphs or signatures of the created world.[25]

## 5 The Sigillum Dei in Heinrich Khunrath's *"Christian-Cabalist" Amphitheatre*

So far our story of Christian Kabbalah has primarily been one of Catholic exponents.[26] However, it is a Lutheran acquaintance of Dee, the German theosopher and alchemist Heinrich Khunrath (1560–1605), who appears to be the first person to publish a work explicitly describing itself as "Christian Cabalist": *The Christian-Cabalist, Divinely Magical and Physico-Chymical Amphitheatre of Eternal Wisdom* (1595 and 1609).[27] Familiar with Agrippa's

---

[24] Peter J. Forshaw, "The Early Alchemical Reception of John Dee's *Monas Hieroglyphica*," *Ambix* 52:3 (2005), 247–269, at 263.

[25] Philip Beitchman, *Alchemy of the Word: Cabala of the Renaissance* (Albany: State University of New York Press, 1998), 242–243.

[26] On Dee's switches from Protestantism to Catholicism and back, plus possible contacts with Familism, see Deborah Harkness, *John Dee's Conversations with Angels: Cabala, Alchemy, and the End of Nature* (Cambridge: Cambridge University Press, 1999), 129, 149.

[27] On Khunrath, see Peter J. Forshaw, "Curious Knowledge and Wonder-Working Wisdom in the Occult Works of Heinrich Khunrath," in *Curiosity and Wonder from the Renaissance to the Enlightenment*, ed. R. J. W. Evans and Alexander Marr (Aldershot: Ashgate, 2006), 107–129. Khunrath's usage is antedated in manuscript, however, by Jean Thénaud (d. 1542) whose *La Saincte et trescrestienne cabale* dates from around 1521. See Blau, *The Christian Interpretation of the Cabala*, 89–97; Wirszubski, *Pico della Mirandola's Encounter*, 185 n.1.

*De Occulta Philosophia*, it is likely that Khunrath deepened his knowledge of Christian Kabbalah through a compendium published while he was studying medicine in Basel: the *Artis Cabalisticæ: hoc est, Reconditae Theologiae et Philosophiae, Scriptorum, Tomus I* (*Volume 1 of the Cabalistic Art, that is, of the Writers of Recondite Theology and Philosophy*, 1587) of Johannes Pistorius of Nidda (1546–1608). This collection has been called the "Bible of Christian Cabala," containing as it does works by Pico, Reuchlin, Rici, Arcangelo da Borgonuovo, Leone Ebreo, and a Latin translation of the *Sefer Yetzirah*.[28]

Khunrath's knowledge of the Kabbalah most clearly reveals itself in the *Amphitheatre*'s engraving of Christ, the *Sigillum Dei* (Seal of God) or *Sigillum Emet* (Seal of Truth). As Raphael Patai remarks, one "has the impression of seeing a complex Jewish emblem written in Hebrew," a central figure (of Christ cruciform) from which radiate eight concentric rings, five in Hebrew letters, forming "a veritable brief anthology of important quotations and names of Jewish religious significance."[29] It includes the *Ein Sof*, ten *sefirot*, ten Names of God and ten angelic orders, the twenty-two letters of the Hebrew alphabet, and the Hebrew text of the Decalogue. The debt Khunrath owes to Reuchlin is nowhere more evident than at the heart of the engraving where five large tongues of flame appear, each bearing one letter of the *wonder-working word* YHSVH.

It appears that we are now quite far from Christian Kabbalah as primarily missionary activity aimed at converting the Jews. For Khunrath, kabbalistic reception of divine revelation is to be used for the recognition of the divine Father and Son and the understanding of what he calls the "Three Books" of Nature, Man, and Scripture, as represented in the best-known engraving from his *Amphitheatre*, the "Oratory-Laboratory." Khunrath's claims of being "ineffably rapt in God" and inspired by "Sophia Enthusiastica" include a new dimension of personal revelation (through dreams and angels) to his kabbalistic experience in the Oratory. In the Laboratory, one of the products of Khunrath's emphasis on the necessary conjunction of Kabbalah, magic, and alchemy is the "Divine" Philosophers' Stone, with its "Physico-Magical, Hyperphysico-magical, Theosophical and Kabbalistic" uses.[30]

---

[28] Secret, *Les Kabbalistes Chrétiennes*, 280.
[29] Patai, *The Jewish Alchemists*, 156.
[30] Forshaw, "Curious Knowledge and Wonder-Working Wisdom," 115, 128; Dan, "Christian Kabbalah in the Renaissance," 639. See Dan, "The Kabbalah of Johannes Reuchlin," p. 62, on the opposition between Kabbalah and mysticism: "the first emphasizes tradition and marginalizes individual experience, whereas the latter includes the notion of an original discovery of a truth by an individual."

## 6 Zoharic and Lurianic Influences: Knorr von Rosenroth's *Kabbala denudata*

Interest in Kabbalah and alchemy reappears in the seventeenth century's most prominent anthology of Jewish and Christian kabbalist texts. With the conviction that the Kabbalah was an original secret revelation that contained all the spiritual evolution of humanity from the creation of the world, and that the Jewish and Christian religions were identical from the point of view of their esoteric core, Christian Knorr von Rosenroth (1631–1689) decided to publish a Latin translation of the most significant parts of the *Zohar*, along with other kabbalistic treatises and commentaries to assist the reader's understanding. This resulted in the publication, in 1677, of the first volume of the *Kabbala denudata, seu doctrina Hebraeorum transcendentalis et metaphysica atque Theologica* (*The Kabbala Unveiled or the transcendental, metaphysical and theological doctrine of the Hebrews*), dedicated "to the Hebrew-, Chymistry-, and Wisdom-loving reader." Whereas previously the most influential Hebrew sources had been the works of medieval authors such as Recanati, Gikatilla, and Abulafia, the *Kabbalah Unveiled* espouses the works of a new form of Kabbalah with a stress on redemption and the millennium, promoting what Scholem calls the "true *theologia mystica* of Judaism."[31]

In keeping with the interests of earlier Christian kabbalists such as Reuchlin and Agrippa, this volume includes a "Key to the Divine Names of the Kabbalah" and an edition of Gikatilla's *Gates of Light*. New, however, are works of the Safed mystic Isaac Luria (1534–1572) and other Lurianic kabbalist works, including a detailed explanation of the Tree of Life and a summary of an unusual Jewish alchemical treatise, the *Esch Mezareph* (*The Refiner's Fire*), giving correspondences between the *sefirot*, planets, and metals, plus several speculative kabbalistic works by the Cambridge Platonist Henry More (1614–1687).

A second volume of the *Kabbalah Unveiled*, the *Liber Sohar restitutus* (*The Book of Splendour restored*, 1684), emphasizes Knorr's missionary intent, beginning with a systematic résumé of the *Zohar's* doctrines, to which is added a Christian interpretation. The same technique is used in another text included in the volume, the *Adumbratio Kabbalae Christianae . . . ad conversionem Judaeorum* (*Outline of Christian Kabbala . . . for the conversion of the Jews*), a dialogue between a "Kabbalist" and a "Christian Philosopher," in which

---

[31] Gershom Scholem, *Major Trends in Jewish Mysticism* (New York: Schocken Books, 1954), 284.

they explain their respective religious doctrines, showing the concordance between the two traditions.

Inspired by the Lurianic Kabbalah with its "optimistic, vitalist philosophy of perfectionism and universal salvation," Rosenroth and his collaborator in the publishing enterprise, Frans Mercurius van Helmont (1614–1699), rejected many of the conventional Christian views of the fall, salvation, and the Trinity, as well as the particularly Protestant focus on divine justice, predestination, man's helplessness, and the concept of an eternal hell. They tended to minimize or allegorize Christ's role in the redemptive process, preferring instead the Lurianic vision of a universe restored to its original perfection through human effort.[32]

This second volume also contains work that would later be of great interest to occult societies such as the Golden Dawn, in particular, a section entitled *Pneumatica cabbalistica*, introducing kabbalistic ideas about spirits, angels and demons, the soul, and the various states and transformations included in the kabbalistic theory of metempsychosis. Also included were Latin translations of Lurianic works, including chapters on angelology, demonology, and the magical creative power of language, describing how pious men can create angels and spirits through prayers. The *Kabbala denudata* was superior to anything that had previously been published on the Kabbalah in a language other than Hebrew, providing a non-Jewish readership with authentic texts that were to be the principal source for Western literature on Kabbalah until the end of the nineteenth century.[33]

## 7 Christian Kabbalah on the Threshold of Modernity: Oetinger and Molitor

Moving to the eighteenth century, the best known representative of Christian Kabbalah is undoubtedly the Lutheran pastor Friedrich Christoph Oetinger (1702–1782), who sought a *philosophia sacra* as a substitute for the systems of profane philosophy developed by thinkers such as Descartes and Hobbes. He found this in various guises, including the philosophy of Leibniz, the Neoplatonically kabbalistic works of Henry More, the writings of Paracelsus and other alchemists, the theosophy of Jacob Boehme (1575–1624), the works

---

[32] Allison P. Coudert, *The Impact of the Kabbalah in the Seventeenth Century: The Life and Thought of Francis Mercury van Helmont (1614–1698)* (Leiden: Brill Academic Publishers, 1999), 345. See especially ch. 6: "Christian Knorr von Rosenroth and the *Kabbalah Denudata*"; eadem, "The Kabbala Denudata: Converting Jews or Seducing Christians," in Pokin and Weiner, *Jewish Christians and Christian Jews*, 73–96.

[33] Scholem, *Kabbalah*, 416.

of the Swedish mystic Emanuel Swedenborg (1688–1772), and in the Jewish Kabbalah. Oetinger was especially drawn to the Lurianic Kabbalah, with the *Etz Hayim* (*Tree of Life*) of Luria's main disciple Hayim Vital (1543–1620), a major source for his *Öffentliches Denckmahl der Lehrtafel einer weyland württembergischen Princeßin Antonia* (*Public Monument of the Didactic Painting of a Former Württemberg Princess Antonia*, 1763).[34] This was his description and analysis of an emblematic triptych commissioned for the Church of the Holy Trinity at Bad Teinach in the Black Forest by Princess Antonia of Württemberg (1613–1679), one of the daughters of the alchemist and occultist Frederick I, Duke of Württemberg. In his commentary on Princess Antonia's *Lehrtafel*, Oetinger sets forth a system of Christian Kabbalah based on his reading of the *Zohar*, containing separate chapters comparing the philosophies of Newton, Boehme, and Swedenborg with that of Kabbalah.

For our final representative of Christian Kabbalah, we are back with a Catholic scholar, in the figure of the German philosopher Franz Josef Molitor (1779–1860). Like Rosenroth and Oetinger before him, Molitor collaborated with Jewish scholars and developed his kabbalistic program over decades of research into primary Jewish sources. His four-volume *Philosophie der Geschichte, oder über die Tradition* (*Philosophy of History, or On Tradition*, 1827–1853) was the nineteenth century's most erudite and profound consideration of the Kabbalah's significance for Christians, earning Scholem's praise as "the crowning and final achievement of the Christian Kabbalah."[35]

## 8 Conclusion

What has become clear is that Scholem's negative image of a Christian Kabbalah primarily engaged in evangelical activity against the Jews requires some modification. While it is justified on the surface by the overt declarations of Pico and Reuchlin (no doubt balancing on a knife edge, ever aware

---

[34] Miklós Vassányi, *Anima Mundi: The Rise of the World Soul Theory in Modern German Philosophy* (Dordrecht: Springer, 2011), 128ff; Eva Johann Schauer, "Friedrich Christoph Oetinger und die kabbalistische Lehrtafel der württembergischen Prinzessin Antonia in Teinach," in *Mathesis, Naturphilosophie und Arkanwissenschaft im Umkreis Friedrich Christoph Oetingers (1702–1782)* ed. Sabine Holtz, Gerhard Betsch, and Eberhard Zwink (Stuttgart: Franz Steiner Verlag, 2005), 165–182. On Oetinger, see also Ernst Benz, *Christian Kabbalah: Neglected Child of Theology*, trans. Kenneth W. Wesche (St. Paul, MN: Grailstone Press, 2004).

[35] Scholem, *Kabbalah*, 200–201; Arthur Verlsuis, *Theosophia: Hidden Dimensions of Christianity* (New York: Lindisfarne Press, 1994), 76. On Molitor, see also Katharina Koch, *Franz Joseph Molitor und die jüdische Tradition: Studien zu den kabbalistischen Quellen der "Philosophie der Geschichte"* (Berlin: Walter de Gruyter, 2006).

of the Inquisition), it misrepresents some of the Christian Kabbalists discussed here, who each had his own motives, ranging from novel biblical interpretation, greater awareness of the prehistory of Christianity, Church reform and the revitalization of religion, to insights into the theories of alchemy and the practices of magic.[36]

Here Dan's more irenic reading should be considered, with the suggestion that even the early Christian kabbalist works included a different, additional message: that non-biblical Jewish sources also held great relevance for their Christian readers, not only as a way of strengthening and upholding their faith, but as a way of discovering a deeper, more profound understanding of the nature of their own religion. True, the aim of conversion often lurked in the background, but with it also the hope of reinvigorating the Christian religion, together with the possibility of personal transformation and spiritual transfiguration. There is surely some historical irony in the fact that it was the Christian kabbalists who were the first to publish and promulgate Jewish esoteric material. With its implication of tolerance and even respect toward the tradition of another religion, their belief in the relevance of Jewish Kabbalah for its Christian counterpart is "very nearly unique in the history of the three scriptural religions."[37]

---

[36] Cf. Yvonne Petry, *Gender, Kabbalah, and the Reformation: The Mystical Theology of Guillaume Postel (1510–1581)* (Leiden: Brill, 2004), 82.
[37] Dan, "The Kabbalah of Johannes Reuchlin," 55–56, 68.

# 14

# PARACELSIANISM

Bruce T. Moran

## 1 Paracelsus and Paracelsianism

Paracelsianism, although consisting of many elements and interpreted in different ways, develops from the thinking of the Swiss German physician, natural philosopher, and alchemist Philippus Areolus Theophrastus Bombastus von Hohenheim, otherwise known as Paracelsus (1493/94– 1541). Following an early education that may have included instruction by his father in the transmutation of metals, Paracelsus began a "great wandering" throughout Europe that brought him into contact with both learned and artisanal communities. Around 1515, he may have received a medical degree at Ferrara, although evidence for this is sketchy. Nevertheless, Paracelsus gained a reputation as a skilled physician; his successful treatment of the well-known humanist printer Johann Froben (ca. 1460–1527) may have been partly responsible for his appointment as city physician and university lecturer at Basel. There he lectured in German, rather than Latin, and his strong criticisms of traditional medicine, which included at one point burning books, led to a hostile reaction from other university physicians and forced his abrupt departure from the city. Controversy followed wherever he went, however. Writings regarding the treatment of syphilis, in which Paracelsus recommended the use of mercury rather than medicaments made of Guajak wood, were denounced by the medical faculty at Leipzig whose dean was a close friend of the merchant family Fugger (the family that held the monopoly on the importation of the wood).

In the 1520s and 1530s, Paracelsus composed a series of texts; several of the most famous are the *Archidoxis, Opus Paragranum, Opus Paramirum, Grosse Wundartzney*, and the incomplete *Astronomia Magna*. These writings and others, most often written in vernacular German, described the bases of a new medical cosmology reviving an ancient view that connected the universe at large (the macrocosm) with the human body (the microcosm). According to Paracelsus, philosophy, astronomy, alchemy, and the virtue of the physician were the pillars that supported true medicine. The physician as philosopher and astronomer needed to recognize that "the firmament is within man"[1] and needed also to understand how each of nature's parts was designed to correspond to specific parts of the human body. Each individual, Paracelsus claimed, contained in him- or herself all of existence, and amounted to a synthesis of physical body, immortal soul, and sidereal (or astral) spirit. The powers or virtues that operated in the world at large also operated in the body. In fact, vital forces penetrated each thing in nature. Astral emanations pressed upon all earthly things and gave them their divinely designated signatures — their outward material signs indicating connections to certain parts of the microcosm. It was one of the principal tasks of the Paracelsian physician to extract those powers from the greater world, usually by means of the art of chemical separation (*ars spagyrica*), and to apply them to specific parts of the body.

Traditions of ancient magic, medieval alchemy, folk medicine, and Renaissance Hermetism influenced the ideas of Paracelsus, and much of his writing took aim at the traditional standard bearers of learned philosophy and medicine: Aristotle, Galen, and Avicenna. Although he referred to the Aristotelian elements of earth, air, fire, and water, Paracelsus defined them as natural wombs within which the first principles (or *tria prima*) of Sulphur, Salt, and Mercury generated particular plants, animals, and minerals with the guidance of an astral spirit. Paracelsus also rejected the traditional notion of an imbalance of bodily humors as the cause of disease. Rather, he thought of diseases as specific entities, identified by particular etiologies that pertained to specific parts of the body. A primary cause of illness was the failure of an internal *archeus*, or inner alchemist, to properly separate purities from impurities in particular organs. When improper separation occurred, that part of the body needed the help of a specific astral power prepared by separating a healing virtue from a corresponding part of nature. In a process that he called *alchemia medica*, Paracelsus described how alchemical techniques, especially those involving distillation, separated spiritual virtues or hidden powers from natural objects and brought them to bear upon diseases in the body. Each illness required a specific remedy, and although medicines might be prepared from plants and animals, mineral remedies were especially potent since they

---

[1] Paracelsus, *Volumen Medicinae Paramirum*, trans. Kurt Leidecker (Baltimore: The Johns Hopkins University Press, 1949), 3.

corresponded best to the sulphurous, saline, and mercurial origins of all things.

Apart from describing a new medical cosmology, Paracelsus also composed philosophical, anthropological, socio-critical, and theological works. All these became part of his intellectual legacy. However, as we will see, interpretations varied about the meaning of those texts, their novelty, and even their authenticity. Debates still rage about them, and make the subject of Paracelsianism the site of an independent intellectual domain.

Like lines of longitude and latitude, the term "Paracelsianism" constitutes a kind of grid that helps us navigate around a certain terrain – in this case, the historical landscape of alchemy, chemical medicine, magic, and mysticism. Unlike lines of longitude and latitude, however, there is no settled agreement concerning the precise location of this grid or whether its lines can even be clearly drawn. If one invokes Paracelsianism as a way of identifying traditions that are solely connected to original ideas unambiguously described by Paracelsus in texts of unquestionable authorship, we might refrain from using the reference at all. On the other hand, we might mean by the term all the interpretations, explications, commentaries, and general discussions based in texts attributed to Paracelsus by authors who refer to Paracelsus as in some fashion relevant to occult, mystical, magical, or practical traditions. If the term is used in this way, then clearly there is a lot to talk about – so much in fact, and so much of it contradictory, that constructing a category such as Paracelsianism becomes a descriptive *refugium miserorum*, a nebulous term ready to hand when nothing more precise springs to mind.

Producing imaginative patterns so as better to comprehend and reason about human actions and experiences is the work of historians. But we have to be careful not to let our imaginations run away with us. Recent scholarship is sensitive to these issues.[2] Some have tried to distinguish "particular" Paracelsianisms on the basis of differing translations and interpretations of Paracelsus's texts. Others admit difficulties in establishing clear-cut categories. The editors involved in the most far-reaching attempt to collect representative examples of early Paracelsianism, Wilhelm Kühlmann and Joachim Telle, have observed that the language of Paracelsus (often obscure

---

[2] References to some of the most useful studies may be found in the Suggestions for Further Reading at the end of this volume. I have also relied on discussions by, among others, Stephen Bamforth, Udo Benzenhöfer, Andrew Cunningham, Ute Gause, Carlos Gilly, Kurt Goldammer, Dietlinde Goltz, Ole Grell, Gundolf Keil, Julian Paulus, Horst Pfefferl, Stephen Pumfrey, Hartmut Rudolph, Heinz Schott, Siegried Wollgast, and Illana Zinguer that appear as individual contributions within edited volumes. References to these collected editions also appear in the Suggestions for Further Reading.

and packed with neologisms) prevented any institutionalized tradition from coming into being.[3] In terms of the texts that relate to Paracelsianism, the editors note that we are not dealing with a clearly authentic authorial *oeuvre*, but with a "mushroom-like proliferating web" of "pseudo or deutero Paracelsica."[4] Practices associated with Paracelsianism have also been recognized as having led separate lives. Some in the early modern era did invoke Paracelsus as an intellectual forerunner, especially in applying chemical principles to medicine and in turning away from ancient humoral pathology. However, strains of chemical medicine existed within traditional alchemy as well as within ancient and Arabic medical practice. Some suspected that even the Paracelsian *tria prima* of Sulphur, Salt, and Mercury had earlier, alchemical roots. The French physician and alchemist Bernard George Penot (ca. 1530– ca. 1620) suggested at one point that there was nothing new in Paracelsus, and that Paracelsus had copied "word for word" what the alchemist Isaac Hollandus had written about the three principles and had also closely followed what the alchemical author Basil Valentine had written about the same.

## 2 Magic and Nature

Sometimes Paracelsus mattered less as a chemical physician than as an advocate of religious and political reform. Some found in him a social revolutionary. Others saw the devil incarnate. In this last sense, being labeled a Paraclesian (*Paracelsista*) was to endure sharp abuse. From some points of view, Paracelsians belonged to a category of "otherness" – one that was forged out of an anxiety about the loss of control over traditional intellectual and linguistic standards, particularly in medicine and philosophy, and a fear that forms of trusted knowledge were under attack. At the beginning of the seventeenth century, the German physician, alchemist, and schoolteacher Andreas Libavius (ca. 1550–1616) distinguished between the perceptions of Paracelsus himself and those of a group he preferred to call Neoparacelsians. Neoparacelsians, he noted, despised the ancients, attacked Galenic medicine, recommended magic along with "Kabbalah," practiced magic by means of signs, words, and characters, and, finally, declared themselves the monarchs of *arcana*. What is characteristic of Paracelsianism in this sense is a subversive epistemology based in magic. Nowhere in the list of Paracelsian

[3] *Der Frühparacelsismus Erster Teil*, ed. Wilhelm Kühlmann and Joachim Telle (Tübingen: Max Niemeyer Verlag, 2001), 4.
[4] *Der Frühparacelsismus Zweiter Teil*, ed. Kühlmann and Telle (Tübingen: Max Niemeyer Verlag, 2004), 5.

characteristics does Libavius mention what some have wished to preserve as the practical center of a Paracelsian tradition, namely, making chemical medicines. The proper name for people who did that, he insisted, was alchemist.

Libavius's depiction may have been harsh and one sided, but it was true that many Paracelsians represented a way of thinking based in magic. According to this worldview, one reflective of older occult traditions, human beings condensed the entire macrocosm within themselves and possessed, as a consequence, an inner knowledge of nature and her powers. As we have seen, Paracelsus thought that each individual contained within him- or herself all existence. Each was a synthesis of physical body, immortal soul, and sidereal (or astral) spirit. For many followers of Paracelsus, that combination had cognitive consequences and made it possible for each person to recognize the vital connections that linked one part of the world to another and, thereafter, to manipulate nature's hidden virtues for specific purposes.

Paracelsus believed that both nature and human beings were magicians. Nature, he thought, disclosed the secret powers within things by means of external signs, or "signatures" (i.e., the actual shape, coloring, texture, etc.) of an object. The physician-magus had learned to read these signs, discovering nature's language through the study of *astronomiam, medicinam, philosophiam, physiognomiam, chiromantiam*, and the like. Thus, one magician taught another, and nature (*Magierin*) revealed to the human being (*Magier*) her secrets. The physician-magus pulled heavenly, vital powers out of nature and then transferred those powers to corrupted parts of the body.[5]

The magical side of Paracelsianism is particularly obvious in the writings of the early seventeenth-century physician Oswald Croll (ca. 1563–1609). In two writings especially, the "Admonitory Preface" to his *Basilica Chymica* (1609) and in a treatise on the doctrine of signs, Croll described essential components of nature's magical structure as well as a method, based in personal experience and revelation, by which such a structure was to be learned. Croll's texts wove together strands of Florentine Neoplatonism, Hermetism, and German mysticism, each of which condensed realms of matter, spirit, and soul into a single divine unity, mixing thereby the sacred with the profane. The physician, Croll argued, needed to know the internal, invisible, or astral structures of things in the greater world and to understand

---

[5] Heinz Schott, "Magie-Glaube-Aberglaube: Zur 'Philosophoa Magna' des Paracelsus," in *Paracelsus und seine internationale Rezeption in der frühen Neuzeit*, ed. Heinz Schott and Ilana Zinguer (Leiden: Brill, 1998), 24–35.

how these related to the organization of the body. Intellectual discovery followed, he claimed, not from reading and interpreting books, or even from accumulated experience, but from personally experiencing the divine – either directly communicated by God through revelation or by becoming awakened to the divine messages concealed in the natural world. For Libavius, the scheme described by Croll was epistemologically dangerous on the one hand, and diabolical on the other. If personal inspiration satisfied for cognitive innovation, Libavius wondered, how could one avoid a multitude of opinions being expressed as a result of personal fantasy? "Take away teachers and books, and allow anyone to philosophize on his own [and] you will have a lovely philosophy indeed." Such a philosophy was the contrivance of the devil, Libavius thought, "so that he may either abolish or pervert every system of learning, and he himself may rule at his own pleasure."[6] From such a perspective, it was easy to link Paracelsians to other personally inspired enthusiasts of the period, such as the Anabaptists, whose views, many claimed, led to social and religious discord.

Paracelsianism, then, gained definition through controversy as it seemed to break with institutionally established social, textual, educational, and linguistic norms. It advocated a revision of methods in acquiring knowledge, especially as related to the knowledge of nature and the body, by arguing for the relevance of personal experience as opposed to the type of book learning that conveyed the concretized views of disciplinary authorities. Its insights were tinged by hermetic and alchemical influences and its expressions were largely directed against academic traditions of Galenism and Aristotelianism. It found fertile soil among social critics and religious dissidents, especially anti-confessional enthusiasts, and it inspired an array of writings defending new sources of intellectual legitimacy in the study of medicine and natural philosophy.

## 3 Problems of Texts, Translations, and Traditions

Depending on the early modern sources, the number of texts supposed to have been written by Paracelsus ranged from around two hundred forty to about four hundred. Some texts were reported to have circulated in manuscript but have never been discovered. Some were supposedly so illegible or contained so many unintelligible signs that they were discarded and never published. Some amounted to fragmentary transcriptions made by students

---

[6] Bruce T. Moran, *Andreas Libavius and the Transformation of Alchemy: Separating Chemical Cultures with Polemical Fire* (Sagamore Beach, ME: Science History Publications, 2007), 219.

and servants. Some were of questionable authenticity even from the start, and some texts lacked parts or whole sections. In establishing traditions of Paracelsianism, the curious thing is that the early editors, translators, and publishers of texts attributed to Paracelsus were, in many respects, more important than Paracelsus himself. Paracelsus wrote at a time when Germans were just deciding on the syntactical rules that would guide their written language. Editors made their own judgments concerning the meaning of obscure words and phrases, and sometimes contrived entirely different wordings in the process of editing and translation. Particularly disturbing were the disparities that peppered the early Latin and German editions of a text called *De Vita Longa*. Modern German translations face the same problems in representing obscure, linguistically tortured phrases, as comparisons of the Paracelsus editions of Karl Sudhoff, Bernard Aschner, and Will Erich Peuckert attest.

Among the early editors, Adam von Bodenstein, Johann Huser (ca. 1545–ca. 1600), Gerhard Dorn (ca. 1530–1584), and Michael Toxites (ca. 1515–1581) stand out most prominently. The early published collections of Huser and Toxites fueled early Paracelsian fervor by combining elements of medical reform with what Joachim Telle called "transconfessional theo-alchemy."[7] To Huser, Paracelsus was the "German Trismegistus," possessing revealed alchemical-cosmological knowledge. Dorn announced Paracelsus as "the philosopher of our time, not undeservedly called thrice great with Trismegistus," and established Paracelsus within the cultural context of medieval and Renaissance alchemical writers.

However, some of the texts referred to by Dorn as directly connected to Paracelsus have origins that are anything but certain. Nevertheless, Dorn used such writings to establish Paracelsus as a kind of irenic-theological alchemist connected to the hermetic *prisca sapientia*. In one work, his *Congeries Paracelsicae Chemiae de Transmutationibus Metallorum* (1581), Dorn interpreted the words of Christ, "my peace I give to you, my peace I leave with you," as a reference to the divinely established order in nature that moved all things toward perfection. Paracelsus, he claimed, viewed the principal *arcanum* in medicine to lie in the transmutation and perfection of natural things and, in this way, had sought the root of peace and all natural harmony established by God within creation. Since celestial spirits combined with elements to produce specific bodies, the Paracelsian physician acted as an alchemist, separating form from matter and reapplying celestially derived

---

[7] Joachim Telle, "Johann Huser in seinen Briefen...," in *Parerga Paracelsica*, ed. Joachim Telle (Stuttgart: Franz Steiner Verlag, 1991), 159–248; 178.

spiritual forms to other parts of the material world. Celestial, life-giving powers were most concentrated in metals. Accordingly, Dorn proclaimed in the name of Paracelsus that a universal medicine drawn from metals and minerals by means of separation could transmute bodies to the greatest degree of perfection, renewing and extending life itself. Adam von Bodenstein, who lost his job as a university physician at Basel following the publication of his own edition of Paracelsian texts, was also motivated by alchemical interests. For him, it was the writings of Arnold of Villanova and Agrippa of Nettesheim that proved convincing and that underscored the theoretical and practical possibility of transmutation.

In the hands of these editors and others, Paracelsianism took on different flavors. In some cases, editors altered Paracelsus's difficult vocabulary or added their own commentaries, arguing for a text's relevance within specific intellectual traditions. Von Bodenstein attempted to make Paracelsus tolerable to Aristotelians while presenting Paracelsus as a harbinger of a "golden age" in which ancient knowledge, once the possession of Hermes, was rediscovered and put to work for a common purpose. Gerhard Dorn and Michael Toxites linked Paracelsus to Hermes and to a tradition of secret knowledge stemming from the hermetic *Emerald Tablet*. At the same time, the French commentator Jacques Gohory (1520–1576) argued that Paracelsus, in addition to being a hermetic *magus*, was also a Neoplatonic philosopher in the tradition of Ficino. Attempts to alter Paracelsian texts for specific social or intellectual purposes have persisted into the modern era as well. In the twentieth century, Paracelsus became an icon of the German racial spirit in the *Blut und Boden* literature of the Nazi regime. In seeking to rehabilitate tainted writings thereafter, the much respected modern editor Kurt Goldammer (1916–1996) openly removed specific references to Jews from the first popular German edition of a Paracelsus text after the war, *Vom Licht der Natur und des Geistes*, published by Reclam as a low-cost pocketbook.[8]

Editors and commentators not only took differing intellectual approaches to Paracelsus's texts but sometimes disapproved of one another's editions. Gohory and the Basel publisher Pietro Perna rejected Dorn's Latin translations, while Dorn himself railed against the deficiencies of Gohory's French renderings. Some parts of Paracelsus's writings were simply untranslatable. Uncertainty abounded concerning what Paracelsus actually wrote, and in this respect part of the experience of Paracelsianism included attempts to create

---

[8] Paracelsus, *Vom Licht der Natur und des Geistes eine Auswahl*, ed. Kurt Goldammer (Stuttgart: Philipp Reclam, 1979), 37.

Paracelsus *lexica* in which obscure references might find some clarity by means of being linked to other citations. Bodenstein was one of the first to offer such an interpretative guide in his text *Onomasticon*, published in 1566 as a supplement to the Paracelsian *Opus Chirurgicum*. Explanatory glossaries accompanied other texts, and further publications by Michael Toxites (one of the most philologically sensitive editors), Leonard Thurneisser, and Gerhard Dorn sought as well to shed light on Paracelsus's linguistic darkness.[9] With each new translation, interpretation, and glossary, another current within the turgid flood of Paracelsianism emerged.

## 4 Severinus and the French Paracelsians

Nevertheless, some currents proved stronger than others, and one particularly strong Paracelsian tradition flowed from a text written by the Danish physician Petrus Severinus (1540/2–1602) called the *Idea medicinae philosophicae* (1571). There, Severinus linked Paracelsian medical theory to ancient authorities and gave shape to a more systematic expression of Paracelsian thinking. He also fashioned a compromise between humoral pathology and chemical cures. It was especially Severinus's notion of seeds, or *semina*, that caught the attention of later commentators. *Semina* were seedlike "reasons" (*rationes seminales*), altogether imperceptible to the senses, possessing the preordained plan for each physical thing. As such, they existed as intermediaries between divine ideas and material bodies. They shared both spiritual and corporeal characteristics, and accounted for both healthy and morbid physical change in the human body. *Semina* were affected by what Severinus called "tinctures." These were pure forms that could be transferred from one thing to another. Such tinctures within *semina* possessed the mechanical knowledge (*scientia mechanica*) of the chemical processes by means of which changes in the body took place. Thus, curing disease occurred by means of "transplantation" (in which the vital tinctures in chemically prepared compounds altered morbid tinctures in the body).[10] Severinus's philosophical medicine was a primary vehicle for disseminating a broad tradition of Paracelsian theory. In the hands of commentators like Johannes Pratensis (b. 1543), Ambrosius Rhodius, Thomas Moffett (1553–1604), and William Davidson of Aberdeen (ca. 1593–ca. 1669), Paracelsian ideas merged both with academic natural philosophy and with the mystical cosmologies

[9] Wilhelm Kühlmann, in Kühlmann and Telle, *Der Frühparacelsisms Zweiter Teil*, 18ff.
[10] Jole Shackelford, *A Philosophical Path for Paracelsian Medicine: The Ideas, Intellectual Context, and Influence of Petrus Severinus: 1540–1602* (Copenhagen: Museum Tusculanum Press, 2004), 183ff.

constructed by Michael Maier (ca. 1568–1622), Robert Fludd (1574–1637), and the early Rosicrucians. In Germany, Daniel Sennert (1572–1637), professor of medicine at Wittenberg, accepted the Paracelain *tria prima*, approved of the doctrine of the macrocosm and the microcosm, developed a notion of "atoms" as formative forces within natural objects, and considered chemical medicaments as the perfection of medicine. All the while he argued for the continued relevance of Galen and Aristotle and did not reject ancient humoral theory.

Paracelsians were often physicians and many Paracelsian physicians found places and patrons at princely courts. The pile of works thought to be directly connected to Paracelsus collected by the Elector of the Palatinate, Ottheinrich, joined alchemical writings at court, including the pseudonymous work of Raymond Lull, and stimulated the interests of the court physician Adam von Bodenstein. Other early Paracelsians turned to the Wittelsbachs in Bavaria, to August of Saxony in Dresden, to the nobility in Bohemia, to the Bishops of Speyer, Salzburg, and Cologne, as well as to members of numerous local noble houses for support and advancement. Gerhard Dorn acquired the protection of the Cardinal de Grenvelle and dedicated writings to the brother of the French king Henry III, François de Valois.

In France, Johannes Guinterius von Andernach (ca. 1497–1574) emphasized a more practical approach to Paracelsian therapeutics. As a prominent medical humanist, a translator of Galen, and respected professor of medicine at Paris, he prepared, in 1571, an enormous text concerning the old and new medicine strongly supportive of chemical medicaments. He argued that the chemical principles Sulphur, Salt, and Mercury differed only slightly from ancient elements and claimed that chemical procedures transformed poisonous matter into wholesome substances. The recently translated French edition of Pietro Andrea Matthioli's (1501–1577) commentary on the works of Dioscorides also spurred debate. The book included reference to the use of stones, minerals, and metals and explained how antimony, which had been described by Paracelsus, could be rendered into an effective purgative.

In Paris, the debate over the internal use of antimony inspired attacks on suspected followers of Paracelsus, and the fear of clandestine support for Paracelsian ideas within the university there led to the prompt condemnation of an early advocate of antimony, Roch le Baillif (*fl*. 1578–1580). Nevertheless, other physicians persuaded by different parts of chemical-Paracelsian philosophy began to appear in Paris shortly thereafter, many returning with the protection of the Huguenot turned Catholic king

Henry of Navarre. Prominent among this new medical entourage were Jean Ribit (ca. 1571–1605), Theodore Turquet de Mayerne (1573–1655), and Joseph Duchesne (ca. 1544–1609), also called Quercetanus. Although each would stir continued medical controversy, the writings of Duchesne became especially expressive of a particular variety of Paracelsian thinking.

Duchesne admitted that the ignorance and faults of some physicians and apothecaries had caused the "chymici" to fall into disrepute, but that this was no reason to condemn an entire art through which the secrets of God became known. Duchesne explained that Paracelsus was no oracle, and that there was much to disagree with in both his philosophy and his theology. Nevertheless, he observed that Paracelsus "teacheth many things almost divinely, in Phisicke [i.e., medicine] which the thankfull posteritie can neither commend and praise sufficientlie."[11] It was Paracelsus the alchemist that Duchesne admired most, and a great part of his dispute with the faculty of medicine at Paris related to his defense of alchemy and metallic transmutation within the context of a Paracelsian-based cosmology. The Paris debates show us how difficult it is to strictly distinguish Paracelsian traditions among chemical physicians. Libavius, who wished to defend the place of alchemy in medicine, ultimately joined the debate as a Duchesne supporter and was immediately condemned as someone who had joined the Paracelsian faction. Regardless of how the intervention was seen by others – especially by one of the leaders of the Parisian medical faculty, Jean Riolan (1539–1606) – Libavius remained no friend to Paracelsus. He could, however, stand with other chemical physicians at Paris and comment about another participant in the dispute, the Paracelsian Turquet de Mayerne. Libavius observed that Mayerne's dignity, like his own, was preserved not by specifically defending Duchesne, but by the effort that each had made to combine Hippocratic and chemical medicine and by their mutual labors in picking out good remedies from Paracelsian manure.

Medical chemists need not have been Paracelsians, unless, of course, it was convenient for their enemies to label them as such. A difference of opinion about the nature of true alchemy had led another doctor at Paris named Pierre Le Paulmier (1568–1610) to attack Libavius as a Paracelsian. Libavius explained in response that simply separating efficacious essences from chemical dregs did not make one a disciple of Paracelsus. If it did, one would have to include Avicenna, Bulcasis, and even members of the Parisian school in that company. In the case of another medical doctor named Nicolas

---

[11] Allen G. Debus, *The Chemical Philosophy: Paracelsian Science and Medicine in the Sixteenth and Seventeenth Centuries* (1977; reprinted, Mineola: Dover Publications, 2002), 149.

Abraham de la Framboisier, the medical faculty at Paris during the reign of Louis XIII seems to have worried about Paracelsian leanings, even though the physician himself rejected "the sect of Paracelsus" and argued that he derived his chemical remedies from Galen and Hippocrates. Suspicions of Paracelsianism in this case were more a matter of religious distrust and envy aroused by apparent royal patronage than a result of precisely defined intellectual commitment.

Despite their problems in France, Duchesne and other French Paracelsians continued to play important roles in the interpretation and transmission of Paracelsianism. After leaving France, Mayerne became chief physician to the English king James I. Elsewhere in England, John Hester (d. 1593) translated the tracts of Duchesne and others. In so doing, he promoted chemical preparations included in works by the Italian physician Leonardo Fioravanti (1518–1588) and the German Philip Herman. Another Englishman, a minister named Thomas Tymme (d. 1620) also translated large sections of Duchesne's works into English, especially his discussions of Paracelsian cosmology. Tymme, like R. Bostock, who defended Paracelsian principles and the macrocosm-microcosm analogy in a book of 1585, drew something spiritual from Paracelsus's works and found there as well an anthropology and natural philosophy removed from, and consequently not indebted to, ancient heathen texts.

## 5 Spiritual Paracelsianism

The spiritual side of Paracelsus had been emphasized as well by early editors. A few, such as Toxites, Dorn, and another defender of Paracelsus, a physician named Samuel Siderocrates, shared in common a connection to the German university town of Tübingen, and each had taken a strong position against the orthodox Lutheranism that flourished there. Because of that connection, early Paracelsian writers within the Tübingen intellectual community may have influenced later Tübingen dissidents probably responsible for composing some of the earliest Rosicrucian writings. In some instances, the spiritual and mystical side of Paracelsus completely swamped Paracelsian chemical-medical philosophy. The mystical interpretation of Paracelsus was especially useful to religious radicals such as Valentin Weigel (1533–1588) and his pseudo-Weigelian imitators. It also influenced trans-confessional theologians such as Johann Arndt (1555–1621) and Christoph Hirsch (i.e., Josephus Stellatus), as well as the early Rosicrucian enthusiast Adam Haselmeyer.

To Haselmeyer, both the mythical Christian Rosencreutz and Paracelsus had promised evangelical freedom to a world of the future, and Haselmeyer proclaimed accordingly a new religion, the *Theophrastia Sancta*, viewed as a kind of perennial religion practiced in occult circles until Paracelsus had publicly proclaimed its meaning. The foundation of the religion was the *tria cabalistica prima*, the three kabbalistic principles of *Bitten, Suchen,* and *Anklopfen* (asking, seeking, and appealing) that Paracelsus had designated in the *Philosophia Sagax* as the means to all natural knowledge. The living word of God sealed within the human being was, on the basis of this theology, far more important than what was written in Scripture. In fact, without the human spirit to enliven it, the Bible itself became a mere a collection of dead letters. To the external trappings of Christendom, some advocated a renewed "church of the spirit" in which the illumination of the spirit found its fulfillment outside a strictly, church-bound Christian context and led to a restoration of knowledge through the possession of pansophic wisdom. The real church thus existed apart from either Protestant or Catholic communities; in constructing such a view, texts associated with Valentin Weigel, the pastor of Zschopau in east Saxony, drew on material ready to hand in the writings of Paracelsus.

At least in part, Weigelian theology comprises yet another strip in the complicated latticework of early Paracelsianism. Treatises and sermons whose content differed substantially from Catholic and mainline Protestant opinion began to appear in the 1570s. In the early seventeenth century, the presses of several publishers churned out "Weigelian" books. Some of those books, however, were not actually written by Weigel and sorting out the genuine from the apocryphal has become a primary task of Weigel scholars ever since. Of those texts most directly linked to Weigel, influences stemming from medieval mystical traditions and, after 1578, from Paracelsian natural philosophy predominated. Other Weigelian texts had a more apocalyptic message, insisted on inward knowledge, and conflated Paracelsus, Kabbalah, and magic. Institutionalized Protestantism made no distinction concerning authorship. It viewed all the writings as consistent with a theology of the inner word and therefore well suited to the mystical ravings of personally enlightened spiritualists and to the subjective epistemologies of religious radicals.

In Paracelsus, Weigel seems to have encountered such notions as the *light of nature* and the *light of grace*. Both were forms of revelation, the first by means of inspired experience, the second by means of direct divine disclosure, and Weigel seems to have based his own views concerning the processes of human understanding upon them. He also found in Paracelsus anthropological notions relating to man as a microcosm of the universe produced from *limus terrae*. Other ideas sharing elements with Paracelsian religious writings were more disturbing. By contrasting a heavenly flesh, which is eternal, to an earthly mortal flesh, Weigel judged that the flesh of Christ was not that of Adam. The flesh of Christ, therefore, was not from the earth, not from the seed of man, but from heaven. Christ had a heavenly body born of Mary, a heavenly Eve.

Paracelsus had stated similar opinions. In his text *Liber de Sancta Trinitate*, which seems to have had an active life in manuscript, Paracelsus described how God was originally alone and without any beginning. Thus, the divine separation into three persons was not eternal, and initially there was only one being, one divinity, one person. God remained alone until he wished to multiply and manifest himself, at which point there came into being three persons, three beings, three qualities and forms, all the while remaining, nonetheless, one God, one creator. Paracelsus also described how God separated a female form from himself, represented as a *himmlische weib* or *frau gottes*, which was understood not as a separate divinity, but the means by which God the Father produced the second person of the Trinity. Embedded here, as well as in the Christologies of other religious writers such as Melchior Hofman (d. 1543) and Casper Schwenkfeld (d. 1561), was a revolutionary and millennial conception of the church. By distancing Christ's flesh from human flesh, Weigel joined those who cast into doubt the possibility of reforming the old Adam. There had to be a new covenant in which the heart would replace the external Jerusalem as the dwelling place of God. To this end, Weigel recognized three stages of the world ending finally in the age of the Holy Spirit. At that time, each person would become a separate Jerusalem and a divine temple, and there would no longer be a need for ordained preachers or other teachers.

Paracelsianism could be aligned with mystics such as Schwenkfeld and Weigel, but it was also appealing to some who took part in more orthodox theological debates surrounding the symbolic interpretation of the Eucharist. For them, it has been argued, Paracelsus became a kind of "Christian Magus" developing a knowledge of God through the study of nature. Despite Protestant links, Catholics too supported the publication of Paracelsian texts. In both theological camps, Paracelsian ideas found fertile ground already prepared by a heritage of Neoplatonic and mystical Renaissance philosophy.

## 6 Later Traditions

Aside from making chemistry relevant to medicine, other themes – philosophical, mystical, and religious – connected later writers to the works and thoughts of Paracelsus. One tradition connected Paracelsus not only to an explanation of disease as specific entities with specific etiologies, rejecting thereby the ancient doctrine of humors, but also annexed Paracelsian notions to explications of physiological processes in the idiom of chemistry. This aspect of what later became known as iatrochemistry developed especially in the seventeenth century in the writings of Jean Baptiste van Helmont (1579–1644), Franciscus de le Boë Sylvius (1614–1672), Raymond Vieussens (ca. 1635–1715), and many others. Expressing a natural philosophy in terms of vitalism and macrocosmic influences and upholding chemical analogies related to the human being inevitably involved reference to Paracelsus. For van Helmont, no part of nature was entirely inert. Especially in a text published posthumously called *Ortus medicinae* (1648), he invoked the (by then well worn) idea of spiritual seeds, or *semina*, and coined new terms such as "gas" and "blas" in attempts to define the spiritual, life-giving, and activating parts of physical existence – some of it innate in bodies, some of it derived from the stars. In some places, aspects of Paracelsian thinking joined in a mixture of new and old medical opinions. By the end of the seventeenth century, Paracelsian views could be found side by side those of Galenists, iatrochemists, and even Cartesians in encyclopedic discussions of the causes and cures of disease.[12] Throughout the same period and beyond, alchemical texts continued to enlist Paracelsus and the *tria prima* in descriptions of vitalist cosmologies and discussions of transmutation. As part of a lineage of magical savants aware of inner relationships and forever maneuvering between matter, spirit, and soul, Paracelsus became a staple reference among esotericists, mystical philosophers, and spiritual alchemists in the eighteenth and nineteenth centuries.

The Neoplatonic and Paracelsian themes combined by the religious mystic and *Philosophus Teutonicus* Jacob Boehme (1575–1624), in numerous prophetic and mystical writings, helped generate thereafter wide currents of Christian theosophy and *Naturphilosophie*. Many of those same themes concerning the spiritual parts of matter and the threefold nature of the human being as composed of body, soul, and spirit continued into the nineteenth and twentieth centuries in the theistic philosophy of Franz von Baader (1765–1841), the works of the post-Romantic poet-alchemist Alexander von Bernus (1880–1965), and in the anthroposophical writings of Rudolf Steiner (1861–1925).

---

[12] For example, *Johannis Dolaei ... Encyclopedia Chirurgica Rationalis...* (Francofurti ad Moenum: sumtibus Friderici Knochii, 1689).

# 15

# ROSICRUCIANISM

## Hereward Tilton

### 1 Introduction: *Gnosis* and Transfiguration in Rosicrucianism

Disparate groups have assumed the Rosicrucian mantle across the four centuries of development of this esoteric current; consequently, the task of defining Rosicrucianism is a challenging one. In both scholarly and esoteric literature, Rosicrucianism has been portrayed as the purveyor of a *gnosis* originating in the ancient gnostic and hermetic milieu, that is to say, an esoteric knowledge promising salvation through the freeing of the spirit from its bondage to matter. The prevalence of this portrayal owes much to the thought of Carl Gustav Jung, who advanced the influential thesis that the alchemical art practiced in Rosicrucian circles was a conduit for such *gnosis*.[1] Jung's view echoes a heterodox Protestant polemic of the seventeenth century, when the Pietist Gottfried Arnold sought to ally Rosicrucianism with the suppressed teachings of a supposedly authentic primitive church.[2]

*Gnosis* is certainly a central motif in the modern construction (and postmodern deconstruction) of Western esotericism as a field of discourse formed by Christian apologetics.[3] Nevertheless, there is little in pre-twentieth-century Rosicrucianism of the world-rejecting flight from matter or heavenly ascent through salvific knowledge that was central to ancient Gnosticism – which like esotericism is a problematic category with origins in a heresiological agenda. Prior to the rise of the neo-gnostic *Lectorium Rosicrucianum* in the 1930s, when the Demiurge emerged among the Neoplatonic cosmologies that were a staple of Rosicrucianism, he was the benevolent architect of Plato rather than the dark creator god of the gnostics. Nor is the presence in the Rosicrucian corpus

---

[1] See Gerhard Wehr's essay on Jung in this volume.
[2] Gottfried Arnold, *Unpartheyische Kirchen- und Ketzer- Historie* (Frankfurt: Thomas Fritsch, 1729).
[3] See Wouter Hanegraaff's contribution on "Gnosis" in this volume.

of other motifs associated with ancient Gnosticism (such as the androgyne and the ouroboros) evidence of a lineage stretching back to antiquity via the gnostic heresy of the Cathars. Rather, these motifs are derived via Boehme and Paracelsus from the alchemical corpus, and their employment by the medieval alchemists cannot be considered proof of the secret practice of a heretical "spiritual alchemy." Jung's references in this regard are not to a consciously transmitted tradition but to a largely unconscious process of collective individuation corresponding to the precession of the equinoxes.[4] As the main conduit of the notion of Rosicrucianism's gnostic lineage, Jung's testimony on this matter must be carefully distinguished from a purely historical enquiry, lest we become unwitting purveyors of an esoteric tradition rather than agents for its historical analysis.

Once this caveat is heeded, the esoteric teachings of the major Rosicrucian groups appear to center less on *gnosis* and more on "transfiguration," that is, on the initiate's achievement of quasi-divine status and powers through the transformation of the human body into a semi-spiritual condition. While some latter-day Rosicrucians have interpreted such transfiguration as a *gnosis*,[5] the sources of this doctrinal element lie primarily in the Christian and alchemical traditions rather than the ancient gnostic milieu. A second and related characteristic of Rosicrucian lore is the notion that the beings thus transfigured have banded together to exert a benevolent influence on the course of world history.

Pseudo-historical fantasies also seem to constitute something of the essence of Rosicrucianism, and they have certainly played a key role in establishing and legitimizing authority within the main Rosicrucian groups considered here. While the task of untangling these fantasies from the historical record is an important one, the urge to demystify should be tempered by an awareness that Rosicrucianism is an esoteric current in which artifacts of the imagination convey truths very different from those of modernity's dominant intellectual paradigms. Moreover, such artifacts may exercise their own considerable influence on the course of history, as the events surrounding the dawn of Rosicrucianism in seventeenth-century Germany reveal.

## 2 Rosicrucian Origins amid the Counter-Reformation

The dawn of Rosicrucianism was heralded across Europe by the publication in 1614 of the anonymous *Fama Fraternitatis*, which described the opening of

---

[4] Carl Gustav Jung, *Aion: Untersuchungen zur Symbolgeschichte* (Zürich: Rascher, 1951).
[5] For example, the *Lectorium Rosicrucianum* and the S.R.I.A., cf. *infra*.

the tomb of Christian Rosenkreutz, the founder of a medieval fraternity of learned monks dedicated to the reformation of theology and the sciences. According to the *Fama*, the *Liber T.* was found clasped in the hands of the "venerable and undecayed" corpse of Rosenkreutz, who was not afflicted by disease but was "summoned by the Spirit of God" in an Enochian fashion.[6] The most treasured of the Rosicrucian fraternity's texts after the Bible, the *Liber T.* contained the intellectual fruits of Rosenkreutz's pilgrimage to Arabia and Africa, where he studied under the wise men of the city of Damcar and the "elemental inhabitants" of Fez.[7] As such, this marvelous book depicted "a microcosm corresponding in all motions to the macrocosm" – just like the burial vault itself, which was lit by "another sun" and structured in accordance with a Neoplatonic cosmology.[8] According to the *Fama*, the *Liber T.* and other works secreted within the tomb held the primordial knowledge granted by God to humanity – alchemy, Kabbalah, and magic – and through their rediscovery "a door will open for Europe" to a new era of the knowledge of God and nature. In this era, it shall no longer be said "something is true according to philosophy, but false according to theology"; rather, the divine signatures in nature will be deciphered by those who recognize that they possess an image of the macrocosm within themselves.[9]

With its promise of the restoration of a *prisca sapientia* or primordial wisdom, the *Fama Fraternitatis* stands within the hermetic tradition inherited by the German late Renaissance from Ficino and the Italian *magi*. However, its chief pedigree is to be found in the work of Paracelsus and pre-Paracelsian alchemy. The prominence of Paracelsian influence is such that the *Fama* tells us that a "dictionary" by the sage of Hohenheim is found within the tomb.[10] This statement gave rise to early suspicions that the *Fama*'s account was allegorical in nature, for the tomb was purportedly closed nine years prior to Paracelsus's birth. Hence the fraternity's *Liber M.*, perused by Paracelsus himself, was held by some to be the *liber mundi* or book of the world, a source of divine revelation equal to Scripture. Likewise, the *Fama*'s description of Rosenkreutz's journey to retrieve the *prisca sapientia* can be read as an allegorical account of the transmission of alchemy and other antique sciences to Europe via the Arabs. The influence of alchemical lore is particularly evident in the motif of the tomb's opening, which bears a close resemblance

---

[6] Johann Valentin Andreae, *Fama Fraternitatis* (Haarlem: Rozekruis Pers, 1998), 92.
[7] Andreae, *Fama*, 74, 76.
[8] Andreae, *Fama*, 88, 90, 92.
[9] Andreae, *Fama*, 72, 98.
[10] Andreae, *Fama*, 92.

to a tale associated with the Arabic *Tabula Smaragdina*, in which the Emerald Tablet is found clasped in the hands of Hermes as he lies in state in his tomb.[11] What is more, Christian Rosenkreutz's perfectly preserved corpse and the 106 years of his life suggested to readers that the Rosicrucian fraternity possessed a transfiguring alchemical panacea, no doubt employed by the brethren in fulfillment of their first law – to heal the sick *gratis*.[12]

The legend of Christian Rosenkreutz related by the *Fama Fraternitatis* and the second manifesto, the *Confessio Fraternitatis* (1615), did more than establish the authority of a religious and natural philosophical program. This clever marriage of allegory with contemporary events such as the 1604 supernova led to a widespread belief in a conspiratorial Protestant fraternity with extraordinary natural magical powers, playing a role equal and opposite to that of the Jesuits in the fractious religious and political affairs of the day. Indeed, the Rosicrucian manifestos and the plethora of published responses they provoked should be understood in the context of rising antagonism between the Protestant Union and Catholic League within the Holy Roman Empire. Nascent Rosicrucianism was nurtured above all by Calvinist Germany, which not only provided a safe haven for modes of thought inimical to the burgeoning Counter-Reformation, but was pervaded by a medievalist nostalgia for a world unriven by the divide between the secular and the sacred.

The historical record points with little equivocation to the source of the manifestos: the "society of intimate friends" surrounding the Tübingen theologian Johann Valentin Andreae and his mentor, the Paracelsian Tobias Hess.[13] Indeed, Andreae had already composed his famous alchemical allegory, the *Chemical Wedding of Christian Rosenkreutz*, by 1607.

Ostensibly describing the seven-day journey of Christian Rosenkreutz to a mysterious royal wedding, the *Chemical Wedding* employs a variety of alchemical symbols, mirroring both the stages of the alchemical process and the progress of the Christian soul's pilgrimage through the world. The origins of the Rose Cross motif are laid bare when Rosenkreutz, summoned to the wedding by an angelic figure, places four roses in his hat and a red band "crosswise" on his shoulders.[14] This may well be an allusion to Andreae's own coat of arms, which features four flowers divided by a cross. However,

---

[11] Pseudo-Albertus Magnus, "Scriptum Alberti super Arborem Aristotelis," *Theatrum Chemicum*, Vol. 2 (Strasbourg: Zetzner, 1659), 458.
[12] Andreae, *Fama*, 82.
[13] Carlos Gilly, *Cimelia Rhodostaurotica* (Amsterdam: In de Pelikaan, 1995), 78–79.
[14] Johann Valentin Andreae, *Chymische Hochzeit: Christiani Rosencreutz. Anno 1459* (Strasbourg: Lazarus Zetzner, 1616), 14.

hermetic symbolism is ambiguous and multivalent in nature, and another likely source for the motif is a tract by Paracelsus, the *Book on the Resurrection and Glorification of Bodies*. There the author portrays the rose as a symbol of the transfiguration or spiritualization of the human body through both the blood of Christ and the Philosopher's Stone, the agent of alchemical transmutation.[15] This portrayal draws in turn on medieval employment of the rose as a symbol of the perfected red Philosopher's Stone, which was understood to be a paradoxical fusion of heavenly spirit and earthly matter. The Stone's nature was likened by the medieval alchemists to the body of the resurrected Christ, a subtle, incorruptible entity akin to the spiritual body received by the faithful on the Day of Judgment.

Some authors have portrayed Andreae's circle as the true "Brethren of the Rosy Cross";[16] however, Andreae himself spoke of the fraternity as a virtual entity, constituted by all those inspired to defend the program of the manifestos.[17] In the eyes of other "insiders" to the virtual nature of early Rosicrucianism, the fraternity was an invisible Christian fellowship in the mystical Franckian sense of "a spiritual and invisible body of all the partakers of Christ."[18]

The statements of the *Confessio Fraternitatis* concerning the invisibility and invulnerability of the Rosicrucian brethren, and those of the *Fama* concerning their near-omniscience, contributed greatly to the potency of the manifestos in the popular imagination. This in turn facilitated the diffusion of conspiracy theories, such as Jesuit accusations that Rosicrucians were seeking world government through an alliance with Islam. Nevertheless, the influence of the manifestos and the prospects for their intellectual and spiritual program soon waned with the descent of the empire into the maelstrom of the Thirty Years War (1618–1648).

3 The *Gold- und Rosenkreutz* and the Counter-Enlightenment

The first sign of Rosicrucianism's eighteenth-century reemergence was the publication in 1710 of *The True and Complete Preparation of the Philosopher's*

---

[15] Paracelsus, *Vita Beata*, Theologische Werke 1 (Berlin: de Gruyter, 2008), 440–457; Roland Edighoffer, "Rosicrucianism I," *Dictionary of Gnosis and Western Esotericism*, Vol. 2, ed. Wouter J. Hanegraaff (Leiden: Brill, 2006), 1012.
[16] Hans Schick, *Das Ältere Rosenkreuzertum* (Berlin: Nordland Verlag, 1942), 69; Gilly, *Cimelia*, 76.
[17] Johann Valentin Andreae, *Turris Babel* (Strasbourg: Lazarus Zetzner, 1619), 37; cf. Hereward Tilton, "*Regni Christi Frater*: Count Michael Maier and the Fraternity R. C.," *Aries: Journal for the Study of Western Esotericism* 2.1 (2001), 3–33.
[18] Tilton, *Regni Christi Frater*.

*Stone*, a tract supposedly stemming from the "Order of the Golden and Rosy Cross" that appeared under the pseudonym of "Sincerus Renatus" ("genuine rebirth"). The author is generally held to be a Silesian pastor by the name of Samuel Richter. It is not clear whether an actual secret society lay behind Richter's work; however, the detailed and sometimes peculiar rules of the order supplied by Richter impart the impression of the existence of a cult based on the spiritualizing, life-extending effects of the Philosopher's Stone.[19]

More evidence – albeit similarly inconclusive – for the emergence of Rosicrucianism as a genuine secret society is supplied by the *Testament of the Fraternity of the Rosy and Gold Cross*, a document of Bohemian provenance written prior to 1735, which reiterates many of the fraternity's rules set forth in Richter's work. It also traces the origins of the *prisca sapientia* to the sons of Noah in the manner of the Renaissance philosopher Francesco Patrizi, and it names Bezalel, chief architect of the tabernacle, as the first imperator of the Rosicrucian Order.[20] The later dovetailing of Rosicrucian and Freemasonic myths of origin was probably facilitated by the prominent place of Bezalel and Solomon within this earlier lineage, and the myths of origin of the Masonic *Gold- und Rosenkreutz* of the later eighteenth century also have recourse to Patrizi's history.[21]

Although the *Testament* also includes chapters on necromancy and the construction of surveillance devices, the predominant concern of the order it describes was the manufacture of the Philosopher's Stone. Following a centuries-old alchemical trope, the author of the *Testament* refers to Moses's creation of an *aurum potabile* or "potable gold" through the pulverization of the Golden Calf.[22] *Aurum potabile* was essentially a liquid form of the Philosopher's Stone, in which an apparently incorruptible substance – gold – had been irrevocably dissolved and its divine virtues made available to human digestion. Hence, in the *Testament* the potion that Moses gave the Israelites to drink is identical with the Philosopher's Stone imparted to every Rosicrucian brother at the end of his seventh year of instruction, which is said to extend his life by a period of sixty years.[23] The plethora of alchemical

---

[19] Sincerus Renatus [Samuel Richter], *Die Warhaffte und vollkommene Bereitung des Philosophischen Steins* (Breslau: Fellgiebel, 1710), 99–106.
[20] *Testamentum der Fraternitet Roseae et Aureae Crucis ... Anno 580* (Vienna: Österreichische Nationalbibliothek, Cod SN 2897), 1–2, 14–15.
[21] Michael Stausberg, "Zoroaster im 18. Jahrhundert: zwischen Aufklärung und Esoterik," in *Aufklärung und Esoterik*, ed. Monika Neugebauer-Wölk (Hamburg: Meiner, 1999), 135–136.
[22] *Testamentum*, 2–3.
[23] *Testamentum*, 26.

recipes and laboratory instructions associated with eighteenth-century Rosicrucianism suggest many such Philosopher's Stones were forms of colloidal gold, that is, gold in a suspended nanoparticular form.[24]

Although they were promulgated in the early seventeenth century as part of what Frances Yates perceived to be a proto-Enlightenment,[25] by the eighteenth century Rosicrucian doctrines had become an anachronism in the face of the advance of mechanistic science and Enlightenment philosophy, which discarded the ambiguous esoteric discourse of alchemy and rejected divine inspiration as a legitimate path to scientific knowledge. From around 1763, the *Gold- und Rosenkreutz* emerged within Freemasonic circles as an absolutist, reactionary force at a time in which aristocratic and ecclesiastical authority was being eroded by a democratic, republican, and materialist radical fringe. Organized into an opaque pyramidal hierarchy, this grouping spread eastward from the German-speaking lands to Hungary, Poland, and Russia, proving attractive not only to conservatives among the nobility and royalty but also to traditionalist clergy. Its emphasis on strict obedience to an unknown authority, which conducted surveillance through informants and control through the confession of personal secrets, reflected a vision of an ideal social order that is more reminiscent of Bentham's *panopticon* than Andreae's utopianism. Indeed, the *Gold- und Rosenkreutz* instruction for circle directors states that the maintenance of oaths of secrecy is itself a means of the initiate's promised transmutation from an earthly to a "spiritual" human.[26]

The Masonic *Gold- und Rosenkreutz*, like its non-Masonic predecessor, portrayed the content of the *prisca sapientia* in terms of natural magic, alchemy, and Kabbalah; these are the concerns of the influential book of emblems associated with the order, the *Secret Symbols of the Rosicrucians*, which presents an amalgam of alchemical-Paracelsian natural philosophy and Christian kabbalistic motifs drawing from the work of early theosophers such as Heinrich Khunrath and Jacob Boehme.[27] Despite its theosophical inclinations, however, the primary interest of the Masonic *Gold- und Rosenkreutz* lay with laboratory alchemy, which it distinguished sharply from "mechanistic" chemistry.[28] It was each initiate's duty to conduct laboratory alchemical

---

[24] Hereward Tilton, "Of Ether and Colloidal Gold: The Making of a Philosophers' Stone," *Esoterica* 9 (2007), www.esoteric.msu.edu/VolumeIX/EsotericaIX.pdf
[25] Frances Yates, *The Rosicrucian Enlightenment* (London: Routledge and Kegan Paul, 1972), 220–233.
[26] Johann Joachim Christoph Bode, *Starke Erweise* (Rome [Leipzig?]: no publisher given, 5555 [1788]), 122–123.
[27] *Geheime Figuren der Rosenkreuzer* (Altona: J. Eckhardt, 1785), 31, 56.
[28] Augustin Anton Pocquieres de Jolyfief, *Der Compaß der Weisen* (Berlin: Christian Ulrich Ringmacher, 1779), 44–45.

experiments and transmit any discoveries to the head of his cell. In the words of an ex-member's exposé, the *Secret History of a Rosicrucian*, the goal of this collective labor was to produce the alchemical agent by which the Rosicrucian's "earthly body is transformed into a spiritual body."[29]

To new initiates of the *Gold- und Rosenkreutz*, their unknown Rosicrucian superiors were not only guardians of the *philosophia perennis* and possessors of the Philosopher's Stone but also transfigured beings in contact with the angels. Hence, the order's leadership derived its authority not only via an unbroken lineage to the first inspired *magi* but also through its vertical proximity to the divine in a cosmos conceived in Neoplatonic terms. Indeed, the documents of the *Gold- und Rosenkreutz* themselves confirm the contention of detractors that the order's myths of origin, doctrine, and structure functioned as the means to political power of a manipulative cabal, the chiefs of which appear to have been the Prussian court intrigants Bischoffwerder and Wöllner.[30]

## 4 Rosicrucianism in a Secular Age

If the *Gold- und Rosenkreutz* can fairly be defined in terms of a medievalist, absolutist reaction to the Enlightenment, its nineteenth-century successors demonstrate a greater accommodation of the ascendant secularizing paradigm through their incorporation of doctrinal elements such as evolutionary theory, proto-psychoanalytic theories of sexuality, women's liberation, and Nietzschean philosophy. While Rosicrucianism during this period constituted an alternative to the Eastern orientation of Blavatskian Theosophy through its focus on the Western esoteric traditions, the influx of Hindu and Buddhist ideas via the nineteenth-century Orientalists also had a considerable impact on the form of Rosicrucian doctrine. Furthermore, growing scholarly interest in ancient Gnosticism was reflected in the increasing prominence of gnostic conceptions within Rosicrucian groups.

Despite these changes in emphasis, the motif of transfiguration and the notion of a band of transfigured beings exerting benevolent influence on world history continued to form the centerpiece of Rosicrucian doctrine. The undermining of the opaque, ambiguous language of alchemy by the more transparent scientific terminology of the modern age went hand-in-hand with a decline in the popularity of laboratory alchemy, which became

---

[29] Heinrich C. Albrecht, *Geheime Geschichte eines Rosenkreuzers* (Hamburg: n.p., 1792), 228.
[30] For a typical polemic against the *Gold- und Rosenkreutz* from the "Enlightened" viewpoint of the Illuminati, see von Löhrbach, *Die theoretischen Brüder* (Athen [Regensburg?]: Montag und Weiß, 1785).

just one among a myriad of magical, mystical, quasi-scientific, and broadly religious paths to Rosicrucian transfiguration. Indeed, alchemical symbolism is encountered more frequently in the modern Rosicrucian literature in the context of a non-laboratory "spiritual alchemy." Particularly influential in this regard were the portraits of medieval alchemy as a mystical proto-Protestant heresy put forward by Mary Atwood and the Freemason Ethan Allen Hitchcock, which left their mark on the *Societas Rosicruciana in Anglia* (S.R.I.A.)[31] and subsequent groups.

Founded in 1867 by Robert Wentworth Little, the S.R.I.A. began as a decidedly middle-class Victorian initiatory society dedicated to the study of mystery religions, Gnosticism, alchemy, the Kabbalah, and Christian mysticism, among other themes deemed beneficial to the elucidation of Freemasonic rites and symbolism.[32] Admitting only Master Masons, its ninefold grade structure derives from that of the *Gold- und Rosenkreutz* and centers on the initiates' rejuvenating mystical encounter with their own mortality – hence the Secret Words of the seventh Adeptus Exemptus grade, *mors janua vitae* ("death is the gate of life" on the "pathway to Divine existence").[33] This encounter is conceptualized with recourse to a neo-gnostic discourse (the divine spark in matter constitutes "the germ of infinite improvement")[34] and a spiritual alchemy whose goal is supposedly identical with that of religion ("spiritualization ... or the redemption of spirit whilst still dwelling in matter").[35] In a work highly regarded by the S.R.I.A., *The Rosicrucians: Their Rites and Mysteries* (1870), Hargrave Jennings wrote of this liberation of the divine spark in terms of an alchemical transfiguration by which the Rosicrucian attains a body of light akin to that of Enoch and Elijah.[36]

Founded in 1888 by S.R.I.A. members William Wynn Westcott and Samuel Liddell Mathers, the influential Hermetic Order of the Golden Dawn differed from its predecessor in its focus on practical magic, as well as its admittance of women and other non-Masons. Nevertheless, it also shared some important similarities with the S.R.I.A.: Headed by three chiefs, its grade system was derived from the *Gold- und Rosenkreutz* and possessed a

---

[31] For example, *Societas Rosicruciana in Anglia: Grade III°. Practicus* (s.l.: s.p., 1953–1965), 22.
[32] William Wynn Westcott, "Historical Account of the Societas Rosicruciana in Anglia, July 11th, 1919," in *Soc. Ros. in Anglia, Metropolitan College: Transactions* (London: The Avondale Press, 1919), 8–11.
[33] *Societas Rosicruciana in Anglia, College of Adepts: Grade VII°. Adeptus Exemptus* (s.l.: s.p., 1953–1965), 4–5.
[34] *Adeptus Exemptus*, 6.
[35] *Practicus*, 24.
[36] Cf. Genesis 5.24, Hebrews 11.5, 2 Kings 2.11, and Matthew 17.1–3.

second division of grades focused on the symbolism of the Rosicrucian vault. The initiatory rituals for the first division of grades or Golden Dawn in the Outer were derived from the infamous Cipher Manuscript, which appears to have been the work of S.R.I.A. Frater Kenneth Mackenzie, left unfinished at his death in 1886.[37] The spiritual path of the initiate detailed therein follows the alchemically conceived Kabbalah derived from the *Aesch-Mezareph* published in the seventeenth-century *Kabbala Denudata*. Enoch and Elijah represent two alternative paths of ascent within this initiatory journey, the aim of which is "to purge matter and exalt it," as the Cipher Manuscript expressly states.[38] Developed by Mathers, the impressive rituals of the Inner Order or *Ordo Rosae Rubeae et Aureae Crucis* were drawn from the account of the discovery of the tomb of Christian Rosenkreutz given in the *Fama Fraternitatis*. Centered on the mysteries of Christ and Osiris, these rituals took place within a microcosmic vault adorned with kabbalistic, alchemical, and astrological symbolism, which also served as a place for individuals to strive for self-transformation through the practice of theurgy.[39]

At its height at the *fin-de-siècle*, the Golden Dawn attained a Bohemian fashionableness, counting among its members William Butler Yeats and the celebrated actress Florence Farr, as well as the noted occultists Arthur Edward Waite and Aleister Crowley. Like the *Gold- und Rosenkreutz*, the Golden Dawn's leadership claimed to possess privileged access to spiritual beings and to represent an unbroken, authentic esoteric lineage. Issued from the upper echelons of an opaque hierarchy, these claims served both to legitimize the order's doctrines and to invest its leaders with personal power. Hence, Mathers declared he was an "ambassador" in astral contact with the Secret Chiefs of the Order, whom he believed to possess "terrible superhuman powers,"[40] while Westcott maintained that the Cipher Manuscript stemmed from an authentic and ancient German Rosicrucian lineage.[41] The manuscript refers to both Brothers and Sisters of the Order, which Westcott claimed was proof "that in older times, as at the present day, women rose to high rank and attainments in the Secret Knowledge of

---

[37] Robert A. Gilbert, "Provenance Unknown: A Tentative Solution to the Riddle of the Cipher Manuscript of the Golden Dawn," in *The Complete Golden Dawn Cipher Manuscript*, ed. Darcy Küntz (Edmonds, WA: Holmes Publishing Group, 1996), 19–25.
[38] Küntz, *The Complete Golden Dawn Cipher Manuscript*, 110.
[39] Cf. the descriptions by Mathers and Westcott in Israel Regardie, *The Complete Golden Dawn System of Magic*, Vol. 5 (Santa Monica: Falcon Press, 1987), 17–28, 29–34.
[40] Samuel Liddell Mathers, *Manifesto*, reprinted in Ellic Howe, *The Magicians of the Golden Dawn* (London: Taylor and Francis, 1972), 129.
[41] V. H. Sapere Aude [William Wynn Westcott], *The Historical Lecture*, in Küntz, *The Golden Dawn Source Book*, 1996), 48; Gilbert, "Provenance Unknown," 17.

the Order."[42] Ironically, in 1903 the Hermetic Order of the Golden Dawn disintegrated amid scandals and disputes arising from its convoluted sexual politics.[43]

## 5 The Twentieth Century: Competing Visions

Rosicrucianism in the twentieth century has a tortuous history of such disputes and schisms, yet a handful of the myriad groups emerged with an international mass following through the exploitation of new methods for promotion and commercialization. The doctrine of Max Heindel's Rosicrucian Fellowship, founded in Seattle in 1909, was largely derived from the teachings of Rudolf Steiner, who at the time of Heindel's visit to Berlin was still a member of the Theosophical Society. The Rosicrucian Fellowship achieved considerable success, in part through Heindel's canny employment of correspondence courses. It seems Heindel was loathe to keep the contents of Steiner's secret teachings to himself and later claimed to have received them directly from an "Elder Brother of the Rose Cross," a transfigured human who visited him in his lodgings in Berlin.[44] Whatever their true origin, these teachings center on the unfolding of divine powers in the human spirit through a series of existences in progressively higher bodies. *Mensch* eventually becomes *Übermensch* through the development of an astral body known variously as the Philosopher's Stone, the Golden Wedding Garment, and the *soma psychikon*, which is akin to the "spiritual body" mentioned in 1 Corinthians 15.44.[45] According to Heindel, the evolution of human civilization is guided by such transfigured beings.

A Dutch splinter group of Heindel's Rosicrucian Fellowship, the *Lectorium Rosicrucianum*, was founded in 1935 by Zwier Leene and his brother Jan (better known by his pen name Jan van Rijckenborgh). With around fifteen thousand members worldwide, this group professes a dualist neo-Catharism, although it also incorporates elements of anthroposophy, Hindu Tantra, and millennialist beliefs in the coming of the Age of Aquarius. It draws directly on ancient gnostic doctrine in its goal of returning the divine spark in humanity to its heavenly origins. The means of this return is again the *soma psychikon*, the

---

[42] Westcott, *The Historical Lecture*, 49.
[43] For more information on the Golden Dawn, see the essay by Egil Asprem in this volume.
[44] Augusta Foss Heindel, *Memoirs about Max Heindel and the Rosicrucian Fellowship* (Oceanside, CA: The Rosicrucian Fellowship, 1997), 3–5.
[45] Max Heindel [Carl Grasshof], *The Rosicrucian Cosmo-Conception* (Chicago: Macoy Publishing, 1910), 516; Max Heindel [Carl Grasshof], *Gleanings of a Mystic* (Oceanside, CA: The Rosicrucian Fellowship, 1922), 181; Max Heindel [Carl Grasshof], *Ancient and Modern Initiation* (London: no publisher given, 1931), 107.

vehicle achieved through transfiguration in the sense of a Christian-gnostic rebirth or "the rebuilding of the original divine man."[46] The individual's moral conduct plays an integral role in his or her journey to transfiguration and includes the observation of biblical strictures, abstention from drugs, and vegetarianism. Although its basic ideas are centuries old, the *Lectorium Rosicrucianum* has recourse to some distinctly modern terminology. For example, to deliver humanity from the perishable dialectical world and its evil rulers, the Aeons, a "new gnostic world-brotherhood" is magically creating a "radiation field" sustained by a system of fire-temples that facilitates the inner liberation of the masses and their binding with the "Christ-radiation."[47]

The doctrine of the largest contemporary Rosicrucian order, the Ancient and Mystical Order Rosae Crucis (AMORC), shares many of the conceptions of its competitors, albeit clothed in slightly different garb. AMORC was founded in New York in 1915 by Harvey Spencer Lewis, who worked in advertising and successfully employed his commercial skills to promote his brainchild. Like the Rosicrucian Fellowship, the success of AMORC has in part been built on the operation of correspondence courses. Remote, astral contact with the Cosmic Masters is possible once the initiate reaches the higher degrees, just as Heindel's Fellowship also promised.[48] Lewis constructed a familiar legitimizing myth: While sojourning in Toulouse, he was initiated into the *Ordo Rosae Crucis* by an old Hierophant R+C, who gave him the task of taking the order's teachings to America.[49] According to Aleister Crowley, the garbled French of the authorizing charter allegedly issued by the Rosicrucians made Lewis "a laughing stock,"[50] but in time he created a successful myth of origin with a focus on the "mystery schools" of Pharaoh Thutmose III. Today, AMORC promotes the evolutionary emergence of a "spiritualized humanity" principally through the use of meditative techniques. While Lewis allegedly performed the alchemical transmutation of zinc into gold in 1916,[51] the order's alchemy is primarily spiritual and in recent decades has taken on distinctly Jungian overtones. As such, it provides

---

[46] Catharose de Petri [Hennie Stok-Huizer], *Transfiguration* (Haarlem: Rozekruis Pers, 1979), 9–14; Jan van Rijckenborgh, *Elementary Philosophy of the Modern Rosycross* (Haarlem: Rozekruis Pers, 1984), 109.
[47] van Rijckenborgh, *Elementary Philosophy*, 104–105.
[48] Harvey Spencer Lewis, *Rosicrucian Manual* (Charleston: Lovett Publishing Co., 1927), 74.
[49] Harvey Spencer Lewis, "History of the Order," *The American Rosae Crucis* 1.7 (1916), 11–15.
[50] Robert Vanloo, "O.T.O. and A.M.O.R.C.," *Noch Mehr Materialien zum O.T.O.* (Munich: Arbeitsgemeinschaft für Religions- und Weltanschauungsfragen, 2000), 76.
[51] Harvey Spencer Lewis, "A Demonstration of Alchemy," *The American Rosae Crucis* 1.7 (1916), 17–20.

a meditative path to psychic integration and the advent of a new "spiritual man" and "spiritual woman."

## 6 Conclusion: A Cabal of the Transfigured

Despite varied sociohistorical contexts, there is evidently a unity in the diversity of Rosicrucian teachings across the four centuries of this esoteric current's existence. The adoption of a subtle or spiritual body through a process of transfiguration is a demonstrably central motif with dual origins in the *coniunctio oppositorum* of alchemy and orthodox Christian teaching on the resurrection body of Christ and the faithful. Although the terminology applied – Invisible Church of Christ, Secret Chiefs, mystic Third Order, Great White Brotherhood, and so on – has been diverse, the notion of a benevolent conspiracy of transfigured or angelic beings has also remained a central component of Rosicrucian doctrine. Access to these beings and their mysteries has often been the reserve of a secretive esoteric hierarchy – and for this reason more than any other, the mantle of Rosicrucianism has lent an authority and legitimacy that at times allows earthly interests to flourish under its cover.

# 16

# JACOB BOEHME AND CHRISTIAN THEOSOPHY

## Glenn Alexander Magee

### 1 Introduction

The term "theosophy" literally means "wisdom of God." This can be interpreted either as "God's wisdom" or as "wisdom about God." As we shall see, this ambiguity is actually crucial to understanding theosophy. Not only are both interpretations correct, in the end – at least in the Christian theosophy of Jacob Boehme – they come to mean the same thing.

The first person to use the term "theosophy" seems to have been Porphyry (ca. 234–ca. 305), and since then the word has been used by many authors in many ways, positively and pejoratively.[1] It is now most famously associated with the Theosophical Society of Madame Blavatsky (1831–1891). However, "Christian theosophy" is something quite distinct from Blavatsky's movement.

Christian theosophy is an early modern, Protestant German mystical movement.[2] It can be seen as a precursor to both German Romanticism and German philosophy, especially Idealism. Indeed, Hegel himself said of Boehme that he was "the first German philosopher; the content of his philosophizing is genuinely German [*echt deutsch*]."[3] The main Christian

---

[1] See Antoine Faivre, *Theosophy, Imagination, Tradition* (Albany: State University of New York Press, 2000), 3.

[2] The idea of an identifiable tradition of Christian theosophy dates back to the seventeenth century. For more information, see Faivre, *Theosophy, Imagination, Tradition*, 10–19; and Wouter Hanegraaff, *Esotericism and the Academy* (Cambridge: Cambridge University Press, 2012), 107–147. It must also be noted in the present context that two of Boehme's most significant interpreters, the Frenchman Louis Claude de Saint-Martin (1743–1803) and the German Franz von Baader (whom I will shortly discuss) were Catholics.

[3] G. W. F. Hegel, *Vorlesungen über die Geschichte der Philosophie* [1805] Vol. 3 (*G. W. F. Hegel Werke*, Vol. 20), ed. Eva Moldenhauer und Karl Markus Michel (Frankfurt am Main: Suhrkamp, 1986), 94.

theosophers are all German, though the movement had a significant influence in England and France.

There is general agreement among scholars as to the intellectual streams that coalesce to form theosophy: medieval German mysticism, alchemy, Paracelsism, and Kabbalism.[4] Of the authors who are recognizably theosophical, some of the early figures include Valentin Weigel (1533–1588), Heinrich Khunrath (1560–1605), and Johann Arndt (1555–1621).[5] The supreme exemplar of the tradition, however, is the famed cobbler of Görlitz, the *philosophicus teutonicus*, Jacob Boehme (1575–1624). Indeed, the Christian theosophical tradition may, for all intents and purposes, be considered the Boehmean tradition, and it is Boehme and his thought that are the focus of this essay.

In the year 1600, Boehme had an experience of mystical *gnosis*. Gazing at a gleam of light reflected in a pewter vessel, he was suddenly opened to an immediate experience of the Being of all beings. He remained silent for twelve years, then began writing the work that would come to be known as *Aurora, oder Morgenröte im Aufgang*. Boehme intended this only as a personal exercise, but he showed the work to friends who then circulated it. In time, he acquired a number of influential admirers, who spread his teachings and acted to protect him. This was necessary, for Boehme was often attacked during his years of literary productivity, principally at the hands of the hateful local pastor Gregorius Richter. During the years 1618 to 1624, Boehme was astonishingly prolific, producing a great number of works and carrying on an extensive correspondence. What were Boehme's influences? There is considerable evidence that he read alchemical works, the writings of Paracelsus and Weigel, and possibly some kabbalistic texts. However, we really do not know when he encountered these. Boehme's friends included a number of Christian kabbalists and Paracelsists.

Initially, Boehme had only a small following in Germany, but he became quite influential in England, first through the translation and publication of his works by John Sparrow (1615–1665), whose editions are still in print. John Pordage (1608–1681) was the center of the first Boehmean movement in England, which gave rise to the Philadelphian Society, led by Jane Leade (1624–1704). Such luminaries as John Milton, Isaac Newton, William Blake, and the Cambridge Platonists read Boehme. His first notable German follower was Johann Georg Gichtel (1638–1710), who published an edition of

---

[4] See Faivre, *Theosophy, Imagination, Tradition*, 7; Arthur Versluis, *Theosophia* (Hudson, NY: Lindesfarne Press, 1994), 98; David Walsh, *The Mysticism of Innerworldly Fulfillment* (Gainesville: The University of Florida Press, 1983), 11.
[5] See Faivre, *Theosophy, Imagination, Tradition*, 6–7, 12–13.

Boehme's writings in 1682 and wrote theosophical works of his own. Other significant early German followers (or sympathizers) include Quirinus Kuhlmann (1651–1689), Friedrich Breckling (1629–1711), and Gottfried Arnold (1666–1714). But Boehme's greatest impact on the history of ideas would come much later.

In the late eighteenth and early nineteenth centuries, Jena became a major center of interest in Boehme. Many of the greatest figures of the German Romantic movement were present in Jena at this time, including F. Schlegel, A. W. Schlegel, Novalis, Ludwig Tieck, and F. W. J. Schelling. All of these men read Boehme. Schelling's interest in Boehme was likely encouraged by his friend Franz von Baader (1765–1841). Often called "Boehmius redivivus," Baader would become the most significant and influential Christian theosophist of the nineteenth century. Boehmean ideas were communicated to Hegel by Schelling in Jena, and they exercised a strong influence on him.[6] Arguably it is through Hegel — whose bastard children include Marxism, existentialism, and certain strains of modern conservatism — that Boehme has had his greatest influence; not just on the history of ideas, but on the formation of the modern world.[7]

Though Hegel admired Boehme, he also called him "a complete barbarian" (*vollkommen Barbar*).[8] This was due to Boehme's peculiar mode of expression, which consists almost entirely in the use of strange, homey images. (The reader will shortly encounter examples of this in abundance.) In addition, his prose style is plodding and awkward. Indeed, "barbaric" is a term one encounters a lot in discussions of Boehme.[9] He is certainly a "barbarian" in that his thought is, as Hegel observed, genuinely Germanic and (as Faivre points out) owes nothing to classical sources. It is thoroughly Teutonic in character; earnest and unsophisticated, utterly lacking in irony or literary pretensions of any kind.

Without question, Boehme is also among the most difficult of mystical authors. The account that follows, which attempts to explain his major ideas,

---

[6] See Glenn Alexander Magee, *Hegel and the Hermetic Tradition* (Ithaca: Cornell University Press, 2008); and Magee, "Hegel's Reception of Jacob Boehme," in *An Introduction to Jacob Boehme*, ed. Ariel Hessayon and Sarah Apetrei (London: Routledge, 2013).
[7] See Walsh, *The Mysticism of Innerworldly Fulfillment*, and also Cyril O'Regan, *Gnostic Apocalypse: Jacob Boehme's Haunted Narrative* (Albany: State University of New York Press, 2001). For more details on Boehme's life, readers should consult Andrew Weeks, *Boehme* (Albany: State University of New York Press, 1991).
[8] Hegel, Vorlesungen über die Geschichte der Philosophie, 92.
[9] See, for example, Alexandre Koyré, *La Philosophie de Jakob Boehme* (Paris: Vrin, 1971), 503; Faivre, *Theosophy, Imagination, Tradition*, 7.

barely scratches the surface. And the reader should proceed with the following authorial admission in mind: *No one* really understands Jacob Boehme.

## 2 The Key to Christian Theosophy

In Hegel's remarks on Boehme, he states that the mystical shoemaker exemplifies the "Protestant principle of placing the intellectual world within one's own heart and in one's self-consciousness gazing upon, knowing, and feeling all that formerly was [conceived as] beyond."[10] The key to Christian theosophy is that it seeks "wisdom about God" by understanding God on analogy with the transformation that takes place in the human soul when we overcome self-will and achieve religious illumination.

Of course, this is immediately quite puzzling. God, after all, is a being, whereas the transformation in the soul is a process. But the recognition of this "problem" is the first step in understanding theosophy, for Boehme does indeed conceive God as in process. However, he is careful to say that this process is atemporal: It does not take place in time. This too is extremely puzzling – nor can it cease to be. In beginning from the experience of spiritual transformation in his own soul and then attempting to know the nature of God, Boehme is trying to put into words the experience of *gnosis*, which can never adequately be expressed. (See the Introduction to this volume, and the entry "Gnosis.")

Of course, an atemporal process is a contradiction in terms. The real process takes place in the soul of the believer, in which the path to illumination unfolds one day at a time. Boehme does indeed write as if an analogous process takes place in God, leading to the creation of the universe. However, he continually reminds us that he writes this way because of the limitations of the human intellect, describing in a piecemeal (*stückweise*) fashion what is in fact one and timeless. Thus, when Boehme writes of stages in the "process" that is God, he is actually writing of inseparable, atemporal moments or aspects of God. The language of "moments" comes from Husserlian phenomenology, and Boehme's procedure is, in fact, phenomenological: He offers us a phenomenology of the human spirit, as it moves from a state of fallenness to a state of illumination and salvation. Then he applies this, by analogy, to God.

In brief, we begin in a condition of radical self-centeredness, holding implicitly that we are all, that there is nothing greater than ourselves. Then

---

[10] Hegel, *Vorlesungen über die Geschichte der Philosophie*, 94. See Magee, "Hegel's Reception of Jacob Boehme."

we discover inside us a conflicting impulse to surrender self-will and open outward in engagement with something greater. These two impulses coexist, and must coexist. The latter would not be felt at all if it were not for the former – and the former continually reasserts itself out of fear of the latter, out of fear of the "loss of self" implied in surrender. One who has become keenly aware of this conflict is tormented by it, at one time falling into self-centeredness, then regretting it and resolving to turn toward the light, then backsliding.

A person in such a condition is headed for a crisis, and for Boehme this comes in the form of the *Schrack*. A term peculiar to him, *Schrack* is often translated into English as "flash," and Boehme writes of it as a fire flash or lightning flash (*Blitz*).[11] This is the spiritual turning point, but Boehme is not entirely clear about what it involves. Most probably, the flash consists in our realization that we are powerless to reconcile the conflict in our souls, that we can really *do* nothing. This desperation precipitates a radical form of surrender, in which we simply give ourselves over to God. We abandon self-will and all vain and covertly self-willed (i.e., self-reliant) attempts to break the power of selfish impulse. "The self" vacates the soul, leaving a vacuum that is filled by God. This event is the "second birth."

What follows is a deep and intense experience of love: a state of intoxicating openness and connectedness to all things. Our egoistic selfhood having departed, we are really *not there* anymore. Yet, in another sense, we are now *truly there*, because we are no longer spiritually opaque and are now fully present to Being. We feel an impulse to express this, to preach, to shout it from the housetops. We feel impelled, in short, to become sayers of Being – as Boehme did when he put pen to paper. In this act, the indwelling spirit of God confronts itself. And the man himself is complete. He becomes a true being – truly substantial and *embodied*. Though his new and true body is not of this material world.

This entire process involves, for Boehme, seven steps – although this will not be clear from the account above. Further, the lines of demarcation are inherently fuzzy, a fact Boehme was well aware of. In any case, what is remarkable is that Boehme essentially takes this understanding of the stages of illumination in the human soul and uses it as a template for understanding God himself, and the process of creation.[12] In acquiring this wisdom about God, we acquire God's wisdom. As we shall see, this is because our

---

[11] On the origins of *Schrack*, see Week's Introduction to Boehme, *Aurora* (Leiden, Netherlands: Brill, 2013), 43.
[12] See Walsh, *The Mysticism of Innerworldly Fulfillment*, 54. See also pp. 51–52, 71.

acquisition of wisdom about God, achieved through self-knowledge, is implicated in God's own awakening – his own self-knowledge.

Readers familiar with other mystical traditions will immediately recognize parallels: In my inmost self I am identical with Absolute Being; insight into my own true self (or soul) thus gives me insight into Absolute Being. However, Boehme does not understand God as a characterless "beyond." Boehme's God is not *Brahman*. Nevertheless, this is essentially the point from which Boehme's God begins.

### 3 *Ungrund*, Three Principles, and Sophia

If we ask why we should believe that knowledge of our own awakening should give us a key to understanding God, Boehme would answer that God is a conscious being (indeed, *the* conscious being). But consciousness arises only through opposition. Consciousness is consciousness *of* something. Furthermore, *self*-consciousness only arises through the encounter with otherness. It is only through encountering an other that opposes or frustrates me in some fashion that I turn inward and reflect on myself. "Nothing may be revealed to itself without opposition," Boehme tells us.[13] If God is a conscious being, then something that is not God must stand opposed to him. The obvious implication is that God requires creation to be conscious. Further, Boehme's logic dictates that God could only be self-conscious through his encounter with this other.

Of course, some will object to Boehme's assumption that God's consciousness is structurally similar to our own. God's consciousness, so they will claim, is radically different: God was perfectly conscious and self-conscious prior to creation. The problem with this claim is simply that a consciousness conscious of nothing is *unconscious*. It is an abuse of language to claim that God, or anything, can be conscious without an other. This sort of empty assertion, which we are supposed to take on faith, is typical of orthodox theology and shows it to be far less rational than Boehme's "irrational" mysticism. Of course, one could take the Aristotelian position that the object of God's consciousness is himself: that he is pure self-consciousness. But then two problems arise. First, how can self-consciousness be achieved without prior consciousness of an other? Second, what can God's self-consciousness really consist in, given that conventional theology insists there is no distinction within God? Every act of self-consciousness involves a division within the subject: "I" think about "my self"; this thought, memory, emotion, and so on.

[13] *The Way to Christ*, Seventh Treatise, "On Divine Contemplation," i. 8.

It is, in fact, precisely by positing distinction within God that Boehme attempts both to explain God's self-consciousness, and to uphold the traditional Judeo-Christian doctrine of the transcendence of God. Boehme does very often speak as if God achieves consciousness through creation. And yet equally often he retreats from this, for this position leads to two problems. First, it suggests that prior to creation God is not conscious, which in turn suggests that God, the supreme being, creates under some kind of compulsion – clearly an unacceptable conclusion. In addressing this problem, Boehme walks a fine line, on the one hand positing a dark, unconscious will within God and simultaneously insisting on God's absolute freedom.

Second, Boehme's position seems to suggest that creation "completes" or perfects God – another dangerous idea. And this implies, further, that creation is part of the Being of God. In *Aurora*, Boehme states that "you must elevate your mind in the spirit and consider how the whole of nature . . . is the body of God [*der Leib Gottes*]."[14] On the other hand, he tells us elsewhere that "The outer world is not God. . . .. The world is merely a being [*Wesen*] in which God is manifesting himself."[15] Of course, there is no real contradiction here: Even if the world is God's body, there is a distinction between the body and the spirit, the animating soul. Nature is God's body, but the body is not all. In *Signatura Rerum* (1622), Boehme compares creation to an apple growing on a tree: Obviously, it is not the tree itself, but it is the fruit of the tree.[16]

And yet questions linger. Isn't it correct to say that producing the fruit is the *telos* (end or goal) of the tree, and that with the emergence of the fruit, the tree completes or perfects itself? Yet in the same text Boehme insists that God did not create in order to perfect himself. This leads to a further, deeper question. Boehme makes it clear that nature is an expression of the Being of God, in the sense that the basic principles informing nature are analogous to the aspects of God's Being. But if nature is an expression of God's Being, what is God apart from this expression? The unexpressed God would seem to be inchoate, merely potential. In short, incomplete and imperfect.

Boehme's first step in addressing these problems looks typically kabbalistic: He distinguishes between God as he is in himself and God as he appears to us, or God manifest. "God as he is in himself" Boehme calls *Ungrund*. Literally, this means "Unground" or "Not-ground." Sometimes it has been translated as "Abyss." Like the *Ein Sof* of the kabbalists, Ungrund is completely without

---

[14] *Aurora*, ii. 16.
[15] *Antistifelius*, ii. 316
[16] *Signatura Rerum* (*SR*), xvi. 1.

form or determination of any kind. *Grund* immediately calls to mind "ground of being," and this is precisely what we expect God to be. But Boehme's choice of *Ungrund* warns us not to predicate even something this indefinite of God.

Indeed, Ungrund is not a being at all. In *Mysterium Magnum* (1623), Boehme tells us, "In his essence [*Wesen*] God is not an essence [*Wesen*]."[17] The German *Wesen* can be translated as "essence" or as "being." Hence, Boehme may be understood here as saying "God in his essence is not a being" (or, "God in his Being is not *a* being"). In other words, as he is in himself God *is not*. In the same text Boehme states, "in the dark nature [within the Ungrund] he is not called God."[18] But how can the supreme being not be a being? How can God not be God? The answer to these riddles is to be found, again, in *Mysterium Magnum*. Just after telling us that "God in his essence is not a being," Boehme writes that God as Ungrund is merely "the power or the understanding for being – as an unfathomable, eternal will in which all is contained, but the same all is only one, and desires to reveal itself."[19] Boehme tells us elsewhere that God "hungers after and covets being [*Wesen*]."[20]

The only Being that God possesses as Ungrund is *becoming*: a pure potentiality for becoming a being (i.e., a thing or substance). As Ungrund, God therefore hovers strangely between Being and not-Being. We cannot say, for example, that God as Ungrund "is" in the sense of "existing" in some primitive sense, for "to exist" literally means to stand forth, emerge, become manifest. But God as Ungrund has not done any of that yet. We are faced with what appears to be an unfathomable mystery: Ungrund, as the primal essence of God and the ground/not-ground of all, is and is not. Boehme says of God "in himself," as Ungrund, "he is nothing and all."[21] While the Ungrund is utterly indeterminate, it contains (potentially) all determinations; it is non-Being, and potentially Being and all beings.

The will to manifest, to become present, can only express itself from a prior condition of concealment or absence. Boehme calls this darkness (*Finsternis*), whereas the will to manifest is light (*Licht*). But the darkness is not simply a state of concealment, it is an opposing will or tendency toward hiddenness. There are thus two conflicting wills within God. Boehme also uses the language of "contraction" and "expansion" to describe these wills,

---

[17] *Mysterium Magnum* (*MM*), vi. 1.
[18] *MM*, vii. 14.
[19] *MM*, vi. 1.
[20] *Six Theosophic Points* (*STP*), i. 27.
[21] *On the Election of Grace*, i. 3.

and "indrawing" and "outgoing." The dark will is contraction: God draws into himself, unconscious and refusing manifestation. This is the "negative moment" within God, and it is also obvious that Boehme is describing the psychology of radical selfishness.

What is remarkable here is the idea of negativity within God. For Boehme, God subsumes not just the negative, but *absolute negativity*: the primal will to close, withdraw, refuse. But, as Pierre Deghaye writes, "Darkness means suffering."[22] God suffers in the dark aspect, as do all beings that are dominated by this quality of selfish, indrawing negativity. But this is a necessary moment in God, and in any being: Beings – of whatever kind – are only individual and substantial by virtue of possessing a "will" to separateness and coherency (i.e., "contraction"). Something is an individual being only in virtue of possessing some aspect, which can change from moment to moment, of hiddenness or absence, out of which it manifests or gives itself. Thus, "closing" or contraction (darkness) is matched by "opening" or expansion (light).

But how does God turn from the darkness to the light? How is this transition made? Through trial by *fire*. After all, how can there be light without fire? "Fire is the origin of light," Boehme says.[23] This brings us to another aspect of selfish will not touched on earlier: anger. Since Boehme's methodology is to argue by analogy from human psychology to theology, we must consider the relation of selfishness and anger in an individual human soul. Very often we find that part of the negative psychology of selfishness is a destructive wrath directed at whatever is not the self, at otherness. Indeed, the desire to harm or destroy that which is other simply because it is other is the essence of evil. And, yes, the "absolute negativity" described above as a moment intrinsic to God is, indeed, evil.

Thus, for Boehme, the indrawing, dark will kindles a fire within God, and this fire is God's wrath or anger (*Grimm, Zorn*). But just as light emerges from fire, so can love emerge from wrath. In human psychology, this happens when the nihilating wrath that follows the anguish of extreme, solipsistic selfishness essentially exhausts itself. What must occur in God for him to become God, and what can occur in a human soul, is an exhaustion of selfish will, leading to a kind of surrender to the light. The light, again, represents an outgoing will to manifest, to "give oneself." This surrender is the birth of love (*Liebe*) within God, but it is also a kind of death.

---

[22] Pierre Deghaye, "Jacob Boehme and His Followers," in *Modern Esoteric Spirituality*, ed. Antoine Faivre and Jacob Needleman (New York: Crossroad, 1995), 219.
[23] *MM*, xxvi. 27.

So far we have discussed two of Boehme's "three principles," darkness and light (although as should now be clear, he has multiple ways of describing them). We have seen that these principles conflict with each other, but that this conflict is necessary and ultimately results in a kind of reconciliation. The third principle, in fact, just is the reconciliation of the first two. Deghaye refers to the "perpetual alternation" of light and darkness as itself constituting the third principle, which is also "our universe."[24] Nature as a whole is to be understood as "attunement" or equilibrium of the two opposing principles. But these three principles are also present in every individual being. If Boehme believes that the Being of God involves his expressing himself in the created world, in an other, this is only possible if the other truly is *other*. As I have said, this is only possible if it is characterized, at the deepest level, by self-will, by the desire to exist for itself. Thus, the dark principle is inherent in the Being of beings; the root of self-will, and the evil that inevitably springs from it, are necessary to existence, and to the self-actualization of God. If God had created all things so that they *must* turn from darkness to the light, then those things would entirely accord with the light-will of God and would not be truly "other" than him.

In speaking of the third principle as "our universe," we must be cautious, however. For Boehme, the birth of God, or God's manifestation, takes place "prior" to the creation of nature. So that the entire drama I have just described – of the fire kindled in darkness, the surrender to the firelight, and the reconciliation of darkness and light – all takes place *within God*.

When God opens to the desire to "give himself," to manifest, he first produces the virgin *Sophia* (Wisdom). Boehme speaks of her as a mirror in which God beholds himself. However, we must be careful in speaking of Sophia as an "image" of God. Faivre points out that "in this period *Bild* meant not only 'image,' but also 'body'" – and he notes that Boehme even employs "image" and "substance" (or being, *Wesen*) interchangeably.[25] Sophia, as the image of God in which he beholds himself, is not an imitation or copy. Instead, she is an *imago*, a mature expression of the Being of God.

A mirror is a means of seeing oneself, and Boehme's treatment of Sophia appears to be a mythic way of speaking about God's self-knowledge. The moment of surrender or self-giving in God paves the way to his self-awareness. The divine surrender is a kind of emptying of all that was contracted and compacted within God as the dark nature. What was within

---

[24] Deghaye, "Jacob Boehme and His Followers," 227.
[25] Faivre, *Theosophy, Imagination, Tradition*, 139.

God was, in fact, *all* – or the potential for all. (Remember: "he is nothing and all.") The potential is always the absent, the hidden, the latent; the actualization of potential is the manifest, the present. For Boehme, it is as if the light produced from the fire in the dark nature (which he refers to as a "dark fire") illuminates the hidden potencies of God.

What God "sees" in Sophia, Boehme's hypostasis of the divine self-knowledge, is the ideas of everything that he can create. These ideas are specifications of his own being, and they are the first stage in creation. Thus, Sophia is consubstantial with God. And this means that if Sophia is the receptacle of the forms of creation, then created nature is a concrete manifestation of God: God come to presence as physical reality. Again, we need to avoid thinking of this as a temporal sequence. But if we are consistent in resisting the temptation to take Boehme's mythic language literally (more consistent, perhaps, than he was), then we must concede that there is no "creation" in the conventional sense at all. Instead, the "act" of creation is really just nature itself: nature understood as the Greeks conceived it, as *phusis*, as a living, growing *process*, rather than simply as a collection of objects (which is the sense conveyed by the Latin *natura*).[26]

The formation of nature out of the *logoi* in Sophia *just is* the process by which each thing "grows toward" its ideal image – and remember that *Bild* (image) is *Wesen* (being). The ideal is manifest in and through the real, spirit through matter. This manifestation is not the process by which the divine produces an image of itself, in the sense of a mere "appearance" issuing from a contrasting "reality." Rather, it is the process by which God emerges from himself, out of concealment, in an eternal recurrence.

Now, the foregoing account has emphasized the emergence of God within the Ungrund in terms of Boehme's three principles. Again, he tells us that these three are present in all of reality: in God and creation. Unsurprisingly, Boehme attempts to identify them with the Christian Trinity, and also with the trinity of elements in Paracelsus: Salt, Sulphur, and Mercury. What remains to be discussed, however, is Boehme's septenary account of God and creation: that of the seven "source spirits" (*Quellgeister*). He also refers to these as "qualities" (*Qualitäten*). The relation between the three principles and the seven qualities has puzzled countless readers. I will attempt to shed some light on these matters in the next section.

---

[26] On *phusis*, see Martin Heidegger, *Introduction to Metaphysics*, trans. Gregory Fried and Richard Polt (New Haven: Yale University Press, 2000), 15–16.

Jacob Boehme and Christian Theosophy   195

## 4 The Seven Source Spirits

Over time, Boehme's attempt to express the inexpressible evolved, just as he believed the inexpressible itself evolves. Thus, we find that he gives multiple formulations of his system of seven qualities. The account that follows is an attempt to amalgamate these.

Boehme makes some points about the seven that never vary. For example, he tells us not just that the seven qualities are interrelated, he speaks of each as "contained" within the others. And in *Aurora* he writes:

> These seven births [*Gebärungen*] in all are none of them the first, second, third, and last; but they are all seven each the first, second, third, fourth, and last. But I must set them down one after the other in a creaturely [*kreatürlicher*] way and manner, otherwise you would not understand it. For the Deity [*Gottheit*] is a wheel [*Rad*] with seven wheels made in one another, wherein one sees neither beginning nor end.[27]

Boehme is suggesting that each of the qualities is an inseparable aspect of what is really an organic whole. Thus, each quality implies the others, and each is what it is only in its relation to the others. Once more, Boehme wants us to understand that he is attempting to express in a piecemeal fashion what is actually One, and is experienced by the mystic *all at once*.

The *First Quality* is Sour or Astringency (*Herb*, or *Herbigkeit*). This is the "darkness" spoken of earlier: the moment in which God contracts himself. It is the "indrawing" that is the foundation of bodily being.

The *Second Quality* is Sweet (*Süss*), the expanding, opening, light force that stands opposed to the dark force of the Sour.

The *Third Quality* is Bitter (*Bitter*), arising from the conflict between the first two. They cannot separate from each other, so these opposing forces coalesce to form a kind of vortex: "They remain in each other as a turning wheel."[28] From this turmoil results a terrible anguish within God, which is a kind of friction. And where there is friction, heat results.

The *Fourth Quality* is *Schrack*, a term discussed earlier. Boehme also calls it lightning (*Blitz*) and heat (*Hitze*; although Boehme may mean this as merely the prelude to the fourth quality: anguish → heat → flash). The Flash is literally central to Boehme's account, flanked by the two triads of qualities 1–3 and 5–7. And it is thus appropriate that he also identifies it with the sun, and with the heart (a traditional alchemical correspondence).[29] In

---
[27] *Aurora*, xxiii. 18, and especially xiii. 71.
[28] *MM*, iii. 15.
[29] See *SR*, iv. 39.

the human soul, the anguished struggle with self-will produces the Flash: a spiritual turning point, a radical surrender that is the birth of Christ in the soul. In *Six Theosophical Points* (1620), Boehme observes that the same process occurs in nature, when things grow and blossom, surrendering themselves in manifestation to the power of the sun.[30] In God, Flash represents an analogous surrender to manifestation. It is in the central sun of the fourth quality that the dark fire becomes a light fire. What had been the energy of anguish "gives up" and releases itself as the bright light of divine manifestation – all in a flash.

The heart-centered, sunlike blaze of self-surrender and "going outwards," ignited by the Flash, just is Love, the *Fifth Quality*. Readers will have noted that there is a structural correspondence between the first, second, and third qualities and Boehme's three principles. Indeed, the three principles provide a kind of template of the dialectic that plays out in the sequence of seven qualities. This template can be expressed as "denying → affirming → reconciling." It repeats itself in qualities 5 through 7, such that 5–7 can be seen as the "reverse" of 1–3. While qualities 1, 2, and 3 map on to principles 1, 2, and 3, in that order, with qualities 5–7 the reverse is the case: Qualities 5, 6, and 7 "express," respectively, principles 3, 2, and 1. The correspondences among the six qualities (excluding number 4, which has nothing to be paired with) are thus as follows: 1/7, 2/6, 3/5. Boehme makes this explicit in *Clavis* – and states that 1/7 is God the Father, 2/6 is the Son, and 3/5 is the Holy Spirit.[31]

It is not difficult to see how the fifth quality is the inversion of the third: It is the dark fire become light fire. While Bitter "reconciles" Sour and Sweet, it does so in a unity of suffering. Via the central Flash, the true reconciliation is achieved in Love. God remains a being unto himself (the Sour is here subsumed as moment), but at the same time he opens outward in the literal externalization of otherness. This is the actualization of the inner potential of God that had remained concealed within the dark quality.

The *Sixth Quality* is Sound (*Ton, Schall*). This is the expression of the preceding spirits, which are all united in Love. In *Signatura Rerum*, Boehme tells us that the seven qualities are repeated throughout all existence in the form of "signatures." These are the "external form of all creatures," and he calls them the "sound, voice, and speech which they utter."[32]

Sound is thus the expression of God's Love through the generation of all forms of nature, each of which is a signature of God himself. Sound is thus

---

[30] *STP*, v. 3–4.
[31] See *Clavis*, ix. 75.
[32] *SR*, i. 14.

equivalent to the *logos* (here in the sense not just of reason or form, but of speech) and thus to Sophia. Just as in its sound a being expresses its essence, so God's sound or voice is an expression of his Being: "And God said, Let there be light." But the sixth quality is merely the "speaking" of God's will to manifest. Again, Boehme links the sixth quality with the second. Like Sweet, Sound is affirming, opening, or "outgoing." However, it is differentiated or specified into a multiplicity of essences or signatures, each of which is an "opening," or form of manifestation.

Manifestation is finally concretized with the *Seventh Quality*, Body (*Leib, Corpus*; Boehme also calls it *Wesen*). Qualities 1–6 are "contained" in the seventh. This means that the seventh is a whole, and 1–6 are the inseparable moments of that whole. When all six "combine" the seventh is "produced": Body comes into being; God achieves corporeal expression in nature. Just how these six are the "formula" for corporality is very obscure. Two things, however, are clear. First, if Boehme means that all beings possess this sevenfold structure, then all beings have both light and dark, hidden and manifest aspects. Indeed, in *Clavis* Boehme characterizes 1–3 as the "dark world," 5–7 as the "light world," and the fourth quality as the "fire world." This means that the three principles I have characterized as "denying → affirming → reconciling" are expressed not just within each of the two triads of spirits (1–3, 5–7) but also in the whole of the sevenfold system. The "middle" spirit, the Flash ("fire world"), is the "reconciling" element in the whole.

It is particularly important to bear in mind Boehme's claim that Body is "one" with the first quality, Sour. Recall that this was the quality of indrawing and self-will. In the alchemical Opus that is God's creation of nature (or, the self-creation of God – it comes to the same thing), the spirits must "compact" themselves to form a body. I remarked earlier that if God's *telos* is to express himself in something that is truly other, then God as Spirit must express himself as body. But everything that is a discrete, individual body is a particular expression of self-will, of the desire to exist for itself. (This is literally true in the case of living things; figuratively true in the case of non-living things.) Thus, the seventh quality "returns to" the first (recall Boehme's image of the wheel). But, to use a German term pregnant with significance, the Sour is *aufgehoben* – canceled, but taken up and preserved. The lowest element within Being – negativity or evil itself – is necessary for the becoming of God and nature, for all that is. Sour is the *prima materia* with which the Opus begins. The result is the Philosopher's Stone: nature itself, the visible expression of the Being of God.

## 5 The Vocation of Man

As we have seen, God is characterized fundamentally by the will to manifest himself – and to manifest himself *to* himself. Boehme maintains that this will is absolutely free, given that there is nothing else to limit it. At the same time, of course, this absolutely free will is at first impotent, just because there is nothing on which it might act – except itself. For Boehme, the expression of God's freedom is in willing his own determination: in moving, in effect, from Ungrund to Grund, to foundation in determinate, individual, bodily being.

However, this can occur only if God expresses himself as a being who may freely choose either to empty his individuality to God or to consciously cling to self-will. Only such a being is truly independent; truly an other to God. Thus, the highest expression of bodily being is that which has the greatest capacity for evil. The worldly manifestation of God can only be fully realized in an individual who freely chooses, in full consciousness, to turn from darkness to light. This, of course, is man: the determinate realization of the inchoate freedom within the indeterminate Ungrund.

For Boehme, Adam (man) is God's replacement for Lucifer, who fell because he wished to be not merely an embodiment of the whole, but the whole itself. Like the fallen angel, man is a perfect microcosm of the whole.[33] In the Garden, Adam possessed the wisdom of God: knowledge of the primordial forms of all things contained within God's great mirror, Sophia. However, Adam possessed this knowledge without consciousness; that is, he did not know that he knew it. And in so far as he remained in this state, Adam could not be an adequate *imago* of God. The divine agent who brings an end to Adam's naïveté is Lucifer, in the form of the serpent. Adam and Eve then eat of the forbidden Tree of the Knowledge of Good and Evil, which represents consciousness of duality or opposition.

The fall of man is the transition from divine – but unconscious – perception of the whole, of the One, to a perception of the multiplicity of things in their separation and division. For Boehme, his vision of 1600 was a momentary recovery of the original standpoint of Adam. When he attempted to express what he had glimpsed in that vision, he could only do so, as he often states, in a piecemeal form, expressing what is One in the form of three or seven. This is a reflection of Adam's fallen state, and Boehme is a child of Adam. Yet in continuously reflecting upon the wisdom of God, Boehme moves toward the very thing Adam lacked: conscious possession of that wisdom. It is thus

---

[33] See *MM*, ii. 5.

only by way of the fall that man can come into possession of theosophy, and God finds a truly adequate incarnation.

Speaking of incarnation, at this point readers may wonder where Christ is in all of this. Boehme states that mere faith that Christ died for our sins is not enough for man's salvation (after all, he says perceptively, "the devil knows this also"[34]). Rather, we must make possible the birth of Christ within ourselves.[35] Christ was a man born of the Virgin, and in Boehme's eyes this means consubstantial with Sophia. And this man died so that we might be born again. Like Christ, we too must die to ourselves, and for ourselves, in order to come to union with Sophia and receive the wisdom of God.

The unconscious darkness, the sleep of self-will, must die in us so that the soul may be awakened. Just as God must die to his dark will before he is born, so man must die to the same dark will in order that he might be born again, in Christ.[36] As is the case with many of the German mystics, Boehme intimates that the birth of Christ in the soul is man becoming Christ, becoming God incarnate. However, salvation is not a permanent condition that, once reached, man simply rests in without further effort. Instead, Boehme portrays man's awakening as a perpetual struggle. And this should come as no surprise to us, as we have seen that for Boehme struggle is written into the very nature of Being itself. As Walsh observes, "The function of Christ [according to Boehme] is no longer simply that of atonement by making reparation for man to God; it now includes the revelation of man's rightful spiritual place in union with the virgin Sophia in whom all things are contained."[37]

For Boehme, salvation no longer consists in mere belief in Christ; salvation is in *becoming wise*. But this salvation is simultaneously the salvation, and realization, of God himself. God begins in absolute concealment and unconsciousness, then manifests. The final, consummating fruit of this manifestation is man, who struggles to "wake up," who becomes aware of himself and of the whole as a reflection of himself. But this just is God's awakening, God's self-knowledge.[38] In man, the unconsciousness of the Ungrund is finally overcome, and God as self-conscious spirit is born in the world.

---

[34] *MM*, li. 43.
[35] See *STP*, vii. 45.
[36] See Basarab Nicolescu, *Science, Meaning, and Evolution* (New York: Parabola Books, 1991), 88.
[37] Walsh, *The Mysticism of Innerwordly Fulfillment*, 102.
[38] See Walsh, *The Mysticism of Innerwordly Fulfillment*, 19.

17

# FREEMASONRY

JAN A. M. SNOEK

1 Introduction

Perhaps the best way to characterize Freemasonry is in terms of what it is not, rather than what it is. First of all, it is not a religion, at least not in the Western sense of the concept. One neither converts to Freemasonry, nor does it have any teachings or dogmas. If a candidate for Freemasonry belongs to a religion, this does not change when he becomes a Freemason. Moreover, the Masonic "work" consists in the initiation rituals that change the status of the candidate, first from an outsider to an Apprentice Freemason, then to a Fellow of the Craft, and finally to the rank of Master Mason. Different systems of so-called "higher degrees," developed in the course of the centuries, offer still more initiation rituals. Although the rituals have changed in the course of time (and in different ways in different countries, producing varying traditions throughout the world), they are guarded as precious treasures, handed down from generation to generation.

However, there exists no official interpretation of the rituals which is held to be universally valid. Every member has the right – and, indeed, the duty – to interpret them in his own way. Consequently, Freemasonry has no particular intrinsic aim. All it aims at is the initiation of new members – on the one hand because it would disappear if it acquired no new members, but much more importantly because Freemasonry simply *is* the practice of these rituals, which are no longer truly secret. Today one can find most of them on the Internet, including the so-called traditional secrets: the words, signs, and hand grips by which the members of a particular degree can recognize one another. The only secret – which will always remain, because it cannot be divulged – is what it is like to experience these rituals as a candidate. Freemasonry, then, is first and foremost a method for inducing a particular kind of experience in candidates. Two methods, in fact, are involved: the initiation method and the allusive method. Three sorts of symbolism also play a role: building symbolism, light symbolism, and center symbolism.

The initiation method involves the use of rituals that belong to the larger class of "rites of passage," which all have three stages: separation, transition, and incorporation.[1] The candidate is first separated from his former status, which puts him in a liminal state in which he has no status at all. After this, a new status is conferred on him. In initiation rituals, these stages are usually symbolically expressed as a process of dying, abiding temporarily in the metaphysical world, and finally being reborn in a new state. Such rituals are known in almost all cultures.

The allusive method is similar to the symbolic approach, but it uses texts instead of images.[2] Within a text, for example that of a ritual, words from one or more sources (the referential corpus) are quoted, but in such a way that someone who does not know the source will not recognize that something is quoted. However, if one knows the referential corpus well, one will recognize it at once. The text quoted is in its turn in some way linked to one or more further texts. For example, if the Bible is used as the referential corpus – as is often the case in Masonic rituals – the footnotes, which have been standardized since the Middle Ages, link certain verses, sometimes in chains of considerable length. If the text pronounced in a Masonic ritual is "[This] blazing star ... goes before us like that Pillar of fire that blazed to guide the people in the desert,"[3] one should not only recognize this as quoting Exodus 13:21–22 but also see the further links to Isaiah 4:5–6, from there to Matthew 2:1–12 and Luke 2:1–20, and from there to Revelation 22:16. None of these biblical passages represents the true meaning of the ritual text, but each one of them may add significance to it, if the person hearing it recognizes the link. It thus may also add a specifically Christian meaning (for someone to whom that would be meaningful) to a text quoted from the Old Testament, without forcing such an interpretation on, for example, a Jewish member.

The most central symbol in Freemasonry is the Temple of Solomon, the building of which is described in 1 Kings 5–9 and 2 Chronicles 2–7. On the one hand, the Bible contains allusive links to other building stories, making it a symbol for, among others, the World (Genesis 1, since the architect of both

---

[1] See Arnold Van Gennep, *Les Rites de Passage* (Paris: Nourry, 1909). English translation by M. B. Vizedom and G. L. Caffee, *The Rites of Passage* (Chicago: University of Chicago Press, 1960).

[2] See Joannes A. M. Snoek, "De allusieve methode / The Allusive Method / La méthode allusive," *Acta Macionica* 9 (1999), 47–70.

[3] Quote from Thomas Wolson [= George Smith], *Le Maçon Démasqué*, 1751, in *The Early French Exposures*, ed. Harry Carr (London: The Quatuor Coronati Lodge, 1971), 442.

is God) and the body of Christ.[4] This Temple, symbolizing the World, is regarded as still incomplete, thus demanding from everyone that he contribute to its completion.

In light symbolism, the opposition between light and darkness is used to represent a number of similar oppositions besides light-darkness: good-bad, happiness-sorrow, and so on. Furthermore, the natural sources of light, the heavenly bodies, all move across the sky from east to west, which makes the East the symbol of the source of light. Since God is supposed to be the source of light, God is also supposed to reside in the East. This symbolism is found, for example, in the symbolic orientation of the lodge room: the Master, representing God (referred to as the Great Architect of the Universe), sits in the East. This is claimed to be so, regardless of the real orientation of the room used. Apprentices and Fellow Crafts are said to travel from the West to the East to search for the Light, whereas Masters travel from the East to the West to spread the Light to the World.

In center symbolism, it is the Center, not the East, that is the place where God resides. The center of the lodge room is marked by a drawing of symbols on the floor, referred to as the Tracing Board. In the eighteenth century, the Master sat directly at the east side of the Tracing Board, combining his position in the East with one in the Center. The candidate "travels" around the Center. Each of these five components of the Masonic method can be found outside Freemasonry, but when all five are found together, one can be rather sure that one is dealing with either Freemasonry proper, or something derived from it.

So far we have seen two of the main roots of Freemasonry: the Christian tradition (the Bible used as referential corpus of the allusive method and initiation rituals) and the stone mason's craft (building symbolism). The third root is Western esotericism, of which many traces can be found in the rituals. For example, the Christian kabbalistic theme of the conversion of the Tetragrammaton of the Old Testament (JHVH) into the Tetragrammaton of the New Testament (INRI) forms a red thread running through many degrees from the first three onward. The perfect stone, which one must become in order to be built into the Temple, was in the British rituals called a "perfect ashlar." It was also understood as the "key stone," referring to both the cornerstone of the temple and the keystone of a vault under the temple. In the eighteenth-century French rituals, this stone was called a "cube," even though one cannot build a building from cubic stones. The reference, no doubt, was to the cube as it occurs in the seventeenth-century emblem

---

[4] See respectively 1 Chronicles 28:19 and John 2:19–21.

books, where it clearly represents the alchemical Philosopher's Stone. Rosicrucianism provided Freemasonry with the concepts of an initiatory brotherhood and of a secret of great value, which must be searched for and kept secret from outsiders. In the end, in Freemasonry this secret is no more than the experience of the initiation rituals, something that cannot be disclosed by any means other than initiation itself.

2 The British Formative Period

Freemasonry has no founder or founding date, and no canonical form. Indeed, around 1600, the time when it can be identified with certainty, at least two distinct forms existed, one in Scotland and one in England. A century and a half later, an Irish form is also present, while in England at least three forms coexisted. Therefore, right from the point it can first be identified by historians, there never was one Freemasonry, but instead a variety of Freemasonries.

The number of theories about the origins of Freemasonry runs into the dozens. Probably the most famous is the thesis first formulated by Robert Freke Gould and his friends in the 1880s. According to this theory, at first there were simple "operative" stonemasons, who had their craft and their lodges but did not "speculate" about their craft or their working tools (i.e., they did not interpret them symbolically). Then, at the beginning of the eighteenth century, more and more "gentlemen masons" became members of the lodges. These men introduced the speculative element, out of which arose modern "speculative" Freemasonry. This theory was regarded as fact for about a century, but we know now that it is wrong. First, Freemasonry significantly predates 1717. Second, the early Freemasons were all but simple folk. The term "Freemason," short for "Freestone Mason," refers to the highest trained members of the craft, the sculptors and architects, who were allowed to work with freestone, the most expensive material. Third, it is also clear now that these freestone masons did speculate about their craft, its tools, and so on. Thus, Freemasonry was speculative right from the start – and that explains precisely why gentlemen masons were interested in it in the first place. They did not introduce the speculative element; rather, they learned it from the stonemasons. Consequently, we should no longer oppose speculative to operative masons, but rather gentlemen masons to stone masons, all of whom were speculative masons, while the latter group was also "operative."

The oldest Masonic documents are the "Old Manuscript Constitutions." Among the oldest are the "Constitutions of the Masons of York" (1352, 1370, 1409), the *Ordonnances des masons de Londres* (1356), the "Constitutions of the Carpenters Guild of Norwich" (1375), the "Regius MS" and the "Cooke MS" (both from between 1425 and 1450), and the *Constituciones artis geometricae secundum Euclidem* (fifteenth century). From 1583 onward, there are more than a hundred. Most of them are English and date from between 1675 and 1725. Especially these later ones often state that they should be read during the "acception" of a candidate. This shows that these were related to the English "acception" (see below), but we do not really know much of the context of the older ones, except that they served to defend the claims of the Freestone Masons on high-level wages.

In 1598 and 1599, William Schaw, the King's Master of Works and General Warden of the Craft, signed new statutes for the lodges of the Masons in Scotland. From the information these texts give, there can be no doubt that these are Masonic lodges, more or less in the modern sense. In the statutes of 1599, Schaw confirmed that the lodge of Edinburgh was the oldest. The lodge of Kilwinning, however, did not agree. It took some years before a successor to Schaw decided that both would receive the status "time immemorial," meaning that no one living could remember a time when the two did not exist. Thus, we must assume that at least these two lodges existed around the middle of the sixteenth century, but possibly earlier.

The archives of the Mason's Company of London go back quite some time. After a gap, they continue from 1619 onward. Almost at once there now occur terms that did not appear before the gap: "the making of Masons" (1621), Masons are "accepted" (1630), and the acception (1645–1647, 1649–1650). There is no reason to assume that the acception was an invention of 1621 only; rather, it had probably been around for some time. In 1646, Elias Ashmole wrote in his diary: "I was made a Free Mason at Warrington in Lancashire." And in 1682 he noted: "I rec[eive]d a Sumons to appe[ar] at a Lodge to be held the next day, at Masons Hall London. . ... I was the Senior Fellow among them (it being 35 years since I was admitted)." All the members mentioned in Ashmole's first entry were senior members of the Mason's Company of London, as well as members of the acception. And from the lodge mentioned in the second entry, we now know that there is a continuous link to the four lodges that James Anderson (in the second edition of his *Constitutions* of 1738) claims to have united in 1716, forming the beginning of the development leading to the "Premier Grand Lodge."

In 1666, workmen from the building trade came to London to begin reconstruction after a great fire destroyed the central parts of the city. Some of them joined the London lodges, which flourished as a result. At the end of 1714, building activity in London came to an end, as no money was left to support it. The workmen departed, leaving the lodges of London with only a few members. According to Anderson's *Constitutions* of 1738, Sir Christopher Wren had been elected Grand Master in 1685. However, in 1716 the lodges in London found "themselves neglected by Sir Christopher Wren." Anderson's complaint is not surprising, if we remember that in 1716 Wren was 84 years old. Still, the lodges believed they had to assemble to discuss their problems. Set against this background, Anderson's story of what happened in 1716 and 1717 makes eminent sense:

> [Four London lodges] and some old Brothers met at the Apple-Tree [Tavern], and having put into the Chair the oldest Master Mason [present] ([making him for that evening what we would] now [call] the Master of a Lodge) they constituted themselves a Grand Lodge pro Tempore in Due Form, and forthwith revived the Quarterly Communication of the Officers of Lodges ([which Quarterly Communications are also sometimes] call'd the Grand Lodge) [and] resolv'd to hold the Annual Assembly and Feast, and then [i.e., at that next Annual Assembly] to chuse a [new] Grand Master from among themselves.[5]

According to Anderson's report (the only account of the event that we have), what happened on St. Johns Day (June 24) in 1717 was definitely not the foundation of a new organization, but simply the continuation of an old one. There can be little doubt that in the decade following this event, the Grand Lodge was reorganized into a form that had not existed in London before. First, it became completely independent from the London Company of Masons. Second, it considerably modified and simplified its ceremonial practice to adapt it to its new, less educated target group, the gentlemen masons. However, there was no significant discontinuity between the Quarterly Communications before and after 1716, apart from the gap caused by Wren's inactivity.

According to Anderson, it was on St. John's Day 1717 that the aforementioned London lodges met and chose Anthony Sayer as their new Grand Master for 1717/18. Soon, the most important and influential members would become John Theophilus Desaguliers, James Anderson, and George Payne. Anderson was a minister of the Church of Scotland. Desaguliers was a minister of the Church of England, assistant to Isaac Newton, and a member of the Royal Society. After Sayer, Payne and Desaguliers became Grand Masters in three successive years during the formative period. In 1721, the

---

[5] James Anderson, *The New Book of Constitutions of the Antient and Honourable Fraternity of Free and Accepted Masons* (London, 1738), 109.

Duke of Montague became the first aristocratic Grand Master. From that point on, all further Grand Masters were aristocrats.

At the end of the seventeenth and the beginning of the eighteenth centuries, the Scottish and English forms of Freemasonry seem to have discovered and influenced each other. As a result, whereas previously they seem to have had only one initiation degree each, there now developed a two-degree system, which we find referenced in Anderson's *Constitutions* of 1723. The acception of London origin had now become the first degree, which the Scotsman Anderson called "Entered Apprentice," whereas the Scottish "Master Mason or Fellow in the Craft" became the second degree, now called "Fellow Craft or Master Mason." In London around 1725, the contents of these two degrees were redistributed over three degrees, now called "Entered Apprentice" (containing part of the old first degree), "Fellow of the Craft" (containing the rest of the old first degree), and "Master Mason" (containing the old second degree). Only one thing could persuade the lodges to work with the new three-grade system: In 1730, its rituals were published as Samuel Prichard's *Masonry Dissected.*

In 1723/24, the Grand Lodge of Ireland was formed; in 1736, the Grand Lodge of Scotland followed. In 1725, the old lodge in the City of York formed itself into the Grand Lodge of All England. When a conflict arose within William Preston's Lodge of Antiquity, the Grand Lodge (the "Moderns") expelled it. In 1779, Preston founded the Grand Lodge of England, South of the River Trent, on a warrant by the York-based Grand Lodge. Within this Grand Lodge, Preston created in 1787 the Ancient and Venerable Order of Harodim. It has now become clear that this Harodim/York tradition of English Freemasonry is the source of most English high degrees, as well as the Royal Order of Scotland and the Adoption Rite.

In the eighteenth century, large numbers of Irish day laborers lived in London. Because of their low social status, they were often not admitted into the lodges of the Premier Grand Lodge. If they were, they must often have been quite surprised at the rituals that took place there. From the 1730s onward, they began forming lodges of their own, which from 1750 to 1752 united in a separate English Grand Lodge, referring to itself as that of the "Antients." Of course, their lodges too needed printed rituals, and thus exposures of these were published in the 1760s. The two most important ones were *Three Distinct Knocks* of 1760 and *Jachin and Boas* of 1762.

After more than half a century of rivalry between the Moderns and the Antients, an attempt was made to merge these two English Grand Lodges. In 1813, they merged into the United Grand Lodge of England and Wales with the Duke of Sussex as Grand Master. The Lodge of Reconciliation was formed to effectuate the merger. In the process, it created new rituals for the United Grand Lodge, which were first published in 1825.

## 3 Freemasonry Conquers the World

In 1720/21, there existed an unofficial lodge in Rotterdam, composed of British Freemasons. However, the spreading of Freemasonry to the Continent and the rest of the world really started after 1725. Lodges were founded in Paris in 1726, Mannheim in 1727 (?), Madrid in 1728, Gibraltar and Bengal in 1729, The Hague in 1734, among many others. Next, other colonial powers, such as France and the Netherlands, started founding lodges in their colonies as well. From 1732 onward, lodges were attached to military regiments.

In 1717, the French concluded an alliance with England. Soon after, everything English became in vogue in France – including Freemasonry. The first lodges in Paris, founded from 1726 onward, were Jacobite ones, probably working within the Harodim tradition. From 1729, however, Hanoverian lodges, working in the tradition of the Moderns, were founded. The first Grand Masters of the French Grand Lodge were British Jacobites. (It was not until 1738 that the first French Grand Master was elected.) The Masons were soon under police investigation, on the orders of the king. In 1737, the police official Hérault succeeded in obtaining a copy of a ritual used by one of the Paris lodges. He published it on December 5 of that year. The following year it was reprinted, together with other materials, as part of a volume titled *La Réception Mystérieuse*.

However, with Freemasonry becoming ever more popular in France, better printed rituals were required. As a result, in 1744 no less than four exposures were published. *Le Secret des Francs-Maçons* by the Abbé Perau gave the rituals for the first two degrees of the tradition of the Moderns, while *Le Catéchisme des Francs-Maçons* by Louis Travenol (writing under the name Leonard Gabanon) added the third degree. Both established a new style of presentation – narrative rather than catechetic – adding much more detail about the rituals than older accounts had contained. The rituals presented in *La Franc-Maçonne* do not seem related to any known Masonic tradition, and it tells the story of the initiation of women in Adoption lodges. *Le Parfait Maçon* presents rituals of the first four degrees of the tradition of the Harodim. In 1745, *Le Sceau Rompu* gave a number of corrections to *Le Secret* and *Le Catéchisme*, after which *L'Ordre des Francs-Maçons Trahi* merged all three into one. Therewith, the French version of the rituals of the Moderns was established, and it was this form that now spread rapidly over the whole of the

European continent, almost completely replacing whatever traditions might have been in place in lodges founded earlier.

The first Masonic knightly order, the *Ordre Sublime des Chevaliers Élus*, was founded in France in 1730 (or shortly after). Around the same time, the first Scots Masons Lodges appeared in England. The Italian painter Jacopo Fabris was initiated into one of them. In 1742, Fabris in his turn founded the Scots Masters lodge L'Union in Berlin. From there, this degree of Scots Master (probably of Harodim origin) spread over the Continent. Soon new degrees were created, especially in France, England (Harodim tradition), and Germany. These degrees were at first mainly practiced in normal lodges, but soon separate bodies (Scots lodges, chapters, etc.) were formed that accumulated a number of these, now called "high degrees" and usually ordered them into a system, or "Rite." Examples of these are the Strict Observance (1751/63–1782, Germany), the Swedish Rite (1756/59, Sweden), the Bavarian Illuminati (1776–1785, Germany), the Rectified Scottish Rite (1778, France), the French or Modern Rite (1786, France), the York Rite (1797, United States), and the Ancient and Accepted Scottish Rite (1801, United States).

In the second half of the eighteenth century, Freemasonry flourished all over the globe. And during this same time, of course, major changes in the Western worldview were underway. In 1789, the French Revolution caused Masonic activity came to a halt in France for ten years. Napoleon then attempted to create a new world order but was defeated in 1815. It is striking to see that in a large number of Western countries, the Masonic rituals were dramatically changed during this period, reflecting a culture that was now predominantly middle class, rather than aristocratic. In Germany, the rituals "Schröder" of 1801 were among the first to reflect this new bourgeois outlook. They were followed by those for the Craft degrees of the Ancient and Accepted Scottish Rite, written in 1804 in Paris. The new rituals for the United Grand Lodge of England, approved in 1816, were marked by a bourgeois moralism that anticipated the Victorian era.

Instead of aiming at inducing a mystical experience in the candidate, the new rituals reflected the conviction that proper moral behavior can be learned simply by the repetitive performance of proper model behavior. For example, in the third degree, the candidate is identified with Hiram Abiff, the architect of the Temple of Solomon, who, according to the Masonic tradition, was murdered shortly before the completion of the work. The eighteenth-century rituals made clear that Hiram was in fact God, so that the candidate experienced a *Unio Mystica*. In the ritual of the Ancient and Accepted Scottish Rite, however, Hiram is reincarnated in the human candidate. In the ritual of the United Grand Lodge of England, Hiram steadfastly refuses to give his murderers the Master's Word, thus showing the model behavior of a man. The Swedish and American rituals escaped this process, at least for a while.

The nineteenth century was the heyday of colonialism, and Freemasonry came to be used as a tool to assimilate conquered peoples to Western culture. Jews had been initiated into lodges from the 1730s onwards, and the first Muslim to be initiated was probably the Persian diplomat Askar Khan Afshar, in Paris in 1808. Both Jews and Muslims knew the most central symbol of Freemasonry, the Temple of Solomon, from their own Holy Scriptures, so that the Masonic ritual could make at least some sense to them. But this was not the case with those of non-Western religious backgrounds. For them, Freemasonry could only mean something if they had assimilated strongly to Western culture. It thus took until the 1840s before the first non-Westerner, a Parsee from India, was initiated. And since Freemasonry is implicitly monotheistic, working "to the Honor of the Grand Architect of the Universe," it took until the 1870s before Hindus were admitted. The majority of the non-Christian members – Jews and Muslims included – seem to have used Freemasonry intentionally as a tool of emancipation, to get recognition from members of the dominant culture with whom they dealt on a daily basis.

## 4 Conclusion: The Social Significance of Freemasonry

During the seventeenth century, the British Isles were almost constantly harassed by civil war over matters both political and religious. By 1720, many intellectual men had had enough. The Masonic lodges were much more interested in the quality of the craftsmanship of their members than in their convictions. Thus, when the lodges reorganized between 1715 and 1725, the gentlemen found them attractive, not in the least because of their intrinsically tolerant attitude. Also, by initiating candidates from different social classes, and adopting the procedure of electing a new Grand Master or a new Master of a lodge, the lodges were in fact experimenting with a form of democracy. As a result, they did promote at least certain aspects of the Enlightenment, although their ritual practice remained at the same time firmly rooted in the Western esoteric tradition.

During the eighteenth and nineteenth centuries, large numbers of "culture bearers" were Freemasons. In the twentieth century, the market for alternative spirituality increased rapidly, while Freemasonry, which had formerly shown a remarkable potential to adapt itself to changing contexts, now predominantly froze into conservatism. Not surprisingly, this resulted in a decline in membership, similar to what happened to the churches. Nevertheless, today several Grand Lodges (such as the Grand Lodge of Women Freemasons in Turkey) are growing. Indeed, because it still advocates tolerance of different political and religious convictions, combined with the possibility of a personal ritual experience of a transcendent dimension of reality, Freemasonry seems far from outmoded.

# 18

# SWEDENBORG AND SWEDENBORGIANISM

## Jane Williams-Hogan

### 1 Introduction

Emanuel Swedenborg (1688–1772) is best known for his theological writings published between 1749 and 1771. The eight-volume *Secrets of Heaven* (1749–1756) was written in Latin and published anonymously in London. According to Swedenborg, this work contained the inner meaning or spiritual sense of Genesis and Exodus and reestablished the link between the spiritual and natural worlds, which he believed had been severely weakened by the decline of the Christian Church.

Revealing these secrets of heaven was Swedenborg's essential mission. He believed that the Lord's *Word*, now unsealed, permitted him to view, as an eyewitness in the spiritual world, the Last Judgment described in Revelation.[1] He recorded these observations in works on *The Last Judgment* (1758 and 1763). In his final work, *True Christianity* (1771), he proclaimed the Second Coming of the Lord Jesus Christ. Swedenborg published a total of eighteen theological titles. Several were multivolume works. *Heaven and Hell* (1758) is perhaps the best known. In *Marriage Love* (1768), he dropped his anonymity for the first time. He signed it "Emanuel Swedenborg, A Swede" and did the same for the remaining three titles he published.

According to Swedenborg's testimony, his call required that he live simultaneously in the spiritual and natural worlds for the last twenty-seven years of his life – an astounding claim. What prepared him for this task, what might possibly lend credence to it, and what has been its impact? I will address each of these questions in turn.

---

[1] Swedenborg referred to the Bible as the Lord's *Word*.

## 2 Swedenborg's Background, Employment, and Philosophical Project

Swedenborg was born on January 29, 1688, in Stockholm. He was the son of Lutheran Bishop Jesper Swedberg (1653–1735) and his wife Sarah Behm Swedberg (1666–1696).[2] His father had a long and illustrious but somewhat controversial career in the church. His mother, who came from a family of iron mine owners, died when he was eight years old. The family moved to Uppsala in 1692, where Swedenborg was raised and attended the university. He graduated in 1709 with a degree in philosophy. His passion, however, was *mathesis* and mechanics. In 1710, he left on a five-year student trip, exploring mathematics and astronomy in England, Holland, and France. He returned in 1715 and launched Sweden's first scientific journal, *Daedalus Hyperboreus* (published 1716–1718). During this period, he worked with Christopher Polhem (1661–1751), the noted Swedish inventor.

In 1716, Swedenborg was appointed an Extraordinary Assessor to the Board of Mines by King Karl XII. The king's death in 1718 delayed his appointment, and Swedenborg was not actually seated on the board until 1724. He worked there diligently until 1747, when he retired to devote himself to his "call." Swedenborg published four philosophical works during this same period: his three-volume, philosophical and metallurgical work *The Principia, Iron,* and *Copper and Brass* (Leipzig and Dresden, 1734); *The Infinite: The Final Cause of Creation* (Leipzig and Dresden, 1734); *The Dynamics of The Soul's Domain* (two volumes, Amsterdam, 1740–1741); and *The Soul's Domain,* (three volumes, The Hague and London, 1744–1745). These works were all part of the same intellectual project, and Swedenborg personally traveled abroad to publish them. Swedenborg began the last work because he was dissatisfied with his first attempt to "show the soul to the very senses."[3] In all these works, he wanted "to demonstrate truths by the analytical method ... [so] an access will be open and a way laid down to faith" for "those who never believe anything but what they can receive with their intellect [reason]."[4]

In Swedenborg's own view, this project failed for two reasons: First, the more he pursued the soul through what he saw as its mirror, the body, the

---

[2] Swedenborg and his siblings were ennobled in 1719 and changed their family name. He will be referred to as Swedenborg throughout this essay.
[3] Emanuel Swedenborg, *The Infinite: The Final Cause of Creation and The Mechanism of the Operation of the Soul and Body* (London: The Swedenborg Society, 1965), 230.
[4] Emanuel Swedenborg, *The Animal Kingdom,* Vol. 1, trans. James John Garth Wilkinson (London: W. Newbery, 1843), 14–15. Reproduced by the Swedenborg Scientific Association, 1960.

farther away it seemed, because the deeper he probed, the greater complexity he found. Nature, the soul's mirror, although profoundly orderly, nonetheless did not reveal its secret. Second, the more Swedenborg searched – even with the advanced analytical principles he had constructed for this purpose – the clearer it became to him that while these principles could indeed shine increasing light on the intricate working of the body, they were not equal to the task of illuminating the soul. Thus, he abandoned this project in 1745.

## 3 Swedenborg's Call and Claim

In addition to the reasons just outlined, Swedenborg also abandoned this course because he believed he had received a "call" to pursue another project, although he was unsure exactly what it involved. He was certain, however, that it was God who was calling. Swedenborg's call came while he was abroad publishing *The Soul's Domain* in The Hague and London (1743–1745). It began in the form of vivid dreams. The dreams started in The Hague in March 1744 and continued after Swedenborg settled in London in May. He wrote in a private journal in October 1744, after months of intense dreams that called him to account for his intellectual hubris and emotional barrenness, "Christ said that I ought not to undertake anything without him."[5] Before returning from London to Sweden in 1745, Swedenborg published a small work titled *The Worship and Love of God*.

In Stockholm, he resumed his work at the College of Mines and began to study the Bible in Hebrew and Latin. In an unpublished manuscript titled *The Messiah About to Come*, Swedenborg assembled passages from the Bible that seemed to speak to him. The manuscript was written in Latin. However, in a note in Swedish on the last page, he stated:

> November 17, 1745. I began to write.
> Lord Jesus Christ, lead me to and on the way on which Thou willest that I shall walk.
> Be ye holy: be ye gifted with the Spirit of God and Christ; and be ye persevering in righteousness. This will be the testimony of the Kingdom of God.[6]

---

[5] *Swedenborg's Journal of Dreams*, ed. William Ross Woofenden (New York: Swedenborg Foundation, 1977), §278.
[6] Emanuel Swedenborg, *The Messiah About to Come, A Posthumous Work*, trans. and ed. Alfred Acton (Bryn Athyn, PA: The Academy of the New Church, 1949), 105.

For the next two years, Swedenborg continued an intensive study of the Bible and wrote more than five thousand pages, which he never published. Among them is an eight-volume work called *The Word Explained*, a Bible index of correspondences, and a diary of his "spiritual experiences."

Through this effort, Swedenborg profoundly changed his understanding of the nature of the Bible, and in particular the story of Genesis. He moved from believing that it recorded the creation of the physical world and humanity to understanding that it told of every human's potential spiritual birth, or what he would term "regeneration."

In 1747, not long after he was offered the position of president at the College of Mines, Swedenborg decided to retire. He wrote to the king, asking that someone else be named in his place. His request was granted, and he was awarded a pension equal to half his salary. He left the college for the last time on July 17 and a week later set sail for Holland.

When Swedenborg boarded the ship at the age of fifty-nine, he was embarking not just on a new journey, but on a new career. Years later, he was to give it a name: "Servant of the Lord Jesus Christ." In January 1748, after a series of experiences in the spiritual world that deepened his understanding of God, Swedenborg changed the name by which he referred to God from "God Messiah" to "the Lord Jesus Christ." The importance of this will be discussed later in the section on Swedenborg's teachings. For the moment, it is sufficient to say that in Christian literature, the idea that Jesus Christ is Lord is relatively commonplace. However, the name "Lord Jesus Christ" is not. After this revelation, Swedenborg continued his studies for another ten months. In the fall of 1748, he decided to move to London, where he would write the first volume of *Secrets of Heaven*.

Swedenborg's call did not result in an immediate announcement of spiritual insight or revelation to a troubled world. Instead, it led instead to a period of study and reflection, similar to the one by which he had prepared himself for the different phases of his philosophical project. What was added in this new preparatory period was prayer – prayer in which he sought guidance from the God he felt called to serve. It is interesting and important to note that the prose he wrote, as a visionary and theologian, was not ecstatic but was instead logical and measured. As Jorge Luis Borges (1899–1986) wrote in his poem, "Emanuel Swedenborg": "In dry Latin he went on listing, the unconditional last things."[7]

---

[7] Jorges Luis Borges, "Swedenborg," in *Emanuel Swedenborg: A Continuing Vision*, ed. Robin Larsen (New York: Swedenborg Foundation, 1988), 353.

## 4 Swedenborg's Theological Period

In September 1749, Swedenborg anonymously published in Latin his first volume of theology, *Arcana Coelestia* or *Secrets of Heaven*. In it he stated:

> The Word in the Old Testament contains secrets of heaven, and every single aspect of it has to do with the Lord, his heaven, the church, faith, and all the tenets of faith; but not a single person sees this in the letter. . . . The truth is, however, that every part of the Old Testament holds an inner message.[8]

He went on to say that this is because the Word is the Lord's and is therefore living, and on that account, divine. "Without this interior life, the Word in its letter is dead."[9] In this, the Word is like a human being, with an inner and outer self. The outer self without the inner is dead, like a body without its soul.[10]

A key aspect related by Swedenborg of the inner wisdom of Genesis is that the six days of creation in the first chapter identify the stages of spiritual growth necessary to achieve a heavenly life in paradise.[11] He further states that no one could know this unless aided by the Lord. He states that the whole of the spiritual realm was opened to him for several years prior to the volume's publication.[12] With these opening paragraphs, Swedenborg's New Christianity made its debut.

The year 1757 was monumental within Swedenborg's theological period. He reported that it was the year that the last judgment took place. Not only had a last judgment been foretold in the biblical book of Revelation, it was generally assumed that it would take place in this world. Swedenborg, however, wrote that because the judgment was spiritual, it took place in the spiritual world, and that what necessitated this judgment was the separation of the life of faith from the life of charity among departed spirits and in the Christian churches on earth. This separation effectively prevented the Lord's love and wisdom from flowing through heaven into the world of spirits and, finally, to men and women on earth. Swedenborg believed that the completion of *Secrets of Heaven*, in which the internal sense of the Word was now visible in the natural world, also allowed light to shine in the spiritual world. This permitted spirits who had been waiting in that world

---

[8] Emanuel Swedenborg, *Secrets of Heaven*, trans. Lisa Hyatt Cooper (West Chester, PA: Swedenborg Foundation, 2010), §1–2.
[9] *Secrets of Heaven*, §3.
[10] *Secrets of Heaven*, §3.
[11] *Secrets of Heaven*, §4.
[12] *Secrets of Heaven*, §5.

because they were uncertain of their true spiritual nature to see it clearly. They now saw their fundamentally good or evil nature and then sought permanent homes for themselves with those who were of a similar disposition, either in heaven or hell. This lifting of the veil in the spiritual world reordered it and allowed spiritual light to flow into the minds of everyone in the world. As a result, according to Swedenborg, human spiritual freedom was restored.

In 1758, Swedenborg traveled to London, where the following works were published: *Heaven and Hell, New Jerusalem, Last Judgment, White Horse,* and *Other Planets.* He requested that one thousand copies of each should be printed.[13] None of these was exegetical in nature. Swedenborg returned to Sweden in 1759, traveling through Gothenburg on his way to Stockholm. In Gothenburg, an event occurred that would identify him as the author of these strange and fascinating religious books that were circulating in Europe. The event occurred on July 19 when Swedenborg was dining at the home of one William Castel. During the dinner, Swedenborg left the company and went out into the garden. On his return, he appeared troubled. When questioned, he reported that a serious fire was burning in a district in southern Stockholm. Over the next two hours, he reported the progress of the fire to the assembled guests. Finally, at eight o'clock, he exclaimed: "Thank God, the fire is extinguished, the third door from my house!"[14]

Given the extraordinary nature of Swedenborg's account, he was summoned by the governor the next day, Sunday, to give a detailed description of what had occurred in Stockholm. Two days later, messengers from Stockholm, more than three hundred miles away, brought news of the fire, and the details they gave confirmed Swedenborg's clairvoyant description. News of this event gradually circulated in Sweden and eventually spread to the Continent.

As he published more books throughout the 1760s, people began to identify Swedenborg, the clairvoyant, as their author. In Amsterdam, in 1763, he published *The Lord, Sacred Scripture, Life, Faith, Supplements,* and *Divine Love and Wisdom*; in 1764, *Divine Providence*; and in 1766, *Revelation Unveiled.* Swedenborg published additional works in Amsterdam during the last years of his life: *Marriage Love* (1768), *Survey* (1769), *Soul-body Interaction* (also 1769), and *True Christianity* (1771). After publishing this last work he traveled to London, where he suffered a stroke in December. Bedridden

---

[13] It should be pointed out that a print run of one thousand copies was substantial in the eighteenth century.
[14] Cyriel O. Sigstedt, *The Swedenborg Epic* (London: Swedenborg Society, 1981), 216.

during his last months, Swedenborg died on March 29, 1772. Shortly before he died, Swedenborg was asked by a friend, a Mr. Thomas Hartley (1709?–1784), whether everything he had written was true. Swedenborg replied, "I have written nothing but the truth."[15] Despite the "dry Latin" of his prose, his works possess a quality that is somehow beguiling and arresting. Otherwise it is hard to account for the need, on the part of some critics, to ridicule and denounce them, often after making initially positive assessments.

## 5 Swedenborg's Teachings

This brief summary covers the topics of God, creation, humanity, freedom, and salvation. Swedenborg's New Christianity is revolutionary. To begin with, it offers a radically new interpretation of the Trinity. The Father, Son, and Holy Spirit are not three distinct persons united in the Godhead, as is taught in traditional Christianity. Instead, *True Christianity* states: "These three, the Father, the Son, and the Holy Spirit, are three essential components of one God. They are one the way our soul, body, and the things we do are one."[16] In addition, the Lord Jesus Christ is the one God of heaven and earth, the Creator of the universe and the Savior of humanity. In *Divine Love and Wisdom*, Swedenborg describes God as life itself, whose divine essence is love and wisdom.[17] God created the universe and humanity from love, by means of wisdom. He created the universe and the world as a finite habitation for humanity. In *Divine Providence*, Swedenborg writes that the end or purpose of that creation was "a heaven for the human race."[18]

What distinguishes humanity from the rest of finite creation is the fact that human beings were created with freedom and rationality so that they could choose to acknowledge God and love him in return.[19] Swedenborg describes love in this way: "The essence of love is that what is ours should belong to someone else. Feeling the joy of someone else as joy within ourselves – that is loving."[20] A loving God longs to be conjoined to his creation, but this is only possible if the desire is mutual, because mutuality is the essence of all love. Love must be freely given and received to be called love. It cannot be forced,

---

[15] Sigstedt, *The Swedenborg Epic*, 431.
[16] Emanuel Swedenborg, *True Christianity*, trans. Jonathan S. Rose (West Chester, PA: Swedenborg Foundation, 2008), §163.
[17] Emanuel Swedenborg, *Divine Love and Wisdom*, trans. George F. Dole (West Chester, PA: Swedenborg Foundation, 2003), §28.
[18] Emanuel Swedenborg, *Divine Providence*, trans. George F. Dole (West Chester, PA: Swedenborg Foundation, 2003), §323.
[19] Swedenborg, *Divine Providence*, §97.
[20] Swedenborg, *Divine Providence*, §47.

demanded, or compelled. Thus, according to Swedenborg, for people to achieve salvation and dwell in God's heaven after death, it is necessary for them to acknowledge the following:

(1) There is one God ... and he is the Lord God the Savior Jesus Christ. (2) Believing in him is a faith that saves. (3) We must not do things that are evil. ... (4) We must do things that are good. ... (5) We must do these things as if we ourselves were doing them, but we must believe that they come from the Lord working with us and through us.[21]

Here we see that in the New Christianity, human beings are granted cooperative efficacy in their own salvation. Human beings, endowed with the gifts of freedom and rationality, construct during their own lifetime their eternal home either in heaven or in hell. In the afterlife, no one is cast into hell, because all freely follow their inmost love to whatever society permits them to find their greatest happiness. This is so because the opening sentence of *Divine Love and Wisdom* states: "Love is our life."[22]

In endowing humanity with freedom, God opened the possibility that he and his way could be rejected. With the gift of freedom, human beings can choose to love themselves and the world more than they love the Lord and the neighbor. Swedenborg's writings teach that not only can this choice be made, but that the history of the world certainly suggests that many, in fact, have chosen to reject God. Over time, this can flood the world with evil, making it difficult for anyone to choose the good. Because the salvation of the human race is God's uppermost concern, he is continually re-presenting himself to humanity through new revelations accommodated to their changing states and the world's spiritual climate, in order to maintain human freedom.

Swedenborg taught that in the beginning, God and humanity dwelled together in mutual love and spoke the same language. Human beings could see spiritual reality in natural things – they understood what corresponded in nature to living spiritual truths. Gradually, however, they began to believe these abilities were self-created, rather than gifts from God. In this way, they ate from the forbidden tree and could no longer live in the garden. Outside the garden, they used their understanding less and less to access spiritual truths

---

[21] Swedenborg, *True Christianity*, §3.
[22] Swedenborg, *Divine Love and Wisdom*, §1. It is important to point out here and, in what follows, that Swedenborg's writings clearly teach that "through the good and truth which are from the Lord all are saved who live in mutual charity, whether they are within the church or without it. (That the Gentiles who are without the church and who are in good are equally saved.)" Swedenborg, *Secrets of Heaven*, §3380.

and employed it instead to control the natural world. As the natural world became the focus, laws were required to maintain social order, and the relationship to spiritual concerns was maintained through ritual. This is exemplified by Moses on Mount Sinai, receiving from Jehovah the Ten Commandments and the laws for the "children of Israel." When ritual lost its spiritual meaning and was practiced essentially for worldly gain, the way to heaven was closed. God came on earth in human form to visibly show "the way, the truth, and the life" (John 14:6). According to Swedenborg, "the Lord came into the world to subjugate the hells and to glorify his human, and the passion on the cross was the final combat whereby he fully conquered the hells and fully glorified his human."[23]

God, in taking on the body through Mary, gained an evil heredity. Armed with his infinite love, during his life he was drawn into internal combat with the hells. He finally overcame them on the cross and, thus, restored human freedom in spiritual matters. According to Swedenborg, this was accomplished by the Lord Jesus Christ, who rose glorified on the third day, for the sake of all humanity. Viewed as the one God of heaven and earth, he has the power to save all who call to him in temptation.

However, after the Council of Nicea, the worship of one God in three persons brought discord to Christianity and ultimately led to a fatal separation of faith and charity at the time of the Reformation. With only a glimmer of spiritual life left in the world, Swedenborg believed he was called to reveal the spiritual life contained in God's Word; to allow God to re-present himself to a humanity that was discontented with mystery and wished to know the workings of both nature and spirit through reason. Swedenborg taught that finite men and women can wrest the secrets from nature with their own God-given powers; however, the secrets of living spirit can only be revealed by the infinite God who is life itself.

Swedenborg stated in his last work, *True Christianity*, that he believed he was called by the Lord to receive the teachings of the New Church in his understanding, and to publish them through the press.[24] While he published his writings and distributed them widely, he never attempted to found a church. He wrote that "now it is permitted to enter with understanding into the mysteries of faith."[25] His works were published, he said, for those who

---

[23] Emanuel Swedenborg, *Doctrine of the Lord*, trans. John F. Potts (West Chester, PA: Swedenborg Foundation, 1997), §12.
[24] Emanuel Swedenborg, *True Christianity*, Vol. 2, trans. Jonathan S. Rose (West Chester, PA: Swedenborg Foundation, 2011), §779.
[25] Swedenborg, *True Christianity*, §508.

saw the Lord in themselves and who wanted to explore spirit with both heart and mind.

Swedenborg's description of the world, created by God's infinite love, is a world of *uses*: a human world of mutual service. This is true both in heaven and on the earth. One of the most important uses, according to Swedenborg, is marriage.

## 6 Swedenborgianism

When Swedenborg died in 1772, perhaps a handful of people had accepted his religious writings as the word of God – a few in Sweden and a few in England. The development of the New Church in these two countries progressed differently because of the different degree of religious freedom in each, and the social class most interested in Swedenborg's religious teachings. In Sweden, the firm control of the Lutheran Church over religious life made the development of Swedenborgian organizations difficult. Several developed nonetheless among the upper class in Sweden at the end of the eighteenth century, although they were short lived. Public confessional Swedenborgianism was not possible until 1874 when freedom of religious association was legalized.

By contrast, much greater religious freedom existed in England and in the English-speaking world generally, so the story of Swedenborgianism in these lands is quite different. Swedenborg's works could be translated from Latin into the vernacular, and this was actually begun before his death. Two men are primarily responsible for the development of the New Church in England: John Clowes (1743–1831) and Robert Hindmarsh (1759–1835). Clowes was an Anglican priest who never left that faith, although he converted many to the New Church. Hindmarsh was a Methodist who was instrumental in establishing a distinct New Church organization. Both men had never met Swedenborg.

In July 1787, men and women in favor of separating from the "old" Christian churches drew up organizational rules, an order of government, and – most importantly – the spiritual principles of the New Church. On July 31, they held their first worship service, which included both holy supper and baptism. With this service, the first New Christian congregation was established. In 1788, the need for an ordained priesthood became apparent. In June of that year, an ordination service was held, and two men thus became the first ministers of the New Church. In 1789, the first General Conference was held in the chapel they had obtained in East Cheap. The purpose of the meeting was to endorse common principles of faith whereby they might establish the General Conference and promote the development of the New Church. Among the seventy or eighty people in attendance at this first General Conference and who signed the principles of agreement were the poet and artist William Blake (1757–1827) and his wife Catherine. While individuals from all classes were drawn to Swedenborg's writings in Great Britain and the British Empire, they took hold primarily among the middle class.

Although issues soon developed within the membership, interest in the New Church continued to grow. Finally in 1810, Swedenborgians were able to agree on both the form of the Conference, congregationalism, and the principles of faith. Almost all Swedenborgian organizations in the world trace their lineage back to the British Conference. By the end of the nineteenth century, there were seventy-three such societies and sixty-three hundred members in Great Britain. The Conference had spread throughout the British Empire as well. There were societies in Australia, New Zealand, and South Africa, which are still in existence. There are nineteen Conference societies in Great Britain today, with a membership of 590.

Swedenborg's religious writings arrived in North America in 1784. Immediate interest in them developed, and groups of readers met in Philadelphia and Boston. The books moved west with the opening of the Northwest Territory, and Cincinnati soon became an important Swedenborgian center. In Philadelphia in 1817, the General Convention was founded, the first of three separate American organizations. Like the British Conference, it was congregational in form. As American society pushed across the continent, so did Swedenborgianism. A Swedenborgian college was established in Urbana, Ohio, in 1853. By 1900, societies were operating coast to coast. The membership total was 6,926. In 2012, twelve associations, made up of multiple societies, had a total membership of 1,531.

Almost from the beginning of the New Church in Great Britain, differences had been brewing about principles of organizational structure. These rose to the surface in the United States after the Civil War. In 1876, another Swedenborgian organization, this one favoring episcopal principles, was established in America. It was called the Academy Movement, and education was an important emphasis for this group. In the 1880s, its members established a college, secondary school, and elementary school outside Philadelphia. For a time, it was possible within the loose structure of the Convention to remain together. However in 1890, a separation occurred whereby 347 members of the Academy Movement withdrew from the Convention. At stake were not only organizational principles but also how Swedenborg's religious writings were to be viewed – as merely inspired or authoritatively revealed. This new movement – later called The General Church of the New Jerusalem – accepted Swedenborg's writings as authoritatively revealed and has been international since its founding. As of this writing, it is a worldwide organization with a membership of 5,368 and a broader community of approximately 20,000 individuals.

In the twentieth century, two additional organizations were established. The Lord's New Church was founded in the United States in 1937, an international group with a current membership of less than one thousand. The other is the New Church of Southern Africa, founded in 1970. This latter group had approximately twenty-five thousand members in 1990. There are also a number of small, independent New Church organizations in many nations in Africa, Asia, and Eastern Europe, as well as in Australia and India.

Swedenborgian groups are found all around the world, and the total number of Swedenborgians in 2014 was approximately fifty thousand. However, Swedenborg's influence cannot be assessed merely by looking at organizational membership figures alone. Since their first publication, Swedenborg's religious writings have influenced a wide range of artists and thinkers: William Blake, Immanuel Kant, Ralph Waldo Emerson, Arthur Conan Doyle, Henry James Sr., Jorge Luis Borges, Carl Jung, Honoré de Balzac, Helen Keller, W. B. Yeats, August Strindberg, and countless others. Obviously the degree of influence is not the same for each person who read and absorbed some of Swedenborg's innovative religious ideas. Nonetheless, their broad cultural impact is undeniable. This speaks well for the "charisma of the book."[26]

---

[26] This is a term developed by the author to identify the locus of "charisma" within Swedenborgianism.

# 19

# MESMER AND ANIMAL MAGNETISM

## Adam Crabtree

### 1 Discovery of Animal Magnetism

In the last quarter of the eighteenth century, Franz Anton Mesmer (1734–1815) devised and promoted a healing method that he called "animal magnetism." For approximately seventy-five years following its initial proclamation in 1779, animal magnetism flourished as a medical and psychological specialty, and for another fifty years it continued to be a system of influence, having a profound impact on medicine, psychology, and psychical research.

The seeds of thought that gave rise to animal magnetism are found in Mesmer's 1766 thesis *Dissertatio physico-medica de planetarum influxu*, which he wrote for his doctorate in medicine at the University of Vienna. Although he chose the title "Physical-medical Dissertation on the Influence of the Planets," Mesmer was not interested in the occult and attempted to develop a theory of human health based on what he believed were purely physical, scientifically observable factors. Here he expounded his belief that just as there are tides in the ocean, so must there be tides in the human organism caused by the celestial bodies. He called this generalized influence "animal gravity." Noting what he considered to be a similarity between gravity and magnetism, Mesmer attempted to cure the sick through the application of iron magnets. Using the terminology of the day, he called the carrier of magnetic influence "magnetic fluid," which he believed was the foundation of life itself and the principle by which organic bodies carry out their vital functions. He asserted that the inhibition of this vital force produced disease. Mesmer therefore developed a technique to remove obstructions to the free flow of magnetic fluid in the body. After a period of experimentation in which he used mineral magnets to dissolve the blocks, he became convinced that the "magnet" of choice in healing is the physician's own body, which is capable of channeling the invisible fluid pervading the universe into the patient's body. This constituted his theory of "animal magnetism."

Mesmer began his healing practice in Vienna, but after coming into conflict with both the medical establishment of that city and the family of one of his patients, he moved to Paris in 1778. There he gave his theory its first complete formulation, set up two clinics, and attempted to gain acceptance for his ideas from the local medical authorities. His hopes were not realized, however. Although Mesmer's ideas and clinics remained popular among the general public, his work eventually came under investigation by two officially appointed commissions and was judged devoid of scientific merit.[1]

In his foundational work, *Memoir on the Discovery of Animal Magnetism*, written in 1779, Mesmer laid out his doctrine of healing through animal magnetism and stated, among other things, that "the facts will show that, following the practical rules that I will establish, this principle can heal disorders of the nerves immediately, and other disorders mediately."[2] Despite this mention of "nerves," Mesmer was not claiming that magnetic healing had a psychological basis. In fact, we look in vain in Mesmer's works for a discussion of anything like states of consciousness. Mesmer was no psychologist. Although he had a flare for the dramatic (background music from the glass harmonica played during healing sessions, the mysterious healing tub or "baquet," purple robes, iron wands, etc.), Mesmer had little interest in the mental side of healing. He had no curiosity about what was going on in the minds of his patients. Mesmer noted that some of his patients "fainted" when being magnetized, but he never asked them about what they were experiencing. Mesmer mentioned "will," but only in connection with the mental attitude of the magnetizer while applying magnetic "passes" (flowing movement of the hands over the body), and he was never noted

---

[1] For details about Mesmer's life and contemporary responses to his ideas, see Jean Vinchon, *Mesmer et son secret* (Paris: Amédés Legrand, 1936); Robert Amadou, *Franz Anton Mesmer: Animal Magnetism* (*Franz-Anton Mesmer: Le magnétisme animal*) (Paris: Payot, 1971); Alan Gauld, *A History of Hypnotism* (Cambridge: Cambridge University Press, 1992); Adam Crabtree, *From Mesmer to Freud: Magnetic Sleep and the Roots of Psychological Healing* (New Haven: Yale University Press, 1993); Frank Pattie, *Mesmer and Animal Magnetism: A Chapter in the History of Medicine* (Hamilton, NY: Edmonston Publishing, 1994); and Bertrand Méheust, *Somnambulism and Mediumship* (*Somnambulisme et médiumnité*), 2 vols. (Le Plessis-Robinson: Institut Synthélabo, 1999). For a bibliography of Mesmer's writings and other works on animal magnetism and related matters, see Adam Crabtree, *Animal Magnetism, Early Hypnotism, and Psychical Research, 1766–1925: An Annotated Bibliography* (White Plains, NY: Kraus International Publications, 1988).

[2] Franz Anton Mesmer, *Memoir on the Discovery of Animal Magnetism* (*Mémoire sur la découverte du magnétisme animal*) (Geneva and Paris: Didot le jeune, 1779), 83.

for his bedside manner, tact, or political savvy. What Mesmer did have was the creative imagination to devise a novel way of thinking about healing and the single-minded drive to gain acceptance for his system in the face of powerful professional opposition. It was left to the Marquis de Puységur, one of Mesmer's most enthusiastic pupils, to take animal magnetism (or "mesmerism" as it came to be called) to its next, more psychological stage.

### 2 Puységur's Approach to Animal Magnetism

In 1784, Armand Marie Jacques de Chastenet, Marquis de Puységur (1751–1825), an aristocrat and artillery officer, took a training course offered by Mesmer in Paris intended to prepare one to do healing work using the techniques of animal magnetism. On returning to his estate at Buzancy near Soissons, Puységur immediately began to practice what he had learned to alleviate the ills of local residents.

Among the first he treated was a peasant of his estate named Victor Race, who was suffering from fever and congestion of the lungs. Puységur noticed that while he was applying the magnetic passes, Victor had fallen asleep. However, his sleep was not a normal one, for Puységur could still communicate with him. In his written account of his experiences, Puységur called this hitherto undefined condition "magnetic sleep": a sleep-waking kind of consciousness. In sharp contrast to Mesmer, who made no inquiries about his patients' state of mind, Puységur showed himself to be quite interested in Victor's subjective experiences. He considered the effects of Victor's ideas on his illness, and he suggested mental images to Victor that he thought would aid in the healing process. Puységur observed that Victor could recognize tunes that Puységur hummed mentally – but he discovered the next day that Victor had no memory of the incident. The words he used to describe this novel state show Puységur's psychological bent: "magnetic sleep," "magnetic crisis," "peaceful sleep," "magnetic state," "state of somnambulism," and "magnetic somnambulism."[3]

The characteristics of magnetic sleep according to Puységur are as follows.

#### a A sleep-waking kind of consciousness

Puységur noted that after administering the magnetic passes, Victor seemed to fall asleep, yet he was also "awake" enough to continue to communicate with him. Puységur used the word "somnambulism" because of the

---

[3] Marquis de Puységur, *Memoir for the History of Animal Magnetism* (Mémoire pour servir à l'histoire et à l'établissement du magnétisme animal) (Paris: Dentu, 1784).

similarity between magnetic sleep and natural sleepwalking or somnambulism. For Puységur, the difference between natural and magnetic somnambulism is that the latter is developed through induction by a magnetizer and results in a special connection or "rapport" with the magnetizer. With natural somnambulism, on the other hand, the subject does not respond to attempts at communication. Natural somnambulists may speak, drink, eat, read, write, distinguish colors, and carry out various other mental tasks, but in contrast to magnetic somnambulists they are not able to connect with others.

*b Rapport and suggestibility*

In a follow-up volume, Puységur wrote about a special connection that occurs between magnetizer and magnetized: "In this state, the ill person enters into a very intimate rapport with the magnetizer, one could almost say he becomes a part of the magnetizer."[4] Magnetic rapport, he said, causes the somnambulist to respond to and obey only the magnetizer and experience the approach of others as so uncomfortable that if anyone else touches the somnambulist, he or she will awaken. Rapport was considered an essential feature of magnetic sleep. It was accompanied by suggestibility, by which the somnambulist would execute tasks at the suggestion of the magnetizer. In practice, magnetic healers often used suggestion to get patients to perform various remedial procedures (e.g., drinking a specific tea at a specific time).

*c Lack of memory, divided consciousness, and change in personality*

Victor found that on the day after his treatment, he could recall nothing of what had happened. Puységur discovered that this amnesia typically followed magnetic sleep, and that it persisted despite his assiduous attempts to "tie their ideas together in their passing from one state to the other." From this, he concluded that "the demarcation is so great that one must regard these two states as two different existences."[5] He also discovered that there was a continuity of memory within the individual in the state of magnetic sleep, and that although the waking person could remember nothing of the magnetic state, the somnambulist could remember both the waking state and all that had occurred in previous magnetic states, indicating that the memory chain of the somnambulist was quite separate from that of the waking person.

---

[4] Marquis de Puységur, *Continuation of Memoirs for the History of Animal Magnetism* (*Suite des mémoires pour servir à l'établissement du magnétisme animal*) (Paris and London: no publisher, 1785), 17.
[5] Puységur, *Memoir*, 90.

Often the somnambulist would speak about himself in the waking state with a certain detachment, as though referring to another person, confirming Puységur's sense that he was dealing with "two different existences" – a phenomenon later referred to as "divided consciousness" or "double consciousness." The two consciousnesses were characterized by a striking contrast in personality traits. Puységur said of Victor that in the magnetized state, he was no longer a naïve peasant who could barely speak a sentence. The transformation of personality was so great and Victor's wisdom so augmented that Puységur found himself relying on the magnetized Victor for advice in his healing work.

### d Paranormal phenomena

Puységur said of Victor, "I do not need to speak to him. I *think* in his presence, and he hears me and answers me."[6] Puységur reported other phenomena that would today be called "paranormal." He wrote of somnambulists who could perceive objects and conditions not available to the senses, exercising a "sixth sense" activated in magnetic sleep. This sense allowed them to diagnose their own illnesses and those of others and to prescribe effective treatments. Puységur speculated that the somnambulist's sixth sense accounted for the lack of memory in their normal state for what happened in the magnetic state: "With six senses (if one can put it that way) they can recall the sensations gained through the five senses, but with five senses, they cannot remember ideas formed with six."[7]

Puységur was in the habit of using this capacity in his somnambulists to help him determine the illness and remedy for the patients who came to him. He was enthusiastic about the potential for good in this sixth sense and had implicit faith in the accuracy of the pronouncements of magnetic somnambulists. Puységur also believed that magnetic somnambulism could be induced at a distance, but he hesitated to do so since he feared this could cause confusion and perhaps harm the magnetic subject.[8]

Puységur's "discovery" of magnetic sleep was a momentous event in the history of psychology. It goes far beyond the scope of this essay to trace the profound effects this innovation had on the development of psychiatry and psychotherapy.[9] I will only say that it resulted in the establishment of a new

---

[6] Puységur, *Memoir*, 35.
[7] Puységur, *Memoir*, 90.
[8] Puységur, *Continuation of Memoirs*, 113.
[9] Puységur developed a remarkably "modern" theory of the nature of emotional disorders. See Marquis de Puységur, *Are Not the Mad, the Insane, Lunatics and the Frenzied Simply Disordered Somnambulists?* (*Les fous, les insensés, les maniaques, et les frénétiques ne seraient-ils que des*

way of explaining mental disturbances and anomalies: what I call the alternate-consciousness paradigm. This new paradigm supplemented two already existing ones: the organic paradigm that conceives of such phenomena in terms of physiological states, and the intrusion paradigm that sees them as the result of the intervention of spirits or the application of magical spells.

Although the introduction of the magnetic-sleep dimension of animal magnetism was momentous for the subsequent development of psychological theory in the West, Puységur did not deny or neglect the fluidic aspect of Mesmer's system, and he continued to use techniques involving magnetic passes in his healing work. He maintained a complex view of mesmeric phenomena and refused to reduce his approach to any one school of thought. This inclusive understanding of animal magnetism contrasts sharply with the attitude of some practitioners in the decades following his death in 1825. The most notable attempt to reduce magnetic phenomena to a simple formula was that of James Braid (1795–1860), who emphasized the fascination-concentration aspect of magnetic sleep and attributed all mesmeric phenomena to the effects of suggestion.[10] Although Braid was not the first to attempt to reduce everything to suggestion, he gave staying power to his speculations by inventing a nomenclature built around his novel term "hypnotism." Although Braid's denatured form of animal magnetism gained considerable support in more conservative medical quarters, it remained doubtful to many that mesmeric phenomena and hypnotism were equivalent.[11]

## 3 Mechanism or Mysticism?

Animal magnetism entered the scene at a time of great intellectual and cultural ferment. Its launching pad was France, which was abuzz with excitement about scientific progress and a lively interest in ideas relating to the potentials of the human spirit. At the same time, a variety of mystical philosophies were much discussed, including the ideas of Emanuel Swedenborg. Churches and local societies promoting Swedenborgianism

---

*somnambules désordonnés?*) (Paris: J. G. Dentu, 1812). For more see Crabtree, *From Mesmer to Freud*, 76–82.

[10] James Braid, *Satanic Agency and Mesmerism Reviewed* (Manchester: Sims and Dinham, Galt and Anderson, 1842), and *Neurypnology: Or the Rationale of Nervous Sleep Considered in Relation with Animal Magnetism* (London: John Churchill, 1843).

[11] See, for example, W. F. Barrett, E. Gurney, and F. W. H. Myers, "First Report of the Committee on Mesmerism," *Proceedings of the Society for Psychical Research*, 1 (1883), 217–229; "Second Report of the Committee on Mesmerism," *Proceedings of the Society for Psychical Research*, 1 (1883), 251–262; and "Appendix to the Report on Mesmerism," *Proceedings of the Society for Psychical Research*, 1 (1883), 284–290.

abounded in the intellectual environment into which mesmerism was introduced. The Martinists, who believed that "the material world was subordinate to a more real spiritual realm in which primitive man once had ruled,"[12] found mesmerism, particularly the Puységurian strain, to be congenial to their speculations. Rosicrucians, millenarianists, Illuminati, and others were drawn to the intriguing idea that a universal superfine fluid was the source of life and health, and somehow under the direction of the human soul.

Despite the fact that Mesmer's ideas were enthusiastically welcomed by these groups, Mesmer himself was not to be counted in their membership. In fact, he rejected the ideas of those who wanted to interpret his theory in occult or mystical terms, insisting that his discovery was an advance in physical science. He made his strongest statement in this regard in his 1799 *Memoir*: "Everything [produced by animal magnetism] can be explained by the mechanical laws of nature, and ... all effects are due to modifications of *matter* and *movement*."[13]

In the course of presenting his theory, Mesmer was at pains to disown anything that might connect it with the occult, in the process rejecting astrology – something he had already done in his doctoral dissertation – as well as the involvement of spirits. The *Memoir* of 1799 gives one the impression that Mesmer believed his theory was getting away from him, being taken over by men with spiritual and/or occult axes to grind. So he devoted the greater part of this work to stating his theory as clearly as possible and opposing it to such "ignorant" and "superstitious" ideas.

His job was not made any easier by the founding of so-called societies of harmony first in Paris and then in the provinces. The Paris society was originally set up to funnel money to Mesmer in compensation for teaching his courses on animal magnetism, but provincial societies were then formed with different aims, focusing much more on the mutual encouragement of practitioners and the development of treatment methods. These provincial societies paid nothing to Mesmer and gradually their connection with him grew weaker. At the same time, the influence of mystical, spiritual, and occult systems, which were often the subject of discussion at meetings, grew stronger.

## 4 Magnetic Magic

In the early nineteenth century, certain thinkers came to see animal magnetism as the continuation of ancient magical traditions. For them, "magic"

---

[12] Robert Darnton, *Mesmerism and the End of the Enlightenment in France* (Cambridge, MA: Harvard University Press, 1968), 69.
[13] Franz Anton Mesmer, *Memoir of F. A. Mesmer, Doctor of Medicine, On His Discoveries* (*Mémoire de F. A. Mesmer, docteur en médecine, sur ses découvertes*) (Paris: Fuchs, 1799), 68.

involved mobilizing the invisible forces of nature. Carl Adolph von Eschenmayer, Joseph Ennemoser, and Baron Jules Du Potet de Sennevoy were influential spokesmen for this view.

Carl Eschenmayer (1768–1852) saw animal magnetism as a practical demonstration of the truth of ancient magical beliefs. He hoped that with the emergence of animal magnetism, magical practices that in the past had been tinged with superstition could at last be correctly understood. Although he took pains to deny that animal magnetism was the product of mysticism, he did believe that it dealt with the same phenomena as the older magical tradition and that, extraordinary as those phenomena might seem, they were nonetheless natural.[14]

Joseph Ennemoser (1787–1854), a professor of medicine with a penchant for anthropology, wrote prolifically on the history of magic and religion. He was a dedicated practitioner of animal magnetism, and his *Instructions in the Practice of Mesmerism* (1852) was one of the best German manuals on the subject. He had a burning interest in the psychological dimensions of magnetic theory and the relationship of occult traditions to mesmeric phenomena. Ennemoser too saw animal magnetism as a way to vindicate the old magic, but unlike Eschenmayer, who denied that spirits intervene in the lives of human beings, Ennemoser was open to this.[15]

The Baron Du Potet de Sennevoy (1796–1881) sensed from his youth that he had an unusual ability to influence people. Having learned the art of magnetization, he believed he had found the vehicle for putting this natural ability into practice. Du Potet came to be considered one of the most notable magnetizers of the nineteenth century. He taught mesmeric technique, and his published lessons went through various editions. He also edited two journals of animal magnetism, the short-lived *Le propagateur du magnétisme animal* and the important *Journal du magnétisme*, and he was instrumental in bringing mesmerism to England.

Inclined more to Mesmer's than to Puységur's approach, Du Potet believed that mesmerism was not so much dependent on the exercise of will as on the automatic action of magnetic fluid. According to Du Potet, the "new" phenomena of animal magnetism had the same source as the magical enchantments of witches and sorcerers in ancient times. Only the form of the phenomena had changed, not their substance, the agent being the same in all. And Du Potet claimed that that agent is *thought before it has become action.*

[14] Carl Adolph von Eschenmayer, *Testing the Seeming Magic of Animal Magnetism* (*Versuch die scheinbare Magie des thierische Magnetismus*) (Stuttgart and Tübingen: J. G. Cotta, 1816).
[15] Joseph Ennemoser, *Introduction to the Practice of Mesmerism* (*Anleitung zur mesmerischen Praxis*) (Stuttgart and Tübingen: J. G. Cotta, 1852), 115–120, 227–229.

Thoughts can be planted in material objects such as seeds and then, at a time intended by the thinker, can make their power felt by persons who come near them. This, he asserted, was the principle that made amulets and blessed tokens effective, and the reason why talismans, altars, and holy places influence those who come into their presence. Du Potet carried out magical demonstrations of this power of thought. For example, he drew lines and symbols with chalk on a wooden floor and used the power of his mind to invest them with a specific meaning. Then he stationed volunteers within the chalked areas and found that they reacted to the lines and symbols exactly as he had intended. Their reactions were so strong and unambiguous that he considered these experiments undeniable proof of his theory. But the power of thought in the sense intended by Du Potet did not derive from mere cogitation. One had to produce a concentration of personal force to empower the thought with the energy to affect another person. Du Potet saw thought as a mental creation invested with a "semi-material" envelope, a creation conceived in the brain and sent out via the fingers into the person or object touched. This, he said, is how magnetizers always operate, although they do not realize what they are doing. He saw magnetism as the agent invested by the soul with the power to affect matter. That is why to be successful in magical (or magnetic) operations, it is necessary for the operator to be vitally energetic and alive, fully alert in every sense – not preoccupied or benumbed by excessive eating or drinking. Du Potet believed that the human will needs to be awakened, and he explicitly associated the awakened power with sexual energy.[16] Du Potet believed that magnetizers were like children playing with adult tools, not knowing how to use them, ignorant of "the substance behind the form ... the key that can open all the locks of nature's laboratories."[17]

## 5 Mesmerism and Spiritism

Puységur was himself quite strongly influenced by the mystical philosophers of the day. In 1785, he organized a society of harmony in Strasbourg called the Harmonic Society of United Friends (Société Harmonique des Amis Réunis), whose purpose was to train magnetizers, treat patients, and report the results. Puységur wrote with appreciation about the Masonic Martinists at Lyon, the work of Cagliostro in Paris and Rome, and the alliance of

---

[16] See Julies Denis Du Potet de Sennevoy, *Magic Revealed, or Principles of Occult Science* (*La magie dévoilée, ou principes de science occulte*) (Paris: Pommeret et Moreau, 1852).
[17] Du Potet, *Magic Revealed*, 254.

Freemasonry with the followers of Swedenborg in Germany and Sweden. He clearly felt a kinship with these metaphysical systems and believed them to be compatible with his version of Mesmer's animal magnetism.

Given this philosophic compatibility, it is not surprising that the Swedenborgian society of Stockholm, called the Exegetic and Philanthropic Society, became heavily involved with magnetic somnambulism and set out to become an associate of the Strasbourg society of harmony. Founded in 1786, the purpose of the Stockholm society was the promotion of the teachings of Swedenborg, whose visions revealed a world of spirits, good and bad, who secretly influence the conduct of ordinary human life. In 1789, the Stockholm society wrote a brief position paper laying out the classical spiritistic view of the phenomena of magnetic somnambulism. It said that the wisdom involved in diagnosis and healing requires an intellectual, spiritual agency beyond the somnambulist himself. Since somnambulists are not aware of acquiring this wisdom through any identifiable experience, the processing must take place in another intelligent agent: a beneficent spirit.

If the Strasbourg society were to take up this challenge, it would have to propose some arena of mental processing that was neither the conscious mind of the somnambulist nor the mind of a spirit. In other words, it would have to posit mental acts that occur within human beings, but outside of and unavailable to consciousness. Needless to say, thinking about magnetic sleep had not yet developed to such a sophisticated stage. As we shall see, it would be much later, when a new form of spiritism (American spiritualism with its table-turning phenomena) met with a more advanced form of animal magnetism (magnetic and hypnotic experiments with double consciousness) that this mystery at the heart of magnetic sleep could be solved.[18]

In the meantime, other forms of magnetic spiritism were developing. Among those whose work in this tradition stands out are Johann Jung-Stilling, Justinus Kerner, Guillaume Billot, and Louis Cahagnet.

## 6 From Spiritualism to Psychotherapy

The receptive climate for the American-based spiritualistic movement was prepared in part by the practice of mesmerism in the popular culture of the day – and in the minds of spiritualists, mesmeric ideas were closely linked with their philosophy.

Spiritualism produced all kinds of remarkable phenomena. One of the most puzzling of these was variously called (in English) "table moving,"

---

[18] See Crabtree, *From Mesmer to Freud*, 236–265.

"table tipping," and so on. It grew directly out of spiritualistic experimentation and became widely practiced from 1853 on. People would gather around a table, usually in the family home, join hands, and invite spirits to communicate. Typically knocks would sound in the table or the table would rise and fall on one leg, producing a percussive sound. The knocks or blows would be interpreted as alphabetic code and messages would be recorded from them. These were seen as telegraphed communications from spirits of the departed.

Along with such phenomena came attempts to explain their cause. If the messages were intelligible, and those who participated had no *conscious* awareness of making them up, from what did they derive? It gradually became apparent that whether the knocks or sounds were produced by a "fluid" or unconscious muscular movements or something else, the mediums involved must somehow be the *unwitting* source of the intelligent communication. How could this be possible? Today it may seem obvious that unconscious mental acts were involved, but at that time no such conception had yet emerged. This kind of explanation requires that there can be nonconscious mental activity concurrent with normal thinking. In the literature of the time, this novel idea was hinted at but not quite attained, with one exception: the anonymously written pamphlet *Second Letter of Grosjean to his Bishop* (*Seconde lettre de Grosjean à son évêque*) written in 1855.[19]

The author speculated that a medium, because of "weakness of the will," can have her thoughts separate into two streams, one conscious and the other hidden from awareness, each with a life of its own. He believed that this second, nonconscious stream of thought was the author of the messages produced in table-moving phenomena. Thirty years later, Pierre Janet would use the ideas in this pamphlet in support of his belief that hysterics have a *subconscious mental life* that is active at the same time as their normal consciousness and affects them in their daily lives.[20]

This theory was crucially important for the development of modern psychodynamic psychotherapy. Up to this point, the alternate consciousness of magnetic sleep could be considered dormant when the person was awake, and active during magnetic sleep. Now it had to be acknowledged that the alternate consciousness was also active when the person was in the normal state, although that activity was unknown and unavailable to waking

---

[19] The author may be Paul Tascher.
[20] The story of this advance in psychological thinking is discussed at length in Crabtree, *From Mesmer to Freud*, 236–265. See also Henri F. Ellenberger, *The Discovery of the Unconscious: The History and Evolution of Dynamic Psychiatry* (New York: Basic Books, 1970), 358–364.

awareness. This new view of the human psyche was first clearly formulated by Frederic Myers[21] and pursued by Pierre Janet and eventually Sigmund Freud.

## 7 Conclusion

Mesmer conceived of animal magnetism as a theory and method for physical healing. Puységur's psychological turn radically altered the evolution of animal-magnetic ideas, drawing attention to the mental states of those who, as a result of mesmeric treatment, experienced a kind of "magnetic sleep," a condition that could be induced at will and employed to enhance the healing process. The result was a complex history with three emerging streams: a physical healing stream, a parapsychological stream, and a psychological stream.[22] From this point of view, the history of mesmerism is a history of the exploration of a variety of human potentials. All three streams produced phenomena not easily integrated into Western culture. To date the most broadly accepted is the psychological stream, with its exploration of the nonconscious mental dimensions of human experience. But it seems fair to say that recognition of the full potential of what was begun by Mesmer and Puységur is yet to come.

---

[21] Frederic W. H. Myers, "Automatic Writing–II," *Proceedings of the Society for Psychical Research*, 3 (1885), 1–63; "Human Personality," *Fortnightly Review*, 38 (1885), 637–655; and "Introduction," in E. Gurney, F. W. H. Myers, and F. Podmore, *Phantasms of the Living*, 2 vols. (London: Trübner, 1886), vol. 1, xxxv–lxxi.

[22] It would probably be appropriate to recognize a fourth: a philosophical stream. Animal magnetism had a substantial influence on the thinking of a number of nineteenth-century philosophers, notably, Hegel, Schelling, Schopenhauer, and Du Prel. See, for example, Glenn Alexander Magee, "Hegel on the Paranormal: Altered States of Consciousness in the Philosophy of Subjective Spirit," *Aries* 8 (2008), 21–36.

# IV

# The Nineteenth Century and Beyond

20

# SPIRITUALISM

Cathy Gutierrez

## 1 Introduction

The religious movement known as Spiritualism was officially inaugurated in 1848 in Hydesville, New York, when two young sisters, Kate and Margaret Fox, attempted to communicate with an apparent poltergeist in their home. Using a laborious version of Morse code called "alphabet raps" (one for "a," two for "b," and so forth), the girls were able to interact with their ghost and question him about the circumstances of his death. Kate and Margaret's enterprising older sister, Leah Fish, began arranging public displays of this new talent and soon discovered that she too had a gift for talking to the dead. Spiritualism changed dramatically over the next fifty-plus years in terms of the modes of communication employed, and it developed a loose theology of earthly and heavenly progression. Nevertheless, the central point of its rituals and literature remained the same: that the living could communicate with those across the threshold of death.

The ability to talk to the residents of heaven functioned effectively as an amateur form of grief counseling: the American Civil War and high infant mortality rates sent the bereaved to séances in droves to learn the fates of their loved ones. Almost without exception, these were happy scenarios with the departed thriving in the afterlife amid relatives and in the company of angels. Children grew up in heaven, completing the life cycles that had been severed on earth. They went to school, grew physically in their spirit bodies, and occasionally even got married in the afterlife. Heaven was a bustling and busy place that was generally portrayed as made up of seven consecutive tiers. Instead of being instantly perfected upon death, the residents of heaven all grew in knowledge and spiritual refinement, advancing through the tiers of heaven and relating the practices and ethics of the afterlife to their living friends and family.

Access to the dead not only gave the grieving assurances about the well-being of their loved ones, it also provided the opportunity to consult the finest minds of history on current topics. William Shakespeare, Benjamin Franklin, Francis Bacon, and Emanuel Swedenborg were among those frequently called on to give advice from beyond the grave. Domestic concerns were usually tended to in the more personal space of a séance in one's home, whereas larger public affairs took place along the lines of the tent revivals that had swept America earlier in the century. Held outdoors or in theaters and auditoriums, these events were open to the public as well as the press and could attract thousands in a single evening. The medium, who functioned as a conduit between the worlds of the living and the dead, would usually enter a trance and let the voice of a visiting spirit speak through her. Since mediums were frequently women, the ability to expound on politics and philosophy was a quiet revolution in culture at the time. As Ann Braude has noted in her seminal work *Radical Spirits*, mediumship was a mixed blessing for women: They were allowed unprecedented influence on the public, but only on the condition that they were entirely passive and understood not even to be present at all. Braude has argued that Spiritualism had a direct impact on women speaking in public, and that the movement for women's rights was positively and directly influenced by this tradition.[1]

Many scholars have commented that communication with the dead is hardly specific to the phenomenon of Spiritualism and that giving it a specific date of origin (such as the year of the Fox sisters' "rappings") artificially separates Spiritualism from a long history of related occurrences. This is undoubtedly true, yet the date is a marker of the ability to self-identify as a spiritualist – as a member of a movement that brought with it a host of new connotations in addition to the core ritual of talking to the dead. While spiritualists resisted the institutionalization of Spiritualism's practices and codification of its beliefs, there was an ethos that permeated the movement and that believers found to be reflected in heaven as well. This ethos could be characterized as unrelentingly progressive, hopeful concerning the future of both science and morality, and most often politically liberal. Heaven served as a cultural model, a place that was not perfect but was advanced in wisdom and spirituality. Communications from those in heaven reflected the fondest hopes of the living, and what the living envisioned in heaven was remarkable for its time: Heaven was completely inclusive of all people regardless of race, religion, or even individual behavior. The idea of hell, a judging God, and

---

[1] Ann Braude, *Radical Spirits: Spiritualism and Women's Rights in Nineteenth-Century America* (Boston: Beacon Press, 1989).

the exclusive claims of Christianity to truth – or those of any religion – were all banished.

The complete inclusivity of heaven marked a sea change in popular thinking about difference and damnation. While most descriptions of heaven did suggest that racial and ethnic others ended up on the lower rungs of heaven, they were generally regarded as equal in spirit, but lacking in the education that was the condition of heavenly progress. Some communications from the dead indicated that spirits continued to practice their various religions in the afterlife, and that the landscape of heaven was dotted with ethnic neighborhoods and temples erected to different faiths. The exclusive truth claims of Christianity were roundly condemned by many mediums as deeply misguided, ultimately leading people to fear the divine. Emma Hardinge, one of the most respected mediums of her day, wryly commented in a trance state that it was unfortunate that according to Christian dogma the ancient Greeks, after having given us science, philosophy, and democracy, were all consigned to hell. Jesus, Buddha, and Confucius, she believed, all existed in heaven as especially wise men on a par with others who were spiritually advanced.

Like all religious movements, Spiritualism developed at the confluence of social, economic, and political events. America had recently experienced what is often called the Second Great Awakening, a series of religious revivals and innovations that changed the character of Protestantism and gave rise to several new articulations of the sacred. The preachers during this epoch were itinerant and often quite charismatic; they made significant changes to the rhetorical style of American religions, introducing an emotional tone that many thought was too informal for the pulpit. Rejecting their forebears' belief in the predestined division of humanity into the saved and the damned, these men sought to induce a dramatic conversion experience in all who heard them. Salvation became universally possible, at least in theory, and the individual became responsible for securing his or her own religious future. This opening of heaven to all Christian believers undoubtedly set the stage for Spiritualism and like-minded liberal denominations to declare an absolute democracy of the dead. While more mainstream factions clung to ideas of Christian exclusivity and the damnation of many, Spiritualists took the egalitarian ethos of the time to its logical extreme: salvation was universally necessary.

The first half of the century also saw the formation of an American middle class and the concomitant changes to daily experience that it brought. The shift from a farm or artisan economy, where the home was the locus of economic activity, to work conducted outside of the household had a profound impact on family structures. Many women in particular found themselves in the unusual position of not being expected to toil for money. Women began to fill their newfound leisure with religious pursuits that quickly took on an overtly political cast. The age of volunteerism had devotees to many causes, foremost temperance, abolition, and the Bible Tract Society. Much energy was also expended on lesser-known causes, many of which were attractive to spiritualists. These ranged from dress reform for women to the treatment of prisoners and asylum inmates. The Second Great Awakening laid the groundwork for women to participate in the public sphere in the service usually of progressive causes.

The conception of heaven as inclusive both reflected and shaped moral codes here on earth. While spiritualists were not unified on any front, in the main they were defenders of progressive political causes such as abolition and women's rights. The equality of race and gender in the afterlife suggested that we could work toward these conditions on earth, and the promise of a heavenly future of equality provided some measure of hope for those who did not get to experience it in life. Spiritualism imagined a democracy in the afterlife where differences remained, but all spirits would advance through education. Heaven reflected the greatest hopes of those on earth — the continuation of individual lives after death and their ties to friends and family, progress through scientific advancement and social reform, and the eventual elimination of inequality.

## 2 Influences

In addition to the cultural atmosphere of the young republic, Spiritualism was thoroughly indebted to a European intellectual legacy that linked it to the Neoplatonic tradition and esoteric currents such as secret societies and ritual magic. Foremost among these influences were the writings of the Swedish mystic Emanuel Swedenborg (1688–1772). His visionary experiences, reported in multiple volumes, described being repeatedly transported to heaven and even other planets, where he was allowed to interact with angels and the dead.

While Swedenborg remained a firm Christian (many of his books are liberally stocked with biblical quotations, and he affirms the existence of hell), the heaven that he described was a far cry from staid and traditional descriptions of static perfection. What he found in his mystical journeys were *three* heavens where the inhabitants were determined by the essential character they possessed while alive, and by whether their primary relationship to the divine had been emotional, intellectual, or spiritual. The spirits of the dead and the angels lived in vibrant societies, each with its own distinct language and activities. The different ways of relating to the divine also implicated different readings of Scripture, which Swedenborg believed had multiple layers of possible meaning with the innermost interpretation bearing no relationship to the actual words on the page.[2]

Spiritualists inherited from Swedenborg not only a many-tiered heaven with constant activity but also two main elements that would affect their daily lived experience. The first was Swedenborg's ideas concerning memory: In his writings, it is not a judging God who determines one's destiny in heaven or hell. Instead, the individual is drawn to one or the other based on memory. On death, human beings discover that in addition to their "exterior" memory (the usual memory that is subject to mistakes and gaps), they also have an "interior" memory that is a perfect recording of their life. This memory is literally stripped off a person at death and watched like a film by the deceased and by the angels. The unflinching evaluation of behavior that results from this experience leads bad people to simply hurl themselves into hell; the others ascend to the heaven to which they are drawn according to their affinity with the sphere's inhabitants. Later, when the Spiritualists had dispensed with hell, Swedenborg's theory of memory provided the answer to the unsettling problem of how to deal with the presence of evil people in heaven. Again, the dead are attracted to the correct sphere of heaven by affinity, but to advance in heaven they must successfully deal with the memory of having committed evil acts.

Swedenborg also believed that the spirits of the dead were married for eternity and that adultery amounted to an alliance with falsehood and would cause one to be condemned to hell. He declared that eternal union and even sexual intercourse are the natural state for all beings in the afterlife including angels. Allowances are made, however, for the unhappily paired on earth, which Swedenborg recognizes as the majority of earthly marriages. At death, everyone will get his or her true mate. Marriage on earth, while important, is provisional. The spiritualists would largely affirm the eternity of romantic love but would use it in pursuit of marriage reform and divorce law. Heavenly couples served as a reminder that earthly arrangements were frequently imperfect or worse, and that divine law demanded that one should be free to search for true love.

The other indispensable influence on Spiritualism was the career of Franz Anton Mesmer (1734–1815), the accidental and eponymous discoverer of mesmerism. This is now generally thought of as a proto-hypnosis, but it came

---

[2] For more information, see the essay "Swedenborg and Swedenborgianism" in this volume.

to serve as the paradigm for the trance state in spiritualist mediumship. One of Mesmer's students, the Marquis de Puységur, discovered that a boy he was treating would fall on occasion into an altered state of consciousness. Moreover, in this second state he was calmer, wiser, and more moral than he was in his usual waking state. As in the case of sleepwalkers, this second self knew all about the waking self, but this knowledge was unidirectional – that is, the waking self was unaware of the second self. Puységur began cultivating this state in all his patients and consulted them about their own medical needs while they were in a trance. Puységur reported some paranormal activity, but this was not his main interest. The artificially induced trance, however, was a natural fit for the mystically inclined. The spiritualists embraced this trance state as the conduit to the afterlife, a higher self that had access to the more ethereal existence of the spirit plane.[3]

Both Swedenborg and Mesmer were men poised between a quasi-mystical, Renaissance vision of the cosmos, in which the divine was infused throughout the universe, and the Enlightenment's love of empiricism. With their strong Neoplatonic influences and their hopes for the technology of the future, spiritualists, too, were enamored with both men and therefore with both worlds.

## 3 Politics

Most but certainly not all spiritualists believed in and often worked toward the progressive politics suggested by contact with heaven. Universal salvation implied that all of humanity was equal in the eyes of the divine or could become so with better education and opportunities. Spiritualists frequently attributed unethical behavior to a climate of misfortune brought about by poverty and ignorance. Curing the causes of social ills would cure the ills themselves, and so the category of sin was replaced by a concept of social injustice. Many spiritualists such as Amy and Isaac Post were ardent abolitionists who worked for the Underground Railroad, and with their fellow radical Quakers hosted speakers such as Frederick Douglass and Sojourner Truth (who became a spiritualist herself later in life). Some African Americans found a consonance between Spiritualism and their own traditional religions and some became mediums. The most famous is the prolific author Paschal Beverly Randolph, who had a successful career as a medium and racial activist before he left the mainstream spiritualists for a more radical branch of esotericism.

---

[3] For more information, see the essay "Mesmer and Animal Magnetism" in this volume.

Issues that affected women were also popular among spiritualists, and marriage reform was central to them. As the institution of marriage within the middle class became less economically based, romantic love came to the fore as the bond between men and women. Intimacy and emotion became the foundation of marriage, and spiritualists further proposed that romantic alliances might be eternal. Called "spiritual affinity," this Swedenborg-inspired theory posited that each individual has a predetermined soul mate, and some writings about heaven even required the pair to be together in order to advance. This emphasis on the importance of romantic love brought many unhappy marriages into sharp focus, and it was apparent to many spiritualists that the laws regarding divorce, child custody, and finances often kept women and children in undesirable and even dangerous circumstances.

In the mind of the public, marriage reform bled easily into the free love movement and Spiritualism came to be associated with this unpopular fringe. Victoria Woodhull, an extraordinary character who was the first woman to run for president of the United States, was head of the Spiritualist Association as well as the most outspoken and infamous advocate of free love. Easily subject to being represented as promoting promiscuity, the free love movement in reality embraced a wide variety of marriage reforms and even endorsed celibacy as a legitimate choice. Woodhull's message was that women stayed in loveless marriages because of money and that this was tantamount to socially sanctioned prostitution. The church and the state were complicit in this sham, and love needed to be freed from the legal system in order to thrive. While Spiritualism was clearly damaged by its association with free love, and most adherents would not have endorsed extreme views about romance, the free love advocates were clearly attracted to Spiritualism's ethos of progress and egalitarianism.

## 4 Science

Since Spiritualism retained a Renaissance worldview in which the divine filled the cosmos rather than ruled over it, nature and the material world were not devalued as base or corrupting. Spiritualists truly wanted science to work with religion rather than to be at odds with it: Science would uncover natural truths that would reaffirm the existence of heaven and significantly improve the earth for the living. The Fox sisters' poltergeist rappings began as an amateur imitation of the telegraph, and the ability to instantly communicate across vast space remained the template for communications with those in heaven. Concepts such as magnetism (à la Mesmer) and electricity were employed often in spiritualist writings, showing a fascination with science even when the understanding of it was far from clear. The idea of the human body as the conduit between worlds was predicated on vague notions of electrical impulses – women, thought to be negatively charged, were attractive to the positively charged heavens.

Spiritualists created machines to aid communication with heaven and to lend credence to their claims that this effort was empirically true and scientifically verifiable. The planchette, still commonly used in Ouija boards, was a simple device to promote communication with the spirits. Similar but significantly more elaborate machines were built that used treadles and wheels with alphabets so that the spirits could spin out words. Many of these machines were designed to eliminate the margin of human error still present with a medium. Robert Hare, a professor of chemistry at the University of Pennsylvania and a famous early convert, was at the forefront of spiritualists who built machines to talk to the dead.

But the dead also sent machines to the living to improve their conditions on earth and to hasten progress. Spirits such as Benjamin Franklin and Antoine Lavoisier reportedly sent instructions for new machines designed to improve the lot of the living. Some of these involved everyday items such as sewing machines and canning devices. Others attempted to control the weather or were political in purpose, such as the ultimate war machine that would promote peace because no one would dare oppose it. Still others, such as the New Motor built in 1853 by the Reverend John Murray Spear in High Rock, Massachusetts, were sent by the spirit world for new but unspecified purposes: At 160 feet tall and built at a cost of two thousand dollars, this machine was supposed to be nothing short of a mechanical messiah – spiritual knowledge come to earth in the form of technology.

As the century wore on, further forms of technology, such as photography, contributed to the spiritualists' hopes that progress would lead eventually to heaven. The apparent objectivity provided by the camera made the advent of ghost photographs extremely convincing. The dead were thought to exist just outside of the normal capacity for eyesight but were able to be captured in photographs. Despite the highly publicized trial of William Mumler for fraud in 1869 – when P. T. Barnum himself showed the judge how ghost photographs could be faked – spiritualists remained convinced of the veracity of this new medium. Mumler was acquitted, "spirit sittings" were popular on both sides of the Atlantic, and such high-profile believers as Mary Todd Lincoln contributed to the conviction that the camera provided a new proof of spiritualist claims.

Influenced from the outset by Mesmer's medical theories as well as others (e.g., homeopathy), spiritualists embraced the science of medicine, serializing new books in their weekly papers and finding adherents among practitioners. Andrew Jackson Davis, a mesmeric trance healer who garnered the movement untold popularity when he supported the Fox sisters, worked as a country doctor. Along with other spiritual healers, he maintained that physical moderation and spiritual development were the keystones to health. The body could be cast into illness out of ignorance and fear – and it could be healed by knowledge, rather than invasive procedures or dubious drugs. Never far from the concept of universal magnetism that tied all of the cosmos together, spiritualists refused to separate the soul from the body, arguing that the health of the latter required knowledge of the former.

Experimenting with trance states, multiple voices from a single source, and unorthodox roles for women, Spiritualism seemed destined to run afoul of nascent psychology. *Harper's Weekly* called for the institutionalization of spiritualists because the movement "created lunatics weekly." Asylums, already swelled to bursting in America, England, and France, began committing people – women in particular – for the diagnosis of "monomania," a now-obsolete label used to describe someone who was sane in all respects except one. These cases almost always involved religious disagreement or experimentation, especially by women. Spiritualists, Shakers, and free thinkers of all sorts were institutionalized by their husbands or other family members in an era when the legal system provided almost no rights for those declared insane. Their writings from the asylum make it apparent that the vast majority of monomaniacs were inconvenient wives caught in a system that simply ignored them. Legal reforms for declared lunatics in England and America significantly improved the conditions of asylums and the rights of those within them, and monomania disappeared as a psychiatric category. Schizophrenia, the nineteenth-century precursor to dissociative disorder, was another common diagnosis for spiritualists.

Mediumship, in particular the capacity of mediums to seemingly manifest multiple identities, raised questions about the nature of consciousness and attracted the attention of psychological theorists. Several iterations of what is now generally called the unconscious were proposed in France, Austria, and England, with second or sometimes even multiple selves being accounted for as psychological rather than spiritual phenomena. In 1843, British surgeon James Braid had made hypnotism therapeutically respectable by divorcing the trance state from any associations with Mesmer and his ideas about animal magnetism. Sympathetic investigators to Spiritualism's claims such as William James and Frederic Myers generally associated themselves with the more intellectually rigorous London-based Society for Psychical Research rather than with run-of-the-mill believers in Spiritualism. While Spiritualism clearly contributed to discussions about the nature of the self and the distinction between religion and pathology, strict materialists such as Sigmund Freud would win the debate for the twentieth century, only to be eclipsed further in the twenty-first with the decline of classical therapy and its replacement by psychoactive drugs. The spiritualists anticipated this usurpation of their claims and fought to interpret altered states as inherently religious and morally superior. But the medicalization of mediumship, combined with economic and cultural trends, conspired to erode the progressive optimism of Spiritualism's heyday.

## 5 Conclusion

Arthur Versluis has characterized Spiritualism as the "exoteric church" of the esoteric tradition. Spiritualism was more mainstream and accessible than secret societies or initiatory groups that practiced ritual magic, but it nevertheless served as an efficient and faithful handmaiden of occult lore. Uniting democratic ideals of egalitarianism with Neoplatonic visions of a ladder of ascent, Spiritualism provided a welcoming and palatable version of esoteric ideals that dismantled Christian damnation and made education the universal goal. Replete with a Renaissance view of nature as infused with the divine and embracing science as a companion to religion, Spiritualism offered an esoteric cosmos stripped of its secrecy.

The overlap between Spiritualism and stricter versions of esotericism may be seen in some of the movements that Spiritualism directly influenced. Theosophy, as expounded by Helena Petrovna Blavatsky, spun off from standard Spiritualism, with Blavatsky claiming that that Spiritualism's "voices of the dead" were actually elemental spirits or "shells" of the dead, a fading form of consciousness no longer tied to the deceased. Blavatsky became a defector from Spiritualism after many years as a successful medium – not because she thought Spiritualism's claims were mistaken but rather because she thought them too modest.

The practice of talking to the dead took on an increasingly theatrical cast over time, and the demands to produce materials and even spirits from the realm of heaven invited charlatans into spiritualist circles. Harry Houdini created contemporary stage magic specifically to debunk the claims of sensational mediums, producing tricks that replicated the antics of séances and blurring the boundaries of what was empirically verifiable. The production of "ectoplasm," a physical substance allegedly from the spirit world and unknown on earth, made the fantastic character of some spiritualist sittings even more pronounced. The movement eventually lost its cohesive theological content and became more individualistic, frequently functioning more as entertainment than as a means to construct a meaningful view of the world.

Current religious movements that are indebted to Spiritualism include the New Age, which combines universalism with religious teachings from Asia, particularly reincarnation and karma. Psychics continue to connect the living to their deceased loved ones and often employ new technologies such as digital photography and the Internet to aid them in this endeavor. Popular culture is rife with fictional depictions of mediums who can talk to the dead or other supernaturally gifted people who can communicate with angels or demons. Implicit in these portrayals is a universal heaven marked by increased knowledge and the ongoing concern of the dead with the affairs of the living. The ethics of inclusion that characterizes so much of current society and ecumenical discourse is the rightful heir of Spiritualism, in which universal progress rather than salvation for the few was believed to govern the universe.

21

# H.P. BLAVATSKY AND THEOSOPHY

## Michael Gomes

## 1 Introduction

With the advent of H. P. Blavatsky's Theosophical Society in 1875, esoteric groups, long limited by coded language and secrecy, moved to what sociologist Edward Tiryakian has termed "the margin of the visible."[1] Through the work of the Theosophical Society, esotericist ideas found an easy conduit into mainstream society. While membership always remained small, its network of lodges served as the means to disseminate its philosophy. This has been a constant throughout modern Theosophy's existence: the primacy of getting the message out not only through lectures and classes, but also by its aggressive publishing program of books, magazines, pamphlets, and leaflets, often distributed free in the tens of thousands. Although Theosophy's initial impetus was for the recovery of an ancient wisdom tradition, it quickly redefined itself as a panacea for society's social and moral ills. Through its message of reincarnation and karma – or hope and responsibility, as Blavatsky defined it – the movement offered the opportunity of taking control of one's destiny and making a change in the world.

## 2 Blavatsky

Modern Theosophy's leading theorist was Helena Petrovna Blavatsky, often referred to as Madame Blavatsky, or by her initials, H. P. B.[2] Born on August 12, 1831, in Ekaterinoslav in Southern Russia (now Dnipropetrovsk in the Ukraine), she was named after her mother, a novelist, and her grandmother,

---

[1] Edward Tiryakian, *On the Margin of the Visible: Sociology, the Esoteric and the Occult* (New York: John Wiley, 1974), 274.
[2] In spite of all the writing about her, no satisfactory biography exists. James A. Santucci's entry on her in *Dictionary of Gnosis and Western Esotericism*, ed. Wouter J. Hanegraaff (Leiden: Brill, 2005), 1:177–185, presents a useful introduction to her career.

248

the Princess Helena Dolgorouky. Her childhood was a series of upheavals, moving from one place to another when her father, Captain Peter von Hahn, a cavalry officer, was transferred. After the death of her mother in 1842, she was sent to live with her maternal grandparents in Saratov, where her grandfather, Andrey Fadeyev, was governor of the province. At the age of seventeen, she surprised everyone by marrying Nikifor Blavatsky, lieutenant governor of the province of Erivan, a man twice her age. After a few months, she abandoned him and left for what would become a life of travel. She reappeared in Russia at the end of 1859, and after a few years she left again until 1872.

According to some accounts, those "veiled years" were spent traveling through Europe with the opera singer Agardi Metrovich, supporting herself by her considerable skills as a pianist. There was also rumor of an illegitimate child. Her own narrative has her meeting her teacher, an Indian who had come with the Nepal delegation to the 1851 Great Exhibition at London's Crystal Palace, on her twentieth birthday, and leaving for North India to join him there. She claims to have traveled as far as Tashi-lhunpo in Tibet, the monastery town where the Panchen Lama resided. In the 1860s, she was again in India, going through Kashmir to Leh in Ladakh and beyond. There is scant evidence for either account, other than the statement of Major General Charles Murray about finding Blavatsky on the Sikkim border in "1854 or '55" when he was stationed there.[3]

How are we to assess Blavatsky's tale of pilgrimage to the wise men of the East? Subsequent European travelers through the Himalayas have born witness to the willingness of learned lamas to take on Western students, but her teachers were not lamas or monks, although there is a strong regard for the Gelugpa tradition of Tibetan Buddhism in their teaching. She credits much of the inspiration for her writings to them, and the bond between teacher and pupil, a form of psychic transmission, as the means of accessing what she wrote about. Whatever the source, some change or transformation took place in her life during these years.

In 1872, she started the Société Spirite in Cairo, Egypt, for the investigation of spiritualist phenomena that had become so popular, but she soon disbanded the group when the medium they hired was found to be cheating. On the eve of her forty-second birthday, she arrived in New York from Paris in the summer of 1873. A year later, she applied for U.S. citizenship, which

---

[3] H. S. Olcott, "Traces of H.P.B." *The Theosophist* 14 (1893): 429–431. Olcott's transcription of Murray's account, marked "correct" by Murray, at the back of his diary for 1893, is printed in *The Theosophist*, December 1949, 190. Murray's Cadet Papers at the India Office Library in London show that he was stationed in the area at that time.

was granted in 1878. Blavatsky came to public attention through a series of articles written by Henry Steel Olcott (1832–1907), a New York lawyer who had been an investigator for the U.S. War Department and was part of the government's investigation of President Lincoln's assassination.[4] Fascinated by news of a family of Vermont farmers who were mediums, Olcott visited them and his reports were published in the *New York Sun* and *New York Daily Graphic*.

Olcott introduced Blavatsky to his readers in the November 27, 1874, *Daily Graphic*, and their acquaintance became a lifelong friendship. She joined him in Philadelphia at the end of 1874 to investigate another case of mediumship; while there, she married an Armenian trader from Russian Georgia. The marriage lasted only a few months, and she returned to New York without him. Blavatsky's emergence among the spiritualists and Olcott's enthusiastic remarks in the book version of his articles gained her lasting identification as a medium. Blavatsky had displayed psychic abilities in her youth. Given to fits of somnambulism, she tells of writing messages from what was believed to be the spirit of an old lady and her son, who had committed suicide, giving intricate details of their lives. On investigation it was found that the woman was still alive, as was her son. This experience contributed to her skepticism about the psychic nature of such communications, and to a lifelong interest in abnormal psychology.

After less than a year among American spiritualists, Blavatsky began to develop a growing antipathy to the movement. Olcott's failure to get the American scientific community interested in studying Spiritualism led him to suggest the formation of a society that would investigate these hidden mysteries of nature and the powers latent in the individual. On September 7, 1875, at a gathering in Blavatsky's rooms in New York to hear George Henry Felt discourse on the lost canon of proportion of the ancients, Olcott made the motion for such an organization. Those interested met the next day, and by October the by-laws for its democratic structure of elected officers and the name "Theosophical Society" were decided on. On November 17, Olcott, who was elected president, delivered his inaugural address at Madison Avenue's Mott Memorial Hall, where the society had rented rooms. Blavatsky, who was in the audience, had been elected corresponding secretary, an office abolished after her death. The Minute Book of the Theosophical Society shows a continued attempt to try and verify

[4] Olcott's contribution is assessed in Michael Gomes, "Olcott, Henry Steel," *Dictionary of Gnosis and Western Esotericism*, 2:894–895; Steven Prothero, *The White Buddhist: The Asian Odyssey of Henry Steel Olcott* (Bloomington: Indiana University Press, 1996), and Gananath Obeyesekere's review of Prothero's book in *The Journal of Buddhist Ethics* 4 (1997).

psychic phenomena under test procedures. The lack of success caused attendance to dwindle until by the end of 1876 the society gave up holding meetings.

Blavatsky's first book, *Isis Unveiled: A Master-key to the Mysteries of Ancient and Modern Science and Theology* (1877), stressed the work of latent powers in the individual and in nature as the real source of spiritualist phenomena. The work further accelerated her loss of support among spiritualists. At the end of 1878, Olcott and Blavatsky went to India to study its philosophy first hand with the reformist Swami Dayananda Saraswati (1824–1883). After corresponding with the head of the Bombay branch of his organization, the Arya Samaj, the two groups briefly merged. However, when Olcott and Blavatsky publicly converted to Buddhism on a tour of Ceylon in 1880, Dayananda denounced their eclectic approach. This did not seem to hinder the growth of the Theosophical Society, which, by 1885, had developed a network of ninety-five branches throughout India and Ceylon and had purchased a permanent headquarters on the banks of the Adyar River in Madras.

The society drew a wide array of Indian scholars, activists, and sympathetic Anglo-Indians, such as A. P. Sinnett (1840–1921), editor of the *Pioneer* newspaper, and A. O. Hume (1829–1912), former secretary to the Government of India. Hume eventually left the Theosophical Society to form the Indian National Congress, which would be instrumental in gaining India's independence. Sinnett remained a lifelong member, writing two of the most widely read books of nineteenth-century Theosophy, *The Occult World* (1881) and *Esoteric Buddhism* (1883), based on his correspondence with Blavatsky's Indian teachers. Olcott's work in Ceylon was no less successful. He traveled the island raising funds for Buddhist schools, and in 1884 he was sent by the islanders to present their grievances to the Home Office in London. During the Theosophists' visit to Europe, news came that two recently dismissed workers from the Adyar headquarters had sold some letters purporting to be from Blavatsky giving them instructions for creating her phenomena.[5]

The appearance of the correspondence in the *Madras Christian College Magazine* drew the attention of the newly formed Society for Psychical Research (SPR), which had set up a committee to gather evidence for Theosophists' accounts of astral travel, the miraculous appearance of letters from Blavatsky's Indian teachers (the Mahatmas, or Masters), and her materialization of various items. A member of the committee, Richard Hodgson,

---

[5] An examination of the events set in motion by Emma and Alexis Coulomb is in Michael Gomes, *The Coulomb Case* (Fullerton, CA: Theosophical History Occasional Papers, 2005).

was sent to India to investigate further. Hodgson's report was damning: Blavatsky's phenomena, he claimed, were the work of accomplices; the letters from the Mahatmas were written by her in an assumed handwriting. In looking for a motive for her actions, he ruled out financial gain or "a morbid yearning for notoriety," settling instead on the theory that her championing of ancient traditions was a diversion for her real work as a Russian spy.[6] The SPR committee endorsed most of Hodgson's conclusions, ending its report with the oft-cited statement: "We regard her neither as the mouthpiece of hidden seers, nor as a mere vulgar adventuress; we think that she has achieved a title to permanent remembrance as one of the most accomplished, ingenious, and interesting imposters in history."[7]

The publication of this report did little to dampen public interest in Theosophy, and its years of growth in the West were still ahead. It did bring an end to the prominence of the Masters and of psychic phenomena in the Theosophical Society and moved it toward a greater focus on the comparative study of the esoteric aspects of philosophy, religion, and science, both Eastern and Western. Blavatsky had wanted to sue the SPR for libel, but the Society's leading members were against doing so.

Blavatsky subsequently resigned her position as corresponding secretary due to illness and left for Europe, where she eventually settled in the small German town of Würzburg. There she turned her attention to writing her major work, *The Secret Doctrine: The Synthesis of Science, Religion, and Philosophy*. More than fifteen hundred pages in print when the two volumes were published in 1888, it aimed at nothing less than chronicling the spiritual, mental, and physical history of humanity and the universe. She resettled in London in the spring of 1887 and drew around her a group of bright young people, including some of the first women college graduates in England, the pioneer of gnostic studies, G. R. S. Mead; the social reformer, Annie Besant; and the Irish poet, William Butler Yeats.

In 1888, Blavatsky started her own school as an Esoteric Section of the Theosophical Society, which she now called "a dead failure," citing the authority of the Mahatmas, who referred to it as a "soulless corpse."[8] This led

---

[6] Richard Hodgson, "Account of Personal Investigations in India, and Discussion of the Authorship of the 'Koot Hoomi' Letters," *SPR Proceedings* 3 (1885), 317. Theosophists, of course, disagreed.

[7] "Report of the Committee Appointed to Investigate Phenomena Connected with the Theosophical Society," *SPR Proceedings* 3 (1885), 207. Over the years the Society for Psychical Research has increasingly distanced itself from this report, pointing out, as stated in their *Proceedings*, that the opinions given represent the views of their authors and not the society.

[8] H. P. Blavatsky, "Preliminary Memorandum of the Esoteric Section," in *Blavatsky Collected Writings [BCW]* (Wheaton, IL: Theosophical Publishing House, 1966–1985), 12:489; *Letters*

her into conflict with Olcott, who saw this as a sectarian move threatening the neutrality of the Theosophical Society. The group became an independent entity, the Eastern School of Theosophy, studying Blavatsky's correspondences of color, number, and sound in relation to her sevenfold system in the microcosm and the macrocosm. But after a year she ceased issuing instructions and turned her attention to the formation of an Inner Group – six men and six women – chosen by her to receive oral instruction. This group seems to have had its problems too. Three months before her death, Blavatsky warned that meetings might cease because of a lack of harmony among participants, a problem in the outer society that she had tried to remedy by teaching select students.[9]

Helena Petrovna Blavatsky died on May 8, 1891, from the effects of the influenza epidemic that was spreading through London. Her death was world news, receiving extensive coverage in the New York and London papers, and throughout India. Among those who attended her cremation was a young Indian law student, Mohandas K. Gandhi, who had been encouraged by two of her pupils to study the *Bhagavad Gita*, a text that would become the basis of his later philosophy.

## 3 Central Concepts of Theosophy

Blavatsky's enduring relevance in the field of esotericism lies in her massive literary output. She started two journals, and her magazine and newspaper pieces are estimated to be close to a thousand. Combined, *Isis Unveiled* and *The Secret Doctrine* run more than twenty-eight hundred pages. She produced two other books: *The Key to Theosophy* (1889) and *The Voice of the Silence* (1889). The former was a manual in question-and-answer form outlining the tenets of Theosophy, especially karma, reincarnation, postmortem states, and Blavatsky's distinctive sevenfold classification of the individual. The latter was a small book based on precepts used by the esoteric school she had come in contact with.[10] It delineated the process of spiritual growth, mixing Hindu and Buddhist concepts, and stressing the mastering of seven *pāramitās*, or virtues, for spiritual success. Her interpretation of the *pāramitās* is reminiscent of Shantideva's treatment in his eighth-century text, the *Bodhicharyāvatara*, a

---

*from the Masters of the Wisdom, First Series*, compiled by C. Jinarajadasa (Adyar: Theosophical Publishing House, 1973), 101.
[9] *The Inner Group Teachings of H.P. Blavatsky*, compiled and annotated by Henk J. Spierenburg, 2nd ed. (San Diego: Point Loma Press, 1995), 74–75.
[10] Both the Ninth Panchen and the Fourteenth Dalai Lamas have written messages for editions of *The Voice of the Silence*.

Buddhist work not then translated. At the time of her death, she was compiling a massive dictionary of esotericism, which was published posthumously as *The Theosophical Glossary* (1892).

Unlike previous works arguing for the existence of an ancient esoteric tradition buried under myth and symbol, *Isis Unveiled* purports to provide the proof for this claim: the survival of its adepts and schools in the present day. *Isis* begins with the words: "The work now submitted to public judgment is the fruit of a somewhat intimate acquaintance with Eastern adepts and study of their science."[11] It is a practitioner's guide effectively defining the tradition. Platonism, Neoplatonism, Paracelsism, mesmerism, Eliphas Lévi's Astral Light, the Emerald Tablet of Hermes, Gnosticism, the Kabbalah, the incarnations of Vishnu, and the laws of Manu are just some of the subjects covered.

Central to Blavatsky's position is the belief that

> Esoteric philosophers held that everything in nature is but a materialization of spirit. The Eternal First Cause is latent spirit, they said, and matter from the beginning.... With the first idea, which emanated from the double-sexed and hitherto inactive Deity, the first motion was communicated to the whole universe, and the electric thrill was instantaneously felt throughout the boundless space. Spirit begat force, and force matter; and thus the latent deity manifested itself as a creative energy.[12]

The nature of the creative impulse is revealed through the idea of cycles, and the first chapter of the book introduces the vast cycles of time, or *yugas*. Their effects in human history are shown by the rise and decline of societies and cultures. Since God is "the universal mind diffused through all things,"[13] the world is seen as a series of spiritual hierarchies, often no more than aspects of impersonal divine force acting in accordance with divine will.

In *The Secret Doctrine*, the creative process is examined in more detail than in *Isis*. "The Eternal Parent," akin to the *Parabrahman* of Indian philosophy and *Ein-Sof* in the Kabbalah, reveals itself through periods of activity and rest. The manifested world is a radiation of this Unknown Cause and is withdrawn back into itself at the end of the cycle. The forms of manifestation are worked out through a series of hierarchies from divine to elemental. Humanity is seen as the crown of creation in this scheme. The Monad, the divine spark, after passing through mineral, vegetable, and animal stages, comes to full self-consciousness in the human, the fourth stage in a sevenfold

---

[11] H. P. Blavatsky, *Isis Unveiled* (New York, 1877), 1:v.
[12] Blavatsky, *Isis Unveiled*, 1:428.
[13] Blavatsky, *Isis Unveiled*, 1:289.

round of development. Present humanity is the fifth human race to inhabit this planet; the previous ones ranged from ethereal unconscious forms to the giants of Lemuria, a continent that existed from India to the South Pacific, and Atlantis, whose Atlantean portion sank thousands of years ago. Blavatsky claimed that a new sixth race, which will develop a sixth sense, will slowly begin to emerge in America.

Many of the concepts in *The Secret Doctrine* had been put forth in the correspondence later published as *The Mahatma Letters to A. P. Sinnett*. The letters, written over a six-year period, from 1880 to 1885, were from Blavatsky's Indian teachers, Morya and Koot Hoomi. The majority of the letters are by Koot Hoomi, a Kashmiri Brahmin who is said to have been educated in Europe, and his writing shows a familiarity with nineteenth-century English science and literature. Blavatsky's Mahatmas possess attributes different from those attributed to them by twentieth-century devotees. As she describes them, they are human beings whose lifespan rarely exceeds a hundred years. The bureaucratic structure of an Inner Government of the World prevalent in the writings of Annie Besant, C. W. Leadbeater, and Alice Bailey, is not found in Blavatsky's work. The most she reveals is that "there is beyond the Himalayas a nucleus of Adepts of various nationalities," and that some of them "remain unknown in their true character even to the average lamas."[14] The adepts are adepts by virtue of the sanctity of their lives and devotion to the welfare of humanity.

The authorship of the letters is usually attributed to Blavatsky. In fact, Richard Hodgson devoted the greater part of his report to an attempt to prove precisely this. William and Harold Hare's 1936 *Who Wrote the Mahatma Letters*, a book-length treatment of the matter, simply recycled Hodgson's conclusions. More recently, the *Journal of the Society for Psychical Research* published the most extensive examination of the entire correspondence to date – a larger selection than had been available to Hodgson – prepared by the noted British handwriting expert Vernon Harrison. His conclusion: Blavatsky was not the writer.[15] K. Paul Johnson in *The Masters Revealed* (1994) has suggested that the Mahatmas were in fact Ranbir Singh, Maharajah of Kashmir, and Thakar Singh Sandhanwalia, cousin of the deposed Maharajah Dalip Singh, both Sikh insurrectionists plotting against British rule. However, correspondence from the Mahatmas continued after the deaths of these two men. Whatever their origin, the Mahatma letters

---

[14] Blavatsky to Franz Hartmann, 2 April 1886, *The Theosophical Quarterly* 23 (April 1926), 324.
[15] Harrison's report in the April 1986 SPR *Journal* is reprinted with a detailed analysis of the script and color plates of the letters in his *H. P. Blavatsky and the S.P.R.* (Pasadena, CA: Theosophical University Press, 1997).

remain a major source for understanding the fundamentals of modern Theosophy, and the complex figure that is H. P. Blavatsky.

One of the main ideas to emerge in the Mahatma letters is the sevenfold classification of the individual: physical body, astral double, vitality, desire, mind, spiritual intuition, and Ātma, the divine spark.[16] At death, only the higher principles survive, constituting the enduring individuality, while the discarded personality dissipates. Between death and rebirth is the intermediate state of *Devachan*, a blissful period absorbing the best of the past life. The regulator of human experience is karma, which is constantly being created by the personality. The spiritual life is put forth as the means of escape from the round of birth and death.

Blavatsky's claims regarding Buddhist esotericism were dismissed by one of the leading Orientalists of her time, F. Max Müller, editor of *The Sacred Books of the East*. His opinion represented the prevailing notions of the day, which viewed the Theravada Buddhism of Ceylon and the Pali texts as the original form of Buddhism, and everything else a corruption. Now that Tibetan Buddhism has been better studied, however, the idea of esoteric Buddhism is accepted and the tradition of wonder-working adepts, the Mahāsiddhas, is acknowledged.

Far more serious is the charge of plagiarism raised by Blavatsky's long-time critic, William Emmette Coleman. A fervent spiritualist, Coleman made a career of attacking Blavatsky and is remembered only for his railings against her. Coleman claimed that the twenty-one hundred quotations in *Isis Unveiled* were derived without acknowledgment from one hundred books.[17] The books he cites were some of the main sources available on the study of myth and symbol at the time. Some – such as S. F. Dunlap's books, which Coleman says supplied Blavatsky with the majority of her material – were extensive collections culled from the works of other writers. Ironically, the same charge had been brought against Coleman himself by another writer, H. W. Burr, who complained that he had passed off translations used by Burr as his own.[18]

The charge of plagiarism against Blavatsky remains undecided because of the difficulty in proving Coleman's claims, especially since the titles he lists are the ones she credits most often in her books. Nor is his accusation of the

---

[16] Blavatsky refined the concept in a later enumeration given to her esoteric students: aura, pattern body, desire, lower mind, higher mind, intuition, and prana.
[17] William Coleman, "The Sources of Madame Blavatsky's Writings," in Vsevolod Solovyov's *A Modern Priestess of Isis*, trans. Walter Leaf (London, 1895; facsimile reprint New York: Arno Press, 1976).
[18] H. W. Burr, *Plagiarism* (Washington, DC, 1881).

wholesale copying of passages as clear-cut as he would like the reader to believe, since anything Blavatsky mined from the sources given was often improved or added to. Blavatsky's last written piece, penned less than two weeks before her death, was in response to Coleman's charges published in a San Francisco spiritualist journal. Acknowledging many defects in her books due to her inexperience as a writer, she cited the quote from Montaigne she had used in *The Secret Doctrine*: "I have here made only a nosegay of culled flowers, and have brought nothing of my own but the string that ties them," adding, "is anyone of my helpers prepared to say that I have not paid full price for the string?"[19]

In spite of her critics, Blavatsky's literary influence during the formative years of the modern Theosophical movement vastly exceeded that of any other author. In the decade between *Isis Unveiled* and *The Secret Doctrine*, A. P. Sinnett's *The Occult World* and *Esoteric Buddhism* were the main source of Theosophical ideas. Issued in America by the respected Boston firm of Houghton and Mifflin – publishers of Emerson and Thoreau – Sinnett's books received wide circulation. Franz Hartmann contributed a number of books on Rosicrucians, Hermeticism, and Paracelsus. Mabel Collins's little book, *Light on the Path* (1884), a guide for spiritual practice, was reprinted countless times. A minor fiction writer, Collins (1851–1927) produced what must be one of the earliest depictions of the trials awaiting a woman on the path, *The Blossom and the Fruit* (1888). Its tone so scandalized Blavatsky that she stepped in and rewrote the ending. The book became required reading for members of Aleister Crowley's occult group, the A∴A∴..

## 4 The Influence of Blavatsky and Theosophy

Often derided and dismissed, Blavatsky nevertheless had an impact that was far-reaching. The first woman with such a presence in a male-dominated field, she opened the way for women as no one else before. Denied the right to vote by society at large, in the Theosophical Society women were allowed to vote and be elected to office. And women would run it after Blavatsky's death: Annie Besant (1847–1933) as president after the death of Olcott, and Katherine Tingley (1847–1929) as head of W. Q. Judge's Theosophical Society in America.

After Blavatsky's death, members including Annie Besant, C. W. Leadbeater, and Alice Bailey took a less aggressive stance against Spiritualism and the churches, and they began integrating both. This caused

[19] H. P. Blavatsky, "My Books," *Lucifer*, May 1891, BCW 13:202.

alarm among some, and a "Back to Blavatsky" movement developed in the twentieth century stressing a return to the study of her writings. Others such as Rudolf Steiner, Anna Kingsford, and Dion Fortune would leave Theosophical terminology behind and form their own groups.[20] Through the writings of Alexandra David-Neel and W. Y. Evans-Wentz, members inspired by Blavatsky's narrative, Tibetan Buddhism would further attract the attention of the West, while Christmas Humphreys and Ernest Wood, with their popular Penguin paperbacks of the 1950s, helped make Buddhism and yoga part of Western culture.

While Blavatsky is often credited with bringing Eastern ideas into the stream of Western esotericism, it was not an undigested assimilation of Hindu and Buddhist concepts. The philosophical positions of those schools were often adapted to the already existing concerns of the Western tradition. This in turn affected the acceptance of these beliefs when the first Hindu and Buddhist practitioners came West. Equally important is the dramatic shift Blavatsky brought about in Western esotericism, previously a textual study abetted by ritual work. Blavatsky's development of a psychology of the mind and reference to Eastern techniques allowed for an interiorization of practice. Meditation, visualization, and the exaltation of consciousness as means to access hidden wisdom have become features of modern esotericism. Nor can one ignore Blavatsky's pioneering work in bringing Western esotericism to India. Through her writings, Indians became aware of the Kabbalah and Hermeticism – quite an achievement considering that, as Wilhelm Halbfass notes, "in traditional Hindu thought and literature, there has been virtually no interest in foreign countries, societies, cultures or religions."[21] Theosophy flourished in India, now its largest membership, and counted among its ranks Jawaharlal Nehru, the first prime minster of independent India.

Drawing on the best of both West and East, the founding of Blavatsky's Theosophical Society in New York helped usher in a new age of American esotericism. Long before anyone else, she saw the fit of Eastern religion and the American temperament. This synthesis would provide a defining marker in the history of esotericism, which until then had been exclusively a European concern. In blurring cultural barriers, Blavatsky created a form that was neither Eastern nor Western but found a global acceptance. With

---

[20] The Theosophical Society would fragment a number of times. Its later history is given in L. H. Leslie-Smith's *100 Years of Modern Occultism* (London: Theosophical History Centre, 1987), and Bruce F. Campbell, *Ancient Wisdom Revived: A History of the Theosophical Movement* (Los Angeles: University of California Press, 1980).

[21] Wilhelm Halbfass, *India and Europe: An Essay in Philosophical Understanding* (Albany: State University of New York Press, 1988), 193.

her ideal of the individual empowered by *gnosis*, she reached back to the Renaissance beliefs of Pico della Mirandola. She presaged the growing movement for a spirituality that could function outside the bounds of organized religion. An expert in myth and symbol, she helped create some of the most enduring images of our time: the mystic East, ancient wisdom, hidden texts, and a secret brotherhood of beneficent guardians.

22

# RUDOLF STEINER AND ANTHROPOSOPHY

## Robert McDermott

### 1 Introduction

Rudolf Steiner (1861–1925) is the founder and teacher of anthroposophy, which derives its name from the Greek *anthropos* (understood by Steiner to mean "ideal human") and *sophia*, which refers to divine feminine wisdom. Anthroposophy overlaps with religion and mysticism in that it is focused on the human experience of the divine, but its emphasis is on a spiritual knowledge that is in principle difficult to attain. Steiner insisted that in theory others could attain the same kind of knowledge that he had. In fact, however, very few have been able to attain the profound secrets of evolution, higher beings, as well as afterlife and rebirth, all of which Steiner claimed to have researched successfully.

Steiner reported his esoteric research in three thousand lectures recorded by stenographers. As he continued to write, lecture, administer, and counsel, he did not have time to revise these lectures for publication. However, Steinerbooks has now undertaken the project of publishing his collected works in 354 volumes. Steiner's writings contain important contributions to philosophy, the natural and social sciences, the arts, education, and the study of Asian and Western spiritual traditions. Steiner is perhaps best known for the Waldorf School movement, consisting of more than one thousand schools in more than one hundred countries. These schools continue to draw guidance from his hundreds of lectures on child development, curriculum, and pedagogy.

Steiner wrote approximately thirty books, beginning in 1891 with *Truth and Knowledge*, his doctoral dissertation in philosophy, and ending in 1924, the year before he died, with his autobiography (which unfortunately covers only up to 1907, therefore before the beginning of the Anthroposophical Society, and before most of his important research).

Steiner was convinced that his *Philosophy of Freedom*, which he wrote in 1894, at age 33, would be the book that would be his most lasting and influential.[1] It seems more likely, however, that his *Theosophy* (1904) and *How to Know Higher Worlds* (1904) might prove more enduring, perhaps because for most readers both are more immediately accessible than *Philosophy of Freedom*.

Rudolf Steiner believed his esoteric mission and research to be a continuation of the tradition associated with the mysterious fifteenth-century esoteric teacher Christian Rosenkreutz. However, he also intended his teaching to be entirely relevant and contemporary, especially given that he set it in direct opposition to the reductionist science of his day. Steiner taught a comprehensive and detailed theory of the evolution of consciousness as a way of demonstrating the need for the transformation of the faculties of thinking, feeling, and willing. He considered the goal of the evolution of human consciousness to be the attainment of universal love and true freedom, and he regarded the incarnation of the Christ as the central event in this process. Steiner's written works and lectures seek to establish that in the past four centuries in the West, humanity gradually lost its previous access to the inner reality of the self and to the inner dimension of the outer world.

In a series of letters to members written in the last year of his life, Steiner offered the following characterization of anthroposophy:

> Anthroposophy is a path of knowledge to guide the spiritual in the human being to the spiritual in the universe. It arises in the human being as a need of the heart, of the life of feeling. It can be justified only inasmuch as it can satisfy this inner need. Only those can acknowledge anthroposophy who find in it what they themselves in their inner lives feel impelled to seek. Only they can be anthroposophists who feel certain questions on the nature of the human being and the universe as an elemental need of life, just as one feels hunger and thirst.
>
> Anthroposophy communicates knowledge that is gained in a spiritual way. Yet it only does so because everyday life, and the science founded on sensation and intellectual activity, lead to a barrier along life's way – a limit where the life of the soul in the human being would die if it could go no further. Everyday life and science do not lead to this limit in such a way as to compel the human being to stop short at it. For at the very frontier where

---

[1] Most recently published as *Intuitive Thinking as a Spiritual Path: A Philosophy of Freedom*, trans. Michael Lipson, introduction by Gertrude Reif Hughes (Great Barrington, MA: Steinerbooks, 1995).

the knowledge derived from sense-perception ceases, there is opened through the human soul itself the further outlook into the spiritual world.[2]

Steiner sought to help human beings develop their spiritual (higher, intuitive) faculties or capacities as a means to gain true and reliable knowledge of the spiritual dimension of the cosmos. According to Steiner, this achievement is possible by a kind of thinking that he describes synonymously as active, loving, spiritual, and free. He tries to show that this new mode of spiritual thinking is at the core of the great advances in science, art, and religion.

According to Steiner, to be a thinking person one must relate lovingly to the universe, earth, the animate world, and to the human person, especially oneself. Steiner intends his ideal of spiritually active thinking as a call to the heart, to the affective and artistic capacities of each person. He develops a concept and method of spiritual, "living" thinking as a contrast to both ordinary intellectualism and to religious faith, neither of which, in his view, develops the capacities essential in this life, in the afterlife, and in future incarnations. In his view, ordinary religious belief is too passive, while scientific knowing is usually limited to the surface, or material level.

## 2 Rudolf Steiner's Life and Work

Rudolf Steiner was born on February 27, 1861, in Croatia, within the Austrian Empire. He spent his early childhood near, and often in, a train station on the Southern Austrian Railway where his father was a station master. It was in this station house when Steiner was eight years old that the ghost of an aunt appeared to him and sought his help. As the young Steiner learned the following day, his aunt had committed suicide. This experience indicated to Steiner that the dead can be in close contact with the living and can need help. When his elementary schoolteacher gave him a geometry book, Steiner found that the pure geometric forms were rather like the world of spiritual forms with which he was already familiar. This discovery convinced him that the experience of the world of spiritual realities, in this case ideal forms, was one that could be shared and communicated.

Steiner attended a scientific high school until age eighteen, later graduating from a polytechnic college in Vienna. During his college years, he was employed as a tutor to a family of boys, the youngest of whom, Otto Specht, had virtually been abandoned by his family because he had hydrocephalus.

[2] Rudolf Steiner, *Anthroposophical Leading Thoughts: Anthroposophy as a Path of Knowledge – the Michael Mystery*, trans. George and Mary Adams (London: Rudolf Steiner Press, 1973), 13.

After two years of patient work, Steiner had the boy learning on a par with those of his age. In later life, Specht became a medical doctor. Steiner's work with Otto Specht would later serve as a model and inspiration for his work as the founder of the Waldorf approach to education – and equally for the Camphill movement, which provides education and community life for individuals in need of special care.

In a brief autobiographical sketch called "The Barr Document," written in 1906, Steiner acknowledges but does not identify by name the spiritual master to whom he was sent by an intermediary, the herb gatherer Feliz Kugetski: "I did not at once meet the M. [master], but first someone sent by him who was completely initiated into the mysteries of the effects of all plants and their connection with the universe and with man's nature."[3]

This herb gatherer gave Steiner his first opportunity to share with another human being the reality of the spiritual world manifest in nature. After this meeting, Steiner's spiritual master, or initiator, gave him the immeasurably difficult task of reversing the fall of Western thought and culture into materialism. He also gave Steiner the specific task of restoring to the West the double concept of karma and rebirth. During the remaining decades of his life, Steiner faithfully carried out these missions, making them his life's work. The first task he set for himself was to establish the philosophical basis for his later esoteric research.

Through his professor of German literature, Steiner began to edit, at age twenty-two, the volume that became *Goethe's Natural Scientific Writings*. At age twenty-five, he wrote *A Theory of Knowledge Implicit in Goethe's World Conception*. In 1891, he received his doctorate in philosophy from the University of Rostock; a year later, he published his dissertation under the title *Truth and Knowledge*. In 1894, he published his primary work in philosophy, *The Philosophy of Freedom*. Because he already believed that he possessed an unusual, and in fact extraordinary, ability to see spiritual realities and to communicate profound spiritual insights, he was eager to establish the philosophical justification for such research. In so doing, he drew on two great streams in German thought: Goethe's "gentle empiricism" and the philosophies of Fichte, Schelling, and Hegel.

Steiner saw the natural philosophy of Goethe, as well as his own esoteric naturalism, as necessary complements to philosophical idealism. This typifies Steiner's habit of synthesis: He often sympathized with diverse and competing positions in such a way as to save and reconcile the positive contributions

---

[3] "Barr Document," in *The New Essential Steiner*, ed. Robert McDermott (Great Barrington, MA: Steinerbooks, 2009), 81.

of each. Both his life and his thought can be seen as attempts to reconcile, and lift to a higher synthesis, such polarities as science and art, matter and spirit, individualism and community.

As Steiner argued in *The Philosophy of Freedom*, to be free is to be capable of thinking one's own intuitive thoughts – not the "thoughts" occasioned by the sensations of the body, and certainly not those promulgated by society, but thoughts generated by one's own spiritual self. He emphasized repeatedly that our faulty (nonspiritual, unfree) thinking is due to alienation from other human beings and from cosmic rhythms. This alienation, both innate and acquired, is characteristic of the present age. It includes an image of the human being that isolates the self from its necessary relations. Steiner sought to show how the thinking characteristic of the past several centuries in the West had led to a disregard for the life of feeling. He sought to critique and replace scientific-rationalistic thinking, which excludes the entire affective dimension of life, and thus denigrates the religious and the artistic.

In 1899, as he later reported in his autobiography, Steiner entered a deep spiritual struggle that led to an experience of the role of Christ in the evolution of consciousness. As a result of this life-transforming experience, his esoteric research was thereafter bathed in the light of the Logos, the Sun Being, or Cosmic Christ. In his autobiography, he described a profoundly transformative event that occurred at this time:

> During the period when my statements about Christianity seemed to contradict my later comments, a conscious knowledge of real Christianity began to dawn within me. Around the turn of the century this seed of knowledge continued to develop. The soul test described here occurred shortly before the beginning of the twentieth century. It was decisive for my soul's development that I stood spiritually before the Mystery of Golgotha[4] in a deep and solemn celebration of knowledge.[5]

Following this experience, and his discovery of "real Christianity," Steiner began to lecture to large audiences of Theosophists. He served as general secretary of the German branch of the Theosophical Society from 1902 until 1909, when he formally separated from the society. This break was virtually forced on him when C. W. Leadbeater and Annie Besant, leaders of the Theosophical Society, announced that the then sixteen-year-old

---

[4] By the Mystery of Golgotha, Steiner intends the events of the last week of the life of Jesus Christ: arrest, execution, "descent into hell," and resurrection from the dead.
[5] Rudolf Steiner, *Autobiography: Chapters in the Course of My Life: 1861–1907*, trans. Rita Stebbing. Chronology, notes, bibliography, Paul Allen. Collected Works, vol. 28 (Great Barrington, MA: Steinerbooks, 2005), 188.

J. Krishnamurti was the vehicle of the reincarnated Master Jesus. Steiner and Besant were unable to collaborate, but one wonders whether he might have been able to collaborate with Madame Blavatsky, had she not died in 1891.[6]

In 1912, Steiner's followers, almost all members of the Theosophical Society, formed the Anthroposophical Society with Steiner as its teacher. In 1913, Steiner laid the foundation stone for the Goetheanum, an enormous wood structure that he designed for an imposing hill in Dornach, near Basel, Switzerland. This architecturally double-cupola structure was named in honor of Goethe and was made of woods from all over Europe and North America. It was under construction for a full decade. Steiner hoped that the Goetheanum would give future generations of open-minded visitors some clues as to the health-giving capacity of spiritually informed arts. This hope was dashed when the Goetheanum building was totally destroyed by an arsonist on New Year's Eve, 1922. In the midst of the ashes, Steiner immediately began to design the second Goetheanum, which was completed after his death.

Marie von Sievers, whom Steiner married in 1914, shared every aspect of his work, particularly in relation to the esoteric renewal of the arts. It seems, however, that Steiner's deepest personal relationship – one that he believed had extended through previous lifetimes – was with Ita Wegman, a Dutch physician with whom he collaborated on medical research for more than two decades.

In response to a request from a young dancer for a new approach to dance, Steiner developed eurythmy, an art of movement intended to strengthen the "subtle body," the etheric aspect of the human being that surrounds and pervades the physical body. Steiner also contributed new methods and innovations in sculpture, architecture, painting, and music. He taught that the etheric, or life-body, is nourished by sculpture and eurythmy, that the soul or astral body is strengthened by painting, and that the "I" or individual spirit is deepened by poetry.

From 1910 to 1913, Steiner wrote four mystery dramas as a way of helping modern Western audiences experience in dramatic form the karma of entwined lives over several incarnations. The economic and social ills of the decade surrounding the First World War led Steiner to develop an elaborate social, political, and economic theory called "the threefold social order," according to which rights and responsibilities fall into three distinct but related groups: the economic, the political, and the cultural. Among the

---

[6] See Rudolf Steiner, *Spiritualism, Madame Blavatsky, and Theosophy: An Eyewitness View of Occult History*, ed. Christopher Bamford (Great Barrington, MA: Steinerbooks, 2001).

many significant implications of this division is the freedom of the cultural sphere from legal and economic control. The cultural sphere, for Steiner, includes religion, education, and the arts, and all other expressions of individual freedom and creativity.

In 1919, in response to a plea from the owner of the Waldorf Astoria Cigarette Factory in Stuttgart for help in educating the children of his employees, Steiner developed a novel educational experiment based on his insights concerning the inner life and development of the child. The Waldorf approach to education is especially significant for its ability to reconcile science and art on the basis of a single source and methodology: active, heartfelt thinking. The Waldorf schools, which constitute the largest non-sectarian private school movement in the world, are characterized by the attempt to integrate the works of head, heart, and hand (or the disciplined cultivation of thinking, feeling, and willing), and by the aim of educating the total child in freedom and responsibility for nature, for the individual, and for the global human community.

In response to requests from doctors for a course of lectures on homeopathic and anthroposophic healing, Steiner classified numerous herbs and other natural substances according to their various healing powers. There are now more than two thousand physicians worldwide who have been trained both in standard medical diagnostic and prescriptive treatment and in anthroposophic healing. Answering the plea of farmers, Steiner lectured extensively on a method of agriculture based on his supersensible knowledge of the spiritual forces operative in the mineral, vegetable, and animal worlds. This method of farming, called biodynamic, is an increasingly influential agricultural alternative to chemically dominated farming.

## 3 Evolution of Consciousness

The spiritual knowledge scattered throughout Steiner's hundreds of volumes includes disclosures – some of them quite startling – concerning such topics as the evolution of the sun, moon, and planets. He describes the role of great spiritual beings such as Krishna, Buddha, and Christ; the two tempters, Lucifer and Ahriman; and the archangel Michael, whom Steiner regards as the regent of the current age. Steiner also includes descriptions of the salient characteristics of Western civilization, which he places in a detailed evolutionary sequence. Steiner discusses historically significant and paradigmatic individuals such as the pharaohs of ancient Egypt, the patriarchs and prophets of Israel, Zoroaster, Plato, and Aristotle, as well as a series of influential Christian personalities and modern Western philosophers and scientists.

Steiner particularly emphasizes the descent of Christ, the "spiritual Sun-Being," into history through the agency of Jesus and several predecessors. When discussing his experience of the Mystery of Golgotha, Steiner explained that his understanding of these events was based entirely on direct vision. He did not claim certitude for his clairvoyant powers; he considered his esoteric research to be work in progress. He refined and deepened his findings throughout his life, and he sought collaborators who could penetrate as deeply as he could into the secrets of humanity and the universe. Steiner apparently believed that he was able to "read" (or to supersensibly "see") the essential events recorded in what is known in the esoteric tradition as the "astral akashic record." He characterizes the evolution of consciousness by a double direction: a steady decrease in human spiritual-intuitive thinking and a corresponding increase in the capacity of, and reliance on, the human intellect.

According to this theory of evolution and devolution, modern Western consciousness lost the clairvoyance it possessed thousands of years ago, but it has gained independence in thinking and in the development of individual consciousness. Steiner details the loss of ancient clairvoyance without regret: It is precisely this loss that made possible the development of intelligence and individual creativity. The real cause for regret, he explains, lies in the failure of modern Western consciousness to develop a thinking capability at once warm and rational, individual and sacred. Steiner sought to help people (particularly Westerners) living in his own time to understand how and why they think, feel, and will as they do. He considered Greek thought to represent a remarkable transition from the old clairvoyance represented by the gods of ancient Greek religion to the possibility of rational, intellectual thinking represented by Socratic inquiry, Platonic dialectic, and Aristotelian logic.

Steiner states that soon after this transition, the Logos, or Christ-Being, incarnated and helped reverse the increasing control of the material world, particularly the grip of materialist thinking on Western consciousness. By entering the body of Jesus of Nazareth, the Logos brought into the earth a spiritual impulse that can help lead humanity to greater freedom and love. Steiner's worldview and spiritual practices are permeated by the Christ impulse but are not constrained by Christian dogma or the ideal of faith. Rather, he teaches that in the present age, the "Christ impulse" serves the ideal of human freedom in thinking and action.

Steiner believed that the separation of mind from nature, as formulated by Descartes in the seventeenth century, is the fundamental life problem of the modern, Western individual. The solution to this problem lies in a new kind of clairvoyance based on an intensely active spiritual thinking. The nature and function of this kind of thinking constitute the spiritual methodology called anthroposophy.

## 4 The Discipline of Spiritual Science

Perhaps Steiner's most significant contribution to contemporary esotericism is the method he provided for acquiring higher or deeper spiritual knowledge. Steiner is distinctive, and perhaps unique, in the degree to which he theorized about his clairvoyant powers and tried to instruct people with ordinary consciousness to develop spiritual intuition.

Steiner intended his research into the spiritual world to exemplify his method and to show the need for solutions that stem from a higher level of spiritual insight. Again, anthroposophy represents a method of spiritual growth and transformation that aims to create an ideal harmony between thinking, feeling, and willing. Steiner recommends rather simple exercises that cultivate these three components of human life and also serve as a basis for the more advanced work of spiritual science. He offers six preconditions for spiritual-esoteric progress:

1. Practice concentrating: gain control of one's thoughts for a few minutes faithfully every day. For example, concentrating for five minutes on a simple object, one that is presumably uninteresting in its own right, for example, a paper clip. Steiner held that it should be possible to experience each new thought as issuing from one's own will and creativity.
2. Practice controlling the will. Steiner recommended performing one positive but relatively insignificant task the same time each day, for example, turning one's ring at 3:00 every afternoon.
3. Practice equanimity: learn to stabilize fluctuations of pleasure and pain, joy and sorrow. Steiner conceived this not as an exercise to weaken one's involvement or concern. Rather, it simply places each event and thought (particularly ones that would ordinarily arouse fear or delight, sympathy or antipathy) under one's conscious control.
4. Practice seeing the positive in all things and events; resist negative criticism.
5. Practice openness to new experiences and ideas; try to overcome one's opposition to a new or strange event or idea simply because it is new.

6. Practice repeating and harmonizing the first five exercises. The first two can be performed at specific points in the day; the third, fourth, and fifth can be practiced throughout one's daily life.[7]

In his *Philosophy of Freedom*, Steiner sought to establish the theoretical and experiential possibility of attaining spiritual or esoteric knowledge. He tried to show the causes of alienated (i.e., unfree, materialistic, superficial) thinking, and the possibility of thinking in a new, creative, original way. He hoped that the result of working conscientiously through his *Philosophy of Freedom* would be none other than what the book's title suggests: to think freely, to intuit ideas and ideals that exist in the spiritual world, of which every free thinker is a part.

*How to Know Higher Worlds* is intended as a kind of handbook for the development of clairvoyant or supersensible perception, the possibility of which Steiner insists on in the opening paragraph:

> There slumber in every human being faculties by means of which individuals can acquire for themselves knowledge of higher worlds. Mystics, Gnostics, Theosophists, all speak of a world of soul and spirit that for them is just as real as the world we see with our physical eyes and touch with our physical hands. At every moment the listener may say: That, of which they speak, I too can learn, if I develop within myself certain powers which today still slumber within me.[8]

Steiner insists that esoteric knowledge is available to anyone who seeks it according to a method established by a genuine spiritual school and by an esoteric teacher disciplined in the methods of that school. Unfortunately, modern Western individuals typically lack the imagination to recognize that their ordinary thinking cannot access spiritual depth. Steiner believed that the widespread inability to experience the thinking, feeling, and willing of others is at the root of national, racial, gender, and generational misunderstandings and violence, and he offered a discipline by which to overcome such alienation and violence. He believed that the development of esoteric capacities usually follows a systematic progression, from intellectual knowing up through imagination, inspiration, and intuition. Each of these three levels of higher knowledge corresponds to a part of the human being: Imagination is a capacity developed by, and in the realm of, the subtle body or life principle (also called the etheric, or formative, principle); inspiration

---

[7] *Start Now! – A Book of Soul and Spiritual Exercises*, ed. Christopher Bamford (Great Barrington, MA: Steinerbooks, 2004), 109–119.
[8] Rudolf Steiner, *How to Know Higher Worlds* (Great Barrington, MA: Steinerbooks, 1994), 13.

corresponds to the astral (or soul) principle; and intuition corresponds to the "I," or the spiritual self.

For Steiner, science and art are equally effective means by which to develop spiritual-thinking capacity. Like other great spiritual figures (e.g., Swedenborg, Goethe, Blake, Emerson, and Sri Aurobindo), Steiner was able to express himself in a wide range of endeavors, including natural science, art, philosophy, and history. He was convinced that meditative or imaginative thinking, according to the method of anthroposophy, can enable one to acquire higher ways of knowing as well as a more fruitful relationship to one's self, to the rest of humanity, and to the universe.

## 5 Karma and Rebirth

At the core of Steiner's teaching concerning karma and rebirth is his claim that human beings have two closely related life histories: waking and sleeping. The beginning of sleep represents a kind of death to the waking biography, just as the beginning of waking consciousness is a kind of death to the sleeping biography. The activity of the soul after its earthly life parallels the activity of the soul during sleep, when the soul and spirit leave the remainder of the sleeping individual – the physical and etheric bodies – and return to the spiritual world for the period of sleep. After death, the sleep biography is relived in an ingenious reversal of the individual's earthly life.

Steiner believed that at death, only the physical body immediately dies. The etheric body, which has recorded the essential qualities of a person's lifetime, presents a detailed summary of this life to the astral body. After it absorbs the panoramic report of the etheric body, the astral body remains in existence for approximately one-third the duration of a person's lifetime. During this time, the astral body, in which is embedded the individual's desires and emotions, continues to seek the kinds of satisfaction it enjoyed on earth. To the extent that it clings to physical and selfish satisfaction, it can only be frustrated. In the second phase of this process, the spirit of the individual relives its entire past life from death to birth, all the while receiving the consequences of its earthly actions as they were experienced by everyone and everything that was the object of their actions. The experiences of these recipients rain down the appropriate sympathies and antipathies on the one who is absorbing the qualities of his or her recent life and preparing for the next life.

The law of karma refers to the complex process by which the enduring qualities of each action and of a full lifetime fashion the possibilities and the tasks of the next moment and the next lifetime. On the basis of the previous life experience, as summarized and reexperienced between death and rebirth, the individual self, or "I," chooses the personal and environmental conditions of its next life. It is the karmic condition of the individual that largely determines the components of the next life, including the "choice" of parents, body, disposition, and capacities, as well as important influences and tasks.

## 6 The Anthroposophical Society

At the 1923 Christmas Foundation Meeting held in Dornach, Switzerland, in the shadow of the ruins of the Goetheanum, Rudolf Steiner founded a public society devoted to esoteric research. To be a member of this society, one need only affirm the kind of research influenced by Rudolf Steiner and conducted at or by the Goetheanum. He also founded an esoteric School of Spiritual Science, members of which are expected to be in the process of transforming the content of such research into a living state of the soul, one that expresses warm and loving truths concerning the full range of human concerns. This school includes the following sections: general anthroposophy, medicine, pedagogy, arts of speech and music, visual arts, letters, mathematics and astronomy, natural science, social sciences, nutrition and agriculture, and the spiritual striving of youth.[9]

---

[9] Some of the ideas in this essay first appeared in my "Steiner and Anthroposophy," in *Modern Esoteric Spirituality*, ed. Antoine Faivre and Jacob Needleman (New York: Crossroad, 1992), 288–310, and in my introduction to *The New Essential Steiner* (Great Barrington, MA: Steinerbooks, 2009), 1–72.

23

# THE GOLDEN DAWN AND THE O.T.O.

EGIL ASPREM

## 1 Introduction: Magic in an Institutional Setting

The Golden Dawn and the O.T.O. share a place in the history of Western esotericism because of their importance in reshaping conceptions of magic and relocating it to the context of institutionalized esoteric societies. While the practice of other occult arts (notably alchemy) has a long institutional history, the practice of ritual magic had typically remained a solitary pursuit. A link between masonry and theurgy had existed in Martinès de Pasqually's (1727–1774) eighteenth-century Order of Élus Coëns, but nineteenth-century occultists tended to view the teaching and practice of magic as an entirely private affair.

Both orders discussed in this essay illustrate a move toward creating new social and institutional sites for magic by reconceptualizing the esoteric order as a vehicle for magical teachings. As sources for the production and dissemination of new syntheses of magic, both the Golden Dawn and the O.T.O. have exerted a profound influence on twentieth-century esoteric trends.

## 2 The Hermetic Order of the Golden Dawn

### a Birth of a Magical Order

During its short lifespan from 1888 to 1903, the "classical" Hermetic Order of the Golden Dawn was the pivotal esoteric order in *fin-de-siècle* Britain. Despite its quick lapse into disorder and schism, it managed to create a social platform for the study and practice of ritual magic, operating four temples in England and one in Paris. Among the better known members were the poet William Butler Yeats; the actresses Florence Farr and Maud Gonne; and Mina Bergson Mathers, the sister of philosopher and Nobel laureate Henri Bergson.

The order was established by a small coterie of London-based Freemasons and occultists. The key founders were the coroner William Wynn Westcott (1848–1925) and Samuel Liddell "MacGregor" Mathers (1854–1918), both members of the Rosicrucian Masonic group Societas Rosicruciana in Anglia (S.R.I.A.). William Robert Woodman (1828–1891), Supreme Magus of the S.R.I.A., was invited in as the third chief, but he died shortly thereafter. The Golden Dawn culled many of its early members from Rosicrucian- and Hermetic-oriented parts of the occult milieu. Like Anna Kingsford's Hermetic Society (then only recently defunct), it presented itself as a decidedly Western alternative to the increasingly Oriental and anti-Christian Theosophical Society, claiming an authentic Rosicrucian heritage and reinstating Egypt as the true origin of perennial wisdom.

The circumstances surrounding the creation of the Golden Dawn's constructed tradition are among the most thoroughly discussed episodes in modern occultism. Briefly, Westcott had come across a manuscript among the papers of the Swedenborgian Rite in 1887, coded in a cipher taken from Johannes Trithemius's *Polygraphiae*. When deciphered, the manuscript revealed a set of notes sketching the outline of five initiation rituals. It also hinted at the existence of an occult order by the name of "Golden Dawn," but it offered nothing to suppose a Rosicrucian connection. Westcott, recognizing the great potential of these notes, provided such a connection by forging a series of letters from one "Fräulein Sprengel." In this spurious correspondence, the mystery lady revealed herself as a Rosicrucian adept ("Sapiens Dominabitur Astris," S.D.A.) in charge of a secretive Rosicrucian Order in Germany, "die Goldene Dämmerung." S.D.A. attested that the lower grades of her order were the ones revealed in the cipher manuscript. The adept was kind enough to provide Westcott with the authority to open a local temple in London, as soon as he could gather two companions to serve as co-chiefs. These would be Mathers and Woodman.

The Rosicrucian connection was likely Westcott's invention, designed to create an air of legitimacy in a milieu obsessed with "tradition." The cipher manuscript, on the other hand, was genuine enough. It was claimed to be of ancient provenance, related to the Rosicrucians in Germany and possibly to ancient Egyptian hermetists. In reality, it was probably written only a few years before, by the recently deceased occultist Kenneth Mackenzie.

In October 1887, Westcott wrote his friend Samuel Liddell Mathers, who spent most of his time studying obscure magical manuscripts in the British Museum, asking for cooperation. If Mathers fleshed out the rituals, they could found and run the order together. He accepted, and things proceeded smoothly from there. In March of the following year, the first initiations into the "Isis-Urania Temple" took place at Mark Mason's Hall, London. Within a year, sixty persons had been introduced to the first degree of Neophyte.

At this point, the order operated initiations into five degrees. In 1892, these were joined by a new "Inner" or Second Order, open on invitation to those possessing the highest Outer grade. The Second Order went under the name *Rosae Rubeae et Aurea Crucis* ("Ruby Rose and the Golden Cross") and had a distinctly Rosicrucian, but also magical, emphasis. Mathers had designed two new initiation rituals, which demanded the construction of a vault that the initiate would recognize as the tomb of Christian Rosenkreutz. For this reason, the Second Order rituals took place in a different location from those of the Outer; additionally, it was desirable that nobody in the Outer Order should have a clue about its existence.

### b Initiations, Magical Doctrines, and Techniques

Westcott once boasted that the Golden Dawn was a school for "classical medieval occult science."[1] But what were the magical teachings of the Golden Dawn actually about? Members of the order only found out gradually, since the theories were taught in steps modeled on the order's initiation structure. In the Outer Order, disciples were handed so-called Knowledge Lectures expounding on the theme and symbolism of each grade. The initiate was gradually taken through a grand synthesis of symbol systems, from alchemy, the Kabbalah, and astrology to the Tarot and the mysterious "Enochian" letter squares.

The Golden Dawn initiation system was composed of ten degrees plus one preliminary Neophyte degree. The structure was borrowed from the S.R.I.A., but it ultimately stemmed from the eighteenth-century German *Gold- und Rosenkreutzer* Order. The grades were divided into three segments: the First or Outer Order, the Second Order, and an obscure Third Order. In the beginning, only the four lower degrees of the Outer Order were worked with initiations. The fifth to seventh degrees (Adeptus Minor, Major, and Exemptus) were originally honorary titles reserved for the chiefs, but they became operative with the creation of Mathers's Second Order. The final three degrees of the Third Order belonged to the mysterious (or mythical) "secret chiefs" and were not attainable in practice.

Except for the preliminary Neophyte grade, the Golden Dawn grades were correlated with the ten *sefirot* of the Kabbalistic Tree of Life, running from the bottom up. The four proper degrees of the Outer Order were

---

[1] Cited in Ellic Howe, *The Magicians of the Golden Dawn: A Documentary History of a Magical Order 1887–1923* (York Beach, ME: Samuel Weiser, 1978), 34.

additionally correlated with the four elements. Progressive initiation in the order thereby took the form of an ascent through the *sefirot*, along with a gradual training of the magician toward mastery of the four elements. This reflects the basic aim of the Golden Dawn: approaching deification through magical ascent.

Doctrinally, a reinterpreted Christian Kabbalah plus the four elements together made up a matrix in which all other occult systems were framed. John Dee's Enochian magical squares, for example, were attributed to the four elements and presented consecutively in the elemental initiations of the Outer Order. On entering the Second Order, the adepts would learn how to apply all this occult knowledge in magical practice. Instructions were circulated in documents called "Flying Rolls," some of which may have been lectures delivered at gatherings, while others are descriptions of procedures and results attained by senior adepts.

Among the first things a magician needed to know were how to consecrate magical weapons and how to ritually "banish" and invoke elemental, planetary and zodiacal forces. There were instructions in divination by means of the Tarot, geomancy, and the casting of horoscopes; others discussed the making and consecration of magical talismans, and instructions in the evocation of spirits, whether angels, demons, planetary intelligences, or elementals. Much of this was borrowed from Agrippa's *De occulta philosophia* (1533), Francis Barrett's *The Magus* (1801), the Greek magical papyri, and revisions of medieval and Renaissance grimoires.

The most fundamental magical technique was based on the concept of "the astral," developed much later. Following the occult theories of Eliphas Lévi, the Golden Dawn taught the existence of "astral realms" paralleling the ordinary, visible world. Familiarity with the astral was fundamental for Golden Dawn magicians: Any successful practice of magic was dependent on the control of astral forces, or action on the astral plane. Access to these dimensions was primarily gained through two techniques known as "scrying" and "traveling in the astral." For scrying, the magician would typically employ certain symbols (e.g., the "Tattwas" or the Enochian letters) as foci for ritual meditations, inducing visions of the astral region to which the particular symbol corresponded. But these visions were passive and only imparted a mirror image of the astral world. When a more active approach was desired, the adept would instead project his or her astral body into the parallel dimensions, traveling around freely, touching objects, performing rituals, and encountering astral entities.

The most common magical experiments were aimed at gaining esoteric knowledge in the astral plane. Other, more operative types of magic, such as the evocation of spirits or the use of talismans, were intended to achieve material ends. For many, the obligatory consecration of magical weapons became the first and the last elaborate ritual they ever performed. The costly and time-consuming nature of larger magical workings may have been one reason. Time and place needed to be calculated and planned according to astrological principles, and magical implements prepared from often exotic and expensive materials. Sometimes it would simply be easier to keep to the next best thing of purely astral work.

## c Downfall and Aftermath

The Golden Dawn disintegrated abruptly around the turn of the century, mainly due to three factors: (1) leadership problems between the distant but authoritarian Mathers and the London Isis-Urania Temple; (2) a controversy among the London adepts over the place of private magical groups within the order; and (3) the scandalous "Horos affair," which damaged the order's reputation beyond repair.

Following a conflict with the respected adept Annie Horniman, Mathers made several choices that were strategically unwise. Westcott had to resign from his office because of suspicions from his employer, leaving Mathers in charge from Paris. In January 1900, the members of the London Isis-Urania Temple had grown so impatient with their erratic and absent leader that they threatened to shut down the temple. Mathers was convinced they planned to restart with Westcott as chief and launched a campaign to discredit his authority. This he did by revealing the truth behind the Fräulein Sprengel letters. Mathers wanted to foster the idea that the only link to the "secret chiefs" of the order ran through him, claiming to be in contact with the real Soror S.D.A. in Paris.

The strategy was short sighted, since it created the suspicion that the order was founded on nothing but lies. Mathers's own extravagant claims about secret chiefs seemed less trustworthy in this light, and instead of support he got demands for proof. Mathers refused to deliver and instead threatened that the secret chiefs would unleash "a deadly and hostile Current of Will" to smite down the rebels, as was promised in the oath of the Neophyte ritual. Mathers sent one of his last allies, a young Aleister Crowley, to London in a final attempt to win the rebels back to the fold. Crowley's eccentric manœuvres failed, however, and instead the rebels expelled Mathers from the order and resumed business independently.

In Paris, Mathers had been in contact with a certain couple named Horos. It was with reference to Mrs. Horos, a "powerful medium," that he claimed to have renewed contact with the secret chiefs. However, the Horos couple turned out to be sly con artists. By appearing as high-degree initiates to Golden Dawn members, they managed to get hold of the order's rituals and used them to set up a scam in London. In September 1901, the couple was arrested on allegations of fraud and rape of a young girl during a bogus Neophyte initiation. The scandal attracted massive press coverage, seriously damaging the integrity of the Golden Dawn, even though the actual order had had nothing to do with it. The Neophyte ritual was made public, ridiculed by the press, and deemed blasphemous by the judges. Many respectable members found it hard to remain associated with the Golden Dawn after this episode.

To make matters worse, an internal conflict emerged over the function of the Second Order and the role of certain small private magical groups that had become popular among its members. A concern that such groups might form "elites within elites" was voiced by Yeats and Horniman, while Florence Farr, who ran the secret "Sphere Group" together with twelve other adepts, defended such practices. The conflict proved impossible to resolve, and the order finally dissolved in 1903.

Several factions nevertheless attempted to carry on the Golden Dawn's "true lineage." Most notable were the Alpha et Omega Lodge in Paris, based on Mathers's temple, and the Stella Matutina, which set up lodges in London, Bristol, and even New Zealand. Several other groups and orders carried on its influence as well, including A. E. Waite's Independent and Rectified Rite, Paul Foster Case's California-based Builders of the Adytum (B.O.T.A.), and Crowley and G. C. Jones's Astron Argon (A∴A∴). The latter two are still active today. After several rounds of exposures and publications of Golden Dawn material throughout the twentieth century, new groups claiming lineage have appeared, together with a wide range of books and instructions.

### 3 Ordo Templi Orientis

The Ordo Templi Orientis (O.T.O.) rivals the Golden Dawn's influence on occultism and conceptions of magic in the twentieth century. Its organizational roots are grounded in the fascination with fringe-masonry, Rosicrucianism, and Templarism in Germany and Austria at the turn of the century. However, its chief impact is related to the new religious movement Thelema, and its English creator and prophet Aleister Crowley (1875–1947). The O.T.O. has been the institutional site for disseminating a novel mix of ideas, doctrines, and practices drawing on Rosicrucianism,

Hermeticism, Golden Dawn ritual magic, neo-Gnosticism, Theosophical teachings, and perhaps most importantly sexual magic.

*a Roots, Foundation, and Early History*

The early history of the order is complicated and contested. We first find references to an Order of Oriental Templars in 1906, in the fringe-Masonic periodical of the German occultist, political activist, and journalist Theodor Reuss (1855–1923), the *Oriflamme*. Yet it was not until 1912 that the existence of an order by the name O.T.O. was officially announced. This announcement further claimed that the order dated as far back as 1895, connecting it with the Austrian paper chemist and occultist Carl Kellner (1851–1905) and yet another secret society, the Hermetic Brotherhood of Light.[2] Although we should view 1912 as the order's formal date of birth, it is nevertheless important to have a look at some prior events.

During the first decade of the 1900s, Reuss had collected a number of charters for mostly "irregular" Masonic rites, including Memphis and Misraim, the Ancient and Accepted Rite, and the Swedenborgian Rite. These systems were tied together by the *Oriflamme* journal. Kellner, often regarded as the "spiritual father" of the O.T.O., had been connected with Reuss's Masonic activities in Berlin before his death in 1905. Together with the Theosophist Franz Hartmann, Reuss and Kellner viewed themselves as the elite "Inner Circle" of this Masonic milieu, boasting that they possessed the secret key to all Masonic mysteries and religious systems. Certainly by 1906, but perhaps earlier, Reuss held that this secret key was of a sexual nature. He may have been influenced by theories on the solar-phallic origin of religion, popular in the late nineteenth century. The influence of Hargrave Jennings's *Phallicism* (1884) is particularly clear; Reuss published it in German as *Lingam-Yoni* in 1906, adding his own introduction. Additionally, the sexual interpretation of religion was widespread in the neo-gnostic movement, particularly in France and Belgium, where the idea had suggested itself from Christian heresiological allegations of gnostic perversities. Reuss did have connections with the neo-gnostics, obtaining charters to run a gnostic Catholic Church in 1908. The combination of Gnosticism and a sexual theory of religion would find its way to the core of the O.T.O. project.

The mysterious Hermetic Brotherhood of Light, which Kellner is said to have come in contact with, appears to have been a Rosicrucian society

---

[2] "Unser Orden," *Jubiläums-Ausgabe der Oriflamme*, September 1912, 15.

established in Boston in 1895, possibly an offshoot of the somewhat better known Hermetic Brotherhood of Luxor.[3] Suggestively, this latter group was known for its sexual teachings, originating with the American spiritualist and occultist Paschal Beverly Randolph (1825–1875). The relation with the Hermetic Brotherhood of Light remains unclear, but it is worth noting that the O.T.O. tends to view itself as a continuation of that nebulous order, allegedly treasuring its secrets in the high degrees. Indeed, parts of the O.T.O. high-degree instructions do contain paraphrases of Randolph's "Mysteries of Eros," suggesting that at least some of the sexual teachings came from this source.[4]

Despite these precursors, the actual formation of the functioning O.T.O. resulted from Reuss's meeting with Aleister Crowley in London in 1912. We have already seen that Crowley was an aspiring magician in the Golden Dawn at the turn of the century. During the interim years, he had traveled the world, spending his inherited money and living the life of an adventurous mountaineer, magician, mystic, and poet. He had founded Thelema, a new magical religion based on *The Book of the Law*, a text he claimed to have "received" from the entity Aiwass on behest of the gods Nuit, Hadit, and Ra-Hoor-Khuit, in Cairo in 1904. Around 1907, he had set up his magical order, the A∴A∴ and established its periodical, *The Equinox*, in 1909. The A∴A∴ and *The Equinox* became the organs through which Crowley promoted Thelema and communicated his ideas on magic, religion, and science, under the banner of "Scientific Illuminism."

When Crowley and Reuss met between 1910 and 1912, Reuss found a man with radical visions similar to his own. The anti-Christian, antibourgeois ideology of Thelema apparently appealed to the political activist. Crowley for his part was looking for new institutional vehicles to promote his ideas. When Reuss offered him the leadership of a British section of the O.T.O., the Mysteria Mystica Maxima (M∴M∴M∴), and the job of rewriting the order's rituals, Crowley eagerly accepted. The process of transforming the O.T.O. into a Thelemic Order followed soon after.

The existence of the O.T.O. was officially announced in the 1912 autumn issues of *Oriflamme* and *The Equinox*. Until 1918, Crowley spent much time writing new rituals and instructions, replacing the traditional Masonic themes with explicitly Thelemic and magical ones. During a stay in Moscow in 1913, he also produced the liturgy of a gnostic Mass for use in

---

[3] Anon., "The Hermetic Brotherhood of Luxor," *The Rosicrucian Brotherhood*, II:4 (1908), 161.
[4] Martin P. Starr, *The Unknown God: W. T. Smith and the Thelemites* (Bollingbrook, IL: Teitan Press, 2003), 25, n. 25.

the Gnostic Catholic Church (Ecclesia Gnostica Catholica, or EGC) that Reuss had obtained charters for back in 1908. In effect, Crowley revived and re-created the gnostic church as well, designed as an ecclesiastical and exoteric counterpart to the esoteric O.T.O., openly worshiping its secrets in religious rituals. The EGC became a veritable "church of magic."

Reuss and Crowley soon mobilized their respective networks to spread charters and set up local lodges. This was, however, an unhappy time for international organizational expansion. When war broke out in 1914, international Masonic networks were dispersed, and publication of the *Oriflamme* was discontinued. Reuss settled near Ascona, Switzerland, where he attempted to launch O.T.O. activities among the utopian spiritual milieu flowering at Monte Verità during the war. Meanwhile, Crowley ran out of money. After emigrating to the United States, he sustained himself as a journalist and editor, while relying on donations from followers. He also engaged in war propaganda for the Germans, although he would later claim it all had been part of a British disinformation strategy. The activities nevertheless damaged the reputation of Crowley's order, even causing a police raid at its London premises in 1917.

During this period, a gulf grew between the two leaders of the order, as Crowley became more dedicated to his role as prophet of a new religion. He may even have attempted to stage a revolt to overthrow Reuss as Outer Head of the Order (OHO) around 1921. Although this failed, Reuss died in 1923 and Crowley finally succeeded him as international chief. Under Crowley's rule, the O.T.O. gradually let go of the Masonic pretensions that had been so important to Reuss, increasingly focusing on the Thelemic mission. Crowley's Thelemic vision for the order was published in 1919, in the so-called *Blue Equinox*. Crowley nevertheless had a hard time establishing the O.T.O. as a potent movement for implementing the radical social, political, and religious reforms he hoped for. His apparent pro-German activities during the war had made it difficult to operate in Britain, and he was losing control over the Continental lodges due to schisms over succession following Reuss's death. With the ascent to power of fascism and National Socialism in Europe, the operation of esoteric orders became increasingly difficult, sometimes attracting direct persecution. As a consequence, the O.T.O. moved most of its activity to the United States. By the mid-1940s, the Agape Lodge in California was the last functioning body of the order worldwide.

## b Doctrines and Ritual of the O.T.O.

The esoteric doctrines of the O.T.O. can be summed up in three key terms: Thelema, solar-phallicism, and sex magic. Although only the first of these aspects is explicit in the lower parts of the O.T.O.'s eleven degrees, the latter two remain tacitly present. It is only in the high degrees, from VII° to XI°, that they become explicit, with elaborate theories and ritual instructions.

Although drastically reformed by Crowley, solar-phallicism and sex magic form the oldest parts of the O.T.O. synthesis. They constituted the "secret key" guarded by Reuss, Kellner, and Hartmann in the early days of the *Oriflamme*. In the journal's 1912 "Jubilaeums-Ausgabe," Reuss openly divulged that the secret of all Masonic ritual was sex magic, and further coupled it with practices of yoga.[5] He explained sex magic as the concentration and transmutation of the "energy of reproduction" (using the yogic term *vayus napa*), the essence of the divine creation process. The point is to employ yogic practices to concentrate the "vital energy" that rests in the subtle counterpart to the reproductive organs, raising them up to the solar plexus, where they are transmuted. This should effect the consummation of "the Great Union" between the male and female aspects of the practitioner.

Although it has become commonplace to view sex magic as an antinomian transgression of conventional mores based largely on a flawed Orientalist understanding of Indian Tantra, it is worth noting that there is little emphasis on these themes in the O.T.O. primary literature.[6] While Reuss insisted on using yogic terms in his brief 1912 exposition, this is less present in high-degree O.T.O. instructions, such as *De natura deorum, De nuptiis secretis, Liber Agape*, and *De arte magica*. While tantric references still occur occasionally, allusions and analogies with Greek, Egyptian, and biblical mythology, and even Christian demonology, are much more common. In place of a focus on transgression, we find attempts at formulating a positive religious stance based on solar-phallicism: God is one; in the macrocosm he is the Sun, simultaneously creator, sustainer, and eventually destroyer of life on our planet; in the microcosm, he is the phallus. In this sense, man is also divine, endowed with godly creative powers, and sex magic thus becomes a sacred art. *De nuptiis secretis*, which deals with sexual magic and devotional practices largely based on masturbation, tells of the Egyptian theogony in which the sun-god Toum creates the other gods by masturbating and ejaculating semen. This account forms a parallel to a ritual in which the magician consecrates himself

---

[5] Theodor Reuss, "Mysteria Mystica Maxima," *Oriflamme* (September 1912), 21–23.
[6] See Hugh Urban, *Magia Sexualis: Sex, Magic, and Liberation in Modern Western Esotericism* (Berkeley: University of California Press, 2006).

as the sun and proceeds to create two talismans, one male and one female, vivified by the magician's sperm. These talismans become new gods, who conjoin and create an entirely new world, replete with elementals and other beings.

The most important high-degree doctrines concern full sexual intercourse. The union of male and female is paramount, celebrated in the gnostic mass and situated as an essential component of magical ceremonies. The mixing of male and female sexual fluids is utilized to produce the alchemical "Elixir of Life," and vaginal intercourse may even be arranged magically to produce a homunculus through procreation. By extension, anal intercourse, whether homosexual or heterosexual, can also be utilized for giving birth to astral entities. Rites based on anal intercourse were Crowley's invention, absent from Reuss's earlier conceptions.

In fact, however, the most novel element that Crowley introduced into the O.T.O. was the framework of Thelema. As presented in *The Book of the Law* and Crowley's numerous commentaries, Thelema (Greek for "will") prophesies the end of "the Aeon of Osiris," a millennia-long period characterized by patriarchal, collectivist religions, and the coming of a new "Aeon of Horus" to replace it. A radical, liberal individualism is the credo of the new aeon, and Thelema is its only proper religion. Its dictum is "Do What Thou Wilt," – however, this is not meant to license indiscriminate indulgence. Crowley explained that Thelemites were bound to discover their single "True Will" and follow it unconditionally. For Crowley, magic is always interwoven with this pursuit; indeed, Thelemic magic becomes a complete "form of life."

We can distinguish at least two roles for Thelema in the O.T.O. First, candidates are taught how to implement Thelemic and magical principles in their lives, as part of initiation and self-realization. Second, the elected high-degree members of the order are committed to promulgating the law and work toward the establishment of a truly Thelemic society. In addition to proselytizing and recruiting new members, this duty would be observed by working the rituals of sex magic, employing the order's esoteric practices to advance its worldly mission.

*c The O.T.O. after Crowley: Aftermath and Influence*

When Crowley died in 1947, he had entrusted the leadership of the order to Karl Germer (1885–1962), the O.T.O.'s Grand Treasurer. Germer had lived in New Jersey since fleeing from war and persecution in Germany. However, his unpleasant encounter with the Nazi regime had left a lasting stain on his psychology. Germer's paranoid leadership style would soon destroy what little was left of O.T.O. activities in the United States. Recruitment came to a halt, the Agape Lodge dissolved during the 1950s, and Germer himself died in 1962 without assigning a successor. This left an unclear situation, which several groups have taken advantage of. Among claimants to the O.T.O. leadership, we find a Swiss O.T.O. group, based on Reuss's lodges from the Ascona period; the Brazilian Societas O.T.O., claiming links with Germer; the British Typhonian O.T.O., run by British occultist Kenneth Grant (1924–2011); and the California-based Caliphate O.T.O. Counted in numbers, presence, and publications, the latter of these groups is by far the most significant.

The Caliphate originated with Grady Louis McMurtry (1918–1985), who met Crowley when he was stationed in England during the Second World War. McMurtry began a process of reassembling the American order after Germer's death. Availing himself of two letters from Crowley appointing McMurtry his representative in the United States, he claimed to be the legitimate chief of the order. McMurtry laid claim to the title of "Caliph," a title for Crowley's successor appearing only in these letters. Much of the Caliphate's later success has been built on victories in the legal system. It was incorporated as a religious, nonprofit organization in 1979 and has since won several trials over rights to the O.T.O. name and copyrights.

The Typhonian O.T.O. is still influential in Great Britain but has received little recognition abroad. In contrast to the Caliphate, which is considered a fairly orthodox Crowleyan movement, the Typhonian branch has notably extended the O.T.O. synthesis by incorporating UFO lore, the Lovecraftian "Cthulhu mythos," and a larger emphasis on Indian Tantrism.

In addition to these continuities, the synthesis of Golden Dawn and O.T.O. magic, resulting from the encounter between Crowley and Reuss, has helped shape the many loosely knit occultist currents associated with Wicca, Satanism, chaos magic, and paganism in its many forms.

# 24

# G.I. GURDJIEFF AND THE FOURTH WAY

## Glenn Alexander Magee

## 1 Life, Writings, and Influence

As is the case with many figures in Western esotericism, the life of George Ivanovich Gurdjieff is shrouded in both mystery and controversy. Seen by some as a sage and others as a charlatan, he is arguably the most influential esoteric teacher of the twentieth century. As we shall see, whether we are approaching Gurdjieff's life, writings, teachings, or legacy, there are no easy answers to be found.

We are not even certain when Gurdjieff was born, but it was likely January 13, ca. 1866. The place of birth was definitely Alexandropol, which at the time was part of the Russian Empire. Gurdjieff's father was Greek, his mother Armenian. The family name was originally Georgiades and was later Slavicized as Gurdjieff. When he was quite young, Gurdjieff's family resettled in Kars near the Turkish border, which had once been part of the Ottoman Empire but was then under Russian control. Because of its location and rich history, Kars exposed the young Gurdjieff to a great variety of cultures and faiths. *Meetings with Remarkable Men*, Gurdjieff's most accessible work, is our chief source of information on his early life, and it contains a number of fascinating stories about his experiences in this mysterious region.

Gurdjieff's father was an *ashiq*, or balladeer, and was a strong influence on him. His parents raised him in the Eastern Orthodox faith, whose theology is almost entirely "mystical," and it is clear that this was a strong influence as well. However, Gurdjieff was no admirer of organized religion, and in later life expressed strong antipathy to the clergy. From a young age, he reacted against both the tendency to rationalism and reductionism in the modern outlook, and the unquestioning faith demanded by religion.

In early adulthood, Gurdjieff set off on what would become roughly two decades of travels, journeying throughout Central Asia and the Middle East in search of wisdom. Our chief source for this period in his life is, again, *Meetings*. Though it must be acknowledged that this is a flawed source, for it contains some anecdotes that strain credulity. Precisely because of this, and because *Meetings* does not fill in all the gaps, there has been a great deal of speculation about Gurdjieff's activities during this time. For example, it has been claimed that he was a spy for the Russians and a tutor to the Dalai Lama. Gurdjieff's own account features him meeting various spiritual teachers, including Sufis, and finding a number of companions along the way, men and women who shared his hunger for truth. He also claimed to have been initiated into a mysterious organization known as the Sarmoung Brotherhood, located in a monastery in the heart of Asia. Scholars differ in their views as to the identity (and existence) of this brotherhood.

In 1912, Gurdjieff appeared in St. Petersburg, Russia, offering himself as a spiritual teacher. By 1914, he had moved to Moscow, and a year later encountered P. D. Ouspensky (1878–1947). A highly intelligent man, Ouspensky was already a successful journalist on esoteric matters and the author of several books. In the work for which he is known best, *In Search of the Miraculous: Fragments of an Unknown Teaching* (hereafter referred to as *Fragments*), Ouspensky offers a vivid account of his first meeting with Gurdjieff in a crowded Moscow café. Like so many influential spiritual teachers, Gurdjieff possessed enormous charisma and made a strong first impression (Ouspensky refers to his "piercing eyes"[1]). Soon, with Ouspensky's help, a group had formed around Gurdjieff. It included the composer Thomas de Hartmann (1885–1956) with whom Gurdjieff would later collaborate on the so-called Gurdjieff – de Hartmann music.

In 1916, with the approach of the Revolution, Gurdjieff and his students headed for Essentuki, located near the base of the Caucasus Mountains. In 1919, they relocated to Tiflis and then were eventually forced to head west, finally ending their travels in Paris. The students accompanying Gurdjieff on these journeys included de Hartmann and his wife Olga, as well as Alexandre and Jeanne de Salzmann. The latter not only became Gurdjieff's principal student but an important spiritual teacher in her own right. Ouspensky, however, did not make the entire journey. He broke with Gurdjieff in 1918, although they remained in contact for several years. He was not the first nor was he the last pupil to feel compelled to leave Gurdjieff. Sometimes it seems clear that Gurdjieff himself instigated these breaks when he felt it was necessary for the individual's further development.

---

[1] P. D. Ouspensky, *In Search of the Miraculous: Fragments of an Unknown Teaching* (New York: Harcourt Brace, 1949), 7.

In 1922, Gurdjieff founded the Institute for the Harmonious Development of Man at the Chateau du Prieuré at Fountainbleau, outside Paris. New students from several countries came to Fountainbleau after news of Gurdjieff's teachings circulated abroad. It was at the Prieuré that Gurdjieff established many of the practices now associated with his school, including the "movements," a complex and difficult form of sacred dance. Gurdjieff reported that he had learned these movements through his experiences with different initiatic schools in his years of spiritual wandering.[2]

Activities at Fountainbleau were more or less brought to a halt by Gurdjieff's disastrous automobile accident in July 1924, which almost claimed his life. His recovery was long and difficult. Physically weakened and also penniless, Gurdjieff decided to begin writing books. He started in December 1924, dictating the first parts of what would become *Beelzebub's Tales to His Grandson* to Olga de Hartmann. This was the projected first part of a series collectively referred to as *All and Everything*. *Beelzebub* was eventually published for the first time in 1950. The second part of the series, *Meetings with Remarkable Men*, was not published until 1963. The third part, *Life Is Only Real Then, When "I Am,"* which Gurdjieff did not (apparently) finish, was published in 1975.

Gurdjieff left the Prieuré in the early 1930s and moved to Paris. He took a number of trips to the United States to raise funds, where he inevitably made a variety of impressions on those who encountered him. But Gurdjieff spent the majority of his time at his flat on the Rue des Colonels-Renard, where he lived out his remaining years. He was apparently able to continue his work unmolested throughout the German occupation. In 1948, he was involved in a second serious car accident, from which he also recovered. But he died on October 29, 1949.

A discussion of Gurdjieff's teachings must inevitably begin with the question of influences, and of the interpretation of his writings. In both cases, we face great challenges. There has been a good deal of speculation concerning the sources of Gurdjieff's ideas. Here I will only mention that there seems to be a clear influence of Eastern Orthodox mysticism, Sufism, and even, surprisingly, Pythagoreanism. It would be wrong, however, to characterize his teachings as a mélange culled from different sources. Gurdjieff himself claimed that he was recovering an ancient esoteric tradition, a Western tradition – and there is some reason to take him at his word on this. He

---

[2] See Jacob Needleman, "G. I. Gurdjieff and His School," in *Modern Esoteric Spirituality*, ed. Antoine Faivre and Jacob Needleman (New York: Crossroad, 1995), 369.

sometimes referred to his philosophy as "esoteric Christianity," but in fact its roots are much older than Christianity.

As to Gurdjieff's writings, they are extraordinarily difficult. In particular, *Beelzebub* is a strange and baffling book. Set on a spaceship, it is ostensibly (as the title implies) an account of Beelzebub's conversations with his grandson, in which he teaches him quite literally "all and everything" (a recent edition is 1,135 pages long). The book is written in a deliberately off-putting style, with extremely complex and confusing sentence structures, and is also filled with peculiar neologisms. These all have specific meanings, but seem calculated to test the reader's patience and commitment.

The truth is that *Beelzebub* is one of the strangest examples of esoteric writing in world literature – "esoteric" both in the sense employed throughout this volume, and in the sense of "hidden." Gurdjieff deliberately obscures his meaning. Indeed, in a conversation about the meaning of *Beelzebub*, Gurdjieff is supposed to have said, "I bury dog." One of his interlocutors took him to mean that he had "buried the bone," but Gurdjieff corrected him: "No. I bury whole dog."[3]

By contrast, *Meetings* and *Life Is Only Real Then, When "I Am"* at least *appear* to be easier to understand, especially the former (which was made into a film in 1979). It is generally believed that all of Gurdjieff's writings are calculated to affect the reader in more than one manner. And this is another way in which they may be said to be esoteric. While they reach the reader on an intellectual level, imparting ideas, they also have a much deeper effect. Gurdjieff states at the beginning of *Beelzebub* that its purpose is to "destroy, mercilessly and without any compromise whatever, in the mentation and feelings of the reader, the beliefs and views, by centuries rooted in him, about everything existing in the world."[4] Over the years, transcripts or summaries of Gurdjieff's lectures and group meetings have also been published. As is the case with many authors, the remarks Gurdjieff delivered orally are often much more accessible than those he prepared for publication.

Still, most readers begin by reading about Gurdjieff, rather than reading Gurdjieff himself. The "standard introduction" for many years has been Ouspensky's *Fragments*. However, *The Reality of Being* by Jeanne de Salzmann (posthumously edited and published in 2010) is arguably a better place to begin, although more challenging than Ouspensky.

---

[3] Edwin Wolfe, "Further Episodes with Gurdjieff," *The Gurdjieff International Review* 6:1 (Spring 2003), http://www.gurdjieff.org/grossman2.htm
[4] G. I. Gurdjieff, *Beelzebub's Tales to His Grandson* (New York: Viking Arkana, 1992), v. It should be noted that this edition is controversial: It is a revision of the original translation published in 1950. Nevertheless, the revision was supervised by Jeanne de Salzmann herself.

Gurdjieff did not just learn from remarkable men, he also influenced them. Mention has already been made of Thomas de Hartmann and Jeanne de Salzmann. Others influenced by Gurdjieff, his students, or Fourth Way teachings include: founder of *The Little Review* Margaret Anderson, mathematician and scientist John G. Bennett, poet T. S. Eliot, filmmaker Alejandro Jodorowsky, writer Katherine Mansfield, psychiatrist Maurice Nicoll, painter Georgia O'Keefe, editor of *The New Age* A. R. Orage, novelist J. B. Priestley, Henry John Sinclair (Lord Pentland), "Mary Poppins" creator P. L. Travers, and architect Frank Lloyd Wright. The degree of influence, of course, is different in each case. Some of these individuals (e.g., Bennett, Nicholl, and Lord Pentland) became teachers of the Gurdjieff Work. Others can only be said to have been on the periphery of the movement (e.g., Eliot, Jodorowsky, and Priestley).

Before his death, Gurdjieff charged Jeanne de Salzmann with the task of carrying on his work, and of creating centers for its study. Accordingly, over time the Gurdjieff Foundations were established in Paris, New York, London, and Caracas. In addition, however, there is a bewildering number of other groups today claiming to teach Gurdjieff's philosophy. Needless to say, these differ greatly in quality, and some are decidedly "cultish." It is the Gurdjieff Foundations established by de Salzmann, and their affiliated groups, that have the strongest claim to be the authentic representatives of Gurdjieff's teachings. Jeanne de Salzmann died in 1990, at the age of 101.

## 2 Ideas

As a spiritual teacher, Gurdjieff did not simply impart doctrines. Instead, he acted on his students in various ways calculated to place them in situations he believed were necessary for their development. Like Socrates, he changed his approach depending on the person or the group he was dealing with, and the circumstances of the moment. The result of this is that we have been left with wildly conflicting accounts both of Gurdjieff's character and of his manner of teaching (hence, the title of Margaret Anderson's 1962 memoir *The Unknowable Gurdjieff*).

Gurdjieff did have a "philosophy," but it was always taught – and still is taught – within the context of a "school": a group of individuals devoted to what is referred to as "the Work," led by one or more teachers. Gurdjieff and his followers are unwavering in their insistence that solitary individuals can accomplish little in the Work. The Gurdjieffian school is not an *ashram*, however; it is not intended as a refuge from life. Here we come to the meaning of what Gurdjieff called the "Fourth Way," which is the term widely used to refer to the movement he founded. The "first way" is that of the fakir, who develops control over his physical body. The way of the monk, the "second way," concentrates chiefly on emotional control. The "third way" is that of the yogi, whose attainments are mainly intellectual. All have two things in common: first, their development is one sided; second, they typically follow their path in separation from worldly affairs, as much as possible.

By contrast, the Fourth Way is that of what Gurdjieff called "the sly man." He does not separate himself from the world; rather, he uses the world as a vehicle for Work on himself. And that Work develops all his aspects: physical, emotional, and intellectual.[5] Gurdjieff's vision of the Fourth Way is not that far removed from the "left-hand path" as conceived by Traditionalist author Julius Evola: the path of "riding the tiger"; of utilizing the world, including even the destructive, disintegrating forces of the present age (the Iron Age, or *Kali Yuga*), as a means to self-transformation.[6] Thus, Gurdjieff schools do not insulate their members from the world.

While the importance of a group and a teacher is heavily emphasized, there is a strong individualist element to the Work as well. Gurdjieff steadfastly resisted the tendency of pupils to treat him as a guru. (This is one of things that make the Fourth Way a path "for the West," as it is often called.) Also, he insisted that pupils *not* take what he said on faith, and verify all claims for themselves. The reason for this is simple: to blindly follow the word of a guru is a form of sleep, which is precisely what the Gurdjieff Work combats.

Indeed, that "man is asleep" is arguably the central tenet of Gurdjieff's philosophy, or at least the logical point to begin an account of it. Gurdjieff emphasizes that human beings as they are (especially in the modern world) are thoroughly mechanical. While they imagine themselves to be conscious and free, in fact they are at the mercy of a variety of forces, and usually completely unaware of this. This is true not just of "ordinary people" but even of the vast majority of intellectuals. "Man is a machine," Gurdjieff tells Ouspensky in *Fragments*. And "he can do nothing."[7] Things simply happen to him.

If you confront people with such claims, they become indignant. No one likes to be told that he is a robot, and everyone thinks he is not only conscious but has a stable sense of personal identity. In fact, Gurdjieff argues that the vast majority of people have no authentic "I" at all and live in a constant state

---

[5] On the "four ways," see Ouspensky, *Fragments*, 44–51.
[6] See Julius Evola, *Ride the Tiger*, trans. Joscelyn Godwin and Constance Fontana (Rochester, VT: Inner Traditions, 2003).
[7] Ouspensky, *Fragments*, 21.

of self-deception about this. Rather, they have many "I's," each of which has been constructed in certain ways, essentially as a result of the same sort of experiences psychoanalysts have described in vivid detail: unmet needs, repressed desires, the internalization of voices of authority, and so forth.

The sense of what Gurdjieff means can easily be seen if we reflect on the fact that frequently we respond to our own deeds as if they had been committed by another person: The "I" that got out of bed in the middle of the night and ate the rest of the pie is not the "I" that loathes the pie-eating "I" the following morning at 9:00. We are ruled by these "I's," each of which we fully identify with in the moment. Each "I" really is like a separate self, and none of them wants to be exposed because that would mean the diminishment of its hold on us. Thus, there is enormous resistance to seeing how we are "taken" by these "I's," how we are really mechanical and unfree. The "I's" have so great an aversion to being exposed to the light that they will throw up all sorts of barriers to "awakening" – including dismissing Gurdjieff's claims as either absurd or as applying only "to other people, but not to me."

As Gurdjieff has described it, the condition of most human beings is clearly one of great suffering – although, again, most are unaware that they suffer. We are deluded in thinking that we will be truly fulfilled when all our needs and desires are satisfied. Since each "I" has its own set of needs and desires, often conflicting, this is obviously a trap. Once we realize this, and truly confront the degree to which we are mechanical, the result is potentially (and quite literally) ego shattering. Some will flee from this, back to the safety of identifying with this "I" or that. Others, however, will be seized by a desire to overcome this condition, as far as possible – to "wake up" and achieve an authentic "I." This desire is a necessary precondition for "Work on oneself," as it is called in the Fourth Way.

In a moment, I will turn to the question of what, specifically, Work consists in. But before doing so, I must note that Gurdjieff ties this "psychological" teaching to an elaborate cosmology involving a diagram called the "Ray of Creation," which shows reality emerging from the Absolute. The Ray of Creation must be understood in terms of what is known as the "law of three" and the "law of the octave." The latter seems strikingly Pythagorean. Gurdjieff argues that the octave of the musical scale (do, re, mi, fa, sol, la, ti, do) corresponds to a cosmic octave governing the emergence of the world from the Absolute, as well as to the stages in the spiritual development of the individual. The law of three holds that every phenomenon exhibits three "forces": active, passive, and neutralizing; or affirming, denying, and reconciling. In Fourth Way teachings, the connection between the law of three and the law of the octave is explicated through the mysterious symbol known as the *enneagram*. To really do justice to Gurdjieff's philosophy, the intricacies of these laws and diagrams would have to be explained in detail. But this is simply not possible in a short introduction. For our purposes, we may focus instead on just one crucial point: Gurdjieff's views on the place of man in creation. First of all, he makes it clear that whether we choose to do the Work and attempt to "wake up" is not a purely personal matter. The Work is not self-improvement, nor is happiness its goal. Instead, Gurdjieff claims that our ability to become conscious plays a crucial role in the life of the cosmos itself. Unfortunately, he also teaches (again, not unlike the Traditionalists) that in the modern period, it is more difficult than ever for us to perform this role.[8]

Gurdjieff and Ouspensky both utilize the language of evolution to describe the process by which individuals can become conscious and play their part in the cosmic scheme. For Gurdjieff, the evolutionary process described by biologists only takes mankind up to a certain point of development. Going further involves, in fact, *resisting* the very physical forces that made our biological evolution possible. In *Fragments*, Ouspensky reports that Gurdjieff told him "The law for man is existence in the circle of mechanical influences, the state of 'man-machine.' The way of the development of hidden possibilities is a way *against nature, against God*."[9] However, this is only possible for certain individuals. Gurdjieff teaches no doctrine of universal salvation. Only individuals of a very special sort can freely and consciously choose to wage war against sleep.

But in what way do these individuals participate in a cosmic process, rather than a purely personal one? To answer this question, we must look more close at what "Work on oneself" consists in, and to the crucial concepts of "remembering the self" and "self-observation." The reader should proceed with the warning that these are difficult ideas to explain, and that there are significant differences of opinion within the Gurdjieff movement about what they mean, and how to discuss them. The following is only one possible interpretation.

Self-remembering, at its most basic level, consists in what we may call "being present."[10] This is the vivid but ineffable sense, which we have all experienced at one time or another, of *being here now*. It is not what is often called today "being in the moment," which seems to simply mean enjoying

---

[8] See Ouspensky, *Fragments*, 309.
[9] Ouspensky, *Fragments*, 47. Italics in original.
[10] See Jeanne de Salzmann, *The Reality of Being* (Boston: Shambhala, 2011), 19.

the present rather than being preoccupied by our cares. Instead, being present means being aware that I am in *this* body, at *this* time, having *this* experience; it involves the sense of being "grounded" in the body, and in the present.

Normally, consciousness is absorbed in some object or situation, and the sense that *I* am conscious and that it is happening *in this body* and *now* simply drops out. In other words, the self is "forgotten." What Gurdjieff means by self-remembering is something like being aware *that* we are aware, or what is called in philosophy *apperception*. This term actually comes up in *Fragments*. Shortly after encountering Gurdjieff, Ouspensky describes the concept of self-remembering to a friend who states dismissively that this is nothing new, it's just apperception.[11] The pretentious friend attributes the concept to Wilhelm Wundt, but of course Wundt derives it from Kant. To be sure, self-remembering and Kantian apperception are not exactly the same thing, but if one defines apperception simply as "awareness that we are aware," this is helpful in getting to Gurdjieff's meaning.

Clearly, then, self-remembering involves a kind of bifurcation in consciousness: I am aware simultaneously of my surroundings, and of myself being aware.[12] This does not mean the same thing as having "internal thoughts" while being aware of external events. Gurdjieff and his followers continually emphasize that true self-remembering is grounded in the body, rather than something that takes place entirely "above the neck." If our awareness of ourselves being aware becomes exclusively a matter of consciousness of our thoughts, then we will involve ourselves in all sorts of distractions and self-deceptions. Indeed, Gurdjieff and those trained by him give explicit instructions on how to ground attention in the body.

Once one is grounded in this way, one practices self-observation. And what is observed are the "centers." Some accounts list four: intellectual (thought), emotional or feeling, moving (all learned actions of the organism such as walking, eating, speaking, etc.), and instinctive (all innate – as opposed to learned – activities of the organism, such as the work of the internal organs, reflexes, and sensations).[13] More often, however, the last two are grouped together as "moving-instinctive center," since they both deal with actions (learned or innate, voluntary or involuntary) of the physical organism.

Each of these centers has its own way of sensing and being, and ideally they should be in harmony. In most people, some kind of disharmony is often

---

[11] Ouspensky, *Fragments*, 121.
[12] See Ouspensky, *Fragments*, 119. See also p. 188.
[13] See P. D. Ouspensky, *The Psychology of Man's Possible Evolution* (New York: Random House, 1950), 25–28.

present, and this usually consists in the overdevelopment of one center. For example, some individuals "live in their heads": They are focused almost entirely on the intellectual center and are numb to the others. This is a common malady of modern people. The practice of self-observation is supposed to reveal these imbalances. It involves noting such things as unnecessary thinking, emotional reactions and our tendency to be "taken" by them, tension in the body, and habitual actions.

Gurdjieff maintains that self-observation requires an unsparing honesty. One will discover all sorts of things to dislike in oneself, and the process can be painful (it is referred to in the Fourth Way as "voluntary suffering"[14]). One habitual action that will frequently take us in the practice of self-observation is the tendency to *judge* what one observes. But Gurdjieff teaches that this is a trap: In judging, one "I" is simply passing sentence on another; and, quite obviously, when we judge we have stopped observing! (Similarly, observation is not "analysis."[15]) Just as one should refrain from judging, so one should also make no attempt to change what is observed. There will be enormous temptation to do this, since much of what one observes about oneself is negative. But Gurdjieff teaches that it is vital to the Work to come to terms with just how mechanical we are, and that most attempts to change are futile.

As a result of such claims, some see Gurdjieff's philosophy as extraordinarily pessimistic. In fact, he does offer hope. The very act of observing our negative qualities creates "space" between our observing selves and those qualities. This means that over time their hold on us may be gradually diminished. Those who are "in the Work" do practice self-observation in meditation (referred to as "sittings"). But since the Fourth Way involves engagement with the world, students practice self-observation in a variety of life contexts. A particular emphasis is placed on observation while engaged in physical work. And the importance of bodily orientation is frequently mentioned: Erect posture is emphasized as conducive to the cultivation of the right sort of attention, as well as the absence of unnecessary physical tension.[16]

Observation, again, involves awareness of all the centers. However, "awareness" is not really the right term. Rather, what Gurdjieff seems to mean is that we should be fully present both *to* and *through* the centers. The ideal is to be aware of the world "out there," but through *all* of the centers –

---

[14] See de Salzmann, *The Reality of Being*, 238–243.
[15] See Ouspensky, *Fragments*, 105.
[16] See de Salzmann, *The Reality of Being*, 49–50, 143.

and, again, to be aware of ourselves *in* all these centers simultaneously (to remember the self).[17] In other words, the Work involves achieving a state in which we are present to the Being of the world, and to our own Being. Taken together, the world "out there" and the one "in here," in ourselves (between which we make an artificial division), are everything. We may therefore say, in sum, that the objective of the Work is simply to be present to *what is*. In Heideggerean terms, we could say that the Gurdjieff work is a *praxis* for the full development of *Dasein* – Heidegger's term for the fundamental nature of humanity as the being who is open to Being-as-such.

However, it must be noted that in the Fourth Way the term "being" has a special, technical meaning. This is reflected, for example, in the title chosen for Jeanne de Salzmann's posthumously published notes, *The Reality of Being*. If one does not understand the connotations of these words in Gurdjieff's teaching, this title may seem vacuous or redundant, but it is neither. In the Fourth Way, the term "being" is usually used to refer to an attribute of man. Gurdjieff and his followers use the word a great deal, and it is often juxtaposed with "knowledge."[18] Gurdjieff states that it is possible for a man to have a great deal of knowledge while having a low level of being. And he says that this is not only common in modern Western culture, it is not even perceived as a problem.[19] What Gurdjieff is referring to is the familiar phenomenon of, say, the professor who possesses a great deal of book learning but who is also petty, absent minded, and neurotic. Or, to take an example of more recent vintage, the techno-wizard who is socially dysfunctional to the point of autism.

It is clear from both examples that "being" is not reducible to "character" (absent mindedness and social ineptitude are not moral failings). Rather, for Gurdjieff being seems to involve a kind of self-possession or self-mastery that cannot be acquired via knowledge, in the sense of the accumulation of facts. However, Gurdjieff also states that *"knowledge* depends on *being."*[20] What is meant by "knowledge" in this context is authentic knowledge, or "knowledge of the whole," as Gurdjieff is quoted as saying in *Fragments*.[21] This is, of course, the conception of wisdom that philosophers have held from Plato to Hegel. The difference is that Western philosophers conceive "knowledge of the whole" as knowledge of a "system" of ideas or concepts that serves to

---

[17] See de Salzmann, *The Reality of Being*, 41.
[18] See, for example, Ouspensky, *Fragments*, 64–68.
[19] Ouspensky, *Fragments*, 65.
[20] Quoted in Ouspensky, *Fragments*, 65. Italics in original.
[21] Ouspensky, *Fragments*, 65.

explain everything. For Gurdjieff, by contrast, knowledge of the whole involves what is sometimes called in the Fourth Way "direct knowing."

Like the concept of mystical *gnosis* (to which it may be equivalent), direct knowing is extraordinarily hard to put into words. Here I will merely suggest that direct knowing may be just what I described earlier as the state of being "present to Being" – present to the Being of the world, and to our own Being. In other worlds, "knowledge of all things" is a direct knowing of the Being of the All.[22] (Is this the same thing as knowing what Gurdjieff terms the Absolute? Perhaps.) Gurdjieff believes that an individual can cultivate his or her "level of being" through the development of this capacity, which involves the harmonization of all the centers. Thus, it is precisely through becoming present to Being that I actualize my own "being" (in Gurdjieff's sense of the word).

But now an important question arises: Just *what is it* that is present to Being? I have said that this state is one in which we are present to both what is "out there" and "in here" simultaneously; present to the All. But what is it in us that does this? It cannot belong to any of the centers – intellectual, emotional, or moving-instinctive – precisely because the attention Gurdjieff wishes us to cultivate observes all of the centers. And so we must ask: What is the "self" that observes? What is the "self" that remembers itself? It is with the asking of these questions that Gurdjieff's philosophy converges with the most profound perennial teachings of mysticism, East and West.

Jacob Needleman writes that "the proper relationship of the three centers ... in the human being is a necessary precondition for the reception and realization of what in the religions of the world has been variously termed the Holy Spirit, Atman, and the Buddha nature."[23] Note that Needleman says "reception and realization." "Reception" implies that something "outside" and distinct from us enters in, whereas "realization" implies that something is born within us, or through us. One frequently finds this ambiguity in the mystics, and the reason is simple. The "self" that remembers itself, that is capable of being present to Being, is *not* myself – where "myself" refers to my individual ego with all its idiosyncratic vices, virtues, and quirks. But beneath that there is another "self" that is capable of *seeing* all of my individual qualities and hence *isn't any of them*. This self is by definition impersonal. Thus, it is "mine" – and not mine. And so it is perfectly reasonable to speak of identification with this self as if it were the *reception* of something distinct from me, since it really is distinct from *me*. But

---

[22] See de Salzmann, *The Reality of Being*, 36.
[23] Needleman, "G. I. Gurdjieff and His School," 370.

it is equally reasonable to speak of it as the *realization* of something already in me, since it is the *real me*.

The Gurdjieff Work appears to be about giving birth to a higher "I" within oneself, and the strong suggestion is that it is through us that the Absolute comes to consciousness of itself. To be present to Being is to be able to say, with Parmenides, "It is." But *what says this* is not an individual, finite being but rather an infinite (not individual, not limited) self to which all finite beings presence themselves. It is the soul of the All – Needleman's Holy Spirit, Atman, or Buddha nature – awakened within an individual human being. It is not "I" that wakes up, in the sense of my individual selfhood or ego. It is something far greater. And yet, again, it *is* "I": the authentic "I" that is occluded by the many finite "I's" spoken of earlier. Thus, the message of the goddess to Parmenides, "It is," ultimately is equivalent to the message God gives to Moses: "I am" (Exodus 3:14). When the authentic "I" in me is able to say "I am," then "my" being (in Gurdjieff's sense) is realized, and Being confronts itself.[24] Hence the title of Gurdjieff's *Life Is Only Real Then, When "I Am,"* as well as the title given to Jeanne de Salzmann's posthumous book *The Reality of Being*.[25]

The Fourth Way claims to teach a clear path to the realization of being. Still, although the path may be clear, it is far from easy. As noted earlier, Gurdjieff holds that the "I's" will fight attempts to observe them and will erect all sorts of barriers and distractions to Work. However, the Fourth Way teaches that resistance is actually useful material for self-observation, and that there can be no progress without it. Observation of resistance continually confronts us with our mechanicalness. This can produce a kind of shock, and a flash of awakening, which can have a profound effect.

Gurdjieff does not, however, promise us enlightenment: There will never come a point when we "wake up" permanently, and Work is no longer necessary. As it is in ordinary life, so it is in the Gurdjieff Work: Awakening is not a constant state, but a continually repeated process of emerging from sleep. Hence the title of Colin Wilson's 1980 book on Gurdjieff, *The War Against Sleep*.[26] For Gurdjieff and his followers, it is a war without end.

---

[24] See de Salzmann, *The Reality of Being*, 60, and especially p. 173.
[25] Gurdjieff also taught that through Work, one could create an "essence" that could survive the death of the body. This is a complicated matter, beyond the scope of the present essay.
[26] See Colin Wilson, *The War Against Sleep: The Philosophy of G.I. Gurdjieff* (Wellingborough, Northamptonshire: Aquarian Press, 1980).

# 25

# C.G. JUNG AND JUNGIANISM

## Gerhard Wehr

### 1 Life and Work

Carl Gustav Jung, the founder of analytical psychology, left behind a life's work that has significant implications for spiritual and religious matters. Jung's writings are often studied by readers who are less interested in professional psychology than in self-understanding. A large number of his writings fall under the rubric of esoteric literature.

Jung was born on July 26, 1875, the son of an Evangelical Reformed minister in the small town of Kesswil, within the Swiss Canton of Thurgau, on Lake Constance. After attending the gymnasium in Basel, he completed his studies in the natural sciences and medicine from 1895 to 1900 at the University of Basel. Jung's decision to devote himself to psychiatry afforded him the opportunity to link his interests in the natural and social sciences. As he reports in his 1962 autobiography *Memories, Dreams, Reflections*, already during his youth he was drawn to the world of the supersensible and transpersonal. Jung participated in spiritualist sittings with a medium (Helene Preiswerk, a member of his mother's family), which led to his 1902 doctoral dissertation, *On the Psychology and Pathology of So-Called Occult Phenomena* (Zur Psychologie und Pathologie sogenannter occulter Phenomena). Jung's time from 1900 to 1909 as an assistant and later chief physician at the psychiatric clinic at Burghölzli (under the direction of Eugen Bleuler) was of great importance to his later medical and psychotherapeutic practice. He studied briefly with Pierre Janet at the famous Salpetrière Clinic in Paris, but it was Sigmund Freud and psychoanalysis that were to make the most important impact on him. In his speaking and writing, Jung advocated

---

Translation by Timothy Dail, revised by the editor. All translations are those of the translator unless specifically noted otherwise. English titles of German-language works have been adopted.

for psychoanalysis, which, at the beginning of the century, was still controversial. However, within a few years he had set his own course and distanced himself from the Freudian school. His analytical psychology placed itself in opposition to psychoanalysis, beginning with a new model of psychological types.

In 1903, Jung married Emma Rauschenbach, the daughter of a Swiss industrialist, and started a family. Around the same time, he opened a highly successful private psychotherapy practice in Küsnacht, near Zurich. He also began publishing numerous works setting forth his theories. It was during this same time that Jung turned to mythology and to the mystical and gnostic traditions. He was also quite interested in the natural philosophy of German Romanticism, in which one already found discussions of the unconscious and the "dark side of the soul" in the early nineteenth century.

The year 1909 would be significant for Jung. He and Freud were invited to lecture at Clark University in Worcester, Massachusetts. This invitation contributed to the growth of Jung's reputation in the Western world. At the same time, it strengthened his high standing in the psychoanalytical movement. Nevertheless, Jung was then also developing his own libido theory, which differed from Freud's in that it did not treat libido as exclusively sexual. This view is found in his major work from 1912, *Wandlungen und Symbole der Libido* (Transformations and Symbols of the Libido) translated into English as *Psychology of the Unconscious*. This led to Jung's break with Freud in 1913, and to his removal from the International Psychoanalytical Association, in which he had acted as president for several years.

By the beginning of the First World War, Jung had reached middle age. For him, it was the period of a penetrating and transformative spiritual experience, which can be characterized as his conflict with the unconscious. A flood of inner images threatened to conquer Jung and to throw him dissociatively into mental instability. These were experiences that drove him, he believed, to the outer reaches of consciousness. At the same time, Jung saw in them the primary material for his future life's work. To bear up under this nightmarish imaginativeness, he was careful to maintain contact with reality. He told himself, "One does not become bright by imagining brightness, but rather by becoming aware of darkness."[1] Departing from conventional psychoanalysis, he no longer saw the unconscious merely as the repository of the forgotten and repressed, which eludes deliberate access. Aside from the personal unconscious, his new conception of the "collective

---

[1] C. G. Jung, *Gesammelte Werke*, Vol. 13, ed. M. Niehus-Jung and L. Hurwitz Ellsner (Olten und Freiburg: Walter, 1978), 215.

unconscious" (i.e., the transpersonal unconscious) became much more important to him, especially in that he saw it as underlying spiritual-religious experience. The collective unconscious manifests itself, for example, in dreams, in which one finds imagery and themes of an archetypal nature. Jung argued that these "archetypes" were not ascribable to personal experience and that analogues were to be found in the fairy tales and myths of peoples throughout the world.

Central to analytical psychology and its understanding of the collective unconscious is the model of archetypes (from the Greek *arche*, beginning, and *typos*, the molded, the originally produced). Jung derived the term linguistically from texts in the *Corpus Hermeticum* and even used it to infer that the designation is present in Greek philosophy as well as in the literature of the Christian Church Fathers (e.g., Augustine). The concept of the archetype underwent a process of clarification within the framework of Jung's psychology. Such a process of evolution was characteristic of him, as Jung did not remain content with mere heuristic suppositions but aimed to get as close to the real nature of the psyche as possible.

Nevertheless, he conceived the archetype as less a "primordial image" than a dynamic and process-like force. Jung himself spoke of archetypes as "mental life forces" (*seelischen Lebensmächte*), which in a peculiar way demand to be recognized and validated. Because the archetype stands as the centerpiece of analytical psychology, individuation takes on a central role as well. In Jung's conception of human nature, "becoming human" cannot merely be the result of biological maturation. It is apparent that the empirical ego is subject to a lifelong spiritual-psychical process of growth whose goal is the archetype of "the self." The center and circumference of this self are determined through its embodiment of a whole or unity of the conscious and unconscious. To this unity – which has the sense of completeness, rather than perfection – belongs the integration of the individual "shadow," that is, one's own unconscious dark side. Just as the shadow is invested in the individual unconscious, there is within the unconscious of the man a psychical feminine, the *anima*. Analogically, in the woman there is the masculine *animus*. Because these are unconscious as well, they are typically projected onto other human beings, which leads to all kinds of problems and misunderstandings. The process of individuation does not merely involve becoming aware of these elements of the psyche. Rather, one must strive for integration in the full sense of the word – and to affirm and bear one's own destiny.

Seen in this way, Jung's conception of the process of individuation exhibits initiatic traits. However, as a psychologist it could not be his concern to offer meditative or contemplative exercises. In conjunction with his personal psychological process at the time of the First World War, in 1916 he nonetheless developed "active imagination" (*Aktive Imagination*). This is a method employed during the phase of advanced therapy through which patients unfold the depth of their own psyche, thereby activating the creative potentials of the unconscious. The individual ego enters into a state of detachment.[2] The therapist must refrain from all interference so that the self can take over the direction during the process, in which images that affect the dream and fantasy life display themselves. Jung, who also occasionally occupied himself with the spiritual exercises of Ignatius of Loyola, followed in this way a directive of the Jesuits, who recommended that instructors of meditation refrain from all interference.

It is no coincidence that in his 1939 English-language commentary on the *Tibetan Book of the Dead*, Jung speaks of the extent to which, as a path to individuation, psychoanalysis constitutes a Western initiatic process. In this context, he addresses the individual forms of the Western and Eastern paths. He describes the *Tibetan Book of the Dead* as "an esoteric book" — esoteric in so far as its understanding requires a special spiritual capacity that one does not readily possess from the first. It is more valid to find one's own path in the form of a spiritually oriented conduct of life, and the experience that results from it. And it is not possible merely through attaining secondhand knowledge of another horizon of consciousness already developed by some spiritual teacher. Jung was also skeptical of an imprudent adoption by Westerners of practices developed by persons living under completely different psychosocial conditions, whether those practices be yoga or so-called theosophical teachings.

According to Jung, both the individual and humanity as a whole find themselves in a process of transformation and maturation of an archetypal nature. According to this way of looking at things, the existential meaning of religiosity, with mysticism and esotericism at its spiritual core, allows itself to be truly authentic. Whereas, by contrast, a theology that is mainly preached or lectured remains lodged in formalism rather than in conscious participation in "divine wisdom." The inefficacy of such theologies and their diminishing appeal are evident everywhere today.

Jung deepened his investigation of the archetypal dimension of the psyche through his study of the gnostic texts of antiquity. His preoccupation with Gnosticism was an important element in his struggles with his own unconscious. Jung's 1916 work *Septem Sermones ad Mortuos* (*Seven Sermons to the Dead*), a text initially withheld from the public, documents this critical,

---

[2] (The word employed here by Professor Wehr is *Gelassenheit* – trans.)

internal psychic process. He felt inwardly compelled to express, in poetic language, the powerful images that arose within him in terms of forms found in the gnostic tradition, in particular those of the Alexandrian gnostic Basilides (117–138 CE). Further images came forth from the depths of the transpersonal unconscious. Jung discovered what a clarifying effect an artistic rendition (painting, for example) can have within the psychotherapeutic process. The images Jung produced included a mandala, which he drew from a strong inner impulse. For Jung, the meaning of images always points beyond their explicit definition, or expression in language.

Jung's encounter and first intellectual exchange with the German Sinologist Richard Wilhelm (1873–1930) became particularly important to him. Wilhelm had made a name for himself as an expert on the East Asian spiritual world and as translator of the *I Ching*. In 1929, Jung contributed a commentary to Wilhelm's translation of the eighth-century Chinese meditation classic *The Secret of the Golden Flower*. Within his more intimate circle of colleagues and students, he invited Indologist Jakob Wilhelm Hauer (1881–1962) of Tübingen to give a course on Kundalini yoga. Jung himself contributed depth-psychological correspondences that illuminated the meaning of this spiritual discipline. His encounter with Indologist Heinrich Zimmer (1890–1943) also contributed to the expansion of Jung's spiritual horizons with a view toward other areas of the Indian spiritual world.

Jung visited India in 1937–1938, and for the first time, as he himself confessed, he found himself under the immediate influence of a truly foreign culture. It was typical of him, however, that he took with him as travel reading the seventeenth-century alchemical text *Theatrum Chemicum*. Jung paid heed to his dreams and was therefore not surprised that alongside his impressive daily experience of the Indian world of temples, he dreamed of the Grail and of occidental Christian symbolism. For him, this was an expression of spiritual-archetypal rootedness, which cannot be extinguished even when the daily life of the traveler abroad is filled with completely alien and exotic images.

Jung's collaboration with Richard Wilhelm and Heinrich Zimmer remained important beyond their early deaths. His association with *The Secret of the Golden Flower*, for which Jung had written a psychological commentary, inspired Jung's work in later life to a great degree. From then on, the world of alchemical symbolism in its illustration of the transpersonal processes of the unconscious opened itself to him. For Jung, alchemy is a centuries-old form of knowledge that can be applied hermeneutically to the unconscious productions of men living today. While gnostic texts contributed helpful insights to Jung's understanding of psychic processes in the first years of his research, only alchemy turned out to be appropriate for a better understanding of spiritual-psychical transformations in the phases of maturation and how they can represent themselves in dreams.

In comparison to the *gnosis* of antiquity, alchemy had an advantage in that the medieval texts and iconographic portrayals were closer to the consciousness of modern human beings than records from the early Christian and pre-Christian eras. This becomes apparent when one takes note of Jung's pertinent works in which he amplifies or enriches images produced by modern people with equivalents from the alchemical tradition. As a psychologist, Jung had to be careful to see that immediate experiences were documented as carefully as possible. That was complicated in the case of early Christian Gnosticism, since in the first half of the twentieth century – before the discoveries of Nag-Hammadi had become known – there were still relatively few original texts available. One had to rely on multiple scattered reports and interpretations from the quill of Christian heresiology, that is, from ecclesiastical enmity.

Moreover, it must be emphasized that in dealing with alchemical material, Jung was not concerned simply to "psychologize" it and to disregard actual alchemical laboratory operations. It was important to Jung to cross the boundaries of a personalist-constructed psychology to derive possibilities for comparison, with whose help psychic processes in their depth dimension might be better understood. As a psychologist, Jung made important contributions to research in intellectual history in general, and to esotericism in particular. This already becomes clear when one sees with what care he compiled and interpreted rare alchemical literature. Jung's research into alchemy stretches from the 1930s up to his late work. Aside from a series of smaller preliminary works, the volume *Psychology and Alchemy* represents an important milestone in his research.

If the descent into his own unconscious gave Jung unexpected insights into psychic reality, it was only his penetration of the multifaceted alchemical tradition that made it possible for him to decipher these highly personal experiences. For Jung, it was a decades-long process of coming to awareness. Jung's contributions to research into alchemy conclude alongside a series of further studies in the posthumously published, two-part work *Mysterium Coniunctionis*, in which he was assisted by his colleague Marie-Louise von Franz.

In light of the significance of archetypes in religious and spiritual contexts, one must in addition discuss Jung's psychological works in their relationship to religion. This topic moved him his entire life – not simply because he grew up in a parsonage, but rather because for Jung the religious signified a reason for being. In this context must be understood the words he had placed over the gate to his house: *Vocatus atque non vocatus, deus aderit* (Summoned or not summoned, God will be present).

Jung opened his 1937 Terry Lectures (later published as *Psychology and Religion*), delivered at Yale University, with the following statement:

> Since religion is incontestably one of the earliest and most universal expressions of the human mind, it is obvious that any psychology which touches upon the psychological structure of human personality cannot avoid taking note of the fact that religion is not only a sociological and historical phenomenon, but also something of considerable personal concern to a great number of individuals.[3]

It is remarkable when one sees Jung, a Protestant, speaking of the extraordinary importance of dogma and ritual, which he validates as "methods of spiritual hygiene." The life of Christ is not a one-time historical occurrence for him. To Jung, who was familiar with the mysticism of Meister Eckhart and Jacob Boehme, the life of Christ in fact happens always and everywhere, because the Christian archetype is interwoven with what it means to be human. Naturally, this is not meant in a narrowly sectarian way. Jung wished to deconstruct traditions of thought that have become historically fixed and rigid, in order to reveal their experiential value.

This becomes clear, for example, in two studies: "A Psychological Approach to the Dogma of the Trinity" (1948) and "Transformation Symbolism in the Mass" (1954). When he was criticized for "psychologizing" religious facts, he responded that by "God" he meant a psychic image, a phenomenon that appears in the human psyche. Jung expressly abstained from making theological pronouncements. On the other hand, if someone accused him of abstraction and of not being faithful to the spiritual experience, then he did not shy away as a layman from responding with a statement of avowal, such as when he confessed to the Catholic theologian Gebhard Frei (in a letter dated January 13, 1948): "Christ is indeed in us and we in him! ... I am thankful to God every day that I am permitted to experience the reality of the *Imago Dei* [man as God's image]. . . . Thanks to this *actus gratiae* [act of grace] my life has meaning, and my inner eye has been opened to the beauty and grandeur of the dogma."[4]

---

[3] C. G. Jung, *Psychology and Religion: West and East*, 2nd ed., *Collected Works*, Vol. 11, trans. R. F. C. Hull (Princeton: Princeton University Press, 1969), 5.

[4] *C. G. Jung Letters*, Vol. 1, ed. Gerhard Adler and Aniela Jaffé, trans. R. F. C. Hull (London: Routledge and Kegan Paul, 1973), 487.

Testimonies such as these show that Jung did not retreat exclusively to the position of a nonpartisan observer and researcher when he dealt with the central themes of religion. He speaks as someone deeply moved, one who was not untouched by the great contents of religious tradition. The darkness of the Old Testament image of God (Yahweh) aroused him at his innermost core. In none of his later works did this become more obvious than in *Answer to Job* (1952). Therein he raised fundamental questions about the image of God, which coincide with essential questions about human existence in relation to the elemental force of the transcendent. Without a doubt, Jung was successful at moving minds again and again.

As to more recent esoteric or mystical figures and movements, Jung principally kept a certain distance from them. In this way, he consciously refrained from seeking out gurus of the status of Ramana Maharshi (1879–1950) during his trip to India, or questioning them in the manner of countless contemporaries, or meditating in their presence. With all due respect for them as holy and honored initiates of the East, Jung came to the following conviction: "I would have felt it as a theft had I attempted to learn from the holy men and to accept their truth for myself. Neither in Europe can I make borrowings from the East, but must shape my life out of myself – out of what my inner being tells me, or what nature brings to me."[5] He reiterated this reliance on that which springs up from one's own psychic ground when speaking of H. P. Blavatsky or Rudolf Steiner; for this reason, he was skeptical of both of them. From personal friends close to the Anthroposophical Society, he received all kinds of inside information about Steiner's followers.

Jung became especially suspicious when observing how otherwise unknowing believers misinterpreted messages of this or that master figure as their own "awareness of higher worlds," instead of working toward an awareness stemming from the depths of their own soul. The spiritual transformation for which one should strive cannot be reached through a method. On the other hand, it is legitimate to place Steiner's work in dialogue with Jung's, so to speak. One would only have to be careful not to blur the fine line between comparison and synthesis, whereby everything is lumped and mixed together, undifferentiated. As always with Jung, the dialogue with representatives of other disciplines was important, especially with theology and the natural sciences.

---

[5] C. G. Jung, *Memories, Dreams, Reflections*, recorded and edited by Aniela Jaffé, trans. Richard and Clara Winston (New York: Random House, 1965), 275.

In this context, one must consider the Eranos Symposia, organized by Olga Froebe-Kapteyn (1881–1962) beginning in 1933 at Lake Maggiore in Switzerland. Here, scholars and scientists from all over the world met to discuss their research and present it to an international audience. In the early years, the symposia dealt mainly with religious studies and esoteric issues, which took center stage, but in later years disciplines of the natural sciences were also discussed. Eranos had its origins in Froebe-Kapteyn's Theosophical "School of Spiritual Research." Following a break with Alice Bailey, Froebe-Kapteyn closed the school and replaced it with the Eranos Symposia. It would chiefly be Jung who set the priorities for Eranos. In terms of his principles, Jung continually placed great emphasis on the liveliness and spontaneity of the psyche, in light of which dogmatic theological systems become superfluous. In this way, a characteristic of the esoteric reveals itself – not in the sense of the "secretive," but rather attentiveness to the inner dimension of experience and reality. For his entire life, Jung advocated for such attentiveness.

It is ultimately worth noting that even the stone erected above Jung's grave at the Küsnacht cemetery unambiguously expresses the spirit and hope for which he lived. The inscription states: *Primus homo de terra terrenus, secundus homo de caelo caelestis* ("The first man is of the earth, earthly; the second man is of heaven, heavenly," 1 Corinthians, 15:47).

## 2 Aspects of the Jungian School

Through his writing and lecturing, C. G. Jung established a school of thought and a therapeutic approach that have been very influential. The development of the Jungian movement had already begun in 1916 with the founding of the Psychological Club (Psychologischer Club) in Zürich. Numerous training schools, the first of which was the C. G. Jung Institute in Küsnacht at Lake Zurich, have charged themselves with the further development of analytical psychology. This process took on various forms. It was contingent on the fact that numerous Freudian and Jungian analysts were forced to emigrate from Europe around the mid-twentieth century, as a result of the rise of fascism. A theory and therapeutic method based on superpersonal and supernational foundations were not permitted in nations under totalitarian regimes. Jung's attitude during the era of National Socialism in Germany is still debatable. Certain ambiguous and unfortunate statements made by Jung damaged his image considerably. He was not even spared the slanderous accusation that he was an anti-Semite. It is easy to overlook the fact that Jung made it possible for Jewish colleagues to remain legally in his psychotherapists' organization in spite of the political consolidation of institutional powers and the alignment of psychoanalytic organizations with National Socialist ideology.

Further, reliable witnesses – such as the leading Jewish Jungian Thomas Kirsch – explicitly confirm Jung's dedication to the disadvantaged and the persecuted. On emigration, a great number of dispossessed analysts found affiliation with the Jung Centers that already existed in the United States. Some, such as Jung's students James and Hilde Kirsch, settled in Los Angeles, affiliating themselves with other refugee Jungians in an organization that eventually became the C. G. Jung Institute of Los Angeles. Erich Neumann (1905–1960), whose works explored the origins of consciousness and the archetype of the Great Mother, became a major figure in analytical psychology in Israel and internationally. He was one of the acclaimed lecturers at the Eranos Symposia.

Concerning the ideas of the Jungian movement, two main streams succeeding Jung are worth mentioning. One is a "classical" formulation, a stream geared more strongly toward developmental psychology. Another stream can be described as oriented more toward archetypal psychology. It deals with the theme of maturation, to which integration of the shadow and spiritual image belong within the framework of the process of individuation. It is a process that starts to appear in midlife and in which one can recognize initiatic traits, somewhat analogous to Nietzsche's aphorism: "You should become who you are."[6]

A further direction of the so-called Jung School gives special attention to the images and symbols produced by the psyche. Here the focus of attention is placed on the archetypal observation of mental facts. Among its representatives is James Hillman, the late editor of the magazine *Spring*, who also became known through his early involvement with the Eranos Symposia. He employed the description "archetypal psychology" in his work. One must also note the important role Jung's ideas have played within the framework of transpersonal psychology, whose representatives pay special attention to spiritual traditions, including the spiritual-religious schools of both East and West. Whether one can also speak, as Richard Noll does, of a pseudo-religious "Jung Cult," which places the psychologist in the gray area of neo-paganism, magic, and so on, remains open for debate.[7] But Jung himself does not deserve to be reduced to the shadow side of the movement he

---

[6] Friedrich Nietzsche, *The Gay Science*, trans. Josefine Nauckhoff (Cambridge: Cambridge University Press, 2001), 152.

[7] See Richard Noll, *The Jung Cult: Origins of a Charismatic Movement* (Princeton: Princeton University Press, 1994).

founded, or the shadow of its followers. (Additionally, there are the shadow projections of some critics.)

The movement that began in the original circle of colleagues of the Psychological Club in Zürich, then as the Zürich C. G. Jung Institute, was advanced over decades with some transformations. Mention must be made of the work of Marie-Louise von Franz and her Research and Training Center for Depth Psychology. Von Franz stressed the importance of not only perpetuating but deepening Jung's approach. Some saw in such a position an attempt to shield the work of the founding father from change, or even falsification through new developments. In any case, such a controversy demonstrates again that Jungianism is a vital, multi-faceted movement.

If, in light of these many accents and innovations, one asks to what extent there are essential commonalities in the post-Jung era, then one must surely point to the importance of Jung's use of alchemical symbolism, with the help of which he described the psychological process of maturation. Aside from the texts mentioned, *Psychology and Alchemy* and *Mysterium Coniunctionis*, the work *Psychology of the Transference* is notable. Other commonalities can be mentioned. These include, in particular, a view of psychic reality based on completeness and individuation that does not only take the individual into account but at the same time looks to a transformation of society. The problems of human beings are not solvable solely by technical or organizational skill – not if damage to the psyche is to be prevented. In light of the globalization and homogenization encompassing virtually all regions today, Jung's work has never been more useful and important.

# 26

# RENÉ GUÉNON AND TRADITIONALISM

## Mark Sedgwick

### 1 Introduction

What is sometimes called "Guénonian Traditionalism" is a school or movement most easily identified by its origin in the writings of the French philosopher René Guénon (1886–1951). Guénonian Traditionalism – distinguished in this essay from other forms of traditionalism by the use of a capital "T" – was originally developed in Paris in the 1920s and has since become widespread and influential. Some Traditionalists today stay close to Guénon's original conceptions and practice, and they may be said to form the Traditionalist school, sometimes now called Integral Traditionalism; others have modified and developed his ideas to the extent that purist Guénonians do not recognize them as fellow Traditionalists. These may be said to be part of the broader Traditionalist movement.

Guénonian Traditionalists of both sorts understand "tradition" in a special sense that distinguishes them from the many other individuals and groups that use the term. For Traditionalists, "tradition" indicates the spiritual wisdom that is conceived as having formed the ancient core of all the great religions and spiritual paths – in effect, the perennial philosophy. The term "perennialist" is also used, both by some Traditionalists to describe themselves and by some outsiders. Traditionalists, however, differ from other perennialists such as Aldous Huxley (who published his *The Perennial Philosophy* in 1944) in their anti-modernism and their insistence on esoteric initiation. Huxley, for example, was interested in neither of these. This insistence is one basis on which Traditionalism may be classed as esoteric; another is the degree to which Traditionalism draws on other esoteric currents discussed in this volume, even though Traditionalists are fiercely critical of most other such currents, which they see as "pseudo-initiatic" or even "counter-initiatic."[1]

---

[1] This summary and the following paragraphs draw on my *Against the Modern World: Traditionalism and the Secret Intellectual History of the Twentieth Century* (New York: Oxford

Traditionalism has a complex doctrine,[2] and a cyclical conception of time borrowed from Hinduism. In the distant first age of the current cycle, spiritual wisdom was widespread and generally accessible; in the current and final age, identified as the *kali yuga* or dark age, spiritual wisdom has almost vanished. The result is what is called modernity, with all its problems. Inevitably, things will degenerate further. During the first age, spiritual wisdom was unified, and there was no distinction between the esoteric and exoteric. In later ages, a distinction developed between these, and the exoteric split into the various religions that we know today. Some of these, including the Catholic Church, then lost their esoteric content. Under these circumstances, the immediate task of Traditionalism is to reveal and recover what remains of the ancient tradition. A related task is to do what can be done under the circumstances.

However, Guénon did not think that much could be done under the circumstances of modernity. At best, a small "elite" might save what could be saved, for themselves and for the new age that would come in the new cycle. Guénonian purists agree, and their activities have thus generally been in the scholarly and spiritual fields. Some Traditionalists – generally rejected by the purists – have, however, seen possibilities for a more general transformation and have thus been active in the political field. At the present time, it is these political Traditionalists who are most widespread and active.

The scholarly activities of certain Traditionalists are impressive in their scope but are mostly ignored by mainstream academia, which generally rejects Traditionalism when it notices it (as it does from time to time), on the grounds that it is methodologically unsound, not to mention tainted with esotericism. Traditionalists, in turn, generally reject academic scholarship,[3] seeing it as incapable of grasping what really matters, and as contributing more to confusion than to clarification. Despite this, some important Traditionalists have been academics, and most Traditionalists are in some sense intellectuals, if only because the complexity of Guénon's work means that it is not easily accessible. Political Traditionalism, however, has been to

---

University Press, 2004), 21–28. In general, my approach has been to cite this book when sources and argument are given there, and to cite other works especially when they are more recent and/or were not included in *Against the Modern World*.

[2] For more detail, see Graham Rooth, *Prophet for a Dark Age: A Companion to the Works of René Guénon* (Eastbourne: Sussex Academic Press, 2008) or William W. Quinn, *The Only Tradition* (Albany: State University of New York Press, 1996).

[3] This includes the historical scholarship in my *Against the Modern World*, as might have been expected. There are, however, exceptions: Traditionalists who believe that an accurate understanding of Traditionalism's past may contribute usefully to its future.

some extent popularized and so in some form reaches a more general audience.

The scholarly activities of Traditionalists have resulted over the years in an impressive number of books and journals and, more recently, publishing houses and Internet sites.[4] Some of the books and articles are dense and technical, intended for other Traditionalists, and may be termed "hard Traditionalism." Others are aimed at a more general audience and are either not explicitly Traditionalist or are merely inspired by Traditionalism, sometimes as no more than one influence among many. These may be termed "soft Traditionalism." Still others are editions and translations of classic non-Western religious texts that meet the highest standards of mainstream academic scholarship.

The spiritual activities of Traditionalists may likewise be termed "hard" or "soft." There have been Traditionalist groups that have established Traditionalist Sufis and Traditionalist Masonic lodges, and there have also been Traditionalists who participate in, and sometimes influence, preexisting groups – again, generally Sufi or Masonic.

The activities of political Traditionalists have been of a non-electoral variety, and at the far right of the standard political spectrum. In the sense in which the terms were used earlier, they have more often been "soft" than "hard," although there are also published works of hard political Traditionalism.

## 2 The Origins of Traditionalism

Guénon's writings rarely disclosed their sources, but his biography and an analysis of his work allow these sources to be reconstructed. Most Traditionalists would dispute such a reconstruction, stressing that the only real source of Traditionalism is tradition itself.

After a provincial childhood, Guénon encountered esotericism when he moved to Paris at the age of eighteen, in 1904. While a student, he became closely involved in the Martinist Order of "Papus" (Gérard Encausse, 1865–1916), itself a development of Theosophy with elements of irregular Masonry.[5] His thought was subsequently influenced principally by his own

---

[4] An analysis of the books and Internet sites, now somewhat outdated, is given on my website www.traditionalists.org

[5] The classic source for Guénon's life is Paul Chacornac, *La vie simple de René Guénon* (Paris: Editions traditionnelles, 1958). There are several later editions and translations. For Papus, see Marie-Sophie André and Christophe Beaufils, *Papus, biographie: la Belle Epoque de l'occultisme* (Paris: Berg International, 1995).

readings of the Vedanta; by a Swedish painter resident in Paris, Ivan Aguéli (1869–1917), who combined Theosophy with Egyptian Sufism; and by a French writer, Count Albert-Eugène de Pouvourville (1861–1940), who combined concern about what would now be called the "clash of civilizations" with what was then called Taoism.[6] It is unclear how Guénon was first introduced to Hindu works, but these were relatively well known in *fin-de-siècle* Paris.

This early period of Guénon's life ended with the disruption of the *fin-de-siècle* esoteric milieu by the First World War, and with Guénon's marriage to a respectable Catholic. Guénon published his first books in 1921, condemning Theosophy and other such currents, under the patronage of the neo-Thomist Catholic theologian and philosopher Jacques Maritain (1882–1973).[7] He also published a book on Hinduism that he had written as a doctoral thesis, but which had been rejected by the Sorbonne – one reason for his and Traditionalism's lasting hostility toward academia. During this period, Guénon worked as a high school philosophy teacher while developing what would become the essential tenets of Traditionalism in numerous articles as well as books.[8]

Between 1927 and 1929, Guénon suffered a number of disasters: He lost his job, his wife died, and his adopted daughter was removed from his care by her family. In 1930, he traveled to Egypt, a country in which he had never previously been much interested, in the company of a wealthy American widow who had proposed to finance a book series he was to edit. However, Guénon broke with the widow and spent the rest of his life in Cairo, never returning to France. He attempted to support himself by his writing but achieved a reasonable standard of living only as a result of gifts from various admirers of his work, the number of which continued to grow.[9]

During this final period of his life, from 1930 until his death in 1951, Guénon lived as a Muslim and followed an Egyptian Sufi Order.[10] His later Muslim admirers date his conversion to Islam to his encounter with the Swedish Sufi Aguéli in 1911, while his later non-Muslim admirers dispute this, stressing his continuing commitment to Masonry even during his Egyptian years. Masonry need not be incompatible with Islam, however,

---

[6] Sedgwick, *Against the Modern World*, 39–50, 56–62.
[7] Nöele Maurice-Denis Boulet, "L'ésotériste René Guénon: Souvenirs et jugements," *La pensée catholique: Cahiers de synthèse* 77 (1962).
[8] A limited selection of these is given in the Suggestions for Further Reading at the end of this volume.
[9] Sedgwick, *Against the Modern World*, 73–80.
[10] Sedgwick, *Against the Modern World*, 76.

and it is clear that Guénon did follow the Shariah scrupulously during this period. There are no traces of any Islamic practice before 1930. Guénon himself denied that he had "converted" to Islam, since it was impossible for anyone who truly understood the perennial philosophy to convert to anything – he had merely "moved in" to Islam.[11]

Guénon's writing in Cairo further developed his earlier themes, but with a new emphasis on initiation, stressing that esoteric initiation (in his own case, Sufism, as well as Masonry) must be within an orthodox exoteric framework (in his own case, Islam). These were the final elements to be added to what might be called the pure doctrine of Guénonian Traditionalism.

Traditionalism is in many ways a typical product of nineteenth-century Western approaches to the spiritual. Like so much else, it is clearly indebted to Theosophy, and through Theosophy to the common fund of Western esotericism. Its emphasis on initiation derives at least in part from Masonry. It also reflects the widespread interest in Oriental spirituality that followed the first translations of Hindu and Sufi works into modern European languages in the 1820s, an interest that may itself be understood in terms of the Romantic Movement and, before that, of Deism.[12]

Traditionalism's understanding of modernity as the result of decline rather than of progress is unusual in a nineteenth-century context, although it is in some ways implicit in the Romantic Movement, even though the idea of decline and degeneration as the basic dynamic of history has always been popular, in Hinduism as well as in many versions of the Golden Age myth. Anti-modernism is, however, fairly typical of the period following the end of the First World War. Spengler's *Decline of the West*, published in 1918, is the best known representative of this trend. Sufism, another important element, was also popular in Europe and America in the interwar years.[13]

However, Traditionalism also owes something to non-Western sources. At the level of detailed doctrine, the Advaita Vedanta is both Guénon's inspiration and source. At the level of practice, Sufism is clearly even more important than Masonry, as the source of the idea that the esoteric path must be followed within the context of orthodox exoteric practice. The relationship between the esoteric path and exoteric practice has been disputed for

[11] Thierry Zarcone, "Relectures et transformations de Soufisme en Occident," *Diogène* 187 (2000), 145–160.
[12] Mark Sedgwick, "Quelques sources du dix-huitième siècle du pluralisme religieux inclusif," in *Etudes d'histoire de l'ésotérisme: mélanges offerts à Jean-Pierre Laurent*, ed. Jean-Pierre Brach and Jérôme Rousse-Lacordaire (Paris: Editions du Cerf, 2007), 49–65.
[13] Mark Sedgwick, "European Neo-Sufi Movements in the Interwar Period," in *Islam in Interwar Europe*, ed. Nathalie Clayer and Eric Germain (New York: Columbia University Press, 2008), 183–215.

centuries in Islam, with Sufis frequently being criticized – sometimes with justification and sometimes without – for ignoring exoteric rules and practice.[14] One response to these criticisms was for Sufis to emphasize the importance of the exoteric Shariah as the vessel that holds the esoteric *Haqiqah* or truth. This approach was taken by Guénon's Sufi shaykh in Cairo, Salama al-Radi.[15]

From an academic perspective, it is far from clear that Sufism as found in the Muslim world involves initiation as understood in the West, but this question has troubled few Traditionalists, most of whom have had no direct contact with the Muslim world or with non-Traditionalist Muslims. Scholars might also question the very concept of "orthodoxy," but again this has rarely troubled the Traditionalists themselves.

## 3 The Initial Reception of Traditionalism

Some of the earliest enthusiasts of Guénon's work came, like him, from the French esoteric and Masonic milieus. Others came from the artistic milieu, some seeking to ground their artistic production in a deeper understanding of reality. Marxism provided an analysis of reality that was attractive to many, and Traditionalism provided its own analysis, attractive to a few.[16]

By the late 1920s, Guénon's work was beginning to be known outside France. His enthusiastic readers from this period who are now well known are mostly those who later played some part in the further development of Traditionalism. One of the first and most important of these was Ananda Coomaraswamy (1877–1947), an Englishman partially of Sri Lankan origin who emigrated to America during the First World War. Coomaraswamy was a distinguished art historian, and the first academic to be a Traditionalist. Guénon's writings turned Coomaraswamy's focus from what was then called Oriental art to the spirituality underlying that art, understood within a Traditionalist framework. Coomaraswamy's main interest was Buddhism, and he worked with Guénon – who he never actually met, but corresponded with at length – to integrate Buddhism into Traditionalism, which had until that point drawn mostly on Hinduism.[17]

---

[14] For the phenomenon, Richard McGregor, "The Problem of Sufism," *Mamluk Studies Review*, 13:2 (2009).
[15] Michael Gilsenan, *Recognizing Islam: Religion and Society in the Modern Middle East* (London: I. B. Tauris, 2000), 233.
[16] Kathleen Ferrick Rosenblatt, *René Daumal: The Life and Work of a Mystic Guide* (Albany: State University of New York Press, 1999), 97–111.
[17] Sedgwick, *Against the Modern World*, 34–36, 51–53.

Another academic enthusiast of Traditionalism was Mircea Eliade (1907–1986), then at the University of Bucharest, who was later in correspondence with Coomaraswamy, and also with a painter and would-be academic in Italy, Baron Julius Evola (1898–1974), a further early enthusiast of Traditionalism. Unlike Coomaraswamy, Eliade did not influence the development of Traditionalism, but Traditionalism may have influenced the development of Eliade. Eliade's mature work is massive and complex and differs from mainstream Traditionalism in important respects, but much of Eliade's basic analysis is arguably derived from Traditionalism.[18]

In the long run, Evola would prove the most important contributor to the development of Traditionalism after Guénon and Coomaraswamy. As Guénon is the origin of Traditionalism as a whole, Evola is the origin of political Traditionalism. Guénon was not Evola's only source – Nietzsche was also a major influence – and Evola never agreed with Guénon's requirement for esoteric initiation within an exoteric framework. His esotericism was more eclectic than Guénon's and included *magia sexualis*, closely linked to his reading of Tantra.[19]

Frithjof Schuon (1907–1998), another Guénon enthusiast, was the Swiss-born son of a German musician and his French wife. Schuon was interested in non-Christian religion as a teenager and dreamed of being a painter, but financial hardship forced him to leave school and take a job in a factory.[20] In later life, he created paintings and poetry that were much admired by his followers.

All these early Traditionalists have similar backgrounds. All had long-standing interests in esotericism, the occult, and non-Western religion, save that neither Eliade nor Schuon were ever much interested in the occult. Aguéli, Coomaraswamy, Evola, and Schuon were interested in art or were artists, often of real talent. Aguéli is well known as a painter today in his native Sweden, if not much outside it, and Evola still features in standard histories of the Dada movement, whose authors often seem unaware of his later career. Coomaraswamy and Eliade were distinguished academics; Guénon and Evola attempted academic careers.[21]

---

[18] Natale Spineto, "Mircea Eliade and 'Traditional Thought,'" in *The International Eliade*, ed. Bryan S. Rennie (Albany: State University of New York Press, 2007), 131–147.
[19] Hugh Urban, *Magia Sexualis: Sex, Magic, and Liberation in Modern Western Esotericism* (Berkeley: University of California Press, 2006), 140–161.
[20] Sedgwick, *Against the Modern World*, 84–85. The classic source for Schuon's life is his autobiography, Frithjof Schuon, *Erinnerungen und Betrachtungen* (Switzerland, privately printed, 1974), but this is almost impossible to obtain.
[21] Sedgwick, *Against the Modern World*, 99.

What seems to have attracted all these early Traditionalists to Guénon's work and to Traditionalism itself is its uncompromising condemnation of a modernity that they had already, for various reasons, rejected. Traditionalism provided an explanation of what was wrong. It also indicated a way forward, or at least a general direction.

## 4 The Development of Traditionalism

The development of Traditionalism by Schuon is closest to Guénon's original vision in that it was spiritual, and initially Sufi. The development of Traditionalism by various Masons was probably also close to Guénon's original vision, but less is known about this. Traditionalist Masonry remains under-researched, partly because of the difficulties that research into Masonry presents for the non-Mason.[22] Evola's development was the furthest from Guénon's vision and – unlike the other developments – took place independently of Guénon.

Schuon was one of a number of Traditionalists who were inspired by Guénon's work to search for a traditional esoteric initiation. He found this at the hands of a well-known Algerian Sufi shaykh, Ahmad al-Alawi (1869–1934), and he used this "initiation" to establish a Swiss branch of al-Alawi's Sufi Order, the Alawiyya, in about 1933. A number of Swiss Traditionalists joined Schuon's branch of the Alawiyya, converting to Islam to do so, but keeping their conversion secret, and modifying the standard practices of Islam somewhat to this end and to facilitate life as a practicing Muslim in Europe. Guénon referred some of those who wrote asking for a recommended initiation to Schuon, and Schuon's Alawiyya grew, establishing branches in France and elsewhere, and losing contact with its Algerian origins.[23] The final size of Schuon's Alawiyya is not known but was probably in the region of one thousand to two thousand people at its height.[24] Its impact was greater than those numbers suggest, however, because many of Schuon's Alawis were writers or academics: Their works of soft Traditionalism reached a wide audience, presenting religious and artistic topics to the reading public within a framework that derived from Traditionalism.[25]

---

[22] One starting point is Denys Roman, *René Guénon et les destins de la franc-maçonnerie* (Paris: Editions de l'Œuvre, 1982).

[23] Sedgwick, *Against the Modern World*, 88–90. See this source for other information on Schuon, following.

[24] This estimate is impressionistic and may be badly wrong. The absolute lower limit is probably five hundred; the total might be much higher.

[25] The best-selling Maryami author in North America was Huston Smith, whose *The World's Religions* sold millions of copies there, although it sold fewer copies in Europe. *The World's*

Schuon is important for establishing the largest and most widespread Sufi Traditionalist organization. He is also important for his development of Guénon's original Traditionalism, identifying Guénon's esoteric perennial philosophy as primordial truth or perennial religion, and developing the concept of the "transcendent unity of religions," including Christianity, which Guénon had rejected more firmly. One result of this development was that even before Guénon's death, Schuon's following began to include non-Muslims, most of whom were Christian; this was the cause of a breach with Guénon.

Schuon's Alawiyya initially combined Traditionalist metaphysics with Sufi initiation within the context of orthodox Islam, just as Guénon himself had. As the years passed, however, the relative importance of Islam declined, a development connected with a series of visions in which Schuon saw the Virgin Mary. These led to an increasing emphasis on the Virgin, and to the renaming of Schuon's Sufi Order, which became the Maryamiyya in Mary's honor. Schuon moved with some of his closest followers to Bloomington, Indiana, in 1981, and elements of Native American religious practice such as the Sun Dance were then added to the original Sufism and to the reverence for the Virgin. The focus on the person of Schuon himself increased. Reports also indicate the practice of sacred nakedness.[26] The Maryamiyya at this point might perhaps have developed into a new religion had not scandal connected with the practice of sacred nakedness and then Schuon's own death intervened.

One member of the Maryamiyya was an Iranian academic, Seyyed Hossein Nasr (b. 1933), the first and most important Traditionalist to be of Muslim origin. Although Nasr followed Schuon and accepted the premise of the transcendent unity of religions, his focus was always on Islam, and he probably knew nothing about the stranger goings-on in Bloomington until scandal broke there. Nasr encountered Traditionalism while studying in the United States, and he established it in prerevolutionary Iran on his return, both in the Philosophy Department at Tehran University and through the well-funded Imperial Iranian Academy of Philosophy, which he headed. In the context of Nasr's Academy, "philosophy" was understood as the perennial philosophy.

---

*Religions*, initially published in 1958 as *The Religions of Man*, predated Smith's encounter with Schuon and owed its perennialist approach to other sources. Later revisions of the book reflect Traditionalism, however, and Smith's later works are more explicitly Traditionalist.

[26] Sedgwick, *Against the Modern World*, 161–177; and Hugh Urban, "A Dance of Masks: The Esoteric Ethics of Frithjof Schuon," in *Crossing Boundaries: Essays on the Ethical Status of Mysticism*, ed. G. William Barnard and Jeffrey J. Kripal (New York: Seven Bridges Press, 2002), 406–440.

Like the early Schuon, Nasr developed Traditionalism in an Islamic context; unlike Schuon, he focused less on the organization of practice and on other religions, and more on scholarship. As well as completing a doctoral degree at Harvard, Nasr studied under some of the leading teachers of mystical philosophy in Iran, and his work combined the Traditionalist framework with greater learning in, and understanding of, a non-Western religious and esoteric tradition than had been possessed by any previous Traditionalist. As a result, his works have been well received in many parts of the Muslim world, as well as in the West.[27] Nasr's close connections with the shah meant that he was obliged to leave Iran when the revolution came. He continued his academic and Traditionalist careers in the United States, gathering a following there, and working with other Muslim Traditionalists, of whom the most important was Martin Lings (1909–2005), an English Sufi who had once been close to Guénon in Cairo.[28]

Just as Schuon established a Traditionalist Sufi Order to provide esoteric initiation within the framework of exoteric Islam, others established Traditionalist Sufi lodges to provide esoteric initiation within an exoteric framework that was, generally, Christian. The number of lodges that followed this approach is not known, but there were perhaps two or three in each major Western country. None grew as large as Schuon's Sufi Order, probably because the organizational structures of Masonry do not accommodate this sort of growth.

Two early Traditionalists were involved in politics, Evola and Eliade. Both were part of milieus of the 1930s that looked for national and spiritual renewal, saw interwar democracy as part of the problem rather than part of the solution, and were firmly opposed to Bolshevism. Eliade was initially a strong supporter of the Legion of the Archangel Michael in Romania, and Evola initially hoped for great things from the Fascist Party in Italy and from the Conservative Revolutionary movement in Germany. The initial difference between the two men was that while Eliade formally supported the legion and wrote on its behalf, he did not develop a Traditionalist political ideology. By contrast, Evola never formally supported fascism but did develop a Traditionalist political ideology. The later difference between the two was that when the implications of such movements began to be apparent to Eliade, he dissociated himself from what degenerated into Romanian Nazism and from political action in general, whereas Evola remained committed for the rest of his life to a political vision that changed

---

[27] Sedgwick, *Against the Modern World*, 154–158.
[28] Sedgwick, *Against the Modern World*, 119.

only in some details. Even though the Conservative Revolutionary movement was destroyed by Hitler, Evola still looked to Germany, where he was involved in official discussions in Berlin on racial questions in 1942.[29] Evola was never, however, a Nazi, regarding Nazi understandings of race as simplistic. Race was incidental to his ideology and was never understood by him in purely biological terms.[30]

The key to Evola's development of Traditionalism was his replacement of Guénon's vision of a tradition in which the Brahmin priest-class had once ruled with a vision of a tradition in which the Kshatriya warrior-class had once ruled. Rather than look for the return of the individual to the former priestly state through initiation as Guénon had, Evola looked for the return of the group to the warrior state through action. To this end, he attempted during the mid-1930s to establish an Italo-German chivalric order, but without success.[31] By the end of the Second World War, his impact on Italian and German policies had been negligible, partly because the fascists considered his views too extreme, and because the Nazis had their own ideology, with which Evola's was not really compatible.

Evola was more influential, however, in the postwar period, partly because he was an ideologist of the Right who was not implicated in what many had come to see as the debacle of fascism. His later works, in which he developed a theory of individual self-realization through political action irrespective of actual effect, proved extremely popular with the rightist terrorists who fought the Italian state, as well as the leftists terrorists during Italy's "years of lead" in the 1960s and 1970s. Evola himself never explicitly endorsed terrorism, but the closest he came to condemning it was to stress that political action without adequate spiritual preparation was pointless.[32]

Evola's analysis of modernity is compatible with mainstream Traditionalism, from which it derives, but his prescriptions are very different. Although interested in esotericism, he did not incorporate esotericism into his work to the same extent that Guénon did. Serious readers of Guénon usually ignore Evola, whereas serious readers of Evola do not ignore Guénon.

---

[29] Sedgwick, *Against the Modern World*, 108.
[30] Sedgwick, *Against the Modern World*, 98–117.
[31] Sedgwick, *Against the Modern World*, 106.
[32] This, at least, is my interpretation of the material quoted in the introduction to Julius Evola, *Cavalcare la Tigre: Den Tiger reiten* (Radeberg: Zeitenwende Verlag, 2006). The introduction, however, comes to the opposite conclusion, and it must be admitted that the case is not clear.

## 5 Traditionalism Today

Traditionalism continues to exist in all its main varieties, but it is political Traditionalism that has enjoyed most growth in recent years. The largest spiritual Traditionalist organization, the Maryamiyya, changed after Schuon's death, splitting into two parts: a perennialist core in Bloomington and a larger network elsewhere in the world, led by Nasr, and focusing almost exclusively on more standard Sufism.[33] Other smaller groups, generally Sufi or Masonic but sometimes Orthodox Christian, are to be found in most Western countries, as are occasional Traditionalists engaged in the academic study of religion.[34] There are also Traditionalist influences within one of Morocco's most important Sufi Orders, the Boutchichiyya,[35] and interest in Traditionalist works, especially Nasr's, grew during the 1990s in Iran and Turkey. Lings became the most influential Sufi Traditionalist in Europe, passing his interest in Traditionalism to Britain's Prince Charles, who combines Traditionalism with other approaches to spirituality and modernity.[36]

The end of Europe's Communist regimes opened new spaces for Traditionalism, notably in Hungary and Romania, where interest in Traditionalism, dating from Eliade's activity in the interwar period, had survived the Ceaușescu years. Traditionalism had even played a small part in Ceaușescu's downfall, since one of the members of the extempore court that condemned him to death, Gelu Voican Voiculescu (b. 1941), had previously been arrested for – among other things – possession of Traditionalist works.

Political Traditionalism has enjoyed a renaissance since the 1990s. One of the most important reasons for this is events in Russia. The origins of Traditionalism there lie in a small group of low-profile Soviet dissidents in the 1960s whose original interest in Gurdjieff shifted to an interest in Evola, Guénon, and other "alternative" writers, some of whose works were available in the Lenin Library in Moscow. Alexander Dugin (b. 1962), a junior member of this group, emerged after the collapse of the Soviet Union as

---

[33] This view is based on reports from various correspondents in 2005–2006 and has not been confirmed by further research.
[34] A brief Internet search will identify many such groups and individuals.
[35] Mark Sedgwick, "In Search of the Counter-Reformation: Anti-Sufi Stereotypes and the Budshishiyya's response," in *An Islamic Reformation?* ed. Charles Kurzman and Michaelle Browers (Lanham, MD: Lexington Books, 2004), 125–146.
[36] See various entries on Prince Charles and Traditionalism on *Traditionalists: A Blog for the Study of Traditionalism and the Traditionalists, moderated by Mark Sedgwick*, http://traditionalistblog.blogspot.com/search/label/United%20Kingdom

Russia's leading political Traditionalist, both generating interest in Traditionalist classics and developing his own eclectic mixture of Evola and other sources, both Western European and Russian. He developed a Traditionalist understanding of Russia as engaged in an inevitable and ultimately apocalyptic contest with modernity, represented by the United States.[37] During the chaotic but somewhat liberal Yeltsin period, Dugin and his followers occupied the margins of Russian politics and cultural life, but as Russian foreign and domestic policies became more "assertive" under Putin, Dugin and the political and intellectual mainstream moved toward each other. Dugin acquired a growing following and influential allies, as well as access to prime-time television. Dugin's views on Russian relations with the West were probably the main cause of his popularity, but he used this popularity to promote the intellectual basis of these views, including Traditionalism.[38] He later established the Center for Conservative Studies at Moscow State University, one of Russia's leading academic institutions, with Evola and Guénon in the curriculum. Guénon had already appeared in the online library of the Institute of Philosophy of the Russian Academy of Sciences.

Dugin's influence in Russia resulted in rightist political circles in other European countries becoming interested both in Dugin himself and in political Traditionalism. Evola became an increasingly popular point of reference in such circles, and also in the Neo-Folk music scene. The extent to which interest in Evola in this arena is related to the growth of political Traditionalism elsewhere is uncertain, as indeed is the extent to which the interest itself should be taken at face value.[39]

## 6 Conclusion: Traditionalism in Perspective

Traditionalism is significant as a development of Western and non-Western esotericism that ultimately produced a new definition of the esoteric as primordial religion, and as the common core of contemporary exoteric religion. Its relationship with mainstream Western esotericism is equivocal: drawing on it for perennialism and initiation, but rejecting it in favor of

---

[37] Sedgwick, *Against the Modern World*, 221–237. See also Marlene Laruelle, "Aleksandr Dugin: A Russian Version of the European Radical Right?" Woodrow Wilson Center, occasional paper #294, 2006.
[38] Mark Sedgwick, Russian translation of *Against the Modern World* (Moscow: New Literary Review, 2014). The Russian translation contains the results of fieldwork performed in Russia after the publication of the original English edition.
[39] Stéphane François, "The Euro-Pagan Scene: Between Paganism and Radical Right," *Journal for the Study of Radicalism* 1:2 (2007), 35–54.

orthodox religion, generally of non-Western origin. Political Traditionalists have been less interested in non-Western religion, preferring European paganism mixed with esotericism in Evola's case, and Russian Orthodoxy mixed with esotericism in Dugin's case. Traditionalism's relationship with mainstream academia is also equivocal, as Traditionalism condemns academia but sometimes prospers there.

Traditionalism has always been a minority interest except when popularized in combination with other philosophies and ideologies, as is the case in Russia today. Traditionalism's greatest source of appeal is probably its condemnation and rejection of modernity, which is common to all Traditionalists from Guénon to Dugin. Given that disenchantment with modernity seems to be an important characteristic of modernity, Traditionalism may be expected to continue to prosper.

# 27

# VIA NEGATIVA IN THE TWENTIETH CENTURY

## Arthur Versluis

## 1 Introduction

The *via negativa* – or mysticism proceeding by way of negation – has a very long history in Christianity. We find it very early, in the work of Basilides, then again, pivotally, in the works of Dionyius the Areopagite, in Eriugena, and again in the high medieval period in Meister Eckhart, in Tauler and in anonymous works such as *The Cloud of Unknowing*. One even finds the *via negativa* hinted at in the works of Jacob Boehme, in particular in his terms *Nichts*, or the Divine Nothing beyond all that exists, and *Ungrund*, or the Not-ground as the means by which being-time comes into existence.[1] One also sees this kind of *via negativa* terminology in the works of English theosophers, notably, John Pordage (1608–1681), who used the word "Chaos" to describe the transcendent plenitude out of which existence emerges.

But by the early modern period, exponents of the *via negativa* for the most part seem to have disappeared. Most of what has come to be termed "Western esotericism" is chiefly occupied with cosmological concerns – alchemical, magical, or related currents predominate. By the eighteenth and nineteenth centuries, one can find almost no exemplars of the *via negativa*, and even in the twentieth century, instances are few and far between. In fact, the absence of *via negativa* from theology or religious philosophy during this period is quite noteworthy. It is only in the mid-twentieth century, in part due to the influx of Asian religious traditions into the West, that we find the *via negativa* beginning to reappear. The *via negativa* is esoteric in a functional sense – that is, its adherents focus on absolute transcendence, which functionally generates an insider/outsider dynamic.

---

[1] See Arthur Versluis, "The Mystery of Böhme's Ungrund," *Studies in Spirituality* 11 (2001), 205–211.

## 2 What Is the *Via negativa*?

Already by the second century, Basilides, the earliest of the Alexandrian Gnostics (ca. 120 CE), and said to be a disciple of St. Matthias and of Glaucias (a disciple of St. Peter), taught a negative mysticism that is quite similar to the central Buddhist work, the Prajnaparamita sutras. Both reject the ultimate value of any analogy in understanding the nature of direct spiritual knowledge: It is not like this, or like that. It is not up or down, black or white, but in the words of the Prajnaparamita sutras, echoing the earliest Buddhist sources, it is "gone-beyond"; that is, it is absolute transcendence of all dualistic knowledge. According to Hippolytus, Basilides emphasized the sheer and utter transcendence of the divine nature, which is not even conceivable by man.[2] Basilides held that prior to creation, "nothing existed": "not matter, nor substance, nor what is insubstantial, nor is absolute, nor composite, nor conceivable, nor inconceivable, nor sensible, nor devoid of senses, nor man, nor angel, nor a god, nor any object with a name, or apprehended by sense, or cognized by intellect."[3]

This tradition of *via negativa* was ridiculed by some of the Ante-Nicene Church Fathers, including Hippolytus, but it was brought into orthodox branches of Christianity largely through the works of the pseudonymous author Dionysius the Areopagite, who probably lived in the fifth century. In his *Mystical Theology*, Dionysius writes lyrically of the "divine dark," of mystical contemplation that goes beyond "all sensation and all intellectual activities," "all non-beings and all beings," and the ecstasy of being raised up into the "divine darkness beyond being." This experience, he writes, is not without intellect, but it is not body, not form, not in space, not visible, not perceivable through the senses.[4] These Dionysian negations also resemble those of the Prajnaparamita sutras but derive from the Platonic tradition.

The Dionysian tradition had a significant influence on both Western and Eastern forms of Christianity. In the West, both the *via negativa* and the *via positiva* (the way of ascent through symbols and images) are cited and recur in the works of many individuals, including John Eriugena (flourished ca. 850 CE), whose *Periphyseon* clearly draws on the Dionysian corpus, citing Eastern fathers such as Maximus the Confessor. Eriugena also translated Dionysius's works and thus made them more available to medieval Europe. He wrote at

---

[2] Hippolytus, *Refutation of All Heresies*, VII.ix
[3] Hippolytus, *Refutation of All Heresies*, VII.ix
[4] See *The Divine Names and Mystical Theology*, trans. John D. Jones (Milwaukee: Marquette University Press, 1999), 211–212, 219–220.

length about what he called the divine "Nothing" that precedes and transcends all being, in this theme following Dionysius but also anticipating such prominent figures as Eckhart, Tauler, Boehme, and many others.[5]

3 Key Exemplars of the *Via negativa* in the Twentieth Century

When we look for examples of the *via negativa* in the twentieth century, however, we do not find many. Of course, a few scholars alluded to the tradition, among them Evelyn Underhill, and there are others who incorporated some elements of the tradition while not necessarily belonging to it. In this category, we could place the Catholic priest Thomas Keating, influential for his "centering prayer." But figures such as these are not really exemplars of the *via negativa* tradition proper. Of these, there are only a few, among them the philosopher Nicholas Berdyaev (1874–1948), Franklin Merrell Wolff (1887–1985), and Bernadette Roberts (b. 1931).

We should also mention here the Hungarian philosopher Béla Hamvas (1897–1968), a remarkable figure who wrote numerous books while under great ideological pressure from the Communist authorities. Strongly criticized by Marxist ideologue Georg Lúkacs, he was forced to live as a laborer, and his books were banned. Among his works, few of which are available in English, are a series of novels, volumes of art and cultural criticism, and sweeping works on the collective human religious inheritance. In a collection of essays entitled *Silentium* (1947), he writes eloquently about mysticism. While Hamvas does not belong exclusively to the *via negativa* current himself (he is more of a perennial philosopher), still his work is at least worth noting here, despite its relative obscurity.[6] But there are other figures who clearly place themselves in the intellectual current of the *via negativa*, and we shall focus on them.

The first of these, philosopher Nicholas Berdyaev, belonged to a relatively wealthy Russian family; by his student years, he was drawn to philosophy. Later, he became deeply involved in the lively religious ferment of what is now called the Russian Silver Age, editing periodicals and writing on a wide range of subjects, all tied to religious themes. In 1924, following the Communist revolution, Berdyaev went into exile in Paris with his wife, where he was to remain. His religious background was Russian Orthodox, and Berdyaev situated himself explicitly in the current of Christian

---

[5] *Periphyseon* 687A, B.
[6] See Béla Hamvas, *Silentium* (Munich: Editio M, 1999). For some information on Hamvas, see www.hamvasbela.org

theosophy whose founding figure is Jacob Boehme (1575–1624).[7] In *Nicolas Berdyaev: Theologian of Prophetic Gnosticism* (1948), Charles Knapp observes, correctly, that Berdyaev did not belong to the Blavatskyan Theosophical Society, which he thought "quite devoid of historic sense or real philosophic, theological, or scientific rigor." Rather, he espoused a mystical theology that had at its center the Dionysian *via negativa*.[8]

In *The Meaning of Creativity* (1914), Berdyaev began to explore his most characteristic subjects, including the nature of human freedom, the power of creativity, and the significance of mysticism. By *Freedom and the Spirit* (1935), he had developed his mature philosophical approach, which has as its center the transcendence of being or the *via negativa*, drawn explicitly from Boehme's concept of the *Ungrund*. This approach reaches its culmination in his important book *The Beginning and the End* (1941/1952). Berdyaev expresses the transcendence of being with the term *meontic*, and in *The Beginning and the End*, we find what was also published as "The Doctrine of the *Ungrund* and Freedom in Jacob Boehme."[9] Berdyaev follows Boehme in emphasizing the centrality of the concept of *Ungrund* for achieving human freedom. *Ungrund* is the undifferentiated source of all existence, and so it is also the source of our primordial human freedom. Modern philosophy and theology in general lack an understanding of this primary concept, and as a result they remain, in Berdyaev's view, disconnected from a profound metaphysical basis for understanding.

Berdyaev is important not least because he applies the Dionysian tradition of *via negativa* (and the Boehmean concept of the *Ungrund*) in a modern philosophical context. He draws from the *via negativa* a thoroughgoing critique of modern philosophical figures and tendencies, and affirms instead his own theological philosophy, for which human creativity and freedom derive from the *meontic* possibility of the *via negativa*. While Berdyaev is not an exponent of the *via negativa* as such, his work establishes the apophatic theological tradition as absolutely central to religious-cultural renewal, and indeed is unique in the twentieth century in injecting the *via negativa* into contemporary philosophical discourse.

---

[7] On Christian theosophy, see Arthur Versluis, *Wisdom's Children: A Christian Esoteric Tradition* (Albany: State University of New York Press, 1999); see also Versluis, *Wisdom's Book: The Sophia Anthology* (St. Paul: Paragon House, 2000).
[8] Charles C. Knapp, "Nicolas Berdyaev: Theologian of Prophetic Gnosticism" (Ph.D. Dissertation, Toronto: 1948), 40.
[9] On this topic, see Knapp, "Nicolas Berdyaev," 275 ff. See Berdyaev's introduction to Jacob Boehme's *Six Theosophic Points* (Ann Arbor: University of Michigan Press, 1958).

Franklin Merrell-Wolff was trained as a mathematician and taught mathematics at the university level. But in the 1930s, while living in California, he underwent a profound series of spiritual experiences. Merrell-Wolff's primary account of his spiritual awakening is to be found in *Pathways through to Space* (1944), which he describes as "a record of transformation in consciousness written down during the actual process itself."[10] During this time, while prospecting for gold in California, Merrell-Wolff read a book detailing the Vedantic metaphysics of Shankara. Then, sitting on a porch swing, he had what he called a "Recognition," after which, he wrote, "I have been repeatedly in the Current of Ambrosia. Often I turn to It with the ease of a subtle movement of thought. Sometimes it breaks out spontaneously."[11] What he called a "Current" could be perceived by others, he wrote, and although he was inspired by Vedanta, he combined Vedantic terms with Western alchemical language: "Emptiness is thus the real Philosopher's Stone which transfers all things to new richnesses; It is the Alkahest that transmutes the base metal of inferior consciousness into the Gold of Higher Consciousness."[12]

Central to Merrell-Wolff's thought is the idea of "consciousness without an object." For instance, in *Philosophy of Consciousness without an Object*, he writes that he had three successive experiences of "Recognition," and "in the third instance, I isolated the subjective moment from the relative manifold of consciousness ... and the result was Emptiness, Darkness, and Silence, i.e., Consciousness with no object."[13] Later, he writes in an aphorism that "Consciousness-without-an-object may be symbolized by a SPACE that is unaffected by the presence or absence of objects, for which there is neither Time nor Timelessness; neither a world-containing Space nor a Spatial Void; neither Tension nor Equilibrium; neither Agony nor Bliss; neither Action nor Rest; and neither Restriction nor Freedom."[14]

Here, as is often the case, Merrell-Wolff expresses himself in clearly apophatic language. But Merrell-Wolff's experiential philosophy is not explicitly indebted to Dionysius, because his primary sources of inspiration are from Asian religious traditions, in particular Shankara and the Buddha. One must also note that Merrell-Wolff associated himself with the Theosophical Society in California. Although he certainly cannot be termed

---

[10] Franklin Merrell-Wolff, *Experience and Philosophy* (Albany: State University of New York Press, 1994), x.
[11] Merrell-Wolff, *Experience and Philosophy*, 7.
[12] Merrell-Wolff, *Experience and Philosophy*, 15.
[13] Merrell-Wolff, *Experience and Philosophy*, 29.
[14] Merrell-Wolff, *Experience and Philosophy*, 314.

a Blavatskyite, he shares with it an indebtedness to Asian religious traditions. This is a significant shift: In the West of the twentieth century, the *via negativa* largely appears as a synthesis of Asian and Western traditions and is not exclusively Western as in earlier centuries.

Clearly, Merrell-Wolff's "Consciousness-without-an-object" belongs to the *via negativa*: It represents the negation/transcendence of sensory and rational forms of knowledge, as well as the realization of a higher state of consciousness marked by bliss and, he tells us, ultimately by intense intellectual power. In keeping with the history of the *via negativa*, Merrell-Wolff does not offer the details of what practices he had undertaken, how specifically he meditated, and so forth. He begins at the point of realization, just as Meister Eckhart did. But unlike Eckhart, Merrell-Wolff does offer a wealth of autobiographical detail and personal reflection.

The Catholic mystic Bernadette Roberts of California is similar in many respects to Merrell-Wolff. Although she claims that her work is off "the beaten path of mystical theology so well-travelled by Christian contemplatives," nonetheless it certainly resembles the *via negativa*.[15] Roberts's writings chronicle her journey into experiences of what she came to call "no-self," or the falling away or disappearance of ego, which she claims to be her unique discovery.[16] However, in *The Experience of No-Self*, she does acknowledge Meister Eckhart as "one who has made the journey [to no-self] and crossed over."[17]

Roberts discusses her progressive realization of no-self in her books *The Experience of No-Self* (1982) and *The Path to No-Self* (1985/rpt. 1991). In the former, Roberts relates that during a two-year period, she "experienced the falling away of everything I can call a self. It was a journey through an unknown passageway that led to a life so new and different that, despite nearly forty years of varied contemplative experiences, I never suspected its existence."[18] She tells us that her journey began with her realization that she had no self, whereupon she experienced a sensation like an elevator falling hundreds of floors. This realization of no-self had a corollary, a realization of no-God: "When there is no personal self, there is no personal God." She

---

[15] See Bernadette Roberts, *The Experience of No-Self: A Contemplative Journey* (Albany: State University of New York Press, 1993), 128.
[16] Bernadette Roberts, *The Path to No-Self: Life at the Center* (Albany: State University of New York Press, 1991), xv.
[17] Roberts, *The Path to No-Self*, 199. After acknowledging Eckhart as one of her predecessors, Roberts then states that "he is unique and unlike any other Christian mystic" (p. 203). This is true but invites the question of whether he nonetheless belongs to a larger current in the Christian tradition, that of the *via negativa*, to which Roberts herself also belongs.
[18] Roberts, *The Experience of No-Self*, 9.

writes that God and self belong together, so "where they went, I have never found out."[19]

By the strictest definition, Roberts's work belongs to the *via negativa*.[20] In the writings of both Meister Eckhart and Roberts, we encounter sheer transcendence. The difference, and this may be a particularly modern difference, is that Roberts's work is strikingly autobiographical in nature; she takes us along with her on her personal journey to no-self. Roberts is not interested in her predecessors and even goes far as to suggest that to read the works of prior mystics is misguided.

Roberts's accounts are quite harrowing, and she does not like to use conventional theological terms, even words such as "God," noting that "I am always reluctant to use the word 'God,' because everybody seems to carry around their own stagnant images and definitions that totally cloud the ability to step outside a narrow, individual frame of reference."[21] Her descriptions are experiential, not theological:

> Initially, with the falling away of all sense of having an interior life, there had been a turning outward to the seeing of Oneness and the falling away of everything particular and individual. The seeing itself was not located within, but first seemed to be like 3D glasses imposed upon my ordinary vision, and later, localized as a seeing "on top of the head."[22]

Robert's experiences of no-self include what she terms a "great passageway," in which she feared madness, and which raised the profound question of *what* is conscious of the disappearance of self. She writes of "Something that is just there, just watching, and 'that' is true life, while all the energies that come and go are not true life. But what is 'that' that remains and observes?"[23]

Roberts's discussion of what she terms no-self is certainly a discussion of negation, but it contains no allusion to Dionysius the Areopagite or other scholarly reference points. It is, rather, an account of her personal struggle to explain what she herself had experienced:

---

[19] Roberts, *The Experience of No-Self*, 25.
[20] Some have expressed skepticism about Roberts's experiences, which some have suggested exemplify "depersonalization disorder" (or DPD). See Daphne Simeon, *Feeling Unreal: Depersonalization Disorder and the Loss of the Self* (New York: Oxford University Press, 2006), in particular, 140–145. Disentangling DPD and the *via negativa* is beyond our scope here.
[21] Roberts, *The Experience of No-Self*, 37
[22] Roberts, *The Experience of No-Self*, 60.
[23] Roberts, *The Experience of No-Self*, 63.

The step beyond no-self is like the dissolution of that which remains when It draws back into Itself as if overcome by Its own intensity. Even though what Is is all that Is, its acts or doing – which is identical with Itself – is not its entirety, for what we ordinarily know of It, is only that which falls into the realm of the known – the created, that is. But there seems to exist a fullness of act that does not fall into the known or created, and to be overcome by this fullness means that at any moment all we know to exist may easily, instantly, and painlessly be dissolved into what Is. I do not understand this mechanism, but I do know this dissolution, this enduring intensity, is the ending and last of all silences.[24]

In such passages, we can see Roberts struggling to express her experiences in comprehensible language; like Merrell-Wolff, she sometimes resorts to unusual capitalization and other devices that highlight the unreliability of linguistic expression.

In *The Path to No-Self*, Roberts describes her experiences, but in a way that is both more abstract and explicitly Christian. However, Roberts rejects a Christ of social works, emphasizing instead that Christ was

a mystic who had the continuous vision of God and whose mission was to share it, give it to others. Few people see it this way; instead, they have exploited Christ's good works to justify their own busy lives, lives without interior vision and therefore lives without Christ. As already said, performance of our duties and responsibilities as human beings, respect for the rights of others, lending a helping hand are what it means to be human; there is nothing particularly Christian about it.[25]

Roberts emphasizes what she terms "the awakening of the inner butterfly," or spiritual vision, even remarking that someone who affirms his own "self-abandonment" in the manner of Henry Suso is roundly condemned, perhaps even crucified, because "unwittingly, he is saying that he is a man without sin!" But in reality, "a man without a self is not about to stand up and say 'I have no sin.' He cannot say this because the truth of the matter is: he has no 'I'."[26] Clearly Roberts is trying to express in new terms an age-old conflict between what we might term exoteric and esoteric Christianities. The *via negativa* is functionally or experientially esoteric and can be misunderstood from an exoteric, dualistic perspective. This is at least one implication of Roberts's point here.

[24] Roberts, *The Experience of No-Self*, 106.
[25] Roberts, *The Path to No-Self*, 124.
[26] Roberts, *The Path to No-Self*, 146.

Although Roberts remains Roman Catholic, the tradition into which she was born, she did spend time with Zen Buddhist contemplatives, and her mysticism does have affinities with Buddhism.[27] In fact, in a later book, *What Is Self?*, she writes that in the Zen Buddhist concepts of *kensho* and *satori*, she finds the closest parallels to her experiences of no-self. It is curious that although she describes herself as a Christian contemplative, she does not readily acknowledge her predecessors in the Christian tradition – figures such as Dionysius, Eckhart, and the author of the *Cloud of Unknowing* – nor does she acknowledge that she belongs to the long-standing tradition of the *via negativa*. Possibly this is because of the experiential dimensions of her work, but the lack of reference is noteworthy all the same.

What else is Roberts writing about, however, if not the *via negativa*? She asserts that one "has no peace until all the energies, will, desires and feelings are totally submitted to the divine – a dark, unrecognized silent void in ourselves."[28] Later, she writes that "the major question is the true nature of 'that' which remains or exists when there is no self or consciousness." Hence "part of the acclimation to the no-self condition is getting around without a bodily experience, or experience of a body. But obviously some type of form remained, a form that was as void as all the forms beheld by the senses." In Buddhist language drawn from the Prajnaparamita sutras, she writes that "Form then IS void and this void IS form."[29] In the end, she may be more comfortable with Buddhist than with Dionysian expressions.

Unlike Berdyaev, who is almost completely indebted to Western traditions, Merrell-Wolff and Roberts represent the emergence of a new, twentieth-century synthesis of East and West. Characteristic of this synthesis is the *via negativa*, which is certainly present as an element in all three of these very different authors. Berdyaev's *via negativa* comes to him in a lineage from Dionysius to Boehme, whereas Merrell-Wolff's is inspired by Vedanta, and Roberts, she insists, is uniquely her own mystic. The presence of Asian influences in the work of Merrell-Wolff and Roberts brings us inevitably to the larger question of Asian-Western cross-pollination.

### 4  *Via negativa* and Asian Religions in Diaspora

It is true that one does not find many exemplars of the *via negativa* in the twentieth century – that is, not many figures whose work can be said to stand

---

[27] Roberts, *The Path to No-Self*, 108.
[28] See Bernadette Roberts, *What Is Self?* (Austin: M. B. Goens, 1989), 22.
[29] Roberts, *What is Self?*, 190.

more or less within the Dionsyian tradition. In one way or another, however, Berdyaev, Merrell-Wolff, and Roberts do express their primary insights in apophatic terms. But it may well be that although the Dionysian apophatic current is not so visible in Christianity any longer, or for that matter in secular modernity, it appears now in a different context, that of East-West synthesis, often in the form of new religions.

In his *The Book of Enlightened Masters: Western Teachers in Eastern Traditions* (1997), Andrew Rawlinson provides biographical introductions to hundreds of Westerners who have taken on the role of spiritual teacher, sometimes in Asian religious traditions, but often as independent syncretic figures. Rawlinson provides entries on traditional Zen teachers such as Robert Aitken (1917–2010), Philip Kapleau (1912–2004), John Daido Loori (1931– 2009), or Jiyu Kennett (1924–1996). A well-known Western author in the Tibetan tradition is Pema Chödrön (b. 1936). There are a great many such figures now, as Buddhism has taken root in the West.[30]

One also finds numerous religious teachers in the West who have been more or less strongly influenced by Asian religious traditions but who also draw on Christian or other Western traditions. Syntheses of this kind became fairly widespread by the end of the twentieth century, more or less after the example of Thomas Merton (1915–1968), the influential Catholic monastic and author. East-West synthesis was made popular by Alan Watts (1915– 1973), author of such books as *Behold the Spirit* (1947) and *Beyond Theology* (1964), which did incorporate elements of negative mysticism. We should note the numerous works by William Johnston (1925–2010), including not only *Christian Zen* (1997) but also *The Mysticism of the Cloud of Unknowing* (2000) and *Mystical Journey: An Autobiography* (2006). Johnston, a Catholic priest in Japan, brings his Zen Buddhist practice to interpretations of classical negative mysticism of the West.

A. H. Almaas (A. Hameed Ali; b. 1944) also incorporates some aspects of the *via negativa* into his mysticism. Almaas is founder of the Ridhwan School, an esoteric group that draws from Tibetan Buddhism and from Sufism, combining various religious teachings with an emphasis on contemporary psychological theory and practice. Almaas draws on some aspects of Buddhism but maintains an emphasis on the self and on psychology. Similar or related teachings drawn in part or primarily from Buddhism are to be found in the work of Ken Wilber (b. 1949). It is not that the *via negativa*

---

[30] The reverse is also true. See, for instance, Keiji Nishitani, *Religion and Nothingness* (Berkeley: University of California Press, 1982), 61–68, for a discussion of negative theology and Eckhart from a Buddhist perspective.

is central to these figures, but rather that one finds instances of it woven into their works.

What these Buddhist-influenced individuals and their groups offer is very much akin to what one finds in *via negativa* texts throughout Christian history, only now appearing in a new religion or a Western Buddhist context. The emergence of Buddhist praxis in the West is understandable, not least because traditionally in the West, esotericism often has been conveyed elliptically, through enigmatic writings and images.[31] In Western esotericism, the individual is on his or her own, whereas in Buddhism, the aspirant is given detailed practical guidance. Likewise, in the history of *via negativa* mysticism, from Basilides and Dionysius all the way through the twentieth century, one finds almost no instances of written practical instruction. The closest might be the anonymous *Cloud of Unknowing*, but even in this instance, the author does not provide the kind of specific instructions and detailed practical guidance that one finds in the various schools of contemporary Buddhism (e.g., posture, breathing, and so forth). Even Bernadette Roberts, who is unprecedented in her autobiographical detail, does not really provide instructions on what practices one ought to undertake to realize no-self.

## 5 Conclusion

The *via negativa*, particularly in its Western context, not only remains esoteric up to and through the twentieth century but arguably becomes even more so. Only a handful of authors clearly exemplify this tradition of Western mysticism in the twentieth century, and even many of those owe as much to Asian religious traditions (in particular Vedanta and Buddhism) as they do to the classical Western *via negativa*. None of these authors – neither Berdyaev, nor Merrell-Wolff, nor Roberts – is widely known or influential, and that fact is itself revealing. While it is an important pattern in the tapestry of Western esotericism, the *via negativa* rarely has been visible in exoteric forms of Western religion, nor has it been acknowledged by them.[32] What is more, despite (or because of) the exponential growth of evangelical forms of Christianity, this tendency toward omission of the *via negativa* continues

---

[31] On the means of transmitting esotericism in the West, see Arthur Versluis, *Restoring Paradise: Western Esotericism, Literature, and Consciousness* (Albany: State University of New York Press, 2004).

[32] "The tapestry of Western esotericism," here, means esotericism as broadly defined in Arthur Versluis, *Magic and Mysticism: An Introduction to Western Esotericism* (Lanham, MD: Rowman and Littlefield, 2007), with the primary characteristic of *gnosis*.

right through the twentieth century and, if anything, becomes more pronounced.

But omission is not obliteration. Marginalized from the beginning of Christianity, the *via negativa* nonetheless is an important aspect of Christian theology, and probably its most esoteric aspect. Western esotericism, historically, has always been fluid and *syncrasic* (i.e., joining practices, not only beliefs), and it is not surprising that we find exactly these characteristics describing the forms that the *via negativa* took during the twentieth century. Apophatic mysticism has much in common with Buddhism, and if the twentieth century is any indication, we should not be surprised to find that in the future, as in the past, the *via negativa* continues to be a creative esoteric juncture of Eastern and Western religions.

28

CONTEMPORARY PAGANISM

CHAS S. CLIFTON

1 Introduction

With few exceptions, such as Feraferia and the Church of All Worlds in the United States (both products of the 1960s), today's Pagan religions present themselves as reviving, reconstructing, or somehow connecting with a pre-Christian past. For example, the founders of modern Wicca initially claimed an unbroken continuity with the Stone Age via a persecuted, underground religious tradition that persisted in England until the 1930s – a claim that owed much to the theories of the English archaeologist Margaret Murray.[1] Other contemporary Pagan leaders and theorists have claimed that earlier forms of their religions can be recovered from fragments of folklore, folk dance, ancient artwork, and mythic tales. *Homo religiosus* prizes that which is ancient, but the actual development of contemporary Paganism primarily occurred in the late nineteenth and twentieth centuries, involving the work of many creative men and women, some of whom merely expressed their own spiritual longings while others sought consciously to create a communal movement – a religion. But before examining this history, let us consider how "Pagan" is defined today.

2 Defining Paganism

Pagan religions, while varied in their expression, offer certain common expressions and family resemblances.[2] These include a view of deity as multiple rather than single; a view of nonhuman nature as valuable in and

[1] Margaret Murray, *The Witch-Cult in Western Europe* (Oxford: Oxford University Press, 1921).
[2] Although the use of lowercase "pagan" to mean irreligious is still used by some, I capitalize Pagan when referring to any self-conscious religious tradition that fits the definitions set forth in this section.

for itself, and not created merely for our use; and a tendency to focus on time as cyclical, rather than as moving toward an apocalypse, last judgment, or final goal. Thus, from the contemporary Pagan's viewpoint, such varied traditions as classical Roman religion, shrine Shinto, Wicca, aspects of Hinduism, and indeed any "indigenous" religion might all be seen as Pagan. Attempting to reduce these multiplicities to their simplest terms, Michael York in *Pagan Theology* offers this broad definition: "an affirmation of interactive and polymorphic sacred relationship by the individual or community with the tangible, sentient, and/or nonempirical."[3]

In other words, for the Pagan, "sacred relationships" may be with tangible objects that evoke holiness, awe, or humility. These might be natural objects or persons – a mountain, a canyon, a tree, an animal – or they may be manmade. They may include other humans, when those persons manifest a deity or a deity's attributes. Pagans may also, of course, enjoy a relationship with "the sacred" expressed in nonempirical form – through contemplation, dreams, visions, and so on. York's definition is drawn broadly enough to include humanism, pantheism, and panentheism. However, the majority of contemporary Pagans follow some sort of polytheism, which is often divided by practitioners themselves into the categories of "hard" and "soft."

A soft polytheism may be summarized by the aphorism of Dion Fortune, an English ceremonial magician and novelist of the early twentieth century: "All gods are one God, and all goddesses are one Goddess, and there is one Initiator [the Higher Self]."[4] It permits the blending of pantheons from different times and cultures, encouraging syncretism and a softening of boundaries between religions traditions. For example, a soft polytheistic Pagan could easily regard the Virgin Mary as yet one more manifestation of the Great Goddess, the Magna Mater. These Pagans are most likely to speak of deity in general as "immanent" rather than "transcendent," an attitude linked to a rejection of hierarchical religious authority in favor of more self-directed authority, as in songwriter Catherine Madsen's 1980s composition "My Heretic Heart," whose refrain is, "My skin, my bones, my heretic heart are my authority," as opposed to "law and scripture, priest and prayer." In some expressions, such as the writing of the Wiccan theologian and novelist Starhawk (Miriam Simos), the proclaimed immanence of deity is linked to utopian-leftist politics, although Wiccans in general may be found across the political spectrum.

[3] Michael York, *Pagan Theology: Paganism as a World Religion* (New York: New York University Press, 2003), 157.
[4] Dion Fortune, *The Sea Priestess* (New York: Samuel Weiser, 1978; originally published 1938), 227.

Hard polytheism, on the other hand, generally characterizes reconstructed Pagan religions, for example, Norse, Slavic, or Hellenic, in which the various pantheons are treated as assemblies of distinct spiritual beings with distinct attributes and personalities, with or without an application of the *Interpretatio graeca*. Hard polytheism is often associated with Paganism of an ethnic (and in Eastern Europe, nationalist) cast, whose adherents state that "these are the gods of our people." Pagans describing themselves as hard polytheists may place great value on learning archaic languages such as Old Irish or Old Norse in order to read the oldest available texts that treat of the pre-Christian religion of a particular region, as well as to perform religious rituals in the language associated with their favored pantheon. Likewise, they will study folk life, create customs, and perform music associated as much as possible with the pre-Christian era. In Latvia and Lithuania, for example, folk music played a key role not only in the creation of national identity but also of contemporary Pagan movements. The Lithuanian Romuva (sanctuary) organization, named for an ancient Pagan Prussian religious site, was founded in 1926, repressed by the Soviet Union, but revived in the 1960s as a nonreligious, folkloric association devoted to the singing of *dainos*, folk tunes believed to contain fragments of pre-Christian religion. Romuva bloomed during the *perestroika* era of the 1980s and after Lithuanian independence openly proclaimed its religious nature, including the performance of religious rituals.[5] In the case of both Latvian and Lithuanian Paganism, emigrant followers in North America were important to sustaining the movement during the decades when the home countries were under Soviet and German domination.

Similarly, contemporary Pagan movements have arisen in Russia, Ukraine, Hungary, and other former Soviet bloc nations. Russian anthropologist Victor Shnirelman, who has written extensively on new Paganism movements in the former Soviet Union, notes that they are often characterized by a defiant anti-foreign (or anti-modernist) message that often includes a large dose of anti-Semitism. Among non-Russian peoples of the former Soviet Union, artists and ethnographers have begun to find inspiration in local pre-Christian religious practices, and to systematize fragments of them. These new Pagans rebel against both Orthodox Christianity's smoothing over of ethnic differences and the central government's Russification of other ethnic groups.[6]

[5] Michael Strmiska, "The Music of the Past in Modern Baltic Paganism," *Nova Religio* 8:3 (2005), 39–58.
[6] Victor A. Shnirelman, "'Christians! Go Home': A Revival of Neo-Paganism between the Baltic Sea and Transcaucasia," *Journal of Contemporary Religion* 17:2 (2002), 197–211.

Whether hard or soft polytheists, followers of most new (and arguably, those not so new) Pagan religions are non-creedal. In the framework created by anthropologist Harvey Whitehouse, who divides religious dynamics into "doctrinal" and "imagistic" modes, they are firmly imagistic. Pagans favor performance over doctrine, and the question "What do you believe?" is apt to be met with either a blank look or the response, "What matters is what we do, not what we believe." The imagistic mode of religiosity, Whitehouse explains, "consists of the tendency ... for revelations to be transmitted through sporadic collective action, evoking multivocal iconic imagery, encoded in memory as distinct episodes, and producing highly cohesive and particularistic social ties."[7] A classic example of this episodic collective action would be the Eleusinian mysteries: They were experienced collectively, involved thousands of initiates over a period of centuries, and were apparently significant life events for most of the *mystai*. The social cohesion they produced was so strong that to this day, we do not know precisely what the mysteries entailed, although they may well have conveyed a teaching about life after death, or reincarnation.

The Abrahamic religions – Judaism, Christianity, and Islam – while including collective action and multivocal imagery, are above all concerned with doctrine, with specified beliefs, and consequently with heresy as well, a concept outside most Pagan religious experience. The contrast of these religious modes offers the potential for numerous interfaith misunderstandings, generally to the detriment of the new Pagans, who lack codified scriptures, credentialed clergy, and weekly worship. In the United States in particular, Pagans seeking to become prison, hospital, or military chaplains have faced numerous institutional barriers not placed in front of clergy of Abrahamic faiths. While some Pagan prison chaplains are in place, the military remains closed, despite the presence of Pagan service members. Only the pressure of a federal lawsuit forced the Veterans Administration to permit distinctive grave markers for Wiccan veterans. (Other Pagan groups are now applying for their own symbols.) What remains unanswered is the question of how the attempt to meet bureaucratic requirements for chaplaincies, and so forth, will in turn transform the Pagan religions, whether they were initially conceived of as mystery cults, as in the case of Wicca, or as re-creations of pre-Christian religion, as in the case of Ásatrú (revived Norse religion), for example.

---

[7] Harvey Whitehouse, *Arguments and Icons: Divergent Modes of Religiosity* (Oxford: Oxford University Press, 2000), 1.

Another significant difference between the contemporary Pagan worldview and that of the Abrahamic faiths is that Pagans generally do not experience a conflict with science. The beginnings of that conflict in the West – arising (in the eighteenth century) from geologists challenging the literalness of the biblical story of the flood, and then (in the nineteenth century) biologists championing the theory of evolution – for the most part predate the contemporary Pagan revival, which is a twentieth-century creation. Today's Pagans do not experience scientific knowledge as a threat to religious authority. Those who perceive deity or "the Goddess" as immanent in creation may feel strongly about the moral implications of applied scientific knowledge, as expressed, for example, through atomic bombs or the side effects of pesticides, but they rarely criticize science itself. If anything, they are likely to accept uncritically some ways in which New Age thinking has absorbed modern science – believing, for example, that quantum physics can show how magic works.

## 3 Origins of Today's Pagan Movements

Today's Pagan religions have multiple roots. Most claim a connection with the past that frequently puts their adherents into confrontation with current scholarship, yet folklorists can see in their practices "responses to novel situations, which take the form of reference to old situations"; in other words, they are "invented traditions," as Eric Hobsbawm defined them.[8] All Pagan religions are built on old texts – and some on forgeries of old texts, such as the works of Iolo Morganwg (1747–1826) for British Druids, or the *Book of Veles* for many Slavic Pagans.[9] Interestingly, Pagan groups that are more or less *sui generis*, such as the Church of Aphrodite, founded by Russian émigré Gleb Botkin in 1939, or Feraferia, founded by Frederick Adams in Southern California in 1967, tend either not to survive their founders or to survive only in a diminished state. (Feraferia, while borrowing much terminology and imagery from classical Greek Paganism, was perhaps too linked to Adams's own utopian ecological vision of "Wilderness Mysteries" to have lasting appeal.[10])

Wicca, the largest form of contemporary Paganism, arose in England around 1951. Its history in the United Kingdom is described in Ronald

---

[8] Eric Hobsbawm, "Introduction," in *The Invention of Tradition*, ed. Eric Hobsbawm and Terence Ranger (Cambridge: Cambridge University Press, 1982), 1–2.
[9] Victor A. Shnirelman, "Ancestral Wisdom and Ethnic Nationalism: A View from Eastern Europe," *The Pomegranate: The International Journal of Pagan Studies* 9:1 (2007).
[10] Chas S. Clifton, *Her Hidden Children: The Rise of Wicca and Paganism in America* (Lanham, MD: Altamira Press, 2006), 142–149.

Hutton's *The Triumph of the Moon: A History of Modern Pagan Witchcraft.*[11] Its roots are multiple. One important root is a nineteenth-century recasting of the figure of the "witch" as an antiauthoritarian and Romantic (and sexy) lover of liberty and freedom who carries on the almost-forgotten worship of Pagan gods.[12] This view dominates two well-known works, *La Sorcière*, by Jules Michelet (1865?), and *Aradia, or The Gospel of the Witches* (1899), by Charles Godfrey Leland, an American folklore collector living in Florence. Both Michelet and Leland (who may have met during the revolutionary days of late 1840s France) rejected any nostalgia for the Middle Ages and were strongly anticlerical, blaming the Roman Catholic Church (erroneously) for the medieval and early modern witch trials. (The church, in fact, was more concerned with heresy than witchcraft, the bulk of trials for witchcraft being conducted by secular governments, often in Protestant lands.)

Another root, of course, is "witchcraft" in the popular sense – the performance of spell casting, divination, and so forth, with little reference to any larger theological framework, also known as "low magic." This form of witchcraft has commonly been believed to be passed on in certain bloodlines, acquired by sexual intercourse with an established witch, or granted through a pact with the Christian Devil. Sometimes referred to as "anthropological witchcraft" to differentiate it from the new Pagan witchcraft religion (Wicca), its history in Western Europe provided both inspiration and problems for the mid-twentieth-century Wiccan witches. Gerald Gardner (1884–1964), chief architect of Wicca, drew on an unorthodox interpretation of the earlier European witch trials advanced by Margaret Murray in the 1920s: that the witches, male and female, were followers of a suppressed Pagan religion and that the Devil before whom they bowed at the witches' sabbath was actually its high priest.[13] If Wicca were to grow as a religion, ideas of witchcraft as an inherited taint or as a perversion of Christianity would have to be cast away. At the same time, the mystique and aura of earlier witchcraft could be applied liberally to the new religious movement, with much description in Gardner's writing of witches organizing like World War II resistance fighters, expecting torture and death if caught practicing their religion.[14]

---

[11] Ronald Hutton, *The Triumph of the Moon: A History of Modern Pagan Witchcraft* (Oxford: Oxford University Press, 1999).
[12] Ronald Hutton, "Modern Pagan Festivals: A Study in the Nature of Tradition," *Folklore* 119 (2008), 251–273.
[13] Murray, *The Witch-Cult in Western Europe*. A similar idea had been advanced in Germany in the 1820s, to different purposes. See Hutton, *Triumph of the Moon*, 136–137.
[14] Gerald Gardner, *Witchcraft Today* (Secaucus, NJ: Citadel Press, 1973), 51–53.

In creating Wicca, Gardner and his associates also drew on Freemasonry and ceremonial magic, the "high magic" of the Renaissance. As Ronald Hutton notes, the rituals of Freemasonry influenced countless other societies and associations throughout the nineteenth century and afterward.[15] From high magic came not only a vocabulary of symbolic forms – most notably the pentagram – but also the attitude of nineteenth-century esoteric practitioners that magic's purpose was the transformation of the magician, not worship of deity.[16] To this combination – the allure of historic witchcraft, the claim of ancient roots, and the techniques of high magic – we may add a matrix of attitudes about nature and humanity that would later create an attraction between Paganism, environmentalism, and feminism.

By contrast, the "reconstructionist" contemporary Pagan groups look chiefly to ancient texts (including, as noted earlier, certain "manufactured" ancient texts) to leapfrog the Christian era. Hellenic and Roman reconstructionists have ample resources in both pre-Christian texts and for learning the languages in which they were written. Norse reconstructions, by contrast, must rely on texts collected and copied by Christians, usually monks or clergy, and thus wrangle over the issue of how "corrupted" these copies are. Some passages, such as the description of the trance seer (*völva*) in the Saga of Erik the Red, have become normative for present-day practitioners.

## 4 Nature Religion and Feminist Influences on Paganism

By the time of the twentieth-century Pagan reemergence, another spiritual current had arrived to challenge the scriptural or creedal faiths: nature religion. As Catherine Albanese described it, "nature religion" was a category that could include Deism as well as "natural" foods, healing methods, and lifestyles.[17]

English Wicca and Druidry both benefited from the so-called Pagan writers of the Victorian and Edwardian periods, who were disenchanted by modernity, especially industrialization, and by a Christianity they found to be both oppressive and increasingly irrelevant.[18] Kenneth Grahame's chapter "The Piper at the Gates of Dawn" from *The Wind in the Willows*, which

---

[15] Hutton, *The Triumph of the Moon*, 58.
[16] Hutton, *The Triumph of the Moon*, 78–79.
[17] Catherine Albanese, *Nature Religion in America* (Chicago: University of Chicago Press, 1990).
[18] Jennifer Hallett, "Wandering Dreams and Social Marches: Varieties of Paganism in Late Victorian and Edwardian England," *The Pomegranate: The International Journal of Pagan Studies* 8:2 (2006), 162.

personifies nature in the form of the god Pan, is typical.[19] Rudyard Kipling's "A Tree Song," from his book of short stories *Puck of Pook's Hill* has actually been incorporated into contemporary Pagan rituals.[20] These "Pagan writers" (as they were labeled by critics) looked for cultural roots in the "eternal" countryside – but different circumstances prevailed in the New World.

Prevented by barriers of language and culture from participating in the religious lives of its native peoples, European settlers in America projected their attitudes onto this new land. While some Puritans saw the indigenous people as devilish inhabitants of a godless wilderness, Americans commonly saw the land as a place of new beginnings, one untainted by European feudalism and clericalism. This attitude contributed to an increasing reliance in the nineteenth century on nature itself as a source of sacred value, an attitude that persists today in the prevalence of outdoor camping festivals in American Paganism. By 1970 – not coincidentally, the year of the first Earth Day – American Pagans, particularly Wiccans, were beginning to refer to theirs as an "earth religion" or "nature religion," drawing on the cultural stream of sacred nature as a way to legitimize religious traditions that lacked scriptures, prophets, and similar elements. This claiming of nature's mantle marked both followers of imported English Wicca and indigenous new Pagan religious movements such as Feraferia ("Wilderness Festival") and the Church of All Worlds, which grew partly from co-founder Tim (now Oberon) Zell's vision of earth as a single organism, with humans and cetaceans as her neo-cortex – a vision he received, not coincidentally, in September 1970.[21] In the 1960s, the members of what became the New Reformed Orthodox Order of the Golden Dawn, a seminal West Coast Pagan group, held outdoor celebrations at the solstices and thought of themselves as Druids before realizing that they had more in common with Gardnerian Wicca. (In the United States, the term "Druid" lost its associations with English, Scottish, or Welsh nationalism and heritage, retaining only a literary association with primeval religion and oak groves.)

Nature religion may be further subdivided into three categories: "cosmic," "Gaian," and "embodied."[22] Cosmic nature religion may be paired with Renaissance high magic, seeking to unify the cosmos in the interests of the practitioner: "As above, so below." Cosmic nature religion, which

---

[19] Kenneth Grahame, *The Wind in the Willows* (London: Methuen, 1908).
[20] Rudyard Kipling, *Puck of Pook's Hill* (London: Macmillan, 1906).
[21] Oberon Zell-Ravenheart, "Theagenesis: The Birth of the Goddess," in *Green Egg Omelette: An Anthology of Art and Articles from the Legendary Pagan Journal*, ed. Oberon Zell-Ravenheart (Franklin Lakes, NJ: New Page Books, 2009).
[22] Clifton, *Her Hidden Children*, 37–70.

concentrates on calendrical and astrological features, organizes worship according to the eight-festival wheel of the year popularized by English Druid Ross Nichols and Gerald Gardner.[23] One of the first attempts to codify Wiccan belief, developed at a 1974 conference in Minneapolis sponsored by the occult publishing house of Llewellyn, opened with this statement: "We practice rites to attune ourselves with the natural rhythms of life forces marked by the full of the Moon and seasonal quarters and cross-quarters."[24] Indeed, it has been observed that the ritual year is more important than gods, goddesses, and spirits to many contemporary Pagans. Studying the relationship of folk music and the Pagan revival, Christopher Chase asks, "If folk music has not bequeathed sacred persons to whom worship and relationship are directed, then what other specific elements (besides nationalism, populism, and identity politics) has it given contemporary Paganism?" He answers that it "seems to have been the ritual year, that 'old time religion.'"[25]

Gaian nature religion concerns itself with the practitioner's relationship to the planet-as-divinity, following Oberon Zell's 1970 vision of "Gaia" as an organism. It could be seen as the spiritual wing of the broader environmental movement, and arguably it is the reason that some monotheist writers attack environmentalism as "false religion." The Gaian vision, however articulated, follows on the heels of Transcendentalism and Swedenborgianism; it was the eighteenth-century mystic Emanuel Swedenborg who enunciated, "All nature is full of confirmation of the Divine." The key difference between Pagan nature religion and its previous manifestations is that most Pagans saw Mother Earth as divine, not merely as metaphor. For Wiccans, the post–Earth Day emphasis on nature religion served to counterbalance the idea of folk witchcraft as spell casting only. By connecting themselves with the spiritual stream of nature as source of sacred value, Wiccans of the 1970s were able to cling to the folk idea of the low magic-working witch, while casting themselves as followers of a religion – nature religion – and thus able to claim the mantle of religious choice and freedom.

Finally, some contemporary Paganisms offer a new theology of the body. Whereas Christianity sought to control the body, European folk witchcraft retained a tradition – emphasized in literary and artistic depictions – of literal transformation into an animal or of flying in one's human form. For many

---

[23] See Hutton, "Modern Pagan Festivals."
[24] Clifton, *Her Hidden Children*, 49.
[25] Christopher Chase, "'Be Pagan Once Again': Folk Music, Heritage, and Socio-Sacred Networks in Contemporary American Paganism," *The Pomegranate: The International Journal of Pagan Studies* 8:2 (2006).

Pagan women in particular, control over their own bodies and their own pleasure is described in religious terms: "It sacralizes the body and the cycles of nature ... [rejecting] any form of authority imposed from without or perceived as coming from a locus of power within the hegemony."[26] Inanna, a Pagan blogger, writes, "For we Pagani, all glory is in embodiment. We don't honor asceticism, chastity, or restraint. There is no reason to deny the pleasures of the flesh."[27] Pagan religionists sometimes embody the gods through trance possession. Wicca also offers a ritualized form of sexual intercourse, usually expressed symbolically through the union of the *athame* (ritual dagger) and chalice, representing the creative powers of the universe. Under some circumstances, ritualists themselves physically unite as representatives of the divine.

For Wicca, in particular, which was cast in 1950s Britain as a surviving Stone Age fertility cult, the religious language of the body ran directly counter to the dualistic spirit expressed in much of Christianity (not to mention by heretics such as the medieval Cathars). It is the most direct expression of Michael York's formula of a sacred relationship with the "tangible" and "sentient." Likewise, the regard for the body in the religion, combined with the rejection of hegemonic authority and a valuing of female religious leadership, was one way in which the new religion of Wicca found common ground with Second Wave feminism. Arguably, America's contributions to the Wiccan movement were the stress on feminism (through such writers as Zsuzsanna Budapest, Starhawk, Margot Adler, and others) and an expanded concept of nature religion. Both have helped Wicca become a world religion, albeit still a small one, moving beyond the English-speaking world to such nations as Germany, Italy, Mexico, Brazil, and India. Not bound by nationalist or ethnic qualifications, Wicca has "experienced an explosive growth in English-speaking countries" and appears poised to thrive in the contemporary religious marketplace, where "in tandem with the weaker social relationships that characterize modern society, there is an increasing tendency for people to 'hand craft' their own individual spirituality."[28]

---

[26] Sabina Magliocco and Holly Tannen, "The *Real* Old-Time Religion: Towards an Aesthetics of Neo-Pagan Song," *Ethnologies* 20:1 (1998), 175–201.
[27] Inanna, "Pagan Values: Pleasure and Beauty," *At the End of Desire*, June 18, 2009, http://attheendofdesire.blogspot.com/2009/06/Pagan-values-pleasure-and-beauty.html
[28] James R. Lewis, "The Pagan Explosion," in *The New Generation Witches: Teenage Witchcraft in Contemporary Culture*, ed. Hannah E. Johnson and Peg Aloi (Aldershot: Ashgate Publishing, 2007).

# 29

# THE NEW AGE

OLAV HAMMER

## 1 Introduction: "The New Age," A Catchall Term?

In modern society, an astounding range of religious or "spiritual" alternatives to organized religion are available. A very incomplete list includes tarot reading, Reiki healing, swimming with dolphins, astrology, (neo-)shamanism, crystal healing, psychic phenomena, the recall of past-life memories, Aura-Soma remedies, fire walking, and various modes of "positive thinking." Among the list of the spiritual, one also finds vast numbers of books, with titles such as *A Course in Miracles*, *Conversations with God*, and *The Celestine Prophecy*. The term "New Age" is often affixed to them all, at least by people who do not personally share any of these interests. Insiders will, on the contrary, often insist that the label is derogatory or even meaningless. Rather than seeing their own beliefs and practices as part of any wider social movement, many hold that they have embarked on a thoroughly individual quest. Scholarly literature hovers uncertainly between the two views, some authors insisting that there is a minimal shared discourse uniting these various practices and ideas, others rejecting "New Age" as a thoroughly vacuous term.[1] One difficulty with the expression is that, in common with many other terms employed in the study of religion, it was a designation coined by the members of a particular religious milieu and has since become employed in a wide and not always compatible variety of ways.

The concept "New Age" is diffuse also because it consists of a combination of a common adjective and an equally common noun and has therefore historically been repeatedly used in contexts that would seem to have few points of contact with the modern concept. William Blake uses the term in a

---

[1] For a discussion of the issues involved, see especially George D. Chryssides, "Defining the New Age," in *Handbook of New Age*, ed. Daren Kemp and James R. Lewis (Leiden: Brill, 2007), 5–24.

publication dated 1804, in a context that has roots in the writings of the eighteenth-century visionary Emanuel Swedenborg, and earlier.[2] Other early references are Warren Felt Evans's book *The New Age and Its Messenger* (1864), and the literary magazine *The New Age* founded in 1894.

New Age as label for a utopian vision with an occultist tinge is a later creation. It originally arose in the 1930s in the Theosophical works of Alice Bailey (e.g., in titles such as *Discipleship in the New Age*) and spread in the years shortly after World War II in connection with the millennialist belief prevalent in certain occultist and UFO-oriented circles that the world was on the brink of a major evolutionary transformation of consciousness. At the time, the phrase "New Age" was not the only way to designate such eschatological views. Astrological symbolism was also prevalent, and the period of global "consciousness revolution" was often identified in literature dating back to the 1960s and earlier as the "Aquarian Age."

Around 1970, the designation New Age began to be regularly affixed to the amalgam of spiritual interests outlined earlier. Millennialism and astrological symbolism were still frequent references, and the various techniques of healing, divination, and so on that were available were often seen as tools that could be used to effect the transformation of consciousness. At this point, using a generic label was still often perceived as quite unproblematic, and New Age was an insider's term. However, the millennial vision of the movement rapidly lost strength; increasingly during the 1980s and beyond, the various concepts and techniques were adopted by people who did not share the vision of a collective transformation.

Wouter Hanegraaff helpfully suggests distinct terms for the two divergent forms of New Age.[3] The social movement that looked forward to a major transformation of human consciousness can be called the New Age in the restricted sense (*sensu stricto*). New Age in the broad sense (*sensu lato*) of the word refers, by contrast, to the wide array of ideas and practices, united by little more than historical links, a partly shared discourse, vague resemblances, and particular settings (e.g., New Age book stores, festivals) where the various interests coexist. Whether these hazy similarities are sufficient to make it meaningful to identify such diverse practices by a shared designation and, if so, whether it is acceptable to use a term abandoned by nearly all who are sympathetic to these practices remain issues about which scholars disagree.

[2] Christoph Bochinger, *"New Age" und moderne Religion: Religionswissenschaftliche Analysen* (Gütersloh: Kaiser, 1994), 280–281.
[3] Wouter J. Hanegraaff, *New Age Religion and Western Culture: Esotericism in the Mirror of Secular Thought* (Leiden: Brill, 1996), 94–103.

It is not my intention here to attempt to solve the questions of coherence and acceptability. These questions are by no means particular to the New Age label, and arguably not even particularly fruitful ones to pose. After all, what non-arbitrary criteria could establish whether two practices are "sufficiently similar" to be labeled Christian, Islamic, or Hindu? Rather, the remainder of this essay will be devoted to outlining a few of the historical links, making the shared discourse explicit, and discussing some potential reasons for the family resemblances connecting an otherwise truly diverse and eclectic set of religious options.

## 2 Precursors, and a First New Age Generation

The 1967 musical *Hair* may have garbled its astrological terminology, but its opening lyrics did express a feeling common to the late 1960s and early 1970s: "This is the dawning of the Age of Aquarius." The "Age of Aquarius" was firmly anchored in countercultural pursuits. The anticipated transformation was to be ushered in by a diverse set of spiritual paths. Astrology, as can be expected from the term itself, held a prominent place. But so did varieties of Hindu philosophy, Zen, mysticism, and also psychedelic drugs, the latter the preferred means to the transformation of consciousness of at least some sectors of the late 1960s spiritual milieu. There is certainly an element of Western esotericism in all of this, but the Age of Aquarius was omnivorous in its spiritual appetites and respected few boundaries.

By the early 1970s, the Age of Aquarius had transformed into the first generation of the New Age. *Books for Inner Development*, a catalogue of literature on the vast variety of books available to those early New Agers, published in 1976 and therefore generously including literature of the immediately preceding years, provides examples of what the spiritually adventurous could sample.[4] Most of the topics would be instantly recognizable to a present-day spiritual seeker. These include alchemy, astrology, biorhythms, Buddhism, Edgar Cayce, color and aura, divination, dreams, the occult properties of gems and stones, psychic healing, humanistic psychology, Indian philosophy, Jewish mysticism, meditation, mythology, parapsychology, reincarnation and karma, Tantra, tarot, UFOs and yoga. There are few readily detectable changes in content from the more countercultural 1960s; even the literature on psychedelics is amply represented, albeit under the somewhat more discrete rubric Consciousness Expansion. The catalogue

---

[4] Cris Popenoe, *Books for Inner Development: The Yes! Guide* (Washington, DC: Random House, 1976).

is also a product of a New Age *sensu stricto*. The jacket blurb clearly indicates that the disparate interests included are paths toward an overarching transformation: "[The author] realized that the changes needed in the society weren't going to happen until changes took place within us."

An interesting, almost postmodern aspect of *Books for Inner Development* is its inclusion of high and low: from scholarly literature, to abstrusely esoteric source texts, and to truly mass-market–oriented titles. Coexisting in the pages of this catalogue are academic works by Frances Yates, editions of works by various Christian and Islamic mystics, Theosophical texts, "channeled" books such as the Urantia Book and Jane Roberts's Seth materials, the collected works of Carl Jung, titles by Gurdjieff and Ouspensky, and some popular and accessibly written books on topics such as health food, sun signs, and psychedelics. While the sun sign and health food literature is ubiquitous also in contemporary New Age bookshops, the intellectual aspiration of a good deal of the literature from the mid-1970s is a distinctive trait of this first generation of New Age. The hope for an imminent transformation of human consciousness was a topic of interest also to numerous individuals with considerable social and cultural capital. The attempt to formulate an intellectually viable vision inspired by spiritual concerns can for example be seen from the New Age science formulated by Fritjof Capra (b. 1939) and other authors who were especially popular in the 1970s and into the 1980s.

Besides being apparent from the literature, the utopian drive of this first generation of the New Age also displayed itself in concrete initiatives, such as the communes and growth centers that were established at the time. Since its inception in the early 1960s, the Findhorn Foundation in Scotland has offered workshops and lectures on spiritual topics and has attracted thousands of short- and long-term residents. The Esalen Institute on the coast of California has similarly functioned as a center for alternative religiosity since the 1960s.

Scientific aspirations and practical attempts to disseminate this utopian vision went hand-in-hand with occultist and mystical concerns inherited from earlier esoteric currents. An example is the early work of David Spangler (b. 1945), whose claim to clairvoyance and connection to the Findhorn Foundation made him a major influence on the first generation of the New Age. His channeled texts from the early 1970s functioned as a conduit for Theosophical ideas into the New Age. Another example is the British writer George Trevelyan (1906–1996), whose book *A Vision of the Aquarian Age* (1977) also helped promote a Theosophically based worldview in New Age circles. Anthroposophy, Jungianism, and the works of Gurdjieff are other esoteric influences on the first New Age generation.

## 3 Elements of a New Age Milieu

Much has changed since the New Age of the early 1970s. The present-day (*sensu lato*) milieu of spiritual seekers is considerably less oriented toward eschatology, and less clearly influenced by Theosophical ideas. It is more of a mass-market audience and arguably even more diverse than was the first generation. Diversity is an inevitable result of the most overt social characteristics of this milieu. In a centralized organization, one will typically find authoritative statements of doctrine. The New Age milieu is so fragmented that no such list of "acceptable views" can be made. What we have are commonly voiced opinions in the literature and among people involved in various loosely organized forms of "spirituality." Furthermore, the diversity of the New Age milieu is connected to its rapid rate of change over time. Books, ideas, and practices that captivated large audiences at one time can be marginalized a few years later. James Redfield sold millions of copies of his novel *The Celestine Prophecy*, published in 1993. After some years, Redfield was largely eclipsed by Neal Donald Walsh's book series *Conversations with God*, the first volume of which appeared in 1995. More recently, the top best-seller in the "alternative spirituality" genre has been Dan Brown's *The Da Vinci Code*, which has perhaps more tenuous links to a New Age form of religiosity, however defined.

Despite the vast variety of individual doctrines and practices, and the rapid rate of change, a few prevalent and more stable themes can be discerned. Perhaps unsurprisingly, these themes tend to gravitate toward matters frequently addressed in non-scriptural or folk religions around the world and are of immediate concern to many: illness, death, misfortune, difficult life choices, and perceived personal shortcomings. Theological and philosophical issues are also treated in the literature, but they play a more subordinate role. New Age therapists can wax eloquent on the beneficial modes of healing that involve "balancing one's energies" but can be remarkably vague when it comes to discussing the nature and origins of these energies.

The matter of most concern to New Age religiosity, judging from the literature, is the perceived shortcomings of our lives. We are, it is suggested, living well below our optimum potential. Fulfilling our potential can, at a minimum, entail good health and a well-functioning life in terms of work and personal relationships. Beyond those basic concerns, New Age literature will often go further and challenge us to overcome suboptimal levels of vitality, creativity, and energy. Self-improvement at various levels and in the most diverse forms appears to be a major topic.

Questions prompted by the quest for health, vitality, and self-improvement are often dealt with by New Agers through various ritual techniques. The specific methods employed in healing vary from the laying on of hands to the use of a variety of ritual substances and objects. Reiki involves the use of the healer's hands. Crystal healing depends on the idea that gems and minerals possess healing properties. Color therapies and Aura-Soma therapy assume that colors influence physical and spiritual well-being. One prominent subset of rituals that promote spiritual self-improvement consists of divinatory practices. Astrology obviously predates the emergence of the New Age by many centuries. However, the interpretations of the various symbols of the birth chart have changed considerably over time and have become steadily more integrated into the New Age focus on the individual, his or her life situation, and inner spiritual change. The difficulties encountered in life are explained in terms of lessons to be worked on and absorbed into the individual's present existence on earth. Other forms of divination, such as the use of tarot cards, also typically concern the spiritual development of the individual.

The specific concepts and rituals involved in healing and self-improvement can be rooted in the personal experience of those who create them. Quite commonly, however, these concepts and methods are held to have a suprahuman origin. In traditional cultures around the world, religious specialists have functioned as links between human beings and what each culture understands to be spiritual reality. The New Age counterpart of this process of prophetic communication is widely known as "channeling." Channeled messages generally convey the idea that we are functioning at suboptimal levels and issue the same sort of call for self-improvement that we encounter in the context of healing and divination. Channeled texts can suggest that fear and guilt, negative thinking, the blockage of spiritual energy, or the forces of rationality and materialism are obstacles to a higher, intuitive mode of thinking and impede us from recognizing our spiritual natures. A related credo that permeates much of the channeled material is that we "create our own reality." If guilt or fear burdens us, our world will be dark and frightening. If we bring out our inner divine selves, however, the world will become filled with apparent miracles.

These basic doctrinal elements were at the core of an early series of channeled messages, set forth in a series of books by Jane Roberts known as the "Seth material." In these works, Roberts (1929–1984) claimed to have channeled the messages of the discarnate entity Seth. Her writings spread through the emerging New Age network throughout the late 1960s and early 1970s and became trend setting for subsequent claims of channeled messages.

They also contain a number of innovative religious ideas and concepts that have been adopted as normative by the wider New Age culture.

A quite different but also very influential channeled text in the contemporary New Age milieu is *A Course in Miracles*. According to this work's founding legend, the text was received by psychologist Helen Schucman (1909–1981) through dictation from an inner voice that she identified as that of Jesus. According to *A Course in Miracles*, our everyday image of physical reality is illusory. Our conventional view of the world shows us a place where human beings are separated from one another and from the divine, and where pain, disease, and disharmony exist. However, this worldview is in reality a projection of our frightened egos.

## 4 Unity in Diversity?

The description given earlier of a loose social milieu where, among other things, New Age science, astrology, healing, and channeling coexist can give the impression of a true anarchy of opinions, where anything goes. Nevertheless, a reasonably coherent underlying set of conceptions can be identified within the various practices and ideas. This underlying core includes a cosmology, a view of human nature, and a set of postulates regarding the nature of spiritual knowledge. Although rarely spelled out in full by insiders, these conceptions can be made explicit as follows.

The entire cosmos is not so much a vast collection of material objects as a great, interconnected web of meaning. The underlying "stuff" of the cosmos is therefore not matter but something intangible, identifiable as "consciousness" or "energy." We humans contain a spark of this energy or consciousness within us, a resource that we can tap into to change reality and create our own worlds. The human being is thus not only a material body but also contains a spiritual element. That such a spiritual component exists is apparent in a variety of contexts. Healing, for instance, addresses our spiritual nature, rather than merely treating isolated physical symptoms. The spiritual aspect of the human constitution can also be invoked in the concept of reincarnation: Each of us is on a journey of spiritual development, in which our true, inner self develops as we incarnate again and again over a series of many lives.

It is also generally held that there are normally invisible vital forces ("energies") that surround and/or permeate the human body, and which the New Age therapist is able to manipulate. Thus, the human aura, a colored sheath said to enclose the physical body, is held by many healers to provide clues to the state of the client's health. The hidden anatomy is often understood to be composed of seven or more centers of vital force, the *chakras*. The body is furthermore perceived as a holistic system. The body as a whole is mirrored in the feet (reflexology), in the outer ears (as in one modern, Western development of acupuncture), and in the eyes (iridology). Theories of Chinese origin, according to which the vital forces flow through channels connecting all parts of the body into an integrated whole, have been eagerly embraced by New Age healers.

But how can we know what a particular tarot card entails for our self-understanding, what a particular crystal will do to our chakras, or what the colors of the aura signal? The New Age literature presupposes a particular view of knowledge. It holds that there are potentially better ways to come to understand ourselves and the world than those that depend on rationality and the intellect. Perhaps we can gain spiritual insight in flashes of intuition. Perhaps there are altered states of consciousness in which we can access knowledge from various highly developed beings, or from a divine part of ourselves. Similar insights into the workings of the cosmos and into our own selves, it is often suggested, were granted to a number of ancient cultures, ranging from Egypt and India to the Native Americas and are confirmed by the most recent developments of Western science, especially quantum mechanics. Ultimately, however, spirituality is not a matter of accepting doctrines formulated by others but rather a highly individual quest that can (and perhaps should) be based primarily on personal experience.

## 5 The New Age as Cultic Milieu?

One reason that has been cited in the scholarly literature for the apparently chaotic plurality of opinions and practices to which the New Age label is often affixed is that the New Age constitutes a cultic milieu.[5] The "cultic milieu," a term coined by Colin Campbell, consists of people who have adopted a variety of beliefs that from the majority point of view may seem more or less unorthodox.[6] They have done so with varying degrees of commitment, without expressing them in an organized setting. The cultic milieu can support unrelated and at times even mutually contradictory beliefs, simply because they share certain important characteristics. For instance, the belief in psychic messages, in astrology, or in the prophecies of Nostradamus constitute minority views that flourish in a society whose

---

[5] Hanegraaff, *New Age Religion*, 14–18.
[6] Colin Campbell, "The Cult, the Cultic Milieu and Secularization," *A Sociological Yearbook of Religion in Britain* 5 (1972), 119–136.

institutions take little notice of them or can attempt to suppress them. People who want to defend the value of such views often do so in defiance of the worldview of the majority and will seek support among others who espouse equally "alternative" ideas.

Colin Campbell contrasts "alternative" or (in his terminology) "deviant" ideas with those that are mainstream or socially accepted. His theory thus appears to presuppose that there is one dominant, nearly monolithic culture, in opposition to an underground of divergent and rather marginalized innovations. Other theories, developed by cultural anthropologists over the past several decades, afford opportunities to understand religious innovation, and thus New Age religiosity, in different terms.

Since at least the 1980s, the representation of cultures as stable systems regulating individual behavior has come under considerable criticism. The assumption that a particular group shares a culture has been seen as masking the hegemony of the dominant strata of that group and as being blind to variability and diversity. Numerous anthropologists have suggested that "culture" is a problematic term, an abstraction created by the anthropologist to describe the manifold things that people do, rather than a monolithic model that people collectively inherit and embody.[7] A useful metaphor to conceptualize this more recent approach to culture and cultural variability is that of culture as a large repertoire of discourses and practices. The repertoire metaphor is helpful in describing both the diversity and the rapid change over time just discussed. Variation, as Fredrik Barth argues, is part of any complex society that encompasses people with different levels of expertise, different received traditions, local variations, different social strata, and various practical interests.[8] Rapid change is the effect of agents with different competences and interests picking different elements from the repertoire, and occasionally adding novel components to it.

A number of constraints on variability and change prevent New Age religiosity (or any other tradition) from becoming entirely devoid of specific content. The constraints include the net composition of the repertoire at any given time, the social and historical context that makes a particular selection from this repertoire relevant, the individual creativity of particular agents, and the ability of dominant players in the religious environment to enforce their own selection on others. Jointly, many of these factors can be summarized in a model of religious supply and demand.

---

[7] For a background to older views of culture and to the debate of the 1980s and 1990s, see Adam Kuper, *Culture: The Anthropologists' Account* (Cambridge, MA: Harvard University Press, 1999).
[8] Fredrik Barth, *Balinese Worlds* (Chicago: University of Chicago Press, 1993), 4–5.

## 6 The Supply and Demand of Religion

The view of the New Age as a set of selections from a vast repertoire of cultural elements has specific consequences. Clearly, not all selections and combinations of cultural elements are equally successful: Some innovations catch on and become major trends, whereas others remain associated with individual people and their closest networks. Two major views of what allows certain movements to grow are supply-side and demand-side theories. Supply-side theories look at the ability of religious movers and shakers to formulate their message in an appealing way. Demand-side theories focus on the preferences of the potential consumers. Since the New Age is a largely unregulated market, the viability of its individual elements is dependent on both aspects, that is, on supply meeting demand. Only to the extent that New Age suppliers supply what consumers require can they hope to make an impact.

The demands of the New Age consumer can be inferred by looking at a list of traits shared by many of the products on offer. Successful New Age innovations will typically be characterized by the following:

1. A sufficient distance from beliefs and practices supported by major social institutions. New Age healing, to take just one example, is often in marked disagreement with the ideals and practices of mainstream medicine.
2. Individualism. As noted earlier, many New Agers see themselves as pursuing an individual spiritual quest.
3. Nostalgia and exoticism. New Agers will typically understand their own doctrines and rituals as rooted in ancient cultures, such as Egypt, India, China, Tibet, or the Native Americas.
4. Needs in the here-and-now, with a particular a focus on the self as functioning suboptimally but embarked on a voyage of self-improvement.
5. Recognizability. Innovations rarely stray too far away from the already acceptable. A new mode of healing that manipulates energies differently will no doubt be better received than a therapy based on concepts of witchcraft and exorcism.

This perspective of the New Age as supply meeting demand has two important and seemingly contrary consequences. The first, conservatism, is readily accounted for by the fact that spokespersons of the New Age generally pick elements from an already existing religious repertoire. Available methods of healing, divination, or channeling will be reformulated or recombined in new ways. Due to this element of recognizability and the conservatism it entails, a historical chain of doctrines and their predecessors can be traced back in time. The second consequence is innovation: As long as the resulting mix of cultural elements attracts customers, it can also contain components that are not selected from the already existing pool. The relationship between the New Age and Western esotericism is a result of this tension between conservatism and innovation.

The conservative aspect of this form of religiosity is evident from the existing literature. Paul Heelas points at predecessors in *fin-de-siècle* occultism, Jungianism, *Lebensreform* movements, and so forth.[9] Hanegraaff pursues the historical roots further back in time and sees the New Age as an eclectic combination of several strands of Western esotericism, ultimately stretching back to the Renaissance, but radically modernized from the eighteenth century onward.[10] Much of the present New Age is prefigured by the ideas and practices created by individuals crucial to this process of modernization, such as Emanuel Swedenborg (1688–1722) and Franz Anton Mesmer (1731–1791). From the mid-nineteenth century on, at least two main currents have come to influence the history of the New Age. The first is Theosophy and its heirs. The second is the "harmonial religions" that followed in the wake of the American mesmerist healer Phineas Parkhurst Quimby (1802–1866). The Theosophical strand leads us to Alice Bailey (1880–1949), where we started our historical journey at the beginning of this essay.

The description given earlier emphasizes the continuity of the emerging New Age of the 1970s with earlier forms of Western esotericism. The innovative aspect should, however, not be underestimated. As long as supply matches demand, there is no inherent mechanism in the New Age milieu that necessarily favors Western esoteric elements over any other sources. Loans from other religious traditions and the various products of individual creativity are equally important ingredients. It can, of course, be argued that the already familiar colors the hitherto unknown to such an extent that even elements borrowed from, for example, Sufism, Tantrism, or shamanism are reinterpreted and become integrated into a Western esoteric framework. Nevertheless, individual beliefs and practices can be picked from anywhere

---

[9] Paul Heelas, *The New Age Movement* (Oxford: Blackwell, 1996), 41–48 *et passim*.
[10] Hanegraaff, *New Age Religion*, esp. chap. 14. Modernization in Hanegraaff's perspective includes the adoption of mechanical causality, an interest in the Orient, the idea of evolution, and psychologization. For a complementary, more sociologically oriented approach to modernization, see Olav Hammer, "New Age Movement" in *Dictionary of Gnosis and Western Esotericism*, ed. Wouter J. Hanegraaff (Leiden: Brill 2005), 855–861.

on the globe, from the Native Americas to Egypt, from China to Polynesia, as long as they fit the specific preoccupations of the New Age.

A case in point is Transcendental Meditation (TM), a practice into which vast numbers of people have been initiated because it addresses the demands outlined earlier. It advocates beliefs and practices that run counter to those supported by major social institutions, such as the educational and scientific communities (e.g., by suggesting that accomplished meditators can overcome the force of gravity); it is individualistic (promising each initiate a uniquely tailor-made mantra), exotic (Indian), centered on the here-and-now needs of the self (from relaxation to increased vitality and creativity), and recognizable (by referring, for example, to scientific evidence for its effectiveness, and blaming "stress" instead of karma as the cause of spiritual malaise). Nevertheless, the historical roots of TM lie in a particular interpretation of Vedantic philosophy, and not with any current of Western esotericism. Paradoxically, although much of the New Age turns out to be affiliated with earlier esoteric currents, it is so for no deeper reason than sheer historical contingency.

# V
# *Common Threads*

# 30

# ALCHEMY

LAWRENCE M. PRINCIPE

## 1 Introduction

Alchemy is a complex and wide-ranging discipline that is difficult to characterize in simple terms. In the course of nearly two millennia, alchemy has appeared in many guises; was formed and reformed by various cultures, ideas, and locales; and was directed toward a variety of goals by its thousands of practitioners. Perhaps the greatest obstacle in gaining an accurate historical understanding of the subject today is the fact that alchemy continues to be misrepresented in many modern accounts. In many quarters, reinterpretations and programmatic reassessments of alchemy that date from the eighteenth to the early twentieth centuries continue to dominate and to be read back onto earlier epochs. Recent scholarship, however, has shown that these latter-day perspectives are historically untenable. Indeed, the past forty years have witnessed a remarkable blossoming of scholarly studies of alchemy, with the felicitous result that we now have access to a vastly more accurate understanding of what alchemy really was at various points in its long history.

A key point to stress at the outset is the internal diversity of alchemy. It is not an unchanging monolithic tradition, although it is sometimes represented as such by both its practitioners and its commentators. This issue becomes especially critical when the question of alchemy's connection to esotericism and mysticism arises. It is true that alchemy can be seen as a "common thread" running through various topics addressed in this volume. Nevertheless, both the degree and the uniformity of those connections are frequently overstated, and their nature misunderstood. The source of the problem is twofold. On the one hand, interpretations of alchemy dating from the Enlightenment and the Victorian era recast the subject into much closer association with topics routinely labeled as "occult" than had ever been the case historically. Thus, many popular treatments of alchemy today, and even some scholarly ones, regularly and rather casually claim that alchemy was "magical," "spiritual," "occult," or "mystical." The general aim of these characterizations has been to define alchemy as something very distinct from chemistry. By doing so, these accounts perpetuate – often unwittingly – the ahistorical claims of uniquely eighteenth- and nineteenth-century interpretations or reformulations of alchemy.

On the other hand, the terms "mysticism" and "esotericism" tend to be employed in so loose and vague a manner that they sometimes fail to retain any precise or consistent meaning. Caught between the opposing forces of the exuberant extravagance of nineteenth-century occultism and the smug aridity of nineteenth- and twentieth-century positivism, these terms (and related ones such as "occult," "magical," and even "scientific") have become so overburdened with accreted connotations that they have come to be deployed more often as terms of opprobrium or approbation than of precise or meaningful description. Their incautious use invites misunderstanding. For example, if we define "esoteric" in its strict sense of "abstruse or secret knowledge possessed only by a small group," then some parts of alchemy are indeed esoteric: In almost all historical contexts, these parts are considered to be *secret* and *privileged* knowledge. Examples include the operational details for making the Philosophers' Stone and for transmuting base metals into gold. Yet even in this strict sense, only *some* parts of alchemy qualify as esoteric: Throughout alchemy's history, most of its basic principles – for example, theories of matter or of the nature, composition, and subterranean production of metals – were readily available and widely known. The situation is similar to that of contemporary physics, where its fundamental principles are easily accessible and known to a broad audience, while its most advanced concepts remain abstruse and incomprehensible to non-physicists, and some applications (e.g., the specifics of constructing nuclear weapons) remain guarded secrets. When we move to usages of the adjective "esoteric" that depend on a link to "esotericism" (a term of nineteenth-century coinage) and thereby relate to specifically religious, spiritual, or occultist currents, then the great majority of alchemy is *not* esoteric at all. A similar argument may be made, *mutatis mutandis*, about "mystical" (in the senses of "mysterious and secret" versus "pertaining to mysticism") and "occult" (in the senses of simply "hidden" versus "pertaining to occultism").

The balance of this essay attempts to clarify these points and to provide a historically accurate presentation of the main features of alchemy and their historical development, with emphasis on alchemy's contact with topics that can be (or have been) classed as esoteric. It surveys the history of alchemy through its four major phases in the West, from its origins in Late Antique

Egypt (100–700 CE), through its elaboration in the Arabic world (750–1400), to its broadest development in Latin Europe (1150–1750), and finally through its period of retrospective evaluation and revivals (after 1750).[1]

## 2 Greco-Egyptian Alchemy

Alchemy's origins lie in Greco-Roman Egypt of the first centuries CE, when two preexistent traditions began to merge. One component was a practical craft tradition of metalworking that included techniques for imitating gold, silver, and other precious materials. Traces of this artisanal tradition survive in the Leiden and Stockholm Papyri, documents dating probably to the third century, which list practical recipes for such things as how to alter the surface color of metals to make them look like silver or gold. The other component was Greek philosophical speculation about the nature of matter and change, intellectual currents dating back to the Presocratics. Thus, alchemy represents, from its beginnings, a fusion of theory and practice, of knowledge and craft, of *epistēmē* and *technē*.

One early witness of this mingling is the *Physika kai mystika* of pseudo-Democritus. The title (probably added later) is often translated as *Physical and Mystical Things*, but it is more accurately rendered as *Natural and Secret Things*. Most of the text, dating probably to the late first or second century CE, contains recipes such as those in the Papyri, but these are interspersed with the refrain "Nature (*physis*) delights in nature, nature conquers nature, nature masters nature." This phrase can be interpreted as the expression of a theoretical principle about how to use and manipulate the properties ("natures") of materials for practical ends.

A full synthesis of the practical and theoretical appears in the writings of Zosimos of Panopolis (*fl.* 300 CE), the most important Greco-Egyptian alchemist. Most of Zosimos's writings are lost; however, surviving fragments describe an array of (often quite sophisticated) apparatus for chemical processes, alongside guiding theoretical principles regarding the nature and composition of metals. Significantly, Zosimos's goal is not the *imitation* of precious metals but rather their real production from baser metals. This process of *transmutation* is undergirded by the theoretical principle that all metals share a common underlying matter and are therefore capable of being interconverted. The process of making gold, or *chrysopoeia*, is to be done by combining baser metals with one or more materials prepared from other

[1] For a fuller account of the history of alchemy, see Lawrence M. Principe, *The Secrets of Alchemy* (Chicago: University of Chicago Press, 2013).

substances. The transmuting agent would later (not before the seventh century) be called the Philosophers' Stone.

Several enduring features of alchemy are established in Zosimos's writings, perhaps none more significant than the commitment to secrecy. Both of alchemy's progenitors incorporated secretive elements. The recipe tradition undoubtedly relied on keeping techniques secret to preserve "proprietary" methods, and the philosophical tradition likewise contained secretive, or privileged, elements – particularly the more esoteric branches of Alexandrian Neoplatonism current in Zosimos's day. A further incentive to secrecy may have been the emperor Diocletian's contemporaneous decree to destroy Egyptian books dealing with "the *cheimeia* of silver and gold."[2] Secrecy manifests itself both in Zosimos and in later alchemy in several ways. Most commonly, substances are not called by their usual names. Instead, *Decknamen* (cover names) are used, and authors often "call a single thing by many names while they call many things by a single name."[3]

Zosimos considers metals to be composed of two substances: a nonvolatile part he calls "body" (*sōma*) and a volatile part he calls "spirit" (*pneuma*). The spirit carries the properties particular to each metal, while the body seems to be common to all metals. The metal's identity thus depends on its spirit; hence, Zosimos uses fire – in distillation, sublimation, volatilization, and so forth – to separate spirits and infuse them into other substances to bring about transmutation. This body-spirit nomenclature for metals naturally leads to (and derives from) a metaphorical linkage with death and the soul of man. Accordingly, Zosimos expresses some technical processes allegorically in the form of dreams (sometimes misleadingly called "visions"). He describes men made of metals, an altar shaped like a chemical vessel, sacrifices, death, and torments. Zosimos draws on details of contemporaneous temple practices for his imagery, but he is likewise clear that these "dreams" are to be interpreted allegorically, as providing technical details or theoretical foundations for practical metallic transmutation. This secretive, allegorizing tendency would become typical of alchemical writing and reached its zenith in early modern Europe.

Gnostic ideas are expressed in Zosimos's *Letter Omega*. (Zosimos's writings were apparently classified according to the Greek alphabet; what we have as the *Letter Omega* is only the preamble to a treatise on apparatuses and furnaces, now lost.) Zosimos attacks rival alchemists who claim that specific materials

---

[2] *Acta sanctorum julii*, 7 vols. (Antwerp, 1719–31), 2:557.
[3] Zosimos, "Twenty-Sixth Epistle," in Benjamin Hallum, "Zosimus Arabus" (Ph.D. dissertation 2008, Warburg Institute), 366.

and techniques are not needed to prepare transmuting tinctures. Zosimos declares that their success is only an illusion produced by daimons. This daimonic trickery is akin to that which – gnostically speaking – tricked Adam into taking on a body, with all its ill effects. Zosimos insists on tinctures that act completely naturally, and that human beings remain free of daimonic influence and the control of fate.

Most of the later Greek alchemical writings are commentaries on the earlier material, often relating it more closely to Greek philosophical speculation. A significant expansion of alchemy dates from the Islamic period. The Arabic world inherited Greek texts and added enormously to their conceptual and practical content.

## 2 Arabic Alchemy

The early period of Arabic authorship produced the *Emerald Tablet*, one of the most revered texts relating to alchemy, attributed to the legendary figure Hermes Trismegistus, a complex layering of Greek and Egyptian mythic figures. Zosimos cited "Hermes" as an authority, and by the tenth century Hermes had grown into the founder of alchemy. The *Tablet* is probably an Arabic composition of the eighth century, although it later appeared in various versions. In all cases, its text is obscure and of debatable meaning but seems to adopt Greek ideas about monism and celestial-terrestrial interrelationships.

The largest set of Arabic alchemical writings is connected to the name Jābir ibn-Hayyān. It is doubtful that Jābir actually existed; these writings are the product of many authors, a "school" of alchemists operating over several generations, from roughly 800 to 1000.[4] "Jābir" presents himself as the favored student of the sixth Shi'ite imam, Ja'far al-Sādiq (700–765). Jabirian writings display features of ninth-century Shi'ite ideas; the earlier linkage of them to the Ikhwān al-Safā' (Brethren of Purity) now seems less tenable.[5] Connection to this Shi'ite sect did however lead to an initiatic style, whereby the author calls readers his sons and promises to reveal privileged knowledge to the worthy. This style was later propagated and developed throughout Latin alchemy, as the earliest Latin authors endeavored to imitate Jabirian literary style. Another literary feature is the "dispersion of knowledge," a

---

[4] Paul Kraus, *Jābir ibn Hayyān: Contribution à l'histoire des idées scientifiques dans l'Islam, Volume I: Le Corpus des écrits jābiriens*, Mémoires de L'Institute d'Égypte 44, (1943) and *Volume II: Jābir et la science grecque*, Mémoires de L'Institute d'Égypte 45, (1942).
[5] Yves Marquet, "La place de l'alchimie dans Les épîtres des Frères de la Pureté," *Chrysopoeia* 7 (2000–2003), 49–59.

technique of secrecy that divides a single process or concept into pieces and scatters the pieces through one or more texts.

Jabirian transmutational theories are often based on the four elements of Empedocles and Aristotle: fire, air, earth, and water. These works, such as the *Book of Seventy*, endeavor to prepare "elixirs" that, when mixed with a base metal, are capable of adjusting the proportions of these elements in the metal to turn it into gold. Other texts adopt the Mercury-Sulphur theory of the early ninth-century *Book of the Secrets of Creation* of Balīnūs. This Mercury-Sulphur theory states that all metals are compounds of two ingredients called Mercury and Sulphur. These two combine in different proportions and degrees of purity to produce the various metals. Gold results from the best Sulphur and Mercury combined in exact proportions. When the Mercury and Sulphur are impure or combined in the wrong ratio, base metals are produced. This theory provides a strong theoretical foundation for transmutation: If all metals share the same ingredients and differ only in the relative proportions and qualities of those ingredients, then purifying the Mercury and Sulphur in lead and adjusting their ratio should produce gold. The Mercury-Sulphur theory would endure until the eighteenth century.

Later Arabic authors, such as al-Rāzī (or Rhazes, ca. 865–923/4) and ibn-Sīnā (Avicenna, ca. 980–1037), would add dramatically to the practical and material repertory of alchemy. Ibn-Sīnā, however, wrote dismissively of the possibility of transmutation, based on his belief in a fundamental difference between natural and artificial products. Nevertheless, many contemporary and subsequent Arabic writers continued to pursue chrysopoeia. The Arabic world also records the appearance of "false alchemists" – those who use alchemy as a pretext for defrauding the unwary with deceptions of various sorts.

## 3 Latin Alchemy

Alchemy came into Europe through translations of Arabic texts, part of a broad translation movement beginning in the twelfth century. By 1300, numerous original Latin compositions had appeared, perhaps none more influential than the *Summa perfectionis*. Its author, possibly the Franciscan lecturer Paul of Taranto, wrote under the name Geber to coopt the authority of Jabir. "Geber" displays extensive knowledge of practical processes and develops an influential quasi-particulate matter theory for explaining chemical phenomena from density to transmutation. While deploying the initiatic tone, Geber's style is predominantly Scholastic: clear, orderly, and without overt secrecy. The earliest Latin alchemical works share this style.

By 1300, transmutational alchemy had become controversial. Some debates focused on intellectual issues such as the limits of human ability and differences between natural and manmade substances.[6] Others drew on linkages between chrysopoeia and dishonest practices, particularly counterfeiting; these links, cited in the Islamic world, became more pronounced in Europe. Accordingly, Dante placed alchemists alongside forgers and counterfeiters in the eighth circle of Hell.[7] In 1317, Pope John XXII issued a decretal skeptical of transmutation and forbidding the sale of artificial metals. Similar decrees followed from secular authorities, motivated by practical concerns over counterfeiting and the debasement of the currency.

Alchemy thereafter became more secretive, employing authorial pseudonyms, *Decknamen*, and allegory more extensively. Many allegories were drawn from Christian concepts. As Zosimos had compared his treatment of metals to torments and sacrifice, so did some Christian authors compare their treatments of materials in making the Philosophers' Stone to Christ's passion, death, and resurrection. Fourteenth-century authors such as John of Rupescissa and pseudo-Arnald of Villanova wrote explicitly that they were describing laboratory operations in metaphorical terms; however, they also *expected* analogical affinities to exist between material and spiritual aspects of the world. Such allegorical speech was later (ca. 1400) cast into pictorial format, giving rise to emblematic depictions of alchemical processes and ideas.[8]

### 4 Early Modern Alchemy (or "Chymistry")

The sixteenth and seventeenth centuries, commonly called the "scientific revolution," saw alchemy's greatest flowering. It is crucial to note, however, that throughout its Arabic and European history, alchemy encompassed more than chrysopoeia. The preparation of an array of chemical materials – pigments, dyes, pharmaceuticals, perfumes, acids, salts, and so forth – as well as theories of material composition also fell under alchemy's rubric. Indeed, until circa 1700 "alchemy" and "chemistry" were largely synonymous terms; hence, historians have suggested using the term "chymistry" to refer to this

---

[6] See William R. Newman, "Technology and Alchemical Debate in the Late Middle Ages," *Isis* 80 (1989), 423–445.
[7] Dante, *La divina commedia*, Canto XXIX.
[8] See Barbara Obrist, *Les débuts de l'imagerie alchimique* (Paris: Le Sycomore, 1982); *Rosarium philosophorum: Ein alchemisches Florilegium des Spätmittelalters*, ed. Joachim Telle, 2 vols. (Weinheim: VCH, 1992).

undifferentiated domain to avoid the connotations now attached to "alchemy" (old and discredited) and "chemistry" (modern and scientific).[9] Chymistry was ubiquitous in early modern Europe. Thousands of practitioners from all ranks of society pursued it for diverse reasons. Some saw chrysopoeia as a "get rich quick" scheme and ruined themselves in its pursuit. Some chymists found employment in princely courts; some signed contracts with rulers to make gold or improve mining extractions – failure under such conditions could result in imprisonment or execution.[10] Still others used chymical techniques and processes (in refining, mining, pharmacy, or other manufactures) to earn a middle-class living. More educated or leisured practitioners engaged in lengthy practical investigations, developing or refining chymical theories and writing scholarly treatises – ranging from straightforward to highly allegorical and secretive. Many respected figures of the scientific revolution also studied chrysopoeia seriously, such as Robert Boyle, John Locke, and Isaac Newton. Chymical emblemata flourished not only as veiled communication but also as learned play and art. Painters depicted chymists at work, and poets and preachers alike borrowed images and concepts – especially those dealing with distillation, purification, and transformation – for use as metaphors in their own works.[11]

Medicinal applications represent an important addition to chymistry. Although originating in the Middle Ages, medical chymistry (iatrochemistry) owes much of its establishment to Theophrastus of Hohenheim, called Paracelsus (1493/94–1541). Paracelsus used chymistry primarily for medicine and was little interested in chrysopoeia. Through *Scheidung* (separation), ordinary materials could be freed of impurities and toxins and transformed into medicines. Paracelsus expanded the Mercury-Sulphur dyad by adding Salt to provide the *tria prima* – a material trinity reflecting the immaterial Trinity. Division of a substance into its *tria prima* and recombination of these

---

[9] William R. Newman and Lawrence M. Principe, "Alchemy vs. Chemistry: The Etymological Origins of a Historiographic Mistake," *Early Science and Medicine* 3 (1998):32–65; also Robert Halleux, *Textes alchimiques* (Turnhout: Brepols, 1979), 43–49.

[10] Tara Nummedal, *Alchemy and Authority in the Holy Roman Empire* (Chicago: University of Chicago Press, 2007); Bruce Moran, *The Alchemical World of the German Court, Sudhoffs Archiv* 29 (Stuttgart: Steiner Verlag, 1991); Pamela H. Smith, *The Business of Alchemy: Science and Culture in the Holy Roman Empire* (Princeton: Princeton University Press, 1994).

[11] Lawrence M. Principe and Lloyd Dewitt, *Transmutations: Alchemy in Art* (Philadelphia: Chemical Heritage Foundation, 2002); Stanton J. Linden, *Darke Hieroglyphicks: Alchemy in English Literature from Chaucer to the Restoration* (Lexington: University Press of Kentucky, 1996); Sylvain Matton, "Thématique alchimique et litterature religieuse dans la France du XVIIe siècle," *Chrysopoeia* 2 (1988), 129–208; Sylvia Fabrizio-Costa, "De quelques emplois des thèmes alchimiques dans l'art oratoire italien du XVIIe siècle," *Chrysopoeia* 3 (1989), 135–162.

purified essentials – a process called *spagyria* – "perfected" the substance, allowing it to manifest its properties most powerfully. Paracelsus's chymical world-system embraced both theology and natural philosophy. Chymical processes provided fundamental models for natural processes in the macrocosm (the world) and the microcosm (the human body). He envisioned everything from digestion to the weather and God's creation of the world out of chaos as chymical processes. Later followers organized Paracelsus's often obscurantist and chaotic system; thus, Paracelsianism proved extremely influential.[12]

Jacob Boehme (1575–1624) deployed Paracelsian language in his complex theology. (The Lutheran cobbler borrowed ideas from astronomy and other disciplines as well.) For Boehme, the *tria prima* are not constituents of material substances but rather aspects of God. Boehme's *Salitter* is a nexus of divine creative powers, while the name refers to sal niter (potassium nitrate), a salt that displays physical properties analogous to the spiritual ones of the divine Salitter.[13] Boehme's terminological borrowings, however, are quite distinct from contemporaneous chymistry.

The relationship between chymistry and religion is complex. While it is often claimed that alchemy bears a special relationship to religion, the links between the two reflect broader interrelationships between religion and *all* early modern natural philosophy. For example, many chrysopoeians called the Philosophers' Stone a *Donum dei* (gift of God); in doing so, they both acknowledged the ultimate source of all good and elevated their knowledge to privileged status. Yet this denomination, understood in the context of contemporaneous piety, does not mean that alchemists viewed the Stone as something spiritual or something acquired miraculously without laboratory work, or that their goals and practices were radically different from those of other contemporaneous practitioners. The Stone's preparation, although considered knowledge of the highest kind, is a *Donum dei* in much the same way as a laborious farmer's harvest, an assiduous scholar's rare knowledge, or a theologian's special insights.

Heinrich Khunrath (ca. 1560–1605) provides another example. While often loosely cited as a "spiritual alchemist," Khunrath was clear about the physical nature of preparing the Stone. Nevertheless, he also asserted the

---

[12] Didier Kahn, *Alchimie et Paracelsisme en France (1567–1625)*, (Geneva: Droz, 2007); Walter Pagel, *Paracelsus: An Introduction to Philosophical Medicine in the Era in the Renaissance* (Basel: Karger, 1958); Allen G. Debus, *The Chemical Philosophy: Paracelsian Science and Medicine in the Sixteenth and Seventeenth Centuries*, 2 vols. (New York: Science History Publications, 1977).
[13] Andrew Weeks, *Boehme: An Intellectual Biography of the Seventeenth Century Philosopher and Mystic* (Albany: State University of New York Press, 1991), esp. pp. 65–69.

value of theurgical practices for gaining knowledge of secrets, and emphasized analogies between physical and spiritual, for example, between the Philosopher's Stone and Christ.[14] Drawing and relying on such analogies was widespread in early modern thought of all kinds.

Despite ubiquitous metaphorical linkages to theological and spiritual matters, the overwhelming majority of chymical books and manuscripts indicate that virtually all early modern alchemists strove to prepare in their workshops a material Philosophers' Stone that operated purely naturally to transmute base metals into gold. Only a few writers envisioned *literal* connections between chymical products and the supernatural. Robert Boyle (1627–1691), for example, sought to prepare the Stone for transmutational and medicinal purposes but also thought that it might facilitate communication with angels.[15]

Early modern chymical practices enriched commerce and medicine, chymical theories provided ideas and concepts for natural philosophy, and chymical experiments revealed the workings of nature. Yet chymistry suffered from a poor public image in the seventeenth century, partly due to the dirty, laborious nature of its practice, and partly due to the long-standing association of chrysopoeia with counterfeiting and fraud.

## 5 Reevaluations and Revivals of Alchemy

The early eighteenth century witnessed the dramatic collapse of chrysopoeia. In 1700, pursuit of transmutation remained strong, but by 1725 it had largely disappeared from view in many (but not all) national contexts. On one hand, the increasing professionalization of chemistry virtually required a repudiation of chrysopoeia, the topic within chymistry that had brought the whole discipline into disrepute. Consequently, period refutations of chrysopoeia depended not on new experiments or theoretical structures disproving transmutation but rather on moral and social denunciations of chrysopoeia as fraud.[16] On the other, the increased role for non-transmutational chymistry (e.g,. in commerce and medicine) meant that the chymically interested

---

[14] Peter Forshaw, "Alchemy in the Amphitheatre: Some Considerations of the Alchemical Content of the Engravings in Heinrich Khunrath's *Amphitheatre of Eternal Wisdom* (1609)" in Jacob Wamberg, *Alchemy and Art* (Copenhagen: Museum Tusculanum Press, 2006), 195–220.

[15] Lawrence M. Principe, *The Aspiring Adept: Robert Boyle and His Alchemical Quest* (Princeton: Princeton University Press, 1998).

[16] On the demise of chrysopoeia, see Lawrence M. Principe, *Wilhelm Homberg and the Transmutations of Chymistry* (forthcoming), and until then, "A Revolution Nobody Noticed? Changes in Early Eighteenth Century Chymistry," in *New Narratives in Eighteenth-Century Chemistry*, ed. Lawrence M. Principe (Dordrecht: Springer, 2007), 1–22.

could easily find more promising activities than seeking the Stone. The result was a sundering of the terms "alchemy" and "chemistry" into nearly their modern connotations. The "chemical" part of chymistry continued into an increasingly accepted and useful scientific discipline; the "alchemical" part was repudiated as delusion and dishonesty.

Enlightenment partisans made alchemy an exemplar of the outdated and unenlightened. They set it in opposition to the new chemistry and regularly associated it with witchcraft, magic, and necromancy. It is largely to this period that we owe the notion of alchemy as magical, superstitious, and foolish. Although the serious pursuit of chrysopoeia greatly diminished, some work continued "underground," including among some prominent chemists; indeed, it persists to this day. One early reemergence occurred in late eighteenth-century German secret societies such as the *Freimaurer* and *Gold- und Rosenkreuzer*. Their alchemical activities included running communal laboratories and republishing alchemical classics. Significantly, their alchemy was predominantly practical – manufacturing pharmaceuticals and seeking the Philosopher's Stone – and thus extended work typical of the seventeenth century.[17]

The greatest rupture in the history of alchemy began in the mid-nineteenth century. In 1850, Mary Anne Atwood claimed that alchemists of earlier ages were really practitioners of Mesmerism or "animal magnetism"– a practice then in vogue in Britain.[18] She claimed that alchemical practice was not physical but spiritual; it had no connection to chemistry but aimed at the purification and development of the practitioner. In self-induced Mesmeric trances, alchemists endeavored "magnetically" to draw in "Ether" and condense it within themselves into an incorporeal Philosophers' Stone, an agent of universal change and advancement.[19] Atwood's reading obviously has no historical validity. Nevertheless, her ideas propagated widely in the subsequent Victorian occult revival. The notion of alchemy as a self-transformative psychic practice originates predominantly with Victorian occultists.[20]

---

[17] Renko Geffarth, *Religion und arkane Hierarchie: der Orden der Gold- und Rosenkreuzer als geheime Kirche im 18. Jahrhundert* (Leiden: Brill, 2007), 242–265; Christopher McIntosh, *The Rose Cross and the Age of Reason: Eighteenth Century Rosicrucianism in Central Europe and Its Relationship to the Enlightenment* (Leiden: Brill, 1992).

[18] Mary Anne Atwood, *A Suggestive Inquiry into the Hermetic Mystery* (London: T. Saunders, 1850); on Mesmerism, see the essay in this volume.

[19] Atwood, *Suggestive Inquiry*, esp. pp. 78–85, 96–98, 162, 454–455.

[20] For more details, Lawrence M. Principe and William R. Newman, "Some Problems in the Historiography of Alchemy," in *Secrets of Nature: Astrology and Alchemy in Early Modern Europe*, ed. William Newman and Anthony Grafton (Cambridge, MA: MIT Press, 2001), 385–434; see especially pp. 388–401.

This Victorian perspective influenced the psychologist Herbert Silberer and, later, the celebrated formulations of Swiss psychoanalyst Carl Gustav Jung. Jung claimed that alchemy deals "not with chemical experimentations as such, but with something resembling psychic processes expressed in pseudo-chemical language."[21] He claimed that alchemy involved a hallucinatory state wherein the alchemists' psyche was "projected" onto their materials. In other words, during laboratory work, alchemists fell into an altered state of consciousness in which their unconscious produced hallucinations reflecting mental contents and activity, not unlike dream images. Thus, Jung claimed that alchemical texts really describe the unconscious, and that the alchemist's "experience had nothing to do with matter in itself."[22]

Jung's views proved enormously influential throughout the twentieth century. While his interpretations may have interest and value as objects of study in their own right, they are not historically valid explanations of alchemy; they have been thoroughly refuted by scholars working in various fields.[23] The extravagant alchemical language and imagery that Jung thought to be "irruptions of the unconscious" have been decoded into replicable laboratory procedures and their *conscious* creation as methods of secrecy has now been well documented.[24]

## 6 Conclusion

Alchemy boasts a rich and diverse history. Careful scholarship of the past forty years has corrected many errors and revealed much new information. There is now no question that alchemy (or chymistry) played a significant

---

[21] Carl Gustav Jung, "Die Erlösungsvorstellungen in der Alchemie," *Eranos-Jahrbuch 1936* (Zurich: Rhein-Verlag, 1937), 13–111; English translation "The Idea of Redemption in Alchemy," in *The Integration of the Personality*, ed. Stanley Dell (New York: Farrar & Rinehart, 1939), 205–280, quotation from p. 210. Jung's contributions on alchemy are in *The Collected Works of Carl Gustav Jung*, 20 vols. (London: Routledge, 1953–79), vol. 9, pt. 2: *Aion*; vol. 12: *Psychology and Alchemy*; vol. 13: *Alchemical Studies*; vol. 14: *Mysterium Coniunctionis*.

[22] Jung, "Idea of Redemption," 206, 213, 215; "Erlösungsvorstellungen," 23–24.

[23] E.g., Obrist, *Les débuts*, 11–21 and 33–36; Principe and Newman, "Some Problems," 401–408; Dan Merkur, "Methodology and the Study of Western Spiritual Alchemy," *Theosophical History* 8 (2000), 53–70; Halleux, *Textes alchimiques*, 55–58.

[24] Lawrence M. Principe, "Apparatus and Reproducibility in Alchemy," in *Instruments and Experimentation in the History of Chemistry*, ed. Frederic L. Holmes and Trevor Levere (Cambridge, MA: MIT Press, 2000), 55–74; William R. Newman, "Decknamen or 'Pseudochemical Language'? Eirenaeus Philalethes and Carl Jung," *Revue d'histoire des sciences* 49 (1996), 159–188; and William R. Newman and Lawrence M. Principe, *Alchemy Tried in the Fire: Starkey, Boyle, and the Fate of Helmontian Chymistry* (Chicago: University of Chicago Press, 2002), especially pp. 177–195.

role in the history of science, contributing to chemical and medical theories and practices, technical production, experimentalism, and the understanding of the natural world. Considerable further work is both needed and now underway to address continuing questions. At present, however, we have learned that we must view "historical alchemy" (from Late Antiquity to the Enlightenment) on its own terms and in its due historical context, rather than reading nineteenth- and twentieth-century developments back into it.

# 31

# ASTROLOGY

Kocku von Stuckrad

## 1 Introduction: Astrology Defined

Astrology (from Greek, "science of the stars") belongs to the oldest cultural phenomena of humankind. Its persistence from antiquity to modernity – despite many transformations and various developments – is remarkable. If we want to define this phenomenon, we can say that, most generally, astrology engages the supposed relationship and correspondences between the heavenly realm (the stars, planets, zodiacal signs, etc.) and the earthly realm. To interpret these correspondences and interrelationships, astrology developed different and often conflicting strategies. On the one hand, astrologers asserted a *causal* influence of heavenly bodies on the sublunar world, which consequently seems to lead to a deterministic or even fatalistic worldview. Ancient Greek philosophers – particularly the Stoics – spoke of the cosmos as a complex network of correspondences and influences, governed by a hidden power. On the other hand, astrologers argued that the stars do not exert influence themselves but that they are mere "signs" or "symbols" of powers that are active throughout the cosmos. The intellectual, religious, and ethical issues that are linked to these alternatives have been part of astrological discussion ever since. Are the heavenly signs simply accompanying the mundane events, or are they responsible for them? And if there is a sympathetic correspondence between the celestial sphere and the earth, does this necessarily imply a deterministic or fatalistic influence?

The answers to these questions evidently challenge philosophical and religious convictions. Particularly in Western scriptural religions, a deterministic interpretation of astrology was often seen as problematic because it seems to eliminate freedom, the prerequisite of moral action and the precondition of redemption, punishment, and sin. Not surprisingly, then, it was the second alternative that gained the upper hand in Western cultural history:

The stars were deprived of their divine power and were seen as mere "instruments of God," their path interpreted as "God's handwriting" (already in Origen's *Philocalia*).[1]

The search for underlying principles in the correspondence between heavenly and earthly realms brought forth several fields of interest that can be distinguished as different areas of astrological practice. Already at an early stage, the prediction of agricultural matters and weather conditions was made on an astrological basis. This could mean that eclipses of the sun and moon, conjunctions of planets, or the paths of individual planets were correlated with climatic conditions. In addition, an astrological theory was developed that purported to predict the outcome of an initiative (a war, business venture, foundation of a city, etc.) on the basis of the horoscope cast for the moment the initiative was undertaken.

The reading of an individual birth chart was a relatively late development (after the fourth century BCE), although in antiquity there already was a complex theory available concerning this field of astrological practice. Usually the individual was the king or another high-ranking person, whose horoscope thus represented not only a forecast of an individual's life course but also that of the political or religious community as well. Although today the main focus of astrological practice is on the interpretation of individual nativities, we should not forget that the move from "mundane astrology" to "individual astrology" happened only after the Renaissance and was further fostered by the development of "psychological astrology" in the twentieth century. I will explain this in more detail when I present a historical overview. Before doing so, however, it is necessary to discuss the relationship between astrology and what is usually referred to as "Western esotericism."

## 2 Astrology and Esoteric Discourse

When we look at publications in the field of Western esotericism, it is striking that despite their different approaches there seems to be little doubt among scholars that astrology is an important part or "discipline" of esotericism. This, however, is by no means self-evident. Why would scholars choose to disconnect astrology from the history of science and philosophy, or from disciplines such as medicine and politics? Questions such as these lead us directly into historical developments that are of quite recent origin. It may

---

[1] See Kocku von Stuckrad, *Das Ringen um die Astrologie: Jüdische und christliche Beiträge zum antiken Zeitverständnis* (Berlin: Walter de Gruyter, 2000), 771–782; Tamson Barton, *Ancient Astrology* (London: Routledge, 1994), 75–76.

even be argued that the lumping together of astrology and esotericism is itself characteristic of a cultural dynamic that came to full fruition after the Enlightenment. In the service of that ideology, astrology was pushed away to the margins of science and reason, a development that served the modern view of Western identity as enlightened, rational, and immune from its religious and mythical past.[2]

In general, the discourses of inclusion and exclusion that have accompanied the process of forming the modern identity have affected the way in which scholars describe the status of astrology. Besides labels such as "pseudo-science" or "superstition," astrology has often been called an "occult science." This term probably originated in the sixteenth century, along with notions of *occulta philosophia*. "Occult," in this context, refers to hidden or secret powers that inform a substantial part of the disciplines lumped together under the rubric "occult sciences" – notably astrology, alchemy, and magic.[3] Twentieth-century scholars turned this rubric from an *emic* (an "insider's") into an *etic* (an "outsider's") category, positing a unity to these various disciplines. While Keith Thomas believed that astrology formed the basis of the occult sciences – and that consequently the "decline" of astrology would inevitably lead to the decline of magic and alchemy – Brian Vickers encouraged this interpretive trend by arguing that all "occult sciences" share a common mentality that is clearly distinguishable from a rational, "scientific" mentality.[4]

However, such a distinction is problematic for several reasons. First, although these disciplines overlap in varied and complex ways, all of them have distinct histories with quite different and complex intersecting trajectories. As William R. Newman and Anthony Grafton put it, "Even during the heyday of Renaissance neoplatonism, astrology and alchemy lived independent lives, despite the vast inkwells devoted to the rhetorical embellishment of occult philosophy."[5] Second, other disciplines and practices had

---

[2] See Charles Zika, *Exorcising Our Demons: Magic, Witchcraft, and Visual Culture in Early Modern Europe* (Leiden: Brill, 2003), 4.
[3] In an influential work, Wayne Shumaker also adds witchcraft to this mélange; see his *The Occult Sciences in the Renaissance: A Study in Intellectual Patterns* (Berkeley: University of California Press, 1972).
[4] Keith Thomas, *Religion and the Decline of Magic: Studies in Popular Beliefs in Sixteenth- and Seventeenth-Century England* (London: Weidenfeld and Nicholson, 1971), 631–632; Brian Vickers, "On the Function of Analogy in the Occult," in *Hermeticism in the Renaissance*, ed. A. G. Debus and Ingrid Merkel (Washington, DC: Folger Books, 1988), 265–292, at p. 286; see also *Occult and Scientific Mentalities in the Renaissance*, ed. Brian Vickers (Cambridge: Cambridge University Press, 1984).
[5] William R. Newman and Anthony Grafton, "Introduction: The Problematic Status of Astrology and Alchemy in Premodern Europe," in *Secrets of Nature: Astrology and Alchemy*

direct and long-standing links to astrology, especially mathematics, philosophy (natural and moral), medicine, historiography, theology, and politics. Configuring astrology with the other so-called occult sciences tends strongly to distort our understanding of its relationship with these other areas of knowledge. Third, the heuristic notion of "hidden powers" continues to remain important within the more "legitimate" sciences, from the scientific revolution to the present. Fourth, it is difficult to demonstrate that astrology is "irrationalism," given that astrology (Latin *ars mathematica*) was part of the curriculum taught in universities until the seventeenth century and that it was based on empirical and rational methods of argumentation.[6]

Indeed, it is important to note that until the eighteenth century, astrology had been intrinsically linked to astronomy, mathematics, natural philosophy, and medicine.[7] Thus, the fact that astrology was subsumed under the artificial category of occult sciences has to do, again, with the formation of a modern self-understanding that seeks to distance itself from these disciplines. But it is precisely in terms of the interface of science, philosophy, religion, and other cultural phenomena that the role of astrology in the West must be understood.

Why then, one might ask, should astrology be studied as part of Western esotericism, mysticism, or Hermeticism? If astrology is closely linked to the history of science, to natural philosophy, and to other cultural domains, it is difficult to escape the impression that connecting it to esotericism is nothing more than a prolongation of the Enlightenment agenda of marginalizing astrology. In fact, as I have argued elsewhere,[8] the entire scholarly field of esotericism should be integrated or even dissolved into an analysis of the dynamics that are operative in European history of culture. Notwithstanding

---

in *Early Modern Europe*, ed. Newman and Grafton (Cambridge, MA, and London: MIT Press, 2001), 26.

[6] I deal with this topic in more detail in *Geschichte der Astrologie: Von den Anfängen bis zur Gegenwart*, 2nd ed. (Munich: C. H. Beck, 2007); see the index for "Empirie" and "Astrologie und wissenschaftliche Methode." Cf. Lynn Thorndike, "The True Place of Astrology in the History of Science," *Isis* 46:3 (1955), 273–278.

[7] See, for instance, H. Darrel Rutkin, "Astrology, Natural Philosophy and the History of Science, ca. 1250–1700: Studies toward an Interpretation of Giovanni Pico della Mirandola's Disputationes adversus astrologiam divinatricem" (Ph.D. dissertation, Indiana University, Bloomington, 2002); Monica Azzolini, "Reading Health in the Stars: Politics and Medical Astrology in Renaissance Milan," in *Horoscopes and Public Spheres: Essays on the History of Astrology*, ed. Günther Oestmann, H. Darrel Rutkin, and Kocku von Stuckrad (Berlin: Walter de Gruyter, 2005), 183–205.

[8] Kocku von Stuckrad, *Locations of Knowledge in Medieval and Early Modern Europe: Esoteric Discourse and Western Identities* (Leiden and Boston: Brill, 2010), particularly chaps. 1–3.

this methodological caution, let us see whether there is more to say about astrology, esotericism, and Hermeticism.

If we conceptualize esotericism as a discourse of "perfect knowledge" involving a dialectic of concealment and revelation, astrology is seen as a means to unlock hidden knowledge of the universe and to grant human beings perfect understanding of the ultimate meaning of existence and of human history. As an example of this, we may consider the concept of the so-called Great Conjunctions of Jupiter and Saturn elaborated by Abū Ma'shar in the ninth century, and subsequently applied to Shi'ite, Jewish, and Christian apocalyptic speculation. But even here, we should not forget that the best astrologers have never claimed that astrology offers perfect understanding or knowledge; rather, astrology has usually been understood to be conjectural or probable knowledge.

When it comes to Hermeticism, a similar observation can be made. There is no reason to assume that astrology as such is hermetic, or that there exist intrinsic links between astrology and Hermeticism.[9] On the other hand, the figure of Hermes Trismegistus has featured prominently in the legitimization of astrological doctrines from antiquity through the twentieth century. Early on, Mercury, Hermes, and Hermes-Thot were credited as significant representatives of astral knowledge. Subsequently, Jews combined this tradition with their understanding of Enoch and Metatron as revelatory entities that knew "the secrets of the heavens." Muslims, for their part, blended this idea with the figure of Idris. The result is a rich and complex literary, iconographic,[10] and magical tradition centering on the figure of Hermes as the revealer of astrological knowledge. Interestingly enough, the authority of Hermes Trismegistus was so strong that leading scholars of the scientific revolution still legitimated their new astronomical models with reference to him. Nicholas Copernicus, for instance, in the tenth chapter of his *De revolutionibus orbium coelestium* (1543), justified the importance of the sun as

---

[9] The only exception perhaps is the doctrine of correspondences that is a basic component of astrology (even if a causal relationship between objects is assumed, see von Stuckrad, *Geschichte der Astrologie*, 16) and at the same time is reminiscent of the alleged Hermetic doctrine of "as above, so below."

[10] The iconographic tradition of the zodiac in the Muslim Middle Ages has been studied by Anna Caiozzo, *Images du ciel d'Orient au Moyen Âge: Une histoire du zodiaque et de ses représentations dans les manuscrits du Proche-Orient musulman* (Paris: Presses de l'Université de Paris-Sorbonne, 2003), with many references to Hermes. An important publication is also Jean-Patrice Boudet, *Entre science et nigromance: Astrologie, divination et magie dans l'Occident médiéval (XIIe–XVe siècle)* (Paris: Publications de la Sorbonne, 2006).

the center of the universe with the assertion of the "Thrice Greatest" that the sun was a "visible god."[11]

The example of Copernicus shows how problematic it is to approach esotericism and Hermeticism as "marginal" or "suppressed" parts of Western culture. When scholars today conceptualize Western esotericism with reference to traditions that have been neglected or marginalized by mainstream culture, they are – unwittingly, to be sure – part of a discursive formation that has taken shape during the past three hundred years. This discourse is characterized by what may be called a "strategy of distancing," or a "process of disjunction." These disjunctive strategies artificially distinguished astrology from astronomy, alchemy from chemistry, magic from science, and so on. Self-evident as these disjunctions may seem to the modern reader, they are in fact of quite recent origin. As scholars, we should not apply the rhetoric of synecdoche here and take relatively recent phenomena as representing the West in all its history.[12]

Astrology should be studied as part of the history of science, philosophy, mathematics, medicine, politics, historiography, art, and religion. Only when it comes to the revelation of hidden, perfect knowledge by means of astrological methods does it make sense to speak of esoteric astrology.

## 3 The History of Astrology in Western Culture: An Overview

The origins of Western astrology lie in the Mesopotamian cultures of the third millennium BCE. From the fifth century BCE onward, both the zodiacal scheme – with twelve zodiacal signs of equal size – and horoscopic astrology were developed. In this process, the influence of Greek mathematics and astronomy played an important role. Later, some elements of Egyptian tradition were adopted, as well. In Imperial Rome, a full-blown astronomical and astrological science was available that is usually referred to as "classical astrology."[13] This tradition was canonized by Claudius Ptolemy (ca. 100–178 CE) in his *Syntaxis mathematica* (for astronomy) and *Tetrabiblos* (for astrology).

Despite the fact that ancient scholars differentiated the calculating and the interpreting branch of the science of the stars, the utter devaluation of

---

[11] See von Stuckrad, *Geschichte der Astrologie*, 255.
[12] For a critique of these approaches to Western esotericism, see von Stuckrad, *Locations of Knowledge*, chap. 3.
[13] As important works on ancient astrology, see Auguste Bouché-Leclercq, *L"astrologie Grecque* (Paris: Ernest Leroux, 1899); Wilhelm Gundel and Hans Georg Gundel, *Astrologumena: Die astrologische Literatur in der Antike und ihre Geschichte* (Wiesbaden: Franz Steiner, 1966); Tamsyn Barton, *Ancient Astrology* (London and New York: Routledge, 1994).

astrology vis-à-vis astronomy is a modern phenomenon that led – in the aftermath of the scientific revolution – to the dismantling of astrology from the accepted sciences. In antiquity, however, astrology held a key position among the reputable sciences. As *ars mathematica* closely connected with astronomy, it made its way into the highest political and philosophical orders of the Roman Empire and became the standard model of interpreting past, present, and future events.[14]

In the Middle Ages, astrological theory – both calculative and interpretative – was expanded on, particularly by Muslim scholars. While Christian astrologers usually clung to a few Latin sources of late antiquity seen as compatible with Christian theology, Muslim and Jewish scholars absorbed theories of Indian astrology, combined them with the Greek and Latin sources of Roman times, and developed complex and mathematically more exact hermeneutical systems. From the ninth century onward, Christian circles increasingly felt the need to catch up with Muslim and Jewish science, and in many monasteries translations of Arabic texts were provided. The interaction between scholars of different religious backgrounds was particularly fruitful in Spain and Italy, leading to a shared astrological field of discourse in the High Middle Ages.

Characterized by a new interest in Platonism and the availability of rediscovered Greek Hermetic texts in Latin translation, the period between 1450 and 1650 can be seen as the pinnacle of astrological research in Europe. Astrology played a decisive role in religious controversies and discussions both intra-faith and interfaith. One example of this is the debate about the cycles of historical development that were interpreted with reference to the cycle of Great Conjunctions between Jupiter and Saturn, a theory mentioned earlier. Already a part of ancient discourse, the theory of the cyclical succession of religions, kingdoms, and powers on the basis of Great Conjunctions was developed by medieval Muslim astrologers. Shi'ite scholars interpreted these events as indications of the return of the "hidden Imam." Jews joined this debate with prognostications of messianic events, and Christians referred to the Great Conjunctions as signs for the second coming of Christ. The interconfessional debate about Luther's horoscope, for instance, was strongly informed by speculations about the messianic impact of Great Conjunctions.

---

[14] On the political influence of astrologers in Rome, see Frederic H. Cramer, *Astrology in Roman Law and Politics* (Philadelphia: American Philosophical Society, 1954). On the dramatic change with regard to the legal status of astrology under the impact of Christian emperors, see Marie Theres Fögen, *Die Enteignung der Wahrsager: Studien zum kaiserlichen Wissensmonopol in der Spätantike* (Frankfurt am Main: Suhrkamp, 1993).

Within an apocalyptic and millennialist mindset, astrology was a key factor in the legitimation of identity and power.[15]

The scientific revolution changed the position of astrology in scholarly discourse. It is often argued that the crisis of astrology was due to the victory of the Copernican heliocentric model of the cosmos, while astrologers still clung to the geocentric Ptolemaic model. This is too simplistic, however.[16] Kepler, for instance, argued in several treatises that the heliocentric model would pose no problem for astrologers, because for astrology it makes no differences *how* the paths of the planets are to be explained. More important for the crisis of astrology, in fact, was that from the seventeenth century onward, radical empiricism gained the upper hand in scientific research. Empiricism led to a rejection of theories involving invisible (occult) powers in nature, and astrologers had serious problems in justifying their concepts of "sympathy" and "correspondences."

In the eighteenth century, astrology in Europe had completely lost its status as a scientific discipline – with the exception of England, where a continuous development of astrology is attested.[17] It was no longer part of university programs, a critical factor of the so-called decline of astrology. The result, however, was not that astrology vanished from intellectual discourse, but that it shifted from the realm of science to that of art and literature. Even before the era of Romanticism, astrology entered those cultural areas, for instance, in the writings of Schiller and Goethe, who made use of astrological symbolism to establish an alternative to Christian monotheism.[18] In the nineteenth century, then, astrology played a role in Romantic concepts of "living nature," concepts that challenged the then-dominant mechanistic materialism.

However, it was the Theosophical Society, founded in 1875, that was chiefly responsible for reawakening interest in astrology on the Continent.

---

[15] See Paola Zambelli, ed., *"Astrologi halluzinati": Stars and the End of the World in Luther's Time* (Berlin: Walter de Gruyter, 1986); Anthony Grafton, *Cardano's Cosmos: The Worlds and Works of a Renaissance Astrologer* (Cambridge, MA: Harvard University Press, 1999).

[16] Aside from the impact of the new scientific paradigms, it is important to note the influence of Pico della Mirandola's harsh refutation of astrology – or certain aspects of astrological theory that he refuted. On the response to Pico's critique, see Steven vanden Broecke, *The Limits of Influence: Pico, Louvain, and the Crisis of Renaissance Astrology* (Leiden and Boston: Brill, 2003).

[17] See Patrick Curry, *Prophecy and Power: Astrology in Early Modern England* (Cambridge: Polity Press, 1989); and his *A Confusion of Prophets: Victorian and Edwardian Astrology* (London: Collins and Brown, 1992).

[18] See Kocku von Stuckrad, "The Function of Horoscopes in Biographical Narrative: Cardano and After," in *Horoscopes and Public Spheres*, 225–240; von Stuckrad, *Geschichte der Astrologie*, 281–286.

The Theosophists developed mystical and karmic readings of astrological concepts that ran counter to the prognostic emphasis of older astrological currents. In the twentieth century, the growth of psychology provided a second major influence on the new appreciation, and reconfiguration of astrology. Now, it was the individual and the inner qualities of the human psyche that came to the fore. Certainly, without C. G. Jung's psychology and its adaptation in New Age culture, the history of astrology in the twentieth century would have been completely different.[19]

Today, the majority of professional astrologers cling to a non-deterministic, psychological concept of astrology. In all Western countries, societies have been founded that strive for the advancement of what they see as serious astrology, in a culture ambivalent about the science of the stars. While astrology is mostly neglected and ridiculed by scholars and scientists today, a significant percentage of the population in Europe and North America nonetheless still believes it can provide guidance in life. It is the task of the scholar of religion to analyze the underlying polemical structures and the discourses of modern identity formation that have led to this state of affairs, rather than taking sides for or against astrology.

---

[19] On modern astrology, see the overview in von Stuckrad, *Geschichte der Astrologie*, 287–368.

# 32

# GNOSIS

## WOUTER J. HANEGRAAFF

TO UNDERSTAND THE ROLE OF *gnosis* IN THE HISTORY OF Western esotericism, we must begin by detaching it from a too close and exclusive association with Gnosticism. *Gnosis* is Greek for "knowledge," and in the Hellenistic milieus of Late Antiquity, it was understood more specifically as a special kind of salvific knowledge by which the soul could be liberated from its material entanglement and regain its unity with the divine Mind.[1] The search for such salvation was by no means limited to gnostics; rather, it seems to have been the central preoccupation of a kind of "trans-confessional" cultic milieu that flourished particularly in Egypt, and whose adherents – whether they were pagans, Jews, or Christians – all interpreted (Middle) Platonic metaphysics in such a way as to transform it into religious worldviews with their own mythologies and ritual practices. This does not mean, however, that they themselves considered their religious beliefs as something new: On the contrary, the common assumption in this period was that the oldest was always best, and therefore the most ancient sages had been closest to divine truth.[2] Accordingly, even Plato himself was not supposed to have been an original thinker, but merely an important link in the chain of transmission of the ancient and universal spiritual wisdom, the origins of which could be traced back to the most ancient "barbarian" peoples of the Orient and their legendary sages: notably Hermes Trismegistus in Egypt and Zoroaster in Persia. To distinguish such perspectives from strictly

---

[1] Note that it would be artificial to consider the noun *gnosis* in isolation: It belongs to a complex semantic field consisting of several related families of words concerned with perception, cognition and intuition. See Brian P. Copenhaver, *Hermetica* (Cambridge: Cambridge University Press, 1992), 96.
[2] Arthur J. Droge, *Homer or Moses: Early Christian Interpretations of the History of Culture* (Tübingen: J. C. B. Mohr, 1989), 9 and *passim*.

philosophical Platonism, they will be referred to here as "Platonic Orientalism."[3]

Scholars have long tended to discuss this entire milieu in rather denigrating terms as an "underworld" of Platonism, a "murky area" full of "sub-philosophical phenomena,"[4] although we are clearly dealing with religious phenomena that should not be judged by the yardstick of philosophical rationalism but deserve to be taken seriously on their own terms. Traditional prejudices in this regard have slowly begun to vanish in recent scholarship, but what still remains is a tendency to focus more or less exclusively on philosophical and doctrinal matters while downplaying or ignoring the fact that when it comes to grasping the true mysteries of divinity, the sources never cease to emphasize the total inadequacy of discursive language.[5] It is precisely this point that is crucial to understanding what *gnosis* is all about. It implies that theoretical discussions about such matters as cosmogony, anthropology or eschatology, no matter how much space may be devoted to them or how interesting they may be to modern scholars, were considered of strictly secondary importance. As formulated in the Hermetic writings, reasoned discourse (*logos*) simply "does not lead as far as the truth."[6]

It follows that one should not expect the relevant sources to describe the contents of *gnosis*: At most, they contain stammering expressions of amazement and awe about a range of spiritual experiences that defy verbalization and can only be hinted at by very inadequate analogies. Rather than direct descriptions of *gnosis*, we find idealized narratives of how it has been attained by exemplary seekers such as Hermes Trismegistus and his pupil Tat. These figures are depicted as going through a series of ecstatic or "altered" states, which allow them to perceive progressively more exalted dimensions of reality beyond what is accessible to the five senses.[7] The direct perception of such spiritual dimensions, by means of "higher senses" equivalent but not identical to bodily hearing and sight, is what *gnosis* was all about. The

---

[3] Coined by John Walbridge, *The Wisdom of the Mystic East: Suhrawardī and Platonic Orientalism* (Albany: State University of New York Press, 2001), the term "Platonic Orientalism" makes explicit what was implied already by André-Jean Festugière, *La révélation d'Hermès Trismégiste*, vol. 1 (Paris: Les Belles Lettres, 1950), 19–44.

[4] John Dillon, *The Middle Platonists: A Study of Platonism 80 B.C. to A.D. 220* (London: Duckworth, 1977), 384; and cf. Majercik, *The Chaldean Oracles: Text, Translation, and Commentary* (Leiden: Brill, 1989), 3–4.

[5] Wouter J. Hanegraaff, "Altered States of Knowledge: The Attainment of Gnōsis in the Hermetica," *The International Journal of the Platonic Tradition* 2 (2008), 128–163; 129–130, and *passim*.

[6] C.H. IX: 10.

[7] See detailed analysis in Hanegraaff, "Altered States."

knowledge attained in this manner was salvific for at least three reasons. First, it is described as freely given from above, as a divine reward from the "realms of light" in response to the pupil's persistent efforts at transcending the realm of the senses and the human passions. Second, it claims to provide direct and irrefutable evidence not only that those realms of light really exist but also that it is possible for the pupil to enter them as his true home. They are no longer something to believe in blindly, or merely speculate and talk about: The pupil *knows*, for he has now seen and heard them himself. Third, the light of the divine realms is believed to be identical to the seeker's own essential nature; hence, the process of return means a radical end to alienation from one's own divine essence. It is not just that the seeker returns to the spiritual light from whence he has come, but he discovers that he *is* that light. This idea of "self knowledge as knowledge of God" is often conveyed by the image of a "divine spark" that has been trapped in matter and is now liberated from it and reunited with its source, but it is important to realize that that is just one possible conceptualization. For example, in the Hermetic *Poimandres*, the same point is made in an entirely different manner, by the dramatic image of the visionary looking for a long time into Poimandres's eyes and realizing that he is looking at himself: divine light looking at divine light.[8]

The Hermetic writings may be seen as paradigmatic of what *gnosis* must have meant in its original late Hellenistic context, but the term and its meaning came to be separated from each other in the later history of Western esotericism. The possibility of gaining direct access to the realms of light by means of ecstatic states was inherent in Platonic Orientalism; therefore, one should not be surprised to see it return in later developments of the same tradition, such as notably the Islamic esotericism of Suhrawardī:

> That there are dominating lights, that the Creator of all is a light, that the archetypes are among the dominating lights – the pure souls have often beheld this to be so when they have detached themselves from their bodily temples.... Whoso questions the truth of this... let him engage in mystical disciplines and service to those visionaries, that perchance he will, as one dazzled by the thunderbolt, see the light blazing in the Kingdom of Power and will witness the heavenly essences and lights that Hermes and Plato beheld.[9]

---

[8] C.H. I: 7–8; and see analysis in Hanegraaff, "Altered States," 139–140.
[9] Suhrawardī, *Ḥikmat al-ishrāq* II.2.165–166, trans. according to Suhrawardī, *The Philosophy of Illumination*, ed. and trans. by John Walbridge and Hossein Ziai (Provo, UT: Brigham Young University Press, 1999), 107–108.

In the Latin West, this tradition was eclipsed for many centuries. The Platonic and Hermetic writings known to the Middle Ages were mainly concerned with philosophical and cosmological problems; even the revival of Platonism (more precisely, of Platonic Orientalism) since the fifteenth century did not initially lead to anything resembling a rehabilitation of *gnosis*. The term was associated much too strongly with the gnostic heresies to be eligible as a positive category, and it is important to realize that in his epochal translation of *Corpus Hermeticum* I–XIV, Marsilio Ficino completely overlooked the special connotations of *gnosis* (translated as *cognitio*) and its cognates.[10] The term and its connotations simply did not register on the screen of Renaissance Platonism and Hermetism.

Nevertheless, it would have been strange if the humanists who were so busy studying and translating the entire referential corpus of Platonic Orientalism – the Hermetica, the *Chaldaean Oracles* (attributed to Zoroaster since George Gemistus Plethon), and a variety of Middle-Platonic and especially Neoplatonic writings – had remained entirely oblivious to its message of salvation. And indeed, although the term *gnosis* is never used, the kind of suprarational ecstatic knowledge to which it refers did become an important theme. One can see this already in the work of Ficino's contemporary Lodovico Lazzarelli, who translated the final three treatises of the *Corpus* and seems to have understood its basic message far better than the great Ficino: For Lazzarelli, the Hermetica were all about attaining salvific knowledge of one's own divine nature and origin by means of an ecstatic ascent back to the realm of light.[11] As for Ficino, his primary reference for the same idea seems to have been not the *Corpus Hermeticum* but Plato's *Phaedrus*, with its description of four divine "frenzies" (*furores*) that allow the famous "chariot of the soul" to make its ascent back to the divine.[12] In various later Renaissance thinkers, one can observe how Hermetic religiosity and the Platonic frenzies were associated to a point of virtual identity.[13] It is therefore reasonable to conclude that in this tradition of "ecstatic religion" on

---

[10] Wouter J. Hanegraaff, "How Hermetic Was Renaissance Hermetism? Reason and Gnosis from Ficino to Foix de Candale," in *Hermetism and Rationality*, ed. Jan Veenstra (Louvain: Peeters, 2010).

[11] See Lazzarelli's *Crater Hermetis*, in Wouter J. Hanegraaff and Ruud M. Bouthoorn, *Lodovico Lazzarelli (1447–1500): The Hermetic Writings and Related Documents* (Tempe: Arizona Center for Medieval and Renaissance Studies, 2005).

[12] Wouter J. Hanegraaff, "The Platonic Frenzies in Marsilio Ficino," in *Myths, Martyrs and Modernity*, ed. Jitse Dijkstra, Justin Kroesen, and Yme Kuiper (Brill: Leiden, 2009), 553–567.

[13] On du Preau and Foix-Candale, see Hanegraaff, "How Hermetic Was Renaissance Hermetism?"; on Agrippa, see Hanegraaff, "Better than Magic: Cornelius Agrippa and Lazzarellian Hermetism," *Magic, Ritual and Witchcraft* 4:1 (2009), 1–25.

Platonic-Hermetic foundations, the Late Antiquity tradition of *gnosis* survived incognito. Due to the wholly negative image of Gnosticism, it was to be expected that connections between Renaissance Platonism-Hermetism and the dualistic heresies of the first centuries would be drawn not by the defenders of the *prisca theologia* but by its critics. During the second half of the sixteenth century, largely under the impact of the witchcraft debate, various forms of anti-Platonism, and Protestant attacks on Roman Catholicism, it became increasingly common for polemicists to imagine historical "lineages of darkness" from Oriental barbarism (Egypt, Persia, Babylonia) to Pythagoras, Plato and Platonism, and from there to Gnosticism.[14] Eventually, this perspective gave rise to full-blown "histories of error" in which the spread of heresy was traced from its origins through the centuries, and up to the present. The culminating examples of this genre, known as "anti-apologeticism,"[15] were Ehregott Daniel Colberg's *Platonisch-Hermetisches Christentum* (1690–1691), which presented contemporary currents such as Paracelsism, Rosicrucianism, and Christian theosophy as latter-day manifestations of the perennial Platonic-Hermetic enemy; and Jacob Brucker's great *Historia Critica Philosophiae* (1742–1744), where it was described as the superstitious shadow of true philosophy.[16]

Interestingly, the virtual founder of the anti-apologetic genre, Jacob Thomasius, discussed the idea of *gnosis* much more explicitly than his successors: His pioneering *Schediasma Historicum* (1665) even carries the term in its full title.[17] For the Protestant Thomasius, *gnosis* was a core element of heresy, referring to the attempt (vain and illegitimate by definition, and closely linked to *curiositas*) to gain knowledge about divine realities by merely human means, independent of the biblical revelation. As such, he demarcated it from two other categories: the legitimate although limited knowledge gained by rational philosophy on the one hand, and the superior knowledge

---

[14] E.g., Johann Weyer, *De praestigiis Daemonum* (1563) II.3; Martin Del Rio, *Disquisitionum magicarum libri sex* (1599) I.3; Giovanni Battista Crispo, *De Platone caute legenda* (1594), Preface.
[15] That is to say, against the Patristic apologetic tradition: see Sicco Lehmann-Brauns, *Weisheit in der Weltgeschichte: Philosophiegeschichte zwischen Barock und Aufklärung* (Tübingen: Max Niemeyer, 2004).
[16] On Colberg, see Lehmann-Brauns, *Weisheit*, 223–265. On Brucker, see Wouter J. Hanegraaff, "Western Esotericism in Enlightenment Historiography: The Importance of Jacob Brucker," in *Constructing Tradition: Means and Myths of Transmission in Western Esotericism*, ed. Andreas Kilcher (Leiden: Brill, 2010).
[17] Jacob Thomasius, *Schediasma Historicum, quo, Occasione Definitiones vetustae, quâ Philosophia dicitur ΓΝΩΣΙΣ ΤΩΝ ΟΝΤΩΝ, varia discutiuntur* ... (Leipzig: Joh. Wittigau 1665); cf. Lehmann-Brauns, *Weisheit*, 21–111.

about divine things revealed by God and received by *pistis* (faith) on the other.[18] In Brucker, this triad corresponded with a distinction between (1) the true religion of biblical revelation, (2) the history of philosophy, and (3) the history of (crypto) pagan religion as the negative counterpart of both, containing essentially everything we nowadays study under the rubric of "Western esotericism." As the history of philosophy established its identity as an independent discipline from the eighteenth century on, it did so by sharply excluding the third category, which became academically homeless for centuries.

In Thomasius's analysis, the search for *gnosis* was highlighted as central to that third category, thus resulting in the suggestion of three essential "paths of knowledge": reason, faith, and *gnosis*. With hindsight, it was only a question of time before authors critical of Enlightenment rationality and science, but unwilling to simply return to Christian orthodoxy, would therefore begin to see *gnosis* in a more positive light.[19] In most such cases, however, the term was used not in the specific sense of a special type of salvific knowledge, but as a general label for the various currents in Late Antiquity (including, but not limited to, Gnosticism) to which we have been referring as Platonic Orientalism. Thus, Jacques Matter, who seems to have invented the term "esotericism," used Gnosticism and *gnosis* as synonyms and described them as "the introduction into Christianity of the cosmological and theosophical systems that had been the chief part of the ancient religions of the Orient."[20] The great historian of Christianity Ferdinand Christian Baur built on Matter's work and defined *gnosis* quite simply as philosophy of religion.[21] This was a smart move, which amounted to turning the third category of the anti-apologists (from Thomasius through Brucker) into a neutral one: The human attempt to investigate the divine mysteries was now presented not as punishable *hubris*, but as a legitimate pursuit that could be traced from the ancient gnostics through Jacob Boehme, culminating in Hegel's system of idealism. That *gnosis* was turning into a positive category in the circles of

[18] See analysis in Lehmann-Brauns, *Weisheit*, 89–99.
[19] As pointed out by Antoine Faivre, the term begins to make its first "timid" appearance in the context of Western esotericism in the early nineteenth century. See Faivre, "Le terme et la notion de 'gnose' dans les courants ésotériques occidentaux modernes (Essai de périodisation)," in *Les textes de Nag Hammadi: Histoire des Religions, Approches contemporaines*, ed. Jean-Pierre Mahé and Paul-Hubert Poirier (Paris: Institut de France, 2010).
[20] Jacques Matter, *Histoire critique du Gnosticisme, et de son influence sur les sectes religieuses et philosophiques des dix premiers siècles de l'ère chrétienne* (1828; 2nd ed., Strasbourg / Paris, 1843), 15.
[21] Ferdinand Christian Baur, *Die christliche Gnosis, oder die christliche Religions-Philosophie in ihrer geschichtlichen Entwicklung* (Tübingen, 1835), vii.

German idealists and admirers of Boehme is also demonstrated by the case of Franz van Baader, who presented "the true *gnosis*" as an alternative to linear causality in several of his essays.[22]

In the occultist milieus of the later nineteenth century, *gnosis* remained a general label for Platonic Orientalism, rather than for some special type of knowledge. Thus, in a chapter with the significant title "Christian Dogmas Derived from Heathen Philosophy," Helena P. Blavatsky declared that although the gnostics were destroyed, "the *Gnosis*, based on the secret science of sciences ... was never without its representatives in any age or country."[23] Examples were, among many others, Zoroaster, Abraham, Henoch, Moses, the three Hermeses Trismegisti, Pythagoras, Plato, Jesus, Philo, and the Kabbalah. Elsewhere, Blavatsky makes clear that for her *gnosis* is simply one of the synonyms of Theosophy.[24] In many later instances of the term in esoteric, occultist, or Traditionalist literature, from Blavatsky to the present, the pattern remains essentially the same: *Gnosis* stands quite generally for "the true wisdom" or "secret science" and its many representatives through the ages, who possessed a superior knowledge about the nature of reality and the divine.[25]

Parallel to the history of the term as such, the incognito survival of *gnosis* as ecstatic religion based on Platonic and Hermetic foundations did not cease with the Renaissance either. The notion of an "internal sense" by means of which the soul can perceive metaphysical realities beyond the realm of the normal senses continued in the *vernünftige Hermetik* of the late eighteenth to the nineteenth centuries, closely connected to the search for a "higher reason" superior to Enlightenment rationality and a "higher knowledge" reaching beyond the domain of natural science.[26] That the appeal to *gnosis* could serve the agendas of the Enlightenment, remarkable though this might seem at first, may be illustrated here using the example of a rationalist paraphrase of the Old Testament published in 1735, where the snake tells Eve: "God knows that you will receive a great illumination when you eat

---

[22] See discussion in Faivre, "La terme et la notion."
[23] H. P. Blavatsky, *Isis Unveiled: A Master-Key to the Mysteries of Ancient and Modern Science and Theology* (1877; reprinted Pasadena: Theosophical University Press, 1972), 38.
[24] H. P. Blavatsky, "What Is Theosophy?," *The Theosophist* 1:1 (1879), 2–5.
[25] Many examples are discussed in Faivre, "La terme et la notion."
[26] Rolf Christian Zimmermann, *Das Weltbild des jungen Goethe: Studien zur Hermetischen Tradition des Deutschen 18. Jahrhunderts* (Munich: Wilhelm Fink, 1969/1979), vol. 1, 11–43; Monika Neugebauer-Wölk, "'Höhere Vernunft' und 'höheres Wissen' als Leitbegriffe in der esoterischen Gesellschaftsbewegung: Vom Nachleben eines Renaissancekonzepts im Jahrhundert der Aufklärung," in *Aufklärung und Esoterik*, ed. Neugebauer-Wölk (Hamburg: Felix Meiner, 1999), 170–210.

from this fruit: yes, you will receive a divine intellect and attain to a higher knowledge."[27] While such a passage clearly served Enlightenment polemics against ecclesiastical dogmatism, criticized for trying to keep man ignorant, it implied a criticism of rationalist dogmatism as well: the limitations of the merely human intellect could be transcended in the attainment of a superior and divine knowledge. Thus, even though the term *gnosis* is not used here, we are dealing with yet another example of a positive reversal of Thomasius's triad.

Just as in Late Antiquity, the attainment of higher knowledge as an alternative to strict rationalism and blind faith still appeared to require an altered state of consciousness. In the late eighteenth century and continuing through the nineteenth, the techniques discovered by Franz Anton Mesmer and his successors appeared to make it possible to induce conditions of artificial sleep, or trance, during which many so-called somnambules claimed spectacular visions of invisible spiritual realms and their inhabitants.[28] In the post-Kantian era, such experiences were often interpreted as proof that the categories of time, space, and causality could be transcended after all, making it possible to gain direct access to the noumenal realm of spirit: In such a manner, it was claimed, one could gain direct experiential knowledge of the metaphysical reality from whence the human soul had come and to which it would return.[29] In the same context, the implicit (and often explicit) polemics against Enlightenment could lead to fascinating mutations of the light versus darkness metaphor. Thus Gotthilf Heinrich von Schubert, a key author in this context, conceptualized the spiritual realms as the "Nightside of Nature": Paradoxically, it was precisely in the dark realm of dream and sleep (often code words for mesmeric trance) that one could find the immediate spiritual illumination that was being obscured by the superficial daytime consciousness of the so-called Enlightenment.[30] And just as in the

---

[27] Johann Lorenz Schmidt, *Die göttlichen Schriften vor den Zeiten des Messie Jesus* ... (Wertheim: J. G. Nehr, 1735), 13, quoted here according to Wilhelm Schmidt-Biggemann, *Theodizee und Tatsachen: Das philosophische Profil der deutschen Aufklärung* (Frankfurt am Main: Suhrkamp, 1988), 88.

[28] Wouter J. Hanegraaff, "Magnetic Gnosis: Somnambulism and the Quest for Absolute Knowledge," in *Die Enzyklopädik der Esoterik: Allwissenheitsmythen und universalwissenschaftliche Modelle in der Esoterik der Neuzeit*, ed. Andreas Kilcher (Paderborn: Wilhelm Fink, 2010).

[29] For an excellent example of such implicit anti-Kantian polemics, see Johann Heinrich Jung-Stilling, *Theorie der Geister-Kunde, in einer Natur-, Vernunft- und Bibelmässigen Beantwortung der Frage: Was von Ahnungen, Gesichten und Geistererscheinungen geglaubt und nicht geglaubt werden müsse* (Nuremberg: Raw'schen Buchhandlung, 1808), 30–32 (§ 45–46).

[30] Gotthilf Heinrich von Schubert, *Ansichten von der Nachtseite der Naturwissenschaft* (Dresden: Arnold, 1808) and *Die Symbolik des Traumes* (1814; facsimile edition Heidelberg: Lambert Schneider, 1968).

context of Late Antiquity, the knowledge thus gained could not be adequately expressed in normal discursive language, such as that of science or philosophy. It could only be experienced directly or, at best, conveyed indirectly and quite vaguely by symbols and images, hieroglyphic "inner languages" of the soul, or numerical abstractions.[31]

As the mesmeric current developed into occultism, practitioners during the nineteenth century began to experiment with any possible technique, whether traditional or novel, by which normal, rational consciousness could be modified so as to gain access to the "higher world." For example, one reads in the early occultist classic *Ghost Land* that trance states "could be induced some times by drugs, vapors, and aromal essences: sometimes by spells, as through music, intently staring into crystals, the eyes of snakes, running water, or other glittering substances; occasionally by intoxications caused by dancing, spinning around, or distracting clamors."[32] By the end of the nineteenth century, experimentation with occult techniques for changing one's consciousness and thereby gaining higher knowledge had become interwoven in complex ways with the emergence of the new science of psychology, leading to a process of "psychologization of religion and sacralization of psychology" that has continued up to the present day.[33] At the same time, the various manifestations of Platonic Orientalism in Late Antiquity had become a major focus of scholarly research, particularly in the context of the *Religionsgeschichtliche Schule* (history of religion school); following a terminological convention that, as pointed out earlier, can be traced back at least to Ferdinand Christian Baur, that field as a whole was often referred to by the generic German label *die Gnosis*.

All these various developments – nineteenth-century occultism (including a strong concern with phallic and solar mythologies[34]), experimentation with altered states of consciousness; clinical psychology; and the scholarly study of Gnosticism, Hermetism, and other manifestations of the Platonic Orientalist

---

[31] Next to Schubert, a classic example is the famous "Seeress of Prevorst." See analysis in Wouter J. Hanegraaff, "A Woman Alone: The Beatification of Friederike Hauffe née Wanner (1801–1829)," in *Women and Miracle Stories*, ed. Anne-Marie Korte (Leiden: Brill, 2001), 211–247.

[32] *Ghost Land, or Researches into the Mysteries of Occultism illustrated in a Series of Autobiographical Sketches*, ed. and trans. Emma Hardinge Britten (1876; facs. repr. Pomeroy: Health Research, no date), 30; and cf. a similar passage on p. 67, which mentions, for example, "mephitic vapors, pungent essences, or narcotics."

[33] Wouter J. Hanegraaff, *New Age Religion and Western Culture* (Albany: State University of New York Press, 1997), 482–513.

[34] As demonstrated in Joscelyn Godwin, *The Theosophical Enlightenment* (Albany: State University of New York Press, 1994).

milieus of late antiquity – came together in the work of Carl Gustav Jung.[35] Jung's famous term "individuation" refers to an arduous process of self-discovery and psychological integration, through confrontation with the archetypal contents of one's personal as well as "collective" unconscious. With explicit reference to gnostic symbolism, it was described by him as an initiatic process ultimately aiming at unification with one's own divine self, or deification. In the wake of Jung's enormous influence in popular culture, particularly after Word War II, his psychological interpretation of ancient Gnosticism (as well as alchemy, seen as a continuation of it[36]) has become certainly the most dominant influence on twentieth- and twenty-first-century esoteric perceptions of *gnosis* as a special kind of "knowledge of the Self as knowledge of God." As an intuitive "knowledge of the heart," it is polemically juxtaposed (as in the days of Jacob Thomasius) against rational and scientific knowledge, as well as against the claims of religious orthodoxy.[37] In the wake of the discovery of the Nag Hammadi library, this essentially Jungian discourse has developed into a significant current of New Age religion, in which newly discovered "sacred texts" such as the *Gospel of Thomas* are interpreted in a selective manner so as to give support to "neo-gnostic" holistic spiritualities.[38] To this, we might add the popularity of Traditionalist assumptions about *gnosis* as a core element of "true" spiritual wisdom, from René Guénon to Fritjof Schuon and their many contemporary sympathizers.[39] Although orthodox Traditionalists reject Jungianism and other forms of psychologized religion as just another modernist perversion, in the broader context of contemporary alternative religion the two perspectives are easily combined by enthusiasts of "inner traditions."[40]

---

[35] On Jung's intellectual roots in contemporary philosophical, scientific, and esoteric culture, see Richard Noll, *The Jung Cult: Origins of a Charismatic Movement* (Princeton: Princeton University Press, 1994).

[36] Robert Segal, "Jung's Fascination with Gnosticism," in *The Allure of Gnosticism*, ed. Segal (Chicago: Open Court, 1995), 26–38, here 26.

[37] Wouter J. Hanegraaff, "Reason, Faith, and Gnosis: Potentials and Problematics of a Typological Construct," in *Clashes of Knowledge: Orthodoxies and Heterodoxies in Science and Religion*, ed. Peter Meusberger et al. (New York: Springer, 2008), 133–144.

[38] Richard Smith, "The Revival of Ancient Gnosis," in *Allure of Gnosticism*, 204–223; and Dylan Burns, "Seeking Ancient Wisdom in the New Age: New Age and Neognostic Commentaries on the Gospel of Thomas," in *Polemical Encounters: Esoteric Discourse and Its Others*, ed. Olav Hammer and Kocku von Stuckrad (Leiden: Brill, 2007), 253–289.

[39] See Faivre, "Le terme et la notion" (discussing, *inter alia*, Guénon's journal *La Gnose*, Schuon's *Sentiers de gnose*, and Jacob Needleman's collective volume *Sword of Gnosis*).

[40] I am referring to the kind of spiritual perspectives represented by a publisher such as Inner Traditions, or the popular journal *Gnosis: A Journal of the Western Inner Traditions* (1985–1999).

Finally, to an extent that may come as a surprise to some, the term *gnosis* has been reunited in contemporary esotericism with its original meaning of "ecstatic" ascent to, direct perception of, and unification with the higher realms of spiritual light. In countless cases, historians will have little trouble recognizing current New Age descriptions of those higher realms as latter-day variations or mutations of the Platonic hierarchies; although the phenomenon remains under-researched, countless groups and individuals today are deeply involved in a range of practices and techniques aimed at gaining experiential access to those invisible spiritual dimensions so as to unite themselves with their own "inner essence" and regain their original divinity.[41] It is easy for scholars to snicker about such aspirations, but although the relevant sources are obviously permeated by the characteristic low-brow jargon of pop science and psychology rather than the philosophical terminology of its ancient counterparts, it is hard to see why the salvific knowledge sought in these contexts should not qualify as *gnosis*.[42]

In closing, a final remark may be in order about the state of academic research on the topic of this essay. Entire libraries can be filled with learned studies of Gnosticism and Hermetism in Late Antiquity, their context in Hellenistic culture, and later historical developments in which their religious perspectives were continued in some manner, up to the present day. However, articles and books devoted specifically to *gnosis* as "knowledge" are virtually nonexistent. In a nutshell: many scholars have attempted to answer the question "what is Gnosticism?" – but answers to the question "what is *gnosis*?" are remarkably scarce. Obviously, this is not meant to deny that one will find at least some discussion of *gnosis* in most monographs on Gnosticism or Hermetism. But typically it is discussed there as merely one element among many others, and not necessarily an important one, especially if compared with the lengthy and detailed analyses of such dimensions as cosmic dualism, various elements of gnostic mythology such as the *heimarmenè*, the *demiurge*, the *archonts*, and so on.[43]

---

[41] For some examples from the New Age movement up to the early 1990s, see Hanegraaff, *New Age Religion*.

[42] The essentialism of contemporary esotericists who would claim that ancient and modern *gnosis* are all one and the same universal spiritual phenomenon is neither more nor less problematic than the academic essentialism according to which ancient *gnosis* was the "real and authentic" article in comparison to which its contemporary parallels (as discussed, for example, by Burns, "Seeking Ancient Wisdom") are just fake surrogates.

[43] For Gnosticism alone, see, for example, the classic studies by Hans Jonas, and important recent monographs such as Michael Williams, *Rethinking "Gnosticism:" An Argument for Dismantling a Dubious Category* (Princeton: Princeton University Press, 1996) or Karen L. King, *What Is Gnosticism?* (Cambridge, MA: Harvard University Press, 2003). The

It is virtually unheard of in serious scholarly literature to see *gnosis* presented as the central core of these types of religion, in relation to which the other dimensions, although obviously important, would be of strictly secondary importance.[44] Admittedly, to pursue such an approach consistently would imply a kind of Copernican revolution in the study of gnostic, hermetic, and esoteric forms of religion, since it would promote *gnosis* from the status of a minor planet to that of the central sun in the religious cosmos under discussion. Radical though it may be, this is precisely what the present contribution would like to suggest.

---

former has precisely one reference to *gnosis* in the index, the latter none at all, although the term is in fact discussed in both works. Garth Fowden does have a special section on *gnosis* in *The Egyptian Hermes: A Historical Approach to the Late Pagan Mind* (Princeton: Princeton University Press, 1986), 105–114.

[44] In sharp contrast, that Gnosticism is all about *gnosis* is the default assumption in much of the popular "spiritual" literature referred to earlier; and this is probably among the major reasons why academics have an instinctive aversion against such suggestions, or at most, pay lip-service to the centrality of *gnosis* without drawing the right conclusions.

# 33

# MAGIC

WOUTER J. HANEGRAAFF

## 1 Introduction

Magic is a wretched subject.[1] Perhaps no other concept in the study of religion has caused so much confusion and frustration among scholars, because it seems to resist all attempts at defining its exact nature, thus causing serious doubts about whether it refers to anything real at all – or if so, in what sense. In spite of all the trouble that the concept has caused, nobody has seemed capable of exorcizing it from the academic vocabulary.[2] Like the monster in cheap horror movies, "magic" always keeps coming back no matter how often one tries to kill it.

To explain this strange situation, we must begin by distinguishing sharply between two ways of understanding magic. On the one hand, we can look at the many different meanings and connotations that the term has acquired in Western culture from antiquity to the present. We will see that this gets us closest to understanding the actual role of magic in the context of Western esotericism. On the other hand, there is the common use of "magic" as a general reified concept that is part of the triad "magic–religion–science." We will see that this latter perspective is the chief cause of all the confusion about the term. Thus, before getting to magic in the history of Western esotericism, we will begin with this second perspective.

## 2 The Reification of "Magic"

Although there are countless academic definitions of magic, they are essentially variations on three extremely influential theories. First, there is the

---

[1] Otto Neugebauer, "The Study of Wretched Subjects," *Isis* 42:2 (1951), 111.
[2] H. S. Versnel, "Some Reflections on the Relation Magic-Religion," *Numen* 38 (1991), 177–197.

"intellectualist" approach, associated with the work of the two famous Victorian armchair anthropologists Edward Burnett Tylor and James G. Frazer.[3] Tylor, the nineteenth-century pioneer of cultural anthropology, defined magic as based on "the error of mistaking ideal analogy for real analogy."[4] In other words, he claimed that it was grounded in the erroneous assumption typical of "primitive man" that things associated in thinking must be connected in actual fact. Frazer integrated Tylor's theory in his famous evolutionist triad, claiming that humanity had progressed from primitive "magic," first to the higher level of "religion," and from there to "science," the highest level of all.

For Frazer, magic actually meant "sympathetic" magic: It was based on the assumption that "things act on each other at a distance through a secret sympathy"[5] (a concept that goes back to Plotinus) or "an invisible ether" (a concept that, ironically, was still very popular in mainstream scientific theorizing even in Frazer's day).[6] The important point to emphasize about the Tylor-Frazer theory is that it holds science, not religion, to be the theoretical opposite of magic: The essence of magic was its belief in merely imaginary analogies, correspondences, and invisible forces, in contrast to the real causal mechanisms basic to science.

The second, "functionalist" theory of magic concentrates on ritual action and is linked to another scholarly couple: the French sociologists Marcel Mauss and Emile Durkheim. For Mauss, the term referred to "any rite that is not part of an organized cult: a rite that is private, secret, mysterious, and ultimately tending towards one that is forbidden."[7] Following a similar line of reasoning, Durkheim defined religious beliefs as shared by, and constitutive of, a social group, which he referred to as a "Church." In contrast, magic was inherently nonsocial: *"There is no Church of Magic."*[8] Functionalist approaches are therefore based on the opposition of magic to religion, not

---

[3] Wouter J. Hanegraaff, "The Emergence of the Academic Science of Magic: The Occult Philosophy in Tylor and Frazer," in *Religion in the Making: The Emergence of the Sciences of Religion*, ed. Arie L. Molendijk and Peter Pels (Leiden: Brill, 1998), 253–275.

[4] Edward Burnett Tylor, *Primitive Culture: Researches into the Development of Mythology, Philosophy, Religion, Language, Art, and Custom* (1871), vol. 1 (London: John Murray, 1913), 116.

[5] James G. Frazer, *The Golden Bough* (1900), vol. 1, 2nd ed. (reprinted London: MacMillan & Co, 1951), 54.

[6] Egil Asprem, "Pondering Imponderables: Occultism in the Mirror of Late Classical Physics," *Aries* 11:2 (2011), 129–165.

[7] Marcel Mauss, "Esquisse d'une théorie générale de la magie," (1901–1902), in Mauss, *Sociologie et anthropologie* (1950; Paris: Quadrige/Presses Universitaires de France, 1995), 16.

[8] Emile Durkheim, *Les formes élémentaires de la vie religieuse* (1912; Paris: Quadrige/Presses Universitaires de France, 1994), 61. Emphasis in original.

science. In Durkheim's opinion, there was "something inherently antireligious about the maneuvers of the magician."[9]

Finally, a third approach is derived from a theoretical concept that is central to the oeuvre of the French philosopher Lucien Lévy-Bruhl (remarkably enough, since he himself saw it as applicable equally to magic and religion). It was based on the perceived contrast between a worldview or mentality grounded in "instrumental causality" (which assumes the presence of secondary causes or mechanisms that mediate between causes and effects) and an alternative one, grounded in "participation" (where causes and effects are seen as associated, or merging, to the point of identity or consubstantiality).[10] While Lévy-Bruhl originally saw participation as typical of "primitive" cultures, he eventually came to understand it as a primary and irreducible constant that is present in any society, including our own. Later scholars came to assume, quite incorrectly, that participation and magic were meant to be equivalent terms, resulting in all kinds of theories that interpret magic as grounded in a "different kind of rationality."[11] In these cases, it is clear that science, not religion, serves as the theoretical opposite of magic: It is all about alternatives to instrumental causality.

The three theoretical approaches linked to the names of Tylor and Frazer, Mauss and Durkheim, and Lévy-Bruhl have been mixed and combined in many different ways, but almost without any exception this has happened within a more general context that has very much been taken for granted, explicitly or implicitly. This is the famous triad "magic-religion-science" itself, with its ambitious suggestion that all forms of human culture can essentially be analyzed in terms of three perspectives or worldviews. The triad has its origin in the period of the Enlightenment, although most of its underlying assumptions go back much further in history, as will be seen. Its point of departure is the relatively unproblematic recognition that "religion" (however defined) is clearly something different from modern science and rationality.

Once this distinction has been made, it is bound to be followed by the further observation that a whole class of phenomena in human culture and society apparently do not fit too well within either of these categories: They

[9] Durkheim, *Les formes élémentaire*, 59–60.
[10] Analysis in Wouter J. Hanegraaff, "How Magic Survived the Disenchantment of the World," *Religion* 33:4 (2003), 357–380, here 371–374.
[11] For example, see Robin Horton, *Patterns of Thought in Africa and the West: Essays on Magic, Religion and Science* (Cambridge: Cambridge University Press, 1993); and see the overview in Tanya M. Luhrmann, *Persuasions of the Witch's Craft: Ritual Magic in Contemporary England* (Cambridge, MA: Harvard University Press, 1989), 345–356.

too appear to be clearly different from science and rationality, and yet one hesitates to call them "religion." If one looks at it more closely, one finds that this third category is in fact a kind of wastebasket filled with materials that have been known by many different names: Next to the term "magic," they have been referred to, or associated with, a whole series of generalizing concepts such as "the occult" (respectively, "occultism," "occult science"), "superstition," "mysticism," "esotericism," "the irrational," "primitive thought," "paganism," "idolatry," "fetishism," and so on. These many terms refer to an even greater variety of practices and ideas, and their association is highly problematic. (For example, what does the invocation of demons have to do with the drawing of horoscopes, or alchemical transmutation with the animation of statues or the making of amulets?) Nevertheless, the idea is that they can all be subsumed under the single unifying label of "magic," thus setting them apart from whatever belongs to the similarly unifying categories called "religion" and "science."

Tacitly assuming the existence of such a triad, scholars and intellectuals have tended to be favorable toward "science and rationality," respectful toward "religion," and quite negative about "magic" (or whatever equivalent term they might use). Now, to get to the core of the problem: It is quite evident that the distinction between magic and religion is a direct legacy from Christian theology and doctrinal polemics. Implicitly or explicitly, religion really meant Christianity (or more precisely, "true" or theologically correct Christianity), whereas magic meant such things as demonic worship and pagan idolatry (i.e., false religion). Clearly, this framework is so transparently normative and biased toward Christian theological agendas that it should never have had a chance to be accepted in a purportedly neutral scholarly framework. But the opposite occurred: It has been adopted as a matter of course by countless academics.

That this could happen so easily and successfully has to do partly with a second historical legacy in addition to the theological one, which has created further confusion. Since the twelfth century, as we will see, intellectuals had begun promoting the idea of *magia naturalis*: magic understood in non-demonic terms, as based on the workings of the hidden (occult) forces of nature, and therefore easier to legitimate theologically. In fact, those who were defending "natural magic" in the early modern period found themselves open to attack from all sides. The Protestant Reformation had given a new sense of urgency to anti-magical polemics, often targeting Roman Catholicism. Many theological critics failed to be convinced by the argument that natural magic was free from demonic influence. And they were now joined by natural philosophers and scientists who accused any defender of magic – natural or not – of obscurantism and irrational superstition. The upshot of this confused debate was that magic always found itself on the wrong side of things, regardless of how it was defined or what arguments were being used against it.

It is therefore quite evident that the magic-religion-science triad relies entirely on normative distinctions between "true" and "false" religion as well as between "true" and "false" science. The fact that, in this context, magic is a polemical category of exclusion, not an unbiased instrument for analysis or a straightforward descriptive label should already be sufficient to discredit it as suitable for scholarly research. But there is more. What makes the triad particularly problematic (although, paradoxically, it is precisely this further weakness that accounts for its enormous popularity) is the almost automatic mental *reification* of the three terms. In other words, it is widely assumed that certain kinds of human thought and behavior really *are* magical in and by themselves, while others *are* religious, and yet others *are* scientific.

Magic, religion, and science come to be perceived as universal categories *sui generis*. And this is what made it possible for them to play a central role in the complex processes of identity formation and "othering" through which the dominant parties in modern Western culture – Christians on the one hand, scientists and rationalist philosophers on the other – have been trying to promote their hegemonic agendas. For example, Protestants might argue that Catholic veneration of images is not really Christian but a form of magic; Catholics, however, might come up with sophisticated arguments to the effect that such practices may look like magic to their opponents but were really a genuine religious practice; and rationalists could argue that all kinds of practices that are seen as supernatural by the common people can really be given a straightforward rational and scientific explanation. The deep irony of the situation is that the very process of reification, as practiced by Christians and rationalists alike, is a perfect example of what Tylor had described as magic! That is to say, it entails the confusion of mental concepts with actual realities, so that what we believe we understand in our mind seems to exist in the external world.[12]

This process of projection makes it possible for magic to be perceived as an ominous and almost omnipresent threat, often leading to alarmist rhetoric:

> It is beneath our feet – and not very far beneath them – here in Europe at the present day. . . . This universal faith, this truly Catholic creed, is a belief in the efficacy of magic. . . . [T]he permanent existence of such a solid layer

[12] Wouter J. Hanegraaff, *Esotericism and the Academy: Rejected Knowledge in Western Culture* (Cambridge: Cambridge University Press 2012), 168.

of savagery beneath the surface of society, and unaffected by the superficial changes of religion and culture [is] a standing menace to civilization. We seem to move on a thin crust which may at any moment be rent by subterranean forces slumbering below.[13]

But reification can work in favor of magic as well. Once the magic-religion-science triad was firmly in place, it became possible for critics of established Christianity and mechanical science – mostly Romantics and their heirs – to idealize magic as a noble worldview of enchantment. Not least through the medium of fiction, such perceptions have become particularly widespread among the general population.

It is undoubtedly *because* of its normative and ideological foundations, not in spite of them, that the magic-religion-science triad has become an indispensable component of how intellectuals have conceptualized modernity. How deeply the reification of magic is ingrained in modernist theory can be seen clearly, for example, in Max Weber's theory of *Entzauberung*, or Disenchantment, as explained in a famous lecture, "Wissenschaft als Beruf" (Science as a Vocation).[14] But it also became essential to the missionary and colonialist enterprise: With constant implicit or explicit reference to traditional heresiological stereotypes about the alleged horrors of paganism, the magic-religion-science triad (particularly understood from an evolutionist perspective) lent intellectual and scientific legitimacy to the project of converting non-European peoples from their supposedly magical superstitions to the superior truths of Christianity, Enlightenment, and science. In short, the rejection of magic became a hallmark of civilization. But here, too, the logic could work in reverse as well: Again, those who were critical of Western civilization could be attracted, precisely for that reason, to magic as an enchanted worldview that was still alive among the "primitives" or "noble savages" and should be revived in the modern world.

We may conclude that precisely because of its status as the "other" both of religion (i.e., Christianity, or more specifically, Protestantism) and science (i.e., a mechanistic worldview with atheistic implications), the category of "magic" since the eighteenth century has become a favorite projection screen for Western hopes and fears. Far from actually recovering or reconstructing any observable or structural reality existing "out there" (in the past or in the present, or on other continents), it *constructs* such a reality on the

---

[13] Frazer, *Golden Bough*, vol. 1, 235–236.
[14] Max Weber, "Wissenschaft als Beruf," in *Wissenschaft als Beruf 1917/1919. Politik als Beruf 1919* (Studienausgabe der Max Weber-Gesamtausgabe Band 1/17; ed. Wolfgang J. Mommsen and Wolfgang Schluchter) (Tübingen: J. C. B. Mohr [Paul Siebeck], 1994), 1–23.

basis of normative and ideological assumptions and agendas. Implicitly or explicitly, its real function is to distinguish "truth" from "error" in terms of a simplifying post-Enlightenment discourse; but this normative and prescriptive function is concealed behind the deceptive claim of mere objective description. The discovery of magic is in fact its creation.

## 3 Concepts of Magic

From a strictly historical point of view, any attempt to write a "history of magic" is therefore misleading in principle: It can only lead to anachronistic distortions that prevent us from perceiving what has actually been going on. What can be written, however, is a history of *concepts* of magic. In any such attempt, one must be continually attentive to the question of *who is speaking*: Are we dealing with a "self-referential" discourse in which people claim to be doing magic themselves or with an "other-referential" discourse in which they claim that others are doing it?[15] In this short essay, it is obviously impossible to make even a preliminary attempt at writing such a history in chronological order. Instead, we will be looking at some of the main concepts of "magic" that have emerged over the course of time. In what follows, we will distinguish between seven categories, but this categorization is not intended to be either final or absolute. It is perfectly possible to expand the list further, and the main reason for presenting it here is to illustrate that a great variety of different practices and beliefs have been called "magic" at one time or another, in some context or other, always according to specific intellectual contexts and contingent factors, so that the attempt to reduce them all to some abstract master category is a hopeless undertaking. This initial list of categories, then, looks as follows:

1. Magic as ancient wisdom
2. Magic as worship of demons
3. Magic as natural philosophy and science
4. Magic as occult philosophy
5. Magic as pseudoscience
6. Magic as an enchanted worldview
7. Magic as psychology

The Greek complex of words relating to magic (μάγος, μαγεία, μαγικός, μαγεύω, etc.) is derived from the Old Persian *magu-*. Its exact meaning is

---

[15] Bernd-Christian Otto, *Magie: Rezeptions- und Diskursgeschichtliche Analysen von der Antike bis zur Neuzeit* (Berlin: De Gruyter, 2011).

unclear, but it must have referred to a religious functionary of some kind. The historical career of the first meaning of magic, *ancient wisdom*, relies to a remarkable extent on only one short reference in Plato's *Alcibiades* I (122a), where Socrates refers to Zoroaster's *mageia* as "the worship of the gods." The passage was quoted by a surprisingly great number of classical authors, and this initial and quite positive understanding of magic survived at least as late as Apuleius in the second century.[16] It underwent an impressive revival in the Renaissance, partly under the influence of George Gemistos Plethon's attribution of the *Chaldean Oracles* to Zoroaster, who became one of the chief authorities of "ancient wisdom" in the context of the *prisca theologia*. Because Zoroaster was also known as the originator of *mageia*, Plethon titled his edition *Magical Sayings of the Magi, Disciples of Zoroaster*, and the result was a widely popular perspective that may conveniently be referred to as *prisca magia*: Here magic was understood very positively as referring to the wisdom of the ancients that had been passed on through history to Plato and the Platonists but had later come to be confused with demonic and superstitious practices of all kinds. It is on this basis, for example, that Cornelius Agrippa wrote his famous *De occulta philosophia* in an attempt to restore magic to its ancient state of honor. It also led to endless repetitions of the apologetic argument that true magic is a good and divine thing but should not be confused with the despicable dark practices of *goetia*.

This brings us to our second category. Even though the term *mageia* may sometimes have been understood in a positive sense in antiquity, it appears to have rapidly lost that status as it acquired most of the negative connotations that already adhered to the native term γόης – whence *goetia*. Such negative understandings were normative in Christian culture since the first centuries, leading to the understanding of magic as *worship of demons*. Christians, of course, argued that those demons were none other than the gods of the pagans; what the latter described as "ancient wisdom" was in fact an idolatrous practice forbidden by the true God. There is no need here to dwell on this second category: The assumption that magic relies on contact with demons is so widespread and well known that it hardly needs further demonstration.

But as already briefly mentioned, the demonic theory of magic came to be contested beginning in the twelfth century, when great numbers of manuscripts concerned with the ancient natural sciences were translated from

[16] Albert F. de Jong, *Traditions of the Magi: Zoroastrianism in Greek and Latin Literature* (Leiden: Brill, 1997), 213 note 29; Otto, *Magie*, chaps. 6–7. On the contested authenticity of the *Alcibiades*, see Nicholas Denyer, "Introduction," in Plato, *Alcibiades* (Cambridge: Cambridge University Press, 2001).

Arabic into Latin. This leads us to our third category. Intellectuals began to argue that many miraculous effects attributed to demonic activity by the common people could in fact be explained in purely natural terms. The scholastic notion of *qualitates occultae* (occult qualities), originating in the Greek ἰδιότητες ἄρρητοι, came to play an important role in this argument. It is not entirely correct to describe the new concept of *magia naturalis* as an attempt to present magic as scientific: More precisely, it was an attempt to protect the study of the ancient sciences against theological censure and thus legitimate them as a serious object of study for natural philosophers.[17]

The rediscovery of the ancient sciences from Arabic sources was joined, since the fifteenth century, by the translation of multiple Greek manuscripts concerned with Platonic and hermetic wisdom, and Hebrew manuscripts concerned with Kabbalah and other forms of Jewish speculation, followed by the unprecedented dissemination of these materials thanks to the invention of printing. As a result, scholars and intellectuals were faced with the daunting task of trying to synthesize a wide variety of ancient and medieval traditions concerned with miraculous effects of all kinds. This brings us to our fourth category. As Jean-Pierre Brach has remarked, "the elaboration of a synthetic approach had, in many cases, the paradoxical effect of partially blurring the basic differences that were assumed to exist between them."[18] In other words, magic in the Renaissance took the form of a syncretic "occult philosophy" that made heroic attempts at achieving the impossible: harmonizing widely divergent materials from Greek, Arabic, and Latin sources, combining Aristotelian with Platonic strands of natural philosophy and metaphysics, convincing theologians that these "pagan" traditions were strictly natural (in spite of multiple references to the involvement of intelligent agents, whether demonic or angelic), and yet presenting this "natural magic" as part of one single, supreme tradition of *religious* wisdom derived from sages such as Zoroaster or Hermes Trismegistus.

This Renaissance project of an "occult philosophy" – the attempt to synthesize an enormous range of textual materials concerned with astrology, alchemy, Kabbalah, *magia naturalis*, and Platonic or hermetic speculation, while presenting them as one single whole – was still very well known during the advent of the Enlightenment and came to be seen by its representatives as the sum total of "traditional error and superstition." While orthodox Christians had already rejected much of it as demon-inspired idolatry and

[17] For the longer argument on *magia naturalis* and *qualitates occultae*, see Hanegraaff, *Esotericism and the Academy*, 170–175, 178–182.
[18] Jean-Pierre Brach, "Magic IV," in *Dictionary of Gnosis and Western Esotericism*, ed. Hanegraaff (Leiden: Brill, 2006), 732.

pagan superstition, representatives of the new science and rational philosophy were bound to perceive it as "pseudoscience" and dismiss it under the convenient label of "magic." This, then, is how the magic-religion-science triad came into existence: The occult philosophy of the Renaissance became the Enlightenment's wastebasket of "rejected knowledge."[19] As we have seen, this fifth understanding of magic was widely adopted as a polemical tool by intellectuals and academics throughout the nineteenth and twentieth centuries.

But whatever the Enlightenment rejected as unacceptable was bound to become attractive to those who criticized or rejected the new forms of philosophical rationalism and mechanical philosophy. As illustrated in exemplary form by a large *History of Magic* published by the Romantic physician Joseph Ennemoser in 1844,[20] it was possible to reinterpret all the contents of the wastebasket in a positive manner and present them as parts of a venerable tradition of ancient wisdom grounded in a thoroughly enchanted view of the world. According to this sixth understanding of magic, nature is full of strange and miraculous powers – "mysterious and incalculable forces" in Max Weber's formulation – that are ultimately grounded in the powers of the soul. This new theory was part and parcel of Mesmerism as interpreted by German Romantics. Next to the "daylight rationality" of the Enlightenment, it claimed that the human mind had a natural connection to the mysterious and much more profound "nightside of nature": the source of dreams, visions, ecstasies, and all the strange powers and abilities that were ignorantly attributed to demons from a perspective of religious superstition and prematurely dismissed as nonsense by narrow-minded rationalists.

German Romantic Mesmerism and its concern with the nightside of nature eventually led to what has been called the "discovery of the unconscious,"[21] and this brings us to our seventh category. As the hard sciences were more and more successful in uncovering the secrets of external nature, the human unconscious – internal nature – became the privileged location of occult or "mysterious and incalculable" forces. The trend toward psychologization of the sacred went hand in hand with a sacralization of psychology; it is emblematic of this development that in late nineteenth-century forms of occultism, and increasingly since the twentieth century, the personal inner development of the practitioner came to be seen as the main goal of magic. Another central heir of German Romantic Mesmerism, Carl

[19] Hanegraaff, *Esotericism and the Academy*, chap. 3.
[20] Hanegraaff, *Esotericism and the Academy*, 260–277.
[21] Henri F. Ellenberger, *The Discovery of the Unconscious: The History and Evolution of Dynamic Psychiatry* (New York: HarperCollins, 1970).

Gustav Jung, developed a highly influential theory of "synchronicity" designed to rehabilitate the *magia naturalis* and occult philosophy of the Renaissance by interpreting it in psychological terms and harmonizing it with quantum physics as a more advanced alternative to post-Newtonian science. This meant, quite literally, that in Jung's perspective, avant-garde physics and depth psychology had joined forces to unmask positivism as "superstition" and announce the return of magic as science!

It bears repeating that the series of seven categories briefly summarized here makes no claim of completeness and might well be expanded further or arranged differently. The point of this discussion is that the term "magic" has continuously been acquiring new meanings and connotations through its long history from antiquity to the present. To the question "what is magic?" one will therefore receive very different answers depending on the historical period in question and the personal agendas of whoever is being asked. There is no convincing way of subsuming all these meanings under one general heading without making arbitrary judgments along the following lines: "Although X is known by the term 'magic,' it is not *really* magic, but although Y is not known by the term 'magic,' it really *is* magic." According to whom, and on what basis? The answer must be obvious by now: according to whoever happens to be speaking, and on the basis of whatever arguments he or she happens to like.

Although there is no such thing as a history of magic, then, it is possible to write a history of the discourse on magic. The only solid foundation for such a history is the detailed analysis of terms and concepts as used in their own context, and a precise investigation of their continuous transformations under the impact of changing historical circumstances.[22] Such a contextual historical analysis is not just possible, but highly important, for the obvious reason that few other terms have been so effective and influential as polemical and apologetic instruments in the formation of Western identities. As such, concepts of "magic" are inextricably entwined not only with the history of modernity but also with the history of how and why Western esotericism has come to be perceived as a distinct field of study.[23] To what extent all the historical concepts of magic are part of the history of esotericism, and to what extent they fall beyond its boundaries, is a tricky question that cannot be answered in general terms. Few scholars would deny that magic as "ancient wisdom" and as "occult philosophy" are proper objects of research in the study of Western esotericism; but when it comes to some other terms,

---

[22] For a pioneering attempt along these lines, see Otto, *Magie*.
[23] For this general argument, see Hanegraaff, *Esotericism and the Academy*.

especially those that are based on what Bernd-Christian Otto calls an "other-referential discourse,"[24] there is bound to be more hesitation.

Whatever one's position in this respect, one thing seems clear: Magic is something to beware of. It is such a powerful concept that most scholars and intellectuals who have come into contact with it have fallen under its spell. Even its strongest enemies appear to have been unable to resist the enchantment and the illusions it produced: It literally caused them to see things that were not there. Had these illusions been no more than empty chimeras, then the problem might not have been too serious. But unfortunately, illusions that are widely believed to be true become potent factors in the real world, as one can see from the limitless literature on magic as a concept *sui generis* and its enormous impact in such domains as religious rhetoric or colonialist politics. Ironically, then, it is appropriate to end this short essay with a warning that will sound uncannily familiar to scholars of magic: Beware of the power of words!

---

[24] Otto, *Magie*, 18–19 and *passim: Selbstbezeichnung* (referring to oneself) versus *Fremdbezeichnung* (referring to others), leading to a positive self-referential discourse ("I am practicing magic") versus a negative other-referential one (*fremdreferentiell* in German; "they are practicing magic"). Cf. Hanegraaff, "Review of Bernd-Christian Otto," *Aries* 14:1 (2014), 114–120.

# 34

## MATHEMATICAL ESOTERICISM

### JEAN-PIERRE BRACH

### 1 Theology, Ethics, Cosmology

"Number symbolism" refers to a "qualitative" approach to number and mathematical objects in general. It is backed by what is known as "correlative thinking"[1] and operates according to a network of analogies linking the quantitative values of mathematical entities to a vast array of correspondences throughout the many levels of the so-called Great Chain of Being.[2] It is also a universal cultural phenomenon, likely to have existed from time immemorial. But it should not be confused with "numerology," a term that has mainly come to designate contemporary methods of a pseudo-divinatory character,[3] which do not concern us here.

Within Western culture, to which we shall limit ourselves in this essay, explicit considerations pertaining to "arithmology" (or qualitative number) first appear with the Greeks – insofar, that is, as extant documents are concerned.

Although it is clear that correlative thinking, mathematical symbolism, and the worldview they both depend on pertain to a type of archaic "wisdom" predating Greek civilization,[4] it is nevertheless the case that the few truly arithmological texts that have come down to us date from no earlier than the late Hellenistic period. Still, one must take into account the fact that the name of Pythagoras (ca. 570–490 BCE) was already synonymous in Ancient Greece with a "philosophy of number." It appears that the Pythagorean

---

[1] Jean-Pierre Brach and Wouter J. Hanegraaff, "Correspondences," in *Dictionary of Gnosis and Western Esotericism*, ed. Wouter J. Hanegraaff (Leiden: Brill, 2005), 275–279.
[2] Arthur O. Lovejoy, *The Great Chain of Being: A Study of the History of an Idea* (Cambridge, MA: Harvard University Press, 1936); Edward P. Mahoney, "Lovejoy and the Hierarchy of Being," *Journal of the History of Ideas* 48 (1987), 211–230.
[3] Eric T. Bell, *Numerology* (New York: Hyperion Press, 1979; originally published 1933).
[4] Walter Burkert, *Lore and Science in Ancient Pythagoreanism* (Cambridge, MA: Harvard University Press, 1972).

school, which vanished around the end of the fourth century BCE, never felt compelled to draw a clear distinction between mathematical research, as we would understand it, and mystical speculations about arithmetic and geometry. Both Proclus[5] (412–485 CE) and Damascius (ca. 470–535 CE) ascribe to Philolaus of Croton[6] (fl. ca 450 BCE), one of the main representatives of the early Pythagorean movement, a discourse on "theological geometry," which correlates the respective angles of the triangle and square to the same number of masculine and feminine Olympian deities, to underline the sovereignty of the duodenary ($3 \times 4$) associated with the supreme god Zeus. This appears to confirm the presence of symbolic perspectives from the beginning of the school, inasmuch as it is feasible to distinguish between supposedly "original" material and later, "traditional" developments.

What appears to us, accordingly, as a mixture of scientific and symbolic perspectives results in a general doctrine of cosmic harmony, partly expressed in mathematical concepts and correspondences that may have exerted a certain influence on Plato. As far as we know, Philolaus's cosmology hinges on the complementarity of the dual principle of Limit and Unlimited, which, through its assimilation to the categories of odd and even, manifests the development of the supreme and universal One both in mathematics and in nature.

The early Pythagorean triple focus on cosmology, ethics, and theology (or on the cosmos, man, and the divine realm), and its relation to number, was retained by later arithmological literature, which also maintained the original insistence on the decad. The number 10 was understood to express the elaboration of the primordial Unity (One), through the agency of the *tetraktys* ($1 + 2 + 3 + 4 = 10$). The Pythagoreans recognized the importance of the first four numbers in the constitution of the primary musical intervals (symbolizing cosmic harmony, expressed by proportion and consonance). The number 4 seems to have been of particular importance to them, as in Philolaus's doctrine of the fourfold cognitive faculties of the soul-harmony. The number 7 was held to be a structural factor of life and nature.

## 2 A Pythagorean Plato?

Even though it has frequently been considered (most especially in the case of the *Timaeus*) as being of Pythagorean inspiration, Plato's philosophical use of

---

[5] *Commentary on the First Book of Euclid's Elements*, trans. G. R. Morrow (Princeton: Princeton University Press, 1970), 173–174; Proclus, *Théologie platonicienne*, ed. and trans. into French by H.-D. Saffrey and L. G. Westerink, 5 vols. (Paris: Les Belles Lettres, 1968–87) (I, 20, 11).

[6] Carl A. Huffman, *Philolaus of Croton Pythagorean and Presocratic: A Commentary on the Fragments and Testimonia with Interpretive Essays* (Cambridge: Cambridge University Press, 1993).

mathematics is for the most part very different in spirit. Whether we consider the *Republic*, or the possibly spurious *Epinomis* (wherein the science of number is said to constitute a fundamental tool in the search for wisdom), or the *Timaeus* and its harmonic cosmogony, traditional numerical analogies (e.g., 7 planets – 7 metals – 7 Gates of Thebes) play almost no part at all.

In the *Timaeus*, mathematical proportions – representing an intermediate order of reality between the intelligible forms and the material *corpus mundi* – actually structure the world-soul which, in turn, imparts a measure of order and musical harmony to the physical universe, inasmuch as it is capable of receiving it. The polyhedral shapes correlated with the four elements and the "All," as well as the minute triangular "particles" they are allegedly composed of, add a geometrical match to the harmonic intervals of the world-soul. They figure among the components of a wider philosophical discourse, which applies mathematics to physics with the aim of providing the rational basis for an account of the genesis and constitution of the material dimension of nature. It is still debated whether or not such tenets in fact echo older Pythagorean speculations, considerably reworked, as do other developments in Plato linking proportional means to political regimes, justice, and social order.[7]

From roughly the second century CE, a widespread philosophical eclecticism makes room also for a neo-Pythagorean current, most often blended with Middle Platonism or Neoplatonism. Writers such as Nicomachus of Gerasa, Moderatus of Gadès, Theon of Smyrna, and Anatolius are eager to include mathematics within the philosophical curriculum and to exploit its supposed potential, from both a symbolic and a scientific perspective, in expanding knowledge and supporting the *ascensio mentis*, the gradual elevation of the soul from earthly concerns toward the divine. This general tendency to view the study of numbers as primarily a spiritual exercise is further reinforced by the fact that late Neoplatonism turns ever more toward theology, as exemplified by thinkers such as Iamblichus (ca. 245–325 CE) and Proclus. If, after Nicomachus and Anatolius,[8] Iamblichus has left us one of the special arithmological tracts referred to earlier,[9] he is also the author of more doctrinal expositions bearing on the natural, ethical, and divine transpositions of

---

[7] *Gorgias*, 508a; *Laws* V, 737c; 744b, and so on.
[8] Nicomachus of Gerasa, Theologoumena arithmeticæ in Photius, *Bibliothèque* [3], ed. and trans. into French by R. Henry (Paris: Les Belles Lettres, 1962), 40–48; Anatolius, On the Decad, trans. Robin Waterfield, *Alexandria: The Journal of Western Cosmological Traditions* 3 (1995), 181–194.
[9] Iamblichus, *Summa Pitagorica*, ed. and translated into Italian by F. Romano, (Milan: Bompiani, 2006; includes the *Theology of Arithmetic*); Iamblichus, *The Theology of Arithmetic*, trans. Robin Waterfield (Grand Rapids, Michigan: Phanes Press, 1988).

arithmetic, which have already been mentioned.[10] Even his ritual approach to religion is not devoid of number-symbolical considerations.

As shown by Gregory Shaw,[11] the isomorphism Iamblichus assumes between the soul and mathematical entities makes possible its participation in the cosmic harmony of the world-soul, while setting up a definite analogy between the soul's ascension through theurgical rites and the pursuit of mathematical knowledge. In this way, numbers are construed as rungs on the spiritual ladder, as well as intelligible entities that the soul must eventually sacrifice in ritual worship, on the noetic plane, before it returns to the gods. Understood as an image of cosmogenesis, or of the descent of the soul into corporeal matter, geometry is equally involved in the symbolization of theurgic activity, the more so since forms or linear shapes are sometimes attributed to the gods themselves, as we have seen.

Equivalents in Greek philosophical culture of the Jewish practice of *gematria*,[12] that is, of taking into account the numerical value of letters (sometimes also their geometrical shape, their rank within the alphabet, or position within a given word), crop up intermittently, for example, in Plutarch's *On the E at Delphi* (ca. 115 CE), the Iamblichan *Theology of Arithmetic*, and some fragments by Theodore of Asine[13] also quoted by Proclus.

For the most part, this conscious attempt at "pythagoreanizing" the philosophical approach to reality belongs to a general, scholarly endeavor both to interpret Plato's doctrines and to secure the status of mathematics amid the official curriculum of the Neoplatonic school. Commentaries on scientific textbooks (by Euclid or Ptolemy, for instance) and the production of manuals (e.g., by Nicomachus) constitute an integral part of this intellectual process, which exerted an extremely significant influence on the medieval and early modern understanding of number.

## 3 The Patristic and Medieval Outlooks

Both contemporary Jewish writers (e.g., Philo of Alexandria, *fl*. first half of the first century CE) and the Greek Church Fathers were confronted with

[10] In lost portions of a tenfold and explicitly neo-Pythagorean *Summa*. See Dominic J. O'Meara, *Pythagoras Revived: Mathematics and Philosophy in Late Antiquity* (Oxford: Clarendon Press, 1989), 30–105, 217–229.
[11] Gregory Shaw, *Theurgy and the Soul: The Neoplatonism of Iamblichus* (University Park: Pennsylvania State University Press, 1995), 189–215.
[12] It should be noted that most of the Neoplatonic philosophers mentioned earlier came in fact from the Middle East.
[13] Wilhelm Deuse, *Theodoros von Asine* (Wiesbaden: O. Harrassowitz, 1973).

the authority of Scripture and the challenge of interpreting it. Above "rational" mathematics or philosophy now stood the "divine inspiration" attributed to the books comprising the Bible. This new outlook necessarily entailed the spiritual relevance of all numbers featured in Holy Writ, which were seen as containing a deeper or hidden meaning. Biblical numbers, moreover, far surpassed those comprised in the Decad sacred to pagan writers. All this meant that number symbolism now had to adapt to much broader materials and perspectives, which in turn pointed to the necessity of elaborating a wider system of hermeneutics, able to take into account the variety of biblical texts and their multilayered hidden meanings.

Even though Irenaeus, Origen, Clement, and Tertullian long preceded him in the practice of arithmology, Augustine (354–430) is a case in point regarding the evolution of number symbolism, an evolution that finds itself, on the whole, faithfully mirrored in his work. This is probably one of the reasons why he rapidly became the foundational Latin authority in the field. Nevertheless, this is relatively surprising since in fact Augustine left no systematic account of his views on arithmology, only a multitude of instances and arguments scattered throughout the bulk of his writings. In sentences that have become famous,[14] Augustine contends that the correct interpretation of numbers and numerical passages in the Bible is essential to the understanding of its spiritual meaning. Invoking the triple authority of Scripture, tradition (the teachings of the Church), and the *ratio numerorum* (analysis of the arithmetical properties of number), he uses arithmology mainly as an exegetical tool[15] designed to shed light on the inner significance of the text and, particularly, on the network of spiritual and messianic correspondences assumed to link both Old and New Testaments.[16]

In the context of this practice, Augustine also manages to attain an excellent balance between the attention given to number as such, as "qualifying" its textual environment, and the importance conceded to the biblical context per se, as the key to the meaning of the numerical figures it contains. Medieval arithmology, in the wake of Augustine, will revolve around this central question of whether to privilege secular knowledge over Christian thought, or vice versa, in interpreting Scripture. These two attitudes are summed up in the two following quotations, the first by Augustine and the

---

[14] See Jean-Pierre Brach, "The Reception of Augustine's Arithmology," in *Oxford Guide to the Historical Reception of Augustine*, ed. Karla Pollmann (Oxford: Oxford University Press, 2013).
[15] A. Quacquarelli, "Recupero della numerologia per la metodica dell'esegesi patristica," *Annali di Storia dell'Esegesi* 2 (1985), 235–249.
[16] *De Trinitate* IV, VI, 10, 47–50 (CSEL, °°).

second by his exact contemporary Ambrose of Milan (although neither of them adhered strictly to a one-sided perspective): "Therefore we cannot say that the number six is perfect because God perfected all his works in six days, but that God perfected his works in six days because the number six is perfect"[17]; and "We do not treat it [i.e., the Septenary] according to the Pythagorean manner or that of the other philosophers, but according to the form and divisions of spiritual grace."[18]

Another key feature of Augustine's arithmology is the frequent display of triadic analogies developed between the Godhead and creation, on the model of the famous quotation of the Book of Wisdom: "Thou hast disposed all things according to measure, number and weight."[19] The Trinitarian structure is therefore being transposed to man and the universe, thus illustrating the ontological participation of creatures in the divine nature. From the Platonic forms and ideal numbers, mathematical archetypes become "essences" in the mind of God, presiding over the manifestation of created beings and constituting the seal of divine wisdom, inasmuch as the material world is actually capable of retaining it. As for the Greek habit of reducing higher numbers to those within the Decad, it is still present, yet now construed as implicating the divine immanence in physical creatures and/ or their return to the Godhead at the end of time.

To give but a few instances of the numerical analogies developed by Augustine, Unity is understood – in traditional fashion – not as a number in the ordinary sense but as an immaterial monad, the most perfect entity aside from God, its immediate origin; 2 denotes separation and the breaking-up of unity, inherent to both love and knowledge; 3 is, of course, referred to the Trinity and is, more generally, the heavenly number of the soul, whereas 4 is that of the body and of the material world, a figure of firmness and solidity; 5 illustrates virginity and the five senses, instruments of the soul; 6 – as we have seen – represents the accomplishment of creation; 7 symbolizes the perfection of creation, imaged by the Sabbath and the gifts of the Holy Ghost; the Kingdom and messianic era are figured by 8, whereas 9 is but the last step before the denary which, as 3 + 7, introduces the Decalogue and expresses the ultimate fulfillment of all things; 12 is, of course, the number of the Apostles, of the Elect ($12 \times 12 = 144$), and of the spreading of the Gospel (3 [Trinity] $\times$ 4 [corners of the world]); 40, of fasting and penance; 50, of the Jubilee, and so forth. Geometrical symbolism is evoked, in turn, in the *De*

---

[17] *De Genesi ad litteram*, IV, 7, ed. and trans. into French by P. Agaësse and A. Solignac, 2 vols. (Paris: Desclée de Brouwer, 1972), 288–299, 635–639.
[18] Ambrosius, *Ep.* XXXI (44, ML), 32–34; (CSEL, 1968, 217 [O. Faller],★★).
[19] *Wis.*, XI, 21.

*quantitate animae*[20] to describe the relations between the soul and body. The characteristics of some elementary, circular, and linear figures (e.g., number and symmetry of angles and sides), progressively reduced to the non-dimensional dot (representing the immaterial soul), illustrate the way the soul permeates the whole body and communicates its properties to the different parts or members of it.

Most later medieval writers who treat number symbolism – from Eucher of Lyon (died ca. 450) to John Scottus Eriugena (died ca. 870) – can be said to be dependent on Augustine. Eriugena is, of course, an important and original thinker, who does not limit himself to reproducing or adapting Augustine's views; he develops some quite personal speculations about the process of emanation of numbers from the uncreated Unity (a process parallel, for him, to that of creation). Eriugena brilliantly synthesizes the Greek tradition of Pseudo-Dionysius the Areopagite (sixth century) and Maximus the Confessor (seventh century), both of whom he translated into Latin, with the Western tradition represented by Augustine himself and his followers (Isidore of Seville and the Carolingians), as well as by the "Latin Platonists" from Macrobius (fourth century) to Martianus Capella (fifth century)[21] and Boethius (d. 524).

With the rise of the great medieval schools and universities, this current of Augustinian arithmology gradually blends within the growing body of available literature and knowledge (mathematical and otherwise), a situation that is already perceptible in Carolingian authors and becomes ever more present from the twelfth century on. A number of factors contribute to dissolve traditional references in the flow of common knowledge. These include the development of theology, of the sciences of the Quadrivium (backed by the literature of Latin Platonism, already accessible to the Carolingians), and of physics,[22] plus the attempts at establishing various fixed sets of rules for the interpretation of scriptural numbers, typical of the Victorine and Cistercian Schools (Hugh of Saint-Victor, Eudes of Morimond, Guillaume d'Auberive).[23] Although now included in, one might say, a much larger library, such references nonetheless still retain their power to influence later writers until the end of the thirteenth century and are eventually rediscovered in the Renaissance.[24]

---

[20] *De Quantitate animae*, ed. W. Hörmann (Vienna: Hoelder-Pichler-Tempski, 1986).
[21] Jean-Pierre Brach, *Il simbolismo dei numeri* (Rome: Arkeios, 1999), 40–43.
[22] For instance, the theological transpositions of physics and arithmetic, mostly based on reinterpretations of the *Timaeus*, within the School of Chartres.
[23] Jean-Pierre Brach, *La symbolique des nombres* (Paris: Presses Universitaires de France, 1994), 41–58.
[24] For example, J. Lauret's *Sylva allegoriarum totius Sanctae Scripturae* (Allegories of Scripture; Barcelona, 1570), in which the *Appendix in sylvam de allegoriis numerorum* (Appendix on

## 4 "Which I have introduced as new, but which is in fact old"

Interest in the qualitative aspects of numbers suddenly regained favor in the Renaissance, in the works of Marsilio Ficino (1433–1499) and perhaps most importantly in those of Giovanni Pico della Mirandola (1463–1494) and Johannes Reuchlin (1455–1522). Nevertheless, it is significant that none of them left a systematic account of the topic in question or wrote a specific treatise about it. Ficino made occasional references to arithmology, as well as to geometrical symbolism,[25] in the context of his various commentaries on Plato,[26] as well as in his *Platonic Theology*.[27]

As early as 1486, in his famous *Oration on the Dignity of Man* (to which the section title refers),[28] Pico claimed to have rediscovered number symbolism as a "new way of philosophizing by numbers," and he made clear his intention of reinstating it as a current of speculation in its own right, almost on a par with Neoplatonism, magic, or Kabbalah[29]. Arithmology, therefore, ceases to be mainly a hermeneutical tool for the interpretation of passages from the Bible and becomes – to a certain extent – an autonomous "art of numbers" capable of addressing problems of cosmology, metaphysics, or theology. In his *Conclusiones* (or *900 Theses*, 1486[30]) and *Apology* (1487), Pico introduces the category of "formal number," implying that mathematical entities – in typical Neoplatonic fashion – possess an independent ontological status. Located in an intermediary level of reality, above the material plane, they are endowed with

---

numerical allegories) still derives its title from Augustine (*numerorum sylva* – "host" of numbers – Serm. CCLXX).

[25] Michael Allen, "Marsilio Ficino: Demonic Mathematics and the Hypotenuse of the Spirit," in *Natural Particulars: Nature and the Disciplines in Renaissance Europe*, ed. Anthony Grafton and Nancy Siraisi (Cambridge, MA: The MIT Press, 1999), 121–137; Stéphane Toussaint, "Mystische Geometrie und Hermetismus in der Renaissance: Ficinus und Cusanus," *Perspektiven der Philosophie* 26 (2000), 339–356.

[26] Michael J. B. Allen, *Nuptial Arithmetic: M. Ficino's Commentary on the Fatal Number in Book VIII of Plato's Republic* (Berkeley: University of California Press, 1994).

[27] Marsilio Ficino, *Platonic Theology*, ed. and trans. by M. J. B. Allen and J. Hankins (Cambridge, MA: Harvard University Press, 2001).

[28] This title is in fact a slightly later attribution; translated by John Herman Randall Jr., in *Renaissance Philosophy of Man*, ed. Ernst Cassirer, Paul Oskar Kristeller, and John H. Randall Jr. (Chicago: Chicago University Press, 1948), 223–254.

[29] The study of the interactions of number symbolism with early modern alchemy, magic, and Christian Kabbalah (as in Agrippa, for instance) would require another essay in itself; see Jean-Pierre Brach, "Number Symbolism," in *Dictionary*, ed. Hanegraaff, 874–883 (see esp. pp. 879–880); J.-P. Brach, *Il simbolismo*, 102–107.

[30] Stephen A. Farmer, *Syncretism in the West: Pico's 900 Theses (1486)* (Tempe, AZ: Medieval and Renaissance Texts and Studies, 1998).

the faculty of bestowing "a power and an efficacy" on natural things that belong to the — less "formal," therefore less "actual" — physical plane of existence.[31] Number is thus assimilated to a secondary cause, active on the material world.[32] Even though he does not make use of the expression "formal number" as such, Reuchlin expresses quite similar views in assimilating in turn the essence of intelligible number to that of the divine intellect. From there (i.e., from the conjunction of the primordial Unity and Binary), number "flows" according to a process of emanation and constitutes, along with its subsequent transformation into *tetractys* and Decad, an intermediary realm that, again, "informs" the physical plane.[33]

Following Pico's and Reuchlin's impulse, and obviously facilitated by the growth of the printing industry, the literature of arithmology enjoyed rapid development from the early sixteenth century into the eighteenth, and even later. It gave birth to different typical subgenres and currents, represented by works that have sometimes become famous. An essentially speculative current is that of the French disciples of Jacques Lefèvre d'Etaples (1460?–1536) who, between 1510 and 1521, in Paris, published several treatises on number symbolism. These authors include Charles de Bovelles (1479–1567), whose philosophical exposition of the ontology of number[34] and of the correlated *elevatio mentis* toward the supreme Unity is supported by geometrical considerations that frequently owe much to Nicholas of Cusa's *Docta ignorantia* (On Learned Ignorance, 1440). Others worth mentioning include Josse Clichtove (1472?–1543) and his theological hermeneutics of biblical numerals,[35] and Gèrard Roussel (1500–1550), who produced a learned arithmological commentary on Boethius's *Arithmetica* (Paris: S. de Colines, 1521). All three of these figures demonstrate the continuity of many trends in the practice of arithmology: for example, the serial examination of the primary positive integers and of their varied correspondences and analogies, interpretation of Scripture, and commentary on scientific or philosophical manuals.

---

[31] Jean-Pierre Brach, "Mathematical Esotericism: Some Perspectives on Renaissance Arithmology," in *Hermes in the Academy. Ten Years' Study of Western Esotericism at the University of Amsterdam*, ed. Wouter J. Hanegraaff and Joyce Pijnenburg (Amsterdam: Amsterdam University Press, 2009), 75–89 (see esp. p. 77, and notes).
[32] Brach, "Mathematical Esotericism."
[33] Brach, "Mathematical Esotericism," 76–77.
[34] Charles de Bovelles, *Liber de XII numeris* (Treatise on the [first] 12 numbers) (Paris: H. Estienne, 1510/11). An ensemble of varied mathematical tracts.
[35] Josse Clichtove, *Opusculum de mystica significatione numerorum* (On the mystical signification of numbers [which are found in Scripture]) (Paris: H. Estienne, 1513).

Another category within arithmological texts is that of the *Summae* or "Encyclopedias." Such volumes were inspired by the atmosphere of the Counter-Reformation and aimed at mobilizing vast resources of erudition to establish the agreement of academic learning with Scripture and Roman Catholic orthodoxy, via the mediation of number symbolism. Pietro Bongo's *Numerorum Mysteria* (1599)[36] and Athanasius Kircher's *Arithmologia* (1665)[37] represent the most well-known examples of such efforts, which have conferred to their topic a wide cultural appeal and relevancy. Other important essays of this kind, but written in a different spirit, include J. Lauret's *Sylva allegoriarum totius Sanctae Scripturae* (Allegories of Scripture; Barcelona, 1570), an interpretation of biblical allegories, including numerical ones, still very much in the medieval tradition (although it makes use of humanist sources such as the works of the Venetian Christian kabbalist Francesco Zorzi, 1466?–1540) and *Denarius pythagoricus*, a compendium of ancient Greek arithmological literature by Johannes Meursius (1579–1639).[38]

At the other end of the scale, we find similar endeavors but limited to the study of a single given number, most often – yet not exclusively – the septenary. Most important in this respect are Alessandro Farra's 1562 *Settenario dell'humana riduttione* (Septenary of the human "reduction" [to wisdom])[39] and Fabio Paolini's 1571 *HEBDOMADES, sive septem de septenario libri* (Hebdomads, or seven books on the septenary).[40] The first deals with the seven degrees of spiritual life leading to the acquisition of divine wisdom, illustrated by seven mythological figures, from Mercury to Orpheus. Its last part makes use of numerical and geometrical analogies, which tend to show how the septenary synthesizes in itself the properties of the other numbers within the Decad. In the course of forty-nine chapters, Paolini concentrates on the interpretation of a verse by Virgil,[41] as well as on the musical scale, which both evoke the number seven. His main purpose – relatively typical of the dominant pursuits of scientific academies of his time, in Northern Italy at

---

[36] Pietro Bongo, *Numerorum Mysteria* (Mysteries of Numbers) (Bergamo: C. Ventura, 1599; reprinted Hildesheim: Olms, 1983).

[37] Athanasius Kircher, *Arithmologia, sive de abditis numerorum mysteriis* (Arithmology, or the hidden mysteries of numbers) (Rome: Varese, 1665). T. Leinkauf, *Mundus combinatus: Studien zur Struktur der Barocken Universal Wissenschaft am Beispiel Athanasius Kirchers SJ (1602–80)* (Akademie Verlag: Berlin, 1993), 192–235.

[38] Johann Meursius (the Elder), *Denarius Pythagoricus* (Pythagorean Decad) (Leiden: J. Maire, 1631).

[39] Venice, C. Zanetti, 1571; Armando Maggi, *Identità e imprese rinascimentale* (Ravenna: Longo, 1998).

[40] Venice, F. Senese, 1589. D. P. Walker, *Spiritual and Demonic Magic from Ficino to Campanella* (University Park: Pennsylvania State University Press, 2003; originally published 1958).

[41] *Aen.* VI, 646.

least – is in fact to study the (sevenfold) ways of correlating music and poetic discourse to natural and celestial magic to retrieve the "miraculous" achievements of the art of Amphion or Orpheus. During the seventeenth (and even eighteenth) century, a number of other treatises concerned with the "mysteries" of a single number were published,[42] thus perpetuating a tradition dating back to Greek antiquity. Their speculative value is unequal, and their contents oftentimes dilettantish and haphazardly compiled.

Following in the wake of Cusa's *Idiota de Mente* (The Layman on the Spirit, 1450), certain thinkers evinced a broader, more general interest in the practical applications of mathematics – even striking up relations with artists and craftsmen – and in doing so insisted on the role and importance of geometry, while evoking the spiritual analogies and transpositions of number and figures. Charles de Bovelles (later Desargues) kept these topics separate in his handbooks of geometry. Luca Pacioli (1445?–1514), on the other hand, added to his *De divina proportione*[43] several tracts of a technical nature, praising sculptors and architects. *De divina proportione* was devoted to the symbolic properties of the geometrical division in mean and extreme ratio (the so-called divine proportion or – later – Golden Section) and of the five Platonic polyhedra of the *Timaeus*, which express for Pacioli the way in which the perfection of divine attributes is mirrored in the fabric of the universe.

In his *Mathematicall Praeface* to the first English translation of Euclid's *Elements*,[44] the famous John Dee also extolled, with didactic precision enhanced by the use of vernacular language, the merit and usefulness of applied mathematics (of which he was himself an inventive practitioner). At the same time, he links mathematics to a superior, "formal" conception of number as deriving its being from the supreme Monad, a conception he inherits mainly from Pico. Number as such is present for Dee as a pattern in the mind of the Creator, in angelic and human intellects, as well as in natural objects.

## 5 Lost in Translation

As we have seen, most of these speculative conceptions of mathematics and number symbolism are supported by a mainly Neoplatonic worldview,

---

[42] All dedicated to the Septenary, with the exception of Antonio Croci's *Breve discorso della perfezione del numero ternario* (Brief Discourse on the Perfection of the Ternary) (Modena: G. Cassiani, 1623), and Erik O. Tormius's *De Ternario* (On the number 3) (Franecker, 1663).
[43] *On the Divine Proportion* (Venice: P. Paganini, 1509).
[44] By H. Billingsley (London: J. Daye, 1570); facsimile ed. of the *Mathematicall Praeface* by Allen G. Debus (New York: Science History Publications, 1975).

which grounds the study of nature and cosmology in ontological and theological perspectives. Like all other esoteric currents of the Renaissance (which it frequently pervades, such as magic, alchemy, and Christian Kabbalah), Pythagorean arithmology is bound to a conception of number as "formal cause." It also depends on the doctrines of the unity of creation, and of "cosmic correspondences" linking the different levels of creation, construed as an organic, living being, mirrored entirely (though obviously on a smaller scale) in man.

The progressive decline of such a worldview within European culture, from the seventeenth century onward, was inevitably accompanied by the increasing marginalization of the currents of thought that depended on it, including, of course, arithmology. Increasingly, number is reduced to the status of a mere logical operator, without any reference to the inner essence of things, therefore rendering meaningless its ancient role as a mediator between the qualitative and quantitative aspects of reality. While concentrating on the geometrical and quantitative aspects of space and objects occupying it, scientists henceforth restrict their efforts to the discovery of a mathematically effective account of nature and of its workings, understood as mechanical constructs submitted to verifiable, quantitative laws, in lieu of a quest for the pattern of natural elements in the mind of God, as expressed by the mystic harmonies of numbers and geometrical proportions.

# 35

# PANPSYCHISM

LEE IRWIN

1 Introduction

The term "panpyschism" is a combination of the Greek *pan*, "all or every," and *psuchê* (or psyche), "breath or soul," implying life-force, mental activity, and an animating spirit inherent in all of nature. The historical morphology of the term is complex and it was not until the Renaissance period that the term panpsychism was first used by Francesco Patrizi in 1591 in an esoteric, philosophical work. Much of what might be interpreted as panpsychism is also interwoven with other late philosophical constructs, such as "pantheism," which was first articulated by John Toland in 1705 as "God or Deity throughout everything"; a bit later, "panentheism" defined by Karl Krause in 1829 as a theological doctrine that "all is in God."[1]

The construction of panpsychism within the history of Western esotericism is a complex of related ideas forming a rich morphological history from which ideas of pantheism and panentheism are not easily separated. Further, the early history of panpsychism is implicit in comparison to much later writings in which the concept becomes explicit (and where psyche is usually interpreted as "mind"), although even in contemporary esotericism, panpsychism tends to cover a range that mediates between implicit theories and explicit definitions.[2] In this essay, I will review some key implicit morphologies of panpsychism within the history Western esotericism and, where possible, indicate where the idea becomes more explicit.

---

[1] For John Toland, see Stephan H. Daniel, *John Toland: His Methods, Manners, and Mind* (Montreal: McGill-Queen's Press, 1984), 211ff.; for Karl Krause, see John W. Cooper, *Panentheism: The Other God of the Philosophers* (Grand Rapids: Baker Academic, 2006), 121–122.

[2] For more on this topic, see Cooper, *Pantheism*, 26–30.

## 2 Panpsychism in Greco-Roman Traditions

The belief that nature is ensouled can be found in early Greek philosophy as a classical source for cosmological speculation in Western esotericism. Applied to the world at large, an implicit panpsychism was constructed as an animate presence or vital soul principle within the world, imbued with mental influences, and often conceived as taking the form of gods or goddesses. Thus, for Thales the world was *enpsychion* or "ensouled" as a great living organism, an animal, within which lesser beings had their own lives and souls. Aristotle cites Thales as the author of the statement "all things are full of gods," implying a panpsychism with strong pantheistic content.[3]

In a related but distinct morphology, Cicero attributes similar panspiritual beliefs to Pythagoras, whose mathematical theory infused the whole of nature with divine number and forms, universally spiritualizing nature.[4] Empedocles combined the creative principles (*archai*) of earlier Greek philosophers into a classic unity of four elements (fire, air, water, and earth, from highest to lowest) as mediated by Love and Strife, thus imbuing the entire cosmos with passion and soul. His dictum that "all things have thought" is an expression of implicit panpsychism.[5] Plato envisioned the world as wrapped in a living soul to mediate the Platonic Forms. In the *Timaeus*, he writes of the World Soul, "she was woven in everywhere and encompassed it ... a divine beginning of endless and reasonable life."[6] Even the atomists such as Democritus, who conjectured on the "unfeeling" atoms that make up nature, identified one particular type of atom, the spherical, as possessing soul and sensitivity. These atoms "permeate everywhere." Thus, since these spherical atoms are the primary cause of motion, nature is to some degree ensouled. Even Aristotle, generally not considered a panpsychist, wrote in a late work that because life comes from the vital power of spirit (*pneuma*), then "all things have soul."[7]

The Stoics also formed diverse morphologies of panpsychism, based primarily on the belief that reason was inherent in nature and the cosmos, arising from the *logoi spermatikoi* or active "seeds of universal reason." These implicit seeds give rise to *pneuma* (spirit) as the active principle (symbolized as

---

[3] Aristotle *De anima* (411a7) in David Skrbina, *Panpsychism in the West* (Cambridge, MA: The MIT Press, 2005), 24–26; Conrad Bonifazi, *The Soul of the World: An Account of the Inwardness of Things* (Lanham, MD: University Press of America, 1978), 2.
[4] Cicero, *De natura deorum* (I, 26–28) in Skrbina, *Panpsychism in the West*, 27.
[5] Empedocles (frag. 103) and Aristotle *De anima* (404b11), in Skrbina, *Panpsychism in the West*, 31–32.
[6] Plato, *Timaeus* (31a–37a).
[7] Aristotle, *Generation of Animals* (736b 29ff.) in Skrbina, *Panpsychism in the West*, 49–50.

air and fire) that animates the world and infuses the passive elements (water and earth) and all beings with cohesion, life, and awareness. The cosmos is "an animal, rational and alive, intelligent" and thus divine. According to Cicero, "the parts of the cosmos ... contain the power of sense perception and reason" and the stars "perceive and have intelligence."[8] For the Stoics, the implicit idea is one of pluralistic panpsychism whereby mind (or psyche) exists in varying degrees, or "parts," as distinct from the more monistic view of Plato in which the World Soul is a single animating principle of all nature. Among Neoplatonists such as Plotinus, the soul is a fundamental unity and "ensouled reason" permeates earth, water, air, and fire; thus, the World Soul is an emanation from the One through Mind (*nous*) such that "there is soul in everything ... covering all realms." Here the panpsychic morphology is both a transcendent principle of unity, order, and intelligence and a lower principle of embodied life and growth, suggesting an emanationist panpsychism.[9] Later Neoplatonists such as Iamblichus and Proclus also held a view of the World Soul as a unitary intelligible medium, hierarchically structured, through which the souls of individuals could reunite with the One, although individual souls must overcome intellectual impediments to attain the higher unity.[10]

One textual source that contributed greatly to the morphologies of panpsychism was the *Corpus Hermeticum* (ca. second and third centuries CE). For example, in Book Ten, Hermes cites from the *General Discourses* that "all souls that wander ... as if separate, are from a single soul, the soul of all"; in Book Eleven, Nous explains to Hermes that "Inwardly, a soul full of mind and god fills the universe and brings it to life. Outwardly, the universe is this great and perfect living thing, the cosmos; inwardly, it is all living things."[11] The *Asclepius (Logos teleios* or "perfect discourse") states "the soul and cosmos being embraced by nature are set in motion by her... these [diverse] forms are also united so that all things appear as one whole" and also "the cosmos is one, the soul is one, and God is one." Here we can see that, as in the Hermetica, both God and soul imbue nature with motion and life and

---

[8] Skrbina, *Panpsychism in the West*, 53–58; Bonifazi, *The Soul of the* World, 4–5.
[9] Plotinus *Enneads* (III 8.4–5, V 15 and VI 7). See Cooper, *Pantheism*, 40–42, who argues that Plotinus holds a panentheist view because God as the One contains but is separate from the world (creation).
[10] Iamblichus, *De Mysteriis* (200, 1–10); Gregory Shaw, *Theurgy and the Soul: The Neoplatonism of Iamblichus* (University Park: Pennsylvania State University Press, 1967), 63–67; also, Cooper, *Pantheism*, 43–44.
[11] Brian Copenhaver, *Hermetica* (New York: Cambridge University Press, 1992), 31, 38, 59–60; Clement Salaman et al., *The Way of Hermes* (Rochester: Inner Traditions, 2000), 47, 53, 75–77.

through the agency of gods and spirits form a living cosmos with ranked ontological order.[12]

During this same period, Greco-Roman alchemists borrowed from Empedocles the "living" four elements and united them with a fifth element (quintessence) to create a pluralistic panpyschism in which soul became a medium for the transmutation of elements. Some alchemical writers such as Zosimos strongly reflected Hermetic themes of both panpsychism and panentheism.[13] Implicit panpsychic ideas are also present in many classic texts of Arabic alchemy, for example, the *Tabula Smaragdina* (Emerald Tablet, ca. 650), even though Islamic theology does not generally support ideas of panpsychism.

## 3 The Renaissance Rediscovery of Panpsychism

Nicholas of Cusa articulates an implicit panpsychic vitalism in his work *De Docta Ignorantia* (1440), where he writes of the *anima mundi* (World Soul) that "it co-exists with matter from which it receives a limitation ... [and is] not separable from things." Soul in this case does not mediate between God and the world but is a universal form containing all other forms known only through things. Thus, God is a synthesis of opposites such that all things are in God and God in all things, while soul reflects the immediate, dynamic bonds between formative elements and all creatures. Such a theory is implicitly panpsychic and panentheist.[14] Many Renaissance thinkers drew on Cusa in forming their cosmological theories, each modifying the theory. In addition, Marsilio Ficino in *De Vita Coelitus Comparanda* (1489) articulated the *prisca theologia* or "ancient theology" of a panpsychic Hermeticism and translated into Latin the *Corpus Hermeticum* (as "Pimander," 1463), providing Renaissance thinkers with a primary panpsychic text for further speculations.[15]

Heinrich Cornelius Agrippa in *De occulta philosophia* (1533) devotes several chapters to the panpsychic idea of the World Soul. He writes, "The world, the heavens, the stars and elements have a soul" and "the world lives, has soul and sense, for it gives life to plants and ... sense to animals." He also writes,

---

[12] *Ascelpius: The Prefect Discourse of Hermes Trismegistus*, ed. and trans. by Clement Salaman (London: Gerald Duckworth & Co., 2007), 54–55.
[13] Howard Jackson, *Zosimos of Panopolis on the Letter of Omega* (Atlanta: Society of Biblical Literature, 1978), passim.
[14] *De Docta Ignorantia* (II, 4, 9), in Bonifazi, *The Soul of the* World, 11.
[15] Kocku von Stuckrad, *Western Esotericism: A Brief History of Secret Knowledge* (London: Equinox Press, 2005), 53–56.

"The Soul of the World fills all things ... knitting together all things, that it might make one frame of the world ... one instrument made of many strings ... with only one breath and life." Here we have a monist expression of the panpsychic idea according to which while all strings or individual souls have vibrancy and reason, yet they all harmonize and unite as One.[16]

Paracelsus also supported the alchemical idea of ensouled nature. Under the concept of Archeus, as *spiritus vitae* (or vital spirit), Paracelsus envisions the perfection of the latent potential of nature in concord with the active capacities of soul. He writes, "The spirit with all its powers is born of God and thus the body of the world [nature] is provided with as many powers as man needs ... each soul encloses [these powers] within itself." Thus through soul, in combination with the agency of Archeus, divine and natural potentials (or "seeds") could be brought to perfection.[17] The Italian naturalist Girolamo Cardano articulated a similar form of panpsychic dualism: Among five principles of nature, soul (*anima*) as the principle of life, inherent in all natural bodies (composed of matter and form), mediates between body and mind (the higher form of soul).[18]

In *Nova de universis philosophia* (1591), Francesco Patrizi explicitly defined *pampsychia* as the necessary, mediating soul (*anima*) that unified the Neoplatonic source of light in its descending illuminations with heavenly, elemental, and worldly bodies. Heavenly bodies (stars) are described as endowed with "mind" and as "animate" as well as endowed with "light, heat, motion," and the "seeds of things." Patrizi further defined soul as an "incorporeal-corporeal" — that is, a real being, alive and rational, imitating higher mind but also with some characteristics of body.[19] Soul in this view, informed by the supersensible through participation in the sensible, is a mediating presence partaking of both supernal mind and living nature. Thus, all of nature is infused with ten grades of soul that mediate higher mind; however, "nature" is further differentiated by explicit qualities that in turn create generic and individual forms of bodies, such that soul is also

---

[16] Henry Cornelius Agrippa, *Three Books of Occult Philosophy*, ed. Donald Tyson (Woodbury: Llewellyn Publications, 1998), 419–421.

[17] Jolande Jacobi, *Paracelsus: Selected Writings* (Princeton: Princeton University Press, 1979), 199; Andrew Weeks, *Paracelsus: Speculative Theory and the Crisis of the Early Reformation* (Albany: State University of New York Press, 1997), 109–110; Bonifazi, *The Soul of the World*, 7–11.

[18] Brian Copenhaver and Charles Schmitt, *Renaissance Philosophy* (New York: Oxford University Press, 1992), 308–309; Skrbina, *Panpsychism in the West*, 67–68.

[19] Benjamin Brickman, "An Introduction to Francesco Patrizi's Nova de Universis Philosophiam" (Ph.D. Dissertation, New York: Columbia University, 1941), 27–30, 40–41, 52–53.

differentiated in each being.[20] The whole cosmos (or *Pancosmia*) is filled with soul, and this includes the inorganic, the elemental, the earth itself, as well as all plants, animals, and humans.[21]

For Patrizi, space, the first created quality of nature, is infinite, unbounded, and limited only by human thought or by local bodies. In the center of this infinity is earth. Maximal space is the primal place of natural creation through minimal constructs, reducible to Pythagorean number, geometry, and volumes. Thus, soul infuses all space and is also manifest through mathematical principles inherent in the creation of form, structure, and elemental bodies created by higher mind and ultimately, by the One-that-is-All. Light and heat then manifest in primordial space, giving birth to a multiplicity of forms and bodies connected by flow or "flux" (a medium of soul) that creates concord or discord between beings.[22] Thus, the entire pancosmia is alive, soulful, infused with divinity and mind, which descends from the divine essence as the highest quality of soul, above and yet within nature. Christianizing the One-All, Patrizi claims that the Deep Divine has three aspects: the Father (*Un'omnia*, Absolute One), the Son (Unity or First Mind, containing all essences and ideas), and the Holy Spirit (Second Mind, containing all souls and beings).[23]

Drawing on Nicholas of Cusa, Giordano Bruno constructed a complex theory of "soul" in a boundless, acentric universe of multiple worlds, suns, and stars. In a universe without a center, Bruno writes that "all things are full of spirits, divine power, God or divinity, and the whole of intelligence and the whole of soul is everywhere." Paying tribute to Pythagoras, he offers the analogy that just as a piece of a broken mirror can reflect an image of the whole, so, too, the "particles of matter" (making up soul) reflect the whole of creation. These atomic "minima" ("seeds" or "tiny worlds") are part of every object, however small, such that even the least corpuscle possesses in itself a

---

[20] Brickman, "An Introduction to Francesco Patrizi's Nova de Universis Philosophiam," 32–35; Skrbina, *Panpsychism in the West*, 70–72; Miguel Granada, "New Visions of the Cosmos," in *The Cambridge Companion to Renaissance Philosophy*, ed. James Hankins (New York: Cambridge University Press, 2007), 275–278.

[21] Paul Oskar Kristeller, *Eight Philosophers of the Italian Renaissance* (Palo Alto: Stanford University Press, 1964), 121–123; Brickman, "An Introduction to Francesco Patrizi's Nova de Universis Philosophiam," 42–43.

[22] Brickman, "An Introduction to Francesco Patrizi's Nova de Universis Philosophiam," 44–51, 56–57; see also Luc Dietz, "Space, Light and Soul in Francesco Patrizi's *Nove De Universis Philosophia* (1591)," in *Natural Particulars: Nature and the Disciplines in Renaissance Europe*, eds. Anthony Grafton and Nancy Siraisi (Cambridge, MA: The MIT Press, 1999), 139–169.

[23] Copenhaver and Schmitt, *Renaissance Philosophy*, 187–195; Brickman, "An Introduction to Francesco Patrizi's Nova de Universis Philosophiam," 36–39, 67–71.

portion of spiritual substance that allows it to become alive. Thus, "the soul of the world, the spirit of the universe, connects and unites everything with everything else." Further, soul as a "universal formal cause" animates the entire infinite universe and "according to the diversity of dispositions of matter and the capacity of material principles, produces different configurations and realizes different potentialities." All of the aspects of nature are ensouled but differentiated; simultaneously, "every soul and spirit has some degree of continuity with universal spirit." For Bruno, panpsychism is an explicit unitary theme in which soul is the vital medium of a vast divine immanence uniting nature, mind, and spirit in continual processes of creation, destruction, and regeneration.[24]

Tommaso Campanella presents us with a late example of a Renaissance theory of implicit panpsychism. He identifies three primaries: power, wisdom, and love as inherent in all things. Power or perhaps better energy is his first principle – the power to be, to maintain being, to sustain existence. Wisdom derives from sensation and perception: As all beings are and perceive, they "know" both themselves and other beings. The primary elements of the world are such knowing beings, with varying degrees of perception and power, and through combination "the heavens are sentient and the earth and animals as well." Further, the world's multitude of beings reflects the image of God, and they are related to one another through divine love. This primary quality of love is fundamental to the joy, power, and awareness of existence; self-knowledge and, more inclusively, knowledge of others result in "change in the sentient body" through a sharing of perceptions, manifest as sympathy and antipathy. The medium of this sharing and communication is soul, individual and universal, "infused by God." Knowledge in this context is a reflective process by which the "higher intellect" is assimilated into that which it contemplates, such that "the world becomes a conscious image of God with all its parts endowed with sense perception." The human being is thus a microcosm, a witness, who can reflect on the macrocosm as a "perfect animal with its own body, spirit, and soul."[25]

[24] Giordano Bruno, *Cause, Principle and Unity and Essays on Magic* (New York: Cambridge University Press, 1998), 5–6, 43–45, 91–92, 111–115, 129–130; Kristeller, *Eight Philosophers*, 127–144; Bonifazi, *The Soul of the World*, 1978: 12–15; Copenhaver and Schmitt, *Renaissance Philosophy*, 314–317; Skrbina, *Panpsychism in the West*, 72–76; also see Ramon Mendoza, *The Acentric Universe: Giordano Bruno's Prelude to Contemporary Cosmology* (Boston: Element Books, 1995), 31, 125–128, *passim*.

[25] John Headley, *Tommaso Campanella and the Transformation of the World* (Princeton: Princeton University Press, 1997), 89–93; Copenhaver, *Hermetica*, 318–328; Skrbina, *Panpsychism in the West*, 77–81; see also D. P. Walker, *Spiritual & Demonic Magic from Ficino to Campanella* (University Park: Pennsylvania State University Press, 2000), 224–229.

## 4 Panpsychism in the Seventeenth and Eighteenth Centuries

The shift from religious to scientific discourse in panpsychic thought is perhaps best illustrated by William Gilbert, who in *De Magnete* (1600) described the force of magnetic attraction as "a power of self-movement which seems to betoken a soul." The inventor of the term "electricity," Gilbert described "electrical bodies" as having a light and spiritual *effluvia* that caused attraction and repulsion. The earth itself was a magnetic body, whose effluvia or "animate force" expressed World Soul. Hence, if all planetary bodies have magnetic fields, they must also "have souls or minds" that they can communicate to other objects, thus magnetizing them. Anthanasius Kircher drew on Gilbert in his three-volume work on magnetism *Magnes, sive De Arte Magnetica* (1641) and also described magnetism as an elementary soul force that was a "secret power of nature" expressing an aspect of the indwelling presence of God.[26] Johannes Kepler wrote that each planet was endowed with an animating force or "soul" that he claimed was magnetic, but whose motions could be calculated with mathematical precision. In his work *Harmonies of the World* (1618), he further claimed that predictable movements of the planets were the "object of some mind" and that "there dwells in the sun simple intellect or *nous* ... the source of every harmony." However, some years later he concluded that the cause of planetary motion was some "corporeal force," that is, a mechanical cause.[27] Thus in Kepler, we can map the rise of measurable mechanics as a causal explanation for motion and life, instead of soul and mind. From this point forward, panpsychism becomes increasingly aligned with esoteric doctrines in the face of growing mechanistic and material explanations of causality.

Cambridge Platonists and esotericists such as Henry More and Ralph Cudworth, both dedicated Protestants, defended a view of nature and matter as a "vital, formative (plastic) ground" of Spirit. Cudworth wrote, "we constantly oppose the generation of souls ... out of dead and senseless matter and assert all souls to be substantial as matter itself." Thus, the "spirit of nature" was a divine power pervading the physical world and sowing "spermatical or vital" seeds, thus giving rise to all natural forms. These "seminal forms" (like Stoic *logoi spermatikoi*) pervade all of "plastic nature" and act from within to shape matter into variable forms – beings, plants, animals, humans – as a "whole corporeal universe ... together in one

---

[26] Skrbina, *Panpsychism in the West*, 76–77; Bonifazi, *The Soul of the World*, 80–82.
[27] Skrbina, *Panpsychism in the West*, 81–82; Bonifazi, *The Soul of the World*, 27–28.

harmony."[28] According to Henry More, the vital conjunction of spirit with matter (or soul with body) was through a shared "vital congruity" that blurred their differences and made each receptive to the other. Soul pervades the entire universe, within all matter, and working through the plastic vitality of nature, it shapes each thing according to the "predispositions and occasions of [its] parts." This soul (or spirit of nature) was the "vicarious power of God" as a shaping power inherent to matter-nature, a power that permeated the entire body of each and every created being. This immanent "spirit of nature" could not be accounted for by mechanical explanations or measurable and observable effects; rather, it reflected a purposeful, spiritual universe "above fortuitous mechanisms."[29]

From this period forward, multiple esotericists developed panpsychic themes in which nature retains a vital, symbolic role as representing an inherent spiritual capacity whose secrets must be uncovered through explicit training. In a general sense, "spiritual alchemy" was conceived in terms of a *coincidentia oppositorum* (coincidence of opposites) in which nature and spirit are conjoined through complex, integrative processes of intellectual and visual symbolism. In the context of an implicit panpsychism, the alchemical *Hieros Gamos* (sacred marriage) expresses a symbolism of "ensouled nature" brought to perfection through the stages of alchemical development. This conjunction reflects the union of physical life with vital consciousness "at every level" and symbolizes the goal of the alchemical *opus*. As stated in one alchemical text, Mother Nature, the most perfect of all God's creations, "moves the bodies above and transmutes the elements below." The alchemist exclaims, "nothing can live without soul and all that exists flows forth from thee [Mother Nature] by virtue of the power of God."[30] Isaac Newton, a practicing alchemist who believed in the immanence of divinity within nature, extolled the Universal Ruler who "governs all things" and who is "everywhere present" substantially, in whom all things were contained and moved, "but in a manner not at all corporeal, utterly unknown to us." In another context, he wrote, "we cannot say that nature is not alive." Thus, divinized, living nature held alchemical secrets

---

[28] Bonifazi, *The Soul of the World*, 54–65.
[29] Skrbina, *Panpsychism in the West*, 85–87; Bonifazi *The Soul of the World*, 65–67.
[30] Unknown author, "A Demonstration of Nature," in *The Hermetic Museum Restored and Enlarged*, ed. Arthur Waite (Newburyport: Samuel Weiser, 1999), 133; Karen-Claire Voss, "Spiritual Alchemy: Interpreting Representative Texts and Images," in *Gnosis and Hermeticism: From Antiquity to Modern Times*, ed. Roelof van den Broek and Wouter Hanegraaff (Albany: State University of New York Press, 1998), 147–181.

that Newton sought to uncover, as expressed in his extensive alchemical writings.[31]

The German theosopher and alchemist Friedrich Christoph Oetinger was another explicit panpsychist. Oetinger's concept of infinite space as the *sensorium dei* (awareness of divinity) was linked to the concept of the first light of creation as "electrical fire" drawn out of chaos by God for creation. This electrical fire (also referred to as *spiritus mundi* or with reference to Paracelsus, as *Archeus*) penetrates all matter as a transformative or "plastic" (*gestaltend*) principle and brings all things to life. As a God-created animating force, electrical fire is a creative, generative power constantly giving birth "within the womb of Nature" to innovation and new forms. As a potentially evolutionary principle, the work of electrical fire was divine self-revelation, the highest expression of which was corporeality and incarnation, "the end of all the ways of God." In referring to the electrical fire, Oetinger wrote, "One may well say that the earth is the mother of the subtlest and rarest essences, and that life lies quiescently in every body ... life is never separable from matter, at the very birth of the atoms, life or spiritual elements were incorporated." In human beings, he writes, "the psychic is electrical, the intellectual supersedes the electrical and yet is so compatible with it that none can define the frontier between them."[32] Franz Anton Mesmer also combined electrical theory with the idea of animal magnetism (animal from *anima*, soul) to describe the "rarefied fluid" that circulated through nature.[33]

## 5 Panpsychism in the Nineteenth and Twentieth Centuries

F. W. J. Schelling in his *Naturphilosophie* emphasized a single underlying force that expressed a panpsychic outlook through the "absolute identity" of spirit and nature. The natural processes of electricity, magnetism, and chemical reaction were "secondary potencies" that acted on the "first potency" of inorganic matter to produce a "third potency" in the form of organic beings who manifested sensitivity in the form of attraction and repulsion. In the human being, these interactive potencies produced self-awareness that was then able to reflect on the entire process. The tension or opposition between spirit and matter was thus reconciled through a graded evolution of stages by

---

[31] Isaac Newton, "Commentary on the Emerald Tablet" in *The Alchemical Reader: From Hermes Trismegistus to Isaac Newton*, ed. Stanton Linden (New York: Cambridge University Press, 2003), 247; Bonifazi, *The Soul of the World*, 45–49; Skrbina, *Panpsychism in the West*, 93–94.
[32] Oetinger as quoted in Bonifazi, *The Soul of the World*, 87–95.
[33] Nicholas Goodrick-Clarke, *The Western Esoteric Traditions: A Historical Introduction* (London: Oxford University Press, 2008), 174–180.

which the latent potency of spirit became manifested in conscious, self-aware beings. Nature functioned through a dynamic process by which absolute Spirit was able to objectify itself in a "higher physics" that was trans-mechanical and gave an ontological affirmation to spiritual potential inherent to nature. Here we can see a panpsychic attitude or, more exactly, an implicit panentheism that emphasizes emergent evolution. Purposeful nature, stimulated by spirit, demonstrated a "continuous striving toward organization," and "spirit, understood as the principle of life, is called soul" – a formless influence of incessant creative activity within nature. As a Christian, Schelling wrote, "the conviction of a genuine unity of God and Nature is the veritable point at which human science is fulfilled."[34]

In *Nanna: On the Soul Life of Plants* (1848), Gustav Fechner wrote of his "day light view" of the world as nature utterly alive and conscious, matter outwardly and spirit inwardly. Spirit and soul were inseparable from matter and nature. For Fechner, souls were inherent to every aspect of nature, with simpler souls below humans and more complex above humans in the planet, the sun, the solar system, and the cosmos overall. Each soul contributed to the complexity and diversity of the whole of nature forming a perfect unity, an ensouled cosmos. He contrasted this view to the "night view" of materialism in which humans were a product of blind forces in a universe of utter darkness. Arguing by analogy, Fechner believed that where there was life, as in human beings, there was also soul. Human consciousness only contributed to the existing consciousness of every plant and animal to create a collective earth consciousness, or earth-soul, that in turn contributed to the living consciousness of the conjoined planets, sun, and moons. Between earth and sun, a special relationship existed through an exchange of light-energy that connected all organic beings in a unitary consciousness. In this "intercourse of light," each organic being contributed its unique quality of awareness to the whole. In turn, this created an "earth system" superior to humanity that maintains the harmony and balance of nature. All organic beings have a degree of inwardness, distinct by species, location, and habitat. God is the unifying matrix of this shared awareness; soul development is a guiding influence in an increasing scale of complexity for each aspect of nature (a cell, a plant, an animal) in "a state of becoming that gives direction to the entire process."[35]

---

[34] Antoine Faivre, *Access to Western Esotericism* (Albany: State University of New York Press, 1994), 82–83, 272–273; Skrbina, *Panpsychism in the West*, 115; *The Soul of the World*, 167–174.

[35] William James, *A Pluralistic Universe* (Glouchester: The Book Depository, 2007 [1909]), 53–71; Skrbina, *Panpsychism in the West*, 122–126; Bonifazi, *The Soul of the World*, 152–158. William James also expressed pluralistic panpsychic beliefs.

In the twentieth century, panpsychism has become a fully explicit concept in the writings of many esotericists influenced by philosophical thought – for example, Alfred P. Sinnett, P. D. Ouspensky, Eileen Garrett, Jane Roberts, and others. At the same time, writers in philosophy and science have also articulated explicit theories of panpsychism – among them Josiah Royce, Henri Bergson, Alfred North Whitehead, Teilhard de Chardin, Gregory Bateson, and others. Many magical societies embraced a pantheistic attitude as they assimilated neo-pagan beliefs about nature.[36] The world as embodying a living, divine presence whose members are conscious and uniquely developed through a multitude of cultural sub-collectives is certainly a fundamental idea in esotericism. The panpsychic perspective on nature as ensouled reflects innumerable morphologies whose contributions to the whole of esotericism only enrich and deepen the potential "convergence of paradigms" that so often contributes to the multilayered nature of esoteric studies.[37]

---

[36] Panpsychism in neo-pagan thought is pervasive. See Graham Harvey, *Contemporary Paganism: Listening People, Speaking Earth* (New York: New York University Press, 1997), 90, 175–176; Denis Carpenter, "Emergent Nature Spirituality: An Examination of the Major Spiritual Contours of the Contemporary Pagan Worldview" in *Magical Religion and Modern Witchcraft*, ed. James R. Lewis (Albany: State University of New York Press, 1996), 50–53.

[37] The "convergence of paradigms" comes from Peter Russell, *From Science to God: A Physicist's Journey into the Mystery of Consciousness* (Novato: New World Library, 2003), 36–38, 116–117.

# 36

# SEXUALITY

## Hugh B. Urban

## 1 Introduction

Sexuality has long held a central place of both symbolic and practical significance in the history of Western esotericism. Indeed, male-female sexual differentiation and the act of sexual union are among the most pervasive, recurring, and multivalent themes running through esoteric traditions from early Gnosticism and Hermeticism down to contemporary occult and magical groups.

The reasons for this frequent association between sexuality and esotericism are not far to seek. If esotericism refers literally to what is hidden, or known only to an intimate few, then sexuality is not surprisingly one of its most common metaphors. Indeed, we might say that, "in some real sense, sex is the secret *par excellence*."[1] And if esotericism involves a complex dialectic of concealment and revelation of secret knowledge, then it finds a close analogue in eroticism, which also involves a subtle dialectic of concealing and revealing. As Elliot Wolfson observes in his study of sexual imagery in Kabbalah, "eroticism and esotericism converge at the point of divergence . . . eroticism ostensibly exposes the concealed and esotericism conceals the exposed."[2]

Similarly, the union of male and female bodies in sexual intercourse is also a common metaphor (and at times a physical vehicle) for the ideal of divine union, for intercourse between the physical and spiritual realms, and for a state of divine androgyny. If sex (from Latin *sexus*) is literally what "divides" or "separates" male from female bodies, then the act of sexual union can serve

---

[1] Wouter J. Hanegraaff and Jeffrey J. Kripal, eds., *Hidden Intercourse: Eros and Sexuality in the History of Western Esotericism* (Leiden: Brill, 2008), xi.
[2] Elliot Wolfson, "Murmuring Secrets: Eroticism and Esotericism in Medieval Kabbalah," in Hanegraaff and Kripal, eds., *Hidden Intercourse*, 65.

as a powerful symbol, or even ritual technique, for the experience of spiritual reintegration. Finally, because esoteric traditions are by definition largely secret, surrounded by layers of concealment and obfuscation, they have also been frequent targets for charges of sexual licentiousness, obscene perversion, and all manner of transgressive rites. Indeed, from the early gnostics down to the medieval heresies, Freemasons, and contemporary occult movements, one of the most frequent (and often fantastic) charges leveled at esoteric traditions is that they are involved in some form of perverse, demonic, or sacrilegious sexual activity.

Since the literature on sexuality and esotericism is vast, in this essay I will focus on just a few of the more representative traditions, exploring three main periods in the history of Western esotericism from roughly the second or third century onward: first, late antique and medieval esoteric traditions such as Hermeticism, Gnosticism, and Kabbalah; second, esoteric currents of the Renaissance and Enlightenment, such as magic, alchemy, and the works of Emanuel Swedenborg; and finally, the modern forms of sexual magic that emerged in America and Europe from the mid-nineteenth century onward, with figures such as Paschal Beverly Randolph and Aleister Crowley. To conclude, I will suggest that these long associations between sexuality and esotericism have continued into the twenty-first century, giving birth to a whole new age of spiritual sexuality – though today often in ironically "exotericized" forms for a mass popular audience.

## 2 "When the Two Are Made One": Sexual Themes in Hermeticism, Gnosticism, and Kabbalah

The symbolism of sexual union is one of the oldest tropes in Western esoteric literature, appearing throughout early Hermetic, Christian, and Jewish traditions alike to express the ineffable nature of the divine, the transmission of secret knowledge, and the experience of mystical union. One of the most explicit examples of this use of sexual imagery is found in the Coptic version of the hermetic text *Asclepius*, which describes sexual union as a "wonderful representation" of the transmission of the holy mysteries. Indeed, sexual union here seems to be a metaphor for esotericism itself and for the nature of hidden, ineffable and secret knowledge: To the uninitiated, it seems disgraceful and shameful; to those who know, it is the most profound experience of divine union itself:

> For when the semen reaches its climax, it leaps forth. In that moment the female receives the strength of the male; the male for his part receives the

strength of the female, while the semen does this. Therefore the mystery of intercourse is performed in secret, in order that the two sexes might not disgrace themselves in front of many who do not experience that reality... if it happens in the presence of those who do not understand the reality [it is] laughable and unbelievable. And, moreover, they are holy mysteries, of both words and deeds, because not only are they not heard, but also they are not seen.[3]

Sexual images of the divine and of spiritual union also appear throughout the large and amorphous body of early Christian literature known as Gnosticism. According to the key Valentinian gnostic text the *Gospel of Philip*, the return of the soul to its true spiritual home is described as a kind of spiritual wedding, the mystery of the "bridal chamber." Death, *Philip* tells us, came into the world through the separation of Eve from Adam in Paradise; therefore, Christ has come to heal this division by reuniting the divided soul with its spiritual counterpart and so give it eternal life. However, as April DeConick has argued, the Valentinians saw the sexual act as more than simply symbolic. At the same time, they revered sexual union as the sacred moment in which the Spirit of God joins with the souls of the parents to produce a child. Thus, the Valentinians also appear to have developed contemplative sexual practices designed to "conceive children whose souls would contain an elect or morally-included 'seed' of the Spirit."[4]

Some of the most complex and profound sexual imagery appears in the Jewish mystical tradition and in the rich body of esoteric texts that comprise the Kabbalah. Kabbalistic literature uses erotic symbolism in a variety of ways, for example, to describe the relationship between the Torah and her lover, the kabbalist, and to describe the relations between different aspects of the divine realm itself. According to most kabbalistic traditions, there is a series of ten divine emanations or potencies (*sefirot*) that radiate from the divine abyss in a succession of male-female pairs. Often the *sefirot* are imagined in the form of a divine (male) body or *anthropos*, complete with its own penis. Much of kabbalistic spiritual practice is aimed at rejoining the male and female aspects of the divine body manifest as the *sefirot*. And because human beings on earth are a mirror of the divine realm above, physical sexual union between husband and wife can also serve as a technique to rejoin the *sefirot* and so assist in the

---

[3] *The Nag Hammadi Library in English*, trans. James R. Robinson (San Francisco: Harper & Row, 1977), 300–301. See Roelof van den Broek, "Sexuality and Sexual Symbolism in Hermetic and Gnostic Thought and Practice," in Hanegraaff and Kripal, eds., *Hidden Intercourse*, 1–21.
[4] April DeConick, "Conceiving Spirits: The Mystery of Valentinian Sex," in Hanegraaff and Kripal, eds., *Hidden Intercourse*, 23.

unification of the male and female aspects of God. In the words of the classic thirteenth-century text the *Zohar*, this union of man and wife in turn symbolizes the union of God with his bride, the community of Israel itself:

> When there is male and female, and he is sanctified in the supernal holiness ... when a man is in the union of male and female, and he intends to be sanctified ... then he is complete and called one without any blemish. Therefore a man should gladden his wife at that time, to invite her to be of one will with him. ... When the two are found as one, then they are one in soul and body.[5]

These texts make it clear, however, that this union is anything but a matter of sexual license or hedonism. On the contrary, this union is not so much antinomian as "hypernomian," as the husband and wife must prepare themselves by strict celibacy for six days "for the Torah's sake, and on Sabbath nights have their conjugal union."[6]

### 3 Eros, Magic, and Conjugial Love in the Renaissance and Enlightenment

Many of these older currents of Hermeticism, Gnosis, and Kabbalah were rediscovered and revived during the European Renaissance, giving birth to a rich new esoteric synthesis. Some of the most important speculations on esoteric sexuality appear in the works of Italian philosophers and magicians such as Marsilio Ficino (1433–1499) and Giordano Bruno (1548–1600). As Ficino wrote in his classic treatise on Love, the forces of Eros and Magic are inextricably intertwined, for both work by the principle of attraction, the drawing together of similar things, which is the very force that holds both the human and body and the entire universe itself together:

> The whole power of Magic is founded on Eros. The way Magic works is to bring things together through their inherent similarity. ... [I]n our body, the brain, the lungs, the heart, the liver, and other organs interact, favor each other, intercommunicate and feel reciprocal pain. From this relationship is born Eros, which is common to them all; from this Eros is born their mutual rapprochement, wherein resides true Magic.[7]

---

[5] *Zohar* III, 81a-b, quoted in Elliot Wolfson, *Circle in the Square* (Albany: State University of New York Press, 1995), 96. See Moshe Idel, "Sexual Metaphors and Praxis in the Kabbalah," in *The Jewish Family: Metaphor and Memory*, ed. David Charles Kramer (New York: Oxford University Press, 1989), 205.

[6] *Zohar* III, 274.

[7] Ficino, *De Amore* VI, 87. See also D. P. Walker, *Spiritual and Demonic Magic from Ficino to Campanella* (London: Warburg Institute, 1968).

If Eros is the attractive power that holds all things together, from the stars in the heavens to a blade of grass on earth, then magic is the art of understanding and manipulating the attractive relationship between parts of the world. The magus is one who is able to know and control the attractive force flowing through the cosmos, just as a lover binds and creates a magic "web" around his beloved.

After Renaissance magic and Kabbalah, probably the most important source of esoteric sexual imagery is found in the alchemical tradition. The Western alchemical tradition can probably be traced back to the third century BCE, although it underwent a major rediscovery and revival in Europe after the twelfth century. By the time of the Renaissance, alchemy had evolved into a rich and highly symbolic tradition, an art aimed not just at the transformation of physical substances but at a kind of spiritual transformation and divine union. Among the most important figures in this spiritual alchemy was the surgeon, chemist, and pioneer of modern medicine Theophrastus Bombastus von Hohenheim, better known as Paracelsus (1493–1541). Drawing on the magical ideas of Renaissance Hermeticism and the new scientific knowledge of the sixteenth century, Paracelsus saw in alchemy not simply a physical process aimed at transforming base metals (such as lead into gold) or even simply a chemical process aimed at achieving the elixir of life but also an esoteric process occurring within the alchemist himself. According to Paracelsus, the goal of the alchemical process, the Philosopher's Stone, is created through the union and transformation of Sulphur and Salt, here compared to Sol and Luna, the cosmic male and female principles. However, to be united they must be joined with a third thing, Mercury, which unites them as spirit completes soul and body. The process is compared to the union of man and woman, who are united by sperm to create a child:

> There are two matters of the Stone, Sol and Luna, formed together in a proper marriage. . . . [A]s we see that the man or the woman, without the seed of both, cannot generate, in the same way our man, Sol and his wife, Luna, cannot conceive . . . without the seed and sperm of both. Hence the philosophers gathered that a third thing was necessary, namely, the animated seed of both. . . . Such a sperm is Mercury, which by the conjunction of both bodies, Sol and Luna, receives their nature into self in union.[8]

The result of this alchemical marriage is nothing less than the birth of the new spiritual being, the hermaphroditic Adam. This perfect man contains his own

---

[8] Paracelsus, *The Aurora of the Philosophers*, trans. Arthur Edward Waite, in *The Hermetic and Alchemical Writings of Paracelsus* (Berkeley: University of California Press, 1976), v.1, 65–66.

female principle hidden within himself, just as Adam originally contained Eve within himself in Paradise: "They called it their Adam, who carries his own invisible Eve hidden in his body, from that moment in which they were united by the power of the Supreme God. ... The matter of the Philosopher's Stone is none other than a fiery and perfect Mercury extracted by Nature and Art; that is the ... true hermaphroditic Adam."[9]

By the seventeenth and eighteenth centuries, these various streams of erotic magic, Kabbalah, and alchemy had begun to flow together and comingle in the midst of the European Enlightenment. One of the most important forefathers of modern sexual magic – and arguably one of the most influential figures in the rise of modern spiritualism and new religious movements – was the Swedish philosopher, politician, scientist, and mystic Emanuel Swedenborg (1688–1772). A key part of Swedenborg's work is devoted to the nature of love in both its spiritual and physical expressions. Indeed, Swedenborg developed a kind of "sexual theology,"[10] centered on the concept of "conjugial love," or the profound spiritual union between man and woman in their innermost selves. Conjugial love, as he defines it, is in fact "the inmost of all loves, and such that partner sees partner in mind (*animus*) and mind (*mens*), so that each partner has the other in himself or herself ... and they thus cohabit in their inmosts."[11] This inner conjugial union, in turn, re-creates the primordial unity of the human being (*homo*) as a total being that contains both male and female within itself: "For the male and female man were so created that from two they may become as one man, or one flesh; and when they become one, then taken together they are a man (*homo*) in his fullness."[12] The key point, however, is that this union is not limited purely to the spiritual plane. Rather, as in the kabbalistic tradition, physical love can also serve as a ladder to this higher state of conjugial love, and, in turn, the spiritual power of conjugial love will then flow back toward and sanctify physical union: "Carnal love can be *holy* because it is the first step on the ladder to true love of God. The 'love of the Sex' may first be 'corporeal' but 'as man was born to become spiritual' it also becomes spiritual."[13] Swedenborg's ideal of conjugial love would have a tremendous

---

[9] Paracelsus, *The Aurora*, v.1, 65–66.
[10] Robert Rix, "William Blake and the Radical Swedenborgians," *Esoterica* 5 (2003), 115. See Marsha Keith Schuchard, "Why Mrs. Blake Cried: Swedenborg, Blake, and the Sexual Basis of Religious Vision," *Esoterica* 2 (2000), 45–93.
[11] Emanuel Swedenborg, *The Spiritual Diary*, trans. George Bush and James Buss (London: James Speirs, 1889), #4408. See Emanuel Swedenborg, *The Delights of Wisdom Pertaining to Conjugial Love* (New York: Swedenborg Foundation, 1938), 70–129.
[12] Swedenborg, *The Delights of Wisdom*, 43.
[13] Rix, "William Blake," 117.

impact on most later esoteric traditions in the West from the eighteenth century onward, inspiring mystical poets such as William Blake, as well as the Spiritualist movements in America and England in the nineteenth century, which continued his vision of spiritual development through physical union.

### 4 Sex Power Is God Power: The Rise of Sexual Magic in the Nineteenth and Twentieth Centuries

While the general association between sexuality and esotericism has a long history, in the West the practice of sexual magic as a specific, detailed technique appears to be a relatively recent invention. While there are traces of erotic magic in medieval Kabbalah and Renaissance alchemy, the more developed art of *magia sexualis* is largely a product of the modern era, beginning in the mid-nineteenth century. There are many important figures who could be mentioned here – ranging from the Italian Traditionalist Julius Evola, to the Russian Satanist Maria de Naglowska, and esoteric orders such as the Fraternitas Saturni and the Hermetic Brotherhood of Luxor. I will focus here primarily on two of the most important, influential, and yet under-studied sexual magicians of the nineteenth and twentieth centuries.

Arguably the most important figure in the development of modern sexual magic was the enigmatic Spiritualist and Rosicrucian Paschal Beverly Randolph (1825–1875). Born the son of a wealthy Virginia landowner and a slave from Madagascar, Randolph was raised a poor, self-taught, free black in New York City. Orphaned at age seven, he ran away from his foster parents as a teenager to travel the world. Eventually Randolph emerged as a leading figure in nineteenth-century Spiritualism, the most famous scryer of his day, as well as an outspoken abolitionist and advocate of women's rights. Today, however, Randolph is best known as America's foremost exponent of magical eroticism or "affectional alchemy." In sexual love, Randolph saw nothing less than "the greatest hope for the regeneration of the world, the key to personal fulfillment as well as a social transformation and the basis of a non-repressive civilization."[14] In the course of his travels through the areas of Jerusalem and Bethlehem, Randolph claimed to have met a group of fakirs (who may have been members of the unorthodox mystical order, the Nusa'iri) and to have been initiated into the mysteries of sexual magic.

---

[14] Franklin Rosemont, Foreword to John Patrick Deveney, *Paschal Beverly Randolph: A Nineteenth-Century Black American Spiritualist, Rosicrucian, and Sex Magician* (Albany: State University of New York Press, 1996), xv.

Whatever his original inspiration, Randolph began to teach a form of sexual magic that would have a profound impact on later Western esotericism. For Randolph, the sexual instinct is the most fundamental power in the universe, the natural attraction between positive and negative forces that flows through and sustains all things. Borrowing the language of magnetic attraction, Randolph sees the male and female as complementary electro-magnetic forces: On the material plane, the male genitals are positive and the female genitals negative; on the mental plane, the female mind is positive and male mind negative. Hence, the two have an innate attraction that is both physical and spiritual.

Because sexual attraction is the most fundamental force in nature, the experience of orgasm is the most important moment in human existence and the key to magical power. As the moment when new life is infused from the spiritual realm into the material, it is the crucial instant when the soul is opened up to the spiritual energies of the cosmos. Anything that one truly wills at that moment can be accomplished as a magical act:

> The moment when a man discharges his seed – his essential self – into a ... womb is the most solemn, energetic and powerful moment he can ever know on earth. ... At the moment his seminal glands open, his nostrils expand, and while the seed is going forth from his soul to her womb, he breathes one of two atmospheres, either fetid damnation from the border spaces or Divine Energy from the heavens. Whatsoever he shall truly will and internally pray for ... that moment the prayer's response comes down.[15]

The tremendous power contained in sexual union can be used for a wide range of both spiritual and materials ends. Randolph lists an array of such uses of sexual magic, which include "increasing the brain and body power of an unborn child"; "influencing one's wife or husband and magnetically controlling them"; "regaining youthful energy"; "Supreme white magic of will, affection or Love"; "furtherance of financial interests, schemes, lotteries, etc."; and ultimately, "the attainment of the loftiest insights possible to the earthly soul."[16]

Randolph's technique of sexual magic, however, was far from a matter of mere sensual self-indulgence. On the contrary, he insisted that sexual magic should be performed only by married couples and safeguarded by moral and physical sanctions. Quite progressive for his time, Randolph also suggested

---

[15] P. B. Randolph, *The Mysteries of Eulis*, manuscript reproduced in Deveney, *Paschal Beverly Randolph*, 339–340.
[16] Randolph, *The Mysteries of Eulis*, 337.

that the female's pleasure was as important as the male's and that sexual magic could only be effective if both partners experienced a simultaneous orgasm. Finally and perhaps most important, Randolph's sexual magic was also tied to a goal of progressive social reform, ideally leading the way to a new, non-repressive civilization. For Randolph, the leading cause of social ills is the abuse of marital and sexual relations, and, therefore, the key to a more egalitarian, liberated society lay in the mutually beneficial power of Love and Affectional Alchemy. In Randolph's words, "it is in every man's power to make his wife love him, and in every wife's to make her husband worship God through her ... if my rules were followed, the social millennium would be at hand."[17]

Randolph's system of sexual magic was enormously influential, giving birth to a wide array of occult movements throughout America, England, and Europe. Many of Randolph's teachings were transmitted to Europe through esoteric orders such as the Hermetic Brotherhood of Luxor, begun by Max Theon and Peter Davidson sometime in the late 1880s. And they later mingled with Eastern-influenced esoteric groups such as the Ordo Templi Orientis (O.T.O.), founded in the 1890s by Theodor Reuss and Carl Kellner, which made sexual magic the central and most powerful secret of its ritual practice. Indeed, for the OTO, "the KEY which opens up all Masonic and Hermetic secrets" is none other than "the teaching of *sexual magic*, and this teaching explains, without exception, all the secrets of Nature, all the symbolism of FREEMASONRY and all systems of religion."[18]

However, arguably the most important sexual magician after Randolph was the controversial occultist and self-proclaimed "Great Beast 666," Aleister Crowley (1875–1947). Reviled by the popular press as the "king of depravity, arch-traitor and drug-fiend," Crowley is today one of the most influential figures in the revival of modern occultism, magic, and neo-pagan witchcraft. Born in 1875, the son of a minister in the highly puritanical Plymouth Brethren sect, Crowley embodied some of the deepest tensions within British Victorian culture as a whole. A child raised in strict Christian morality, he would later gravitate to the magical arts and to extremes of sexual transgression. Crowley's first great revelation occurred in Egypt in 1904, when he claimed to have come into contact with his Guardian Angel and to have received the *Book of the Law* or *Liber Legis*. The key to Crowley's

---

[17] Randolph, *The Mysteries of Eulis*, 107; Randolph, *The Immortality of Love: Unveiling the Secret Arcanum of Affectional Alchemy* (Quakertown, PA: Beverly Hall Corp., 1978 [1874]), e, 169.

[18] Theodor Reuss, "Mysteria Mystica Maxima," *Jubilaeums-Ausgabe der Oriflamme* (1912), 21. See Hugh B. Urban, *Magia Sexualis: Sex, Magic and Liberation in Modern Western Esotericism* (Berkeley: University of California Press, 2005), chaps. 2 and 4.

new law is the principle of *Thelema*, derived from the Greek meaning "Will," and his central maxim: "Do what thou wilt shall be the whole of the law." In place of servile submission to some imaginary God in the sky, the law of Thelema is the full affirmation of the individual will and of the individual self as the "centre of the cosmos."[19]

Central to Crowley's new law of Thelema – and also the primary reason for the scandalous reputation that surrounds him – is his practice of sexual magic. For Crowley (as for his contemporaries such as Freud), sex is the most powerful force in human nature and the fullest expression of the will. But it has been stupidly repressed by social and religious institutions, thus giving birth to all manner of social and psychological ills. In fact, the "sexual instinct is ennobling," and most social evils are largely "produced by suppressions" and by "the feeling that sex is shameful and the sense of sin."[20]

Crowley's sexual magic itself is a complex melding of both Eastern and Western traditions. In fact, Crowley was one of the most important figures in the transmission of Yoga and the sexual techniques of Hindu Tantra to the West – though in a somewhat garbled form and with significant transformations.[21] But he also combined his knowledge of yoga and Tantra with the tradition of Western esoteric sexuality, as transmitted by Randolph and his followers in groups such as the Hermetic Brotherhood of Luxor and the Ordo Templi Orientis. Beginning in 1910, Crowley became closely involved with the O.T.O. and soon emerged as its most infamous leader. According to Crowley, sexual magic is the most powerful and most secret form of ritual magic, for it unleashes the raw power of human creativity, which has the potential to bring into being anything one desires: "If this secret, which is a scientific secret, were perfectly understood ... there would be nothing which the human imagination can conceive that could not be realized. If it were desired to have an element of atomic weight six times that of uranium, that element could be produced."[22]

In striking contrast to both Randolph and the early O.T.O., however, Crowley emphasized forms of sexuality that were considered quite "deviant" by late Victorian moral standards. In contrast to Randolph's insistence on

---

[19] Aleister Crowley, *The Confessions of Aleister Crowley: An Autohagiography* (New York: Hill and Wang, 1969), 873, 939. See Crowley, *The Law Is for All: The Authorized Popular Commentary on Liber AL sub figura CCII, the Book of the Law* (Tempe, AZ: New Falcon, 1996); Lawrence Sutin, *Do What Thou Wilt: A Life of Aleister Crowley* (New York: St. Martin's Press, 2000).
[20] Crowley, *The Confessions*, 874–875.
[21] Hugh B. Urban, "Unleashing the Beast: Aleister Crowley, Tantra and Sex Magic in Late Victorian England," *Esoterica* 5 (2003), 138–192.
[22] Crowley, *The Confessions*, 767.

heterosexual marriage and strict moral codes, Crowley made use of sexual techniques that were explicitly transgressive as the ultimate keys to magical power. Crowley's revised O.T.O. system of initiations included a series of eleven grades, the eight and eleventh of which involved autoerotic and homosexual intercourse – acts considered both antisocial and self-destructive by the standards of late Victorian morality. Indeed, during his most transgressive period of magical practice while at his Abbey of Thelema in Sicily in the 1920s, Crowley engaged in all manner of radical magical techniques, including bestiality, animal sacrifice, and consumption of blood and excrement, exploiting both sexual and moral transgression as a profound source of magical power.[23] Whereas Randolph had hoped to free the power of sexual love to create a more harmonious, egalitarian society, Crowley hoped to unleash the power of sexual transgression to tear down the repressive Victorian Christian world in which he was raised and create a wholly new one in its place, based solely on the law of Thelema: "Crowley came to believe that he was a new magical messiah – the Lord of the New Aeon – whose doctrine would supersede ... other outmoded religions which had constructed barriers to spiritual freedom. For him the basis of this freedom was sexuality."[24]

## 5 Conclusions: The "Exotericization" of Sexual Magic in the Twenty-First Century

In the wake of Randolph's sexual magic and Crowley's explicitly transgressive practices, a wide range of new forms of esoteric sexuality began to flourish in the late twentieth and early twenty-first centuries. If Randolph had let the "genie" of sexual mysticism out of the bottle, bringing ancient ideas of esoteric sexuality to nineteenth-century America, Crowley broadcast the most transgressive forms of sexual magic to a twentieth-century audience of spiritual consumers. Despite his infamous reputation, Crowley in particular was to have a tremendous impact on virtually all later forms of magic, neo-paganism, and Satanism from the mid-twentieth century onward. We can see direct links, for example, between Crowley's sexual magic and the Great Rite performed by Gerald Gardner and the early

---

[23] See Hugh B. Urban, "The Power of the Impure: Transgression, Violence and Secrecy in Bengali Shakta Tantra and Modern Western Magic," *Numen* 50:3 (2003), 269–308; Sutin, *Do What Thou Wilt*, 265, 288.

[24] Nevill Drury, *The History of Magic in the Modern Age* (New York: Carroll & Graf, 2000), 95. See Aleister Crowley, *The Book of Lies, Which Is Also Falsely Called Breaks* (New York: Samuel Weiser, 1952), 100.

Wiccan covens in mid-twentieth-century England (which included both a symbolic union of male and female and a literal practice of ritual intercourse).[25] We can also see Crowley's influence in the sexual magic performed by Anton Szandor LaVey and the early Church of Satan in the 1960s and 1970s. Even today, Crowley's influence can be seen in more radical movements, such as Chaos Magic, which employ an array of esoteric and often explicitly transgressive sexual practices among other magical techniques.

By the turn of the twenty-first century, the mystical and occult dimensions of sexuality had ceased to be particularly "esoteric." On the contrary, they had begun to appear quite openly on the shelves of bookstores and on countless websites proliferating in cyberspace. Virtually all of these combine a loose mixture of Crowley-style sexual magic with a garbled version of Hindu Tantra, usually with a dash of *Kama Sutra* and *The Joy of Sex* thrown in for good measure. Today we find hundreds of books bearing titles such as *Modern Sex Magick: Secrets of Erotic Spirituality* and *Sex Magic, Tantra and Tarot*; indeed, the more erotically challenged among us can now even consult the *Complete Idiot's Guide to Tantric Sex*. Meanwhile, a mere click of the mouse can bring us "A Sex Magic Primer," the "Church of Tantra," and "Kama Sutra Sex Magic." Ironically, the once elusive secret of sexuality, the source of so many accusations and so much esoteric symbolism, has now become quite exoteric and widely available to a new audience of spiritual consumers.

---

[25] Urban, *Magia Sexualis*, 163–180. See Janet and Stewart Farrar, *A Witches' Bible: The Complete Witches' Handbook* (Custer, WA: Phoenix, 1966), 32–33; Doreen Valiente, *Witchcraft for Tomorrow* (Blaine, WA: Phoenix, 1978), 137–139.

# SUGGESTIONS FOR FURTHER READING

## General Works Treating Western Mysticism

Carmody, Denise Lardner and John Tully Carmody. *Mysticism: Holiness East and West.* Oxford: Oxford University Press, 1996.
Happold, F. C. *Mysticism: A Study and an Anthology.* (Rev. ed.) London: Penguin, 1991.
Harmless, S. J., William. *Mystics.* Oxford: Oxford University Press, 2007.
James, William. *The Varieties of Religious Experience.* (Orig. pub. 1902.) New York: Penguin Classics, 1982.
McGinn, Bernard. *The Presence of God: A History of Western Christian Mysticism.* 5 vols. New York: Crossroad, 1991–2012.
Otto, Rudolf. *Mysticism East and West.* Trans. Bertha L. Bracey and Richenda C. Payne. New York: Meridian Books, 1957.
Stace, W. T. *Mysticism and Philosophy.* (Orig. pub. 1960.) Los Angeles: Tarcher, 1987.
Underhill, Evelyn. *Mysticism: The Nature and Development of Spiritual Consciousness.* London: Methuen, 1911.
Weeks, Andrew. *German Mysticism from Hildegard of Bingen to Ludwig Wittgenstein.* Albany: State University of New York Press, 1993.
Wehr, Gerhard. *Esoterisches Christentum (Aspekte, Impulse, Konsequenzen).* Stuttgart: E. Klett, 1975.
Zaehner, R. C. *Mysticism: Sacred and Profane.* Oxford: Clarendon Press, 1957.

## General Works Treating Western Esotericism

Amadou, Robert. *L'Occultisme: Esquisse d'un monde vivant.* (Expanded ed.) Paris: Chanteloup, 1987.
Broek, Roelof van den and Antoine Faivre (eds.). *Gnosis and Hermeticism: From Antiquity to Modern Times.* Albany: State University of New York Press, 1998.
Faivre, Antoine. *Access to Western Esotericism.* Albany: State University of New York Press, 1994.

*Western Esotericism: A Concise History*. Albany: State University of New York Press, 2010.
Faivre, Antoine and Jacob Needleman (eds.). *Modern Esoteric Spirituality*. New York: Crossroad, 1995.
Godwin, Joscelyn. *The Golden Thread: The Ageless Wisdom of the Western Mystery Traditions*. Wheaton, IL: Quest Books, 2007.
Goodrick-Clarke, Nicholas. *The Western Esoteric Traditions: A Historical Introduction*. Oxford: Oxford University Press, 2008.
Hanegraaff, Wouter J. (ed.) in collaboration with Antoine Faivre, Roelof van den Broek, and Jean-Pierre Brach. *Dictionary of Gnosis and Western Esotericism*. Leiden: Brill, 2005.
Hanegraaff, Wouter J. *Esotericism and the Academy: Rejected Knowledge in Western Culture*. Cambridge: Cambridge University Press, 2012.
Stuckrad, Kocku von. *Western Esotericism: A Brief History of Secret Knowledge*. 2nd ed. London: Routledge, 2014.
Versluis, Arthur. *Magic and Mysticism: An Introduction to Western Esoteric Traditions*. Lanham, MD: Rowman and Littlefield, 2007.
Yates, Frances. *Giordano Bruno and the Hermetic Tradition*. London: Routledge and Kegan Paul, 1964.

# I Antiquity

## *Ancient Mysteries*

Burkert, Walter. *Ancient Mystery Cults*. Cambridge, MA: Harvard University Press, 1987.
Kerenyi, Carl. *Eleusis: Archetypal Image of Mother and Daughter*. Trans. Ralph Mannheim. New York: Pantheon Books, 1967.
   *Dionysus: Archetypal Image of Indestructible Life*. Trans. Ralph Mannheim. Bollingen Series LXV. 2. Princeton: Princeton University Press, 1976.
Meyer, Marvin W. (ed.). *The Ancient Mysteries: A Source Book*. San Francisco: Harper & Row, 1987.
Mylonas, George E. *Eleusis and the Eleusinian Mysteries*. Princeton: Princeton University Press, 1961.
Otto, Walter F. "The Meaning of the Eleusinian Mysteries," in *The Mysteries: Papers from the Eranos Yearbooks*. Ed. Joseph Campbell. Princeton: Princeton University Press, 1955.
Stein, Charles. *Persephone Unveiled: Seeing the Goddess and Freeing Your Soul*. Berkeley: North Atlantic Books, 2006.
Ulansey, David. *The Origins of the Mithraic Mysteries: Cosmology & Salvation in the Ancient World*. Oxford: Oxford University Press, 1989.
Wasson, Gordon R., Albert Hoffman, and Carl A. P. Ruck. *The Road to Eleusis: Unveiling the Secrets of the Mysteries*. Berkeley: North Atlantic Books, 2008.
West, M. L. *The Orphic Poems*. New York: Oxford University Press, 1983.

## Pythagoras and Pythagoreanism

Bamford, Christopher (ed.). *Homage to Pythagoras: Rediscovering Sacred Science*. Hudson, NY: Lindisfarne Press, 1994.
Burkert, Walter. *Lore and Science in Ancient Pythagoreanism*. Cambridge, MA: Harvard University Press, 1972.
Gorman, Peter. *Pythagoras: A Life*. London: Routledge & Kegan Paul, 1979.
Guthrie, Kenneth Sylvan. *The Pythagorean Sourcebook and Library*. Ed. David Fideler. Grand Rapids, MI: Phanes Press, 1987.
Iamblichus (attrib.). *The Theology of Arithmetic: On the Mystical, Mathematical, and Cosmological Symbolism of the First Ten Numbers*. Trans. Robin Waterfield. Grand Rapids, MI: Phanes Press, 1988.
Riedweg, Christoph. *Pythagoras: His Life, Teaching, and Influence*. Trans. Steven Rendall. Ithaca: Cornell University Press, 2005.
Strohmeier, John and Peter Westbrook. *Divine Harmony: The Life and Teachings of Pythagoras*. Berkeley: Berkeley Hills Books, 1999.

## Parmenides and Empedocles

Cherniss, Harold. *Aristotle's Criticism of Presocratic Philosophy*. Baltimore: Johns Hopkins University Press, 1964.
Detienne, Marcel and Jean Pierre Vernant. *Cunning Intelligence in Greek Culture and Society*. Trans. Janet Lloyd. Chicago: University of Chicago Press, 1991.
Gallop, David. *Parmenides of Elea*. Toronto: University of Toronto Press, 2000.
Kingsley, Peter. *Ancient Philosophy, Mystery, and Magic*. Oxford: Oxford University Press, 1995.
*In the Dark Places of Wisdom*. Inverness, CA: Golden Sufi Press, 1999.
*Reality*. Inverness, CA: Golden Sufi Press, 2003.
Kirk, G. S., J. E. Raven, and M. Schofield. *The Presocratic Philosophers*. Cambridge: Cambridge University Press, 2003.
Marciano, M. Laura Gemelli. "Images and Experience: At the Roots of Parmenides'*Aletheia*." *Ancient Philosophy* 28 (2008): 21–48.
Mourelatos, Alexander P. D. *The Route of Parmenides*. Las Vegas: Parmenides Publishing, 2007.
Vernant, Jean Pierre. *Myth and Thought among the Greeks*. Trans. Janet Lloyd and Jeff Fort. Brooklyn: Zone Books, 1988.
*Mortals and Immortals*. Ed. Froma I. Zeitlin. Princeton: Princeton University Press, 1991.

## Plato, Plotinus, and Neoplatonism

Aubry, Gwenaëlle. *Plotin. Traité 53 (I, 1). Introduction, traduction, commentaire et notes*. Paris: Vrin, 2004.
*Dieu sans la puissance. Dunamis et energeia chez Aristote et chez Plotin*. Paris: Vrin, 2006.

"L'impératif mystique: notes sur le détachement de soi chez Plotin et Maître Eckhart," in *Maître Eckhart*. Ed. Julie Casteigt. Paris: Cerf, 2012.
Brisson, Luc. *How Philosophers Saved Myths: Allegorical Interpretation and Classical Mythology*. Trans. Catherine Tihanyi. Chicago: University of Chicago Press, 2004.
Dodds, Eric Robertson. *The Greeks and the Irrational*. Los Angeles: University of California Press, 1951.
Hadot, Pierre. *Plotin. Traité 38 (VI, 7)*, Introduction, traduction, commentaire et notes. Paris: Cerf, 1987.
*Plotin. Traité 9 (VI, 9)*, Introduction, traduction, commentaire et notes. Paris: Cerf, 1994.
*Philosophy as a Way of Life*. Ed. Donald I. Davidson. Trans. Michael Chase. Oxford: Blackwell Publishing, 1995.
*Etudes de philosophie ancienne*. Paris: Les Belles Lettres, 1998.
*Plotinus, or the Simplicity of Vision*. Trans. Michael Chase. Chicago: University of Chicago Press, 1998.
*Plotin, Porphyre. Etudes néoplatoniciennes*. Paris: Les Belles Lettres, 1999.
"Shamanism and Greek Philosophy," in *The Concept of Shamanism: Uses and Abuses*. Ed. Henri-Paul Francfort and Roberte Hamayon. Budapest: Akademiai Kiado, 2001.
*What Is Ancient Philosophy?* Trans. Michael Chase. Cambridge, MA: Belknap Press, 2004.

## Hermetism and Gnosticism

Broek, Roelof van den. "Hermes Trismegistus I: Antiquity," "Hermetic Literature I: Antiquity," and "Hermetism," in Hanegraaff (ed.), *Dictionary of Gnosis and Western Esotericism*.
*Gnostic Religion in Antiquity*. Cambridge: Cambridge University Press, 2013.
Copenhaver, Brian. *Hermetica. The Greek Corpus Hermeticum and the Latin Asclepius in a New English Translation, with Notes and Introduction*. Cambridge: Cambridge University Press, 1992.
Festugière, A.-J. *La révélation d'Hermès Trismégiste*, 4 vols. Paris: Gabalda, 1944–1954.
Filoramo, Giovanni. *A History of Gnosticism*. Trans. Anthony Alcock. Cambridge, MA: Blackwell, 1990.
Fowden, Garth. *The Egyptian Hermes: A Historical Approach to the Late Pagan Mind*. Princeton: Princeton University Press, 1993.
Kasser, Rodolfe and Gregor Wurst (eds.). *The Gospel of Judas, Critical Edition*. Washington, DC: National Geographic Society, 2007.
Lucentini, P., I. Parri, and V. Perrone Compagni (eds.). *Hermetism from Late Antiquity to Humanism*. Turnhout: Brepols, 2003.
Mahé J.-P. *Hermès en Haute-Égypte. Les textes hermétiques de Nag Hammadi et leurs parallèles grecs et latins*, 2 vols. (Bibliothèque Copte de Nag Hammadi, Section « Textes », 3 and 7). Québec: Les Presses de l'Université Laval, 1978–1982 (in vol. 1 NHC VI, 6: *L'Ogdoade et l'Ennéade*, and NHC VI, 7: *Prière d'action des grâces*; in vol 2 NHC VI, 8, 8a: *Le fragment du* Discours Parfait, *Les* Définitions hermétiques arméniennes).
Meyer, Marvin W. (ed.). *The Nag Hammadi Scriptures: The International Edition*. San Francisco: HarperCollins, 2007.

Nock, A. D. and A.-J. Festugière (eds.). *Corpus Hermeticum*. 4 vols. Paris: Les Belles Lettres, 1945–1954.
Robinson, James M. (ed.). *The Coptic Gnostic Library*. 5 vols. Leiden: Brill, 1975–1996.
Rudolph, Kurt. *Gnosis: The Nature and History of Gnosticism*. San Francisco: Harper, 1987.

## Early Jewish Mysticism

Alexander, Philip S. *Mystical Texts: Songs of the Sabbath Sacrifice and Related Manuscripts*. London: T&T Clark, 2006.
Arbel, Vita Daphna. *Beholders of Divine Secrets: Mysticism and Myth in the Hekhalot and Merkavah Literature*. Albany: State University of New York Press, 2003.
Dan, Joseph. *The Ancient Jewish Mysticism*. Tel Aviv: MOD Books, 1993.
Davila, James R. *Descenders to the Chariot: The People Behind the Hekhalot Literature*. Leiden: Brill, 2001.
DeConick, April D. "What Is Early Jewish and Christian Mysticism?" in *Paradise Now: Essays on Early Jewish and Christian Mysticism*. Ed. April D. DeConick. Atlanta: Society of Biblical Literature, 2006.
Elior, Rachel. *The Three Temples: On the Emergence of Jewish Mysticism*. Oxford: Littman Library of Jewish Civilization, 2004.
Halperin, David J. *The Faces of the Chariot: Early Jewish Responses to Ezekiel's Vision*. Tübingen: Mohr Siebeck, 1988.
Himmelfarb, Martha. *Ascent to Heaven in Jewish and Christian Apocalypses*. New York: Oxford University Press, 1993.
Lesses, Rebecca M. *Ritual Practices to Gain Power: Angels, Incantations, and Revelation in Early Jewish Mysticism*. Harrisburg: Trinity Press International, 1998.
Rowland, Christopher, and Christopher Morray-Jones. *The Mystery of God: Early Jewish Mysticism and the New Testament*. Leiden: Brill, 2009.
Schäfer, Peter. *The Hidden and Manifest God: Some Major Themes in Early Jewish Mysticism*. Albany: State University of New York Press, 1992.
*The Origins of Jewish Mysticism*. Tübingen: Mohr Siebeck, 2009.
Scholem, Gershom. *Jewish Gnosticism, Merkabah Mysticism, and Talmudic Tradition*. New York: Jewish Theological Seminary, 1965.
*Major Trends in Jewish Mysticism*. (Orig. pub. 1941.) New York: Schocken, 1974.
Segal, Alan F. *Two Powers in Heaven: Early Rabbinic Reports about Christianity and Gnosticism*. Leiden: Brill, 1977.
Wolfson, Elliot R. *Through a Speculum That Shines: Vision and Imagination in Medieval Jewish Mysticism*. Princeton: Princeton University Press, 1997.

## Early Christian Mysticism

Cohn-Sherbok, Dan, and Lavinia Cohn-Sherbok. *Jewish and Christian Mysticism: An Introduction*. New York: Continuum, 1994.
DeConick, April D. "Heavenly Temple Traditions and Valentinian Worship: A Case for First-Century Christology in the Second Century," in *The Jewish Roots of Christological Monotheism*. Ed. Carey C. Newman et al. Leiden: Brill, 1999.

Voices of the Mystics: Early Christian Discourse in the Gospels of John and Thomas and Other Ancient Christian Literature. Sheffield: Sheffield Academic Press, 2001.

Recovering the Original Gospel of Thomas: A History of the Gospel and Its Growth. London: T&T Clark, 2005.

"Mysticism and the Gospel of Thomas," in *Das Thomasevangelium: Entstehung-Rezeption-Theologie*. Ed. Jörg Frey et al. Berlin: de Gruyter, 2008.

Egan, Harvey D. *An Anthology of Christian Mysticism*. 2nd ed. Collegeville: Liturgical Press, 1996.

Fossum, Jarl E. *The Image of the Invisible God: Essays on the Influence of Jewish Mysticism on Early Christology*. Göttingen: Vandenhoeck and Ruprecht, 1995.

Louth, Andrew. *The Origins of the Christian Mystical Tradition from Plato to Denys*. Oxford: Clarendon Press, 1981.

Orlov, Andrei. *The Enoch-Metatron Tradition*. Tübingen: Mohr Siebeck, 2005.

Rowland, Christopher. *The Open Heaven: A Study of Apocalyptic in Judaism and Early Christianity*. London: SPCK, 1982.

Schweitzer, Albert. *The Mysticism of Paul the Apostle*. Trans. William Montgomery. Baltimore: The John Hopkins University Press, 1998.

Segal, Alan F. *Paul the Convert: The Apostolate and Apostasy of Saul the Pharisee*. New Haven: Yale University Press, 1990.

*Life After Death: A History of the Afterlife in the Religions of the West*. New York: Doubleday, 2004.

## II The Middle Ages

### Sufism

Böwering, Gerhard. *The Mystical Vision of Existence in Classical Islam: The Quranic Hermeneutics of the Sufi Sahl at-Tustari (d. 283/896)*. Berlin: de Gruyter, 1980.

Chittick, William C. *Sufism: A Short Introduction*. Oxford: Oneworld, 2000.

Corbin, Henry. *Spiritual Body and Celestial Earth: From Mazdean Iran to Shi'ite Iran*. Princeton: Princeton University Press, 1977.

Ernst, Carl. *The Shambhala Guide to Sufism*. Boston: Shambhala, 1997.

Izutsu, Toshihiko. *Sufism and Taoism*. Berkeley: University of California Press, 1984.

Knysh, Alexander. *Islamic Mysticism: A Short History*. Leiden: Brill, 2000.

Lings, Martin. *What Is Sufism?* Berkeley: University of California Press, 1975.

Nasr, Seyyed Hossein. *The Garden of Truth*. San Francisco: HarperOne, 2007.

Renard, J. *Knowledge of God in Classical Sufism*. Mahwah, NJ: Paulist Press, 2004.

Ritter, Hellmut. *The Ocean of the Soul: Man, the World, and God in the Stories of Farīd al-Dīn ʿAṭṭār*. Leiden: Brill, 2003.

Schimmel, Annemarie. *Mystical Dimensions of Islam*. Chapel Hill: University of North Carolina Press, 1975.

Schuon, Frithjof. *Sufism: Veil and Quintessence*. Bloomington, IN: World Wisdom Books, 1981.

## Kabbalah

Dan, Joseph. *Kabbalah: A Very Short Introduction*. New York: Oxford University Press, 2006.
Hallamish, Moshe. *An Introduction to the Kabbalah*. Trans. Ruth Bar-Ilan and Ora Wiskind-Elper. Albany: State University of New York Press, 1999.
Heschel, Abraham Joshua. *The Sabbath: Its Meaning for Modern Man*. New York: Farrar, Straus and Young, 1951.
Huss, Boaz. "The Mystification of Kabbalah and the Myth of Jewish Mysticism" [Hebrew]. *Pe'amim* 110 (2007), 9–30.
Idel, Moshe. *Kabbalah: New Perspectives*. New Haven: Yale University Press, 1988.
—— *Absorbing Perfections: Kabbalah and Interpretation*. New Haven: Yale University Press, 2002.
Matt, Daniel C. *The Essential Kabbalah: The Heart of Jewish Mysticism*. San Francisco: HarperCollins, 1996.
Ogren, Brian. *Renaissance and Rebirth: Reincarnation in Early Modern Italian Kabbalah*. Boston and Leiden: Brill, 2009.
Scholem, Gershom. *The Messianic Idea in Judaism and Other Essays on Jewish Spirituality*. New York: Schocken Books, 1971.
—— *Origins of the Kabbalah*. Ed. R. J. Zwi Werblowsky. Trans. Allan Arkush. Princeton: Princeton University Press, 1987.
Wolfson, Elliot R. *Language, Eros, Being: Kabbalistic Hermeneutics and Poetic Imagination*. New York: Fordham University Press, 2005.
—— *Venturing Beyond: Law and Morality in Kabbalistic Mysticism*. New York: Oxford University Press, 2006.

## Medieval Christian Mysticism

Augustine. *Confessions*. Trans. Henry Chadwick. Oxford: Oxford University Press, 1991.
Bernard of Clairvaux. *Selected Works*. Trans. G. R. Evans. Mahwah, NJ: Paulist Press, 1987.
Bonaventure. *The Mind's Journey to God*. Trans. Philotheus Boehner. Indianapolis: Hackett, 1993.
Eckhart, Meister. *The Essential Sermons, Commentaries, Treatises, and Defense*. Trans. Edmund Colledge and Bernard McGinn. Mahwah, NJ: Paulist Press, 1981.
—— *Teacher and Preacher*. Trans. Bernard McGinn, Frank Tobin, and Elvira Borgstadt. Mahwah, NJ: Paulist Press, 1986.
Eriugena, John Scotus. *Periphyseon: On the Division of Nature*. Trans. Myra I. Uhlfelder. Indianapolis: Bobbs-Merrill, 1976.
Gerson, Jean. *Early Works*. Trans. Brian Patrick McGuire. Mahwah, NJ: Paulist Press, 1998.
Jantzen, Grace. *Power, Gender and Christian Mysticism*. Cambridge: Cambridge University Press, 1995.
McGinn, Bernard. *The Presence of God: A History of Western Christian Mysticism*. Op. cit.
—— (ed.). *The Essential Writings of Christian Mysticism*. New York: Random House, 2006.

Nicholas of Cusa. *Selected Spiritual Writings*. Trans. H. Lawrence Bond. Mahwah, NJ: Paulist Press, 1997.
Sells, Michael. *Mystical Languages of Unsaying*. Chicago: University of Chicago Press, 1993.
Turner, Denys. *The Darkness of God: Negativity in Christian Mysticism*. Cambridge: Cambridge University Press, 1995.

## Hildegard of Bingen and Women's Mysticism

Bynum, Caroline Walker. *Fragmentation and Redemption: Essays on Gender and the Human Body in Medieval Religion*. New York: Zone Books, 1991.
Elisabeth of Schönau. *The Complete Works*. Trans. Anne L. Clark. Mahwah, NJ: Paulist Press, 2000.
Gertrude of Helfta, *The Herald of Divine Love*. Trans. Margaret Winkworth. Mahwah, NJ: Paulist Press, 1993.
Hadewijch. *The Complete Works*. Trans. Columba Hart. Mahwah, NJ: Paulist Press, 1980.
Hildegard of Bingen. *Scivias*. Trans. Columba Hart and Jane Bishop. Mahwah, NJ: Paulist Press, 1990.
 *Symphonia*. Trans. Barbara Newman. 2nd ed. Ithaca: Cornell University Press, 1998.
 *Book of Divine Works*. Trans. Priscilla Throop. Charlotte, VT: MedievalMS, 2009.
Hollywood, Amy. *The Soul as Virgin Wife: Mechthild of Magdeburg, Marguerite Porete, and Meister Eckhart*. Notre Dame: University of Notre Dame Press, 1995.
Jantzen, Grace M. *Power, Gender, and Christian Mysticism*. Cambridge: Cambridge University Press, 1995.
Newman, Barbara. *St. Hildegard's Theology of the Feminine*. Berkeley: University of California Press, 1987.
 *From Virile Woman to Woman Christ: Studies in Medieval Women and Literature*. Philadelphia: University of Pennsylvania Press, 1995.
 (ed.). *Voice of the Living Light: Hildegard of Bingen and Her World*. Berkeley: University of California Press, 1998.
Porete, Marguerite. *The Mirror of Simple Souls*. Trans. Ellen L. Babinsky. Mahwah, NJ: Paulist Press, 1993.

# III The Renaissance and Early Modernity

## Renaissance Hermetism

Broek, Roelof van den, and C. van Heertum (eds.). *From Poimandres to Jacob Böhme: Gnosis, Hermetism and the Christian Tradition*. Amsterdam: In de Pelikan, 2000.
Faivre, Antoine and F. Tristan (eds.). *Présence d'Hermès Trismégiste* (Cahiers de l'Hermétisme). Paris: Albin Michel, 1988.
Faivre, Antoine. *The Eternal Hermes: From Greek God to Alchemical Magus*. Grand Rapids: Phanes Press, 1995. Rev. and expanded ed.: *I volti di Ermete*. Rome: Atanor, 2001.

Gentile, S. and C. Gilly (eds.). *Marsilio Ficino and the Return of Hermes Trismegisto (bilingual English and Italian)*. Florence: Biblioteca Mediciana Laurenciana, and Amsterdam: Biblioteca Philosophica Hermetica, 1999.
Gilly, C. and C. van Heertum (eds.). *Magic, Alchemy and Science 15th–18th Centuries: The Influence of Hermes Trismegistus*, 2 vols. (bilingual English and Italian). Florence: Centro di della Edifimi, 2002.
Godwin, J. *The Pagan Dream of the Renaissance*. London: Thames & Hudson, 2002.
Hanegraaff, Wouter J. and R. M. Bouthoorn. *Ludovico Lazarelli (1447–1500). The Hermetic Writings and Related Documents* (Medieval and Renaissance Texts and Studies, vol. 281). Tempe: Arizona Center for Medieval and Renaissance Studies, 2005.
Merkel, Ingrid and Allen G. Debus (eds.). *Hermeticism and the Renaissance. Intellectual History and the Occult in Early Modern Europe*. London and Missisauga, ONT: Associated University Presses, 1988.
Shumaker, Wayne. *The Occult Sciences in the Renaissance: A Study in Intellectual Pattern*. Berkeley: University of California Press 1972.
Walker, D. P. *The Ancient Theology: Studies in Christian Platonism from the 15th to the 18th Century*. London: Duckworth, 1972.
Westman, R. S. and J. E. McGuire. *Hermeticism and the Scientific Revolution*. Los Angeles: William A. Clark Memorial Library, 1977.
Yates, Frances. *Giordano Bruno and the Hermetic Tradition*. London: Routledge and Kegan Paul, 1964.

## Christian Kabbalah

Beitchman, Philip. *Alchemy of the Word: Cabala of the Renaissance*. Albany: State University of New York Press, 1998.
Benz, Ernst. *Christian Kabbalah: Neglected Child of Theology*. Trans. Kenneth W. Wesche. St. Paul: Grailstone Press, 2004.
Blau, Joseph Leon. *The Christian Interpretation of the Cabala in the Renaissance*. New York: Columbia University Press, 1944.
Coudert, Allison P. *The Impact of the Kabbalah in the Seventeenth Century: The Life and Thought of Francis Mercury van Helmont (1614–1698)*. Leiden: Brill, 1999.
Dan, Joseph (ed.). *The Christian Kabbalah: Jewish Mystical Books & Their Christian Interpreters*. Cambridge, MA: Harvard College Library, 1997.
Farmer, Steven A. *Syncretism in the West: Pico's 900 Theses (1486): The Evolution of Traditional Religious and Philosophical Systems*. Tempe, AZ: Medieval & Renaissance Texts & Studies, 1998.
Popkin, R. H. and G. M. Weiner (eds.). *Jewish Christians and Christian Jews*. Dordrecht: Kluwer Academic Publishers, 1993.
Reuchlin, Johann. *On the Art of the Kabbalah*. Trans. Martin and Sarah Goodman. Lincoln: University of Nebraska Press, 1983.
Schmidt-Biggemann, Wilhelm (ed.). *Christliche Kabbala*. Ostfildern: Jan Thorbecke Verlag, 2003.
Secret, François. *Les Kabbalistes Chrétiens de la Renaissance*. Paris: Dunod, 1964.

## Paracelsianism

Ball, Philip. *The Devil's Doctor: Paracelsus and the World of Renaissance Magic and Science.* London: William Heinemann, 2006.
Debus, Allen. *The English Paracelsians.* New York: F. Watts, 1965.
*The Chemical Philosophy: Paracelsian Science and Medicine in the Sixteenth and Seventeenth Centuries.* (Orig. pub. 1977.) Mineola, NY: Dover, 2002.
Dilg, Peter and Harmut Rudolph. *Neue Beiträge zur Paracelsus-Forschung.* Stuttgart: Akademie der Diözese Rottenburg-Stuttgart, 1995.
Goldammer, Kurt. *Paracelsus: Natur und Offenbarung.* Hannover-Kirchrode: Oppermann, 1953.
Goldammer, Kurt and Rosemarie Dilg-Frank (eds.). *Kreatur und Cosmos: internationale Beiträge zur Paracelsusforschung.* Stuttgart/New York: Fischer, 1981.
Grell, Ole Peter (ed.). *Paracelsus: The Man, His Reputation.* Leiden: Brill, 1998.
Kühlmann, Wilhelm and Joachim Telle (eds.). *Der Frühparacelsismus.* Tübingen: Max Niemeyer Verlag, 2001(*Erster Teil*), 2004 (*Zweiter Teil*), 2013 (*Dritter Theil*).
Moran, Bruce T. *Andreas Libavius and the Transformation of Alchemy: Separating Chemical Cultures with Polemical Fire.* Sagamore Beach, MA: Science History Publications, 2007.
Pagel, Walter. *Paracelsus: An Introduction to Philosophical Medicine in the Era of the Renaissance.* Basel: S. Karger, 1958.
Scholtz, Gerhild and Charles Gunnoe Jr. (eds.). *Paracelsian Moments: Science, Medicine, and Astrology in Early Modern Europe.* Kirksville: Truman State University Press, 2003.
Schott, Heinz and Ilana Zinguer (eds.). *Paracelsus und seine internationale Rezeption in der frühen Neuzeit.* Leiden: Brill, 1998.
Telle, Joachim (ed.). *Parerga Paracelsica.* Stuttgart: Franz Steiner Verlag, 1991.
Webster, Charles. *Paracelsus: Medicine, Magic and Mission at the End of Time.* New Haven: Yale University Press, 2008.
Weeks, Andrew. *Paracelsus: Speculative Theory and the Crisis of the Early Reformation.* Albany: State University of New York Press, 1997.
*Valentin Weigel (1533–1588) German Religious Dissenter, Speculative Theorist, and Advocate of Tolerance.* Albany: State University of New York Press, 2000.
(ed.). *Paracelsus: Essential Theoretical Writings.* Leiden: Brill, 2007.
Zimmermann, Volker (ed.). *Paracelsus: Das Werk – die Rezeption.* Stuttgart: Franz Steiner Verlag, 1995.

## Rosicrucianism

Edighoffer, Roland. *Les Rose-Croix et la Crise de la Conscience européenne au XVIIe siècle.* Paris: Editions Dervy, 1998.
Geffarth, Renko D. *Religion und arcane Hierarchie: Der Orden der Gold- und Rosenkreuzer als Geheime Kirche im 18. Jahrhundert.* Leiden: Brill, 2007.
Gilly, Carlos. *Adam Haslmayr: Der erste Verkünder der Manifeste der Rosenkreuzer.* Amsterdam: In de Pelikaan, 1995.
McIntosh, Christopher. *The Rosicrucians: The History, Mythology, and Rituals of an Esoteric Order.* York Beach, ME: Samuel Weiser, 1998.

Tilton, Hereward. *The Quest for the Phoenix: Spiritual Alchemy and Rosicrucianism in the Work of Count Michael Maier (1569–1622)*. Berlin: Walter de Gruyter, 2003.
Vanloo, Robert. *Les Rose-Croix du Nouveau Monde, aux sources du rosicrucianisme moderne*. Paris: Claire Vigne, 1996.

## Jacob Boehme and Christian Theosophy

Boehme, Jacob. *Sämtliche Schriften*. 11 vols. Ed. Will-Erich Peuckert and August Faust. Stuttgart: Fromanns Verlag, 1955–1961.
*Aurora (Morgen Röte im Auffgang, 1612)*. Trans. Andrew Weeks et al. Leiden: Brill, 2013.
*Mysterium Magnum*. Trans. John Sparrow. London, 1654. Ed. C. J. Barker. 2 vols. London: John M. Watkins, 1924.
*Six Theosophic Points and Other Writings*. Trans. John Rolleston Earle. Introduction by Nicholas Berdyaev. Ann Arbor: University of Michigan Press, 1958.
Faivre, Antoine. *Theosophy, Imagination, Tradition*. Trans. Christine Rhone. Albany: State University of New York Press, 2000.
Hessayon, Ariel and Sarah Apetrei (eds.). *An Introduction to Jacob Boehme: Four Centuries of Thought and Reception*. London: Routledge, 2013.
Nicolescu, Basarab. *Science, Meaning, and Evolution: The Cosmology of Jacob Boehme*. New York: Parabola Books, 1991.
Versluis, Arthur. *Wisdom's Children: A Christian Esoteric Tradition*. Albany: State University of New York Press, 1999.
Walsh, David. *The Mysticism of Innerworldly Fulfillment: A Study of Jacob Boehme*. Gainesville: University of Florida Press, 1983.
Waterfield, Robin (ed.). *Jacob Boehme*. Berkeley: North Atlantic Books, 2001. (Selections and commentary.)
Weeks, Andrew. *Boehme: An Intellectual Biography of the Seventeenth-Century Philosopher and Mystic*. Albany: State University of New York Press, 1991.

## Freemasonry

Bogdan, Henrik and Jan A. M. Snoek (eds.). *Handbook of Freemasonry*. Leiden: Brill, 2014.
Carr, Harry (ed.). *The Early French Exposures*. London: The Quatuor Coronati Lodge, 1971.
Hamill, John. *The Craft: A History of English Freemasonry*, Wellingborough: Crucible, 1986. Second ed.: *The History of English Freemasonry*, 1994.
Hasselmann, Kristiane. *Die Rituale der Freimaurer. Zur Konstitution eines bürgerlichen Habitus im England des 18. Jahrhunderts*. Transcript. Bielefeld, 2009.
Lefebvre-Filleau, Jean-Paul. *La franc-maçonnerie française: Une naissance tumultueuse (1720–1750)*. Caen: Maître Jacques, 2000.
Prescott, Andrew. "The Old Charges Revisited." *Transactions of the Lodge of Research* 2429 (2005), 25–38.
Snoek, Joannes A. M. *Initiations. A Methodological Approach to the Application of Classification and Definition Theory in the Study of Rituals*. Pijnacker: Dutch Efficiency Bureau, 1987.

"De allusieve methode / The Allusive Method / La méthode allusive." *Acta Macionica* 9 (1999), 47–70.

"A Manuscript Version of Hérault's Ritual" in *Ésotérisme, Gnoses & Imaginaire Symbolique: Mélanges offerts à Antoine Faivre* (Gnostica 3). Ed. Richard Caron et al. Leuven: Peeters, 2001.

"The Earliest Development of Masonic Degrees and Rituals: Hamill versus Stevenson" in *The Social Impact of Freemasonry on the Modern Western World* (The Canonbury Papers 1). Ed. M. D. J. Scanlan. London: CMRC, 2002.

"Printing Masonic Secrets – Oral and Written Transmission of the Masonic Tradition" in *Alströmersymposiet 2003. Fördragsdokumentation*. Ed. Henrik Bogdan. Göteborg: Frimureriska Forskningsgruppen i Göteborg, 2003.

"Researching Freemasonry: Where Are We?" *Journal for Research into Freemasonry and Fraternalism* 1:2 (2010), 225–246.

*Initiating Women in Freemasonry*. Leiden: Brill, 2012.

Stevenson, David. *The Origins of Freemasonry: Scotland's Century, 1590–1710*. Cambridge: Cambridge University Press, 1988.

## Swedenborg and Swedenborgianism

Block, Marguerite Beck. *The New Church in the New World: A Study of Swedenborgianism in America*. New York: Henry Holt, 1932.

Rose, Jonathan, S. et al. (eds.). *Emanuel Swedenborg: Essays for the New Century Edition on His Life, Work, and Impact*. West Chester, PA: Swedenborg Foundation, 2005.

Sigstedt, Cyriel O. *The Swedenborg Epic: The Life and Works of Emanuel Swedenborg*. London: Swedenborg Society, 1981.

Swedenborg, Emanuel. *The Letters and Memorials of Emanuel Swedenborg*. Vols. 1 & 2. Trans. and ed. Alfred Acton. Bryn Athyn, PA: Swedenborg Scientific Association, 1948, 1955.

Synnestvedt, Dan (ed.). *The World Transformed: Swedenborg and the Last Judgment*. Bryn Athyn, PA: Bryn Athyn College Press, 2011.

Tofel, Rudolph L. (trans. and ed.). *Documents concerning the Life and Character of Emanuel Swedenborg*. Vols. 1–3. London: Swedenborg Society, 1875, 1890.

Warren, Samuel M. *A Compendium of the Theological Writings of Emanuel Swedenborg*. West Chester, PA: Swedenborg Foundation, 2009.

Williams-Hogan, Jane. "A New Church in a Disenchanted World: A Study in the Formation and Development of the General Conference of the New Church in Great Britain." Ann Arbor: University Microfilms International, 1985.

"Emanuel Swedenborg," in Hanegraaff (ed.), *Dictionary of Gnosis and Western Esotericism*.

"Swedenborgianism," in *Introduction to New and Alternative Religions in America*. Vol. 3. Ed. Eugene V. Gallagher and Michael Ashcraft. Westport, CT: Greenwood Press, 2006, 1–25.

## Mesmer and Animal Magnetism

Crabtree, Adam. *From Mesmer to Freud: Magnetic Sleep and the Roots of Psychological Healing*. New Haven: Yale University Press, 1993.

Darnton, Robert. *Mesmerism and the End of the Enlightenment in France.* Cambridge, MA: Harvard University Press, 1968
Ellenberger, Henri. *The Discovery of the Unconscious: The History and Evolution of Dynamic Psychiatry.* New York: Basic Books, 1970.
Gauld, Alan. *A History of Hypnotism.* Cambridge: Cambridge University Press, 1992.
Mesmer, Franz Anton. *Mesmerism, a Translation of the Original Medical and Scientific Writings of F. A. Mesmer, M.D.* Trans. George Bloch. Los Altos, CA: William Kaufman, 1980.
Pattie, Frank. *Mesmer and Animal Magnetism: A Chapter in the History of Medicine.* Hamilton, NY: Edmonston Publishing Inc., 1994.
Winter, Alison. *Mesmerized: Powers of Mind in Victorian Britain.* Chicago: University of Chicago Press, 1998.

## IV The Nineteenth Century and Beyond

### Spiritualism

Braude, Ann. *Radical Spirits: Spiritualism and Women's Rights in Nineteenth-Century America.* Boston: Beacon Press, 1989.
Chéroux, Clément and Andreas Fischer (eds.). *The Perfect Medium: Photography and the Occult.* New Haven: Yale University Press, 2004.
Cox, Robert S. *Body and Soul: A Sympathetic History of American Spiritualism.* Charlottesville: University of Virginia Press, 2003.
Edmonds, John W. and George T. Dexter. *Spiritualism.* 2 vols. New York: Partridge and Britain, 1855.
Hardinge, Emma. *Modern American Spiritualism.* New York: Published by the author, 1870. (Also published under the name Emma Hardinge Britten.)
Hare, Robert. *Experimental Investigations of the Spirit Manifestations: Demonstrating the Existence of Spirits and Their Communion with Mortals.* New York: Partridge and Brittan, 1856.
Hatch, Cora L. V. *Discourses on Religion, Morals, Philosophy, and Metaphysics.* New York: B. F. Hatch, 1858.
Mumler, William H. *The Personal Experiences of William H. Mumler in Spirit Photography.* Boston: Colby and Rich, 1875.
Swedenborg, Emanuel. *Love in Marriage: A Translation of Emanuel Swedenborg's "The Sensible Joy in Married Love; and the Foolish Pleasures of Illicit Love."* Trans. David F. Gladish. New York: Swedenborg Foundation, Inc., 1992

### H. P. Blavatsky and Theosophy

Barker, A. Trevor (ed.). *The Mahatma Letters to A. P. Sinnett.* London, 1923, Pasadena, CA: Theosophical University Press, 1975; chronological edition, Adyar, India: Theosophical Publishing House, 1998.
Blavatsky, H. P. *The Key to Theosophy.* London, 1889. Facsimile reprint, Los Angeles: Theosophy Co., 1987.

*The Voice of the Silence: Being Chosen Fragments from the Book of the Golden Precepts.* London, 1889. Peking, China: Chinese Buddhist Research Society, 1927.
*Blavatsky Collected Writings.* 15 vols. Wheaton, IL: Theosophical Publishing House, 1966–1985.
*Isis Unveiled: A Master-key to the Mysteries of Ancient and Modern Science and Theology.* 2 vols. New York, 1877. Wheaton, IL: Theosophical Publishing House, 1976.
*The Secret Doctrine: The Synthesis of Science, Religion, and Philosophy.* 2 vols. London, 1888, facsimile reprint, Pasadena, CA: Theosophical University Press, 1988.
*The Letters of H. P. Blavatsky.* Vol. 1. Ed. John Algeo and Adele Algeo. Wheaton, IL: Quest Books, 2003.
*The Secret Doctrine Commentaries: The Unpublished 1889 Instructions.* Ed. Michael Gomes. The Hague: I.S.I.S. Foundation, 2010.
*Esoteric Instructions.* Ed. Michael Gomes. Chennai, India: Theosophical Publishing House, 2015.
Campbell, Bruce F. *Ancient Wisdom Revived: A History of the Theosophical Movement.* Berkeley, CA: University of California Press, 1980.
Gomes, Michael. *The Dawning of the Theosophical Movement.* Wheaton, IL: Quest Books, 1987.
*Theosophy in the Nineteenth Century: An Annotated Bibliography.* New York: Garland Publishing, 1994.
Kuhn, Alvin Boyd. *Theosophy: A Revival of Ancient Wisdom.* New York: Henry Holt, 1930.

## Rudolf Steiner and Anthroposophy

Barnes, Henry. *A Life for the Spirit: Rudolf Steiner in the Crosscurrents of Our Time.* Great Barrington, MA: Steinerbooks, 1997.
Lachman, Gary. *Rudolf Steiner: An Introduction to His Life and Work.* New York: Tarcher, 2007.
Lindenberg, Christoph. *Rudolf Steiner: A Biography.* Great Barrington, MA: Steiner Books, 2012.
McDermott, Robert (ed.). *The New Essential Steiner: An Introduction to Rudolf Steiner for the 21st Century.* Great Barrington, MA: Steinerbooks, 2009.
Steiner, Rudolf. *How to Know Higher Worlds: A Modern Path of Initiation.* Trans. Christopher Bamford. Great Barrington, MA: Steinerbooks, 1994.
*Theosophy: An Introduction to the Spiritual Processes in Human Life and in the Cosmos.* Trans. Catherine E. Creeger. Great Barrington, MA: Steinerbooks, 1994.
*Intuitive Thinking as a Spiritual Path: A Philosophy of Freedom.* Trans. Michael Lipson. Great Barrington, MA: Steinerbooks, 1995.
*An Outline of Esoteric Science.* Trans. Catherine E. Creeger. Great Barrington, MA: Steinerbooks, 1997.

## The Golden Dawn and the O.T.O.

Crowley, Aleister. *The Confessions of Aleister Crowley.* London: Arcana, 1989.
Godwin, Joscelyn. *The Theosophical Enlightenment.* Albany: State University of New York Press, 1994.

Howe, Ellic. *The Magicians of the Golden Dawn: A Documentary History of a Magical Order 1887–1923.* York Beach, ME: Samuel Weiser, 1978.
Howe, Ellic and Helmut Möller. *Merlinus Peregrinus: Vom Untergrund des Abendlandes.* Würzburg: Köningshausen and Neumann, 1986.
King, Francis (ed.). *The Secret Rituals of the O.T.O.* London: C. W. Daniel Co., 1973.
Küntz, Darcy (ed.). *The Complete Golden Dawn Cipher Manuscript.* Edmonds, WA: Holmes Publishing Group, 1996.
Naylor, A. R. (ed.). *O.T.O. Rituals and Sex Magick.* Thame: IHO Books, 1999.
Owen, Alex. *The Place of Enchantment: British Occultism and the Culture of the Modern.* Chicago: University of Chicago Press, 2004.
Pasi, Marco. "Ordo Templi Orientis," in Hanegraaff (ed.), *Dictionary of Gnosis and Western Esotericism.*
Regardie, Israel (ed.). *The Golden Dawn. The Original Account of the Teachings, Rites and Ceremonies of the Hermetic Order of the Golden Dawn.* (Orig. ed. 1937–1940.) St. Paul, MN: Llewellyn Publications, 1989.
Starr, Martin P. *The Unknown God: W. T. Smith and the Thelemites.* Bollingbrook: Teitan Press, 2003.

## G. I. Gurdjieff and the Fourth Way

Gurdjieff, G. I. *Meetings with Remarkable Men.* (Orig. pub. 1963.) Trans. A. R. Orage (rev.). New York: Viking Arkana, 1985.
 *Beelzebub's Tales to His Grandson.* (Orig. pub. 1950.) No translator named. New York: Viking Arkana, 1992.
 *Life Is Only Real Then, When "I Am."* (Orig. pub. 1975.) No translator named. New York: Viking Arkana, 1999.
Moore, James. *Gurdjieff: The Anatomy of a Myth.* Boston: Element Books, 1991.
Needleman, Jacob and George Baker (eds.). *Gurdjieff: Essays and Reflections on the Man and His Teaching.* New York: Bloomsbury, 1998.
Ouspensky, P. D. *In Search of the Miraculous: Fragments of an Unknown Teaching.* New York: Harcourt Brace, 1949.
 *The Psychology of Man's Possible Evolution.* New York: Random House, 1950.
Salzmann, Jeanne de. *The Reality of Being.* No translator named. Boston: Shambhala, 2010.
Sinclair, Frank R. *Without Benefit of Clergy: Some Personal Footnotes to the Gurdjieff Teaching.* 2nd ed. Published by the author, 2009.
Webb, James. *The Harmonious Circle: The Lives and Work of G. I. Gurdjieff, P. D. Ouspensky, and Their Followers.* New York: Putnam, 1980.

## C. G. Jung and Jungianism

Bair, Deirde. *Jung: A Biography.* New York: Little, Brown, 2003.
Edinger, Edward. *Ego and Archetype.* Boston: Shambhala, 1992.
Jacobi, Jolande. *The Psychology of C. G. Jung.* Trans. Ralph Manheim. New Haven: Yale University Press, 1973.

Jaffé, Aniela. *The Myth of Meaning in the Work of C. G. Jung*. Trans. R. F. C. Hull. Einsiedeln, Switzerland: Daimon Verlag, 1984.
Jung, C. G. *Memories, Dreams, Reflections*. Recorded and ed. Aniela Jaffé. Trans. Richard and Clara Winston. New York: Random House, 1965.
*Gesammelte Werke*. 20 vols. Mannheim: Patmos Verlag, 2011. English translation: *Collected Works*. 20 vols. Trans. R. F. C. Hull (except Vol. 2, trans. Leopold Stein and Diana Riviere). Princeton: Princeton University Press, 1969.
Jung, C. G. (ed.). *Man and His Symbols*. New York: Dell Books, 1968.
Kirsch, Thomas B.: *The Jungians: A Comparative and Historical Perspective*. London: Routledge, 2001.
Neumann, Erich. *The Origins and History of Consciousness*. Trans. R. F. C. Hull. Princeton: Princeton University Press, 2014.
Samuels, Andrew. *Jung and the Post-Jungians*. London: Routledge, 2014.
Wehr, Gerhard. *Jung: A Biography*. Trans. David M. Weeks. Boston: Shambhala, 2001.
*Jung and Steiner: The Birth of a New Psychology*. Trans. Magdalene Jaeckel. Great Barrington, MA: Anthroposophic Press, 2002.

## *René Guénon and Traditionalism*

Evola, Julius. *The Path of Cinnabar*. Trans. Sergio Knipe. London: Arkos, 2010.
*Revolt Against the Modern World*. Trans. Guido Stucco. Rochester, VT: Inner Traditions, 1995.
Guénon, René. *Orient et Occident*. Paris: Payot, 1924.
*The Crisis of the Modern World*. Trans. Marco Pallis et al. Hillsdale, NY: Sophia Perennis, 2001.
*The Reign of Quantity and the Signs of the Times*. Trans. Lord Northbourne. Hillsdale, NY: Sophia Perennis, 2001.
*Introduction to the Study of the Hindu Doctrines*. Trans. Marco Pallis. Hillsdale, NY: Sophia Perennis, 2004.
Nasr, Seyyed Hossein. "Intellectual Autobiography," in *The Philosophy of Seyyed Hossein Nasr*. Ed. Lewis E. Hahn. Chicago: Open Court, 2001.
Quinn, William W. *The Only Tradition*. Albany: State University of New York Press, 1996.
Rooth, Graham. *Prophet for a Dark Age: A Companion to the Works of René Guénon*. Eastbourne: Sussex Academic Press, 2008.
Schuon, Frithjof. *The Transcendent Unity of Religions*. Trans. Peter Townsend. Wheaton, IL: Quest Books, 1984.
*Understanding Islam: A New Translation with Selected Letters*. Trans. Mark Perry and Jean-Pierre Lafouge. Bloomington: World Wisdom, 2011.
Sedgwick, Mark. *Against the Modern World: Traditionalism and the Secret Intellectual History of the Twentieth Century*. New York: Oxford University Press, 2004.
"European Neo-Sufi Movements in the Interwar Period," in *Islam in Inter-war Europe*. Ed. Nathalie Clayer and Eric Germain. New York: Columbia University Press, 2008.
Wasserstrom, Steven M. *Religion after Religion: Gershom Scholem, Mircea Eliade, and Henry Corbin at Eranos*. Princeton: Princeton University Press, 1999.

Waterfield, Robin. *René Guénon and the Future of the West: The Life and Writings of a 20th-century Metaphysician.* Napa Valley: Crucible Press, 1987.

## Via negativa *in the Twentieth Century*

Johnston, William. *Christian Zen.* New York: Harper, 1971.
———. *Christian Mysticism Today.* San Francisco: Harper, 1984.
———. *The Mysticism of the Cloud of Unknowing.* New York: Fordham University Press, 2000.
Merrell-Wolff, Franklin. *Experience and Philosophy.* Albany: State University of New York Press, 1994.
Nishitani, Keiji. *Religion and Nothingness.* Berkeley: University of California Press, 1982.
Pseudo-Dionysius. *The Divine Names and Mystical Theology.* Trans. John D. Jones. Milwaukee: Marquette University Press, 1999.
Roberts, Bernadette. *What Is Self?* Austin: M. B. Goens, 1989.
———. *The Path to No-Self: Life at the Center.* Albany: State University of New York Press, 1991.
———. *The Experience of No-Self: A Contemplative Journey.* Albany: State University of New York Press, 1993.
Versluis, Arthur. *Magic and Mysticism: An Introduction to Western Esotericism.* Lanham, MD: Rowman and Littlefield, 2007.
———. *Wisdom's Children: A Christian Esoteric Tradition.* Albany: State University of New York Press, 1999.

## Contemporary Paganism

Albanese, Catherine. *Nature Religion in America.* Chicago: University of Chicago Press, 1990.
Chase, Christopher. "'Be Pagan Once Again': Folk Music, Heritage, and Socio-Sacred Networks in Contemporary American Paganism." *The Pomegranate: The International Journal of Pagan Studies* 8:2 (2006), 146–160.
Clifton, Chas S. *Her Hidden Children: The Rise of Wicca and Paganism in America.* Lanham, MD: AltaMira Press, 2006.
Fortune, Dion. *The Sea Priestess.* (Orig. pub. 1938.) York Beach, ME: Samuel Weiser, 1978.
Gardner, Gerald. *Witchcraft Today.* Secaucus, NJ: Citadel Press, 1973.
Hallett, Jennifer. "Wandering Dreams and Social Marches: Varieties of Paganism in Late Victorian and Edwardian England." *The Pomegranate: The International Journal of Pagan Studies* 8:2 (2006), 161–183.
Hobsbawm, Eric. "Introduction," in *The Invention of Tradition.* Ed. Eric Hobsbawm and Terence Ranger. Cambridge: Cambridge University Press, 1982.
Hutton, Ronald. *The Triumph of the Moon: A History of Modern Pagan Witchcraft.* Oxford: Oxford University Press, 1999.
———. "Modern Pagan Festivals: A Study in the Nature of Tradition." *Folklore* 119 (2008), 251–273.

Blood and Mistletoe: The History of the Druids in Britain. New Haven: Yale University Press, 2009.
Lewis, James R. "The Pagan Explosion," in *The New Generation Witches: Teenage Witchcraft in Contemporary Culture*. Ed. Hannah E. Johnson and Peg Aloi. Aldershot: Ashgate, 2007.
Murray, Margaret. *The Witch-Cult in Western Europe*. Oxford: Oxford University Press, 1921.
Shnirelman, Victor A. "'Christians! Go Home': A Revival of Neo-Paganism between the Baltic Sea and Transcaucasia." *Journal of Contemporary Religion* 17:2 (2002), 197–211.
"Ancestral Wisdom and Ethnic Nationalism: A View from Eastern Europe." *The Pomegranate: The International Journal of Pagan Studies* 9:1 (2007), 41–61.
Strmiska, Michael. "The Music of the Past in Modern Baltic Paganism." *Nova Religio* 8:3 (2005), 39–58.
Whitehouse, Harvey. *Arguments and Icons: Divergent Modes of Religiosity*. Oxford: Oxford University Press, 2000.
York, Michael. *Pagan Theology: Paganism as a World Religion*. New York: New York University Press, 2003.
Zell-Ravenheart, Oberon. "Theagenesis: The Birth of the Goddess," in *Green Egg Omelette: An Anthology of Art and Articles from the Legendary Pagan Journal*. Ed. Oberon Zell-Ravenheart. Franklin Lakes, NJ: New Page Books, 2009, 90–95.

## The New Age

Bochinger, Christoph. *"New Age" und moderne Religion: Religionswissenschaftliche Analysen*. Gütersloh: Kaiser, 1994.
Hammer, Olav. *Claiming Knowledge: Strategies of Epistemology from Theosophy to the New Age*. Leiden: Brill, 2000.
"New Age Movement," in Hanegraaff, (ed.), *Dictionary of Gnosis and Western Esotericism*.
Hanegraaff, Wouter J. *New Age Religion and Western Culture: Esotericism in the Mirror of Secular Thought*. Leiden: Brill, 1996.
Heelas, Paul. *The New Age Movement: The Celebration of the Self and the Sacralization of Modernity*. Oxford: Blackwell, 1996.
Kemp, Daren. *New Age: A Guide*. Edinburgh: Edinburgh University Press, 2004.
Kemp, Daren and James R. Lewis (eds.). *Handbook of New Age*. Leiden: Brill, 2007.
Lewis, James R. and J. Gordon Melton (eds.). *Perspectives on the New Age*. Albany: State University of New York Press, 1992.
Rothstein, Mikael (ed.). *New Age Religion and Globalization*. Aarhus: Aarhus University Press, 2001.
Sutcliffe, Steven and Marion Bowman. *Beyond New Age: Exploring Alternative Spirituality*. Edinburgh: Edinburgh University Press, 2000.
Wood, Matthew. *Possession, Power and the New Age: Ambiguities of Authority in Neoliberal Societies*. Aldershot: Ashgate, 2007.
York, Michael. *The Emerging Network: A Sociology of the New Age and Neo-Pagan Movements*. Lanham, MD: Rowman & Littlefield, 1995.

## V Common Threads

### Alchemy

Halleux, Robert. *Les textes alchimiques*. Turnhout: Brepols, 1979.
Kraus, Paul. *Jābir ibn Hayyān: Contribution à l'histoire des idées scientifiques dans l'Islam,* Volume I: *Le Corpus des écrits jābiriens, Mémoires de L'Institute d'Égypte* 44 (1943) and Volume II: *Jābir et la science grecque, Mémoires de L'Institute d'Égypte* 45 (1942).
Mertens, Michèle. *Les alchimistes grecs IV, i: Zosime de Panopolis, Mémoires authentiques*. Paris: Les Belles Lettres, 2002.
Moran, Bruce. *Distilling Knowledge: Alchemy, Chemistry, and the Scientific Revolution*. Cambridge, MA: Harvard University Press, 2005.
Newman, William R. *Atoms and Alchemy*. Chicago: University of Chicago Press, 2006.
Obrist, Barbara. *Les débuts de l'imagerie alchimique: XIVe-Xve siècles*. Paris: Le Sycomore, 1982.
Priesner, Claus and Karin Figala. *Alchimie: Lexicon einer hermetischen Wissenschaft*. Munich: C. H. Beck Verlag, 1998.
Principe, Lawrence M. *The Aspiring Adept: Robert Boyle and His Alchemical Quest*. Princeton: Princeton University Press, 1998.
*The Secrets of Alchemy*. Chicago: University of Chicago Press, 2013.
Principe, Lawrence M. and William R. Newman. "Some Problems in the Historiography of Alchemy," in *Secrets of Nature: Astrology and Alchemy in Early Modern Europe*. Ed. William Newman and Anthony Grafton. Cambridge, MA: MIT Press, 2001.

### Astrology

Barton, Tamsyn. *Ancient Astrology*. London and New York: Routledge, 1994.
Broecke, Steven van den. *The Limits of Influence: Pico, Louvain, and the Crisis of Renaissance Astrology*. Leiden: Brill, 2003.
Curry, Patrick. *Prophecy and Power: Astrology in Early Modern England*. Cambridge: Polity Press, 1989.
*A Confusion of Prophets: Victorian and Edwardian Astrology*. London: Collins and Brown, 1992.
Garin, Eugenio. *Astrology in the Renaissance: The Zodiac of Life*. London: Routledge and Kegan Paul, 1983.
Grafton, Anthony. *Cardano's Cosmos: The Worlds and Works of a Renaissance Astrologer*. Cambridge, MA: Harvard University Press, 1999.
Howe, Ellic. *Urania's Children: The Strange World of the Astrologers*. London: Kimber, 1967.
Klibansky, Raymond, Erwin Panofsky, and Fritz Saxl. *Saturn and Melancholy: Studies in the History of Natural Philosophy, Religion, and Art*. New York: Basic Books, 1964.
Newman, William R. and Anthony Grafton. "Introduction: The Problematic Status of Astrology and Alchemy in Premodern Europe," in Newman and Grafton, *Secrets of Nature: Astrology and Alchemy in Early Modern Europe*.
Oestmann, Günther, H. Darrel Rutkin, and Kocku von Stuckrad (eds.). *Horoscopes and Public Spheres: Essays on the History of Astrology*. Berlin: Walter de Gruyter, 2005.

Stuckrad, Kocku von. *Das Ringen um die Astrologie: Jüdische und christliche Beiträge zum antiken Zeitverständnis*. Berlin: Walter de Gruyter, 2000.
*History of Astrology: From Earliest Times to the Present*. London: Equinox, 2010. Rev. translation of the German edition: *Geschichte der Astrologie: Von den Anfängen bis zur Gegenwart*. 2nd ed. Munich: C. H. Beck, 2007.
*Locations of Knowledge in Medieval and Early Modern Europe: Esoteric Discourse and Western Identities*. Leiden: Brill, 2010.
Vickers, Brian (ed.). *Occult and Scientific Mentalities in the Renaissance*. Cambridge: Cambridge University Press, 1984.
Zika, Charles. *Exorcising Our Demons: Magic, Witchcraft, and Visual Culture in Early Modern Europe*. Leiden: Brill, 2003.

## Gnosis

Faivre, Antoine. "Le terme et la notion de 'gnose' dans les courants ésotériques occidentaux modernes (Essai de périodisation)," in *Les textes de Nag Hammadi: Histoire des Religions, Approches contemporaines*. Ed. Jean-Pierre Mahé and Paul-Hubert Poirier. Paris: Institut de France, 2010.
Fowden, Garth. *The Egyptian Hermes: A Historical Approach to the Late Pagan Mind*. Princeton: Princeton University Press, 1986.
Hanegraaff, Wouter J. "Altered States of Knowledge: The Attainment of Gnōsis in the Hermetica." *The International Journal of the Platonic Tradition* 2 (2008), 128–163.

## Magic

Hanegraaff, Wouter J., Fritz Graf, Claire Fanger, Frank Klaassen, and Jean-Pierre Brach. "Magic I-V," in Hanegraaff, (ed.), *Dictionary of Gnosis and Western Esotericism*.
Hanegraaff, Wouter J., *Esotericism and the Academy: Rejected Knowledge in Western Culture*. Cambridge: Cambridge University Press, 2012.
Otto, Bernd-Christian. *Magie: Rezeptions- und Diskursgeschichtliche Analysen von der Antike bis zur Neuzeit*. Berlin: De Gruyter, 2011.
Pasi, Marco. "Magic," in *The Brill Dictionary of Religion*. Ed. Kocku von Stuckrad. Vol. 3. Leiden: Brill, 2007.
Styers, Randall, *Making Magic: Religion, Magic, and Science in the Modern World*. Oxford: Oxford University Press 2004.

## Mathematical Esotericism

Clulee, Nicholas H. *John Dee's Natural Philosophy*. London: Routledge, 1988.
Counet, Jean-Marie. *Mathématiques et dialectique chez Nicolas de Cues*. Paris: Vrin, 2000.
Gersh, Stephen. *From Iamblichus to Eriugena*. Leiden: Brill, 1978.
Giangiulio, Maurizio (ed.). *Pitagora. Le Opere e le Testimonianze*. 2 vols. Milan: Oscar Mondadori, 2002.
Godwin, Joscelyn. *Harmonies of Heaven and Earth*. London: Thames & Hudson, 1987.

Guthrie, Kenneth S. *The Pythagorean Sourcebook and Library*. Ed. David Fideler. Grand Rapids, MI: Phanes Press, 1987.
Høyrup, Jens. *In Measure, Number and Weight. Studies in Mathematics and Culture*. Albany: State University of New York Press, 1994.
Meyer, Heinz. *Die Zahlenallegorese im Mittelalter. Methode und Gebrauch*. Munich: W. Fink, 1975.
Meyer, Heinz and Rudolf Suntrup. *Lexikon der Mittelalterlichen Zahlenbedeutungen*. Munich: W. Fink, 1987.
Navia, Luis E. *Pythagoras. An Annotated Bibliography*. London: Garland, 1990.
Schimmel, Annemarie. *The Mystery of Numbers*. Oxford: Oxford University Press, 1993.
Surles, Robert L. (ed.). *Medieval Numerology: A Book of Essays*. London: Garland, 1993.
Zimmermann, Albert (ed.). *Mensura. Mass, Zahl, Zahlensymbolik im Mittelalter*. 2 vols. Berlin: de Gruyter, 1983–1984.

## *Panpsychism*

Bonifazi, Conrad. *The Soul of the World: An Account of the Inwardness of Things*. Lanham, MD: University Press of America, 1978.
Harvey, Graham. *Contemporary Paganism: Listening People, Speaking Earth*. New York: New York University Press, 1997.
Mendoza, Ramon. *The Acentric Universe: Giordano Bruno's Prelude to Contemporary Cosmology*. Boston: Element Books, 1995.
Skrbina, David. *Panpsychism in the West*. Cambridge, MA: The MIT Press, 2005.

## *Sexuality*

Hanegraaff, Wouter J. and Jeffrey J. Kripal (eds.). *Hidden Intercourse: Eros and Sexuality in the History of Western Esotericism*. Leiden: Brill, 2008.
Urban, Hugh B. *Magia Sexualis: Sex, Magic and Liberation in Modern Western Esotericism*. Berkeley: University of California Press, 2005.
Versluis, Arthur. *The Secret History of Western Sexual Mysticism: Sacred Practices and Spiritual Marriage*. Rochester: Destiny Books, 2008.

# INDEX

A∴A∴, 279
Abaris the Hyperborean, 15, 18, 43
Abraham ben David of Posquieres, 99
Abū Bakr, 85
Abulafia, Abraham, 99, 144, 152
Accademia Pitagora, 24
Adler, Margot, 343
Afshar, Askar Khan, 209
Aglaophemus, 134
Agrippa, Henricus Cornelius, 137, 138, 148, 149, 150–151, 152, 163, 275, 400, 412, 420–421
Aguéli, Ivan, 311, 314
Ahriman, 266
Aitken, Robert, 331
Albanese, Catherine, 340
Albert the Great, 112–113
Alchemy, xiii, xviii, xix, xxi, xxiv–xxv, xxvi, xxix, xxxi, xxxii, 23, 133, 141, 149, 157, 158, 159, 162, 166, 170, 171, 172, 173, 174, 175, 177, 178, 179, 180, 185, 195, 197, 203, 272, 274, 282, 301–302, 326, 346, 359–371, 374, 377, 412, 416, 425, 430, 433, 434, 435, 437
Alemanno, Yohanan, 99
Alexander VI, Pope, 136
Al-Alawi, Ahmad, 315
Al-Ghazālī, 85–86, 87, 92, 93
Almaas, A.H. (A. Hameed Ali), 331
Al-Radi, Salama, 313
Al-Razi, Muhammad ibn Zakariya, 364
Al-Sādiq, Ja'far, 363
Ambrose of Milan, 410
Amesius, 56
Amphion, 415
Anatolius, 407
Anaximander, 13

Ancient and Mystical Order Rosae Crucis (AMORC), 182–183
Andernach, Johannes Guinterius von, 165
Anderson, James, 204, 205
Anderson, Margaret, 288
Animal Magnetism, xxi, 223–234, 243, 245, 369, 426
Andreae, Johann Valentin, 174, 175, 177
Angelology, 153
Anthroposophy, 170, 260–271, 347
Antonia, Princess of Württemberg, 154
Aphrodite, 33
Apollo, 18, 36
Apollonius of Tyana, 14
Apophatic theology, *see Via negativa*
Apuleius, 134, 400
Aquarian Age, the, 181, 345, 346
Aquinas, St. Thomas, 112
Arya Samaj, 251
Archetypes, Jungian, 299
Archytas of Tarentum, 17
Aristeas, 43
Aristophanes, 99
Aristotle, xxiii, xxv–xxvi, xxvii, 16, 17, 26, 32, 33, 47, 84, 113, 140, 141, 157, 165, 267, 364, 418
Armentano, Amedeo, 23, 24
Arndt, Johann, 167, 185
Arnold, Gottfried, 171, 186
Arnold of Villanova, 163
Ásatrú, 337
Aschner, Bernard, 162
Ashmole, Elias, 204
Association for the Study of Esotericism, xv
Astrology, xiii, xviii, xxvii, xxix, xxx, xxxi, xxxii, xxxv, 19, 49, 50, 137, 150, 180, 229, 274, 344, 345, 346, 349, 372–380

463

Atlantis, 255
Atwood, Mary Anne, 179, 369
Augustine of Hippo, 20, 108–109, 110, 112, 116–117, 409–410, 411
Aurobindo Ghose, 270
Avicenna, 87, 157, 166, 364
Azriel of Gerona, 97

Baader, Franz von, 170, 184, 186, 387
Bacon, Francis, xxxiv, 238
Bahya ibn Paquda, 97
Bailey, Alice, 257, 305, 345, 354
Baldini, Bacchio, 136
Balīnūs, 364
Balsamo, Joseph, see Cagliostro, Count Alessandro di
Balzac, Honoré de, 222
Barnum, P.T., 244
Barrett, Francis, 275
Barth, Fredrik, 352
Basilides, 301, 322, 323, 332
Bateson, Gregory, 428
Baubo, 6
Baur, Ferdinand Christian, 386, 389
Becker, Judith, 119
Beguines, the, 112, 113, 126–129
Benedict of Nursia, 110
Bennett, John G., 288
Bentham, Jeremy, 177
Berdyaev, Nicholas, 324–325, 330, 331, 332
Bergson, Henri, 272, 428
Bernard of Clairvaux, 110–111, 112, 113, 116, 117
Bernus, Alexander von, 170
Besant, Annie, 252, 255, 257, 264, 265
Bezazel, 176
Bible, 19, 66, 95, 96, 100–106, 138, 151, 168, 173, 201, 202, 211, 213, 214, 215, 240, 241, 409, 412, 413, 414, 431, 432
Billot, Guillaume, 232
Biodynamic farming, 266
Bischoffwerder, Johann Rudolf von, 178
Blake, William, xiv, 22, 185, 221, 222, 270, 344, 435
Blavatsky, Helena Petrovna, 178, 184, 246, 248–259, 265, 304, 387
Bleuler, Eugen, 297
Bodenstein, Adam von, 162, 163, 164, 165
Boehme, Jacob, xiv, xvii, xviii, xix, xxviii, xxxiv, 141, 153, 154, 170, 172, 177, 184–199, 303, 322, 324, 325, 330, 367, 386, 387

Boethius, 20, 411, 413
Bonaventure, 112, 116
Bongo, Pietro, 414
Borges, Jorge Luis, 214, 222
Borgonuovo, Arcangelo da, 147, 151
Bostock, R., 167
Botkin, Gleb, 338
Botticelli, Sandro, 136
Bouthoorn, R.M., 136
Bovelles, Charles de, 413, 415
Boyle, Robert, 366, 368
Brach, Jean-Pierre, xiv, 401
Braid, James, 228, 245
Braude, Ann, 238
Breckling, Friedrich, 186
Brethren of Purity, 20
Brown, Dan, 348
Brucker, Jacob, 385, 386
Bruno, Giordano, xix, 139–140, 422–423, 432
Budapest, Zsuzsanna, 343
Buddha, see Gautama Buddha
Buddhism, 178, 251, 253–254, 256, 258, 313, 323, 330, 331, 332, 333, 346
Burkert, Walter, 5, 14, 15
Burr, H.W., 256

Cagliostro, Count Alessandro di, 231
Cahagnet, Louis, 232
Calcidius, 20
Cambridge Platonists, the, 152, 185, 424
Cambyses, 14
Campanella, Tommaso, 423
Campbell, Colin, 351, 352
Capella, Martianus, 20, 411
Capra, Fritjof, 347
Carcopino, Jérôme, 19
Cardano, Girolamo, 421
Casaubon, Isaac, 141
Casaubon, Méric, 150
Castel, William, 216
Catharism, 172, 181, 343
Cayce, Edgar, 346
Caxton, William, 134
Ceaușescu, Nicolai, 319
Censorinus, 20, 21
Certeau, Michel de, 39
*Chaldean Oracles*, 39, 46–47, 48, 384, 400
Champier, Symphorien, 137
Channeling, 347, 349, 350, 353
Chaos magic, 283, 440
Charles, Prince of Wales, 319

Chase, Christopher, 342
Chödrön, Pema, 331
Christianity, xix, xxvii, 4, 10, 20, 45, 58, 69–79, 107–117, 118–129, 143–155, 168, 172, 182, 183, 184–199, 201, 202, 211–222, 239, 264, 287, 316, 323, 330, 331, 333, 337, 340, 342, 343, 379, 386, 396, 398, 430
Christian Kabbalah, 22, 136, 143–155, 177, 185, 202, 275, 412, 414, 416
Christian theosophy, xiii, xvii, xix, 139, 170, 184–199, 324–325, 385
Chrysopoeia, 361–362, 364, 365, 366, 367, 368, 369
Church of All Worlds, 334
Church of Satan, 440
Cicero, 19, 418, 419
Clement VIII, Pope, 140
Clement of Alexandria, 54, 55, 409
Clichtove, Josse, 413
Clowes, John, 220
Coincidence of opposites, xvii, 87, 115, 425
Colberg, Ehregott Daniel, 385
Coleman, William Emmette, 256
Collective unconscious, the, 298–299
Collins, Mabel, 257
Communism, see Marxism
Confucius, 13, 239
Coomaraswamy, Ananda, 313, 314
Copernicus, Nicholas, 137, 376, 377
Corbin, Henry, xxxii, 12, 89, 90
Corpus Hermeticum, see Hermetica
Correspondences, xxi, xxiii, xxiv, xxviii, xxix, xxx, xxxi, 376, 379, 394, 406
Cosimo de' Medici, 134
Cosmic sympathies, xxi, xxiii, xxiv, xxviii, xxix, xxx, xxxi, 379
Coulomb, Alexis, 251
Coulomb, Emma, 251
Counter-Enlightenment, 175–178
Counter-Reformation, 172–175, 414
Creuzer, Georg Friedrich, 24
Croesus, 8
Croll, Oswald, xxv, 160, 161
Crowley, Aleister, 180, 182, 257, 276, 277, 279–283, 430, 437–440
Crystal healing, 344
Cthulhu mythos, 283
Cudworth, Ralph, 424

D'Auberive, Guillaume, 411
Dalai Lama, 285

Damascius, 20, 44, 46–48, 406
Dan, Joseph, 145, 155
Dante, 23, 365
David-Neel, Alexandra, 258
Davidson, Peter, 437
Davidson, William, 164
Davis, Andrew Jackson, 245
DeConick, April, 431
Dee, John, 140, 149, 275, 415
Deghaye, Pierre, 192
Demeter, 3, 4, 5, 6, 7, 8, 10, 11
Demiurge, the, 57, 171, 391
Democritus, 418
Demonology, 153
Denys the Areopagite, see Pseudo-Dionysius
Desaguliers, John Theophilus, 205
Descartes, René, 153, 268
Diocletian, Emperor of Rome, 362
Dionysus, 3, 4, 6, 7, 10, 11, 42
Dioscorides, 165
Diotima, 39
Divination, xxxi, xxxii, 19, 275, 339, 345, 346, 349, 353
D'Olivet, Fabre, 22–23, 24
Dorn, Gerhard, 162–164, 165, 167
Douglas, Frederick, 242
Doyle, Arthur Conan, 222
Druidry, 340
Duchesne, Joseph, 166, 167
Dugin, Alexander, 319–320, 321
Dunlap, S.F., 256
Du Potet de Sennevoy, Baron Jules, 230–231
Du Préau, Gabriel, 138
Durkheim, Emile, 394, 395

Eastern School of Theosophy, 253
Ebreo, Leone, 99, 151
Eckhart von Hochheim, xvii, 46, 112–114, 115, 116, 128, 303, 322, 324, 327, 328, 330, 331
Edward VI, King, 140
*Ein-Sof*, 97–98, 100, 104, 151, 190, 254
Elements, see Four elements
Eleusis, Mysteries of, xv, xvi-xvii, 3–10, 41, 337
Eliade, Mircea, xxxii, 314, 317
Elijah, 180
Eliot, T.S., 288
Elisabeth of Schönau, 124–125
Elizabeth I, Queen, 140
*Emerald Tablet*, 136, 138, 163, 174, 254, 363, 420
Emerson, Ralph Waldo, 222, 257, 270
Empedocles, 17, 26–37, 43, 364, 418, 420

Encausse, Gérard (Papus), 310
Enlightenment, the, xix, xx, xxii, xxvi, xxvii, xxviii, xxxiii, 38, 177, 178, 209, 242, 369, 371, 374, 375, 386, 387, 388, 395, 398, 401, 402, 430, 434
Ennemoser, Joseph, 230
Enoch, 180
Enoch ben Yared, 65
Enochian magic, 149, 274, 275
Environmentalism, 340, 342
Epimenides, 43
Epiphanius of Salamis, 54
Eranos Symposia, 305, 306
Eriugena, John Scotus, xvii, 109–110, 113, 115, 116, 322, 323, 411
Eros, 39–40, 279, 432–433
Esalen Institute, 347
Eschatology, 71, 74, 77, 78, 86, 348, 382
Eschenmayer, Carl Adolph von, 230
Eucher of Lyon, 411
Euclid, 408, 415
Eudes of Morimond, 411
European Society for the Study of Western Esotericism, xiv-xv
Eurythmy, 265
Evans, Warren Felt, 345
Evans-Wentz, W.Y., 258
Everard, John, 141
Evola, Baron Julius, 23, 289, 314, 315, 317–318, 319, 320, 435
Existentialism, 186

Faivre, Antoine, xiv, xx-xxii, xxiv, xxv, xxvi, 186, 193, 386
Farīd al-Dīn ʿAṭṭār, 93
Farr, Florence, 180, 272, 277
Farra, Alessandro, 414
Fechner, Gustav, 427
Feminism, 340, 343
Feraferia, 334, 338, 341
Ferdinand I of Aragon, 135
Fichte, J.G., 263
Ficino, Marsilio, xix, xxiii, xxiv, xxviii, 21, 22, 134, 135, 136, 137, 139, 143, 163, 173, 384, 412, 420, 432
Fideler, David, 18
Figulus, Nigidius, 19
Findhorn Foundation, 347
Fioravanti, Leonardo, 167
Fisch, Leah, 237
Fludd, Robert, 165

Fortune, Dion, 258, 335
Four elements, xxiii, 157, 165, 275, 418
Fourth Way, the, 284–296
Foix-Candale, François, 139
Fowden, Garth, 392
Fox, Kate, 237, 243, 245
Fox, Margaret, 237, 243, 245
Francis of Assisi, 111–112
Franck, Sebastian, 138, 175
Franklin, Benjamin, 238, 244
Franz, Marie-Louise von, 302, 307
Fratellanza Terapeutica Magica di Myriam, 24
Fraternitas Saturni, 435
Frazer, James G., 394, 395
Freemasonry, xiii, 22, 23, 176, 179, 200–210, 272, 273, 278, 310, 311, 312, 315, 317, 340, 369, 430, 437
Frei, Gebhard, 303
French Revolution, the, 208
Freud, Sigmund, 234, 246, 297, 298
Froben, Johann, 156
Froebe-Kapteyn, Olga, 305

Gabriel, 85
Galante, Livius, 141
Galen of Pergamon, 141, 157, 165, 167
Gallus, Thomas, 115
Ganay, Germain de, 138
Gandhi, Mohandas K., 253
Gardner, Gerald, 339, 342, 439
Garrett, Eileen, 428
Gautama Buddha, 13, 239, 266, 295, 296, 326
Geber, 141, 364
Gematria, xxxi, 18, 146, 408
Geomancy, 275
Germer, Karl, 282
Gerson, Jean, 114–115
Gertrude of Helfta, 125–126, 127
Gichtel, Johann Georg, 185
Gikatilla, Joseph, 148, 152
Gilbert, William, 424
Giorgio, Francesco, 21, 137, 147, 148
Giovanni da Correggio, 135
Glaucius, 323
Gnosis, xvi, xvii, xviii, xxix, xxx, xxxi, xxxv, 55, 171, 185, 187, 295, 302, 381–392
Gnosticism, xix, 49, 54–58, 171, 178, 179, 254, 278, 300–301, 302, 323, 381, 385, 386, 389, 390, 391, 392, 429, 430, 431, 432
Goethe, Johann Wolfgang von, xiv, xx, 263, 265, 270, 379

*Goetia*, 400
Gohory, Jacques, 163
Goldammer, Kurt, 163
Golden Dawn, *see* Hermetic Order of the Golden Dawn
Golding, Arthur, 139
Gold- und Rosenkreutz, 175–178, 179, 274, 369
Gonne, Maud, 272
Goodrick-Clarke, Nicholas, xiv
Gould, Robert Freke, 203
Grafton, Anthony, 374
Grahame, Kenneth, 340
Grant, Kenneth, 283
Gregorius XIV, Pope, 140
Gruppo di Ur, 23
Guénon, René, xxii, xxiii, 23, 308–321, 390
Gurdjieff, G.I., 284–296, 319, 347
Gutierrez, Cathy, xvi

Haase, Rudolf, 25
Hades, 6
Hadewijch, 126–128
Hadot, Pierre, 43, 45
Halbfass, Wilhelm, 258
Hamvas, Béla, 324
Hanegraaff, Wouter J., xiv, xvi, xix, xxii, xxvi, xxvii, xxviii, xxx, 136, 142, 345, 354
Hardenberg, Georg Philipp Friedrich Freiherr von, *see* Novalis
Hardinge, Emma, 239
Hare, Harold, 255
Hare, Robert, 243
Hare, William, 255
Harrison, Anna, 126
Hartmann, Franz, 278, 281
Hartmann, Olga de, 285, 286
Hartmann, Thomas de, 285, 288
Haselmayer, Adam, 167–168
Hauer, Jakob Wilhelm, 301
Heelas, Paul, 354
Hegel, G.W.F., xiv, xxxiii, 184, 186, 187, 263, 294, 386
Heindel, Max, 181
Hekate, 6
Hekhalot literature, 59–68
Helios, 11
Hephaistos, 10
Herakles, 4
Herman, Philip, 167

Hermes Trismegistus, xix, 20, 49–54, 133, 134, 136, 137, 138, 139, 140, 143, 144, 174, 363, 376, 381, 382, 383, 401
Hermetic Academy, xv
Hermetic Brotherhood of Luxor, 435, 437, 438
Hermetic Order of the Golden Dawn, xiv, 153, 179–180, 272–277, 278
Hermetica, xxxiv, 49–54, 84, 133–134, 135, 137, 138, 139, 140, 141, 299, 419–420
Hermeticism, *see* Hermetism
Hermetism, xiii, xix, xxvii, 49–54, 133–142, 157, 160, 171, 257, 258, 278, 384, 385, 389, 391, 420, 429, 430, 432
Hermotimus, 43
Herodotus, 13
Heschel, Abraham Joshua, 95
Hesiod, 11, 29, 48
Hess, Tobias, 174
Hester, John, 167
*Hesychia*, 36
Heumann, August, xxv
Hierocles of Alexandria, 16
Hildegard of Bingen, xvii, 120–124
Hillman, James, 306
Hindmarsh, Robert, 220
Hinduism, 178, 181, 253, 258, 309, 311, 312, 313, 335, 346, 438, 440
Hippocrates, 141, 167
Hippolytus, 323
Hiram Abiff, 208–209
Hirsch, Christoph, 167
Historicism, xxxii, xxxiii–xxxiv
Hitchcock, Ethan Allen, 179
Hitler, Adolf, 318
Hobbes, Thomas, 153
Hobsbawm, Eric, 338
Hodgson, Richard, 251–252, 255
Hofman, Melchior, 169
Hohenheim, Philippus Aureolus Theophrastus Bombastus von, *see* Paracelsus
Hollandus, Isaac, 159
Hollywood, Amy, 128
Homeopathy, 266
Homer, 29, 36, 48
Hoomi, Koot, 255
Hoomi, Morya, 255
Horoscopes, casting of, 275, 373, 377, 396
Horniman, Annie, 276, 277
Horowitz, Shabbetai Sheftel, 103
Houdini, Harry, 246
Hugh of St. Victor, 110, 411

Humanism, 138, 335
Hume, A.O., 251
Humphreys, Christmas, 258
Huser, Johann, 162
Husserl, Edmund, 187
Hutton, Ronald, 338–339, 340
Huxley, Aldous, 308
Hypnotism, 228
Hyppolytus of Rome, 54

Iamblichus, 13, 16, 19–20, 22, 39, 44, 47, 48, 407, 408, 419
Ibn ʿArabī, 87, 90, 91, 94
Ibn Taymiyya, 88
Illuminati, the, 178, 208, 229
Inanna, 343
Indian National Congress, 251
Inner Traditions Publishing, 390
Irenaeus of Lyons, 54, 409
Isaac the Blind, 97, 103, 104
Isidore of Seville, 411
Isis, 3, 136
Isis and Osiris, Mysteries of, 10–11
Islam, 10, 83–94, 311, 316, 337

Jābir ibn-Hayyān, 363
James I, King, 167
James, Henry, 222
James, William, 107, 245, 427
Janet, Pierre, 233, 234, 297
Jennings, Hargrave, 179, 278
Jesus Christ, 56, 57, 58, 70, 71, 72, 74, 75, 76, 77, 78, 79, 112, 120, 125, 126, 127, 135, 136, 146, 153, 162, 175, 180, 183, 196, 199, 211, 213, 214, 217, 219, 239, 261, 264, 265, 266, 267, 303, 329, 365, 368, 378, 387, 431
Jodorowsky, Alejandro, 288
John XXII, Pope, 365
John of Patmos, 70
John of Rupescissa, 365
Johnson, Paul K., 255
Johnston, William, 331
Joly, Henry, 43
Jonas, Hans, 391
Judaism, 10, 59–68, 95–106, 152, 337, 430
Judge, W.Q., 257
Julian, Emperor of Rome, 12
Julian of Norwich, 115
Julian the Theurgist, 47
Jung, C.G., xxii, xxiv, xxvii, 171, 172, 182, 222, 297–307, 347, 354, 370, 380, 390, 402–403

Jung, Emma, 298
Jungianism, xxiv, 182, 297–307, 347
Jung-Stilling, Johann, 232
Justinian, Emperor of Rome, 20

Kabbalah (see also Christian Kabbalah), xiii, xvii, xix, xxxi, xxxv, 19, 23, 95–106, 134, 137, 159, 168, 173, 177, 179, 180, 185, 190, 254, 258, 274, 387, 401, 412, 429, 430, 431–432, 433, 434, 435
Kali Yuga, 289, 309
Kant, Immanuel, xiv, xx, xxxiii, 38, 41, 115, 222, 292
Kapleau, Philip, 331
Karl XII, King, 212
Kayser, Hans, 25
Keating, Thomas, 324
Keller, Helen, 222
Kellner, Carl, 278, 281, 437
Kempe, Margery, 129
Kennett, Jiyu, 331
Kepler, Johannes, 21, 379, 424
Kerenyi, Carl, 8
Kerner, Justinus, 232
Khunrath, Heinrich, xxv, 150, 177, 185, 367
Kingsford, Anna, 258
Kipling, Rudyard, 341
Kircher, Athanasius, 414, 424
Kirsch, Hilde, 306
Kirsch, James, 306
Kirsch, Thomas, 306
Knapp, Charles, 325
Koran, 84, 85, 86, 87, 88, 89, 90, 92, 93, 94
Krause, Karl, 417
Kremmerz, Giuliano, 24
Krishna, 266
Krishnamurti, Jiddu, 265
Kristeller, Paul Otto, xiv
Kugetski, Feliz, 263
Kuhlmann, Quirinius, 186
Kühlmann, Wilhelm, 158

Lactantius, 52
Laertius, Diogenes, 16
La Framboisier, Nicholas Abraham de, 167
Lao Tse, 13
Lauret, J., 414
LaVey, Anton Szandor, 440
Lavoisier, Antoine, 244
Lazzarelli, Lodovico, 135–136, 137, 138, 139, 384

# INDEX

Leadbetter, C.W., 255, 257, 264
Leade, Jane, 185
Le Baillif, Roch, 165
Lectorium Rosicrucianum, 181–182
Leene, Jan, 181
Leene, Zwier, 181
Lefevre d'Etaples, Jacques, 136, 137, 413
Leland, Charles Godfrey, 339
Left-Hand Path, the, 289
Leibniz, Gottfried Wilhelm, 153
Leonardo da Pistoia, 134
Le Paulmier, Pierre, 166
Lévi, Eliphas, 254, 275
Lévy-Bruhl, Lucien, 395
Lewis, Harvey Spencer, 182
Libavius, Andreas, 159, 160, 161, 166
Lincoln, Abraham, 250
Lincoln, Mary Todd, 244
Lings, Martin, 317, 319
Little, Robert Wentworth, 179
Living nature, *see* Cosmic sympathies
Locke, John, 366
*Logos*, 76, 134, 135, 197, 264, 267
Loori, John Daido, 331
Louis XIII, King, 167
Lovecraft, H.P., 283
Loyola, St. Ignatius, 300
Lucifer, 198, 266
Lúkacs, George, 324
Lull, Ramon, 143, 165
Luria, Isaac, 96, 152
Luther, Martin, 378
Lutheranism, *see* Protestantism

Macaulay, Anne, 18
Mackenzie, Kenneth, 180, 273
Macrobius, 20, 411
Macrocosm-microcosm correspondence, xvii, xxix, xxx, xxxi, 89, 157, 160, 165, 167, 168, 173, 253, 281, 367
Madsen, Catherine, 335
Magic, xiii, xviii, xxi, xxiii, xxv, xxviii, xxix, xxx, xxxi, xxxii, xxxv, 43, 63, 144, 145, 153, 157, 158, 159, 160, 168, 173, 177, 229–231, 272–283, 339, 340, 341, 369, 374, 377, 393–404, 412, 416, 429, 430, 432, 433, 440
Maharshi, Ramana, 304
Mahavira, 13
Maier, Michael, 165
Maimonides, Moses, 97
Manchester, Peter, 26

Mansfield, Katherine, 288
Maritain, Jacques, 311
Marxism, 186, 313, 319, 324
Mary I, Queen, 140
Mary, the Virgin, 123, 125, 136, 169, 199, 219, 316, 335
Ma'shar, Abū, 376
Masonry, *see* Freemasonry
Mathematical esotericism, xiii, xxviii, xxix, xxxv, 22, 100, 101, 405–416
Mathers, Mina Bergson, 272
Mathers, Samuel Liddell, 179, 180, 273, 274, 276, 277
Matter, Jacques, 386
Matthias, Saint, 323
Matthioli, Pietro Andrea, 165
Mauss, Marcel, 394, 395
Maximilian I, Emperor, 148
Maximus the Confessor, 323, 411
Mayerne, Theodore Turquet de, 166, 167
McClain, Ernest, 18
McDermott, Robert A., xv
McGinn, Bernard, 111
McMurtry, Grady Louis, 283
Mead, G.R.S., 252
Meister Eckhart, *see* Eckhart von Hochheim
Merkavah mysticism, 59–68
Merrell-Wolfe, Franklin, 324, 326–327, 329, 330, 331, 332
Merton, Thomas, 331
Mesmer, Franz Anton, 223–225, 228, 229, 241–242, 243, 245, 354, 388, 426
Mesmerism, xiii, 223–234, 241–242, 254, 369, 402
Metatron, 65
Metempsychosis, *see* Reincarnation
Methodological agnosticism, xxxii, xxxiii–xxxiv
Michael, Archangel, 266
Michelet, Jules, 339
Michell, John, 18
Middle Platonism, 47, 407
Millennialism, 345
Milton, John, 185
Mithras, 3
Mithras, Mysteries of, 10
Moderatus of Gadès, 407
Modernity, xx, xxiii–xxvii, 107, 172, 309, 312, 315, 318, 319, 320, 321, 331, 340, 398, 403
Moffett, Thomas, 164
Molitor, Franz Josef, xxiii, 154

Montaigne, Michel de, 257
Mordekhai of Chernobyl, 100
More, Henry, 152, 153, 424, 425
Morganwg, Iolo, 338
Moses, 19, 87, 95, 96, 102, 135, 136, 137, 176, 219, 296, 387
Moshe de Leon, 102
Muhammad, the Prophet, 83, 85, 89, 91, 92, 93
Mumler, William, 244
*Mundus imaginalis*, 89, 90
Murray, Charles, 249
Murray, Margaret, 334, 339
Musaeus, 44
Myers, Frederic, 234, 245
Mystery rites, 3–12
Mysticism, nature of, xv, xviii, xxix, 9–10, 27, 38–39, 45–46, 59, 61–62, 68, 69, 75, 77, 92, 96, 107, 111, 114–115, 116, 118, 322–333, 360

Nag Hammadi Codex, 50, 55, 56, 302, 390
Naglowska, Maria de, 435
Nahmanides, 102, 105
Nasr, Seyyed Hossein, 316–317, 319
Necromancy, xxviii, 369
Needleman, Jacob, 295, 296
Nehru, Jawaharlal, 258
Neoplatonism, 19, 39, 42, 43, 44–48, 69, 97, 113, 148, 160, 169, 170, 171, 173, 178, 240, 242, 254, 362, 374, 384, 407, 408, 412, 415, 419, 421
Neumann, Erich, 306
New Age, the, 122, 247, 338, 344–355, 380, 390, 391
Newman, Barbara, 123, 128
Newman, William R., 374
Newton, Isaac, xiv, xx, 21–22, 154, 185, 205, 366, 425–426
Nicoll, Maurice, 288
Nicholas of Cusa, 115–116, 413, 415, 420, 422
Nichols, Ross, 342
Nicholson, R.A., 83
Nicomachus of Gerasa, 19, 407, 408
Nietzsche, Friedrich, 178, 306, 314
Noah, 176
Noll, Heinrich, 141
Noll, Richard, 306
Nostradamus, 351
Novalis (Georg Philipp Friedrich Freiherr von Hardenberg), 186

Number symbolism, *see* Mathematical esotericism
Numenius of Apamea, 19
Numerology, *see* Mathematical esotericism

Occultism, xiii, xxix, xxxi, 23, 24, 158, 160, 223, 229, 230, 246, 272, 273, 274, 275, 277, 283, 314, 354, 359, 360, 369, 374, 375, 387, 389, 396, 399, 401, 402, 403, 429, 430, 437
Oetinger, Friedrich Christoph, 153, 426
O'Keefe, Georgia, 288
Olcott, Henry Steel, 249, 250, 251, 253, 257
Orage, A.R., 288
Ordo Templi Orientis, 272, 277–283, 437, 438
Origen, 109, 409
Orpheus, 3, 39, 42, 43, 44, 47, 134, 139, 144, 414, 415
Orpheus, Mysteries of, 11–12, 19, 47
Orphism, 14, 38, 42, 43, 48, 144
Osiris, 3, 180
O.T.O. *see*, Ordo Templi Orientis
Ottheinrich, Elector of the Palatinate, 165
Otto, Bernd-Christian, 404
Otto, Rudolf, 107
Ouspensky, P.D., 285, 287, 291, 292, 347, 428

Pacioli, Luca, 415
Paganism, xxvii, xxviii, 283, 321, 334–343, 398
Panentheism, 335, 417, 420
Panpsychism, xxviii, 417–428
Pantheism, 335, 417
Panteo, Giovanni Agostino, 149
Papus, *see* Encausse, Gérard
Paracelsus (Philippus Aureolus Theophrastus Bombastus von Hohenheim) xix, xxv, xxviii, 141, 153, 156–170, 172, 173, 175, 185, 194, 257, 366–367, 421, 426, 433
Paracelsianism, xxi, xxv, 156–170, 185, 254, 385
Parmenides, xvii, xxvii, 8, 26–37, 296
Patai, Raphael, 151
Patrizi, Francesco, 140, 176, 417, 421–422
Paul of Taranto, *see* Geber
Paul the Apostle, 70, 71, 72, 73, 74, 75, 76, 78
Paulini, Fabio, 414
Payne, George, 205
Penot, Bernard George, 159
Perennial philosophy, *see* *Philosophia perennis*
Perna, Pietro, 163
Persephone, 3, 4, 5, 7, 8, 9, 29
Peter, Saint, 323
Peuckert, Will Erich, 162

Phanes, 11
Pherecydes of Syros, 13
Philadelphian Society, the, 185
Philo of Alexandria, 19, 67, 387, 408
Philolaus of Croton, 17, 134, 406
Philosopher's Stone, 175, 176, 178, 181, 197, 326, 360, 362, 365, 367, 369, 433, 434
*Philosophia perennis*, 136–137, 178, 308, 312, 316
Pico della Mirandola, Giovanni, xix, xxviii, 21, 135, 136, 143–145, 147, 148, 149, 150, 151, 154, 259, 379, 412, 413, 415
Pinturicchio (Bernardino di Betto), 136
Pistorius, Johannes, 151
Plato, xvii, xix, xxvi, xxxiii, xxxiv, 15, 16, 17, 18, 20, 21, 26, 27, 29, 31, 32, 36, 38–44, 45, 47, 134, 136, 143, 171, 266, 294, 381, 383, 384, 385, 387, 400, 412, 418, 419
Platonic orientalism, xix, 382, 383, 384, 386, 387, 389, 406–408
Plessis-Mornay, Philippe du, 139
Plethon, George Gemistus, 384, 400
Pliny the Elder, xxx-xxxi, 21
Plotinus, xvii, xix, 19–20, 39, 44–46, 47, 48, 56, 84, 108, 143, 394, 419
Plutarch, 408
Polhem, Christopher, 212
Pontano, Giovanni, 135
Pordage, John, 185, 322
Porete, Marguerite, 128
Porphyry, 13, 19–20, 39, 44, 46–48, 56, 184
Poseidon, 10
Post, Amy, 242
Post, Isaac, 242
Pouvourville, Count Albert-Eugène de, 311
Pratensis, Johannes, 164
Preston, William, 206
Prichard, Samuel, 206
Priestley, J.B., 288
Principe, Lawrence, xxiv
*Prisca sapientia*, 162, 173, 176
*Prisca theologia*, 137, 143, 385, 400
Proclus, 11, 20, 44, 48, 113, 406, 407, 408, 419
Protestantism, xix, xxvii, 138, 167, 184, 187, 239, 385, 396, 398
Psellus, Michael, 134
Pseudo-Arnald of Villanova, 365
Pseudo-Democritus, 361
Pseudo-Dionysius, xvii, 69, 109, 112, 115, 322, 323, 325, 326, 328, 330, 331, 332, 411
Ptolemy, Claudius, 54, 377, 408
Puritanism, 140, 341, 437

Putin, Vladimir, 320
Puységur, Marquis de, 225–228, 229, 231, 234, 242
Pythagoras, xxviii, 13–25, 39, 43, 47, 134, 144, 385, 387, 405, 418, 422
Pythagoreanism, 13–25, 38, 43, 48, 148, 150, 286, 290, 406, 407, 408, 416, 422
Pytheas of Massilia, 15

Quercetanus, *see* Mayerne, Theodore Turquet de
Quimby, Phineas Parkhurst, 354
Quintilianus, Aristeides, 20

Race, Victor, 225, 226, 227
Raine, Kathleen, 22
Ranbir Singh, Maharajah of Kashmir, 255
Randolph, Paschal Beverly, 242, 279, 430, 435–437, 438, 439
Rawlinson, Andrew, 331
Recanati, Menahem, 144, 152
Redfield, James, 348
Reformation, the, 219, 396
Reghini, Arturo, 23, 24
Reiki healing, 344, 349
Reincarnation, 14
Relativism, xxxii
Religionism, xxxii, xxxiv
Renaissance, xiii, xiv, xix, xxiii, xxviii, 133–142, 143, 144, 146, 147, 157, 162, 169, 173, 242, 243, 246, 259, 275, 340, 341, 354, 373, 374, 384, 385, 387, 400, 401, 402, 403, 411, 412, 416, 417, 420–423, 430, 432–434, 435
Reuchlin, Johann, 145–147, 148, 150, 151, 152, 154, 412, 413
Reuss, Theodor, 278, 280, 281, 282, 283, 437
Rhodius, Ambrosius, 164
Ribit, Jean, 166
Richard of St. Victor, 110
Richter, Gregorius, 185
Richter, Samuel, 176
Ricius, Paulus, 147–148, 151
Riolan, Jean, 166
Rito Filosofico Italiano, 23
Roberts, Bernadette, 324, 327–330, 331, 332
Roberts, Jane, 347, 349, 428
Rolle, Richard, 115
Romanticism, 184, 298, 312, 379, 398
Rosenkreutz, Christian, 167, 173, 174, 180, 261, 274
Rosenroth, Christian Knorr von, 152, 154

Rosicrucian Fellowship, 181, 182
Rosicrucianism, xiii, 167, 171–183, 203, 229, 257, 273, 277, 385, 435
Rossel, Hannibal, 140
Roussel, Gèrard, 413
Royce, Josiah, 428
Rūmī, 90
Ruusbroec, John, 114

Sabians, the, 20
Sacred geometry, *see* Mathematical Esotericism
Saint-Martin, Louis Claude de, 184
Salzmann, Alexandre de, 285
Salzmann, Jeanne de, 285, 287, 288, 294, 296
Samothrace, Mysteries of, 10–11
Sandhanwalia, Thakar Singh, 255
Saraswati, Swami Dayananda, 251
Sarmoung Brotherhood, 285
Satanism, 283, 439, 440
Sayer, Anthony, 205
Schäfer, Peter, 60
Schaw, William, 204
Schelling, F.W.J., xiv, 186, 263, 426–427
Schiller, Friedrich, 379
Schlegel, August Wilhelm, 186
Schlegel, Friedrich, 186
Scholem, Gershom, xvi, 143, 148, 152, 154
Schubert, Gotthilf Heinrich von, 388
Schucman, Helen, 350
Schuon, Frithjof, 314, 315–316, 390
Schwenkfeld, Casper, 169
Scripture, *see* Bible
Secret, François, xiv
*Sefirot*, 97–98, 100, 103, 104, 105, 144, 151, 152, 274, 275, 431
Sennert, Daniel, 165
Sethians, the, 57
Severinus, Petrus, 164
Sex magic, *see* Sexuality
Sexuality, 429–440
Shaivism, xvii
Shakespeare, William, 238
Shamanism, xxviii, 3, 15, 43, 344, 354
Shankara, 326
Shaw, Gregory, 408
*Shekhinah*, 64, 106
Shumaker, Wayne, 374
Siderocrates, Samuel, 167
Sidney, Sir Philip, 139, 140
Sievers, Marie von, 265
Silberer, Herbert, 370

Simon ben Eleazar, 147
Simplicius, 20
Sinclair, Henry John (Lord Pentland), 288
Sinnett, A.P., 251, 257, 428
Societas Rosicruciana in Anglia (S.R.I.A.), 179–180, 273, 274
Société Spirite, 249
Society for Psychical Research (S.P.R.), 246, 251, 252
Socrates, xx, 17, 40, 43, 288
Sodalizio Pitagorico, 23
Solomon, 176
Solon, 8
Sophia (Wisdom), 57, 193, 194, 197, 198, 199, 260
Spangler, David, 347
Sparrow, John, 185
Spear, John Murray, 244
Specht, Otto, 262
Spengler, Oswald, 312
Spiritualism, xiii, xvi, xviii, xxv, xxviii, xxix, 232–234, 237–247, 249, 250, 251, 257, 297, 435
*Spiritus mundi*, xxiii
Starhawk (Miriam Simos), 335, 343
Stein, Charles, xvii
Steiner, Rudolf, 170, 181, 257, 260–271, 304
Stellatus, Josephus, *see* Hirsch, Christoph
Stobaeus, 133
Stoicism, 51, 372, 418–419, 424
Steuco, Agostino, 137
Strauss, Leo, xiv, xxxiv
Strindberg, August, xiv, 222
Stuckrad, Kocku von, xx, xxii
Sudhoff, Karl, 162
Sufism, xvii, 83–94, 285, 286, 310, 312, 313, 315, 316, 319, 331, 354
Suhrawardī, Shahab al-Din Yahya ibn Habash, 383
Suso, Henry, 114, 329
Sylvius, Franciscus de le Boë, 170
Syrianus, 44
Swedenborg, Emanuel, xiv, 154, 211–222, 228, 232, 238, 240, 241, 242, 270, 342, 345, 354, 430, 434–435

*Tabula Smaragdina*, *see* Emerald Tablet
Talemarianus, Petrus, 23
Tantra, xvii, 23, 181, 281, 283, 346, 354, 438, 440
Taoism, xvii, 23, 311

Tardieu, Michel, 20
Tarot, 274, 275, 344, 346, 349, 351
Tascher, Paul, 233
Tattwas, 275
Tauler, John, 114, 324
Taylor, Thomas, 22
Teilhard de Chardin, Pierre, 428
Telepathy, xxv
Telle, Joachim, 158, 162
Templarism, 277
Tertullian, 409
Thales, 13, 418
Thelema, 277, 279, 281, 282, 438
Thénaud, Jean, 150
Theodore of Asine, 408
Theon, Max, 437
Theon of Smyrna, 19, 407
Theosophy (The Theosophical Society), 178, 181, 184, 246, 248–259, 264, 265, 273, 278, 310, 311, 325, 326, 345, 347, 348, 354, 379–380
Theurgy, 47, 272, 368, 387, 408
Thimus, Albert Freiherr von, 24
Thom, Alexander, 15
Thomas, Keith, 374
Thomasius, Jacob, 385, 386, 388, 390
Thoreau, Henry David, 257
Thoth, 49, 133, 140
Thurneisser, Leonard, 164
Thutmose III, Pharaoh, 182
Tieck, Ludwig, 186
Tingley, Katherine, 257
Tiryakian, Edward, 248
Titans, the, 42
Toland, John, 417
Torah, *see* Bible
Toxites, Michael, 162, 163, 164, 167
Traditionalism, 291, 308–321, 390
Transcendental Meditation, 355
Transmigration of souls, *see* Reincarnation
Travenol, Louis, 207
Travers, P.L., 288
Trevelyan, George, 347
Trinity, Christian, 108, 112, 113, 122, 139, 145, 147, 153, 154, 169, 194, 217
Trithemius, Johann, 138
Truth, Sojourner, 242
Turnèbe, Adrien, 139
Tylor, Edward Burnett, 394, 395, 397
Tymme, Thomas, 167

UFO lore, 283, 345, 346
Underhill, Evelyn, 107, 324
*Ungrund*, 190–191, 194, 198, 199, 322, 325
*Unio mystica*, 62, 65, 208

Valentine, Basil, 159
Valentinians, the, 55, 57, 58, 76, 431
Valentinus, 56
Van Beyerland, Abraham Willemsz, 141
Van Helmont, Frans Mercurius, 153
Van Helmont, Jean Baptiste, 170
Van Rijckenborgh, Jan, *see* Leene, Jan
Vedanta, xvii, 311, 312, 326, 330, 332
Vellozo, Dario de Castro, 24
Vernant, Jean-Pierre, 41
Versluis, Arthur, xv, 246
*Via negativa*, 69, 97, 322–333
Vickers, Brian, 374
Vieussens, Raymond, 170
Virgil, 23, 414
Vishnu, 254
*Visio dei*, 72, 79
Vital, Hayim, 154
Voiculescu, Gelu Voican, 319

Waite, Arthur Edward, 180, 277
Waldorf School movement, 260, 263, 266
Walsh, David, 199
Walsh, Neal Donald, 348
Watts, Alan, 331
Weber, Max, 398, 402
Wegman, Ita, 265
Weigel, Valentin, 139, 167, 168–169, 185
Westcott, William Wynn, 179, 180, 273, 274
Western Esotericism, mysticism and, xxix–xxxii
Western Esotericism, nature of, xiii, xvi, xviii–xxxii, 142, 171, 320–321, 322, 360, 373–377, 386, 428
Westman, Robert S., 142
Whitehead, Alfred North, 428
Whitehouse, Harvey, 337
Wicca, 283, 334, 335, 337, 338–340, 341, 342, 343, 440
Wilber, Ken, 331
Wilhelm, Richard, 301
William of Orange, 139
Wilson, Colin, 296
Wiszubski, Chaim, 145
Witchcraft, xxxi, 339, 340, 342, 369, 385
Wolfson, Elliot, 429

Wöllner, Johann Christoph von, 178
Wood, Ernest, 258
Woodhull, Victoria, 243
Woodman, William Robert, 273
Woodville, Anthony, 134
Wren, Christopher, 205
Wright, Frank Lloyd, 288
Wundt, Wilhelm, 292

Yates, Frances, xiv, 142, 177, 347
Yeats, W.B., xiv, 180, 222, 252, 272, 277
Yeltsin, Boris, 320

Yoga, 258, 281, 300, 301, 346, 438
York, Michael, 343

Zarathustra, *see* Zoroaster
Zell, Oberon, 341, 342
Zen Buddhism, xvii, 330, 331, 346
Zeus, 11, 42, 406
Zimmer, Heinrich, 301
Zosimos of Panopolis, 361–363, 365, 420
Zoroaster, 13, 139, 143, 144, 266, 384, 387, 400, 401
Zorzi, Francesco, 414

For EU product safety concerns, contact us at Calle de José Abascal, 56–1°,
28003 Madrid, Spain or eugpsr@cambridge.org.

www.ingramcontent.com/pod-product-compliance
Ingram Content Group UK Ltd.
Pitfield, Milton Keynes, MK11 3LW, UK
UKHW022249220326
469255UK00019B/435